THE ATLANTIC SLAVE TRADE AND BRITISH ABOLITION, 1760–1810

CAMBRIDGE COMMONWEALTH SERIES

Published in association with the Managers of the Cambridge University Smuts Memorial Fund for the Advancement of Commonwealth Studies

General Editor: E. T. Stokes, Smuts Professor of the History of the British Commonwealth, University of Cambridge

Titles published by the Cambridge University Press
John S. Galbraith: *Mackinnon and East Africa, 1878–1895*
G. Andrew Maguire: *Toward 'Uhuru' in Tanzania*
Ged Martin: *The Durham Report and British Policy*
Ronald Robinson (editor): *Developing the Third World*

Titles published by Macmillan
Roger Anstey: *The Atlantic Slave Trade and British Abolition, 1760–1810*
Partha Sarathi Gupta: *Imperialism and the British Labour Movement, 1914–1964*

The Atlantic Slave Trade and British Abolition 1760–1810

ROGER ANSTEY

M

First published 1975 by
THE MACMILLAN PRESS LTD
London and Basingstoke
Associated companies in New York
Dublin, Melbourne, Johannesburg and Madras

SBN 333 14846 0

Printed in Great Britain by
Cox & Wyman Ltd
London, Fakenham and Reading

To
Charles, Rosalind and Louise

Contents

List of Maps

List of Plates

Foreword

Few phenomena of modern history have cast so long a shadow as that of black slavery or branded themselves so deeply in the historical consciousness of both Africa and the Western world. Inevitably it has left a trail of controversy, not least among historians, who take violently opposed views of the internal effects of the slave trade upon Africa, who magnify or disparage its role in the Atlantic economy, and who assign widely differing explanations of British moves to secure its abolition. It is symptomatic of the paradox of much of our contemporary intellectual culture that under the influence of historical materialism it should instinctively deny an autonomous role to ideology while remaining itself so ideologically oriented. Yet the central statement of this viewpoint, Eric Williams' celebrated *Capitalism and Slavery*, undoubtedly threw a salutary douche of cold water over the smug complacency that had hitherto infected the received accounts of British abolition. The argument that British abolition, far from being an act of pure disinterested benevolence, fell into line with the country's economic interests and with the change from commercial to industrial capitalism has never been fully countered. The more exaggerated elements in his thesis have been duly assailed. That the profits of the slave trade should have been sufficiently large and well-directed to power the Industrial Revolution is a hypothesis as far-fetched as that which sees the wealth accumulated from the plunder of Bengal after the battle of Plassey as the main source of investment capital. Yet when purged of such exaggerated claims Williams' argument remains formidable. As D. B. Davis has acknowledged: 'It is . . . difficult . . . to get around the simple fact that no country thought of abolishing the slave trade until its economic value had considerably declined.'

Hence in assessing the weight of the different influences which

brought about British abolition, the question of the overall volume
and profitability of the traffic remains of critical importance, and
this book is the latest example of historians' attempts to bring precision tools to rough and obdurate statistical material. But this
remains only part of the larger problem.

In seeking a satisfactory alternative to historical materialism
Max Weber accepted that the groundwork of decisive historical
change was an alteration in the technological basis of society. Yet
the passage from one mode of production to another was not an
automatic affair but depended essentially on the convergence of an
independent ideological factor. Conversely the materialist argument has seen the thought of the Enlightenment and Evangelical
Revival as derivative in a determinist sense from economic forces,
and consequently as playing only a secondary role in bringing about
the abolition of the slave traffic. Roger Anstey does not engage
directly in what can all too easily become a narrow and stultifying
controversy which concentrates its attention on a few selective
aspects of the issue. The first task of the historian is to rescue
the past from the present and to recover its own attitudes free
from our own contemporary prepossessions. Yet his work fits
naturally into the larger historical conspectus.

In the light of current historical views the success of the British
abolition movement looks all the more remarkable. Williams'
gaze was bounded by the limits of formal empire and his attention
concentrated on Britain as the leader of the Industrial Revolution
and of the modern capitalist free-labour economy. But this preoccupation with the British case has tended to obscure the fact
that, so far from the Industrial Revolution rendering the old
mercantilist slave-trading economy anachronistic, it gave the latter
a fresh and fuller lease of life. The sudden expansion in the supply
of raw cotton and the rapid expansion of export markets for the
Lancashire textile industry could be accomplished only by floating the new industrial capitalism over a greatly enlarged mercantilist base. The pumping-in of State-monopoly opium into China
from the British possessions in India, so enabling the British to
use strong-arm methods to close the circle of exchange through
the China tea trade and to open up India as a market for the new
manufactured textiles, was a deployment of mercantilist power
in the pursuit of profit that dwarfed in scale anything practised
earlier by the West in Asia. Similarly, the forced growth of the

slave plantation economy in the southern United States from the 1790s in order to supply Lancashire's raw cotton requirements far outdistanced the earlier use of slavery in the small West Indian islands. Hence the paradox that after British abolition in 1807 the volume of the slave traffic conducted between Africa and the Americas still continued at a high level. Britain could not opt out of this process entirely. A thinly-disguised system of unfree labour had to be tolerated to maintain the labour supply of the old plantations, and everywhere within the limits of the Empire in which some new form of plantation industry developed, whether in Mauritius, or Trinidad, or Fiji, the State had to allow labour procurement and working arrangements in which new indenture often seemed old slavery writ small.

Yet the importance of British abolition remains undiminished. We have come increasingly to recognise how large was the gap between Free Trade ideology and actual practice and to emphasise that despite tariff reductions Britain retained down to the 1850s an essentially protectionist and in many ways mercantilist economy. Only with the onset of the second Industrial Revolution in the latter half of the nineteenth century could the West as a whole dispense with its mercantilist base. The surprise is not that American slavery was abolished so late but that British slavery was abolished so early. So far from according with British economic needs the abolition of the trade in 1807 was historically artificial and premature.

The attitude of mind that brought it about can only partially be sought in the inheritance of the Enlightenment, whose doctrines affected the public mind far more powerfully in France and North America than in Britain. The religious conviction of Evangelical and Quaker is nearer to its centre. But above all, it was this conviction embodied in a persistent and dedicated political pressure group acting under particular political circumstances that enabled Britain to take time by the forelock and anticipate the downswing of his scythe. This is Professor Anstey's story, and it is significant that ultimately he should give so large a place to the role of political history and to set out in detail for the first time the full connected sequence of events that gave Wilberforce and his followers victory in 1807.

Having divided his academic career after leaving Cambridge between West Africa and Britain, Professor Anstey brings to his task the personal qualifications of having studied the slave trade and its abolition from the two vital centres of historical action. It is fitting that his work should find a place in a Cambridge series devoted to exploring that untidy but deep-rooted set of relationships we know as the Commonwealth.

ERIC STOKES

Acknowledgements

Over the years that this book has been in the making I have received financial help from the University of Durham and University of Kent (Humanities Faculty) Research Funds, from the Duke University African Studies Committee, the Twenty-Seven Foundation and from the American Philosophical Society. To all of these bodies I am profoundly grateful for I could not have otherwise undertaken the considerable travelling necessary.

I should like warmly to thank the librarians or directors of the following institutions for allowing me to consult manuscript collections under their care: Boston, Mass., Public Library, the British Museum, Duke University Library, the Essex Institute, Friends House Library, the Quaker Collection at Haverford College, the House of Lords Record Office, Henry E. Huntington Library, Keele University Library, the John Rylands Library and the Earl of Crawford, Lambeth Palace Library, the National Library of Wales, the Pennsylvania Historical Society, the Public Record Office, the Rijks Archief, Middleburg, the US National Archives, the West India Committee, Wigan Public Library and the Library of Yale University.

I am equally grateful to C. E. Wrangham, Esq., CBE, for allowing me to consult his important collection of Wilberforce manuscripts and to John A. Woods and the late W. B. Hamilton for graciously allowing me to use their own valuable transcripts of the Sharp and Dropmore MSS respectively. I was also granted reading privileges in a number of the above libraries and would like to thank the librarians of Cambridge University Library, the Institute of Historical Research and the Peabody Museum for extending similar facilities. A debt of a different order is no less real: it is to Anne Collins, who displayed great patience and accuracy in the typing, and re-typing, of nearly the whole of this manuscript.

The longer one lives, the more grateful one becomes to friends, colleagues and workers in related fields for comment and help of very varied kinds. To name these, even though the list can not be exhaustive, is not the wooden exercise which a list may imply but a real expression of gratitude: Alan Armstrong, Norman Bennett, Peter Bird, Christine Bolt, Pierre Boulle, Edwin B. Bronner, George E. Brooks, Ronald Butler, the late W. L. Burn, Jack and Gillian Cell, Dorrie Clark, Michael Craton, Philip D. Curtin, K. G. Davies, Ralph Davis, Grayson Ditchfield, David Eltis, Stanley Engerman, John Fage, Betty Fladeland, Christopher Fyfe, Leonard Geddes, Eugene Genovese, Richard Gray, Sv. E. Green-Pedersen, Peter Hampshire, Malcolm Jack, the late Abbé L. Jadin, Mark Kinkead-Weekes, Herbert S. Klein, Bob Kubicek, E. Phillip LeVeen, Wm Roger Louis, Leland Lyons, Patrick C. Manning, Christine Marsh, Walter Minchinton, Vivienne Mylne, David Ormrod, John Pollock, Johannes Postma, James A. Rawley, Mary Reckord, Duncan Rice, David Richardson, Frank Sanderson, Eric Saxton, R. S. Sheridan, George Shepperson, E. A. Smith, Jean Stengers, David Turley, John Walsh, Jim Walvin, W. R. Ward, W. A. Whitehouse and Robin Winks.

The General Editor of the Cambridge Commonwealth Series, Professor Eric Stokes, made many perceptive comments on the manuscript and I am very grateful to him for his insights and patience. I owe an especial debt of gratitude to three scholars working in fields closely related to my own. The late W. B. Hamilton, by inviting me to Duke University and by lending me his personal microfilm copy of the invaluable Wilberforce–Grenville correspondence from the Dropmore manuscripts, provided me with a really major insight – indeed, 'breakthrough' would not be too strong a word. This extreme kindness was followed by numerous perceptive comments on my manuscript as it progressed. In the last stages before completing my manuscript I had the belated pleasure of meeting Seymour Drescher of the University of Pittsburgh and to him I owe not only much encouragement but also detailed and valuable criticism of the manuscript. He has also most kindly allowed me to quote from his manuscript, *A Case of Econocide: Economic Development and the Abolition of the Slave Trade* prior to publication. When work on my book was barely begun David Brion Davis most generously gave me vital leads to sources and in subsequent correspondence and meetings has given help and comment of a value beyond description, and bestowed numerous kindnesses, quite beyond my ability ever to repay. He has also most kindly allowed me to cite his forthcoming *The Problem of Slavery in the Age of Revolution 1770–1823*. These debts are quite apart from what sections of this book owe to David Davis, *The Problem of Slavery in Western Culture*. Of course, I add the usual disclaimer about the responsibility of others for the present book's faults.

My last debt is to my wife: never, I rejoice to say, does she read a line of what her husband writes – unless requested. But when asked, she comments with such unerring perception and felicity that it is to this, and to her infinite patience and understanding, that much of any quality that this book may have is due.

ROGER ANSTEY

Kingston
Canterbury
Kent
April 1974

Abbreviations

A & P	Accounts and Papers (Parliamentary Papers)
BMAddMSS	British Museum Additional Manuscripts
BT	Board of Trade Papers in the Public Record Office
CHBE	Cambridge History of the British Empire
CO	Colonial Office Records in the Public Record Office
DNB	Dictionary of National Biography
Dropmore MSS (WBH)	Photocopies of the Dropmore MSS *kindly made available by the late W. B. Hamilton*
EHR	English Historical Review
FO	Foreign Office Papers in the Public Record Office
HCA	High Court of Admiralty Papers in the Public Record Office
HMC	Historical Manuscripts Commission
JAH	Journal of African History
SP	Sessional Papers (Parliamentary Papers)
Sharp Transcripts (JAW)	Transcripts from the Sharp MSS *kindly made available by Dr J. A. Woods*
T	Treasury Records in the Public Record Office

Introduction

For a very long time one of the greatest involuntary migrations of all time, the Atlantic slave trade, commanded little scholarly attention.[1] Everyone knew that it had been an abomination, that its volume had been enormous and its profits prodigious. Recently some, at least, of the cherished assumptions have begun to be questioned: one area which has begun to command attention is that of the volume and flows of the trade, but the no less important question of the trade's profitability has still not attracted much serious study. Absence of studies of profitability, however, had not inhibited historians from asserting that the profits of the slave trade had been of major importance in the formation of the capital required to launch the British Industrial Revolution. As for the impact of the slave trade on the continent which had been its source of supply the easy assumption that that impact had been uniformly devastating at least had for excuse that the question of impact was not one which could seriously be pursued as long as the serious study of African history had not begun.

Evidently there is much important work to do.

On any reckoning the volume of the Atlantic slave trade reached its maximum extent in the half century after 1760 whilst this same period evidently has a particular importance in regard to the question of the use of its profits to help capitalise industrial development. Again, the study of the African impact of the slave trade, reflecting the publication of a significant number of monographs in the last twenty-five years, is a meaningful exercise for this same period, for the years 1761–1810.

A whole series of initial questions pose themselves. Who provided the ships, how much did slaving expeditions cost and in

[1] The major exception is Elizabeth Donnan's massive and meticulous *Documents Illustrative of the History of the Slave Trade to America* 4 vols. (New York, 1929).

what goods did the slavers trade? Which were the favoured parts of the African coast and how was the trade on that coast carried on? What were conditions on the 'middle passage' and what was the extent of mortality amongst both slaves and crews? The construction of a volume estimate was, for the British trade, a key to the gauging of its profitability; for the first time it was possible to suggest an approach which answered the key question of whether the slave trade was really as hugely profitable as it is commonly reckoned to have been. Profitability established, a brief further exercise enabled a decisive answer to be given to the proposition that the profits of the British slave trade contributed largely to capital formation in the Industrial Revolution.

As for Africa herself, what was the relative drain from the different regions of the coast, what was the demographic impact and what the effect on political and economic institutions?

As the slave trade reached its all-time peak the process of ending the trade began. The first major expression of the process, the movement for abolition of the British slave trade, culminating in success in 1806–07, is the theme of the remainder of this book. For the present writer, the study of British abolition is of particular interest because it involves assessment of the relative importance of ideas, of religious 'enthusiasm', of national interest and of political circumstances. In older, simpler days, such an assessment would have been regarded as redundant for had not Lecky said it all when he wrote, 'The unweary, unostentatious, and inglorious crusade of England against slavery may probably be regarded as among the three or four perfectly virtuous pages comprised in this history of nations'.[2]

The mass of Englishmen probably continue to believe, with Lecky, that it was William Wilberforce and his Evangelical and Quaker helpers who were essentially responsible first for the abolition of the British slave trade in 1806–07, then for the ending of British Caribbean slavery in 1833, and finally for the campaign against the continuing foreign slave trade. The whole achievement, it would probably be added, was wholly creditable to Wilberforce, his friends and successors, and only less to their country. Nor is this just a matter of a layman's interpretation, of a firmly established chapter of the Englishman's history, for it would also

[2] W. E. H. Lecky, *A History of European Morals*, 6th ed. (London, 1884) II 153.

seem that, at the scholarly level, the dictum of Lecky was only a slight extreme form of the view commonly held until about the midway point of the present century. For instance, in Professor Coupland's notable writings on the abolition[3] there was awareness of the change in intellectual attitudes to slavery which the eighteenth century had produced, and there was some recognition of the political and economic context of abolition: but the weight in his interpretation was on the portrayal of the episode as the first great victory of the humanitarian movement. It is true that in Franz Hochstetter, *Die wirtschaftlichen und politischen Motive für die Abschaffung des britischen Sklavenhandels im Jahre 1806– 1807* (Leipzig, 1905), there had been an economic interpretation of British abolition containing many important insights (insights which the present writer hastens to acknowledge), but it seems to have passed largely unnoticed as, in this respect, did C. L. R. James in *The Black Jacobins: Toussaint l'Ouverture and the San Domingo Revolution* (1938) wherein was propounded an ingenious explanation of how humanitarian motives were subordinated to economic in the Younger Pitt's conduct of abolition in the 1790s.[4]

When in 1944 Dr Eric Williams launched a comprehensive attack on what had become a traditional view it was therefore the first attack really to command notice. For the author of *Capitalism and Slavery*[5] the perspectives of historians like Coupland, C. M. MacInnes[6] and F. J. Klingberg[7] were all wrong. The role of the humanitarians, the key figures in what Williams saw as a parade of virtue, had been 'seriously misunderstood and grossly exaggerated by men who have sacrificed scholarship to sentimentality and, like the scholastics of old, placed faith before reason and evidence.'[8] Positively, and in Williams' own words, *Capitalism and Slavery* was 'strictly an economic study of the role of Negro slavery and the slave trade in providing the capital which financed

[3] R. Coupland, *Wilberforce* (Oxford, 1923), *The British Anti-Slavery Movement* (London, 1933), and 'The Abolition of the Slave Trade', *C.H.B.E.* II 188–216.

[4] See 51–54 of the revised edition (New York, 1963).

[5] First published at Chapel Hill, N.C., and subsequently frequently reissued by different publishers. All references hereafter are to the New York 1961 edition.

[6] *England and Slavery* (London, 1934).

[7] *The Anti-Slavery Movement in England* (New Haven and London, 1926).

[8] Williams, *Capitalism and Slavery*, 178.

the Industrial Revolution in England and of mature industrial capitalism in destroying the slave system'.[9] More particularly, Williams argued that during the Napoleonic Wars many of the traditional supporters of the old system of imperial protection were deserting the West Indian interest, whilst at the same time there was overproduction of British sugar in relation to available markets. As a result 'overproduction in 1807 demanded abolition' – just as, Williams went on to say, 'overproduction in 1833 demanded emancipation', whilst the two events were 'inseparable' from the ending of the sugar preference in 1846.[10] Williams' thesis, appealing in its simplicity and in the way in which it invoked universals as the key to understanding, and because it cohered with widely held preconceptions, commonly commanded instant assent.[11] The approach symbolised by Coupland, on the other hand, because its assumptions about piety and politics came to be regarded as too complacent, has more and more been regarded as 'old hat'. Whilst Coupland and his school were the avowed target of Williams, *Capitalism and Slavery* itself was criticised by G. R. Mellor in *British Imperial Trusteeship, 1783–1856* (1951), and subjected to a critique by the present writer in 1968.[12]

At another level of the whole theme of slavery and abolition David B. Davis in 1966, in *The Problem of Slavery in Western Culture* (Ithaca), published a study of attitudes to slavery up to the 1770s. As a result of Davis' outstanding work understanding

[9] Ibid., vii.

[10] Ibid., especially 123–5, 136, 145–53. The last quotations are from 136 and 152.

[11] See, e.g., Carter G. Woodson's review of *Capitalism and Slavery* in the *Journal of Negro History*, xxx (1945) 93–5 and, perhaps more significantly, the recommendations and prefaces contributed by distinguished historians to later reissues of the book.

[12] Roger Anstey, 'Capitalism and Slavery: a Critique', *Economic History Review*, 2nd ser., xxi (1968) no. 2, 307–20. See also John D. Hargreaves, 'Synopsis of a Critique of Eric Williams, *Capitalism and Slavery*', *The Transatlantic Slave Trade from West Africa* (Centre of African Studies, Edinburgh University, duplicated and privately distributed, 1965) 30–32, together with the report of discussion, 33–43. For comment on Williams in a much wider context see Eugene D. Genovese, 'Materialism and Idealism in the History of Negro Slavery in the Americas', *Slavery in the New World: A Reader in Comparative History*, ed. Laura Foner and Eugene D. Genovese (Englewood Cliffs, 1969) 238–55.

of the development of anti-slavery thought has increased dramatically: it remains the case that one *must* explore ideas from one's own perspective and at moderate length, in order for any judgement about the relative importance of ideas in the success of anti-slavery to be credible.[13] Rounded exploration and analysis of eighteenth-century thought will not be attempted: but it will be asked if the climate of opinion changed in any way significant for the growth of anti-slavery conviction, and what philosophical views specifically about slavery were formulated? Were anti-slavery opinions evident in the wider forum of literature and was there any relevance in theological developments during the century? Even if the answers to these questions prove strikingly positive it would be premature to assume that any change in philosophical views of slavery had even a major, still less a preponderant, importance. Other factors must first be investigated: how far can the groups which loom so importantly in traditional accounts of the abolition, Quakers and Evangelicals, be regarded as the actual dynamic of reform? To this end searching inquiry must be made, especially into their theology.

Finally, in Part Four of this book, the bearing of political and economic pressures and circumstances on the accomplishment of abolition will be assessed. Underlying this whole last section is the truth, evident but frequently forgotten, that for the contention that this or that force, or combination of forces, was responsible for abolition to be substantiated, the impingement of that force, or forces, on the political process must be demonstrated. It was law and statute which brought the British slave trade to an end and that was a product of the political process. An important part of the approach to the politics of abolition is through the question: 'Why was the abolition campaign for so long – nineteen years from 1787 – unsuccessful, and why did it triumph when it did, namely in 1806–7?' But there are other even more specific questions. What was the origin, nature, composition and strength of the abolition movement, both in the country and in Parliament? How did the movement act politically, and what were its relations with government, and with Pitt, Prime Minister for most of the

---

[13] For an adumbration of the treatment of these matters see Roger Anstey, 'A Re-Interpretation of the Abolition of the British Slave Trade, 1806–1807', *The English Historical Review*, LXXXVII (Apr 1972) no. 343, 304–32.

period up until early 1806? What can be said about Pitt's disputed role in the abolition attempt? Was he sincere and, if so, how can his relative ineffectiveness be explained? How did a matter such as abolition rate in the constitutional conventions of the day, and does the answer to this question perhaps help to explain the delay in achieving abolition? Can the delay in achieving abolition be explained in the often voiced terms of a strong West Indian interest, well represented in Parliament, and was the abolition struggle as a whole a Manichean affair between abolitionists and West Indians, or to be explained in terms of a wider conflict between interest groups – acting, as some would wish to add, as the vehicles of historical necessity? What was the strength and organisation of the West Indian group, and where did both they and their abolitionist foes stand in regard to other reforming causes? Can any economic forces and pressure groups demanding abolition be identified?

Success came, of course, to the abolition cause in 1806–7. The possibility that abolition came essentially as a necessary expression of the change from Protection to Free Trade, that is of a structural change in the British economy, must be considered. Also to be reckoned with is the possible effect of the slump in West Indian prosperity from about 1804 onwards and of the possible loss by the West Indians of some of their ancient charm. No one disputes that the fortuitous succession of the Ministry of All the Talents in February 1806 was important: this importance must be evaluated in terms of the relations between abolitionists and the new ministry and of particular new political and economic circumstances which may have made success possible. Finally, and subsuming much else, the political strategy of the Talents Ministry must be investigated and laid bare.

Within these covers, then, the European and American export slave trade from Africa in the last half-century of the trade's unfettered existence will be studied, together with the first great check upon it, the British abolition of 1806–7. Subsequent volumes will treat of the second great check, abolition by the United States, of the way in which other powers gradually abandoned the trade, and of the major onslaught on slavery itself which began with the ending of British Caribbean slavery in 1833.

PART ONE

PART ONE

1 The Atlantic Slave Trade, 1761–1810

The eighteenth-century world could look back on slavery and trading in slaves as institutions accepted and practised from time immemorial. The Middle Ages knew a lively trade in slaves around the shores of the Mediterranean and the Black Sea, a trade of which both Christians and Moslems were victims, but in which African Negroes also involuntarily shared. Reaching the Mediterranean as items of barter in the thriving trans-Saharan trade they might find themselves as bondsmen in Catalonia or Aragon, or fieldhands in the sugar plantations of Cyprus.[1] Then from the mid-fifteenth century, as Portuguese navigators drove down the West African coast in their quest for riches and the route to India, and somewhat as an afterthought, a sea-borne trade to Portugal began, a trade in which Spanish captains also joined.[2] Thus by the time that the European conquests in the New World came to generate their own demand for slaves, the European states initially involved, Portugal and Spain, could not only draw on a heritage in which slavery was accepted, but had recently developed their own independent access to the lands which supplied slaves.

Just as Spain, and, with the subsequent discovery of Brazil, Portugal, resorted to the import of African slaves because the Indians failed to adapt to forced labour, and their own citizens were insufficient or too proud, so the British in the Americas found, as early as the mid-seventeenth century, that neither the native inhabitants of their possessions or such white labour as they could get were sufficient for their plantations. Their answer was the same: just as Africans had been imported into Spanish America

[1] David Brion Davis, *The Problem of Slavery in Western Culture* (Ithaca, 1966) 41–6.
[2] A. M. Luttrell, 'Slavery and Slaving in the Portuguese Atlantic (to about 1500)', *The Transatlantic Slave Trade from West Africa* 66 ff.

from at least as early as 1502, so they were now introduced in growing numbers into the British Caribbean islands and southern
colonies of the North American mainland. Nor were the British
strangers to the slave trade for they had had such share in the
supply of slaves to Spanish America as smuggling could give them,
since the first successful slaving voyage of Sir John Hawkins in
1562. The British attempt to entrust the trade to a chartered company, the Royal African Company, founded in 1672, was never
really successful.[3] Although the company had a role in the slave
trade right through the eighteenth century it was increasingly as
the subsidised custodian of a line of forts on the Gold Coast. The
essential role was fulfilled by independent slave traders coming
originally from London, Bristol, Liverpool, and a few small ports
like Lancaster, in descending order of importance. By the mid-
eighteenth century, however, the share of Liverpool was steadily
climbing and that of London and Bristol declining.[4]

From the mid-seventeenth century the Dutch and the French
(not to mention minor carriers like the Danes, the Swedes and
the Brandenburgers) had likewise entered the slave trade as their
own transatlantic empires grew. Spain, on the other hand, was
able only erratically to import slaves for her colonies in her own
ships. The fact that it was British slave ships which primarily made
up the Spanish supply points to a sometimes overlooked feature
of the slave trade, namely that even in a mercantilist age there
was much legal, quasi-legal or illegal carrying of slaves to the
colonies of one nation by the slavers of another. For periods the
Dutch and even the Danes were important in the supply of
European colonies other than their own, but over the years the
British were most persistent and successful in supplying the needs
of foreigners.

The slave trade can for many purposes be studied of and for
itself: but it was no less a part of a triangular trade, a trade which
included the sale of manufactures in Africa, which up to the mid-
eighteenth century included the physical carriage home to Europe
of tropical produce, and which was complicated by the fact that
slave ships frequently traded in items like camwood, gum and ivory
at the same time as they sought slaves. Our concern will be the

---

[3] See K. G. Davies, *The Royal African Company* (London, 1957), for the
history of the company's rise and fall.

[4] C. N. Parkinson, *The Rise of the Port of Liverpool* (Liverpool, 1952) 93–6.

study of the slave trade but in the context of the triangular trade of which it was a part. From the vantage point of the later twentieth century we can see that as the slave trade entered the later part of the eighteenth century it entered upon its last half-century of unfettered life – the process of abolition began in 1806. We shall see in due course that even at the time when our more detailed study of the trade begins, intellectual currents strongly inimical to slavery were flowing strongly in Europe. But it was still possible for men of the age to wish or reason away the difficulties which had always confronted Classical and Christian Europe as it was confronted with slavery's starkest contradiction, that, in Professor Davis' words, it demanded that one 'treat men of one's own tribe as no more than animals'.[5] Only if slaves could be defined as coming from outside the group could this psychological dilemma be avoided, or at least eased. Had not Aristotle written that 'From the hour of their birth, some are marked out for subjection, others for rule';[6] and had not the Christian Church and medieval and early modern philosophy accepted slavery and somehow kept its contradictions in check?[7] The institution thus condoned had duly brought into being a vast trade to serve it. What, then, can be said about the organisation of the slave trade in the later part of the eighteenth century?

The initial requirement of a merchant resolved upon a slaving voyage was capital. The amount required varied with the age and size of the ship – it might be under 50 tons or over 500 – and with the style of outfitting and the choice of cargo. On Dutch slave ships in the later eighteenth century the average 'outset', i.e. initial capital costs plus voyage expenses subsequently incurred, was £8857 sterling[8] whilst the average figure for British slave ships, slightly less – may be taken as £8,534.[9] In the French slave trade

[5] Davis, *Problem of Slavery*, 47.

[6] Quoted in ibid., 70.

[7] For the extended study of attitudes to slavery up to the early eighteenth century see ibid., chapters i–ix.

[8] W. S. Unger, 'Bijdragen tot de Geschiedenis van de Nederlandse Slavenhandel: ii De Slavenhendel der Middelburgsche Commercie Compagnie, 1732–1808', *Economisch-historisch Jaarboek*, xxviii (1961) 87–9. The calculation is based on the very full summaries of balance sheets of the 101 voyages undertaken by the Middleburg Company between 1732 and 1797.

[9] See Table 1, p. 47 below.

95 Nantes slavers in the years 1763–93 averaged 245,627 livres per ship,[10] or £9,825, whilst an estimate of the La Rochelle Chamber of Commerce in 1761 put the figure at 242,500 livres, of £9,700 per slave ship.[11]

Whence did the capital come? In the sense that we have quite good samples of the names of owners of English slave ships we know who provided the capital and can even discern a common pattern of ownership in the three English ports.[12] In the period 1789–91 the London slave trade totalled 50 voyages, for 28 of which three partnerships – Anthony Calvert, Thomas King and William Camden; Richard Miles and J. B. Weuves; and John and Alexander Anderson – and one individual, William Collow, were responsible. The Bristol pattern, though similar, was less tidy, for the partnerships in which the leading slave merchants figured frequently varied, but such names, in particular, as Thomas Jones, James Jones, Charles Harford, John Anderson, James Rogers and Sir James Laroche Bt constantly recur. Even a casual glance at the Liverpool lists reveals the frequent recurrence of such partnerships as Thomas Tarleton, John Tarleton, Daniel Backhouse and Clayton Tarleton, as William Harper and Robert Brade, as William Boats, Thomas Seaman and James Percival, and of such individuals entrepreneurs as John Dawson,[13] and this impression is strengthened by the analysis made by an anonymous Liverpool author of 1797 when he claimed that in the eleven years 1783–93 30% of the houses engaged in the slave trade of that port employed 57% of the ships.[14]

This picture of a significant degree of concentration in owner-

---

[10] Jean Meyer, *L'Armement nantais dans la Deuxieme Moitié du XVIII Siècle* (Paris, 1969) 299–302. The £ sterling was worth about 25 livres.

[11] D. Rinchon, *Le Trafic Négrier* (Paris and Brussels, 1638) 78–9.

[12] *A. & P.*, 1792, xxxv (768), 'Vessels cleared out to the Coast of Africa for Slaves.'

[13] Dawson is well known for his partnership in the slave-trading firm of Baker and Dawson. It seems, however, that the partnership was dissolved in 1788–89 for the Liverpool Port Registers show that Baker sold his share in four jointly owned vessels to Dawson in those years (Register Nos. 37/86, 54/87, 64 and 143/87, in Robert Craig and Rupert Jarvis, *Liverpool Registry of Merchant Ships*, Chetham Society, vol. xv, 3rd series, Manchester, 1967.

[14] *Liverpool and Slavery: an Historical Account of the Liverpool–African Slave Trade. Was it the Cause of the Prosperity of the Town?* By a Genuine 'Dicky Sam', re-issue (Newcastle-upon-Tyne, 1969) 113–14.

ship is abundantly confirmed by an analysis of ownership of Liverpool ships in the single year 1790, made by a knowledgeable Liverpool merchant, Robert Norris, and communicated as his considered opinion to the Commons Select Committee on the Slave Trade. He showed that out of 141 Liverpool ships engaged in the slave trade, 97, or 69%, were owned by 33% of the owners, i.e. by 14 out of 40.[15] The capital investment in ships, outfitting and cargo ranged from the £156,699 (including insurance at 6%) of John Dawson to the £2,311 of Crosbie and Greenwood; from 19 vessels, eight of which appear to have been employed as tenders on the African coast, to one. Norris' estimate of the total Liverpool investment in ships, outfitting and cargo in 1790 was £1,088,526.[16] We have no breakdown for the London and Bristol slave trade, but application of the average figure for investment in the decade 1781–90 of £8,356[17] would give to London's 15 ships £125,340 and to Bristol's 28 £233,968,[18] a total of £1,447,834 for the three British ports.[19]

If we have only this limited, and one port, one year, breakdown

[15] *A. & P.*, 1790, xxix (698). Minutes of Evidence: Select Committee on the Slave Trade 500–09, Accounts of Vessels employed in the Liverpool Slave Trade. In the Register-General of Shipping lists for clearances, 1789–91 (*A. & P.*, 1792, xxxv (768)), the owners of slavers merely appear as a list of the partners involved in each enterprise, without any indication of their respective shares. This mode of recording obscures the fact that there were nuclear slave trading firms who sometimes took in extra partners for particular voyages, or who might invite a probably minor contribution from a man considerably involved in the venture of his own house. It is the merit of Norris' list that, on the basis of his intimate knowledge, he identified the nucleus of slave trading firms. In two other lists of the ownership of Liverpool vessels for 1798 and 1799, the work of 'consolidation' appears to have been attempted, but not as thoroughly as by Norris. These are in Gomer Williams, *History of the Liverpool Privateers and Letters of Marque with an Account of the Liverpool Slave Trade* (London, 1897) 681–5, and *Liverpool and Slavery*, 120–29, respectively: both are reprinted in Donnan, *Documents*, ii 642–9.

[16] *A. & P.*, 1790, xxix (698), 500–09. One owner entered an item of £4020 in respect of slaves owned, and Norris' total has been reduced by this amount.

[17] See Table 1, p. 47 below.

[18] *A. & P.*, 1792, xxxv (768).

[19] This does not include any provision for offices, warehouses, etc., or other fixed installations, but it does include the tenders and boats used on the African coast in two cases, possibly the only firms who had such.

of capital in the British slave trade we do possess evidence on the ownership of capital of some relative importance. Craig and Jarvis have shown that the socio-economic pattern of overall ship ownership at Liverpool at the end of the eighteenth century was markedly different from a then comparable port, Whitehaven. In the former, 80% of all owners were merchants and another 12 or 13% were from maritime backgrounds (probably for the most part captains who had shares in the voyages they undertook). In Whitehaven, on the other hand (apparently at much the same time), 40% of all owners came from a wide spread of maritime interests, 30% were professional men, yeomen, widows or spinsters and only 30% from the world of business, and these very widely spread so as to include, for example, pawnbrokers and milliners.[20] We can perhaps conclude that in the most important English slaving port the slave trade followed the frequent pattern whereby it was mainly capitalised from the profits of earlier ventures and other, probably overseas, trades in which the slave merchant might also be engaged. At the same time, not all slave trading profits can be assumed to have been available for reinvestment in the trade: some, according to opportunity, would have gone into other enterprises.

As regards the concentration of capital in the French slave trade, a random statistic for Honfleur in 1787 shows that of its nineteen slavers dispatched that year, ten were sent out by one company five by another and four by a third – suggesting a highly concentrated ownership even though it is likely that individual investors provided a part of the subscription to those voyages. At Le Havre in the same year there was rather less concentration of ownership.[21] In Nantes, the most important single port engaged in the French slave trade, the concentration of capital was already marked by 1760, two-thirds of outfittings between 1740 and 1760 being put down to four names only.[22] Calculations by Jean Meyer

---

[20] Craig and Jarvis, *Liverpool Registry*, xxxix 201–2, Table 26, see also ibid., 195, Table 20, for a list of investors in 4000 tons or more of Liverpool shipping, registered between 1786 and 1804, which lists the tonnage pertaining to each. Many of the 67 names are of men we know to have been active in the slave trade.

[21] *B.T.* 6/7. Navires du Port de Honfleur destinés pour le Commerce de Guinée et Côte d'Afrique, 1787, and similar list for Le Havre.

[22] Jean Meyer, 'Le Commerce négrier nantais, 1772–1792', *Annales, Economies, Sociétés, Civilisations*, xv (1960) 123; Pierre H. Boulle, 'Slave

covering the Caribbean and American as well as the slave trades, and spanning the years 1694–1792, show that of a total of 6,300 voyages on which there was adequate information (about one-sixth of which were in the slave trade) 115–120 families were responsible for 2200 voyages, and 76 families for a further 4092. Of this latter number, 1725 were sent out by 125 noble families. The capital itself was of local origin but much of it appears to have been reinvestment of earlier profits from overseas voyages.[23]

The vessels engaged in the slave trade might be ships, barques, snows or brigs[24] and were typically of 150 to 300 tons. By the early years of the nineteenth century some approached 600 tons but in all periods some were unbelievably small. Thus the appropriately termed *Little Ben* owned by Robert Bostock, which cleared from Liverpool in 1791, could claim a mere 27 tons.[25] By the second half of the eighteenth century slavers were usually of a special construction, since the nature of their human cargoes demanded decks rather than holds. On the voyage out to Africa, however, a slave ship was freighted with the goods required for the purchase of slaves. Into the purchase and selection of these goods went much skill and knowledge, for, as we shall see, the attractiveness of the assortment of the goods on offer to the African and European traders on the coast was of considerable importance if slaves were to be obtained without the long delays which were the main cause

[23] Meyer, *L'Armement Nantais*, 90–92, 250.

[24] The last three terms obviously describe types of rig: 'ship' was a term particularly applied to three-masted square-rigged vessels.

[25] *A. & P.*, 1792 xxxv (768). The average tonnage of 94 Liverpool ships clearing for the slave trade in 1796 was 199 (*S.P.* 1801–02, IV, Account of Vessels cleared out from Liverpool to Africa for Slaves, 1796–1802; 44 Havre slavers in 1787 averaged 232 tons (*B.T.* 6/7). More freakish was Thomas Clarkson's observation in 1787 of a vessel of 11 tons putting out for a slave trading voyage. Built as a pleasure boat on the Severn with accommodation for six persons it was 'said to be destined to carry thirty slaves'. Another of 25 tons was to carry seventy (Thomas Clarkson, *The History of the Rise, Progress and Accomplishment of the Abolition of the Slave Trade* (reissue, London, 1968) I 327–36. This was before Dolben's Act of 1789 which was the first of the measures which restricted the number of slaves that could be carried.

Trade, Commercial Organisation and Industrial Growth in Eighteenth-Century Nantes', Revue Française d'histoire d'outre mer, LIX (1972), no. 214. 85–9.

of expense, and of mortality amongst crews and amongst the slave cargoes, as they were gradually built up. The goods consisted of malt, spirits, brandy, rum, muskets, gunpowder, flints, knives, brass manufactures, earthenware, hats and different descriptions of cotton cloth. This last was by our period an important element in the assortment and more and more consisted of Lancashire cotton manufacturers as opposed to the re-exported Indian cotton cloth, which had been an earlier staple of the trade, but whose original names, as *nicannee* or *cashtoe,* were still retained.[26] The cargo of a Bristol ship, the *Pilgrim,* which cleared for Africa in 1790 gives an idea of the quantity and assortment of goods. The first item of all is explained by the use of the iron bar on extensive portions of the African coast as a unit of measurement in what we shall see to be an intricately contrived barter trade.

> 1858 bars English iron, 40 casks corn spirits, 65 chests muskets, 2 casks felt hats, 11 casks gun flints, 1 cask wrought iron knives, 5 butts cotton, 4 tubs 10 casks brass manufacture, 3 crates 500 pieces earthenware, 40 puncheon beans, 14,850 kegs gunpowder, 12 butts 1 trunk East India goods, 4 chests bugles, 12 cases calicoes, 2 puncheon rum, 15 dozen bottles wine.[27]

Normally loading of the cargo was probably completed in the port of origin but it was sometimes convenient for English slave ships to pick up certain types of spirit on the Continent on their outward voyage. Captain Crow, for instance, on his voyages of 1790 and 1794, went first to Rotterdam and Jersey, respectively, for spirits.[28] This, of course, was because spirits were more cheaply produced in the Netherlands and France, and it follows from this

[26] One reason for the rise of Liverpool over Bristol and London – and, indeed, something which gave her an important edge over Continenta slave traders – was the easy accessibility of Lancashire cotton goods. The West Country woollens, to which Bristol had convenient access, were naturally less attractive to customers than cotton cloth (Parkinson, *Rise of the Port of Liverpool*, 94).

[27] Printed in W. E. Minchinton, *The Trade of Bristol in the Eighteenth Century,* reissue (Bristol, 1966) 60. A butt was a container for liquid or dry goods of 15 to 22 cwt and a puncheon a large cask.

[28] Hugh Crow, *Memoirs,* reissue (London, 1970), 32 and 46. Jersey must clearly have been an entrepôt for this, as it was for many other products, as a result of the disturbed trading patterns, and massive illicit trading, of the Revolutionary and Napoleonic wars.

that these nations – indeed all other nations engaged in the slave trade – made up their cargoes with significant national variations depending on what had the cheapest prime cost.[29]

For the English slave merchant there could also be other advantages in going first to a foreign port, advantages of a more significant kind than the mere acquisition of spirits or other goods more cheaply. Thus in the 1780s an unknown but significant number of English ships were employed in the French slave trade, attracted by a tonnage bounty, a premium on slaves sold, and a higher market price for slaves in the French colonies to which they by this means had unfettered access. Although crews were largely French, 'the real interest belongs either in part, or in the whole to British subjects . . ., the circumstance which commands the whole' being 'the great advantage we have in capital'.[30] During the truce which followed the Peace of Amiens a significant number of British slavers also wore the Dutch flag in order, primarily, to avoid the limitation on the number of slaves allowed to be carried in British ships, a limitation which had been further stiffened in 1799.[31] Recourse to American and Danish colours was also

[29] For the cargoes of French slavers see D. Rinchon, *Le Trafic Négrier*, 99–104, 114–18; for American slavers, with a consistent emphasis on New England rum, see 15 inventories in Donnan, *Documents*, III 337–9.

[30] *A. & P.*, 1789, xxvi (646a), Report of the Privy Council Committee on the Slave Trade, pt VI, France. Note also *Sharp Transcripts* (*J.A.W.*), Granville Sharp to John Sharp, 14 Jan 1792, where the writer refers to the grant by the French Government of 'enormous bounties for the fitting out of slave ships, which induced Barber and other infamous slave traders from England to settle in France'.

[31] *H.C.A.* 10/31, Dutch Prize Assignation Book. In the High Court of Admiralty Papers is a return which is a long list of Dutch vessels captured by the Royal Navy as prizes in the weeks following the resumption of hostilities with France and her satellite Batavia in mid-May 1803. What attracts particular attention is that some 44 of the vessels have English names, the names of their masters' have a distinctly Anglo-Saxon ring and they near unfailingly were allowed to take bail at Liverpool, or Bristol. The suspicion that these were not really Dutch vessels hardened not a little and when it transpired that the name of one of these vessels was – *John Bull!* Collation with lists of British vessels clearing for the slave trade from British ports reveals that a number of these 'Dutch' prizes had cleared as British vessels participating in the slave trade, often three or four weeks before capture. On the other hand, between four and six of the prizes appear probably not to have cleared as British slavers even though their appearance on clearance lists before or after indicates that they were British slavers. The question therefore arises as to the extent of

made,[32] but we do not know in what circumstances and on what scale. Normally the ship and cargo seem to have been insured, the rate in peacetime, for English trade, for example, amounting to 6% and for the French trade to $6\frac{1}{2}$%.[33]

Size for size a vessel in the slave trade carried a larger crew than ordinary. Mortality on the voyage and the need to attend and guard the slaves seem to have been the reasons for this. It does not seem to have been difficult to recruit masters, mates and even surgeons, for whom there were financial or career inducements, but the known high mortality amongst crews, and the reputation which some slave ship captains apparently had for exceptional brutality, often made the enlistment of seamen difficult. In such a situation the only seamen who enlisted voluntarily, in the English slave trade at any rate, were the young or the innocent. Others were lured on board by 'crimping', a system of collusion between masters and innkeepers of which Thomas Clarkson gained a

---

[32] James Stephen, *The Dangers of the Country* (London, 1807) 187 n. Stephen's practice as a lawyer in the Prize Court gave him unrivalled knowledge of the intricacies of the 'flag of convenience' game, an expedient so widespread that it may well have resulted in branches of the slave trade being unrecorded, or under-recorded.

[33] *A. & P.*, 1790, xxix (698) 500–09; Rinchon, *Le Trafic Négrier*, 154–7. The French contract Rinchon prints covers the whole voyage, the slaves being valued in terms of the cost price of the goods for which they were exchanged. (See Appendix 2, below.) It seems that in the English trade a separate insurance might be taken out against the loss of slaves on the middle passage, apparently at their market valuation. Rates rose sharply in wartime – Crow quotes 15 guineas per cent (*Memoirs*, 135–6).

---

the iceberg of which these cases were perhaps the tip. A document in the *Liverpool Papers* (*B.M. Add. MSS. 38416*, folio 315) explains the use of the Dutch flag. An English firm at Rotterdam, James Crawford and Co., printed the document for circulation in Liverpool under date of 28 July 1802. The document gave detailed information on how a British slaver should avail himself of the cover of the Dutch flag, *quoted the favourable opinion of the Law Officers of the Crown* as to the legality of the enterprise, and implied that the firm of Crawford and Co. could safely be entrusted with the matter! In the assurance of legality, and in its indication that the main advantages of this ploy 'consist in their being no limitations as to the Number of Negroes in their Ships, and also in the certainty of getting home Freight to Holland', and in exemption from Dutch duties, we surely have grounds for postulating wide British recourse to this device in the ensuing months.

thorough and convincing knowledge at Bristol by personal investigation.

> At about twelve at night we generally set out, and were employed till two and sometimes three in the morning. He [Thompson, Clarkson's guide, himself an innkeeper, but not involved in crimping for the slave trade] led me from one of those public houses to another, which the mates of the slave vessels used to frequent to pick up their hands. These houses were in Marsh Street, and most of them were then kept by Irishmen.... Music, dancing, rioting, drunkenness, and profane swearing, were kept up from night to night. The young mariner, if a stranger to the port, and unacquainted with the nature of the Slave Trade, was sure to be picked up. The novelty of the voyages, the superiority of the wages in this over any other trades, and the privileges of various kinds, were set before him. Gulled in this manner he was frequently enticed to the boat, which was waiting to carry him away. If these prospects did not attract him, he was plied with liquor till he became intoxicated, when a bargain was made over him between the landlord and the mate.... Seamen also were boarded in these houses, who, when the slave-ships were going out, but at no other time, were encouraged to spend more than they had money to pay for; and to these ... but one alternative was given, namely a slave-vessel, or gaol....

Clarkson adds that he 'was no less than nineteen times occupied in making these hateful rounds', and found essentially the same system – Captain Crow also attested it –[34] when he subsequently investigated at Liverpool.[35]

The wages which a seaman on a slave ship was articled to receive were, if higher than in other trades, still modest. Captain John Newton records that 'Fore the mast' men on his last slaving voyage

[34] Crow, *Memoirs*, 90. 'Besides these expenses [wages], three to four pounds were given as crimpage for all seamen'. This sum, however, was in the context of a wage level four or five times higher than usual as a result of the acute shortage of seamen in the Napoleonic wars, and of inflation.

[35] Clarkson, *History*, I 322–4, 393–4; James Morley, a witness before the Select Committee into the slave trade, confirmed the notoriety of the Marsh Street innkeepers, having himself helped to take off seamen shanghaied in this way (*A. & P.*, 1790, xxx (699) 160).

in 753 received £1–8s. per month at a time when a sailor on an East Indiaman received five shillings a month less. Captains and first mates on slave ships, on the other hand, received much lower wages than the officers in the same Indiaman – Newton's wage was £5 per month and the First Mate's £4:[36] but they more than made up for this by their commission, or agreed percentage of the price received for the slave cargo – a typical enough £257–3–11 on Newton's second voyage.[37] Alternatively, and much more in the earlier part of our period, they might receive commission on goods sold on the coast plus the entire proceeds of a small number of 'privilege' slaves whom they were allowed to carry. Crow gives wage levels for 1805–6 which show they had increased four or five fold by that time,[38] but much of this increase must have been a result of the severe shortage of men experienced during the war and of inflation. Whatever the level, it appears that seamen were often compelled to take some of their wages in fluctuating and relatively debased West Indian currencies.[39]

Before sailing, captains were given written instructions by their owners, instructions which might be amended by subsequent letters sent out on other slavers, or, say, on West Indiamen for collection from a slave factor on a given island at which the slave captain had been instructed to call. Much of the letters of instruction was generalities and even a specific injunction to buy 'as many good merchantable young slaves as you can',[40] as a Rhode Island captain was once, and typically, told, was wont to be overridden by what was available. The most meaningful part of the instructions was in respect of the part of the African coast to which the captain should proceed, and of the transatlantic market or markets which he should try. Thus in 1789 a Liverpool slave trader, Robert

[36] John Newton, *The Journal of a Slave Trader*, ed. Bernard Martin and Mark Spurrell (London, 1962) 85–7.

[37] Ibid., 87. Newton was certainly well content with this for he wrote to his wife during that voyage, after arrival in the West Indies, 'Most of the cargo is sold, and at a good price. I hope the loss upon the voyage will prove inconsiderable.' But he adds: 'and I believe my own interest in it will be better than in the former [voyage]' (John Newton, *Letters to a Wife* (London, 1793) i 183).

[38] Crow, *Memoirs*, 90.

[39] Clarkson, *History*, i 394.

[40] Sailing Orders to Capt. John Peck of the *Prince George* by Isaac Fuller and Samuel Moses, 29 Oct. 1762, *The Commerce of Rhode Island*, Massachusetts Historical Collections, 7th ser., vol. IX (Boston, 1914), i 96.

Bostock, wrote to one of his captains when he was still on the Windward Coast, saying: 'I have Wrote you to Barbadoes to the care of Messrs. Griffith & Applewhaite if your Cargo is Healthfull and they will not give you £36, £37 or £38 per Head all round for your Slaves you are to proceed to Kingston in Jamaica ... and deliver your Cargo to the Gent[n] that will give you the best Price and shortest Sighted Bills and Quickest dispatch.'[41] Occasionally owners might not hesitate to enjoin fraud: 'Worter yr Rum as much as possible and sell as much by the short mesuer as you can,' a Newport, R.I., owner told his captain in the 1760s.[42]

The most direct track for slave ships bound from Europe to the African coast, what the French called the *petite route,* was to strike the Canary Islands in the first instance and then to pass by the Cape Verde Islands and then make land as required, but usually by Cape Palmas, the point where the coastline turns in an easterly direction. Thereafter the slaver followed the coast unless bound for Gabon, or the coast to the south, when it would usually cut south-east, perhaps calling at San Thomé for refreshment. Between March and August, however, this route was less and less easy the farther down the coast one wanted to go on account of the set of the S.E. Trades, and it seems that in these months vessels for the Congo and Angola, at any rate, sailed down to about 27° S. Latitude, and well out into the Atlantic, the so-called *grande route,* and then struck E.N.E. to the African coast.[43] Such phrases as 'make land as required' obscure the fact that eighteenth-century navigation was a chancy and anxious business. Given clear weather, latitude could be found by taking the angle of the sun at noon, but longitude had to be found by a dead reckoning which depended on compass and crude log and which had to allow for the effect of wind and currents. The first leg of a slaver's voyage, if not without danger, was none the less subject only to the normal hazards of the sea. It could take from as little as five weeks to fifteen

[41] Quoted in J. H. Hodson, 'The Letter Book of Robert Bostock, a Merchant in the Liverpool Slave Trade, 1789–1792', *The Liverpool Bulletin,* III (1953) 41 and passim.

[42] Quoted in W. B. Weeden, *Economic and Social History of New England, 1620–1789* (Boston and New York, 1890) II 465.

[43] Crow, *Memoirs,* 183–4; Abbé Raynal, *A Philosophical and Political History of the Settlements and Trade of the Europeans in the East and West Indies,* trans. J. O. Justamond (London, 1783) bk. XI, vol. 6, 97; Rinchon, *Le Trafic Négrier,* 86–8.

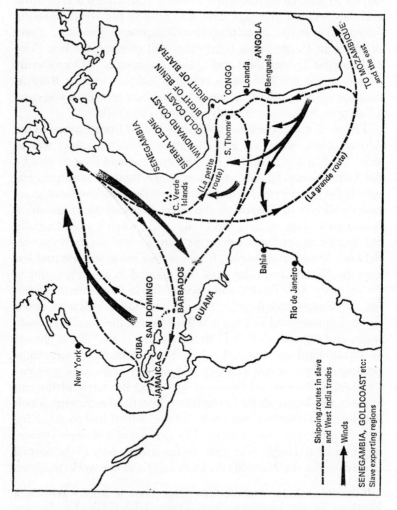

MAP 1. The Atlantic slave trade, slave exporting
regions and maritime routes

or more, depending not so much on the point on the coast aimed for, as the set of the wind.[44]

There were two broad modes of trading – directly with the resident European or mulatto traders, or with African traders under the ageis of established political authority. The first mode could, of course, only be followed in those areas where these foreign traders were established and that establishment, in its turn, could only take place where African political authority was powerless to prevent it or where it was tolerated for the sake of the advantages which it conferred. At the humblest end of the scale was a man like Nics Owen, an Irishman, who, in what proved to be a last attempt to re-establish his family's shattered fortune, began slave trading in the Sherbro region of Sierra Leone in 1754. His capital was trivial, apparently because he and the companions with whom he initially arrived had been deprived of all but life in revenge for the actions of a Dutch captain who had detained and ill-used free members of the coastal people concerned.[45] Owen never seems to have possessed more than a long boat and the scale of his operations can hardly ever have looked like enabling him significantly 'to enlarge my fortune by honest means'.[46] It was, rather, that 'if any of the blacks comes I buy their commodities at as cheap a rate as I can, which enables me to trade aboard the ships once or twice a month, which just keeps me from sinking in the principle stock'.[47] Even this fragile commerce depended on the local people continuing to believe that he had 'ability to do them service',[48] and when a ship appeared determined to trade on

[44] A study of English slaving voyages in 1791 gave the following dura tions for the first leg. The size of the sample is in brackets.

Senegambia (1) 67	Bight of Benin (1) 82
Sierra Leone (8) 70	Bight of Biafra (39) 77
Windward Coast (5) 70	Congo/Angola (6) 90
Gold Coast (3) 71	Unknown (15) 89
	Overall (78) 79

House of Lords Record Office ([Manuscript] Return to an Order of the Right Honourable the House of Lords dated the 10th of July 1799 (Henceforward *Lords A List*).

[45] Nicholas Owen, *Journal of a Slave Dealer: a View of Some Remarkable Accidents in the Life of Nics. Owen on the Coast of Africa and America from the year 1746 to the year 1757*, ed. Eveline C. Martin (London, 1930), 37.

[46] Ibid., 5.

[47] Ibid., 85.

[48] Ibid., 77.

its own account his vulnerability was evident indeed. 'The Sierra Leone brig is arrived, to the great detriment of us traders, who depend upon the good will of the natives for our trade, for the least affront now will keep them from your house, since they know there's a vessel at hand with the best of goods.'[49]

But there were expatriate traders more powerful than this. In the same region was Henry Tucker, a mulatto, who had six or seven wives and numerous children, but who had travelled in Europe and who in many ways lived after the English manner.

> His strength consists of his own slaves and their children, who have built a town about him and serve as his *gremetos* [retainers] upon all occasions. This man bears the character of a fair trader among the Europeans, but to the contrary among the blacks.[50] His riches set him above the kings and his numerous people above being surprised by war; almost all the blacks owe him money, which brings a dread of being stopt [*sic*] upon that account, so that he is esteemed and feared by all who have the misfortune to be in his power.[51]

Tucker also owned a large plantation, one purpose of which was probably to grow the food which was bought by slave ships to supplement the slaves' diet on the middle passage.[52]

It may be that Tucker owed nothing to African tolerance, but it is conceivable that he had at least cemented his position by taking a wife, or wives, from politically important families. Certainly this is what another European trader, Clow by name, who had first resided at Cape Mount and then moved up to one of the Plantanes islands off the Sherbro mouth, had done, for the lady is described as 'a person of some consequence in her own country'.[53] In the Gold Coast, too, union with important local

---

[49] Ibid., 104.

[50] Newton spoke of 'my friend Harry' at Sherbro and adds in a footnote: 'Henry Tucker – there are various spellings of the name, a mulatto, at Shebar, was the man with whom I had the largest connection in business, and by whom I was never deceived' (Newton, *Letters to a Wife*, 229).

[51] Owen, *Journal*, 76.

[52] *A. & P.*, 1790, xxix (698) 587, Evidence of Falconbridge.

[53] Newton, *Authentic Narrative*, 57. This is the woman whom Newton called simply 'P.I.', explaining that these letters conveyed the sound of her name, and who had so terribly ill-treated him during his twelve

families was an important aid to power and wealth, as the career
of Richard Brew illustrates.[54] In contrast, however, to the situation on the borders of Sierra Leone and the Windward coast,
where there was no established European political authority, the
traders on the Gold Coast operated in the protective shadow of
the forts.

Whether under the protecting hand of European authority, as
in Angola, part of Senegal, and on the Gold Coast, or left to their
own devices, as in the Sierra Leone/Windward Coast and Congo
region, resident European or mulatto traders sometimes had a
central role in the slave trade, and a mode of trading developed
accordingly. By whatever means presented itself, contact was
made with likely vendors of slaves, men with whom trade had
previously been done being naturally sought out if possible. 'Pitched
upon Andrew Ross and Peter Freeman [two of several traders
who had come abroad] . . . for my principals, and sent them on
shore with goods for rice, and to look out for slaves', ran a typical
entry in Newton's log.[55] The grant of credit, indeed, seems usually
to have been a part of the commercial relationship by the late
eighteenth century – and it was accorded to African slave traders
as well as to resident European slave merchants. Such business was
often accompanied by the giving of presents, and by 'washmouth',
the civility whereby spirits were offered and cirrhosis of the liver
amply encouraged. But dealings with European or mulatto traders
who owed no tight allegiance to established African political
authority were not characterised by the elaborate system of customs
payments which marked out this trade from trade conducted
under the aegis of African political authorities. Here there was
much more elaboration and large payments had to be made to a
king and his officials before the slave captain was allowed to start
trading. At Bonny the King, or regent, would come off himself to
'break trade', being received with much formality and, by Captain

[54] See Margaret Priestley, *West African Trade and Coast Society: A Family
Study* (London, 1969) especially 106–13.
[55] Newton, *Journal of a Slave Trader*, 28.

---

months' service with Clow, denying him food, water and medicine, and
leaving him to the comfort even of slaves – or of the mastery of the first
six books of Euclid (the solitary author Newton had with him) by working out his theorems on the sand. (Ibid., and Newton, *Journal of a Slave
Trader*, x–xi).

Crow at any rate, with a salute of seven guns. The value of the goods paid over in 'customs', and probably for certain services, was put by Crow in the 1790s at £400 for each ship.[56] The process, as it took place on the Gambia river, is described by the master of a slave ship.

> When a ship arrives in the River Gambia she comes to an anchor at Gillofree Port, in the Kingdom of Barra, opposite James Fort on James's Island. . . . You send your boat on shore to acquaint the Alkaide or Mayor of the town of your arrival; he in common returns with the boat, and receives from you anchorage-money. Ten gallons of liquor for the king, value 30s., and two iron bars for himself, value 7s., and perhaps presents, a few bottles of wine, beer, cyder, etc. He immediately despatches messengers with the liquor as above to the king, informing him that such vessel is arrived, and only wants to pay his Customs, intending to proceed up the river. The king consults his councillors for a proper day to receive the same, and sends word to the Alkaide accordingly. After a detention of four, five, six and seven days, he sends his people to receive his Custom, 140 bars in merchandise, amount sterling on an average £16.

The appointment of interpreters and other necessary intermediaries is then made, at a certain rate.[57] In the more straightforward case of trade with the Kingdom of Dahomey through the port of Whydah, Archibald Dalzell lists in extensive detail, even to the cost of washerwomen and a 'gong-gong beater', the customs there payable, and rates them at the equivalent of £368,[58] close to the Bonny figure.

Such a procedure was unavoidable, then, in places like Bonny, Calabar, Whydah, the Gambia – broadly speaking, that is to say,

[56] Crow, *Memoirs*, 43. Capt. Fraser, who also had much experience of the Bonny trade indicates that the actual handing over of the customs to the King took place when slaving was completed (*A. & P.*, 1790, xxix (698) 20–1).

[57] *A. & P.*, 1789, lxxxiv (646a), pt i (Privy Council Report), Captain Heatley.

[58] Ibid., pt i, Mr Dalzell. For a brief description of an essentially similar process at Loango, Malemba and Cabinda, north of the Congo mouth, see Phyllis Martin, 'The Trade of Loango in the Seventeenth Century and Eighteenth Century', in Richard Gray and David Birmingham (eds.), *Pre-Colonial African Trade* (London, 1970) 154–5; and Rinchon, *Trafic Négrier*, 107, 119–25.

in areas where trade was closely regulated by African political authority. It did not take place in the 'ship' or 'boat' trade carried on with European or mulatto traders, or with petty African traders not under tight political control. The actual business of slave trading also showed variation of a different kind. As Captain Fraser put it: 'On some parts of the Windward and Grain coasts the trade is a mere barter, giving a certain quantity of goods for slaves, according to their appearance, without the intervention of any nominal value.'[59] Although the concluding phrase is highly significant, as apparently denoting an exception from the rule, it appears, again from Fraser's testimony, that trade on the Loango coast might also be 'mere barter'.[60] But in most places where the trade was carried on between European slavers and Africans, there was an agreed standard of value. We have already seen that the standard on the Gambia was the 'bar'. Originally prized as a raw material for iron manufacture, it was an iron bar rather like a stair-rod. Its convenience of handling, and more or less standard size and composition, sometimes transformed it into a medium of exchange also. The bar was also the standard from as far north as Senegal and down to Cape Mount, and again, though in this region it was a brass-rod and was sometimes known as a 'copper', in the Niger delta. From Cape Mount to Cape Palmas, on the southern Windward coast, the unit was the 'piece' (of cloth), whilst from about 1772 onwards on the Gold Coast and along to Whydah the unit was the (trade) ounce or its sixteenth part, the 'ackey'.[61]

---

[59] *A. & P.*, 1790, xxix (698) 23.

[60] Ibid., 9. Fraser was certainly aware of the existence of raffia cloth as a kind of currency on this coast, but implied that it was not suitable for use in transactions involving considerable value (Ibid., 7).

[61] John Matthews, *A Voyage to the River Sierra Leone* (1788), reissue (London, 1966) 141.

The 'ounce' originally signified the amount of goods that could be exchanged for one ounce of gold. It was generally reckoned that this amount of goods would cost about 40s. In Europe, or half the European value of the gold, so the institution of the ounce tended to build in a 'mark-up' for the European trader. Note that the division of the ounce into 16 ackeys made it more flexible. See on this, and for the above section as a whole, Marion Johnson, 'The Ounce in Eighteenth Century West African Trade,' *Journal of African History*, vii (1966) no. 2, 197–214. This valuable article both corrects and clarifies Karl Polanyi, 'Sortings and "Ounce Trade" in the West African Slave Trade', *Journal of African History*, v (1964) no. 3, 381–93.

The standard at Lagos is uncertain, but at Benin, by the late eighteenth century, the standard was a 'cloth', i.e. a standard length of Benin cloth.[62] And though Captain Fraser asserted that his trade on the Loango coast was pure barter, it is clear from the records of the French slave trade that there was a common standard there also, the 'piece'.[63] Once such a standard had evolved all trade goods could be expressed in terms of that standard. Thus at Galam on the Senegal river, in the mid-eighteenth century, one piece of Blue Baft, or one musket, were rated at 8 bars (of 4 livres), whilst at the other extreme 2 lbs. of gunpowder or 80 gunflints were rated at 1 bar.[64] Implicit in such a development is the concept of 'sortings' or assortment, whereby a substantial purchase, such as was a slave, would command not merely a certain number of bars, but bars made up of goods in a specified assortment. In the highly individual ship or boat trade of areas like the Windward Coast there was negotiation at each sale both about the number of bars per slave and the assortment which was to make up each bar. Thus Newton speaks of paying a varying number of bars for slaves – 70 bars on one occasion and 60 bars on two,[65] 63 for a woman slave 'though she had a very bad mouth'[66] and for another 'the excessive price of 86 bars'.[67] At the same time Newton makes it clear that the nature of the assortment making up the bar was a vital factor in trade. Thus a rival captain's superior assortment enabled him 'to bear away all the trade here from a vessel that has only a common assortment'[68] whilst three months later, conceivably because there was no longer competition from this superior assortment, Newton was able to make slave vendors 'take a more equal assortment than they have hitherto done'.[69] By 'equal' is meant a – to him – more favourable balance between goods whose prime

[62] A. F. C. Ryder, *Benin and the Europeans, 1485–1897* (London, 1969) 207–8.

[63] Rinchon, *Trafic Négrier*, 104–5.

[64] T. S. Ashton (ed.), *Letters of a West African Trader, Edward Grace, 1767–70* (London, 1950) 40.

[65] Newton, *Journal of a Slave Trader*, 24.

[66] Ibid., 28–9.

[67] Ibid., 29.

[68] Ibid., p. 13. To take a further example amongst many, several Nantes slaving voyages were recognised as having failed in the mid-sixties 'because they were badly assorted' (Quoted in P. Rinchon, *Les Armements Négriers au XVIII*[e] Siècle (Brussels, 1956) 35.

[69] Newton, *Journal of a Slave Trader*, 24.

cost (in Europe) was high in relation to equivalents accepted on the coast and goods whose prime cost was low. A combination of goods was frequently preferred by the African or resident European party to the transaction and this gave scope for the exercise of entrepreneurial skill. Professor Polanyi expands the significance of Newton's corrective action when he points out that, although the amount of a particular good which was to equal a bar might tend to remain the same, at least in some places, owing to the inertia of convention, the sortings system permitted the slave trader to maximise his profit by slanting the assortment in favour of those goods whose prime cost was low.[70] Polanyi also argues that at Whydah the rates at which all the different imported trade goods might be exchanged for slaves was set by the King or his officer, and that subsequent bargaining was restricted to the amounts and proportions of the goods chosen from the assortments.[71] This claim is also made of Calabar, though without evidence, but it appears to be the way things were done at Benin in the late eighteenth century.[72] Certainly there is no evidence that absence of bargaining over individual purchases was universal. We have noted the variation in the slave prices on the Windward Coast whilst Heatley's account of commercial procedure in Gambia where trade was carried on under the aegis of African political authority, makes it clear that the price of a slave, as well as the assortment of goods making up a bar, was negotiated directly with the owner. The difference between this negotiation and the dealings on shipboard of the type carried on by Newton, or by Nics Owen, was merely one of scale. One commercial negotiation, in the former case, sufficed for more slaves simply because the seller had more to sell, though certainly there was a presumption that batches of slaves offered subsequently to the first batch would command the same price. 'Price and principal articles once fixed upon,' said Heatley, 'it seldom varies . . .'[73]

For the student, as for the participants, there was much more to slave trading than simple understanding of the mechanisms of

[70] Polanyi, 'Sortings and "Ounce Trade"', 385. Polanyi's article is a little expanded in his *Dahomey and the Slave Trade* (Seattle and London, 1966) ch. 10. For the desirability of pushing one ingredient in an assortment more than another see also *Letters of a West African Trader*, 23.

[71] Polanyi, 'Sortings and "Ounce Trade"', 384–5.

[72] Ryder, *Benin and the Europeans*, 209.

[73] *A. & P.*, 1789, xxvi (646a), pt i, Capt. Heatley's evidence.

exchange and assortments. All accounts speak of the infinite worry and considerable hazard of slaving, and not least, of the worry of waiting when trade was slack. 'Ye trade is so very dull it is actuly a noof to make a man Creasey', wrote a Rhode Island captain[74] in an intriguing eighteenth-century variant of American English. It was a fact of hard experience that the dangerous period for the crew of a slaver was while the ship was waiting cargo on the coast. To minimise this risk the French trader Van Alstein, for instance, recommended that the officer with the best knowledge of the coast be sent off on a quite prolonged reconnaissance in a shallop to note availability of slaves, of competing slavers, etc., at the various points on the coast, whilst the slaver remained a little way out to sea.[75] Some slaving firms seem to have had resident agents and sometimes their own small boats permanently on the coast,[76] or up the rivers, as with the British on the Gambia,[77] a manifestation of the principle more obviously apparent in the Gold Coast forts. Slaves could be gradually collected and would thus be available for loading without a long delay. In a closely controlled trade, as at Bonny, the ships that had been waiting longest might be given the preference as fresh slaves became available,[78] but their wait was still likely to be almost four months. Only if a cargo was waiting, or if a slave captain happened to find few competitors, or if the portion of the coast was not heavily slaved, was the stay brief, and none of these conditions were common by the later eighteenth century. Something over four months seems to have been usual in the English trade.[79] Whilst in a place like Calabar, given that trade was once begun, the slave ship just had to wait while the

[74] Quoted in *Commerce of Rhode Island*, 1 60.

[75] Rinchon, *Trafic Négrier*, 106, 160.

[76] Crow, *Memoirs*, 34; *A. & P.*, 1790, xxix (698) 503. The firms were John Dawson and John and Thomas Hodgson and Co., respectively.

[77] P. Labarthe, *Voyage au Senegal pendant les années 1784 et 1785* (Paris, 1802) 120.

[78] Crow, *Memoirs*, 142; much the same happened on the Loango coast, but for rather different reasons (Rinchon, *Trafic Négrier*, 106–7).

[79] The *Lords A List* gives these figures, in days, for average stay on the coast in 1791. The size of the sample is in brackets:

Senegambia (1) 70	Bight of Benin (1) 124
Sierra Leone (8) 200	Bight of Biafra (35) 118
Windward Coast (5) 155	Congo and Angola (5) 67
Gold Coast (3) 138	Unknown (13) 126
	Overall (71) 128

complement of slaves was slowly loaded, in the unregulated conditions of the Windward Coast the slave captain either had to wait for vendors to come on board or had to open business with them himself. In the second case, it was almost implicit that the slaves were not immediately available and the request that the slave captain provide the prospective vendor with trade goods on trust was almost automatic. Moreover, this was a trade where many slave captains made fraud a daily practice. As Newton testified, with 'many of our people',

> not an article that is capable of diminution or adulturation is delivered genuine or entire. The spirits are lowered by water. False heads are put into the kegs that contain the gunpowder; . . . The linen and cotton cloths are opened, and two or three yards . . . cut off, not from the end, but out of the middle, where it is not so readily noticed.[80]

This being so, the slave captain was hardly likely to expect better conduct in return, yet he often had to risk his stock on trust or would be unable to make enough purchases in due time. The very landing of goods on shore was subject to the hazard of the surf, whilst many were the muskets, blue bafts and worsteds given on credit to purchase slaves for one slave ship but then traded to buy slaves for another. To meet the lack of confidence it was general, on important sections of the coast, certainly in Angola and on the Windward Coast, to leave 'pawns', usually a relation of the African trader, on board the slave ship against his return with the promised slaves.[81] But even this arrangement did not always work out satisfactorily.[82]

If a slave captain sought to reduce delay by sending his own ship's boats into the creeks and estuaries of the coast he ran the risk not so much of 'palavers' with Africans tempted by the vulnerability of a small boat, though these were frequent, but of

[80] John Newton, *Thoughts upon the African Slave Trade* (London, 1788), reprinted in *Journal of a Slave Trader*, 106.

[81] *A. & P.*, 1790, xxix (698) 15–16. Evidence of Captain Fraser.

[82] E.g., if the value of the pawn as a slave was not equal to the value of the goods. But even when genuinely forfeited there seems to have been a reluctance – perhaps born of hopes to do business with the same trader on a future voyage – to actually carry the pawn off, for slave-ship captains often transferred pawns to another slaver on leaving the coast (*A. & P.*, 1789, xxvi (646a) pt ii, A. Dalzell's evidence).

sharply raising the incidence of death and illness amongst his crew. The absences of days and even weeks in open boats wrought deadly work amongst the crews, and Newton records an occasion when one of his boats only got back to the ship because of the exertions of the women slaves who were its cargo.[83] It was whilst on the coast that 'epidemical fevers and fluxes' (dysentery) were contracted and here lies the origin of the high death rate amongst the crews of slavers: 21·6% of the original crews of 350 Liverpool and Bristol slavers between 1784 and 1790 died.[84]

Once the slaves were on board in any number the problem of keeping them secure arose – indeed, it was most acute whilst the ship remained on the coast and in sight of land, when escape still seemed a prospect. When below on the slave deck men slaves at any rate were kept shackled in pairs, left wrist to right wrist and left leg to right leg, and when on the upper deck a looser form of shackling was usual. But even shackles could be forced and mutinies were frequent. Newton experienced a slave rising on both of the voyages he made as master.

> *Monday 11th December* [1752] . . . By the favour of Divine Providence made a timely discovery to-day that the slaves were forming a plot for an insurrection. Surprized two of them attempting to get off their irons, and upon farther search in their rooms, upon the information of 3 of the boys, found some knives, stones, shot, etc., and a cold chisel. Upon enquiring there appeared 8 principally concerned to move in projecting the mischief and 4 boys in supplying them with the above instruments. Put the boys in irons and slightly in the thumbscrews to urge them to a full confession. . . .
> *Tuesday 12th December* . . . In the morning examined the men slaves and punished 6 of the principal, put 4 of them in collars.[85]

---

[83] Newton, *Journal of a Slave Trader*, 29–30.

[84] *A. & P.*, 1790–91, xxxiv (748) 276–81. Abstracts of Muster Rolls.

[85] Newton, *Journal of a Slave Trader*, 71. But cf. Newton's remark in his later *Thoughts upon the Slave Trade*, 103–4, by which time he had become convinced of the trade's uniquity. When a slave divulges a plot for a mutiny 'the traitor to the cause of liberty is caressed, rewarded, and deemed an honest fellow. The patriots, who formed and animated the plan, if they can be found out, must be treated as villains, and punished. to intimidate the rest.'

Most of the provisions, for slaves as well as crew, were brought out in the original cargo, but some captains in some parts of the coast brought in yams and even fruit, and sometimes such produce, together with the substantial quantities of water needed and wood for firing, were hard to come by. But eventually the sails used as awnings over the upper deck were unbent, the anchor checked to see that it was clear, final debts, hopefully, regulated. When a favourable wind caressed the slave ship she put to sea, and even in the unemotional pages of ships' logs there is commonly a felt note of relief as the captain records the circumstance. Amongst the slaves, however, reactions were somewhat different. The situation of the plantation slave scarcely encouraged the writing of autobiography, but we do have one slave's reaction to a slaveship.

The first object which saluted my eyes when I arrived on the coast was the sea, and a slave ship which was then riding at anchor and waiting for its cargo. These filled me with astonishment, which was soon converted into terror when I was carried on board. I was immediately handled and tossed up to see if I were sound by some of the crew, and I was now persuaded that I had gotten into a world of bad spirits and that they were going to kill me. Their complexions too differing so much from ours, their long hair and the language they spoke (which was very different from any I had ever heard) united to confirm me in this belief. Indeed such were the horrors of my views and fears at the moment that, if ten thousand worlds had been my own, I would have freely parted with them all to have exchanged my condition with that of the meanest slave in my own country. When I looked round the ship too and saw a large furnace or copper boiling and a multitude of black people of every description chained together, every one of their countenances expressing dejection and sorrow, I no longer doubted of my fate; and quite overpowered with horror and anguish, I fell motionless on the deck and fainted. When I recovered a little I found some black people about me, who I believed were some of those who had brought me on board and had been receiving their pay; they talked to me in order to cheer me, but all in vain. I asked them if we were not to be eaten by those white men with horrible looks, red faces, and loose hair. They told me I was not, and one of the crew brought me a small portion of spirituous liquor in a wine glass, but being afraid of him I would not take it out of his hand. One of the blacks therefore took it from him and gave it to me, and I took a little down my palate, which instead of reviving me, as they thought it would, threw me into the greatest consternation at the strange feeling it produced, having never tasted such any liquor before. Soon after this the blacks who brought me on board went off, and left me abandoned to despair.[86]

Once the middle passage had begun the concern of the captain was simply to get his cargo to market. Navigation and the care of the slaves were therefore his main worries. Getting away from the African coast might be difficult but for most of the year, the S.E. Trades, once they had been picked up, would take the vessel, more or less before the wind, across the Atlantic. There was still, of course, the fear of being becalmed if the wind dropped away or, conversely, of storms. A normal voyage took about eight weeks, the duration being largely determined by the time it took to strike into the Trades.[87] From the point of view of the slave-ship captain the bringing of the cargo to market was a function of storage, the maintenance of security and the preservation of health. Storage was usually on shelves which divided the slave deck horizontally, leaving only a passage way in the middle. There were separate rooms for men, women and boys. The total headroom was only about five feet and so the slaves had headroom of precisely half that. Up until the late 1780s slave merchants worked on a ratio of at least two slaves per ton, but in 1788 British slavers were limited to five slaves per three tons up to 207 tons registered burthen, and one slave per ton thereafter. In 1799 there was a further limitation to approximately one per ton. Even after regulation, slavers were pretty tightly packed, and the provision of air ports, gratings and the occasional ventilator (not favoured because they took

---

[86] *Equiano's Travels*, ed. Paul Edwards (London, 1967) 25–6.
[87] This is apparent from the following sample of passage times in 1791:

Senegambia (1) 13 days	Bight of Biafra (35) 57 days
Sierra Leone (8) 40 days	Congo and Angola (6) 49 days
Windward Coast (5) 65 days	Unknown (13) 57 days
Gold Coast (3) 78 days	Overall (72) 53 days
Bight of Benin (1) 57 days	(*Lords A List*)

up too much space) was usually insufficient in hot weather, whilst the 'windsail', or crude device for forcing air through the slave deck, was dependent on sufficient wind. In bad weather as many orifices as possible had to be closed, and the windsail unbent. If slave mutinies were most common whilst the slaver was still on the coast, they were not infrequent during the passage. To prevent them the men slaves were usually kept shackled in pairs, whilst below, or by a loose chain when on deck, but were sometimes released during the crossing if it was felt that they had become reconciled to their fate. The women and the boys were not normally shackled.

Security to be absolute would have been self-defeating. The slaves had to be kept in health and for this food was the first requisite. Two meals a day were normal but occasionally three seem to have been given. If two, one would often be composed of 'country provisions' and especially yams or rice, whilst the other would consist of foods like barley, corn and biscuit and, rarely, meat, the whole being boiled up into 'a warm mess'. To one or both meals a garnishing of pepper, palm oil or stock fish might be added. We possess an account of the total provisions consumed on the 50 day middle passages of the *Brothers,* Captain Sherwood, in 1789, when the diet per day, per head worked out at about 3 lb. 10 oz. of yam, 10 oz. of biscuit, $3\frac{1}{2}$ oz. of beans, 2 oz. of flour, a large but unspecifiable amount of salt beef (this was unusual), together with a plantain or a head of Indian corn on three days out of five.[88] In addition to this a mouth wash of lime juice or vinegar was commonly given at the morning meal, to prevent scurvy, and water in abundance, always provided enough had been taken on board. Exercise was regarded as necessary and this was induced through 'dancing'. Defenders of the trade contrived to suggest this was a kind of pastoral idyll with good cheer on deck, a beautiful clime and, no doubt, gambolling dolphins looking on approvingly. In practice the dance consisted of jumping up and down, rhythmical to the extent that loose shackles permitted, with the laggards encouraged by a cat-o'-nine-tails.

Unless the weather was bad, the slaves were kept on deck through the day, returning below decks after dinner, the evening meal. During their absence the slave deck was scrubbed out, disinfected with vinegar and lime juice, and dried out by burning

[88] *A. & P.*, 1790, xxix (698) 494, Captain Sherwood's evidence.

tar, tobacco or brimstone in fire pans. Most English slave ships carried a surgeon but not American vessels. If a slave fell sick from fever, or dysentery or other cause he was removed to the 'hospital', usually a bare compartment set apart for the purpose, and given medicine and wine. Remembering the limitations of eighteenth-century medical skill his chances of recovery cannot have been materially better if the physic were prescribed by a surgeon rather than administered, when there was no surgeon, according to 'a book of directions' which was normally carried. Recovery was a chancy thing but losses on any scale nearly always stemmed from an epidemic of dysentery, measles or smallpox, as exacerbated by deficiency of provisions and hygiene, and protraction of the voyage. Occasionally a slave resolutely refused to live in captivity and resisted flogging and forcible feeding – to make this possible a *speculum oris*, or a bolus knife, was first inserted – sufficiently to die.[89] That overcrowding was a factor affecting mortality is attested by the reduction in the death rate after the commencement of regulation in the English slave trade. To the statistics of that mortality we now turn.

Figures for mortality, as for most other things to do with the English slave trade, are more systematic from 1789 than before but the evidence which several captains of slave ships gave to the Privy Council Committee in 1789 gives us quite a good random sample. From 1789 onwards we have much better information, consisting of large samples for several years, based either on the collation of masters' and surgeons' logs, or on Customs entries in the West Indies. The result is the following mortality rate for the British trade, projected figures being bracketed:

[89] This composite picture of conditions on a slave ship is derived from many sources, but see especially Newton, *Journal of a Slave Trader*, passim; *A. & P.*, 1789, xxvi (646a) pt ii. Evidence of Sir George Young, Thomas Eldred, James Penny, Robert Norris, Alexander Falconbridge, Archibald Dalzell, Captain Hall, Robert Heatley, John Anderson, James Bowen, William James and David Henderson; *A. & P.*, 1790, xxix (698), Evidence of James Fraser, Captain Sherwood and Mr Wilson (All of these had been engaged in the slave trade save for one who was a naval officer who had served on the West African coast [Sir George Young]); Rinchon, *Trafic Négrier*, 161–4, 201–8.

	%		%
1761–68	[8·5]	1793	5·5
1769–87	8·5	1794	3·2
1788	[9·6]	1795	2·7
1789	9·6	1796	3·4
1790	[9·6]	1797	4·2
1791	9·5	1798–1807	[4·0][90]
1792	8·4		

These figures suggest that the restrictions imposed by Dolben's Act, coupled as they were with provision for the payment of premiums to the master and surgeon when mortality was less than 3%,[91] were effective enough to more than halve the death rate – though there was a puzzling five years before the death rate dropped sharply. For the slave trade of the other European nations involved, none of which imposed official restrictions or the same kind of inducements, a level of 10% is probably correct for the half century as a whole.[92]

Consciously mirroring the attitudes of most Europeans up to the later years of the eighteenth century – and the views of the African coastal kings and traders also – we have presented the Atlantic slave trade principally as a business venture, as an economic phenomenon. But is an explanation on this level justified since it would seem to ignore the brutalities and atrocities attendant on the trade? A distinction must, in fact, be made between brutality and atrocity. What would certainly now be, and possibly then was, regarded as brutal was certainly accepted as necessary. Life was more overtly brutish than now, a truism evident not least in the relative treatment of seamen and slaves. Harsh treatment of sailors was the rule and not only on slave ships. Newton himself, who in his tempestuous youth had been flogged for desertion from a man of war, merely suffered what thousands of others had suffered, and, when captain of a slaver, there was little difference in the punishments he meted out to refractory seamen and refractory slaves – both stood to be put in irons, whilst the former were

[90] See Appendix 1 for the basis of these calculations.

[91] £100 to the master and £50 to the surgeon on each cargo when mortality was less than 2%, and half these amounts if the mortality were between 2% and 3%.

[92] See Appendix 1.

given the 'cat'[93] and a few of the latter, as we have seen, put 'slightly' in thumbscrews. Nor did the quarters of slaves and sailors differ greatly. Lacking clothing, the slaves suffered greatly in cold weather, but at least had shelter below. So full was a slave ship, however, that the crew might totally lack shelter, nor might they be much better clad, or any better fed – after all, they were not being taken to market! The treatment of both slaves and crew depended basically on the captain, and there were both good and bad, but Clarkson revealed an important truth about the slave trade when he demonstrated from the ships' muster rolls that the death rate amongst the crews of slavers was nearly twice that of the slaves,[94] a rate which was subsequently confirmed by the Inspector-General of the Customs.[95]

But apart from frequent harshness and brutality there was a separate order of ill-treatment which can only be termed atrocity. Thus a Captain Williams would personally flog slaves who refused to eat, 'delighting in such operations', and severely beat women slaves who refused to sleep with him. He deprived sick sailors of their victuals and took the hammock away from one to be the shroud of another; he assaulted the chief mate, knocked the surgeon unconscious and narrowly avoided killing his own (obnoxious) son who served as cabin boy.[96] Again, the captain of the *Zong,* in 1781, threw 132 of his slave cargo overboard, when threatened by an epidemic, having taken good care to confirm that the slaves were covered by the insurance.[97] Seventeen years earlier in 1764, Captain Marshall of the *Black Joke* vented his sadism on a child. One Isaac Parker described the incident to the Commons Select Committee, and there seems no reason to disbelieve him.

[93] Newton, *Journal of a Slave Trader*, 87–8.

[94] *A. & P.*, 1789, xxvi (646a), pt ii, Thomas Clarkson's Evidence.

[95] *A. & P.*, 1790–91, xxxiv (748) 276–81. Of 12,263 original crew members on 350 Liverpool and Bristol slavers, 1784–90, 2643 died on the voyage – i.e. 21·6%.

[96] *A. & P.*, 1789, xxvi (646a) pt ii, Evidence of James Arnold (the surgeon in question) who brought suit against Williams in the King's Bench. For another instance of ill-treatment of the crew see A. Falconbridge, *An Account of the Slave Trade on the Coast of Africa* (London, 1788), 39–50.

[97] Described in, amongst other places, R. Coupland, *The British Anti-Slavery Movement* (London, 1933), 59–60.

What were the circumstances of this child's ill-treatment? The child took sulk and would not eat . . . the captain took the child up in his hand, and flogged it with the cat. Do you remember anything more about this child? Yes; the child had swelled feet; the captain desired the cook to put on some water to heat to see if he could abate the swelling, and it was done. He then ordered the child's feet to be put into the water, and the cook putting his finger into the water, said, 'Sir, it is too hot'. The captain said, 'Damn it, never mind it, put the feet in,' and so doing the skin and nails came off, and he got some sweet oil and cloths and wrapped round the feet in order to take the fire out of them; and I myself bathed the feet with oil, and wrapped cloths around; and laying the child on the quarter deck in the afternoon at mess time, I gave the child some victuals, but it would not eat; the captain took the child up again, and flogged it, and said, 'Damn you, I will make you eat,' and so he continued in that way for four or five days at mess time, when the child would not eat, and flogged it, and he tied a log of mango, eighteen or twenty inches long, and about twelve or thirteen pound weight, to the child by a string round its neck. The last time he took the child up and flogged it, and let it drop out of his hands, 'Damn you (says he) I will make you eat, or I will be the death of you;' and in three quarters of an hour after that the child died. He would not suffer any of the people that were on the quarter deck to heave the child overboard, but he called the mother of the child to heave it overboard. She was not willing to do so, and I think he flogged her; but I am sure that he beat her in some way for refusing to throw the child overboard; at last he made her take the child up, and she took it in her hand, and went to the ship's side, holding her head on one side, because she would not see the child go out of her hand, and she dropped the child overboard. She seemed to be very sorry, and cried for several hours.

It comes as an added horror to learn the age of the child – nine months.[98] It is possibly significant that such men treated their crews at least as badly as their slaves; captains of this type may well have been found in other trades as well. It is no less likely that the whole *ambiance* of the slave ship loosened such constraints as

[98] *A. & P.*, 1790, xxx (699), 122–4, 127, Evidence of Isaac Parker.

those to which they were otherwise subject. But atrocity, in the above senses, was surely exceptional in the degree that sadism is exceptional. For most captains, mates and surgeons an elementary self-interest sufficed to ensure a modium of care, albeit harshly exercised on occasions, for their slaves in their holds. Self-interest, even before the additional premiums provided for in Dolben's Act were considerable. As one slave-captain, Captain Fraser, put it.

> If any of the slaves die, the surgeon loses [on] his head money [usually one shilling for each slave sold], and the Captain [on] his commission; if the slaves are brought in bad order to market, they average low, and the officers' privilege slaves, which are generally paid them on an average with the cargo, are of less value to them.[99]

Captain Heatley put it more succinctly: 'Reason will surely allow (tho' the officers may have no merit) that motives of interest point out the necessity of doing all that is done in treatment and attention.'[100]

The slaver captain's commercial responsibilities were not at an end when, after careful soundings and anxious care to recognise whatever promontory came into view, he eventually made a landfall in the Americas. But in his next task, the sale of the slaves, he was usually referred by his owners to a slave factor. Thus Edward Grace instructed Captain Williamson to take his slave cargo to Barbados 'where Messrs. John and Thomas Tipping will take up the sloop, dispose of the slaves and procure you a freight home'.[101] Sometimes there was a quick sale, sometimes the market was glutted and a weary master and crew had to sail on to some other port or island in hope of finding a better vent, and with a cargo on whom confinement and duress might well be seriously beginning to tell. There were three modes of selling the slaves. A slave factor might purchase the slaves, or some of them, on his own

---

[99] *A. & P.*, 1790, xxix (698) 29. Fraser explains that captains' commissions were increasingly paid on the proceeds in the West Indies, rather than by giving them a commission on goods sold on the coast, plus privilege slaves, as in former days. For the similar treatment of French captains see Rinchon, *Trafic Négrier*, 168–70.

[100] *A. & P.*, 1789, xxvi (646a) pt ii, Capt. Heatley's evidence.

[101] Grace to Williamson, 25 July 1768, in *Letters of a West African Trader*, 25.

account and then sell them off 'retail' as local planters came to him. Or there might be an auction, especially of the sick, the aged and the young. Finally there was the 'scramble', a free-for-all whereby slaves were sold at one price and, at a given signal, the prospective purchasers rushed on board the ship, seized what they could and encircled their purchases with a piece of cloth.[102] Under such a system any families that might have been enslaved were likely to be broken up, though a few captains tried to sell flesh and blood together. Let Equiano describe the process – he had every right to do so. In his case the slaves had previously been sorted into groups.

> We were sold after their usual manner, which is this: on a signal given (as the beat of a drum) the buyers rush at once into the yard where the slaves are confined, and make choice of that parcel they like best. The noise and clamour with which this is attended and the eagerness visible in the countenances of the buyers serve not a little to increase the apprehensions of the terrified Africans, who may well be supposed to consider them as the ministers of that destruction to which they think themselves devoted. In this manner, without scruple, are relations and friends separated, most of them never to see each other again.[103]

There was much variation in the price which slaves might command, variation in supply and demand from market to market, age, sex and condition constituting the variables. Representative, since British slave traders sold to most transatlantic markets, are the estimated average prices gained for slaves by British slavers in the five decades 1761–1807, namely £29, £35, £36, £50 and £60.[104]

In the early days of the slave trade it was triangular in the fullest sense, namely with a cargo carried on each leg. By the 1760s however, it had become general for English slave traders to take the bulk of the proceeds of the sale of Negroes in a bill of exchange though they continued to take 'on freight' such procedure as might be available without prolonged waiting.[105] The West Indiamen

---

[102] *Liverpool and Slavery*, 47–51.

[103] *Equiano's Travels*, 31–32.

[104] See Table 1, p. 47 below.

[105] See pp. 42, 45 below for a brief discussion of this point, but note meanwhile that the *Lords A List* was intended to include particulars of the cargoes of slave ships on their way home from the West Indies, but failed to

specially built for the direct trade could carry bulk freight more economically than vessels built basically to carry slaves, and could better arrange the timing of its voyage to fit in with the season when homeward cargoes of produce were on offer. Dutch slave ships, to give a contrary case, stuck consistently to the old pattern, and the longer duration of their voyages – eighteen months seems to have been the rule[106] as against just over twelve months for the English[107] – was almost certainly due to spending a longer time waiting cargo. Full or empty the slave ship turned eastwards across the Atlantic. Hazard by storm was still a lively risk, especially for a vessel whose sails and rigging and crew were no longer fresh. But with luck some landmark like the old Head of Kinsale on the south-western tip of Ireland, or Ushant, was sighted, and that gave the near prospect of dropping anchor in the Mersey or finding safe moorings in Nantes. The crew were paid off and the completion of voyage accounts put in hand. Another voyage in an age-old commerce had come to an end. Some of those who had served in the slave trade rebelled against its cruelties: many more saw it, like Nics Owen, as a way of enlarging fortune 'by honest means' or, as Newton said of men of his age, 'accounted [it] a genteel employment'.[108] 'An African Merchant', writing in 1772, was conscious that the slave trade was in some danger from those who 'under the specious plea of establishing universal freedom, endeavour to strike at the root of this trade'. But, he went on, the African trade was 'the foundation of our commerce, the support of our colonies, the life of our

---

[106] Unger, 'Bijdragen', 162, 164.
[107] *A. & P.*, 1790–91, xxxiv (748) 281.
[108] Newton, *Authentic Narrative*, 148.

---

do so for a somewhat curious reason, conveyed in a note attached to the return: 'The column which in pursuance of your Lordships' order should have contained the particular cargoes of the African ships that departed from the West India islands is of necessity left blank as it unfortunately happened that the accounts transmitted home by the Collectors and Comptrollers of the respective islands were stolen out of the office at the Customs House about three years ago by a clerk who sold them for waste paper . . .' There is a stark note in the way in which the note continues – 'for which offence he was ordered to be prosecuted; but was afterwards, in consideration of some compassionate circumstances forgiven on consideration that he should transport himself to the coast of Africa, where he died soon after.'

navigation, and first cause of our national industry and riches.'[109] Before we go on to examine that movement to abolish the trade which 'an African Merchant' was already beginning to fear, we must note how extensive it actually was, and determine what order of profits it generated.

[109] An African Merchant, *A Treatise upon the Trade from Great Britain to Africa, humbly recommended to the Attention of Government* (London, 1772) 7.

2 The Profitability of the Slave Trade, 1761–1810

Until recently it was universally supposed that the Atlantic slave trade, over the three and a half centuries of its life, was both vast and extremely profitable. As Philip Curtin pointed out in his masterly *The Atlantic Slave Trade: a Census*, the consensus of guesses was that slave imports to the Americas ran out at between fifteen and twenty million but a figure of forty million, or even higher, was sometimes claimed. The only twentieth-century attempt – by Noel Deerr – to construct an overall estimate had an outcome significantly lower – 11,970,000 slaves imported – but was tucked away in *A History of Sugar* (London, 1949-50, 2 vols). Curtin's conclusion is that the total of *imports* is 'extremely unlikely' to 'turn out to be less than eight million, or more than 10,500,000'; Curtin's actual totals come to 9,566,000 imported – but he is reluctant to invest that figure with particular significance[1] As regards the period 1761–1810 Curtin's *export* total is 3,338,300.[2]

Our own calculations result in figures somewhat higher. They are tabulated below by national sector, with Curtin's export figure shown in brackets.

Carrier	Exported	Imported
Britain	1,535,622 (1,385,300)	1,428,701
Portugal	1,055,700 (1,010,400)	950,130
France	595,881 (545,300)	539,379
13 Colonies/ U.S.A.	294,900 (166,900)	265,410
Netherlands	116,416 (173,600)	102,097
Denmark	59,896 (56,800)	53,906
Total	3,658,415 (3,338,300)	3,339,623

[1] Philip D. Curtin, *The Atlantic Slave Trade: a Census* (Wisconsin, 1969) 8–13, 87, 268.

[2] Ibid., 142, 200, 211–13.

For the British trade it will be convenient also to give a decennial breakdown:

Period	Exported	Imported
1761–70	311,294	284,834
1771–80	254,691	233,042
1781–90	323,446	294,865
1791–1800	419,571	398,404
1801–07	226,620	217,556
Total	1,535,622	1,428,701

Note: The figure for slaves imported in the British, French and Dutch trades is a calculated figure: in the case of the other carriers 10% mortality has been assumed. See Appendix 1.

Sources: The (detailed) calculations on the British trade are contained in Roger Anstey, 'The Volume and Profitability of the British Slave Trade, 1761–1807', *Race and Slavery in the Western Hemisphere: Quantitative Studies*, ed. Stanley Engerman and Eugene D. Genovese (Princeton, N.J., 1974), but differ to the marginal extent that it subsequently proved possible to add in figures for the Lancaster and Whitehaven trades in the sixties and seventies. The estimates for the other national sectors will, it is hoped, be published shortly. They draw on published work to a fair extent but include, notably, a re-working of the evidence on the French and American slave trades.

There were other carriers in the trade – notably Swedes and Brandenburgers – but from the paucity of references to them in the literature their involvement can only have been small; it is difficult to believe that their contribution could raise the total export figure to above 3,700,000. Our figure – 3,658,400, when rounded to the nearest hundred – is 9·6 per cent higher than Curtin's total for the period. When one recalls that many conjectures have run out at a level two or three times higher than the estimates of Curtin and ourself, the significant thing is much more the similarity than the difference. Moreover, our version is well within Curtin's own range of tolerable error.

That the slave trade was highly profitable has long been the accepted wisdom. General books on the subject vie with each other in choice of extravagant adjectives appropriate to their large claims. Monographs, if still imprecise, can be almost as expansive. Thus, for example, Wadsworth and Mann in *The Cotton Trade and Industrial Lancashire* speak of the 'large fortunes [which] were to be made in the slave trade', and cite a contemporary opinion, albeit of the late seventeenth century, that in respect of the far less profitable direct West India trade, a merchant still recovered his money if one ship in three came safely home, that he made a good profit if two returned, and that on average only one voyage in five miscarried.[3] This is in fact to say that profits averaged 140 per cent in the West India trade and something over and above this in the slave trade. Eric Williams in *Capitalism and Slavery* is a little undecided: he cites approvingly the contemporary opinion reported by Wadsworth and Mann[4] – but also cites another, late eighteenth-century Liverpool estimate that slave-trading profits accruing to the merchants of that town between 1783 and 1793 amounted to over 30 per cent.[5] A distinguished historian of ideas, Peter Gay, asserts that at about this same period aggregate profits were between 30 per cent and 40 per cent[6] – a view which is significant in that Gay clearly believes himself to be expressing the received wisdom on that matter. Indeed, the 30–40 per cent estimate has been widely reproduced,[7] partly no doubt because it appears in Donnan.[8] Its origin, however, is a Liverpool observer writing in 1797 and quoted in *Liverpool and Slavery* (1884) who calculated that a decade earlier the profit on the Liverpool slave trade was upwards of 30 per cent.[9] Nor has the conclusion that profitability was high merely the significance of a sombre commentary on human nature, for the triangular trade, of which the slave trade was an integral part, has for half a century, at least, been regarded as an important source of the capital which made possible the Industrial Revolution. 'The triangular trade',

[3] A. P. Wadsworth and Julia de L. Mann, *The Cotton Trade and Industrial Lancashire* (Manchester, 1931), 148, 151, 225.

[4] Williams, *Capitalism and Slavery*, 36–7. Williams implies that the contemporary opinion related to the late eighteenth century whereas it is clear from Wadsworth and Mann that it is a judgement pertaining to a century earlier.

[5] Ibid., 36.

[6] Peter Gay, *The Enlightenment: an Interpretation. Volume II: The Science of Freedom* (New York, 1969), 420.

[7] For example by Wadsworth and Mann, *The Cotton Trade and Lancashire*, 228; Gomer Williams, *History of the Liverpool Privateers*, 598; and is implied in Basil Davidson, *Black Mother* (London, 1961) 78, which otherwise strikes a cautious note about slave trading profits.

[8] Donnan, *Documents*, II 625–7.

[9] *Liverpool and Slavery*, 111.

wrote Eric Williams, 'made an enormous contribution to Britain's industrial development. The profits from this trade fertilised the entire productive system of the country.'[10]

The volume estimate previously noted is a key to the important task of gauging the return on the slave trade. This is quite simply because whereas there are too few complete and compatible voyage accounts to rate as a sufficient sample, there is much more evidence about the separate components of the voyage account. Here the wealth of evidence may be on slave prices; there it may be on voyage costs; elsewhere it may be valuable on, say, depreciation. An illuminating way to maximise the use of this relatively abundant partial evidence is to relate it to the units which feature in the volume estimate, the slave and the ton, and in this manner to surmount the problem of absence of sufficient complete voyage accounts.

Given, then, the volume estimates from which to start, we can immediately link volume to what is, on the whole, good evidence of the slave trader's main return – the price paid for his slaves in the Caribbean. For the first three decades under our view we have good evidence – some thirty-four indications, usually of 'prices round' (expressed in pound sterling, or readily convertible thereto), for the decade 1761–70, forty-four for the following decade, and twenty-nine for the period 1781–90. There is therefore a firm basis for attributing to those decades average prices for newly-landed slaves of £29, £35 and £36 respectively. For the 'nineties, when there are seven indications only, but of which one is an excellent tabulation of purchases of 196 new slaves by the Worthy Park plantation in Jamaica, between 1792 and 1797, we must postulate £50, and for the years 1801–07, when there are again seven indications, we must suggest £60.[11]

---

[10] Williams, *Capitalism and Slavery*, 105. See also 63: 'It was only the capital accumulation of Liverpool which called the population of Lancashire into existence and stimulated the manufacturers of Manchester. That capital accumulation came from the slave trade, whose importance was appreciated more by contemporaries than by later historians'. In this section, it should be noted, Williams is stressing the regional role of profits from the slave trade. Elsewhere he is careful to observe that profits from the triangular trade were not the only source of capital for the Industrial Revolution (see 52 and 98); P. Mantoux, *The Industrial Revolution in the Eighteenth Century*, New Impression (London, 1962) 107–8.

[11] See Appendix 2.

We have thus arrived at the basic element of one of the major components of an overall voyage account: but that gross sale price was subject to significant deductions. The first category of deductions was those made in the West Indies – the captain's, mates' and surgeon's commissions, the commission payable to the slave factor and on the remitting home of the bills of exchange given in payment for the slaves and various disbursements made by the ship's captain. These deductions range from 16 per cent to 20·2 per cent and average 18·3 per cent.[12] We shall take 18 per cent as the norm.

The next deduction results from the financial structure of the British slave trade at this period. Although slavers often brought home part cargoes of West India produce, the need to avoid a long waiting period in the Caribbean had, from about mid-century, combined with the ever more common practice of freighting the tropical staples home in specially built West Indiamen much to reduce the share of slave ships in this trade. In any event, for that substantial portion of the British slave-trading fleet which supplied foreigners, there could be no question of a return lading in foreign-grown tropical produce which the Frenchman or Spaniard, at least in theory, jealously preserved for himself, and which could in any event not have gained admittance at a British port without chicanery too complex to sustain. Slavers which had taken their cargoes to British islands, and only those, commonly did have a part cargo of tropical produce and less often a full hold – but this was simply 'on freight' for a planter who was consigning the produce to his British commission agent: the remittance home of the major part of the net proceeds of slave sales was thenceforward made in bills of exchange which, says Richard Sheridan, 'probably accounted for the Bulk of the returns after 1750'.[13] Now the bill of exchange was not payable immediately

[12] See Appendix 2.

[13] R. B. Sheridan, 'The Commercial and Financial Organisation of the British Slave Trade, 1750–1807', *Economic History Review*, 2nd series, XI, no. 2 (1958) 252–3. See also *A. & P.*, 1789, XXVI (646a), pt IV, no. 1, where evidence of the Assemblies and Agents of the West Indian Colonies is summarised: 'The ships bringing negroes from Africa are not generally employed in transporting the produce of the West India islands, and . . . the number of such vessels, which are employed in transporting produce, bears little or no proportion to the whole'. For the origins of the Commission system see K. G. Davies, 'The Origins of the Commission System

upon receipt, but at so many months sight. We must therefore include an item for discounting as a deduction from the net remittance home. A slave merchant, James Jones, claimed in 1788 that a slave trader 'is on average two years out of his Money',[14] and Thomas Clarkson, who investigated the working of the slave trade for himself, assessed the average 'sight' of the bills at twenty-four months. Other good evidence supports this figure, save for the decade 1761–70 for which we have come across no sets of bills averaging more than twelve months.[15] The discount rate for the

[14] *B.M. Add. MSS. 38416*, ff. 154–5, Jones to Hawkesbury [26 July 1788].

[15] Thomas Clarkson, *Essay on the Impolicy of the African Slave Trade* (London, 1788) 28. Clarkson goes on to show that the average point in time at which the slave trader had to meet the bills by which he had financed the voyage was thirteen months after the voyage had begun. If this is adjusted to take account of the quite considerable cash outgoing, which all voyage accounts show were made before the voyage began, the point becomes zero + nine months. Coincidentally, it was at approximately this point that the bills of exchange for slave sales were tendered in the West Indies. For the further evidence on the period of bills see *Davies-Davenport MSS, R.R.* 57/1, Voyage Accounts of Hawke (1780), *R.R.* 57/3, of *May* (1772 and 1773), and *R.R.* 57/4, of *Badger* (177); *Liverpool and Slavery*, 115; see also Sheridan, 'Organisation of the British Slave Trade', 253–63 passim. Thomas Tobin, who as a young man had captained a slave ship between about 1798 and 1807, told the Commons Select Committee on the Slave Trade in 1848 that 'the payments were made in one, two, and three years' bills, and unless they were rich houses they could not do anything with those bills' (*S.P.* 1847–8, xxii (536) 3rd Report of Select Committee on Slave Trade, para 5690, Evidence of Thomas Tobin). The various evidence of the sight of bills drawn

in the West India Trade', *Transactions of the Royal Historical Society*, 5th series, ii (1952) 89–107. In 'The Triangular Trade', *Business History*, iii (1960) 1–7, J. E. Merritt argued that in the eighteenth century the physical transport of goods on the third leg of the triangular voyage 'would seem to be the exception rather than the rule' (ibid., 3). But in an as yet unpublished critique of the Merritt thesis, which he has kindly made available to me, Professor Minchinton demonstrates, *inter alia*, that in the later eighteenth century, as far as British transatlantic colonies were concerned, slaver ships nearly always brought home cargo, but usually only a part cargo. Moreover, this was 'on freight', the net proceeds of the slave sales being remitted in bills of exchange. My own study of the Jamaica Naval Office lists, the most significant of those which survive, and even they are not complete, confirms Minchinton's conclusion about part cargoes. *C.O.* 142/18 (1762–65); *C.O.* 142/17 (1766–69); *C.O.* 142/19 (1782–84).

two-year period which is postulated from 1771 onwards has been taken as 10 per cent in the years of peace, and 12 per cent in the wartime years, namely 1761–62, 1776–82, 1793–1801 and 1804–07,[16] and as 5 per cent and 6 per cent per annum respectively for the one-year period in the 'sixties. Decennial discount rate are therefore 5·2 per cent, 11 per cent, 10·4 per cent, 11·6 per cent and 11·4 per cent.

The final item on the credit side of the account is the written-down or residual value of the slave ship and its equipment on its return to the home port. Only sometimes do series of voyage accounts reveal the value of a ship and its outfit on its return but some thirteen voyage accounts, estimates, or the equivalents – which appear to contain a balancing spread of both new and old ships – indicate written-down value of ship and equipment at the termination of a voyage. These values can then be adjusted for price changes and averaged over the total tonnage. The resulting residual value per ton figure can then, in turn, be adjusted for each decade so that for the five decades we have, respectively, £5·4, £6·0, £6·4, £7·6 and £9·5 per ton.[17]

On the debit side the principal items were the ship and its

[16] See S. Homer, *A History of Interest Rates* (New Brunswick, 1963) 163–4, 181–6.

[17] *Davies-Davenport MSS. R.R.* 57/1, *Hawke*, 1780 and 1781, *R.R.*, 57/3 *May* 1772 and 1774, *R.R.* 57/4, *Badger*, 1774 and *R.R.* 57/6, *Swift*, 1770; four voyage estimates in *B.T.* 6/7; Parkinson, 'Slaver's Accounts', 148–9 (*Plumper*, 1768), Hodson, *Bostock Letter Book*, 56–7 (*Little Ben*, 1792). We also include evidence from one voyage of a Dutch slaver, because so meticulously accounted (W. S. Unger, 'Bijdragen Tot de Geschiedenis van de Nederlandse Slavenhandel: 2. De Slavenhandel der Middelburgsche Commercie Compagnie, 1732–1808', *Economisch-Historisch Jaarbock, 1958*, 108. Where tonnages were not given, these were worked out by application of the average of slaves per ton landed during the decade.

for slaves landed, mostly in South Carolina, between 1761 and 1773, given in Donnan, *Documents*, IV, 378–466, tends to speak of bills in equal combination of 6, 9 and 12, or 9, 12 and 15 months sight. But in 1774, there is an instance of 12, 15 and 18 months sight (Ibid., III 296) and in 1777, in St Lucia, of 24, 36 and 42 months (Ibid, III 330). Note also Bradbury Parkinson's observation that 'these bills frequently ran for years' ('A Slaver's Accounts', *Accounting Research* III (1951) 146). For our purposes, inability to obtain a discount does not matter: to have the prior use of his money the slave merchant would have had to borrow at the going rate for an average period of two years.

equipment, the cargo, wages, provisions, customs, insurance and miscellaneous expenses. There is extensive evidence on ship and outfit costs but because it relates particularly to 1787 and 1790 respectively it must be adjusted in accordance with the movement in prices and insurance rates and the two-stage introduction of restriction on the numbers of slaves that could be carried. The conclusion of the extensive calculations made in Appendix 3 is the following outset cost per ton for the successive decades – £45·8, £51·7, £52·2, £55·0, £53·4.

It may be objected that accounting on this basis ignores two important items. The first is the profit on West India produce brought home on the third leg of the triangular voyage, and the second the profit of such African produce as ivory, camwood and gum which slavers sometimes bought if opportunity offered. But as regards the first objection, we have already seen that by the beginning of our period it was not all slavers that came home from the Caribbean with cargo, and that this was usually a part cargo only, and 'on freight'. Arguably the return from a pedestrian transaction of this kind would not have much more than balanced the heightened cost of the longer voyage that is implied by the necessity of waiting for cargo. The other practice, the inclusion of African produce in a slaver's homeward cargo, doubtless was as common as Hyde, Parkinson and Marriner assert it to have been.[18] We are not concerned with the profitability of this trade, as such, for it was, though an integral part of the trade of slave ships, distinguishable from the trade in slaves. In balance-sheet terms, however, a proportion of the voyage capital must be attributed to this African commerce and the outset of the slaving enterprise correspondingly reduced. The evidence regarding the relative importance of this commerce in ivory, redwood, etc., is not entirely satisfactory, but it suggests that it should be rated at 5 per cent.[19]

We can now project such figures as the amount of capital investment in the slave trade, the yield on that capital, both in money and as a percentage on the amount invested in the voyage. The primary purpose of these calculations has been to arrive at the return to the slave trader, but an only slight refinement can

[18] Francis E. Hyde, Bradbury B. Parkinson and Sheila Marriner, 'The Nature and Profitability of the Liverpool Slave Trade', *Economic History Review*, 2nd series, v (1952–53) 372.
[19] See Appendix 4.

indicate the contribution of the slave trade to national resource growth. The main component of this is simply the slave traders' profit, but to this must be added the discounting percentage since this is a transaction within the metropolitan economy.

The profit level of just under 10 per cent which is advanced in Table 1[20] – albeit good – will surprise those who assume that the slave trade must have been profitable beyond the dreams of avarice. Of course the apparent precision engendered by decimal points in the decennial profit percentages is a false precision: one's instinct is that there could be error of plus 25 or minus 50 per cent in the final percentage levels. And because of the paucity of indications of slave prices the conclusion for the years 1801–07 is the most fragile. Profitability may not, in fact, have taken such a sharp down-turn. On the other hand, the much quoted, conflicting and apparently well-founded contemporary estimate of 30 per cent plus was based on an average slave price of £50 whereas our quite considerable sample of slave prices points to an average price for the period in question, the years 1783–93, ten pounds lower – which makes a decisive difference.[21] Moreover, some knowledgeable contemporaries reached conclusions about profitability either lower or much the same as our own. Thomas Clarkson, who made a close investigation of the slave trade, believed that between 1763 and 1772 the Liverpool slave trade, at any rate, was running at a loss, and observed that in the 'seventies Liverpool slave merchants failed for the sum of £710,000. He admitted that, in the American War, 'the adventurer, who escaped the ships of the enemy, made his fortune but since the peace the trade has returned to its former state; and it is considered as a fact, at the ports where it is carried on, that it is a losing trade at the present day'. People only continued in the trade, Clarkson concluded, because they saw it as a

---

[20] A similar table has recently been published in my article, 'The Volume and Profitability of the British Slave Trade, 1761–1807, *Race and Slavery in the Western Hemisphere*, ed. Stanley Engerman and Eugene D. Genovese (Princeton, 1974). As far as profitability is concerned the current chapter incorporates revisions made in the light of further study and research. The difference in the working is mainly caused by a reduction in the discount rate postulated for the 1760s and by an increase in the average gross sale price for slaves in the decade 1791–1800. (The table below also includes the allowance for tonnage in the Lancaster and Whitehaven slave trades already referred to, but this makes no significant difference to profitability).

[21] 'Eye-Witness' in *Liverpool and Slavery*, 100–11.

TABLE 1. Volume and Profitability of the British Slave Trade 1761–1807

	1	2	3	4	5	6	7	8	9	10	11	12	13	14
	Voyages	Tons	Slaves landed	Slaves landed per ton £	Average gross sale price £	Gross receipts on slaves £	Net receipts (82%) £	Net receipts after discounting £	Residual value less 5% for produce £	Total credit £ (cols. 8+9)	Outset less 5% for produce ≠	Profit £	% profit	Resource increment £ (cols. 7+9 − col. 11)
1761–70	1368	153,006	284,834	1·86	29	8,260,186	6,773,353	6,421,139	784,921	7,206,060	6,657,291	548,769	8·2	900,983
1771–80	1080	120,652	233,042	1·93	35	8,156,470	6,688,305	5,952,591	687,716	6,640,307	5,925,823	714,484	12·1	1,450,198
1781–90	998	159,757	294,865	1·85	36	10,615,140	8,704,415	7,799,156	971,323	8,770,479	7,922,350	848,129	10·7	1,753,388
1791–1800	1341	278,537	393,404	1·43	50	19,920,200	16,334,564	14,439,755	2,011,037	16,450,792	14,553,558	1,897,234	13·0	3,792,043
1801–07	906	218,690	217,556	0·99	60	13,053,360	10,703,755	9,483,527	1,973,677	11,457,204	11,094,144	363,060	3·3	1,583,288
Aggregates	5693	930,642	1,428,701	1·54	42	60,005,356	49,204,392	44,096,168	6,428,674	50,524,842	46,153,166	4,371,676	9·5	9,479,900

lottery.[22] Another well-informed contemporary observer, Lord Hawkesbury, chairman of the Privy Council Committee of Enquiry into the Slave Trade, formed his own opinion on the profitability of the slave trade, and concluded that 'it is a matter of much doubt whether the excess of the gains after deducting the losses incurred in the trade have exceeded the advantages to be derived by other commerce'.[23] Quantified, this must mean an aggregate return of between 5 and 10 per cent. The slave traders themselves bring oblique support to our figure by believing that the profits *ought* to run out at rather over 10 per cent.[24] J. J. Sell in his *Versuch einer Geschichte des Negersklavenhandels* (1791) suggested a figure of 9 per cent and this was later accepted by Franz Hochstetter, writing in the early twentieth century, as about right for the later years of the British slave trade.[25] Much more recently, Phillip LeVeen, working along lines quite different from our own, has propounded an identical profit rate of 9·5 per cent round about 1800.[26]

It is surely unlikely that better evidence will ever show the slave trade to have been, in this period, a bonanza, or even that it could be made to show a return 'upwards of thirty per cent profitability'. The circumstantial evidence for discrediting the notion of a bonanza is in any event powerful. In a trade with open access, reports of rich pickings must inevitably have led to a rush of investment. The supply of slaves would be unequal to the new demand and prices would rise. Various market forces, such as a decline in sugar prices would, probably sooner than later, mean difficulty in disposing of the slaves at a good, or any, profit, and the probability of a loss. If high profits look improbable on circumstantial as well as statistical grounds, there is strong analogical evidence for the proposition that the British slave trade could have

[22] Clarkson, *Impolicy*, 29–30.
[23] Preface to Privy Council Report.
[24] *B.M. Add. MSS. 38416*, f. 103. Opinion of Tarleton.
[25] Franz Hochstetter, 'Die wirtschaftichen and politischen Motive für die Abschaffung des britischen Sklavenhandels im Jahre 1806/1807, in G. Schmoller and M. Sering (eds.), *Staats- und Sozialwissenschaftliche Forschungen*, xxv, pt 1 (Leipzig, 1905) 63.
[26] E.P. LeVeen, 'British Slave Trade Suppression Policies, 1821–1865: Impact and Implication (University of Chicago Ph.D., Dissertation, 1971) p. 28, Table 3. I am most indebted to Dr LeVeen for making available to me a copy of his thesis.

sustained a much lower overall rate of return. This will be apparent when we come to study the experience of the French and Dutch slave trades.

We are now in a position to turn to the question of the contribution of slave-trading profits to the capital requirements of the Industrial Revolution in Britain.[27] The amount of slave-trade 'profits', in the sense of resource increment, according to our estimate, was slightly over £9,000,000 in almost half a century and the annual average will be marginally rounded down to £200,000. Now by 1800 the national ratio of investment to national income, according to Deane and Cole, was about 7 per cent, and in our crude calculation we will take this figure as constant for the half-century. National income, again following Deane and Cole, rose from £130 m. c. 1770 to £232 m. in 1801;[28] we shall assume an average of £180 m. for the whole period. Total national investment was therefore, at 7 per cent. £12,600,000 per annum. If we assume that the proportion of slave-trading profits invested followed the national 7 per cent ratio, then £14,000 per annum was invested – which is 0·11 per cent of total national investment. An alternative assumption is theoretically credible, namely that all the profits of the slave trade were invested. In this event the contribution of the slave trade to total national investment rises sharply, but still to the not very dizzy height of 1·59 per cent. A further theoretical assumption is that all invested slave-trade profits (7 per cent of the whole) went into the formation of industrial capital. In our period this sector amounted to about 20 per cent of the total, i.e. £2,520,000 per annum, and so invested slave-trade profits would amount to 0·56 per cent of this. Of course, this percentage would rise dramatically if we assumed that all slave-trade profits were put into industrial capital formation, namely to 7·94 per cent. There are varying implausibilities about all of the last three of these four possibilities, especially when we

[27] See Stanley L. Engerman, 'The Slave Trade and British Capital Formation in the Eighteenth Century: A Comment on the Williams Thesis', *The Business History Review*, XLVI no. 4 (Winter 1972) 430–43. I am most grateful to Dr Engerman for sending me a copy of his article before publication and I am indebted to him for thus suggesting to me the line of approach to the study of the role of slaving profits in the Industrial Revolution.

[28] Phyllis Deane and W. A. Cole, *British Economic Growth 1688–1959* (Cambridge, 1964) 259–64, 156 and 282.

recall the lure of land and of the funds, the concern to diversify into other trades, and the need of the slave trader to eat. There is one sense in which these negative judgements can be qualified. Liverpool, the principal slaving port, was of course the port of Lancashire and the cotton industry. It is not unreasonable to suggest that geographical propinquity would result in a relatively large proportion of this capital formation in Lancashire cotton coming from the profits of a major activity of Liverpool. If slave-trading profits of nearly all three British ports (i.e. with no deduction in respect of London and Bristol) were applied to cotton, and with the knowledge that the capital stock in the industry increased by about £400,000 per annum from 1780 onwards,[29] we can assess the contribution made by slave-trading profits firstly on the assumption that 7 per cent of slave trading profits were invested, and secondly, that all profits were invested. The results are 3·5 per cent and 50 per cent respectively. Credible though the notion of a significant flow of slave-trading profits into cotton is, this latter figure can only stem from a number of extreme assumptions and can be dismissed. The *prima facie* case, urged by Williams and others, for some special contribution of slave-trading profits to capital formation in cotton remains, but to be really significant such a contribution would need to be shown – apart from being regionally and industrially concentrated – to be related to the proposition that outside capital infusion was relatively low (most industrial investment being financed, it has been argued, from profits) so that the importance of slave-trade capital in relation to all outside capital would have manifestly been greater. It might also be necessary to 'play linkages and the multiplier effect' and assume that slave-trade capital went into rapidly expanding and highly profitable industries.

This is not to say that there is no possibility of the slave trade having had some positive relationship to the Industrial Revolution: Dr Boulle, as we shall see,[30] has recently demonstrated that

---

[29] Ibid., 262. Cf. the relatively recent brief discussions of the role of slave trade and plantation profits in capital formation in the Industrial Revolution in T. S. Ashton, *An Economic History of England: The Eighteenth Century* (London, 1955) 125, and M. W. Flinn, *Origins of the Industrial Revolution* (London, 1969) 46.

[30] See p. 55 below.

the demands of the Nantes slave trade for large quantities of goods with which to purchase slaves led to the construction of large factories in the area of the port. It may be that the British slave trade could be shown to have had precisely that role. But meanwhile, and in terms of the way in which the proposition about the effect of the British slave trade on the British Industrial Revolution is conventionally stated, we must urge that the most credible contribution of slave-trade profits to capital formation is – at 0·11 per cent of annual investment – derisory enough for the myth of the vital importance of the slave trade in financing the Industrial Revolution to be demolished.

The West Indian plantation economy and its role in capital formation in Britain, is a different case, and one which it is only marginally relevant to consider. Suffice it to say that here, too, recent scholarship would seem to show that this contribution cannot have been considerable. Indeed it is possible that there was a net movement of capital and resources in the reverse direction.[31] The larger question of the value of the West Indian slave economy to the nation (as opposed to the question of its profitability to individuals), and its bearing upon abolition is one of considerable interest, but it is not one on which we have to enter in detail here. A confirmation that the West Indies were, and were seen by contemporaries to be, in Ragatz's words, 'tottering from structural weakness',[32] would constitute a firmer basis for emphasising an element of deep-rooted economic change in the interpretation of abolition. A demonstration that the relative value of the West Indies to the imperial economy was perceived by a majority of contemporaries at least not to be declining would mean that any case for explaining the abolition of 1806–07 in terms of fundamental economic change was seriously, if not fatally, undermined.

[31] See R. B. Sheridan, 'The Wealth of Jamaica in the Eighteenth Century', *Economic History Review*, 2nd series, xviii (Aug. 1965) 292–311, and 'A Rejoinder', ibid., xxi (Apr. 1968) 46–61; R. P. Thomas, 'The Sugar Colonies of the Old Empire: Profit or Loss for Great Britain', ibid., xxi (Apr. 1968) 30–45; Richard Pares, 'The Economic Factors in the History of the Empire', ibid. vii (1936–37) 119–44; K. G. Davies, 'Essays in Bibliography and Criticism xliv, Empire and Capital', ibid., xiii (1960–61) 105–10.

[32] L. J. Ragatz, *The Fall of the Planter Class in the British Caribbean, 1763–1833* (New York, 1928) 206.

On this whole question Dr Seymour Drescher has recently demonstrated that the Ragatz–Williams image of West Indian decline is ill-founded. A wide range of data – which men of the time may be deemed capable of having assimilated intuitively – show that 'in terms of overseas trade, the British West Indies were far more valuable to Britain during the period of intense debate on Imperial slave trade (1788–1807), and on the world slave trade (1814–20), than during the period 1720–75 when there had been no organised agitation or pressure against the trade'. Moreover, 'from the vantage point of British trade, the potential of the slave system was greater in 1804–14 than it had been at the outset of the great public opinion campaigns against the slave trade between 1788–92, or any other point in the eighteenth century'. In short, 'neither Imperial nor world economic and demographic trends indicated a British advantage in destroying, abandoning or neglecting her slave system between 1787–1807'.[33] Important as a brilliant demolition job that Drescher's work is, we shall demonstrate in the last section of this book that a pragmatic approach to the role of the West Indies in the imperial economy is all that is necessary in the economic dimension of our explanation of the successful carriage of abolition. What was important at the politico-economic level was that a fortuitous politico-economic conjuncture in the Napoleonic Wars made the vital West Indian re-exports of sugar and other tropical produce so hard to sell that the national interest suffered heavily. It was this circumstance that the abolitionists were able skilfully to utilise, and which persuaded the political nation that the national interest would positively be furthered by what was presented as principally a politico-economic measure of abolition in 1806. The 1806 measure could be so presented because it ended the British supply of slaves to rivals and enemies – who

[33] I am greatly indebted to Dr Drescher for allowing me to read, and quote from, his forthcoming *A Case of Econocide: British Abolition and Economic Development*. Very striking, for instance, is the invocation of B. R. Mitchell and Phyllis Deane, *Abstract of British Historical Statistics* (Cambridge, 1962) 309–11, to show that the percentage share of the total of the imports and exports of the British West Indies in the total long distance trade of Britain was never as high prior to the quinquennium 1768–72 as it was in that period, when it was 17·7%, and that it was higher than that in every succeeding quinquennium up to 1813–17. The peaks were 21·0% in 1778–82, 20·2% in 1798–1802, 20·8% in 1803–07 and 20·9% in 1808–12.

then beat the British Caribbean producers in competition on the Continental market, and the supply to conquered colonies – which would later compete with the older British islands in the likely event of being restored to their original owners at the peace. That much vaunted economic cause of abolition, overproduction, only has validity in the sense that it arose because of an 'unnatural' denial of access to Continental markets, was only acute because of the war, only related to the 1806 measure, and was a problem whose solution was conceived in terms of cutting down one's rivals' production rather than one's own. Neither in respect of the 1806 measure nor the 1807 measure did any other economic factors play a significant role – save in the qualified sense that it was much easier, in 1807, to abolish the supply of slaves to the old British islands once the supply of their rivals had been much reduced by the 1806 measure. Of any positive connection between structural change in the imperial economy and abolition there is absolutely no sign.

Evidence of the profitability of two other national sectors of the slave trade in our period – the French and the Dutch – is also available. This evidence is valuable both in its own right and as rendering the more credible the level attributed to the British slave trade. The most detailed study of the economics of the French trade has been the recent work of Meyer on the Nantes slave trade in which he has made extensive use of voyage accounts to make a precise delineation of a number of voyages and to suggest the broad characteristics of the trade. There are two important differences between the French and British trades. Firstly, the French trade cannot be separated from the triangular trade as a whole since French slavers still normally brought home a sizeable cargo of Caribbean produce – though not normally to the full value of the slaves sold. More importantly, bills owing to the slave trader were much slower in being paid. Ten or even twenty years was common before all the payments owing were received; only after this kind of period had elapsed was the laconic 'rien à espérer' written in the ledger. As Meyer points out, this makes the conversion of gross profits into an annual profit rate difficult, since even a high profit, if spread over a period of years running into double figures, would be likely to appear derisively misleading, if expressed as a simple annual average. Normally, however, there was a pronounced 'tail' in these profits, that is to say the major part of the returns would be received in a shorter period. Meyer's method is, necessarily arbitrarily, to determine the number of years taken for the major part of the profits to come in and to add this to the years taken for amortisation of the original capital. Thus an annual profit rate is arrived at by dividing gross profits, less the 'tail'; by the number of years necessary to amortise the capital plus the number of years taken to produce the major part of the profits. On this basis, the best annual return of one leading Nantes slave-trader was on his share in the voyage of the *Maréchal de Luxembourg*, commenced in 1768 – 7·54 per cent. Meyer cites no higher annual profit than this for a slaving voyage, whereas another case works out at about 3·5 per cent per annum and a third at 2·2 per cent. He does, however, offer a summary of the profit performance of the brothers Chaurand, who had major shares in eleven slaving voyages sent out between 1782 and 1785. In the event the Revolutionary War supervened at the very point when a prolonged amortisation was only just complete and the profits had barely begun to come in, and the actual annual rate of profit was only about 0·1 per cent. Meyer calculates that in normal conditions the return would have been about 100 per cent, spread over, one may conclude, about 13–14 years, or about 7·5 per cent per annum.[34] But, one may ask rhetorically, how many 14-year periods of peace had Europe known since 1730? The French slave trade, though it *may* have been more profitable in mid-century, was certainly less profitable even than the British in the years after 1760. (Interestingly Meyer shows that the direct trade to and from the West Indies was more lucrative than the slave trade.)[35] Perry Viles, on the basis of scattered evidence from the Bordeaux and La Rochelle slave trades in this period, and of a review of the relatively abundant literature on the Nantes slave trade, concludes that the most successful family firms could do no better than 6 per cent per annum whilst other investors might get as little as 1 per cent.[36]

The question of the possible role of the profits of the French slave – or, more precisely, triangular – trade in metropolitan

[34] Jean Meyer, *L'Armement Nantais, dans la Deuxième Moitié du XVIIIᵉ Siècle* (Paris, 1969) 205–48.

[35] Ibid. 224.

[36] Perry Viles, 'The Slaving Interest in the Atlantic Ports 1763–1792', *French Historical Studies*, VII 4 (Autumn 1972) 533.

capital formation does not, of course, arise. At least it does not arise in the way in which, as we have seen, it is claimed to have been important in England. It is not so much that the profits were trivial as that France's Industrial Revolution was delayed until the mid-nineteenth century. But if the Nantes slave trade could not have had this kind of role, Pierre Boulle has recently demonstrated that between 1730 and 1755 the demands of the Nantes slave trade for more cheaply produced trade goods, and the availability of capital from profits of the triangular trade, did lead to a significant rise of large-scale industry in the Nantes area. In part the geographical isolation and fiscal position of Nantes, but more immediately the serious effect of the Seven Years War on the Atlantic trade of Nantes, nipped this development in the bud.[37] None the less, it is significant in itself and suggests a line of investigation into the role of the *British* slave trade as a stimulus to industrialisation in virtue of the demands of the trade itself – a line of inquiry begun by Eric Williams,[38] and more promising, perhaps, than the traditional focus on the role of slave trading profits in the economy generally.

There is startlingly good evidence on the profitability of the Dutch slave trade – or, more precisely, of the largest Dutch company involved, the *Middelburgsche Commercie Compagnie*. The most meticulous accounts imaginable have been preserved, and have been worked upon and to some extent processed by the Dutch scholar, Dr Unger. From the near complete series of voyage accounts of sixty-six slaving voyages of the Middleburg company between 1761 and 1800 (there are equally full accounts of a further 35 voyages between 1732 and 1760) Unger has tabulated, in Flemish Pounds, the original capital investment and voyage expenses, on the one hand, and returns on the other. In the case of the Middleburg company a cargo of produce was always brought home, having been purchased with the proceeds of the sale of the slaves, which in their turn had been bought by the trade goods

---

[37] Pierre M. Boulle 'Slave Trade, commercial organisation and industrial growth in Eighteenth Century Nantes,' *Revue Française d'Histoire d'Outre-Mer*, vol. LIX, no. 214, 1er trimestre, 1972, 70–112. Boulle is here reinforcing and developing a thesis earlier propounded by Gaston Martin in *Nantes au XVIII siècle: l'ére des Négriers, 1714–1774* (Paris, 1931) 15–16, 23–24 and 155–56 and 'Capital et travail à Nantes au cours du XVIII siècle', *Revue d'historie economique et sociale*, XVIII (1930) 52–8.

[38] Williams, *Capitalism and Slavery*, 58–73, 78–84.

initially sent out, thus completing the cycle.[39] We are therefore
here concerned not just with the slave trade but rather with the
triangular trade. From the tabulation so thoroughly worked out
by Unger it is readily possible to work out profit and loss over
the four decades of our period for which, though in decline,
the Dutch slave trade lasted. There are, of course, the voyages
that looked highly profitable, such as that of the *Het Vergenoogen*
which returned 37·38 per cent on an investment of £23,507,
Flemish (£13,432 Sterling)[40] in 1786–87, but against such seemingly lucrative ventures must be set the fact that, since voyages
always took over twelve months, the profit is much lower when expressed as an annual rate of return. On the other hand there could
be losses at the level of the 59·41 per cent sustained by the *De
Geertruida en Christina* in 1783–85 (likewise lower when expressed
at an annual rate). To remark the chance of high reward and the
possibility of serious loss is to pinpoint an attitude to risk which had
to exist if the slave trade, with all its hazards, was to be carried
on at all. But at another level the significant thing is the overall
return on capital. This can be shown in decennial divisions for
each of the four decades in our period that the trade lasted. The
samples for the 'eighties and 'nineties, however, are too small to
be very meaningful, and compensatory depth will be lent to the
demonstration by adding the figures for the two immediately pre-

[39] 'We get from the account-current a detailed picture of the financial
results. First *the debit side:* foremost we see an account of the costs of the
building of the ship, sometimes stating the measurements and the con-
tents of the cargo. At the end of the voyage the value hereof is written on
the credit side, which will be put under debit with the next voyage. Then
follow the accounts and "homecoming expenses", next the purchase of
the cargo and the expenses on the return cargo. In *Credit*: the yield of the
imported and sold return goods ... (as specified in the accompanying
Captain's statement which lists the successive transactions on the voyage)
... and the above-mentioned book value of the ship.' (W. S. Unger,
'Bijdragen van de Nederlandse Slavenhandel: De Slavenhandel der
Middelburgsche Commercie Compagnie, 1732–1808', *Economisch-Historisch
Jaarboek* (The Hague), vol. xxviii (1961) 106–7).

[40] Assuming an exchange rate of 35 Flemish shillings to the pound
sterling. This was the approximate rate in 1811 (Patrick Kelly, *Universal
Cambist and Commercial Instructor being a General Treatise on Exchange including
the Monies, Coins, Weights and Measures of all trading Nations and Colonies*
(London, 1811) i 35 and 276, ii 9). This was about the rate in much of
the eighteenth century according to J. Castaing, *Course of the Exchange*. I
am indebted to Dr D. Ormrod for a summary of part thereof.

ceding decades. Both voyage profit and loss and annual profit and loss are included, the latter being arrived at proportionately by averaging total voyage duration in each decade.

TABLE 2 Profit and Loss in the Triangular Trade of the Middleburg Company 1741–1800[41]

Period	Outlay (Flemish £)	Profit/ loss (Flemish £)	% Return loss	Av. voyage length (months)	% Annual return/ loss	No. of voyages
1741–50	110,934	− 479	− 0·43	16	−0·32	10
1751–60	282,603	+32,393	+11·46	17	+8·09	22
1761–70	511,543	+36,376	+ 7·11	17	+5·07	33
1771–80	425,036	− 615	− 0·14	18	−0·09	24
1781–90	132,932	− 4934	− 3·73	24	−1·87	6
1791–1800	76,134	− 6530	− 8·58	32	−3·21	3
1741–1800	1,538,642	+56,211	+ 3·65	17[a]	+2·58	98
1761–1800	1,145,105	+24,657	+ 2·15	18[a]	+1·43	66

[a] = This ignores the much extended voyage times in the two decades 1781–1800.

As to profitability then it seems clear that neither the French nor the Dutch, the only two other carriers in respect of whom evidence is available, could attain the British profit level of just under 10 per cent. And if that latter figure, even if one allows for substantial error in it, demolishes the common supposition that the slave trade showed a consistently high return of between, say, 30 per cent and all that avarice could wish, the fact that the Dutch deemed it worth while to continue in a trade whose return in our period, at an annual rate, was 1·43 per cent and that the French accepted voyage profits, likewise adjusted, of 1 per cent to 6 per cent or 7 per cent suggests that the return on the British trade was regarded as good.[42]

But what was the impact of the slave trade in Africa?

[41] Distilled from Unger, 'Bijdragen', II, 87–91.

[42] In the light of valuable contributions by Dr Johannes Postma and Mr Sven E. Green-Pedersen, respectively, to the Sixth International Eonomic History Conference at Copenhagen, in August 1974, it is clear that our volume figures for the Dutch export slave trade should be revised upwards to 143,000 and for the Danish trade downwards to c.33,350— modifications which, taken together, cancel each other out as far as our overall volume figure is concerned. Authoritative observations by Dr Pieter Emmer and Dr David Richardson could suggest that the profitability of the Middleburg Company's triangular trade was even lower than is argued above.

3 The Impact of the Atlantic Slave Trade on Africa

In the last chapter, and to some extent in the first chapter, the slave trade was considered primarily as a phenomenon in the European economy. In noting volume and measuring profitability the unit has been the various European – and the American – national sectors of the trade. In considering the question from an African angle, however, it is more significant to discern the total impact of the Atlantic slave trade on, and as between, the different regions of the African coast. These regions, as usefully defined by Curtin, are Senegambia, Sierra Leone, the Windward Coast the Gold Coast, the Bight of Benin, the Bight of Biafra, Congo/Angola and Mozambique. The three largest carriers were Britain, Portugal and France for between them they were responsible for about 85 per cent of the slave trade in our period. For these dominant slave trading powers the peak decade, overall, was 1781–90 but this decade was not the peak for Sierra Leone, the Windward Coast, the Gold Coast and the Bight of Biafra. Their high points came, respectively, in 1771–80, still earlier in 1761–70, and in 1791–1800 for the last two. As to changes in the coastal distribution there was a clear shift eastwards and southwards in the centre of gravity of the slave trade as between the beginning and end of the period. The percentage share of Senegambia, Sierra Leone and the Windward Coast, taken together, dropped by about two-thirds; the Gold Coast share increased by about a sixth whilst the Bight of Benin trade dropped by a fifth; and the proportion of the trade claimed by the Bight of Biafra remained about the same, as did the Mozambique share in the three decades for which it was projected. The really marked change was the 50 per cent upward swing in the Congo/Angola trade. This pattern would not be

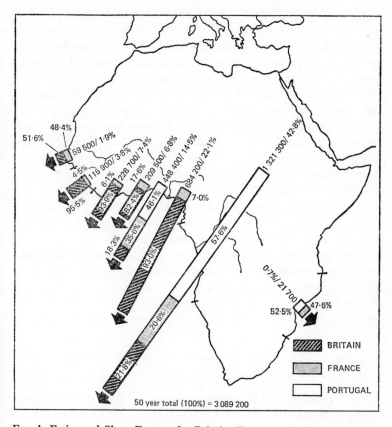

FIG. 1. Estimated Slave Exports by Britain, France and Portugal, 1761–1810, by Regional Volume and Percentages, and by National Percentages within each Region.

strikingly different if the last decade, in which France's share of the trade was miniscule and during which Britain withdrew from the trade, was ignored. The effect of incorporating a regional breakdown of the Dutch, Danish and American slave trades would probably, it may be hazarded, be to augment slightly the shares of the regions westwards of the Gold Coast and of Congo/Angola and Mozambique and to increase rather more the share of the Gold Coast. In static terms the fifty year exports of the three major slave carriers were as indicated on Figure 1.[1]

[1] The coast-regional breakdown of the British slave trade is detailed and justified in my paper in *Race and Slavery in the Western Hemisphere,*

Whence did the slaves come? How were they acquired? And how did they reach the coast? What were the conditions of successful trading, and what light is thrown on the connections between the slave trade and African political and economic development? What were the demographic effects of the slave trade?[2] Although the first three questions may usefully be subsumed in one these are all large questions and the research upon them is at a relatively early stage. Many of the answers attempted here will therefore be tentative and none will be founded on other than existing published work. Furthermore, we shall confine ourselves to three regions, Congo/Angola, Bight of Biafra and Bight of Benin and their hinterlands: but, after all, these regions did account for over three-quarters of the total slave trade during our period.

For the slave trade to attain any volume over the long term a supply network had to be created. Originally the immediate neighbours of the coastal peoples, or of European colonies and settlements, constituted sufficient catchment areas but, most strikingly in the case of Congo/Angola, this had long ceased to be the case by the middle of the eighteenth century for the main source of slaves was now far in the interior. In David Birmingham's words,

> during the course of the eighteenth century the focal point of
> the slave supply in West Central Africa continued to move east-

[2] For a treatment of most of these themes see Basil Davidson, *Black Mother* (London, 1961) 104–43, 179–222.

---

albeit as a breakdown of a volume estimate of the British trade which excluded the (small)Lancaster and Whitehaven trades. These calculations have been revised so as to take these branches of the slave trade into account. Although our overall total is different (see p. 38 above) the percentage coastal distribution of the French trade follows Curtin, *Census*, 211, but the distribution as well as the volume of the Portuguese slave trade has been modified particularly in the light of Herbert S. Klein's work on the Angolan trade in 'The Portuguese Slave Trade from Angola in the Eighteenth Century', *The Journal of Economic History*, xxxii, no. 4 (Dec 1972) 894–18. The difference in the total volume of the British, French and Portuguese slave trades, 1761–1810, in Figure 1 as compared with the total on p. 38 is principally a result of the fact that a portion of the French and Portuguese trades as summarised there is categorised is of unknown coastal origin. Pending publication elsewhere I shall be happy to make available to students of the slave trade my quite extensive calculations on volume and coastal distribution.

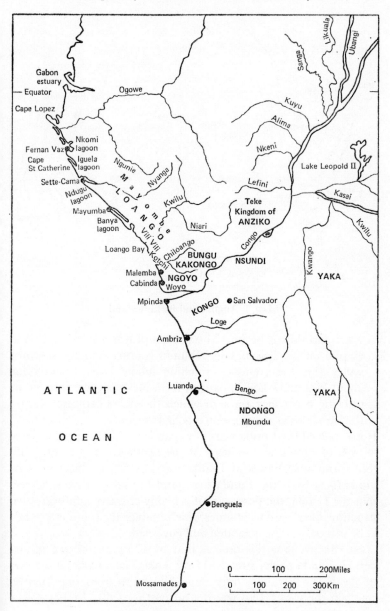

MAP 2. West Central Africa

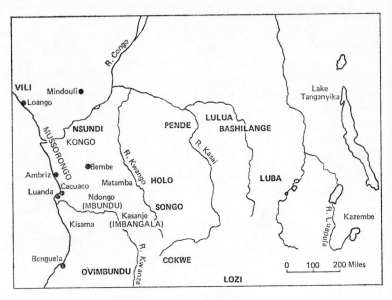

MAP 3. Angola and its hinterland

ward and shifted beyond Matamba and Kasanje to the Lunda empire on the Kasai. The Mbundu country and the Kwanza valley [i.e. the country stretching inland from Luanda for about 200 miles ESE] changed from being a generating point to being a corridor through which the slaves captured during the Lunda wars of expansion reached the sea.[3]

It was indeed the Lunda wars of expansion which opened up new sources of supply in the heart of the continent. It was not only that formidable bands of Lunda warriors fanned out like *conquistadores* from the Lunda heartland but also, as we shall see, that the Lunda, the possessors of a highly effective administrative structure, developed techniques which enabled the conquered lands to be successfully incorporated and governed.

So effective was this process that by 1750, on the eve of our period, Lunda power stretched from Lake Tanganyika in the east to the River Kwango, only some 300 miles from the Atlantic coast, in the west.[4] This was the farthest west that Lunda power

[3] David Birmingham, *Trade and Conflict in Angola: the Mbundu and their Neighbours under the Influence of the Portuguese, 1483–1790* (Oxford, 1966) 133.

[4] J. Vansina, *The Kingdoms of the Savanna* (Madison, 1966) 70.

reached, but it was not a simple case of expanding up to the frontier with Angola. For if the Lunda empire on the one hand and the coastal colonies or states on the other were two major political entities there was also a third situated, literally, between them. This consisted of a group of Yaka states, of Lunda origin,[5] whose western boundaries were from some 100 to 400 miles inland from the coast and which (excluding two small enclaves) extended in a broken line from the middle Kwango in the north to the inside bend of the Cunene river, well below Benguela, in the south. The importance for the slave trade of these various states was great. Already by the end of the seventeenth century two of them, Kasanje and Matamba, had established themselves as intermediaries between Angola and the Lunda peoples. It was through them that Angola received its main supply of slaves, and only through them, since they were always able to prevent the Portuguese entering into direct relations with the Lunda and so, between them, enjoyed a monopoly position. During most of the eighteenth century, despite a war with Matamba lasting intermittently from 1739 to 1744, the Portuguese were unable to break, or even significantly reduce, the power of the inland intermediaries, nor, because of the emergence of Ovimbundu states as intermediaries to the south, to establish a more southerly direct link with the interior.[6]

The African states to the north – Loango, Kakongo, Ngoy, together with Soyo, Mbamba and other successor 'states' of the old Congo Kingdom[7] – also had to trade through the Matamba and Kasanje intermediaries, but to a lesser degree. This was because although the Congo/Loango area obtained some of its slaves from the slave markets of Matamba and Kasanje, it also had sources of supply within the triangle bounded by the coast, the Congo river and the Equator, as well as from regional networks converging on Stanley Pool and from as far north as the

---

[5] Ibid., 50–53 and map on p. 237.

[6] Birmingham, *Trade and Conflict in Angola*, 133–61 passim; Vansina, *Kingdoms of the Savanna*, 65 (map), 83–84, 124, 180, 197–207; J. L. Vellut, 'Relations internationales du Moyen-Kwango et de l'Angola dans la deuxième moitié du XVIIIe siècle;' *Etudes d'Histoire africaine*, I (1970) 86–99.

[7] Defeat at the Battle of Ambuila in 1665 marks the substantial end of the original Congo Kingdom.

Ubangi, and possibly along the Kasai, an alternative route from Lunda territory.[8] Within this whole northerly region there were shifts in the balance of economic power within our period. Loango, which up until the mid-eighteenth century was the most important slave trading state, thereafter saw its trade decline at the expense of Malemba, Cabinda, the Congo estuary ports and the coast to the south down even beyond Ambriz to Mossula, which last was really in Angola but which was effectively independent. Paralleling this development there was within Angola frequent rivalry between Luanda merchants and those of Benguela,[9] whilst overall there was endemic rivalry between the colony of Angola and the whole region to the north (which in Portuguese eyes was under Portuguese suzerainty anyway). During our period this rivalry came to a head in two episodes. The first occasion was in 1759, when after two decades of leisurely debate, the Portuguese went ahead with the construction of a fort at Nkoje, some 150 miles E.N.E. of Luanda. The whole purpose of this enterprise was to seek to block the trade route from Matamba and Kasanje to San Salvador precisely because the northward flow of slaves along this route threatened the trade of Angola. As David Birmingham suggests, a decrease of a third to a quarter in Luanda slave exports from 1768 onwards, as compared with the years before 1759, indicates that the founding of the fort, and the campaigns which ensued, were only successful in the very short run.[10] The second episode was when Portugal attempted a coastal approach to the problem of competition from the north. Thus in 1783 she established a fort at Cabinda itself in an attempt to monopolise the trade of the Loango coast, but this venture too was unsuccess-

---

[8] Phyllis M. Martin, *The External Trade of the Loango Coast, 1576–1870; the Effects of Changing Commercial Relations on the Vili Kingdom of Loango* (Oxford 1972) 117–35; J. Vansina, 'Long-Distance Trade Routes in Central Africa'; *J.A.H.*, III (1962) no. 3, 379–82; Birmingham, *Trade and Conflict in Angola*, 156–57. In his review of *Trade and Conflict in Angola*, in *J.A.H.*, VIII (1967) 547, Vansina asserts that it is unlikely that the Lunda sent slaves by canoe along the Lulua and Kasai rivers to the Loango coast. The river Ogowé, entering the sea at Cape Lopez, began to develop a significant slave traffic in the 1760s and 1770s. (K. David Patterson, 'Early Knowledge of the Ogowé River and the American Exploration of 1854', *International Journal of African Historical Studies* V (1972) no. 1, 75.)

[9] Birmingham, *Trade and Conflict in Angola*, 140–1.

[10] Ibid., 142, 150–5.

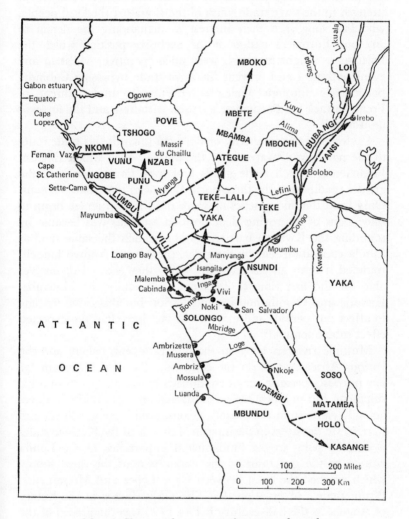

MAP 4. Slave trade routes and sources of supply

ful. By delaying until the end of the American War of Independence Portugal lost what chance she had of consolidating her position before the British, French and Dutch returned in strength to the slave trade south of the Equator; the local people, who had long seen their interest as demanding the denial to any one European nation of the exclusive position which the Portuguese sought to assert, were unco-operative, whilst in any event nothing could prevent the slave trade bypassing Cabinda, particularly through Malemba. Eventually under threat of French attack the Portuguese garrison withdrew and the fort was destroyed.[11]

Underlying this sensitivity of Portugal towards this trade route to the north was awareness of the marked edge which English, French and Dutch trade goods had over Portuguese, and the greater readiness of the three north European powers to sell guns. Only from the mid-nineties onwards did the Portuguese begin to show signs of improving their position and this was because by rounding the Kwango barrier – and at much the same time as Lunda expedition sent by the ruler, the Mwata Yamvo himself, rounded it from an easterly direction – they showed themselves able for the first time to challenge successfully the Malemba, Kasanje and Ovimbundu intermediaries: but this came too late to affect our period (and may not in fact have had the expected effect subsequently).[12]

Multiple rivalries between the one European colony and the various African states on the coast are of course important for our purposes because they determined the coastal points of slave shipment. But to repeat, as we must, that only a minority of slaves actually came from the coastal regions, even largely defined, and to reiterate the stress on the intermediary role of the Kwango states is only to point to the fundamental importance of the Lunda empire as the generator of the major part of the slave supply which reached the coast between Cape Lopez and Mossamedes. Birmingham's observation that 'the major factor in the history of Angola in the half-century before 1790 was the arrival of the Lunda empire at the peak of its trading power'[13] must be expanded so as to refer also, and only less, to the effect of Lunda power on

[11] Ibid., 157–8; Martin, *Trade of the Loango Coast*, 87–91.
[12] Birmingham, *Trade and Conflict in Angola*, 161.
[13] Ibid., 148.

states to the north of Angola, and must not be taken to mean that Lunda power was less important after 1790. To the role of the Lunda empire and the trade routes which connected it with the Atlantic coast we must now turn.

As early as the mid-seventeenth century trade routes into the Lunda sphere were in being. Portuguese traders went to reside at Kasanje where they sold goods to, and bought slaves from the Jaga. They in turn organised caravans of European goods, including some guns, to the Mwata Yamvo at his capital, obtaining ivory and slaves in return. The Mwata Yamvo also dispatched his own caravans and because the trade was officially recognised and protected it tapped in its turn the regional trade and tribute networks of the Lunda empire. The whole process must have been much facilitated during the eighteenth century for it was probably then that the centralisation of the Mwata Yamvo's authority took place. Perhaps the great significance of these trade routes is most strikingly attested by the extension which was made after 1740 to the capital of the kingdom of Kazembe, in present-day Katanga, whence connection was made with trade routes to the East coast.[14] To attest the existence of trade routes and to amplify this with significant but fragmentary evidence of slaves passing along these routes from far in the interior of the continent is only a partial explanation of how, in the words of Richard Gray and David Birmingham, the Lunda empire 'grew in the eighteenth century to be one of Africa's largest suppliers of slaves to the outside world'.[15] Another part of the explanation, as one might expect, lies in the Lunda system of government.

Already by the sixteenth century Lunda villages were linked in a loose but unified political unit by the institutionalisation of the original blood relationships between village chiefs, that is by perpetual kinship. In the generation following the conquest of the Lunda by the Luba in the sixteenth century the political structure of the Lunda–Luba kingdom was amplified and strengthened. Ruling a group of villages, linked internally by ties of

[14] Vansina, *Kingdoms of the Savanna*, 83–4; Vansina, *Long-Distance Trade Routes*, 382–3; I. Cunnison, 'Kazembe and the Portuguese, 1798–1832', *J.A.H.*, II (1961) no. 1, 62–5.

[15] Richard Gray and David Birmingham, 'Some Economic and Political Consequences of Trade in Central and Eastern Africa in the Pre-Colonial Period', *Pre-Colonial African Trade: Essays on Trade in Central and Eastern Africa before 1900*, ed. Gray and Birmingham (London, 1970) 15.

perpetual kinship between their chiefs, whose authority derived in part from their supernatural functions, was the elder of the headmen (*mbay*). These elders were grouped in turn into political districts governed by a *cilool* who was nominated by the King on the proposition of the *mbay* group. Under the supervision of another official, the *yikeezy*, the *cilool* was the main channel of administration between the provinces and the Lunda capital, and was particularly concerned with tax collection and forwarding. At the centre the Mwata Yamvo had sacred attributes and was assisted by office-holders, divided into groups, members of one group of whom were linked both to the King and to different *cilool* by ties of perpetual kinship. There were also other links between centre and provinces whose function, again, was mainly to do with tribute. Tribute was paid at specified times and either in food or in a region's specialised products. Linked to, and as important as, the concept of perpetual kinship was the concept of positional succession such that

> a successor inherited not only an office but also the personal status of the deceased, including his name and kinship relationships. Thus, ancient kinship relations were re-enacted every generation. . . . These mechanisms proved to be extremely useful; they divorced the political structure from the real descent structure since they were not bound to any principle of descent in particular. . . . [Moreover] the mechanisms could be diffused without necessitating any changes in the existing social structures, which explains why so many Central African cultures could take over the system with little or no cultural resistance.

A further part of the explanation of why the Lunda were able to maintain authority over other peoples is that the imposition of a Lunda *cilool* over hereditary local chiefs (whose authority was confirmed) had all the advantages of indirect rule. Underlying all was the strength of a conception of kingship[16] which was derived partly from religion and strengthened by it.

Now in this analysis of the Lunda system of government one of the features to which Jan Vansina attaches particular importance – and he also cites Professor Daniel Biebuyck in his support – is the role of tribute. It is highly indicative of its importance that as

[16] Vansina, *Kingdoms of the Savanna*, 78–83.

late as 1875, when Lunda power was past its peak, the Lunda capital of 8,000 to 10,000 inhabitants was fed entirely on food brought in payment of tribute.[17] Richard Gray and David Birmingham develop this theme by suggesting the broad lines of how tribute, and the relationship of which it was a part, could have done much to ensure a constant supply of slaves. Slave raiding, they say, was often an early phase in the development of a slave-trading state but

> it is followed by a much more important phase in which tribute becomes the key to the supply of slaves. The ability of African rulers to obtain slaves by taxation may emphasise a key difference between African and Western European states. . . . The manner in which a [African] chief commanded the productive services of his subjects was complex, but an understanding of it is probably the key to understanding the Central African tribute system and the methods used to accumulate slaves for export. The relationship between chief and subject went through various shades, father and son, householder and retainer, landlord and villein, master and slave, warlord and captive. Within this range the chief might on occasion be persuaded to exchange the services of subjects for material returns; if he thought that the guns, cloth, drink, and tobacco which traders offered him for a subject whom they would take away into slavery, more than outweighed that subject's life work as a producer at home, he might indulge in slave-trading. The alternative would usually be to forgo any prospect of acquiring exotic goods, thus clearly making the temptation to indulge in such traffic very great. The opportunities for gaining durable material wealth from the slave trade obviously encouraged rulers to expand their possessions and increase the number of people over whom they ruled. Such expansion often took place by warfare which initially provided prisoners of war, a ready source of slaves, and subsequently provided new subjects on whom taxes could be levied in the form of men. One further advantage which a ruler gained from expanding his fief derived from his position as the final arbiter in judicial matters; it was he who could condemn recalcitrants, or alleged recalcitrants, to be sold into foreign bondage. This use of judicial processes to obtain export slaves

[17] Ibid., 82.

may have been a major factor in the trade, and inevitably put pressures on the administration of justice which tended to warp pre-existing values.[18]

All of this has clear implications for the relationship between slave trading and political and economic development, but before drawing these out we must consider the question of whence the slaves came in the second of the three regions which we are studying, the Bight of Biafra.

According to an impressionistic estimate based on first-hand knowledge of the Niger Delta in the years 1786-1800, four-fifths of the slaves exported through Bonny,[19] a Delta port heavily involved in the slave trade, came from the Ibo hinterland. If one modifies this conjecture, suggesting that the Ibo hinterland is likely to have featured to much the same extent in the slave trade of all the Delta ports and of Old Calabar, then it becomes an approximation which may not be very much too high for what, we should also remember, was the crucial part of the whole Bight of Biafra.[20] Thoroughly to test this conjecture would require good evidence on the tribal origins of slaves carried away in our period. Such evidence we do not have but Curtin and Vansina have processed evidence from the mid-nineteenth century to yield conclusions which, tentatively and as a possible guide only, we may apply to our earlier period – a period which, after all, does span the eighteenth and nineteenth centuries. The first part of the evidence in question is the research of a mid-nineteenth-century linguist, employed by the Church Missionary Society in Sierra Leone. As part of a language survey which he carried out among recaptives in Freetown and vicinity (i.e. Africans settled in the colony after being liberated from slave ships by the Royal Navy) in 1849, S. W. Koelle listed the name of the homeland of each of his informants

[18] Gray and Birmingham, *Economic and Political Consequences of Trade in Africa*, 18–19. Cf. A. J. H. Latham's useful distinction between the different functions slavery could fulfil in 'Currency, Credit and Capitalism on the Cross River in the Pre-Colonial Era,' *J.A.H.*, XII (1971) no. 4, 604.

[19] J. Adams, *Sketches taken during Ten Voyages to Africa between the Years 1786 and 1800* (London, 1822), 38.

[20] Cf. the view of David Northrup that in the second half of the eighteenth century a half or more of the slaves taken from the Bight of Biafra were Ibo ('The Growth of Trade among the Igbo before 1800', *J.A.H.*, XIII (1972) no. 2, 232).

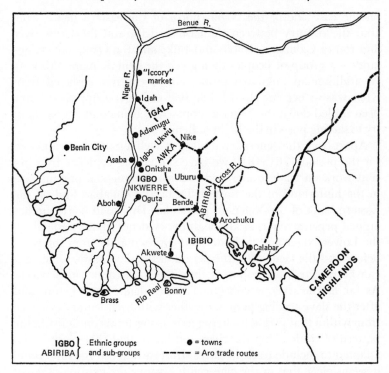

Map 5. South-eastern Nigeria in the first half of the
nineteenth century

and the number of fellow countrymen whom the informant knew
to be resident in the colony.

Koelle's survey is supplemented by the Sierra Leone census of
1848 in which the tribal origins of some 36 per cent of the colony's
population were recorded, albeit in the cruder categorisation of the
larger tribes only; this census has likewise been processed by Curtin
and Vansina. Koelle listed no less than some 160 languages and
his work is therefore a much more accurate guide to the size of
smaller groups: but his informants could not quantify the number
of representatives of the larger groups, such as the Ibo, and so, as
Curtin and Vansina point out, the two lists are complementary.
Taken together the lists show that whilst some slaves had come
from as far north as the Lake Chad region there were three main
catchment areas for slaves in the Bight of Biafra trade: these were

on the east side of the Niger, north of the eastern delta – the Ibo; the country between the eastern delta and the Cross river and round Calabar – Ibibio and Efik; and the Cameroon Highlands – a group of peoples then given the generic name 'Mokos'. In addition an unknown proportion of captives enslaved from what was to become the Middle Belt of Nigeria appear to have been traded down the Niger as opposed to being sent across country to slaving ports in the Bight of Benin.[21]

Apart from the general credibility of such a pattern as valid also for the period 1761–1810 we have supporting evidence from recent work on trade routes and politico–commercial organisation in the hinterland of the Eastern Delta and Calabar, and on the Eastern bank of the Niger. In particular, Dr David Northrup has argued persuasively that although the evidence about trade along the Lower Niger and its hinterland comes mainly from the years before and the years after the period of the slave trade some light can be directed, as he puts it, into the dark tunnel in between. As far as the river is concerned the evidence from before and after the slave trading period, together with fragmentary evidence from within that period itself, suggests a long-term continuity in the pattern of trade along the river and hence that that pattern was adapted to include trade in slaves. In regard to the Ibo hinterland it seems clear that in the eighteenth century pre-existing regional trade networks were put together into a marketing grid by an enterprising people, the Aro, principally in order to supply the demand for slaves and to profit from it. The origins of the Aro are obscure but they are a mixture of Ibo, Ibibio and Cross River peoples who at some point in their past acquired an Ibibio shrine at Arochuku, the so-called 'Long Juju'. The religious function which they thereby acquired gave them, in accordance with Ibo tradition, status and privileges which they put to use also for commercial ends. Thus the Long Juju at Arochuku became the supreme oracle and arbitrator of disputes amongst both the Ibo and their southern neighbours – and the Aro established colonies throughout the hinterland of the Delta and left bank of the

[21] Philip D. Curtin and Jan Vansina, 'Sources of the Nineteenth Century Atlantic Slave Trade', *J.A.H.*, v (1964) no. 2, 185–208. The conclusions and most of the statistical basis, with revisions, of this article are incorporated in Curtin, *Census*, 251–7, 289–8. The material on the Sierra Leone census, however, has not been included in this latter source.

Lower Niger and generally used their religious prestige and military and economic power to establish a network of markets and fairs.[22] W. R. G. Horton gives an instance of how the Aro acquired slaves when he points to their alliance with the people of Nike: astride an Aro trade route they were a relatively wealthy people who either used their wealth to buy slaves from an adjacent land-starved and over-populated people or else seized them by force through the agency of mercenaries supplied by the Aro.[23] A. J. H. Latham makes the further point that the possession of guns played an important part in the development of Aro power and that since guns were not imported into Old Calabar until 1713 the rise of the Aro probably took place in the middle years of the century[24] – on the eve, that is, of our period. Thus old Calabar and the more easterly states of the Eastern Delta were well situated to tap the Aro trade routes whilst traders from Brass-Nembe, as follows from their geographical position, traded to and from the markets up the Lower Niger itself.[25] These Delta traders, as we shall see, themselves constituted an adaptation of Delta politico-commercial institutions in response to the opportunities of the slave trade. As many authorities have pointed out, descent groups developed into trading houses, enhancing their power and numbers by marriages and most of all by acquiring slaves. Houses of this kind – equipped, archetypally, with war and trading canoes manned by warriors and numerous slaves – were eminently capable of driving and protecting a trade with traders from neighbouring peoples.[26]

[22] Northrup, 'Trade among the Igbo', 217–36.

[23] W. R. G. Horton, 'The Ohu System of Slavery in a Northern Ibo Village-Group', *Africa*, xxvi (1956) 17–28, quoted in Northrup, 'Trade among the Igbo', 235.

[24] A. J. H. Latham, *Old Calabar 1600–1891: The Impact of the International Economy upon a Traditional Society* (Oxford, 1973), 27.

[25] See especially, E. J. Alagoa, 'The Niger Delta States and their Neighbours, 1600–1800', *The History of West Africa*, vol. i, ed. J. F. Ade Ajayi and Michael Crowder (London, 1971) 270–71, 295, 298–300. Note also in this whole connection the same author's 'Long-Distance Trade and States in the Niger Delta,' *J.A.H.*, xi (1970) no. 3, 319–29.

[26] K. O. Dike, *Trade and Politics in the Niger Delta*, 1830–1885 (Oxford, 1956) 34–7; Daryll Forde (ed.), *Efik Traders of Old Calabar* (London, 1956) passim; G. I. Jones, *The Trading States of the Oil Rivers* (London, 1963), passim; Latham, *Old Calabar*, 31–34; Alagoa, 'The Niger Delta States and their Neighbours', 280–82.

In short, then, the evidence indicates that, in our period, although an unspecified number of slaves from the Nigerian Middle Belt reached the sea in the Bight of Biafra, most came from the area bounded by the Niger, the Benue and the Cross rivers, together with a sizeable contribution from the Cameroon Highlands. The strong evidence about trade routes and political and commercial organisation in the region makes it all the more credible that the slave trade of this kind could have been generated.

Bight of Benin slaving ports in the years 1761–1810 were principally Whydah, Porto Novo, Epe and Badagry, whilst some slaves were probably shipped from the coast near Benin itself.[27] The question of the provenance of the great bulk of these involuntary emigrants is bound up with political rivalries and changes among the Yoruba and Aja peoples of the area. Since 1730 the kingdom of Dahomey had been a tributary of Oyo and under King Agaja and his successor, Tegbesu, Dahomey had become committed to the slave trade both as its principal economic activity and as a royal monopoly. The state of Dahomey was therefore particularly involved in all aspects of the slave trade and not least the acquisition of slaves. By the time of his death in 1766 Tegbesu's direction of affairs had been crowned with some success, and not least because trade with Oyo permitted him to secure slaves for export. Significantly for the future, however, Dahomean slave raids into the hinterland had not been successful, partly because the army had been neglected; when, therefore, Oyo chose to export slaves through the ports to the east of Whydah, outside Dahomey, the Dahomean slave trade was to prove very vulnerable indeed. Already by 1765 the trade through Porto Novo had displayed a striking increase and in the late seventies Abiodun, the new Alafin of Oyo, a trader by profession, decided to reorganise and consolidate the Oyo trade route to the coast and channel the trade through this more easterly port, much more under his influence. Henceforth slaves from the Oyo empire which previously had fed Whydah as well as Epe, Porto Novo and Badagry now went exclusively to Porto Novo. Deprived of slaves from Oyo, its major source, Dahomey tried to make up the deficiency by more raiding but, as before, its army was unequal to the task. Henceforward the Dahomean slave trade through Whydah could only prosper in

[27] A. F. C. Ryder, *Benin and the Europeans.*

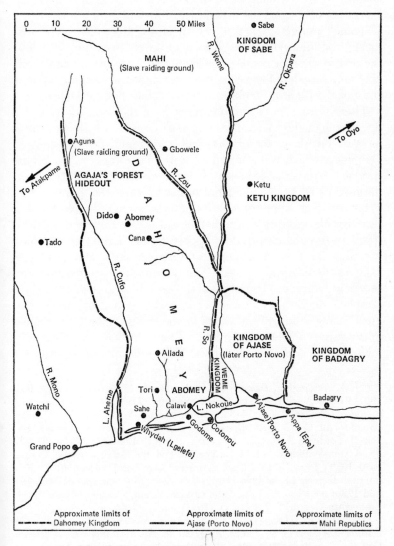

MAP 6. Dahomey Kingdom and its neighbours
after the 1730 settlement

measure as Oyo was unable to enforce her new policy. Even the collapse of the Oyo empire in the 1790s brought no improvement but rather confirmed the superiority of the old arrangement when Dahomey purchased her slaves, in effect, from Oyo. The disturbed conditions of the last decade of the eighteenth century and the first of the nineteenth perodically and transiently made available new supplies of slaves at the coast, but it was on the western coast of the Bight of Benin as a whole rather than at Dahomey.[28]

There were thus two major features of the slave trade in the interior: namely an empire, the Oyo empire, which generated most of the slaves for export, and a kingdom, the kingdom of Dahomey, which was committed to the slave trade as the mainstay of the national economy. It is not clear where all the slaves disposed of by Oyo came from but suzerainty over Borgu up to 1783 and over Nupe up to 1789 or 1790 apparently produced a considerable number – whether by tribute or raiding over their frontiers, or enhanced trading opportunities – is not clear.[29] Raiding over the eastern frontiers of Oyo probably also produced captives for subsequent sale.[30] The fact that the Middle Belt was producing substantial numbers of slaves in the years before Koelle's sample is doubtful evidence for our earlier period because of the great changes and disturbances in the lands of the Oyo empire in the earlier nineteenth century.[31] The disturbances immediately following the decline of Oyo in the 1790s must also have produced

---

[28] I. A. Akinjogbin, *Dahomey and its Neighbours, 1708–1818* (Cambridge, 1967) 91–194 passim; see also C. W. Newbury, *The Western Slave Coast and its Rulers* (Oxford, 1961) 15–33, and P. Morton-Williams, 'The Yoruba Kingdom of Oyo,' *West African Kingdoms in the Nineteenth Century*, ed. Daryll Forde and P. M. Kaberry, reprint (London, 1971), 37–42. P. Morton-Williams, 'The Oyo Yoruba and the Atlantic Slave Trade, 1670–1830', *Journal of the Historical Society of Nigeria* III (1964), I, 40–41. For internal disputes in the Oyo kingdom leading up to the *coup d'état* in the mid-1790s see R. C. C. Law, 'The Constitutional Troubles of Oyo in the Eighteenth Century,' *J.A.H.*, XII (1971) no. 1, 25–44.

[29] Akinjogbin, *Dahomey and its Neighbours*, 81, 75; P. C. Lloyd, *The Political Development of Yoruba Kingdoms in the Eighteenth and Nineteenth Centuries* (London, 1971, Royal Anthropological Institute Occasional Paper No. 31) 14.

[30] Morton-Williams, 'Yoruba Kingdom of Oyo', 36.

[31] Curtin, *Census*, 254; Curtin and Vansina, 'Sources of the Nineteenth Century Slave Trade, 195; Morton-Williams, 'Yoruba Kingdom of Oyo', 41–4.

captives for export. Whatever the obscurity cloaking this last matter it is abundantly clear that few slaves could be found in the Dahomean hinterland despite the numerous efforts of the Dahomean army, despite the fact that Dahomey was a state geared to the prosecution of the slave trade. The fact was that the Dahomean hinterland was a very limited one indeed. In the later eighteenth century Ashanti and Dagomba, then its tributary, closed off access to the west[32] and Dahomey never penetrated to, or by northward leading routes tapped, the Middle Niger. When supplies from Oyo were cut off, therefore, Dahomey, a kingdom which dominated an area no more than about 200 miles deep and 150 miles broad, had no hope of retaining a serious stake in the export slave trade as long as these external constraints endured.

A retrospective comparison may now enable us to discern some at least of the conditions necessary for successful slave trading. First of all, the African coastal kingdom, or for that matter the European colony of Angola, had to have an appropriate political and commercial organisation. In so far as in the later eighteenth century it was still occasionally possible to acquire slaves by trade or warfare from closely adjacent peoples the level of appropriateness did not need to be sophisticated. Little sophistication was necessary, for instance, when Dahomey went to war with Little Popo, Porto Novo and Badagry between 1791 and 1795,[33] or to obtain slaves in the course of the frequent strife between the successor 'states' of the old Congo kingdom.[34] But by the second half of the eighteenth century appropriate organisation increasingly meant a combination of military power, economic resources and institutional adaptation sufficient to carry European trade goods into the interior and exchange them for slaves. By definition the slave-trading kingdoms on the coast possessed this capability, whether it was the Dahomey royal monopoly, which channelled slaves between the interior markets with Oyo and Whydah, or between slave raiding grounds and Whydah; or the trading houses of the Niger Delta states and Old Calabar, sometimes trading

[32] Ivor Wilks, 'The Mossi and Akan States, 1500–1800', *History of West Africa*, I 385.

[33] Akinjogbin, *Dahomey and its Neighbours*, 181.

[34] L. Jadin, 'Relations sur le royaume du Congo de P. Raimondo da Dicomano, missionaire de 1791 à 1795', *Bulletin de l'Académie Royale des Sciences Coloniales*, III (1957) no. 2, 326–8; Martin, *Trade of the Loango Coast*, 130.

with markets up the Niger and nearly always tapping the Aro trading grid either on the banks of the river or inland from the Delta; or the states of the Loango coast, the Congo river and the Congo coast either dispatching caravans to trade with the Teke on Stanley Pool or trading with Matamba and Kasanje; or the Portuguese and Brazilian merchants of Luanda and Benguela equipping and sending expeditions to the same inland intermediaries. Porto Novo was the obvious exception in that she was essentially just the seaward end of a trading system controlled from Old Oyo.

The second condition was that there had to be an interior trading network of some kind with which traders from the coast could establish connection. The importance of this is proved negatively by the case of Dahomey. Of course, if her military resources had been vastly greater and more effective they might have secured for her a sufficient supply of slaves for export – though in the long run this would still have been because this military strength would have permitted her to intrude herself into a trading network. As it was, her slave trade declined into insignificance when Oyo decided to discontinue the sale to Dahomey of slaves obtained from tributaries, border warfare and commercial transactions. A more enduring network was the Aro trading grid, extending some 250 miles inland and one which produced a remarkably steady flow of slaves throughout our period. As to the Congo/Angola region we can at least point to locations like Stanley Pool and San Salvador as conspicuous meeting points of trade routes up from the coast with a trading network, about which we know regrettably little, stretching along the Congo river and some of its tributaries to a distance of at least some 600 miles into the interior. Of all the interior trading networks the one by which slaves from the Lunda empire were exchanged with the Yaka intermediaries was the most interesting and extensive: in our relative ignorance about it, however, it can only be a matter of speculation as to whether it generated the same high proportion of, say, the slaves who were eventually shipped from Luanda and Benguela as the Aro network generated of those who were exported from the Niger Delta ports and Old Calabar. It remains a point of major significance that it was precisely those regions of the African coast, the Niger Delta and Congo/Angola respectively, which were linked to trading networks in the interior – the Aro, Congo and Lunda networks – which were able to yield up, until 1800, a large and increasing supply of slaves.

Consideration of the demographic evidence may shed light both on the ability of Africa, and of the Niger Delta hinterland and West Central Africa in particular, to generate slaves in this manner, and on the demographic effects of doing so.

It must be stressed that the demography of pre-colonial Africa is short on hard evidence and abounds in analogically derived reasoning, backward projection and sheer speculation. Recent work by Professor John Fage, however, provides a basis for commentary on the export figures we have adduced from the two crucial areas of Biafra and Congo/Angola. Anything other than round figures would, in this context, convey a quite unwarranted impression of precision: we shall take 14,000 per annum as the average annual slave export from the Bight of Biafra between 1761 and 1810 (a figure derived from the coastal distribution of the trade of the three main carriers and rounded up to the very limited degree appropriate for the slight additional American trade) and 30,000 per annum for Congo/Angola (a figure similarly derived but with more of a weighting to cover the significant Dutch and American trade). John Fage, by working backwards from twentieth-century censuses and population estimates for West Africa, by taking account of Curtin's decennial slave export figures, in the years before 1850, and assuming progressive growth in the average annual rate of natural increase from the *c*.1500 low of 1·2 per 1,000 implicit in Carr-Saunders and other demographers, to the high levels of the middle and later twentieth century, has produced an exponential curve which postulates a West African population of *c*.25,000,000 in 1700. Relating this figure to Curtin's slave export figures for 1701–1810, which Fage aggregates at 40,000 a year, Fage points out that this represents a rate of loss which is not outstandingly high and which, more important, is of much the same order of magnitude as the likely natural growth rate of 1·6 per thousand.[35] Let us now take the assumption that

[35] J. D. Fage, 'The Effect of the Export Slave Trade on African Populations: a Paper for Discussion' (Unpublished paper given at the African Studies Association of the United Kingdom Conference, September 1972) and cited by Professor Fage's kind permission. In this paper Fage develops an approach which he initiated in 'Slavery and the Slave Trade in the Context of West African History', *J.A.H.*, x (1969) no. 3, 393–404. Fage makes the important point that since only about one-third of slaves

this rate of loss, namely 1:625, would merely cancel out the natural growth rate and apply it first to the Bight of Biafra trade in order to throw light on the question of the likely geographical extent of the Biafra catchment area. This ratio means that the population necessary to sustain without overall loss an annual drain of 14,000 slaves is 8,750,000 and the question which then poses itself is whether it is credible that the later eighteenth-century population of what in crude terms we may identify with Eastern Nigeria and West Cameroon, i.e. the main area whence we know slaves to have come, could have been of this magnitude. Alternatively, do these demographic assumptions rather demand that we postulate a significantly wider catchment area?

The combined area of E. Nigeria and W. Cameroon is 46,538 square miles so an eighteenth-century population of 8,750,000 would mean a density per square mile of 188. The more the catchment area was confined to E. Nigeria and W. Cameroon the more one might venture the comment that with a population density of 188 per square mile there would have been a considerable induce-ment to export slaves as one obvious means of reducing pressure on resources. After all, this was roughly the density of the rural population of Europe at the same time[36] and that rural population was arguably more efficient and therefore better able to support itself, and at the same time was beginning to show a blend of need and readiness to migrate to the towns. On the other hand it might be argued that an agricultural economy in the then state of techno-logical development, even recalling the assumption that natural population increase was being taken off by the slave trade, just could not have had so dense a population.[37] Moreover, if Fage's projection of West Africa's population in 1850 (a year some ten years after the end of serious slave trading in the Biafra region) –

[36] See C. Clark, *Population Growth and Land Use* (London, 1967) 289, Diagram VIIIA.

[37] The fact that the 1963/65 population density of E. Nigeria and W. Cameroon was 289 per square mile hardly seems to shed much light on the problem. All population figures, unless otherwise specified, and all figures of surface area, are from *Africa South to the Sahara, 1971* (London, 1971).

exported were women, and since African men who could afford it were polygynous, the effect of slave exports would not have been as great as if equal numbers of the sexes had been taken. On the other hand it was men and women of child-bearing age who were mostly exported.

a projection made by jobbing back from twentieth-century estimates – were applied to E. Nigeria and W. Cameroon the result
would be a population of 4,300,000. Such a figure is only about
one half the level required for the region, on the given assumptions,
to have withstood the slave trade without a net population loss.

If a wider catchment area is to be postulated it would seem
from other evidence that it can only have been a highly uncertain
area of what in colonial terminology was N. Nigeria. If slave
exports originated over this added area of 281,782 square miles as
well, a population density figure of 27 per square mile would
result. Secondly, if Fage's projection of West African population
in 1850 were applied to E. Nigeria, W. Cameroon and N. Nigeria,
the putative population would have been 13,800,000 – a figure
well above that required for the slave trade to cause no net loss.

The difficulty, of course, is that there is only limited knowledge
of what parts of what was to become N. Nigeria supplied the slave
trade. But the balance of the evidence strongly suggests that if the
slave trade drew to any great extent on N. Nigeria, and we know
from other evidence that slaves come in some number from this
region, as well as upon E. Nigeria and the W. Cameroon, to which
other evidence points to as the major source of supply, then the
trade need have caused no net loss of population in the territories
affected. Of course, particular areas might have been heavily
exploited and so would have suffered accordingly. In short the
application of Fage's proposition of what drain by slave exports
the West African population could sustain without overall loss
to the particular – and important – case of the Bight of Biafra
would seem to confirm other evidence that the area east of the
Niger and south of the Benue was the main catchment area, but
that significant quantities of slaves were also emanating from
farther north, and that overall there was clearly an exportable
'surplus'.

In the case of Congo/Angola the use to which demographic
calculations can be put is different. Firstly, they provide confirmation of the very far-flung nature of the trade routes along which
the slaves passed. The population necessary to provide annual
slave exports of 30,000, without net loss, would, on the Fage for-
mula, have been 18,750,000. Now even if we took *c.*1970 population figures it would take an area comprising Gabon, Congo–
Brazzaville, Angola and all save three of Zaire's nine provinces

to produce a population akin (actually 19,319,640) to the 18,750,000 postulated.[38] Now in fact the catchment area defined above, save for the arguable exclusion of Katanga, constitutes the area whence slaves actually were taken in our period; a further striking implication of the stated premises is that population growth between the later eighteenth and later twentieth centuries would have been slight – a mere 3%. Now this minimal increase contrasts with a West African population growth of 144% between 1910 and 1965 and, on Fage's calculations, of 215% between 1850 and 1965.[39] Given the known factors making for rapid growth by the mid-twentieth century at the latest, the conclusion must be either that the population dipped between the later eighteenth and later twentieth centuries, or that the eighteenth-century Atlantic slave trade had already reduced population below the 18,750,000 necessary for its maintenance, or a combination of both explanations. Certainly both the French and Belgian Congo (Congo-Brazzaville and Zaire) probably experienced sharp population loss in the nineteenth and early twentieth centuries not least because of monstrous labour exactions. On the other hand the Arab slave trade, considerable as it was in Central Africa from about 1810 onwards, hardly affected our catchment area as it has been defined. The Atlantic slave trade from West Central Africa persisted on a large scale until the mid-nineteenth century, though the annual average was probably smaller after 1810, the closing year of our period, than before.[40] On balance it would seem that the Atlantic slave trade, particularly before 1810, is likely to have been an important cause of population decline. All in all the impression which the demographic evidence and the known influences on population change give is that in Congo/Angola, unlike in the other major exporting region, the Bight of Biafra, the slave trade probably was an important cause of population decline.[41]

[38] The six Zaire provinces included are Kongo Central, Kinshasa, Equateur, Kasai Occidental, Kasai Oriental and Bandundu.
[39] Fage, 'Effect of the Export Slave Trade'. His 1910 and 1965 figures are from censuses and estimates, and the 1850 figures from projection.
[40] See Curtin, *Census*, 269.
[41] Christopher Wrigley, 'Historicism in Africa', *African Affairs*, vol. 70, no. 279 (April 1971) 114, suggests that there is 'a consensus of demographers that the "normal" rate of increase in pre-industrial and pre-medical societies lay between five and ten per thousand and that periodic

What light does this modest comparative study of the implication of the export slave trade within Africa throw on the connection between the slave trade and African political and economic development? An important part of the answer is clear and almost banal: African states which gained from participation in the slave trade did so because of their power, and the suitability, or adaptability, of their institutions; the losers lost for the converse of these reasons. Well before our period the winners, and doubtless some of the losers, probably in most cases conditioned to it by the existence of domestic slavery, and in parts of the West African savanna by an export slave across the Sahara, had accepted the slave trade as the means of satisfying individual and collective wants. In some cases institutions were so appropriate to a particular requirement or requirements of the slave trade that adaptation of function was minimal: it is likely that the use of the pre-existing Lunda tribute system for the obtaining of slaves, and a pre-existing political control to ensure safe passage of caravans, was a case of this. At the other extreme, or so it would seem from limited knowledge of them, the Aro owed their rise to power and wealth above all to the adaptation of their institutions to take all possible advantage from the slave trade. An important representative case somewhere in between are the peoples of the Niger Delta. It seems clear in their case that long-distance trading networks existed before the coming of the Europeans, let alone before the advent of the export slave trade, but it is unclear how far change in the political institutions preceded, was caused by, or was accelerated by the demands of the slave trade. In any event a feature of these states was their strong monarchies; how far this strength had emerged before the period of the slave trade is uncertain but at the very least the increase of business with European traders, in dealing with whom a person endowed with authority was required, must have enhanced the kingly office. Again, the process whereby lineage heads, by engaging in long-distance trade, became heads rather of trading

---

calamities would reduce the long term rate to less than five'. If a natural growth rate of up to 5 per thousand were applied to the Bight of Biafra hinterland it would of course emphasise still more its ability to produce the given slave export without net population loss. If such higher growth rate were assumed in the Congo/Angola hinterland the result would be that a drain of 30,000 per annum could have been sustained by a population very much lower than 18,750,000.

houses may well have begun before the slave-trading period: but that trade, because of its scale, must have increased, the political and economic importance, as it did the number, of those trading houses. It seems clear that although the prior existence of the trading house was an important reason why the Delta peoples moved into the supply of the European slave trade, the volume of the slave trade brought about a major change in the whole nature of the house. Lineage and kinship could no longer provide that rapid recruitment of the human resources which a house required if it was to take full advantage of the new competitive opportunity; some of the slaves therefore were retained in the trading houses and integrated into them. So determined and successful was this acculturation – a slave could rise to become head of a house – that it considerably augmented the power of the houses and, within limits, of the state. In short although the export slave trade took root and prospered because appropriate institutions existed, those institutions were also apt for further modification, the whole process serving to enhance the power and wealth of the peoples concerned.[42]

Although they do not appear to have been analysed from the perspective of anthropology and oral tradition, but only of contemporary European sources – which makes comparison with the more broadly based studies of the Delta peoples difficult – there seems to be a limited resemblance between Cabinda, Malamba, and possibly other states in that region, and those of the Delta. Thus brokers, the royally appointed middlemen in the trade with the Europeans, became powerful, rich and important, and a man like Andriz Samba of Cabinda, who in the 1780s was reported to have a following of 700 freemen and slaves, was surely much like the head of a Niger Delta trading house. Again, as in the Delta states, the king through officials closely regulated the trade with the Europeans.

But although states in this region throve on the slave trade because of the appropriateness or adaptability of their institutions, they manifest a further facet of the connection between participa-

---

[42] G. I. Jones, *Trading States of the Oil Rivers*, passim; Alagoa, *Niger Delta States and their Neighbours*, passim; Alagoa, *Long-Distance Trade and States in the Niger Delta*, 319–29; E. J. Alagoa, 'The Development of Institutions in the States of the Eastern Niger Delta', *J.A.H.*, xii (1971) no. 2, 269–78. For Old Calabar see Latham, *Old Calabar*, 24–51.

tion in the slave trade and economic and political development. This is that already by the middle of our period the process of adaptation in the core kingdom of Loango had, so to say, gone too far. That is to say, by the 1780s the brokers and the officials concerned in relations with European slave traders – and officials were often brokers as well – had become the key figures in Loango society. Not only was the power and prestige of princes, unless they became brokers, reduced, but so also was that of the *Maloango*. One effect of this was that his control of his kingdom beyond Loango Bay was increasingly challenged by officials who had the real power, so much so that one must begin to refer to Kakongo and Ngoyo, with their outlets at Malemba and Cabinda respectively, as quasi-independent states.[43] In broad comparative terms, however, it is important to remember that the very powerful kingdom of Benin did not owe its strength to a participation in the slave trade which was not on a large scale at this time.[44]

What of the negative side of our proposition? What of the losers? Some of those who might be so defined are not obviously such. But because the grip of the Kwango states and competition from the north were such as to prevent her obtaining adequate supplies of slaves from the interior in the later eighteenth century, Angola, in a relative sense, falls into this category. So more strikingly, if still unexpectedly, does Dahomey. In her case, although the dominant institution of a strong monarchy lent itself to the adoption of the slave trade as the basis of the national economy, inadequate military power, in relation both to Oyo and to the smaller peoples in the immediate hinterland, meant that her hopes were disappointed, her development as a state distorted. Some smaller potential losers avoided that fate either by withdrawal into impenetrable high ground or by moving into defensible towns.[45] Numerous groups, however, like Dahomey's weaker neighbours, like many Ibo groups, like many Lunda tributaries must have been subject to *all* and not just some of the modes of enslavement as

[43] Martin, *External Trade of the Loango Coast*, 158–71.

[44] Ryder, *Benin and the Europeans*, 198.

[45] For a likely example of this in the Nupe kingdom see Michael Mason, 'Population Density and "Slave Raiding" – The Case of the Middle Belt of Nigeria', *J.A.H.*, x (1969) no. 4, 557, and M. B. Gleave and R. M. Prothero, 'Population Density and "Slave Raiding" – A Comment', ibid., xii (1971) no. 2, 319–24.

Dr Paul Hair defines them on the basis of the recorded experience of Koelle's informants – war, kidnapping, as a result of judicial process, sale by relatives or superiors, and sale for debt.[46] John Fage has ventured an overall generalisation about the political effects of the slave trade and it is one with which, with three reservations, one can agree. 'On the whole it is probably true to say that the operation of the slave trade may have tended to integrate, strengthen and develop unitary, territorial political authority, but to weaken or destroy more segmentary societies.'[47] The first reservation is that, on the evidence of the kingdom of Loango, the process of adaptation whereby the state was able to take full advantage of the slave trade could unleash a process of social and political change culminating in the decline of the power of the King and of central authority.

The second reservation is more substantial and it is that Fage's comment does not take account of the possibility, urged by Dr Walter Rodney for the Upper Guinea coast (Senegambia and Sierra Leone), that the slave trade led to the maturing of 'incipient class contradictions . . . at the expense of communal solidarity'. Rodney continues:

> When one traces the exploitation of the majority of the society by the dominant layer, then the full extent of the destruction wrought by the slave trade on the society is revealed.
>
> The African ruling class in relation to its own subjects was no longer carrying out the functions of maintaining order and policing the states, these being incompatible with the mode of production adopted in response to the lure of European goods.[48]

The last charge can hardly be applied to the regions that have been considered in this chapter, save in two senses. It seems likely that a tendency to use legal process to provide slaves for buyers was a result of the slave trade, but that this was not the source of many slaves; any substantial use of this technique would have

[46] These modes are listed in descending order of frequency in Koelle's sample, namely 34%, 30%, 11%, 7% and 7%. P. E. H. Hair, 'The Enslavement of Koelle's Informants', *J.A.H.*, vi (1965) no. 2, 193–203.

[47] Fage, 'Slavery and the Slave Trade in West African History', 402.

[48] Walter Rodney, *A History of the Upper Guinea Coast, 1545–1800* (Oxford, 1970) 257–8.

weakened the power of the chief concerned. Secondly, it may be that where subordinate chiefs had tribute to pay, as perhaps in the Lunda empire, they would pay in slaves, though presumably as a result of raiding *other* peoples whenever possible. As to the maturing of 'incipient class contradictions' and the exploitation of the majority . . . by the 'dominant layer', one may note that class differentials are not necessarily class contradictions, save to a Marxist, and that 'dominant layer' is an imprecise concept. What, after all, is the dominant layer in an American sandwich? Or what the dominant layer in, say, Calabar society? Is it the King, or the *Ekpe* society, or the house-heads? As far as the important Delta states and Calabar are concerned external trade, and especially the slave trade, led to enhanced differentiation of political and economic function as between King and house-heads and as between house-head and house members, but not necessarily to class contradiction. Indeed, the vertical division of society into houses, together with the rapid acculturation of slaves suggests, rather, that *for those states* the slave trade led neither to exploitation nor to class contradiction. In Loango, as has been seen, a clear effect of the slave trade was the rise of provincial officials at the expense of the King, but an aspect of this development was that the new men could not be checked if they oppressed individual freemen – and this oppression could take the form of an increased resort to enslavement as a form of punishment. In Dahomey, it appears that the important development was the concentration of power into the hands of the King but the effect was to enhance the homogeneity of the state and not to open up class contradictions within it.

The third reservation is of a quite different kind, namely that the question of the effect of the slave trade on Africa is not to be assessed exclusively, or even primarily, by its impact on African socieites 'treated as collectivities'.[49] Historians are under a danger here: they are rightly and properly accustomed to the study of the rise and fall of states but, as Christopher Wrigley has pointed out, a constraint of the period of African decolonisation has been that 'both the partial apologists and the whole-hearted opponents of colonialism concurred in writing about Africa's past in terms of the construction and expansion of governmental systems and in seeing it as moving always to its grand climacteric, the emergence

[49] Wrigley, 'Historicism in Africa', 114.

of the New Independent States of the later twentieth century'.[50]
The limitations of this approach are made clear by a kind of judgement which it encourages, namely that the African chief who sold
people for gin is, to use a crudity which this perspective, carried
to extremes, deserves, metamorphosed into a 'good King' because
he strengthened the structure of his state. The most sobering corrective – and the last word – lies with Equiano as he describes his
capture:

> One day, when all our people were gone out to their works as
> usual, and only I and my dear sister were left to mind the house,
> two men and a woman got over our walls, and in a moment
> seized us both; and, without giving us time to cry out, or make
> resistance, they stopped our mouths, and ran off with us to the
> nearest wood. Here they tied our hands, and continued to carry
> us as far as they could, till night came on, when we reached a
> small house, where the robbers halted for refreshment and spent
> the night. We were then unbound; but were unable to take any
> food; and, being quite overpowered by fatigue and grief, our
> only relief was some sleep, which allayed our misfortune for a
> short time. The next morning we left the house, and continued
> travelling all the day. For a long time we kept to the woods, but
> at last we came into a road which I believed I knew. I had now
> some hopes of being delivered; for we had advanced but a little
> way before I discovered some people at a distance, on which I
> began to cry out for their assistance; but my cries had no other
> effect than to make them tie me faster and stop my mouth, and
> then they put me into a large sack. They also stopped my sister's
> mouth, and tied her hands; and in this manner we proceeded
> till we were out of the sight of those people. . . . The next day
> proved a day of greater sorrow than I had yet experienced;
> for my sister and I were separated, while we lay clasped in each
> other's arms: it was in vain that we besought them not to part
> us: she was torn from me, and immediately carried away, while
> I was left in a state of distraction not to be described.[51]

The next chapter begins the consideration of the process whereby
European thought came to condemn the slave trade, to whose
horrors Equiano's experience movingly points.

[50] Ibid., 118.
[51] *Equiano's Travels*, 16–17.

PART TWO

4 Eighteenth-Century Thought and Anti-Slavery

'The point at which we have now arrived,' writes Professor Sir Herbert Butterfield, referring to the culmination of the scientific revolution of the seventeenth century in Newton's synthesis of astronomy and mechanics, 'must stand as one of the great moments in the history of human experience.'[1] Concentrating on the study of motion Newton had explained motion, whether on earth or in the heavens, by laws of stark and beautiful simplicity. But it is a corollary of the new scientific philosophy which concerns us: so great was the wonder at the structure of the world and of the universe, as revealed by the new science, that there is delight in it because it is so wonderful, rather than any concern to change it. The new science, in other words, came for the time being to the support of age-long conservatism in the reverencing of what existed. Pope, a mirror of his age, captures this attitude in his principal philosophical poem, the *Essay on Man*.

> All are but parts of one stupendous whole,
> whose body nature is and God the soul . . .
> All nature is but art, unknown to thee;
> All chance, direction, which thou canst not see;
> All discord, harmony not understood;
> All partial evil, universal good.
> And, spite of pride, in erring reason's spite,
> One truth is clear, *whatever is is right.*[2]

[1] H. Butterfield, *The Origins of Modern Science* (London, 1950) 143.
[2] Alexander Pope, *Essay on Man*, Epistle I, lines 268–9, 289–94. Cf. Arthur O. Lovejoy, 'Cosmical piety and the sort of Romantic delight in the world which can arise, not from any belief in its adaptation to man's need or hopes, but from its infinite richness and diversity as a spectacle,

Nor do the different ranks of a society thus ordered desire change:

> The rich is happy in the plenty given,
> The poor contents him with the care of heaven.
> See the blind beggar dance, the cripple sing.
> The sot a hero, lunatic a King;[3]

And even if the different ranks did desire change, such a desire would be redundant when

> ... jarring interests of themselves create
> The according music of a well-mix'd state.[4]

Here then is no sense of the desirability, nor belief in the possibility of changing the accepted order of things. A cast of mind cradled in a sense of wonder at the Newtonian universe allowed that sense to be carried over into and to inform the view of the world of men. The early eighteenth-century concept of that age-old piece of intellectual furniture, the Great Chain of Being, combined to support a static view of human institutions. In the words of Arthur O. Lovejoy, author of the classical study of that concept, 'the limitations of each species of creature, which define its place in the scale, are indispensable to that infinite differentiation of things in which the "fullness" of the universe consists, and are therefore necessary to the realisation of the greatest of goods'.[5] Not only can man not complain because denied the endowments necessary to greater excellence, but 'if all partial evils are required by the universal good, and if the universe is and always has been perfectly good, we cannot expect that any of the partial evils will disappear'.[6] Furthermore, the universe being the best of all systems, and the object of the Infinite Wisdom being to attain the maximum of variety by means of inequality, human society is only well constituted if it reflects this principle. Pope, once more, puts it succinctly in his well-known lines:

---

[3] *Essay on Man* Epistle II, lines 265–8.
[4] Ibid., Epistle III, lines 293–4.
[5] Lovejoy, *Great Chain of Being*, 216.
[6] Ibid., 245.

---

the prodigious sweep of the complex and tragic drama which it exhibits ... was by no means unfamiliar in the early eighteenth century' (*The Great Chain of Being*, New York, 1965, 205–6).

> Order is Heav'n's first law; and this confest,
> Some are, and must be, greater than the rest,
> More rich, more wise.[7]

Or, in the more belated words of Soame Jenyns, author of *A Free Inquiry into the Nature and Origin of Evil* (1757):

> The universe resembles a large and well-regulated family, in which all the officers and servants, and even the domestic animals, are subservient to each other in a proper subordination; each enjoys the privileges and perquisites peculiar to his place, and at the same time contributes, by that just subordination, to the magnificence and happiness of the whole.[8]

As the eighteenth century opened, attitudes to slavery were wholly consonant with the attitudes which we have just seen. Certainly Christian Europe had long known a tension between the Aristotelian dictum that from the hour of their birth 'some are marked out for subjection' and the awareness that slavery involved the treatment of one's own species as animals. The outcome of the tension was that the institution of slavery was condoned and rendered less unpalatable by an emphasis on the need to treat slaves well.[9] But as the eighteenth century opened there was nothing in the work of the philosophical luminaries of the previous century to suggest other than continued acceptance of slavery. As David Davis concludes at the end of the first part of his masterly study of attitudes to slavery in Western Culture,

> We must conclude, then, that the thought of Grotius, Hobbes, Pufendorf, and Locke, while preparing the way for the secular theories of the Enlightenment, provided little basis for criticising Europe's policy of supporting and extending slavery in the New World. The ancient Stoic dualism of slavery and nature, which had been embodied in Christian doctrine, might have served as a foundation for anti-slavery thought as soon as men sought to develop a theory of politics on natural principles. But despite the early lead of Jean Bodin, political thought in the

[7] *Essay on Man*, Epistle IV, lines 49–51.
[8] Quoted in Lovejoy, op. cit., 207.
[9] For a profound and wide ranging study of European attitudes to slavery see David Brion Davis, *The Problem of Slavery in Western Culture* (Ithaca, 1966).

seventeenth century did not move in the direction of abolitionism. To be sure, the most original minds no longer justified human bondage as the dark fruit of sin or as a disciplinary force in the divine government of the world. But for Grotius, Hobbes and Pufendorf the divine order had been at least partly replaced by a system of law or power in which slavery was a rational and harmonius element. This, after all, was in the great tradition of Plato, Aristotle, and Aquinas. For Locke, on the other hand, original sin had been replaced by a supposedly willful act which required that the slave be forever excluded from the paradisial compact and worked, in the sweat of his brow, for the benefit of others. And from this secular hell there was apparently no redemption.[10]

As for theological attitudes, men evidently believed that to question the ethical basis of slavery, given a fallen world, would be to question God's purposes. Slavery, after all, had been permitted in Scripture.[11]

The world of the late eighteenth century was quite different. The French Revolution manifested the most radical change in values and institutions that Christendom had yet known. Traditional authority was dethroned; Christianity was dismissed with a scorn which demonstrated the Jacobins' belief that the dismissal was final, whilst the whole life of the revolutionary state attested the belief that society could be given a different direction. In England, after an initial heady exaltation, there were few who wanted change to go so far and so fast: but the very force of Burke's condemnation of the 'presumption' of men in supposing they have made discoveries in the realm of morality, government and in ideas of liberty, and his scorn of their 'pert loquacity' in giving voice to their claim,[12] testifies to the existence of a different attitude to change than that professed by Newton and Pope.

Included in the change of values was a clear shift in attitudes towards subject peoples. Even people generally opposed to radical change in the state – Burke is a striking example – believed British

---

[10] Ibid., 121.

[11] Ibid., 89–92.

[12] Charles Parkin, *The Moral Basis of Burke's Political Thought*, reissue (New York, 1968) 120.

policy towards the Americans to be immoral and thus called into question the whole nature of imperial power. And despite its disreputable overtones, the impeachment of Warren Hastings revealed a stirring of new ideas about the proper treatment of non-Europeans. The age was passing when a Clive, returning from India greatly enriched, could be surprised at his own moderation.

Nowhere is the change of view more marked than in attitudes towards slavery and the slave trade. The plain fact is that little serious intellectual defence of slavery was any longer being attempted. Liverpool representatives might speak of enslavement as rescue from a far worse condition, planters might wax eloquent on the humanity of the provision made for slaves on their plantations and slave captains depict the middle passage as a pastoral idyll: but the emphasis on the treatment of the slaves was an admission of the weakness of such attempts as were made to justify slavery as an institution. Nor was it simply the case that intellectual justification of slavery was no longer much attempted for if this had been the case the institution might have continued indefinitely of its own momentum. Rather, a positive change had occurred. Nearly every school of thought which dealt with ethical problems had, from about the middle of the century, come up with specific condemnations of slavery sometimes persuasively encapsulated in a corpus of moral or legal philosophy. And very varied were these schools. Gisborne wrote his widely read *Principles of Moral Philosophy* (1789) not least to counter the doctrine of expediency propounded by Paley in *The Principles of Moral and Political Philosophy* (1785); but both condemned slavery and the slave trade. A major segment of French Enlightenment opinion, and especially the Abbé Raynal, whose work was very influential in England, was hostile to slavery: so, opposed in almost everything else, was John Wesley. Dr Johnson strongly opposed slavery; so did Rousseau whom Johnson detested.

This change must be explored a little further, and it may be as well to spell out the mode of exploration, and its limits. It is *not* our purpose to argue that a change in moral and intellectual attitudes to slavery is a sufficient explanation of abolition – that first great triumph of the anti-slavery cause. The aim is the much more limited one of arguing that the content of received wisdom had so altered by the 1780s that educated men and the political nation, provided they had no direct interest in the slave system, would be likely to regard slavery and the slave trade as morally condemned, as no longer philosophically defensible. They might, it can reasonably be inferred, even be prepared to support abolition, provided that they had no direct interest in the slave system, provided that they could be assured that the national interest would not thereby be significantly harmed, and to the extent that anything so novel as a positive measure of institutional reform could command support. The role which is to be credited to a change in ideas is therefore noteworthy but limited. The limitation of this approach is that it does not explain, save incidentally, *why* philosophical attitudes to slavery developed in the way they did during the eighteenth century: but the approach will demonstrate a major shift in attitudes towards slavery during the course of the eighteenth century and will also make this shift the more credible by relating it to the simultaneous elaboration of concepts with latent anti-slavery implications. Of course, just as Boswell differed from Johnson on the question of slavery, there were men like Boswell who tried to breast the prevailing current – but it was the prevailing current. A more dramatic role was the achievement of the two religious groups in the abolition movement, Quakers and Evangelicals. Though influenced by the currents of thought of their age, their inspiration was essentially religious. That inspiration will be investigated in some depth because it produced a new, four-square, theologically based condemnation of slavery and a dynamic of faith and action which largely created and sustained the abolition campaign. The protracted failure, and then the success of abolition will be explained by close examination of the political process, the political context, and, not least, the brilliant abolitionist insight into the way in which a particular, fortuitous conjuncture in Britain's politico–economic situation could be utilised to push abolition through.

In summarising the development of eighteenth-century thought, as it relates to reform and to anti-slavery, three concepts – liberty, benevolence and happiness – particularly repay attention. This is, of course, not to suggest that the intellectual history of the century is to be seen exclusively in these terms: its preoccupations were far wider than this. But the development of the three concepts, during roughly the first three-quarters of the century, manifests a cast of thought which is increasingly incompatible with slavery and which leans tentatively towards the possibility and desirability of appropriate reforms. In tracing the rise of anti-slavery thought, therefore, the development of ideas of liberty, benevolence and happiness has an unequalled importance. Not all the philosophers of the age are significantly concerned with all of these ideas and they vary in the attention which they devote to the one or to the other. But if in some cases a concern with these ideas is of restricted importance in the context of the philosophers' thought as a whole, this is of little significance in the context of the clear overall tendency.

If this demonstration, albeit elementary, went no further than this it would be significant; and it would remain so even though it can of course be shown that, for example, an idea of liberty had not necessarily automatic reference to Negro slavery, and that men were sometimes specifically dispensed from supposing that a particular concept of liberty meant either abolition of the slave trade or emancipation of slaves. But in fact, as will be seen, the generalised eighteenth-century change in ideas is usually accompanied by a specific condemnation of Negro slavery.

Ideological development in the eighteenth century was, though less obviously, theological as well as philosophical; and so certain theological changes will also claim our attention. Examination of both philosophical and theological change is also called for by the need to explain the inheritance from their age which was a part of the Evangelical and Quaker world-view, and which, because it was a common heritage, enabled these core groups in the abolitionist camp, the Evangelicals and the Quakers, to speak meaningfully to their age, because in a language which it understood. Finally, the prevalence of relevant concepts in literature will be cited as evidence that changes in ideas were not confined to the leaders of thought.

The philosophers to be considered are Hutcheson, Montesquieu, Burke, Ferguson, Beattie, Wallace, Blackstone, Paley and Adam Smith, with briefer mentions of Foster and Millar, and with a summary glance at *philosophes* of the French Enlightenment. There is a logic in this sequence only to the extent that Hutcheson and Montesquieu's work was seminal and inspired in varying measure a number of the others. Neither their philosophical method nor their quality as philosophers has significance for our inquiry *per se*; what is important is the degree of shared emphasis and common conclusion, from whatever starting-point. It would in a sense not matter if the selection were more partial and random than it is; in fact there are only three major exclusions from the list – Berkeley, Butler and Hume. But Berkeley, in his published writings, was mainly interested in the theory of knowledge; Butler did not move into the area where discussion of slavery was called for; and Hume expressed no view on the principle of it either, though certainly a natural development of his thought could have been in the direction of an expedient justification of slavery, partly because he inclined to a belief in the natural inferiority of the Negro.[13] But more than balancing this is the clear drift of a substantial section of his essay 'Of the Populousness of Ancient Nations'. It is hard to believe that the view that domestic slavery was 'more cruel and oppressive than any civil subjection whatsoever'[14] could ever be reconciled with a defence of slavery. But in any event, Hume's actual influence, because of his reputed atheism, was probably in inverse proportion to his philosophical eminence.

Philosopher, Presbyterian divine and academic, Francis Hutcheson is chiefly known for *An Inquiry into the Original of Our Ideas of Beauty and Virtue* (1725) and for the lengthier *System of Moral Philosophy* which was only published in 1755, after the author's death, though manuscript copies had circulated amongst his friends during his lifetime.[15] His initial concern is with happiness: as he writes in the opening paragraph of the *System of Moral Philosophy*: 'The intention of Moral Philosophy is to direct men to that course of action which tends most effectually to promote their greatest happiness and perfection . . .'[16] But, of course, happiness is not served by indulgence, nor attained through hedonism and once that superficially simple road is forsaken Hutcheson is led, via the notion of the moral sense, to connect happiness with benevolence. From observation and from self-analysis he concludes that man is, to quote David Brion Davis'

[13] David Hume, 'Of National Characters', *Essays Moral, Political and Literary*, re-issue (London, 1904) 213 fn.

[14] 'Of the Populousness of Ancient Nations', ibid., 386.

[15] Caroline Robbins, *The Eighteenth-Century Commonwealthman: Studies in the Transmission, Development and Circumstances of English Liberal Thought from the Restoration of Charles II until the War with the Thirteen Colonies* (Cambridge, Mass., 1959) 185–6.

[16] Hutcheson, *Moral Philosophy*, bk I, chap. 1, sec. i.

description 'a skilfully balanced mechanism of senses and passions'.[17] However, what Hutcheson terms 'two grand determinations' are of particular importance, 'one towards our own great happiness, the other towards the greatest general good'.[18] Goodness, he goes on, does not consist in the pleasurable feelings which come from feeling sympathy, is not to be identified with that which brings advantage, or with fitness and congruity, or usefulness but it is the object of immediate apprehension, of 'a natural and immediate determination to approve certain affections, and actions consequent upon them; or a natural sense of immediate excellence in them'. This 'determination' Hutcheson terms the moral sense.[19] So central to his thought is this concept that Hutcheson is sometimes known as the architect of moral sense philosophy. This is perhaps the more understandable when we see the dominant role which Hutcheson accords to the moral sense, for from its very nature, it 'appears to be designed for regulating and controlling all our powers'.[20]

Hutcheson, like Shaftesbury who was in so many ways his mentor and from whom Hutcheson drew a good deal, considers the situation when there is conflict between the two 'grand determinations' – self-interest and the desire for our own greatest happiness, on the one hand, and 'a desire of communicating happiness, an ultimate goodwill', on the other. Hutcheson's answer is an assertion of benevolence of an active, even dynamic kind.

> The moral faculty at once points out and recommends the glorious, the amiable part; not by suggesting prospects of future interests of a sublime sort by pleasures of self-approbation, or of praise. It recommends the generous part by an immediate undefinable perception; it approves the kind of ardour of the heart in the sacrificing even life itself, and that even in those who have no hopes of surviving, or no attention to a future life in another world. And thus, where the moral sense is in its full vigour, it makes the generous determination to publick happiness the supreme one in the soul, with that commanding power which it is naturally destined to exercise.[21]

[17] Davis, *Problem of Slavery* 375.
[18] Hutcheson, *Moral Philosophy*, bk I, chap. 3, sec. vi.
[19] Ibid., bk I, chap. 4, secs. i–iv.
[20] Ibid., bk I, chap. 4, sec. vi.
[21] Ibid., Preface (Wm Leechman), xliv–xlvii; bk I, chap. 4, sec. xii.

Hutcheson's view of liberty rests principally on his unequivocal assertion of the right of resistance.

> In all governments, even the most absolute, the natural end of the trust is acknowledged on all sides to be the prosperity and safety of the whole body. . . . The subjects must have a right of resistance, as the trust is broken, beside the manifest plea of necessity.[22]

An important characteristic, indeed the strength of Hutcheson's denial of an absolute authority is that he applies it consistently. Fathers cannot act tyrannically towards their children[23] nor husbands towards their wives – indeed marriage is 'plainly declared to be a state of equal partnership' with the husband having no 'perfect right of government' though generally possessed 'of superior strength both of body and mind'.[24] Masters, likewise, have only limited rights over servants.[25] At this point the mode of Hutcheson's reasoning necessarily leads him to a brief but incisive examination of slavery, where he makes what is essentially the same appeal to nature.

> Men differ much from each other in wisdom, virtue, beauty and strength; but the lowest of them, who have the use of reason, differ in this from the brutes, that by fore-thought and reflection they are capable of incomparably greater happiness or misery. Scarce any man can be happy who sees that all his enjoyments are precarious, and depending on the will of others of whose kind intentions he can have no assurance. All men have strong desires of liberty and property, have notions of right, and strong natural impulses to marriage, families, and offspring, and earnest desires of their safety.

The especially able may be better fitted to rule but they have no prescriptive right to rule by force.

> . . . permanent power assumed by force over the fortunes of others must generally tend to the misery of the whole. . . . We must therefore conclude, that no endowments, natural or ac-

[22] Ibid., bk III, chap. 7, sec. iii.
[23] Ibid., bk III, chap. 2.
[24] Ibid., bk III, chap. 1, sec vii.
[25] Ibid., bk III, chap. 3. sec. i.

quired, can give a perfect right to assume power over others, without their consent.[26]

As to that major defence of slavery, the supposed right to enslave captives taken in war, Hutcheson is at his most scathing, reserving, indeed, for the end of this paragraph one of his few exclamation marks.

A set of inaccurate popular phrases blind us in these matters. Captives owe their lives and all to the purchasers, say they. Just in the same manner, we, our nobles, and princes, often owe our lives to mid-wives, chirurgeons, physicians, fellow-soldiers, servants, neighbours: one who was the means of preserving a man's life is not therefore entitled to make him a slave, and sell him as a piece of goods. Strange, that in any nation where a sense of liberty prevails, where the Christian religion is professed, custom and high prospects of gain can so stupify the consciences of men, and all sense of natural justice, that they can hear such computations made about the value of their fellow-men, and their liberty without abhorrence and indignation![27]

Forthright though Hutcheson's denunciation was he perhaps turned aside such wrath as his utopianism may have aroused by the exceptions which he was prepared to concede. Society was justified, on grounds of utility and public policy, in keeping idlers and vagabonds in perpetual servitude if they consistently failed to support their families and themselves. Another exception is particularly interesting for, though it no less attests the immorality of perpetual slavery, it provides the bones of a possible justification of the Atlantic, and other, slave trades.

'Tis further pleaded, that in some barbarous nations, unless the captives were bought for slaves they would all be murthered. They therefore owe their lives, and all they can do to their purchasers; and so do their children who would not otherways have come into life. But this whole plea is no more than that of *negotium utile gestum*, to which any civilized nation is bound by humanity; 'tis a prudent expensive office done for the service of others without a gratuitous intention; and this founds no

[26] Ibid., bk II, chap. 5, secs. ii–iii.
[27] Ibid., bk II, chap. 14, sec. iii.

other right than that to full compensation of all charges and labour employed for the benefit of others. Thus suppose a merchant buys an hundred such slaves; so that his whole charges on the voyage, and prime cost of the captives, adding also a reasonable merchant's profit upon the stock employed, amount to a thousand pounds. These captives are his debtors jointly for this sum; and as soon as the value of their labours beyond their maintenance amounts to this sum, and the legal interest from the time it was advanced, they have a right to be free; and this it would do in ten or twelve years, tho' a third part of them died; and then all his claim, or that of any one under him, would cease.[28]

Significant though this qualification was, one must recall that the slave trade as carried on in the eighteenth century was geared to the notion of perpetual slavery. The force of Hutcheson's qualifications was arguably, therefore, more likely to command for his doctrines a hearing than to blunt their essential and undeniable point.[29]

Liberty, happiness, benevolence – all are qualities extolled by Hutcheson. His doctrine of liberty has little room for Negro slavery just as the invocation of happiness as a goal of man necessarily condemns the institution. Moreover, the call to active benevolence implicity threatens the very existence of slavery. It may not be too much to say, with Wylie Sypher, that 'the modern attitude to slavery originates in Hutcheson's humanitarian attack on Aristotle'.[30]

It is a truism that the writings of Charles-Louis de Secondat, Baron de Montesquieu, and especially *L'Esprit des Lois,* first published in 1748, greatly reinforced the idea of civil and political liberty in the eighteenth century and so by implication undermined slavery. But the fact that Montesquieu had something specific to say about Negro slavery combined with the method and the appeal of his work to give that work an important place in the study of the development of anti-slavery thought. As the dispassionate scholar

[28] Ibid., bk II, chap. 14, sec. iii.

[29] For Hutcheson's views on slavery and liberty see also ibid., bk III, chap. 3, secs. ii–v; Davis, *Problem of Slavery,* 374–8; Robbins, *Eighteenth-Century Commonwealthman,* 185–96; and Wylie Sypher, 'Hutcheson and the "Classical" Theory of Slavery', *Journal of Negro History,* xxiv (July 1939) 263–80.

[30] Sypher, 'Hutcheson and Slavery', 280.

studying the history and environment of different peoples to arrive at what he claims as facts, Montesquieu's feeling for liberty comes out especially strongly when he proceeds to the study of the English constitution. England's lack of an indivisible sovereign authority resulted from a functional division of power into executive, legislative and judicial and it was precisely this division which commended itself to Montesquieu as constituting the secret of English liberty. As he himself put it:

> When the legislative and executive powers are united in the same person, or in the same body of magistrates, there can be no liberty; because apprehensions may arise, lest the same monarch or senate should enact tyrannical laws, to execute them in a tyrannical manner.
> Again, there is no liberty, if the judiciary power be not separated from legislative and executive.[31]

Here in short is the well-known theory of the separation of powers as the essential condition of civil and political liberty.[32]

Like Hutcheson, Montesquieu feels the need to comment upon slavery. In his section on slavery he is under a certain tension for on first principles he was passionately against slavery and yet had to admit, as the student of comparative culture, that there were countries where it existed as a kind of ecological response. He opens his section on slavery with the resounding words:

> Slavery, properly so called, is the establishment of a right which gives to one man such a power over another as renders him absolute master of his life and fortune. The state of slavery is in its own nature bad. It is neither useful to the master nor to the slave; not to the slave, because he can do nothing through a motive of virtue; nor to the master, because by having an unlimited authority over his slaves he insensibly accustoms himself to the want of all moral virtues, and thence becomes fierce, hasty, severe, choleric, voluptuous, and cruel.[33]

[31] C.-L. de S. Montesquieu, *L'Esprit des Lois*, bk xi, chap. 6. This and other translations are from the London edition of 1878, ed. J. V. Prichard and trans. by Thomas Nugent.

[32] For Montesquieu's thought as it relates to liberty see also F. T. H. Fletcher, *Montesquieu and English Politics, 1750–1800* (London, 1939) 12–14, and C. P. Courtney, *Montesquieu and Burke* (Oxford, 1963) 13–21.

[33] *Esprit des Lois*, bk xv, chap. 1.

Montesquieu denies the classical Aristotelian affirmation that some men are slaves by nature and asserts that all men are born equal. But here he has to confront the fact that slavery actually does exist in some countries.

> But as all men are born equal, slavery must be accounted un-natural, though in some countries it is founded on natural reason; and a wide difference ought to be made between such countries, and those in which even natural reason rejects it, as in Europe, where it has been so happily abolished.[34]

Thus Montesquieu is obliged to address himself to the regulation of slavery in those countries where it has a kind of organic existence. This he proceeds to do by urging that the laws must both ameliorate the condition of slavery and guard against its dangers. It may be possible to discern a certain dilemma when Montesquieu comes to the examination of Negro slavery which was presumably 'natural' in terms of physical environment but unnecessary and wrong in terms of the culture of the slave-owning class – people of European origin in whose native continent slavery was regarded as improper on both of these counts. Perhaps this is why he takes refuge in irony in this, the best known of his passages on slavery, which deserves quotation at some length.

> Were I to vindicate our right to make slaves of the Negroes, these should be my arguments:–
>
> The Europeans, having extinguished the Americans, were obliged to make slaves of the Africans, for clearing such vast tracts of land.
>
> Sugar would be too dear if the plants which produce it were cultivated by any other than slaves . . .
>
> It is hardly to be believed that God, who is a wise Being, should place a soul, especially a good soul, in such a black ugly body . . .
>
> The Negroes prefer a glass necklace to that gold which white nations so highly value. Can there be a greater proof of their wanting common sense?
>
> It is impossible for us to suppose these creatures to be men, because, allowing them to be men, a suspicion would follow that we ourselves are not Christians.[35]

[34] Ibid., bk xv, chap. 7.
[35] Ibid., bk xv, chap. 5. Montesquieu's discussion of slavery as a whole

As late as one hundred and fifty years after *L'Esprit des Lois* was published, an editor could so misunderstand, and so take out of context, this section on Negro slavery that he presented clear irony as literal statement, as an infirmity of a noble mind.[36] At the other extreme it would be wrong to represent Montesquieu's concern as exclusively with liberty. In its essence *L'Esprit des Lois* is a study of the nature of law and of political constitutions with major use of the comparative method. Furthermore, the virtue of liberty is not established in any very telling way; it appears indeed that the only attempt to found liberty in some sense on the nature of things is of a somewhat incidental kind. In a consideration of laws in relation to commerce, our author contrasts the situation of the people of the north, where nature has been more sparing, with those of regions where nature has been more bountiful, and feels justified in the distinctly flimsy conclusion that 'the people of the north have need of liberty, for this can best procure them the means of satisfying all those wants which they have received from nature'.[37]

All of this does not alter the fact that Montesquieu was early seen as a great apostle of liberty. An important reason is that because his whole work was put out as a feat of historical and scientific method, it was possible for his clear preference for liberty to be taken as empirically – in a broad sense – validated when in reality that preference stemmed more from preconceived principle. Phrases in his preface and opening chapter show how this guileless deception could take place: 'I have not drawn my principles from my prejudices, but from the nature of things';[38] 'the more we enter into particulars, the more we shall perceive the certainty of the principles on which they are founded';[39] 'Laws, in their most general signification, are the necessary relations arising from the nature of things'.[40] And who could not feel that proven finality lay in a work which had taken twenty years to complete, which had been many times abandoned and many times begun, and

---

[36] Davis, *Problem of Slavery*, 403.
[37] *Esprit des Lois*, bk XXI, chap. 3.
[38] Ibid., Preface.
[39] Ibid.
[40] Ibid., bk I, chap. 1.

---

is contained in the nineteen chapters of Book XV. See also Fletcher, *Montesquieu and English Politics*, 228–30, 277.

whose author had a thousand times committed discarded pages to the winds.[41]

At first sight it might seem that whatever the appeal of Montesquieu it could not also be a call to action in the same way as Hutcheson's active benevolence was a call. In the *Esprit des Lois* there is no essential departure from the caution displayed earlier in the *Lettre Persane:* 'It is sometimes necessary to change certain laws. But the case is rare, and, when it arises, one must only intervene with a trembling hand.'[42] None the less for at least four reasons Montesquieu's writings were a considerable stimulus to reform in England. In asserting that though the *esprit général* of a nation was shaped in the first place by purely physical forces like climate, it must increasingly be moulded by moral ideas, Montesquieu was establishing a modest ground for the operation of moral idealism.[43] Secondly, a justification of change in the laws necessarily lies in a tension between the *esprit général* and positive laws. Could it not frequently be argued in particular cases that such a tension did exist and that it was the duty of the legislator to effect reconciliation by changing the law? Thirdly, and principally in regard to slavery, Montesquieu was challenging existing practice in a quite specific way, and it was a challenge which seemed to spring full-armed from a theory of law and politics clad with all the majesty of an empirically based system perfected by a man of immense repute. Montesquieu, as E. L. Vaughan said, was 'the first man in the front rank of reputation to denounce the wickedness of the whole business; the first to open the struggle which was not carried to final triumph until more than a century after his death'.[44] Fourthly, an impressive body of English and Scots legal and moral philosophers drew from Montesquieu a more direct exhortation to reform, and particularly the abolition of slavery, than in some cases was justified by the words of the master himself.[45] This could not prevent their work enjoying all the prestige of its avowed inspirer, and it will be the subject of a subsequent section to trace this important development.

[41] Ibid., bk xi, chap 6.

[42] Quoted in Courtney, *Montesquieu and Burke.* 9, but here translated.

[43] Courtney, *Montesquieu and Burke*, 23.

[44] Quoted in Fletcher, *Montesquieu and English Politics*, 229. For Montesquieu's contribution to anti-slavery thought see David Davis' penetrating analysis in *Problem of Slavery*, 394–96, 402–08.

[45] Ibid., 48–50.

Edmund Burke, though he drew upon other sources and his own genius, was also one who avowed much to Montesquieu. Political and civil liberty, happiness, and reform which would strengthen or enhance each, were amongst Burke's great concerns. Regarding the first, as he showed in his speech on conciliation in 1775, Burke discerned in the American colonies a national spirit of liberty stemming from the constitutional traditions of the mother country, from the fact of geographical separation and from other physical and moral causes. But though formally Burke might merely acknowledge and analyse, this development of liberty, once explained in terms of Montesquieu's *esprit général* and analysis of political development, was inevitably justified by it.[46] The spirit of liberty explained was the spirit of liberty defended. In domestic politics Burke's attempt to clip the power of the executive by a measure of parliamentary reform, and by otherwise limiting the powers of ministers, could not be other than advocacy of liberty in an important area. England's mixed constitution, Burke valued precisely because of its effectiveness as a defence of the liberties which that constitution was intended to preserve.

Burke's role in the impeachment of Warren Hastings is well known but we perhaps have to remind ourselves that Burke was concerned to attack what he believed to be despotism, the antithesis of liberty. Explicit, too, in this, as other areas of Burke's activity, is a concern with the happiness of the governed on the part of the governor. 'When a British governor is sent abroad, he is sent to pursue the good of the people, as much as possible in the spirit of the laws of this country, which in all respects intend their conservation, their happiness, and their prosperity.'[47] It is not the guilt or innocence of Hastings which matters but 'whether millions of mankind shall be made miserable, or happy'.[48]

As one might expect, Burke approaches reform with 'the trembling hand' which any disciple of Montesquieu was likely to share. He is none the less led to espouse it in particular cases, and the case of India illustrates the basis of his advocacy of reform. Interference, implicitly reform, is justified not merely when it can be demonstrated that there are abuses in administration, for there

[46] Courtney, *Montesquieu and Burke*, 93–9.
[47] Quoted in ibid., 138.
[48] Quoted in ibid., 134; see also 133.

are necessary abuses in all governments, but when certain conditions are fulfilled, namely that the object affected is 'great and
important'; that the abuse is 'a great abuse'; that it is 'utterly in-
curable in the body as it now stands constituted'.[49] Burke's justification of reform at a more philosophical level closely follows
Montesquieu in his teaching that law must reflect the *esprit général*
of the people for Burke rested much of his attack on Hastings and
the East India Company on an exhaustive dissection of geographical factors pertaining to India and of its social system, of religion,
manners and custom, all designed to show that the rule of the
company had ignored the culture and inclinations of the people.
Speaking of the Hindus, he says, 'If we undertake to govern the
inhabitants of such a country, we must govern them upon their
own principles and maxims, and not upon ours'.[50] To put it another way, a sufficiently bad failure to rest law on the *esprit général*
is itself a justification of reform.

Nor is it without significance that this last area in which Burke
advocated reform was one where non-Europeans were centrally
involved. And Burke does not stop short there, does not remain
silent on the question of slavery itself. Admittedly, the invocation
of a people's 'own principles and maxims' could lead to a respect
even for laws which permitted slavery, but this was of course
neither a necessary justification of the slave trade nor of servitude
to Europeans, and it was not a conclusion which Burke drew. As
early as 1780 he had drawn up a plan for ameliorating both the
slave trade and colonial slavery and though, in this spirit, he still
saw merit in abolishing the slave trade gradually in 1792,[51] he did
specifically support Wilberforce in his motions for total abolition
of 12 May 1789 and 19 April 1791. Interestingly, he testifies to
his dual conviction that law must reflect the spirit of the people
and that the development of that spirit can be appropriately
encouraged. Sending Dundas a specific plan for gradual abolition,
following carriage in principle of such a measure in 1792, Burke
writes: 'It required also much perseverance and address to excite
the spirit which has been excited without doors, and which has
carried it through. The greatest eloquence ever displayed in the

[49] Ibid., 132–3.

[50] Ibid., 135. This section on India is principally based on ibid., 127–41.

[51] Burke to Dundas, Easter Monday, 1792, quoted in Burke, *Collected
Works*, 1852 ed., v, 587.

House has been employed to second the efforts which have been made abroad.'[52]

Burke, then, gives his own amplification of the notions of liberty, happiness and reform. He was concerned with political and civil liberty in American, English and Indian contexts; the happiness of the governed was an avowed criterion of good government; and a careful case was made for reform when political institutions permitted despotism to deny liberty, or when political and civil liberty required reinforcement. And for Burke it was in the logic of his thought to support abolition. If a man of the eminence Burke came to attain with the publication of *Reflections on the Revolution in France* in 1790 had refrained from supporting slavery and the slave trade, those institutions would by his abstention have been weakened; in fact, he opposed the slave trade and thereby lent to abolition the support of his considerable reputation.

Burke, though much influenced by Montesquieu, also drew heavily on other springs as well as on his own genius. But a number of other British, or more especially Scottish, thinkers drew more unreservedly on Montesquieu, though with them there was also other inspiration, especially that of Hutcheson. Adam Ferguson, the first of these, followed Montesquieu in the study of the history of nations, beginning with the characteristics of human nature, and tracing human history through 'the History of Rude Nations' to refinement and into decline and corruption. Fletcher describes civil liberty, as 'his great obsession'[53] and this does not seem exaggerated. Imparting emotion to liberty by contrasting it with (political) slavery, he regards liberty as the jewel of political society and gives it a scope whose comprehensiveness is only apparently belied by the mundane language which Ferguson here uses.

The benefits arising from liberty are . . . not the fruits of a virtue, and of a goodness, which operate in the breast of one man, but the communication of virtue itself to many; and such a distribution of functions in civil society, as gives to members the exercises and occupations which pertain to their nature.[54]

[52] Ibid.
[53] Fletcher, *Montesquieu and English Politics*, 47.
[54] A. Ferguson, *Essay on Civil Society* (1767), reissue, ed. D. Forbes (Edinburgh, 1966) 270.

About happiness and benevolence, Ferguson's language is warmer, even cloying.

> It should seem, therefore, to be the happiness of man, to make his social dispositions the ruling spring of his occupations; to state himself as the member of a community, for whose general good his heart may glow with an ardent zeal . . .[55]
>
> Man is, by nature, the member of a community . . . and if the public good be the principal object with individuals, it is likewise true, that the happiness of individuals is the great end of civil society; for in what sense can a public enjoy any good, if its members, considered apart, be unhappy?[56]

As one might perhaps expect from the antithesis between liberty and political slavery in his *Essay on Civil Society* (1767), Ferguson broadens his condemnation of slavery in his *Institutes of Moral Philosophy* published two years later. On the argument that no compact could exist prior to the establishment of society, Ferguson reasoned that no one could be born into a state of slavery.

> No one is born a slave; because every one is born with all his original rights. No one can become a slave, because no one, from being a person, can, in the language of the Roman law, become a thing or subject of property. The supposed property of the master in the slave, therefore, is a matter of usurpation, not of right.[57]

Ferguson is commonly regarded as a clear rather than a profound thinker but the excellence of his style and the manner in which his inquiry followed – some contemporaries thought it rivalled – Montesquieu, gave him a wide audience.[58] Three other British scholars of the second half of the eighteenth century were also particularly inspired by Montesquieu: the first two of these, James Beattie and George Wallace, were Scotsmen.

Beattie's *Elements of Moral Science* (1790–93) is a wide-ranging inquiry of a kind which the eighteenth century knew well. Starting with Psychology, Beattie progresses through Natural Theology and Moral Philosophy to Economics and Politics, and ends with

[55] Ibid., 54.
[56] Ibid., 57·8.
[57] Quoted in Fletcher, *Montesquieu and English Politics*, 234.
[58] Ibid., 44–8.

a section on Logic. Its method is empirical inquiry, though not of so exhaustive a kind as one finds in a fellow divine like Hutcheson, for Beattie is less concerned to keep the two sides of his being, the philosopher and the theologian, apart.[59] There is a certain complacency about his somewhat naturalistic assumptions, 'What is the moral law of nature? is a question that has often been proposed. That (I could answer) is incumbent on us by the law of our nature, which, after candid inquiry, our reason and conscience declare to be right.'[60]

In his section on politics, Beattie follows Montesquieu closely and we find the same delineation of types of government, the same definition and opinion of the British constitution, and an implied, rather than an outspoken, concern for liberty. 'In a free country,' he says, virtually translating Montesquieu, 'every violation of law is an attack upon the public liberty.'[61] On Benevolence he is explicit, after the manner of Hutcheson, and even lyrical.

> We are all by nature brethren . . . and equally dependent on the great author of our being . . . and from one another we daily receive, or may receive, important services. These considerations recommend the great duty of universal benevolence, which is not more beneficial to others than to ourselves; for it makes us happy in our own minds, and amiable in the eyes of all who know us . . .[62]

But it is his treatment of slavery which is most striking. This is not because it is strongly original, though there are new touches, but because it is lengthy and, more curiously, because it constitutes all but twenty-two of the seventy-four pages which comprise the section on Economics, the balance being devoted to observations on relationships within the family. Much of his space is devoted to demolition, after Montesquieu, of the classical argument for slavery but he then proceeds to take a number of common defences of slavery and demolish them also. He concludes with an engagingly Christian and humane statement.

---

[59] 'The moral law of nature is promulgated to man by his reason and conscience; and is ascertained and enforced, by revelation' (James Beattie, *Elements of Moral Science*, 3rd ed. (Edinburgh, 1817) II 82).

[60] Beattie, *Moral Science*, II 82–3.

[61] Ibid., II 162.

[62] Ibid., I 398–9. See also I 180–84.

We have therefore every reason, that the case admits of, to believe, that all the men upon earth, whatever be their colour, are
our brethren, and neighbours: and if so, both reason and Scripture declare, that it is our duty to love them, and to do unto
them as we would that they should do unto us. And if natural
peculiarities of *shape* and *stature* as well as *colour,* may be
accounted for, as I think they may, from the foregoing principles; it follows, that Laplanders, Samoeydes, Esquimaux, the
Hurons, the Chinese, and the American and Asiatic, as well
as Africans, Indians, and, in a word, all the inhabitants of this
globe, who have reason, speech, and erect figure, must be
considered as one great family, and as informed with souls
of the same order, whatever slight variations may appear in
their bodies.[63]

Beattie, then, is significant for the considerable space he devoted
to attacking slavery in his scheme and for the fact that he saw
amelioration and gradual abolition – he later became an out-and-
out abolitionist – as a prime charge on the benevolence to which
he attached such importance.

Like Beattie, the young Scottish advocate George Wallace saw
Montesquieu primarily as the source of a new humanitarian philosophy but, being a man of the law, developed his theme in more
legal terms. He published his great work, *System of the Principles
of the Laws of Scotland,* in 1760 and made no secret of the fact
that his guiding principle – that civil must be founded upon
natural law – came from Montesquieu – but interprets it much
more dogmatically than Montesquieu, claiming that any positive
law which transgresses against the law of nature must be unjust.
Here indeed is a foundation for a whole platform of reforms for it
exploits that tension between the *esprit général* and positive law
which we have already discussed. Wallace drew a number of
conclusions from the immediate premises 'that all inequality, all
dependence, all servility, all superiority, all subjection, all pre-
eminence, which is not *necessary* to the welfare of society, is unnatural; and that, if it could, it ought to be destroyed.' Mankind
should be reduced to as near absolute equality as possible – here
is a striking readiness to bring on change – and this conclusion
necessarily carried with it the further one 'that an institution, so

---

[63] Ibid., III 65.

unnatural and so inhuman as that of slavery, ought to be abolished'.

The immediate appeal of Wallace's book was for various reasons limited, but, as David Brion Davis has recently shown, it was the source of Louis De Jaucort's influential article on the slave trade in the *Encyclopédie, ou dictionnaire raisonné des sciences, des arts et des métiers* (1765), and one of several inspirations of the important Quaker abolitionist, Anthony Benezet.[64]

What Wallace did for Scottish law, Blackstone did for English law in his *Commentaries on the Laws of England*. In this four-volume work, the author's Oxford lectures in book form, Blackstone traces the historical development of English Law in its many aspects. Clearly such an approach coheres with Montesquieu and indeed borrows a good deal from the Frenchman, but Blackstone emphasises the common law, which he describes as 'the first ground and chief corner stone of the laws of England',[65] ethnic mixing and the influence of kings and princes, rather than specifically interpreting English law as displaying a uniquely happy relationship between an *esprit général* and positive law. None the less Montesquieu's sense of felicity at the excellencies of the English constitution is very much present in Blackstone – indeed, coming from a native the observation that 'happily for us of this island, the British constitution has long remained, and I trust will long continue, a standing exception to the truth of this observation (that governments can not endure)'[66] passes over into complacency. There is also the quintessential emphasis on liberty. Volume four closes with the exhortation to men of substance in England that 'The protection of THE LIBERTY OF BRITAIN is a duty which they owe to themselves, who enjoy it; to their ancestors, who transmitted it down; and to the posterity, who will claim at their hands this, the best birthright, and noblest inheritence of mankind.'[67]

There are also some close and more particular correspondences,

---

[64] For Wallace see Fletcher, *Montesquieu and English Politics*, 48–50, 230–31, and David Brion Davis, 'New Sidelights on Early Anti-Slavery Radicalism', *William and Mary Quarterly*, 3rd series, xxviii, no. 4 (Oct 1971), 585–94. The extracts are from Wallace, *Law of Scotland*, as quoted in Davis, 'Anti-Slavery Radicalism', 588–9.

[65] W. Blackstone, *Commentaries on the Laws of England* (1966 reissue, London, of the 1st ed. with supplements, Oxford, 1765–69) i 73.

[66] Ibid., i 50.

[67] Ibid., iv 436.

and none more interesting for our purpose than the treatment of slavery. Blackstone follows Montesquieu almost slavishly but merits extended quotation because he played the dominant role in mediating Montesquieu's ideas to England. Unoriginal though Blackstone's arguments were, they come over as compulsive conclusion from premises of pristine simplicity, whilst we must also remind ourselves of the obvious – that Blackstone was lecturing and writing in *English*.

And indeed it is repugnant to reason, and the principles of natural law that such a state (slavery) should subsist anywhere. The three originals of the right of slavery assigned by Justinian, are all of them built upon false foundations. As, first, slavery is held to arise '*jure gentium*', from a state of captivity in war; . . . The conqueror, say the civilians, had a right to the life of his captive; and, having spared that, has a right to deal with him as he pleases. But it is an untrue position, when taken generally, that, by the law of nature or nations, a man may kill his enemy: he has only a right to kill him, in particular cases; in cases of absolute necessity for self-defence; and it is plain this absolute necessity did not subsist, since the victor did not actually kill him, but made him prisoner. War is itself justifiable only on principles of self-preservation; and therefore it gives no other right over prisoners, but merely to disable them from doing harm to us, by confining their persons: much less can it give a right to kill, torture, abuse, plunder or even to enslave, an enemy, when the war is over. Since therefore the right of *making* slaves by captivity, depends on a supposed right of slaughter, that foundation failing, the consequence drawn from it must fail likewise. But, secondly, it is said that slavery may begin '*jure civili*'; when one man sells himself to another. This, if only meant of contracts to serve or work for another, is very just: but when applied to strict slavery . . . is also impossible. Every sale implies a price . . . an equivalent given to the seller in lieu of what he transfers to the buyer: but what equivalent can be given for life, and liberty, both of which (in absolute slavery) are held to be in the master's disposal? His property also, the very price he seems to receive, devolves *ipso facto* to his master, the instant he becomes his slave. In this case therefore the buyer gives nothing, and the seller receives nothing: of what validity then can a sale be, which destroys the very principles upon which all sales are founded. Lastly, we are told, that besides these two ways by which slaves . . . are acquired, they may also be hereditary . . . the children of acquired slaves are . . . by a negative kind of birthright, slaves also. But this being built on the two former rights must fall together with them. If neither captivity, nor the sale of oneself, can by the law of nature and reason, reduce the parent to slavery, much less can it reduce the offspring.[68]

It is interesting that this demonstration is immediately followed by the repetition of the claim already made that 'upon these principles the law of England abhors, and will not endure the existence of slavery within this nation',[69] and that Blackstone further observed that 'a slave or Negro, the moment he lands in England, falls under the protection of the laws, and with regard to all natural rights becomes *eo instanti* a freeman'. This last sentence was more distinctly qualified in the third and subsequent editions than was the case in the first:[70] but what matters for our present purpose is the general and pronounced anti-slavery tone of Blackstone's argument. Moreover, the method that argument also had the prestige of Montesquieu to commend it, whilst the condemnation of slavery was enshrined in a corpus of ideas which of themselves implied condemnation of slavery and had the very greatest appeal to the thoughtful Englishman of the eighteenth century.

William Paley is claimed by F. T. H. Fletcher to be one of Montesquieu's four principal interpreters. The Frenchman's influence

[68] Ibid., I 411–2.

[69] This first appears in ibid., I 123.

[70] Professor David Davis has pointed out that in the first edition this assertion was accompanied by the important qualification that 'with regard to any right which the master may have acquired, by contract or the like, to the perpetual service of John or Thomas, this will remain in exactly the same state as before'. It follows that the modification in the third edition of the sentence which suggests a slave becomes a freeman on setting foot on English soil, quoted above to '. . . falls under the protection of the laws, and so far becomes a freeman; though the master's right to his service may probably [changed to 'possibly' in the fourth edition] still continue' is less of a new qualification than has sometimes been suggested. This point will be made in Chapter 9 of Davis, *The Problem of Slavery in the Age of Revolution, 1770–1823*, and I am indebted to him for allowing me to consult his MS. in draft.

is certainly evident in *The Principles of Moral and Political Philosophy* (1785), and particularly in Book VI, entitled 'Elements of Political Knowledge', but theology was not a concern of Montesquieu as it was of Paley, who published three widely acclaimed theological works between 1785 and 1802, and it is as theologian that Paley is and was principally known. In praising Paley's mathematical ability – he had been senior wrangler at Cambridge – Leslie Stephen somewhat patronises his subject, one of his many non-heroes; 'Paley shows everywhere that masculine, but rigid, intellect which finds its natural element in mathematical study. He is the very type of the clear and receptive, rather than originative, reasoners who are predestined to success in competitive examinations.'[71] It remains true that Paley was not a profound or original thinker but his synthetic *apologia* for Christianity was an achievement and brought him many readers.[72] It is therefore important that his work included what by now was a conventional assertion of the virtues of moderate liberty, an emphasis upon the duty of benevolence and an uncompromising invocation of happiness as the principle of utility. It is even more important for our purpose that this very influential writer comes out with a condemnation of slavery – indeed, says Clarkson, he 'must be considered as having been a considerable influence in interesting the mind of the public in favour of the oppressed Africans'.[73] Under the law of nature, slavery could exist as a result of crime, of debt or of captivity, but Paley specifically indicts the slave *trade* of his day, that 'upon the coast of Africa' as 'not excused by these principles'. In the immediate, however, and following Montesquieu, emancipation must be gradual for a rapid and complete liberation would be disastrous for mankind as a whole. In the peroration to this section Paley portrays slavery as already *démodé*:

By the mild diffusion of its [Christianity's] light and influence, the minds of men are insensibly prepared to perceive and correct

[71] Stephen, *History of English Thought in the Eighteenth Century*, 3rd ed. (London, 1902) I 407–8. See I 407–20 and II 121–5 for a discussion of Paley.

[72] '*The Moral Philosophy* was adopted early by some of the colleges in our universities into the system of their education. It soon found its way also into most of the private libraries of the kingdom; and it was, besides, generally read and approved' (Clarkson, *History of the Abolition*, I 94).

[73] Ibid.

the enormities, which folly, or wickedness, or accident, have introduced into their public establishments. In this way the Greek and Roman slavery, and since these, the feudal tyranny, has declined before it. And we trust that, as the knowledge and authority of the same religion advance in the world, they will banish what remains of this odious institution.[74]

Thus moderate liberty and anti-slavery, benevolence and utility are all extolled. Nor are they extolled simply as isolated goods but as parts of an ordered philosophy.

In any survey of thinkers who contributed to the formidable intellectual attack upon slavery in eighteenth-century Britain, Adam Smith would readily be included. Extolled or vilified for his application of the two principles of self-interest and natural liberty to economic affairs, Smith was also known for the condemnation of slavery in *The Wealth of Nations* (1776).

The experience of all ages and nations, I believe, demonstrates that the work done by slaves, though it appears to cost only their maintenance, is in the end the dearest of any. A person who can acquire no property, can have no other interest but to eat as much, and to labour as little as possible. Whatever work he does beyond what is sufficient to purchase his own maintenance can be squeezed out of him by violence only, and not by any interest of his own.[75]

Certainly Smith's attack on slavery was impressive because it rested on his two guiding principles: but it gained even greater strength from being cradled also in an original moral philosophy, worked out in *The Theory of Moral Sentiments* (1759). The basis of that philosophy lay in a principle of sympathetic association.

As our sense, therefore, of the propriety of conduct arises from what I shall call a direct sympathy with the affection and motives of the person who acts, so our sense of its merit arises from what I shall call an indirect sympathy with the gratitude of the person who is ... acted upon.[76]

[74] William Paley, *The Principles of Moral and Political Philosophy*, in *Works* (London, 1828) I 87–8.

[75] Adam Smith, *An Inquiry into the Nature and Causes of the Wealth of Nations*, de. E. R. A. Seligman (London, 1920) 345.

[76] Adam Smith, *The Theory of Moral Sentiments*, ed. E. G. West (New York, 1969) 105.

To this principle Smith joins the now almost conventional, utilitarian principle of happiness and further asserts that 'an invisible hand' – which is an important part of Smith's idea of Providence – preserves harmony between the two principles.

> The rich . . . are led by an invisible hand to make nearly the same distribution of the necessaries of life which would have been made had the earth been divided into equal portions among all its inhabitants; and thus, without intending it, without knowing it, advance the interest of the society and afford means to the multiplication of the species. When Providence divided the earth among a few lordly masters, it neither forgot nor abandoned those who seemed to have been left out in the partition. These last, too, enjoy their share of all that it produces.[77]

Smith's moral philosophy and his economic philosophy therefore have the considerable appeal of being related parts of a system of thought – as well as being properly empirical and profiting from an evident association with Montesquieu and Hutcheson. In intellectual circles in Scotland, at any rate, there was familiarity with the outline of further parts of Smith's system, for the lecture he gave at Glasgow, as well as covering the moral philosophy and the political economy out of which grew *The Theory of Moral Sentiments* and *The Wealth of Nations*, also included natural theology and a study of the general principles of law and government.[78] Smith's opposition to slavery, therefore, came with the backing of a whole world-view – and it included a stinging criticism of the African slave trade.

> There is not a Negro from the coast of Africa who does not . . . possess a degree of magnanimity which the soul of his sordid master is too often scarce capable of receiving. Fortune never exerted more cruelly her empire over mankind than when he subjected those nations of heroes to the refuse of the goals of Europe, to wretches who possess the virtues neither of the countries which they come from, nor of those which they go to, and

[77] Ibid., 264–5.
[78] E. G. West, *Adam Smith: the Man and His Works* (New York, 1969), 62–3.

whose levity, brutality and baseness, so justly expose them to the contempt of the vanquished.[79]

Hutcheson, Montesquieu, Burke, Ferguson, Beattie, Wallace, Blackstone, Paley, Adam Smith – to these one might add James Foster whose *Discourses on All the Principal Branches of Natural Religion and Social Virtue* (London, 1749) drew largely on Hutcheson, and condemned slavery,[80] whilst there was a differently founded condemnation in John Millar, *The Origin of the Distinction of Ranks; or an Inquiry into the circumstances which gave Rise to its Influence and Authority in the Different Members of Societies* (London, 1771).[81] Varied though these philosophical exercises were, broadly speaking liberty was extolled: and slavery was thereby condemned; happiness was the great principle of utility: slavery thereby could only be found wanting; the duty of benevolence was asserted: a heightened response to the poor and the outcast was thereby induced.

And all these authorities condemned Negro slavery.

Like their English counterparts the *philosophes* emphasised individual and civil liberty, together with liberty of conscience, speech, publication, of commerce and of industry: their approach to liberty differed in that they enjoyed less of it, had to claim that which in a measure the English already had, and so of necessity appeared hostile to government and the established order. Happiness as the principle of utility was their obsession whilst their intense concern with *bienfaisance* – a word coined by the Abbé de Saint Pierre in 1725 to describe man's disinterested impulse to do good to his fellow creatures[82] – would be merely cloying if there was not so much evidence that it was often a genuine spring

---

[79] Smith, *Theory of Moral Sentiments*, 299–300. On Smith see also Davis, *Problem of Slavery*, 433–5.

[80] References to slavery are in II, 152–8– see also Robbins, *Eighteenth Century Commonwealthman*, 242–6; Davis, *Problem of Slavery*, 378–9.

[81] See especially 344–62 of 3rd ed., (1778); Robbins, *Eighteenth-Century Commonwealthman*, 215; Davis, *Problem of Slavery*, 435–7. Note also the condemnation of slavery in a work of a different order, William Robertson's *History of America* (2nd ed., London, 1778). He described the slave trade as 'an odious commerce no less repugnant to the feelings of humanity than to the principles of religion'.

[82] P. Hazard, *European Thought in the Eighteenth Century*, trans. J. Lewis May (London, 1954), 170–71.

of action.[83] 'Virtue', said Voltaire, 'consists of doing good to one's fellow men',[84] whilst Daniel Mornet asserts that beneficence was the 'dominant principle' of the social code of the *philosophes*.[85] We shall later see how very much this is borne out in some of the most notable literature of the French Enlightenment.

It was Rousseau who made the most fundamental attack on slavery. Conceived as a part of his radical attack on the injustices of the existing social order as a whole he repeated Montesquieu's arguments against the validity of self-sale and of the enslavement of captives, but also went beyond them. Men were born free and equal and so slavery could only stand condemned.[86] Rousseau thus can conclude in *Le Contrat Social* (1762):

So, from whatever aspect we regard the question, the right of slavery is null and void, not only as being illegitimate, but also because it is absurd and meaningless. The words *slave* and *right* contradict each other, and are mutually exclusive. It will always be equally foolish for a man to say to a man or to a people: 'I make with you a convention wholly at your expense and wholly to my advantage; I shall keep it as long as I like, and you will keep it as long as I like.'[87]

Rather as Rousseau went beyond Montesquieu, so in two articles by the Chevalier de Jaucourt, in the famed *Encyclopédie, ou dictionnaire raisonné des sciences, des arts et des métiers*, Montesquieu's ideas were amplified and strengthened.[88] In the second, which was inspired, as we have seen, by George Wallace, Montes-

[83] D. Mornet, *French Thought in the Eighteenth Century*, trans. L. M. Levin, Hamden, Conn. (1969), passim.

[84] Quoted in ibid., 77.

[85] Ibid., 233. Or one of the three virtues, the other two being Tolerance and Humanity, of the 'new morality' of the *philosophes* (Hazard, *European Thought in the Eighteenth Century*, 169–71).

[86] Davis, *Problem of Slavery*, 431–5, 417; Davis goes on to suggest that because Rousseau's attack on slavery was also an attack on all forms of authority and subordination he may well have encouraged conservative resistance to anti-slavery.

[87] J. J. Rousseau, *Le Contrat Social*, bk i, chap. iv. This translation is that of G. D. H. Cole in the Everyman edition of *The Social Contract* (London, 1968).

[88] The first article, entitled 'Esclavage' appeared in 1755; the second, 'Traite des Nègres', in 1765 (Davis, *Problem of Slavery*, 415–16).

Slaver taking in Negroes

Slaves forced to dance to keep them healthy on the middle passage

Lord Grenville (1759–1834)

William Wilberforce

James Stephen (1758–1832)

The Sharp family and friends on their musical barge
Granville Sharp is seated centre-left

Thomas Clarkson

Henry Thornton

quieu's qualifications regarding institutional differences were cast aside (a notable case of Montesquieu's disciples going farther than their master) and slavery unconditionally condemned in terms of simple natural rights philosophy. Negro slaves have the right to be free because they can not truly have lost their freedom.[89]

'By 1765, then,' says David Davis, 'a radical anti-slavery manifesto had been embodied in the great summa of the French Enlightenment.'[90] Davis goes on to add that from 1770 onwards anti-slavery moved more into the foreground of the Enlightenment with the appearance of the Abbé Raynal's *Histoire philosophique et politique des établissements et du commerce des Européens dans les deux Indes*.[91] Only a part of the work deals with slavery but it is significant as bringing together many of the Enlightenment's views on that question, just as the work was a collaborative enterprise in which Diderot, d'Holbach, and others played an important part.[92] Essentially here was a whole segment of human history – Europe's relations with black and brown men – examined in the searching ray of reason which must condemn Negro slavery as affront to natural liberty which 'after reason [is] the distinguishing characteristic of man'.[93] But it is suggested that slavery has in fact always existed. 'Yes, but are we to listen to the suggestions of interest, of infatuation and of barbarism rather than those of reason and of justice?'[94] But Negroes are a type of humanity born for slavery; on the contrary, we have reduced them to a condition which merely gives that appearance. But Negroes were born as some particular person's slaves: on the contrary, there can be no property in human beings. But the slave has voluntarily sold himself into slavery: not so, 'No one hath the right of selling himself; because he hath no right to accede to everything which an unjust, violent and depraved master might require of him. He

[89] Davis, *Problem of Slavery*, 415–17.

[90] Ibid., 417.

[91] First published in 1770, there were numerous editions. Our references will be to the English edition of 1783, entitled *A Philosophical and Political History of the Settlements and Trade of the Europeans in the East and West Indies* (London), trans. J. O. Justamond.

[92] E. D. Seeber, *Anti-Slavery Opinion in France during the Second Half of the Eighteenth Century* (Baltimore and Oxford, 1937).

[93] Raynal, *History of the Europeans in the East and West Indies*.

[94] Ibid., bk II, vol. v, 296.

is the property of God, who is his first master, and from whose authority he is never released.'[95]

In this way Raynal dismisses all the pro-slavery arguments – the rights of captors in war; the right over criminals; that Negroes are happier in America than in their homeland; that in Europe and America the people are slaves anyway; that enslavement is justified by conversion of the slave to Christianity. Raynal's passion mounts as his argument develops.

> Let us, therefore, hasten to substitute the light of reason and the sentiments of nature to (sic) the blind ferociousness of our ancestors. Let us break the bonds of so many victims to our mercenary principles, should we even be obliged to discard a commerce which is founded only on injustice, and the object to which is luxury.[96]

Other passages were yet more declamatory than this and condemned the European colonial record for the calamities which it brought, for its inhumanity – notably slavery – and for 'the most atrocious of all trades that in slaves'.[97]

Negro slavery was also attacked by other figures of the French Enlightenment: by Voltaire in his *Dictionnaire Philosophique* (1764) – though somewhat equivocally;[98] by Turgot in his *Réflexions sur la formation et la distribution des richesses*,[99] on grounds of cost as well as natural rights and humanity; by Louis-Sebastian Mercier in the 1786 augmented edition of *L'An deux mille quatre cent quarante*[100]; and by Condorcet in *Réflexions sur l'esclavage des nègres,* especially in the second edition of 1788.[101] In an age when educated Englishmen read French, books published in France enjoyed a circulation in England. Beyond this, the more important works, at least, of the leading French authors were

[95] Ibid., bk II, vol. v, 299.

[96] Ibid., bk II, vol. v, 304.

[97] Ibid. bk I, vol. I, 210; bk XIX, vol. VIII, 367, 370–71.

[98] Voltaire, *Philosophical Dictionary* (London, 1824) VI 104–11; Davis, *Problem of Slavery*, 392, 402; Seeber, *Anti-Slavery Opinion in France*, 38–40, 65–6, 69, 81, 108–9.

[99] First published in the periodical *Ephémérides du citoyen* in 1767 and in a new edition in 1788 (Seeber, *Anti-Slavery Opinion in France*, 101, 142).

[100] Ibid., 147–8.

[101] Ibid., 144–5.

translated into English.[102] The most striking case of this was Raynal's *Histoire des Européens dans les deux Indes,* for Dallas D. Irvine has pointed out that between 1776 and 1806 the work appeared in no less than fifteen English editions. This certainly entitles us to regard it as the best known to British readers of the anti-slavery manifesto of the French Enlightenment: indeed, we may judge it to have enjoyed a comparable influence to Adam Smith's *The Wealth of Nations* on the grounds that this native product went through precisely the same number of editions in the same period.[103]

It is evident that given philosophical conclusions command assent in measure as the mode of reasoning behind them is convincing. To the extent therefore that the eighteenth century claimed a more scientific approach as its own – the founding upon that method of conclusions latently or directly hostile to slavery would considerably strengthen their appeal. Hutcheson reflected this certainty when he observed that the maxims which disciplined and more searching inquiry was laying bare were no less than the 'laws of nature, and the system of collecting of them is called the LAW OF NATURE'.[104] Not only was latent or specific anti-slavery teaching to this extent commended because of the philosophical method used: it was also commended because, as far as the British thinkers whom we have considered are concerned, their thought was usually presented as at least compatible with Christian belief. This is particularly the case with Hutcheson, Burke, Beattie, Paley and Foster, but none of those whom we have considered appear to have regarded his philosophy as incompatible with Christianity. Professor A. R. Humphreys draws out the significance of this coherence between Christianity and eighteenth-century British philosophy when he writes:

> This new, confident, natural philosophy [reasserts] the mediaval belief in omniscient, infinitely wise, divine superintendence. In a sense the Augustans had all the advantages; with traditional confidence in God's purposes they could enjoy a new intellectual

[102] Including not only the works of Rousseau and Voltaire but the contributions of Turgot and Mercier just noticed.

[103] Dallas D. Irvine, 'The Abbé Raynal and British Humanitarianism', *Journal of Modern History*, III (1931) 575–7.

[104] Hutcheson, *Moral Philosophy*, bk I, chap 1, sec. i. See also *Problem of Slavery*, 405–6.

technique of enquiry (science) which seemed progressively to reveal those purposes as more convincingly admirable.[105]

There are clear limitations to the approach we have taken to eighteenth-century ideas as they relate to anti-slavery. In the idea of Nature[106] and Justice, for instance, there are other keys. Neither do any of the overall studies of eighteenth-century[107] intellectual history single out the concepts of liberty, benevolence and happiness in the kind of way which has been followed above: nor are they necessarily a natural grouping in terms of the thought of an individual, a school or an age. Nevertheless these concepts are always accepted as goods even when not explicitly considered and extolled, and we have concentrated on them because it was appropriate for our purpose to do so whereas it has not been so for most other students of the age. What cannot be in dispute is the striking unanimity in the condemnation of slavery by philosophers of great diversity; what cannot be gainsaid is that none of any rank defended the institution. Positive espousal of reform as a means of bringing institutions and practice into accord with changed values and theory is a less marked note in the philosophy of the age, but it is there. A major recent study of the Enlightenment (as a total European movement) takes the case of abolition as an early subject of the Enlightenment's zeal. Let us note, and provisionally accept, Peter Gay's assessment of its role.

> But while the philosophes [the term is here used in its general sense, and not just in relation to the French Enlightenment], as so often, did little more than to express advanced opinion in their own time, they were in its vanguard ...
>
> The philosophes' views on slavery are predictable and anything but systematic: they are generally exclamations, rarely thoroughgoing analyses. Well-meaning, often vague, they read rather like an automatic response to human misery that speaks well for the philosophes' intentions but hardly amounts to a crusade ...

[105] A. R. Humphreys, 'The Social Setting', *Pelican Guide to English Literature, IV, from Dryden to Johnson*, ed. B. Ford (London, 1970), 38.

[106] See Basil Willey, *The Eighteenth Century Background: Studies on the idea of Nature in the Thought of the Period*, 7th impression (London, 1961).

[107] See notably Hazard, *European Thought in the Eighteenth Century*; E. Halévy, *The Growth of Philosophic Radicalism* 4th ed. (London, 1952); Peter Gay, *The Enlightenment: An Interpretation*, vol. II. *The Science of Freedom*.

In general, though, the men of the Enlightenment helped to change men's thinking on the subject; early in the field and eloquent in their revulsion, they swelled anti-slavery sentiment from a trickle to a respectable stream of opinion that would grow, at the end of the century, with their help, into the torrent of abolitionism.[108]

In tracing eighteenth-century thought on slavery and in seeking to observe indications of a more positive disposition towards change and reform it is not sufficient to restrict ourselves to moral, legal and political philosophy – even with the rider that in Britain, at any rate, there was normally a reinforcing compatibility with religion. Theology had its own contribution to make and to that we must now turn.

[108] Ibid., 409–10.

5 Theology and Reform

In the previous chapter it was argued that two of the concepts which the age particularly valued – liberty and happiness – were, because of the way they were defined and amplified, such as to call Negro slavery into question; and it was demonstrated that most of the influential thinkers of the century specifically condemned that slavery. Sometimes the very intensity of the attack constituted some momentum towards reform whilst the positive definition accorded to benevolence was also such as to encourage the challenging of slavery and the slave trade. Furthermore, there was in the tautness between the *esprit général* and positive law a spring of reform. But what role had theology in the development of anti-slavery thought or in the emergence of a disposition to reform?

Two theological developments played a part in producing a cast of mind prepared to contemplate reform. Firstly it was in the bosom of latitudinarian theology, at least as much as in philosophy, that the concept of benevolence in its characteristic eighteenth-century meaning originated; and because this related to the larger area of religious life and practice, rather than to the more restricted area of philosophy, benevolence can be presented as a sturdier, as a less rarified, growth. Secondly, it was in a development of the doctrine of Providence, namely in the emergence of a concept of progressive revelation, that an important origin of the idea of progress is to be found; and such an idea at least points to institutional change.

Various other developments of the idea of Providence, very different one from another as they were, combined to give added weight to the traditional idea of God as immanent in his world through the operation of His Providence. Since this general Providence of God normally worked, as James Stephen later put it, through 'natural causes' and through mundane sanctions, a highly moral view of desirable conduct – between nations and collectivities as well as individuals – was implied. Arguably, an implication of such a belief is to place a premium on the discernment of right moral conduct, and to induce men, in following the paths of righteousness, to contemplate the possibility that the path might sometimes lead in new directions. But more importantly, once a given line of conduct was branded as evil, an awareness of the formidable sanctions of Providence flooded in to persuade men to eschew that conduct. Finally, and to look ahead to a further stage in the development of our thesis, when we come to see the important role of Evangelicals and Quakers as active agents of reform, as the actual instigators of abolition, we must notice that the theology of their age formed part of their inheritance, that it constituted a part of the base whence they struck out, and a corpus of commonly held ideas to which they could appeal.

At the most profound level of all, the roots of the concept of benevolence obviously lie deep in the simple New Testament injunction to love one's neighbour, but two developments of the later seventeenth century led men to give it a distinctive meaning. Revulsion from Calvinism as a potent source of religious conflict was also revulsion from its gloomy teaching of man's utter depravity. The other force leading in the same direction was quite different; it was the reaction against Hobbes' insistence that man's natural passions were such that, without an all-powerful government, man would be in a state of perpetual conflict with his fellows. This last insistence had so many distasteful implications that, together with the sombreness of Calvin's teaching about man, it led the Latitudinarians to emphasise that, though he was tainted by sin, man still had a natural duty towards, and affection for, his kind. As Professor R. S. Crane has pointed out, there is abundant testimony to the prevalence of such a view of benevolence from before the beginning of the eighteenth century. Take this passage from a divine who was extremely influential for a hundred years after he wrote, Isaac Barrow.

We are indispensably obliged to these duties, because the best of our natural inclinations prompt us to the performance of them, especially those of pity and benignity, which are manifestly discernable in all, but most powerful and vigorous in the best natures; and which, questionless, by the most wise and good Author of our beings were implanted therein both as monitors to direct, and as spurs to incite us to the performance of our duty. For the same bowels, that, in our want of necessary sustenance, do by a lively sense of pain inform us there, and instigate us to provide against it, do in like manner greviously resent the distresses of another, and thereby admonish us of our duty, and provoke us to relieve them. Even the stories of calamities, that in ages long since past have happened to persons nowise related to us, yea, the fabulous reports of tragical events, do (even against the bent of our wills, and all resistance of reason) melt our hearts with compassion, and draw tears from our eyes; and thereby evidently signify that general sympathy which naturally intercedes between all men, since we can neither see, nor hear of, nor imagine another's grief, without being afflicted ourselves. Antipathies may be natural to wild beasts . . . but to rational creatures they are wholly unnatural.[1]

An unnamed preacher of 1720 put more succinctly what had now become common stock of trade.

God has implanted in our very Frame and Make, a compassionate Sense of the Sufferings and Misfortunes of other People, which disposes us to contribute to their relief; so that when we see any of our Fellow-Creatures in Circumstances of Distress, we are naturally I had almost said, mechanically inclined to be helpful to them.[2]

The divine went on to speak of the pleasure which such virtuous action gave, a pleasure which was elsewhere described as so intense as to be almost sensual. Here then we have the origin, the religious origin, of the idea of benevolence in its characteristic eighteenth-century sense.[3]

There are numerous statements of the manner in which the early eighteenth century understood the ordinary or general Provi-

[1] Quoted in R. S. Crane, 'Genealogy of the "Man of Feeling"', *The Idea of the Humanities and Other Essays Critical and Historical* (Chicago, 1967) I 206, to whom I am indebted for the explanation of the origins of benevolence. See also Davis, *Problem of Slavery*, 348–9.

[2] Quoted in Crane, 'The Man of Feeling', 209.

[3] For further demonstration of the central importance of benevolence in Latitudinarian theology see M. C. Battestin, *The Moral Basis of Fielding's Art* (Middletown, Conn., 1964) 14–25, and 52–84 passim.

dence of God. Pope captures the common view, albeit complacently, in some lines of the *Essay on Man*

> But HEAV'N's great view is One, and that the Whole.
> That counter-works each folly and caprice;
> That disappoints th'effect of ev'ry vice;
> That, happy frailties to all apply'd,
> Shame to the virgin, to the matron pride,
> Fear to the statesman, rashness to the chief,
> To Kings presumption, and to crowds belief;
> That, Virtue's ends from Vanity can raise,
> Which seeks no interest, no reward but praise;
> And builds on wants, and on defects of mind,
> The joy, the peace, the glory of Mankind.[4]

A more direct statement is found in one of Archbishop Tillotson's sermons devoted to the demonstration of the proposition that 'Religion and Virtue are the great causes of public happiness and prosperity'. One of his vindications of this truth, 'long enough experienced in the world' but requiring to be restated 'because the fashion of the age is to call everything into question', is from the justice of Providence. As distinct from the operation of divine justice upon individuals – which consists in the conferring of felicity or anguish in the next world as well, sometimes, as in the experience of reward or punishment in this – nations, having no other worldly continuation, must receive justice on earth:

> In the usual course of his providence he recompenseth religious and virtuous nations with temporal blessings and prosperity . . . But the general and crying Sins of a Nation cannot hope to escape publick judgments, unless they be prevented by a general repentance. God may defer his judgments for a time, and give a people a longer space of repentance, he may stay 'till the iniquities of a Nation be full, but sooner or later they have reason to expect his vengeance.

To this vindication Tillotson joined a fairly conventional argument from 'the natural tendency of the thing'.[5]

[4] Pope, *Essay on Man*, Epistle II, lines 238–48.
[5] Archbishop Tillotson, Sermon III, 'The Advantage of Religion to Societies'. *Works* (London, 1728) I 35–7.

The theme of a general Providence was likewise taken up by the Latitudinarians in that the cardinal article of their faith was belief in the existence of God and in the world as his handiwork, and with Providence as the surest testimony to his wisdom and power.[6] In the moral philosophers whom we have already studied there was at least tacit acceptance, and in men like Hutcheson, Beattie and Paley a positive emphasis, to use Hutcheson's phrase, on 'a Governing Mind presiding in this world'.[7] The first respect in which the doctrine of the Providence of God undergoes extensive development during the century, has been brilliantly demonstrated by Professor R. S. Crane. He sums up the nature and importance of this development by pointing to the work of a group of Anglican apologists, writing between 1699 and 1745, whose concern was 'to vindicate the beneficence of God's providence and especially to combat deism by reinterpreting the history of revelation itself, and consequently of the whole spiritual and moral experience of mankind, in terms of a continuous and necessary movement from worse to better'.[8]

The idea of progressive revelation had a long and respectable history in Christian theology but it appears that it was a particular tenet of Deism which led to the development of the idea in the first half of the eighteenth century. This was the deistic assertion that 'any religion necessary for salvation must be one that has always and everywhere been known to men'.[9] Belief in divine Providence and in Christianity were impugned by the 'arbitrary and inequitable temporal distribution of moral good and religious enlightenment which the church's doctrine seems to imply'.[10] The challenge was first taken up by John Edwards in a work of 1699[11] where he reasoned that 'it seems good to the All-wise Creator to

[6] G. R. Cragg, *Reason and Authority in the Eighteenth Century* (Cambridge, 1964), 43–61.

[7] Cf. Wm Paley, *Natural Theology* in *Works* (London, 1828) II 192: 'the degree of beneficence, of benevolent intention, and of power, exercised in the construction of sensitive beings, goes strongly in favour, not only of a creative, but of a continuing care, that is, of a ruling providence.'

[8] R. S. Crane, 'Anglican Apologetics and the Idea of Progress, 1699–1745', *The Idea of the Humanities*, I 215–6.

[9] Ibid., 224.

[10] Ibid.

[11] *A Compleat History or Survey of All the Dispensations and Methods of Religion, from the Beginning of the World to the Consummation of All Things: as Represented in the Old and New Testament.*

reveal the knowledge of himself by degrees, to discover his will as it were by parcels'[12] and went to argue from the analogy of the law of human knowledge: 'can there by any Reason given why God should not prosper *Religion* as well as *Arts*? Why we may not look for increase of knowledge in the Church, as well as in matters that relate only to Nature? Why there may not be a Perfection of Understanding in the one, as well as in the other?'[13] Edward's line of argument was taken further forty years later by William Worthington in his suggestively entitled *An Essay on the Scheme and Conduct, Procedure and Extent of Man's Redemption, Wherein is Shewn from the Holy Scriptures, that this Great Work Is to be accomplished gradually* (1743). Still in the context of refuting the Deists Worthington sought to meet objections to the doctrine of Providence on the grounds that it permitted natural and moral evils by arguing that the divine plan was progressively to eliminate evils until mankind 'shall at length arrive at such a pitch of Proficiency under the Gospel Dispensation that there shall be no Remains left of Sin or Evil of any kind'.[14] This will come about because 'every thing has a tendency to its own Perfection'[15] and God is all-wise and all-good and will surely assist his creatures to overcome the (superable) effects of the Fall. Certainly man may yet choose evil but

> it is most reasonable to suppose, that reasonable Creatures, after the continued experience of the Benefits of Good, and In-conveniences of Evil, will at last perceive their true Interest, and act accordingly – that after Vibrating for a Time from one Extreme to the other, the Centre of moral Oscillation will at length be fix'd.[16]

Christianity, then, and by virtue of it human nature were in 'a growing progressive state'[17] presided over and made possible by a Providence which tailored its dispensations to the ability of men to profit from them.[18]

The most important exponent of the new progressivist doctrine

[12] Quoted in Crane, 'Anglican Apologetics and Progress'. 226.
[13] Quoted in ibid., 229.
[14] Quoted in ibid., 239–40.
[15] Quoted in ibid., 243.
[16] Quoted in ibid., 246.
[17] Quoted in ibid., 248.
[18] Ibid., 239–51.

was Bishop Edmund Law. The book in which it was worked out was made up of three discourses and published under the title *Considerations on the State of the World with Regard to the Theory of Religion in Three Parts: I. Want of Universality in Natural and Revealed Religion, No Just Objection against Either; II. The Scheme of Divine Providence with Regard to the Time and Manner of the Several Dispensations of Revealed Religion, More Especially of the Christian; III. The Progress of Natural Religion and Science, or the Continual Improvement of the World in General* (1745). Still on a battle ground of the Deists' choosing Law brings a new rejoinder to the familiar and still central deistic claim that only a religious belief which can be shown to have been held everywhere, at all times and by all men can possess authority. It stems from an associationist psychology, which necessarily held that since conceptions are derived by association from experience, understanding of religious truths must be related to that experience at any given time, an experience, that is, of an increasing amount of knowledge. In short, God

> has all along acted equally for the good of Mankind in Matters of Religion, though in very different manners according to their different Circumstances and Capacities; that his several Dispensations have been gradually open'd so as regularly to rise out of and improve upon each other; and that the State of Knowledge and Perfection in the World has hitherto been perpetually *increasing*.[19]

Nor, of course, is the significance of this purely historical: rather, if religion 'has hitherto been really progressive, we find good reason to expect the same still farther'.[20] As one might expect, Law shared the now almost commonplace view of development in knowledge of the Arts and Sciences so that, in Crane's words, 'because of the necessary interconnectedness of all forms of knowledge, progress became a general law of human life'.[21]

Similar ideas, deriving in part from Law, came from the pens of men such as David Hartley,[22] John Gordon, Archdeacon of

[19] Quoted in ibid., 270.

[20] Quoted in ibid., 274.

[21] Ibid., 273. Crane's section on Law is made up of pp. 251–75 of his paper.

[22] *Observations on Man, His Frame, His Duty, and His Expectations* (London, 1749).

Lincoln[23] and Joseph Priestley in the decades immediately after 1745. Thus Priestley instructed his students at the Warrington Academy on 'an attention to Divine Providence in the Conduct of Human Affairs' and did so in these terms:

> Let the person . . . who would trace the conduct of Divine Providence, attend to every advantage which the present age enjoys above ancient times, and see whether he cannot perceive marks of things being in a progress towards a state of greater perfection. . . . A thousand circumstances shew how inferior the ancients were to the moderns in religious knowledge, in science in general, in government, in laws, both the laws of nations, and those of particular states, in arts, in commerce, in the conveniences of life, in manners, and, in consequence of all these, in *happiness*.[24]

In short here was a conception of progress as the manifestation of a great providential design and as such different from the belief in progress as originating exclusively in the Enlightenment's modest faith in what would flow from the application of scientific reason to human problems.[25] Here is an important intellectual development and one which at the same time gave a fresh dimension to the idea of Providence.[26]

---

[23] *A New Estimate of Manners and Principles: Being a Comparison between Ancient and Modern Times in the Three Great Articles of Knowledge, Happiness and Virtue* (London, 1760).

[24] Quoted in Crane, 'Anglican Apologetics and Progress', 284 n. My indebtedness to Professor Crane is again evident, in this case to pp. 274–87.

[25] The classic study is J. B. Bury, *The Idea of Progress* (London, 1920). For an expansive view of how *philosophes* envisaged the notion of progress see, e.g., Leo Gershoy, *From Despotism to Revolution, 1763–1789* (New York and London, 1944) 203–5, but compare Gay's observation that 'at least until the nineteenth century it was easier for a Christian than for a philosophe to construct a theory of progress,' and see on this question pp. 912–115 of his *The Enlightenment: an Interpretation*. vol. ii: *The Science of Freedom*.

[26] Just as the idea of Providence underwent this significant development so there took place an analagous development in the idea of the Chain of Being. The earlier idea, we have seen, was that all potentiality of being of the graded links of the Chain had already been fulfilled. This, and the necessarily static view of the world which was implied, was now replaced by the idea that there must, rather, be the potentiality of an infinitude of intermediate members between any two members. Here is, in fact, an

The second development of the idea of Providence is found in the work of the major empirical philosopher, Bishop Berkeley. The philosophical core of Berkeley's work is found in his *Essay towards a New Theory of Vision* (1709), in which he concluded that visible objects are a system of signs of tangible matter; in the *Treatise Concerning the Principles of Human Knowledge* (1710) and especially in the *Dialogues of Hylas and Philonus* (1713), where he concludes that visible and tangible objects are a system of sensible signs of absent objects of sense; whilst in all three of the foregoing is the conclusion that this system of signs, which cannot exist without a percipient, is a sensible expression of the divine ideas, presence and providence.[27] The nature of Berkeley's idea of Providence needs to be drawn out further. From the premiss that 'sensible things cannot exist otherwise than in a mind or spirit' Berkeley concludes not that they have no real existence but that, repeating Berkeley's own italics '*there must be some other mind wherein they exist*'. This has brought Berkeley to the essence of his position on Providence: 'As sure, therefore, as the sensible world really exists, so sure is there an infinite omnipresent Spirit, who contains and supports it.'[28] This omnipresent spirit is no other than the 'being of a God' of whom Berkeley says elsewhere in the *Dialogues of Hylas and Philonus*:

> When I say the being of a *God*, I do not mean an obscure general cause of things, whereof we have no conception, but *God*, in the strict and proper sense of the word, a Being whose spirituality, omnipresence, providence, omniscience, infinite power and goodness, are as conspicuous as the existence of

[27] G. Berkeley, *Works*, ed. A. C. Fraser (Oxford, 1871), Editor's Preface, vol. I 4, and passim.
[28] Berkeley, 'The Second Dialogue between Hylas and Philonus', *Works*, I 304.

---

evolutionist idea of the Chain of Being which admits progress to the scene. As the poet, Mark Akenside, expressed it:

> in their stations all may persevere
> To climb the ascent of being, and approach
> For ever nearer to the life divine.

(Lovejoy, *Great Chain of Being*, 242–68. The Akenside quotation is on p. 265.)

sensible things, of which . . . there is no more reason to doubt than of our own being.[29]

In the fourth of the Dialogues in *Alciphron, or the Minute Philosopher*, Berkeley develops further one dimension of his idea of providence by putting it forward as the foundation of practical morals. His 'optic language', or theory of vision, because of the infinity and complexity of observed 'signs'

> doth set forth and testify the immediate operation . . . of one wise, good and provident Spirit, which directs and rules and governs the world. . . . This visual language proves, not a Creator merely, but a provident Governor, actually and intimately present, and attentive to all our interests and motions, who watches over our conduct, and takes care of our minutest actions and designs throughout the whole course of our lives, informing, admonishing, and directing incessantly, in a most evident and sensible manner.[30]

The excitement which Berkeley generated and appreciation of his considerable philosophical contribution seem to have been confined to philosophers for the most part. None the less it cannot have entirely been overlooked then, as we should not overlook now, that Berkeley's primary concern was to prove the reality of a providential God. It is significant that the full form of the title of the *Theory of Vision or Visual Language* adds the words *shewing the immediate presence and Providence of a Deity, vindicated and explained*.

Like Berkeley, Bishop Butler was a philosopher who felt called to Christian apologetics, in a sceptical age,[31] whilst his best-known and widely influential book, *The Analogy of Religion* (1736), has been coupled with Berkeley's *Alciphron* – and with the *Pensées* of Pascal – as a truly remarkable work of religious philosophy. This widely read writer is also explicit on the subject of Providence, particularly in the *Analogy*; his conclusions on the subject are,

[29] Berkeley, 'The Third Dialogue between Hylas and Philonus', *Works*, I 354.

[30] Berkeley, 'Alciphron, or the Minute Philosopher', *Works*, II 157–8.

[31] It is of Butler that the (probably apocryphal) story is told that he refused elevation to the province of Canterbury because the corruption of the times was such that the end of all things must surely supervene before he could take up that office.

of course, arrived at by the method of analogy and amount to a clear doctrine of Providence and moral government, which can be succinctly put in his own words.

> that God governs the World by general fixt Laws, that he has endued us with Capacities of reflecting upon the Constitution of things, and forseeing the good and bad consequences of our Behaviour; plainly implies some Sort of Moral Government.[32]

> And, since the certain natural Course of Things is the Conduct of Providence or the Government of God, though carried on by the Instrumentality of Men, Mankind find themselves placed by Him in such Circumstances as that they are unavoidably accountable for their Behaviour, in the view of their being mischevious, or eminently beneficial to Society.[33]

> Christianity is not only . . . a new Promulgation of God's general Providence, as righteous Governor and Judge of the World; but it contains also a Revelation of a particular Dispensation of Providence, carrying on by his Son and Spirit, for the Recovery and Salvation of Mankind.[34]

> The moral Government of God is exercised by gradually conducting things so in the Course of his Providence, that every one, at length and upon the whole, shall receive according to his Deserts; and neither Fraud nor Violence, but Truth and Right, shall finally prevail. Christianity is a particular Scheme under this general Plan of Providence.[35]

Butler, then, like Berkeley, had something distinctive to say about Providence and, though in a different way, it was central in his thinking. And if only because his whole system of thought was more obviously congenial to the mid-eighteenth century, and was not the tax on credibility which Berkeley appeared to be, Butler was clearly more widely read.

The fourth development in the idea of Providence is found in the writings of Edmund Burke; the way to the understanding of

[32] Joseph Butler, *The Analogy of Religion Natural and Revealed to the Constitution and Course of Nature*, 2nd ed. (London, 1736) 72.

[33] Ibid., 73.

[34] Ibid., 220.

[35] Ibid., 272

this is to comprehend Burke's notion of what he calls the concrete reason, a concept which he defines principally in the context of his polemic against the French Revolution, and in contrast to what he terms the 'critical reason' manifested in that movement. The concrete reason appeals to the common experience of mankind but also does much more, namely claims for itself a very close relationship to the idea of a providential order. The essence of this concrete reason is that it recognises its dependence on a higher reason, though the concrete reason is only imperfectly aware of that higher reason; that higher reason, moreover, 'a reason which is not our own', is nothing less than the objective reason of the moral order. Burke, of course, develops at length the contrast between the disasters to which the unrelated ideal principles of the abstract reason lead and the sure guide constituted by just prejudice, and instinct and historical experience. He insists, however, that the concrete reason is not discerned in this way alone: it is also founded on theological disclosure; it is, in his resounding phrase, 'the known march of the ordinary Providence of God'. Burke's insistence on the importance of the providential plan is stressed by Professor Cobban.

> Burke . . . sees the divine plan in the actual appearances of the world, in the positive events of experience, and to him any system of politics that denies this faith, is atheist, outcast. When Burke gives expression to the religious view of life it is in very striking terms, and the comparative infrequency of such reference must lead us to underestimate their importance . . . a careful study of his opinions on practically any point will lead to the same implicit foundation.[36]

It may seem at first sight that Burke's well-known emphasis on the sanctity of prescription must both hallow everything that exists and exclude change and reform. In fact he argues the case

[36] A. Cobban, *Edmund Burke and the Revolt against the Eighteenth Century* (London, 1962) 92–3. Cf. R. R. Fennessy, *Burke, Paine and the Rights of Man* (The Hague, 1963) 55: 'For Burke the temporal process itself, the unfolding of history, comes to have a moral value. The human race, as it organises itself concretely in space and perpetuates itself in time, constitutes an objective order which is under divine guidance.' Burke's convictions about the unfolding of Providence are more particularly spelled out in H. F. V. Somerset (ed.), *A Notebook of Edmund Burke* (Cambridge, 1957).

for reform and does so in terms also of a providential purpose. Change, as in nature, is necessary for survival; reform is a natural renovation, a response to the demands of the moral order in the existing situation, a response, that is, to the pressure of the imma-nent providential order. Belief in the embodiment of the provi-dential order in the past is inseparable from belief in its latent presence in the present, and the creative moral effort which must be the response to it – even though it can be felt only and not defined – is the practicable virtue which God has put within our reach.[37]

Burke is then not only much concerned with the preservation and extension of liberty and happiness, but sees these goals pointed to by the wisdom of the ages, and in process of realisation by a superintending Providence.

Evidence is not lacking that the view of Providence as consti-tuting moral government was widely held. In April 1749 the saintly Philip Doddridge, on the day appointed for national thanks-giving following the successful conclusion of the War of the Austrian Succession, preached as his sermon 'Reflection on the Conduct of Divine Providence in the Course and Conclusion of the late war'. This was a somewhat complacent elaboration on the set of the wind which permitted the English armies to be brought back from the Continent and defeat the Jacobite rising; for us the interesting thing is that the sermon has all the flavour of an address given on a public occasion and expressing beliefs already generally held by the congregation rather than teachings peculiar to the preacher.[38] There is a more general statement of the role of Providence in two verses of a hymn by Isaac Watts, mentor and near contemporary of Doddridge:

> The thunders of his hand
> Keep the whole world in awe;
> His wrath and justice stand
> To guard his holy law;
>
> . . .

[37] For Burke and Providence, in addition to the sources already used, see Charles Parkin's important *The Moral Basis of Burke's Political Thought* (Cambridge, 1956), especially 109–30.

[38] Philip Doddridge, *Reflection on the Conduct of Divine Providence in the Course and Conclusion of the late War: a Sermon preached at Northampton on April 25, 1749.*

Through all his mighty works
Amazing wisdom shines,
Confounds the powers of hell,
And breaks their dark designs;
Strong is His arm, and shall fulfil
His great decrees and sovereign will.[39]

Sentiments such as these are common and an interesting development of the theme is the way in which contemporary paraphrases of the psalms and other scriptures were 'providentialised' beyond the original text.[40] Yet more striking evidence of a general belief in Providence is Doddridge's observation in the very different context of his *Rise and Progress of Religion in the Soul*. There he identifies the subject of his appeal to seek true Christianity by speaking of him as a nominal Christian who believes in 'the Existence and Providence of God, and the Truth of Christianity, as a Revelation from him'. Here is a definition which Doddridge clearly assumes fits a great many people.[41]

There is little doubt that in the eighteenth century belief in Providence as the moral government of the universe was general.[42]

The theological contribution to the development of anti-slavery was important. We have sought to argue three points. Firstly, the springs of the idea of benevolence are found at least as much in theology as in moral philosophy; and because theology, as mediated by works of piety and devotion, and by even the eighteenth-century pulpit, was more widely influential upon attitudes than philosophy with its more rarified quality, the distinction has some importance. Behind our second point is the fact that we manifestly err if we attribute to the eighteenth-century *philosohes* too unqualified an embracing of the belief in progress. For all the

[39] This hymn may be found, amongst other places in *The Methodist Hymn Book* (London, 1933) no. 58.

[40] Cf. e.g. Psalm 36, 'High in the Heavens Eternal God . . . (*Congregational Praise* (London, 1951) no. 51, and Isaiah Chap. 40 (ibid., no. 53). I am indebted to Professor W. A. Whitehouse for making this point.

[41] Philip Doddridge, *The Rise and Progress of Religion in the Soul*, 10th ed. (London, 1771) 13.

[42] There is interesting and possibly unexpected evidence of the prevalence of belief in Providence in the definition of *Théiste* in the *Dictionnaire Philosophique* (1764): 'The difficulties connected with the idea of Providence do not shake his faith . . . He deems that this Providence extends to all places and to all ages' (Quoted in Hazard, *European Thought in The Eighteenth Century*, 403–4).

headiness of Condorcet's *Esquisse d'un tableau historique des progrès de l'esprit humain* (1794) the belief was more modest than many have supposed. The importance of the theological origins of progressive revelation as a dispensation of Providence and as a major dimension of belief in progress, of the possibility of reform in human institutions, is therefore evident. Thirdly, the importance of the idea of a general Providence to the eighteenth-century mind has been stressed. Here the cardinal truth is that men of the age saw an immanent divine sanction on evil and saw it very clearly even if they were not devout or pious men. Whilst slavery was tolerated, albeit uneasily, in Christendom, the idea of a providential judgement had no relevance to it (save in the sense that the notion of Providence was rigidified or vulgarised so as to justify slavery): but once slavery began to be morally condemned, consciousness of the sanctions of Providence came heavily into the scales against it. Nations which perpetrated or condoned slavery came to be seen as subject to the retributory justice of God; only so could the moral order be preserved. Testimony not merely to the continuing but to the enhanced importance of the idea of Providence is found in the major, if widely varying developments of it in Berkeley, Butler and Burke, whilst a host of sometimes throw-away lines in literature and poetry likewise attest its importance.[43]

Thus mainstream theology of the first three-quarters of the eighteenth century had nothing new to say about the morality of slavery: it seems, indeed, not to have disassociated itself from the negative implications of the old identification of slavery and sin and from the old view of slavery as justified because used as a punishment in the divine scheme. The theological contribution was, rather, in its contribution to an impetus of reform. The strength of that impetus is uncertain and it should be observed that in another area in which reform was, from the end of the third quarter of the century onwards, being canvassed, namely parlia-

---

[43] See, e.g., the prevalence of the idea of Providence in Richardson's *Pamela;* in E. Young, *Night Thoughts*, Night IX, The Consolation; in Benjamin Stillingfleet, *Some Thoughts Occasioned by the late Earthquakes* (1750), quoted in Hoxie Fairchild, *Religious Trends in English Poetry* (New York, 1958) II 70; in Akenside's, *Pleasures of the Imagination*, quoted in Lovejoy, *The Great Chain of Being*, 264–5; in Richard Savage, *Of Public Spirit in Regard to Public Works* (1737), quoted in Clarkson, *History of the Abolition*, I 54 and in a different extract in Sypher, *Guinea's Captive Kings*, 165.

mentary reform, the appeal to many was not the appeal of reform in the modern meaning, but the appeal of 're-forming', that is of re-creating an earlier, purer form, as in the concern to act against rotten boroughs.[44] But even if its momentum was limited, the impetus of reform must command attention for what it was. At the end of the day our overall interpretation of abolition does not demand, as far as the realm of ideas is concerned, that there should have been a strong demonstrable, ideological pressure for reform – as distinct, from a prevailing conviction that slavery stood condemned.

[44] Cf. John Cannon, *Parliamentary Reform, 1640–1832* (Cambridge, 1973).

6 Anti-Slavery Values in Literature

More direct evidence of the appeal of notions of liberty, benevolence and happiness, as elaborated in eighteenth-century thought, is to be found in literature. The approach, the concern of the poet or novelist is evidently very different from that of the moral philosopher but their work attests even more convincingly what concerns our age. As to liberty, just as Lien Chi Altangi, Goldsmith's Chinese visitor to England, asserted that 'Liberty is echoed in all their assemblies',[1] the eighteenth century gave a due meed of attention to the idea, philosophising about it in the manner of Richard Savage in his *Epistle to Sir Robert Walpole*:

> From Liberty each nobler science sprung,
> A Bacon brighten'd, and a Spenser sung;
> A Clarke and Locke new tracts of truth explore,
> And Newton reaches heights unknown before.[2]

James Thomson, also, was moved, as he told his patron, Frederick, Prince of Wales, 'to trace Liberty from the first ages down to her excellent establishment in Great Britain' in a poem of five parts.[3] What was extolled was liberty with a divine sanction and at once the secret of the political health and stability which England uniquely enjoyed and the germ of creative intellectual activity of many kinds.[4]

Benevolence in eighteenth-century poetry and literature, which is largely synonymous with sensibility, appears to have three dimensions: the exploration and analysis of the feeling; an ethical

[1] Goldsmith, *The Citizen of the World* (1762) Letter IV.
[2] Quoted in Humphreys, 'The Social Setting', 32.
[3] In James Thomson, *Works*, Aldine Edition (London, 1867), II 3–135.
[4] Ibid.; see also Wm. Collins, *Ode to Liberty* (1746) and Oliver Goldsmith, *The Traveller* (1764).

imperative which made the good heart the moral touchstone and source of outgoing goodness and began to see ethical significance in the power to react emotionally to the good and the pain of others; and the cultivation of a high and delicate feeling, that is, sentimentalism. It is the second of these which concerns us, and it is commonly related to the quest for happiness. Thus in Thomson's poem, *Liberty,* we find:

> An active Flood of *universal Love*
> Must swell the Breast. First in Effusion wide,
> The restless Spirit roves Creation round,
> And seizes every Being: Stronger then
> It tends to *Life*, what'en the kindred search
> Of Bliss ally: then, more collected still,
> It urges Human-kind: a Passion grown,
> At last, the central Parent-Public calls
> It's utmost Effort forth, awakes each Sense,
> The Comely, Grand and Tender. Without this,
> This awful Part, shook from sublimer Powers
> Than those of *Self*, this HEAVEN infus'd Delight,
> This *moral Gravitation,* rushing prone
> To press the public Good, MY System soon,
> Traverse, to several *selfish* Centers drawn
> Will reel to Ruin.[5]

Henry Fielding makes a similar point in prose in one of his authorial soliloquies in *Tom Jones*:

I desire philosophers to grant, that there is in some (I believe in many) human breasts, a kind and benevolent disposition, which is gratified by contributing to the happiness of others. That in this gratification alone, as in friendship, in parental and filial affection, and indeed in general philanthropy, there is a great and exquisite delight.[6]

There is no need to labour the omnipresence of benevolence – and of benevolence as the primary source of happiness – in the authors of the age: we find it in Richardson's heroine, Pamela, in the

[5] James Thomson, *Liberty*, v, lines 245–60, quoted in A. D. McKillop, *The Background of the Seasons* (Hamden, Conn., 1961) 38.

[6] Henry Fielding, *Tom Jones*, bk vi, chap. 1, For Goldsmith this was 'the luxury of doing good' (*The Traveller*).

novel of that name, as she fulfils the duties of her married state, in his hero, Sir Charles Grandison, in the novel named after him: as the 'energizing principle' in Fielding's Heartfree, Tom Jones, Squire Allworthy, Captain Booth, Doctor Harrison and pre-eminently Parson Adams.[7] And we see it no less in Julie, the heroine of Rousseau's *La Nouvelle Heloïse*, than in the introspection of Rousseau's fierce opponent, Dr Johnson. 'Afternoon spent cheerfully and elegantly,' he wrote, 'in the general exercise and cultivation of benevolence.'[8] Benevolence, indeed, and the happiness which the practice of it induced, were major components of the century's definition of goodness. Of the appeal of sensibility which was so similar to benevolence we have striking evidence. Harriet Byron wept at the simple reflection that there could be such a man in the world as Sir Charles Grandison; Lady Bradshaigh retired to bed and cried for days on end at the history of *Clarissa*; and doubtless there was English reaction to the frequently translated *La Nouvelle Heloïse*[9] akin to that of the future general Thiébault who was reduced to 'howling like a wild beast'.[10]

We have a more surprising testimony to the wide dissemination even of works of philosophy in John Newton's testimony that during his tempestuous youth as a seaman he picked up a copy of the second volume of Shaftesbury's *Characteristicks* in a bookshop at Middleburg. Moreover, the effect upon him was considerable: 'The style and manner gave me great pleasure in reading. . . . I so much admired the pictures of virtue and benevolence as drawn by Lord Shaftesbury.'[11] The appeal of eighteenth-century literature in England was extensive. *Pamela,* for example, went through five editions in its first year and *Clarissa* through four between 1748 and 1759. James Lackington, a self-made bookseller, wrote in the 1780s of the 'general desire for *Reading* now so prevalent among the inferior orders of society' and observed that in the pre-

[7] 'Formulated as early as *The Champion* Fielding's version of the familiar benevolist concept of good nature remains the substance of his definition of the moral man' (M. C. Battestin, *The Moral Basis of Fielding's Art*, 54. But see the whole of Chapter v also (52–84).

[8] Boswell, *Life of Johnson*, 1280.

[9] J. Voisine, *J.-J. Rousseau en Angleterre à l'Epoque Romantique* (Paris, 1956) 72.

[10] Mornet, *French Thought in the Eighteenth Century*, 214–5.

[11] Newton, *Authentic Narrative*, 20, 24.

ceding two decades there had been a more than fourfold increase in the sale of books, especially among farmers and the poorer country people.[12]

A final testimony to the vogue of benevolence is the large scale of private philanthropy in the eighteenth century.[13] A contemporary, Sir F. M. Eden, suggested at least £6 million as the annual volume of private charity in the last years of the eighteenth century, and another, P. Colquhoun, possibly as a result of more searching inquiry, suggested an annual figure of £4 for public and private charity together in the very early nineteenth century. Fielding, who had seen much of life in the raw in his capacity of chief magistrate of Westminster, believed that 'charity is the very characteristic virtue at this time. I believe we may challenge the whole world to parallel the examples which we have of late given of this sensible, this noble, this Christian virtue.'[14]

One expression of sensibility was especially important for the rise of anti-slavery sentiment. This was the development of appreciation of man's essential virtue in his primitive state – the cult of the noble savage – from the later seventeenth century onwards. Of early importance was the Yarico and Inkle legend. Taking may forms since the first version of the story in the mid-seventeenth century it stemmed from the tale of Yarico, an Indian girl in Barbados, and of considerable beauty, who sheltered a white sailor, Inkle, a survivor from shipwreck. They fall in love and spend months together in an idyllic tropical paradise; eventually a European vessel takes them on board – whereupon Inkle sells Yarico into slavery. Although in its early forms the tale was not concerned to dramatise the horrors of slavery, it came to be appropriated by anti-slavery writers in the middle eighteenth century with Yarico, in some cases, a Negro virgin. The tale was translated

[12] Quoted in F. C. Gill, *The Romantic Movement and Methodism* (London, 1954) 104–5. See also R. A. Humphreys' conclusion that the reading public 'under the Hanoverian Kings stretched widely, until from the 1740s onwards the heady influence of popular enthusiasm could spread literary reputations with unprecedented contagion' (Humphreys, 'The Social Setting', 19).

[13] Cited in David Owen, *English Philanthropy, 1660–1960* (Cambridge, Mass., 1965) 100–01.

[14] Quoted in ibid., 11. See also ibid., 1–133 and M. J. Quinlan, *Victorian Prelude: a History of English Manners, 1700–1830* (London, 1965) 1–100 passim.

into eight languages and inspired some forty separate works during the eighteenth century.[15] Even more important, because it invited more complex responses, was Mrs Aphra Behn's novel, *Oroonoko; or the History of the Royal Slave,* first published in 1688. During a colourful career, which included spying for England during the Anglo-Dutch war of 1665–67, and imprisonment for debt, Aphra Behn visited Surinam and subsequently claimed that *Oroonoko* was a true story, part of which she had witnessed herself whilst there. Oroonoko, an African prince of perfect masculinity, had fallen in love with Imoinda, 'the beautiful black Venus to our young Mars'. Educated by a French tutor, as well as by English traders, the prince excelled in 'the highest passions of Love and Gallantry', expressive, we are told, of his true greatness of soul. This idyll is interrupted, however, for Imoinda is summoned to the harem of her aged King: Oroonoko none the less consummates his love with her but the two are discovered. Imoinda is sold into slavery and taken to Surinam whilst some time later Oroonoko is treacherously kidnapped by an English captain and likewise taken to Surinam, where the lovers are reunited. Given unusual liberties by a kindly master, Oroonoko was promised his own and Imoinda's freedom, but grew restive at delay. He is meanwhile taught both some Roman history and the elements of Christianity, but reveals that he has come to despise the latter by the terms in which he eventually incites his fellow slaves to revolt. The rising, however, cracks and Oroonoko surrenders on a promise of pardon, immediately repudiated. He is subjected to an atrocious whipping by his captors an subsequently condemned to death, but the two lovers slip away and remain free just long enough for Oroonoko to kill Imoinda after a final embrace. He himself remains unmoved whilst being put to death with appalling cruelty.[16]

Aphra Behn's hope was that her pen was sufficient to make her hero's 'glorious name to survive to all ages, with that of the brave, the beautiful and the constant Imoinda':[17] to the extent that her hope was fulfilled it was primarily through stage adaptations of

[15] Wylie Sypher, *Guinea's Captive Kings: British Anti-Slavery Literature of the XVIIIth Century,* 122 ff; Davis, *Problem of Slavery,* 10–13.

[16] Aphra Behn, *Oroonoko: the Royal Slave* in E. A. Baker (ed.), *The Novels of Mrs. Aphra Behn* (London, 1905) 1–81. See also Davis, *Problem of Slavery,* 472–7 and Sypher, *Guinea's Captive Kings,* 108–21.

[17] Behn, *Oroonoko,* 81.

the novel by Thomas Southerne and John Hawkesworth, the former being performed nearly every year for a century after 1696.[18] Just as in the original of the Yarico and Inkle story there was no explicit or intended attack on slavery – indeed Mrs Behn's hero offered 'either gold, or a vast quantity of slaves' for his own freedom.[19] The fact remains that in Southerne's play there could be no doubt that Negroes were the heroes and Europeans the villains. But, as David Davis has convincingly argued, 'the story's significance went beyond its verisimilitude'.[20] Traditional arguments justifying slavery on the grounds of the savagery, paganism and idolatry of Africans

> would remain convincing unless Europeans came to think of the African as a man of feeling whose desire for liberty and capacity for a moral life could not be extinguished by the most oppressive environment. The great question, then, was whether the literary imagination could build a bridge of sympathy and understanding across the enormous gulf that divided primitive and civilized cultures. . . . Europeans could conceptualize the meaning of enslavement only in the familiar terms that increasingly aroused a sensitive response from the middle class: the separation of young lovers; the heartless betrayal of an innocent girl; the unjust punishment of a faithful servant. And no matter how stylised the literary Negro was to become, his great prototype, Oroonoko, was more realistic than critics have imagined.[21]

[18] Sypher, *Guinea's Captive Kings*, 109–10, 116.
[19] Behn, *Oroonoko*, 47.
[20] Davis, *Problem of Slavery*, 478.
[21] Ibid., 473–4. Davis develops this theme further: 'the noble savage and the suffering slave who arouses only sympathy and tears . . . both . . . played essential roles in conditioning anti-slavery opinion. If the Negro was a terrifying avenger, returning blow for blow, demanding as many drops of blood as he had shed through centuries of oppression, he struck a response in one part of the white man's nature. This would be how the European should want to act if he were a slave. But if the Negro patiently accepted flagellation and torture; if he cut his own throat, like Raynal's "Quazy", rather than resist his master's unjust punishment, if he hung in a cage, like the slave described by Crèvecoeur, appealing pathetically for water, his eyes pecked out by birds – he struck an equally important response of pity and fascination. This was, after all, the way Christians were supposed to behave. In both postures he challenged the traditional ideal of Christian servitude as a relationship of reciprocal love and obligation' (ibid., 480–81).

We must stress that there was no automatic necessity for primitivism and the cult of the noble savage to have developed an anti-slavery ethos. The *genre* is clearly subject both to the dangers of a primitivistic revel and of a sentimentality which restricted itself to feeling the exquisite throb of benevolence.[22] In Sypher's words 'the noble Negro, begot of primitivism and fostered by sensibility, is a creature ill fitted to humanitarian purpose'. But he immediately adds the vital qualification: 'in any century but the eighteenth'.[23] In that century the *genre* interacted with a heightened awareness of liberty, humanity, and equality to produce a considerable volume of anti-slavery sentiment in drama, fiction and verse,[24] and in so doing it made an original and significant contribution to the creation of an awareness of the evils of slavery and to the formation of an opinion which condemned it. Philip Curtin, commenting on the importance of the theme of the noble savage for British thought about Africa, says that 'it certainly helped to form a vague and positive image of the "good African" and it was widely used by the anti-slave trade publicists for exactly this purpose. On the other hand it was very much a literary convention, not a rationally supported affirmation about savage life'. (As to 'rationally supported affirmation', Curtin shows that the variants of the dominant monogenesis school (i.e. that humanity was a single creation) saw the varieties of mankind, which were distinguished not least by skin colour, as arranged in hierarchic order – in conformity with the Great Chain of Being.

The unconscious assumption in all these ideas was that God had created man 'in His image', which was necessarily the image of the biologist. Other varieties must therefore be worse varieties,

[22] In a lower key, the West Indian James Grainger in his poem, *The Sugar Cane* (1764), could express conventional benevolism but accept slavery and simply commend kind treatment as more profitable (Sypher, *Guinea's Captive Kings*, 105, 168–75). For the contrast between Bryan Edwards' sentimentality and the realm of his historical writing see ibid., 5-7, 42-4.

[23] Sypher, *Guinea's Captive Kings*, 155.

[24] Ibid., 156. 'Most anti-slavery poetry was narrowly occasional; yet, the wrongs of Africa were a theme peremptory enough to almost every thoughtful eighteenth-century muse, and onslaughts against slaves were not infrequent in poems of consequence. The rime doggerel of anti-slavery usually reproached the avaricious European, appealed to dogmas of liberty or equality, envisioned pseudo-Africa, and exalted the Noble Negro.'

and thus 'degenerations' from the original stock. Even at its worst, however, the usual monogenetic view allowed all races a place in humanity, and peoples who had 'degenerated' in a few thousand years might well 'improve' again in a relatively short time.

The rise of the theory of polygenesis (that each race was a separate creation), especially as one of its early champions was Edward Long, who was positively concerned to justify slavery, strengthened the existing tendency to regard Europeans and their culture as manifestly superior and Negro race and culture as manifestly inferior. Even polygenesis, however, allowed Negroes souls, and though the predominant cast of biological thought had strong overtones of racial pride one may conclude that there was nothing in it to inhibit, or at least strongly to inhibit, humanitarian action against slavery and the slave trade.)[25]

Anti-slavery sentiment cradled in primitivism is very apparent in, for example, James Scott in his *Odes on Several Subjects* (1761), where he depicts how a Negro slave in his slumbers

> Recalls the joys he felt of old,
> When wand'ring with his sable Maid,
> Thro' groves of vegetable gold,
> He clasp'd her yielding to his raptur'd breast,
> And free from guile his honest Soul exprest.[26]

Here a clear contrast is drawn between an idealised primitive state and a slavery from which there can only be an escape in dreams. We find a more direct condemnation of slavery and the slave trade, from a similar perspective, in the epilogue of Isaac Bickerstaffe's *The Padlock,* a play which had an exceptional popularity from its first performance in 1768, spoken by Mungo, a black servant.

> But I was born in Aric's tawny strand,
> And you in fair Britannia's fairer land.
> Comes freedom, then, from colour? – Blush with shame!
> And let strong Nature's crimson mark your blame.
> I speak to Britons – Britons, then, behold
> A man by Britons *snar'd,* and *seiz'd,* and *sold!*

[25] Philip D. Curtin, *The Image of Africa: British Ideas and Action, 1780–1850* (Madison, 1964) 34–57. Quotations are from 51 and 41.

[26] Quoted in Hoxie Fairchild, *Religious Trends in English Poetry*, II, 225.

> And yet no British statute damns the deed,
> Nor do the more than murd'rous villains bleed.[27]

A final case of this type of anti-slavery poetry might be *The Dying Negro* (1773). Usually attributed to Thomas Day, it seems to have been written in part by his friend John Bicknell.[28] It was inspired by a report of a Negro in London who had run away from his master and received baptism so that he might marry a white woman, a fellow servant, but who was seized and put aboard ship in the Thames, whereupon he killed himself.

> Curst be the winds, and curst the tides that bore
> These European robbers to our shore! . . .[29]

The expression in contemporary literature,[30] poetry and drama of anti-slavery themes gave a heightened awareness of slavery for,

[27] Quoted in Thomas Clarkson, *The History of the Rise, Progress and Accomplishment of the Abolition of the African Slave-Trade by the British Parliament* (London, 1808) I 81. See also Sypher, *Guinea's Captive Kings*, 236–7.

[28] The connection was indeed close for Day joined with Bicknell in obtaining two infants from an orphanage with a view to training them 'upon philosophical principles' and under conditions of the utmost propriety, as possible marriage partners. This particular experiment, the chronicler must reluctantly record, failed as far as Day was concerned – though perhaps his expectations were too high, since Bicknell appears to have found one of the girls, Sabrina, eminently satisfactory. Day's matrimonial attempts were long unsuccessful: a lady he met at Salisbury was not responsive to the suggestion that they should lead a married life 'sequestered in some secret grove' whilst another was put off by Day's refusal to cut his hair. Eventually, however, he married an heiress who, with what feminists must surely regard as stark perversity, loved him to distraction. He, in his turn, took legal steps to preserve her fortune to herself lest she should tire of the union. The rest of his life Day spent in authorship – *Sandford and Merton* is his best-known work – in farming, giving religious instruction, and brief involvement in the campaign for political reform of the Constitutional Society. It is not inappropriate that he should have complemented his on the whole engaging eccentricities by building his house by first constructing solid walls and then knocking out doors and windows. Nor is it without significance in explaining the eventual success of abolition that the abolitionist ranks abounded in idiosyncratic characters.

[9] Sypher, *Guinea's Captive Kings*, 177–80; Thomas Day, *The Dying Negro, a Poetical Epistle* (London, 1773). The poem does not appear to have been reprinted.

[30] In anti-slavery fiction the supplementary 'Remarks concerning the Inhabitants of Africa' included in the 1783 reprint of Helenus Scott's *Adventures of a Rupee* (1782) may not be untypical of a line commonly

by making it possible to imagine what it was like to be a slave, directness and intensity was lent to the propositions of reason, whilst a theme expressed in novels, in verse, and in the theatre reached a wider public than when confined to philosophy. Thus philosophical, intellectual condemnation of slavery was accompanied by a relatively widely disseminated sensitivity to it and a generally hostile verdict upon it.

It would be foolish to assert that the major significance of all eighteenth-century British philosophers and of French *philosophes* was that they demanded the abolition of slavery. It would be no less foolish to claim that we have studied in depth the development of their individual thought and the interconnections between their philosophies. Our aim has been the more modest one of demonstrating that, however much the thinkers of the century differed amongst themselves, there was much common ground between them in what in both a general and a particular sense pertained to anti-slavery. It has been shewn that they attached much importance to liberty and tended to extend the definition of it; that a belief in benevolence, in its eighteenth-century sense, was general among them; that happiness as the particular expression of the principle of utility was frequently invoked as a criterion; that there was much more often than not, or was felt to be, a compatibility between the teachings of moral philosophy and of revealed religion; and that the one believed in a moral order, the other in a compatible idea of a providential order. The more emphasis given to liberty and happiness, the more condemned and isolated did the slave system appear. Moreover, slavery was specifically condemned with near unanimity by the leading moral philosophers of the day. The import is, secondly, that the emphasis on benevolence and the invoking of the principles of nature and utility were themselves marks of a growing disposition to effect change in the area of natural, civil and political liberty, by legislative action. And the development was furthered by the development of a dynamic out of a static concept of the Chain of Being.

---

taken. '. . . By our means, thousands of happy men are transported to a distant country, to groan in servitude. . . . These are the blessings which our trade diffuses in Africa (Quoted in Sypher, *Guinea's Captive Kings*, p. 275).

The relevance of theological developments to anti-slavery reform lay in the theological origins and religious dimension of the powerful idea of benevolence; in the reinforcement of belief in a providential moral order as a sanction on conduct, including the conduct required by new moral discernment; and in that important root of the idea of progress which consisted in the belief in revelation as progressive, with the necessary corollary that the Christian was called to new commitment as he received new revelation. Literature, mainly through the anti-slavery implications of the noble savage theme, and through its reflexion – appropriation, even – of ideas of liberty and benevolence, sharpened and extended awareness of the problem of slavery, and made its own contribution to the emergence of anti-slavery conviction. What all these developments meant for the age is suggested in a passage in the *Annual Register* for 1788 which celebrates what the writer saw as the imminent victory of virtue and, significantly, does so as an immediate preliminary to narrating the recent introduction of an abolition motion into parliament.

> It was long a kind of problem in philosophy, whether or not the human species collectively, like the intellectual powers of the individual, were in a state of gradual progress; or whether, according to an opinion of no mean antiquity, there be nothing new under the sun, and the virtues and vices of different ages be so nicely balanced, that no one of them deserves to be preferred to another. *This problem is hastening fast to a decision. Liberty, humanity and science are daily extending, and bid fair to render despotism, cruelty and ignorance subjects of historical memory, not of actual observation. A considerable part of this proof of this was exhibited in the English parliament during its present session* (when an abolition motion was purposed) (My italics)[31]

By the end of the eighteenth century, then – indeed it was substantially true by the end of the third quarter – little serious intellectual defence of slavery was any longer being offered. But for all the important, theological and literary developments of the century we must certainly take account of the insight which has suggested that the slave trade, slavery and abolition were essentially questions where, in Millar's words, 'Fortune perhaps never produced a situation more calculated to ridicule a liberal hypo-

[31] *Annual Register* (1788) 108–9.

thesis, or to show how little the conduct of men is at bottom directed by any philosophical principles'.[32] Certainly we do not wish to argue that changes in ideas produced automatic or necessary change in the realm of action. In the next stage of our arguement we shall seek to demonstrate that it was mainly religious conviction, insight and zeal – 'enthusiasm', in a word – which made it possible for anti-slavery feeling to be subsumed in a crusade against the slave trade. But there *was* nevertheless profound significance in the manner in which intellectual attitudes to slavery and change had altered, both in itself and because abolitionists thereby had a complex of ideas to which to appeal.

[32] J. Millar, *The Origin of the Distinction of Ranks*, 360. Millar was here belabouring the Americans for their inconsistency in claiming political liberty whilst defending Negro slavery.

PART THREE

7 The Evangelical World-View

In the late eighteenth and early nineteenth centuries, Evangelicals were beginning to emerge in a self-conscious way both within and without the Established Church. From the circumstance that they lived close together in Clapham, or frequently visited it, the leading Anglican Evangelicals have been collectively christened the 'Clapham Sect'. E. M. Forster, in his sympathetic and evocative biography of Marianne Thornton, his great-aunt, defines the membership of the 'sect' as Henry Thornton, Marianne's father, an M.P. and a wealthy banker; the Reverend John Venn, rector of Clapham; Charles Grant, a director of the East India Company; William Wilberforce, M.P. for Yorkshire; Isaac Milner, Dean of Carlisle and Provost of Queen's College, Cambridge; Zachary Macaulay, effective founder of the Sierra Leone colony and subsequently editor of the Evangelical periodical, *The Christian Observer*; Thomas Babington (after whom Zachary Macaulay's famous son was named), a country gentleman, philanthropist and M.P., Lord Teignmouth, who, as Sir John Shore, had been Governor-General of India; Hannah More, philanthropist, poet and writer, and formerly member of Dr Johnson's circle; and James Stephen, a lawyer who practised in the Prize Appeal Court of the Privy Council. Between almost all of the families in this group there were cross-ties of affection, and, frequently, of marriage.[1]

A name not included by Forster is that of Granville Sharp. Certainly Sharp's warm involvement with a family of brothers and sister, his residence away from Clapham – albeit 'a few bow-shots' – together with some differences in his theology and devotional practice and more in his politics, made him a less integral member of the Clapham Sect: but James Stephen's son, Sir James

[1] E. M. Forster, *Marianne Thornton, 1797–1877* (London, 1956) 35–48.

Stephen, himself brought up at Clapham and firmly in the Evangelical succession, regarded Sharp as one of the Clapham Sect, whilst he is also listed in the memorial tablet to the sect in Clapham parish church.[2] With qualifications, then, we shall treat Sharp as a member of the Evangelical core-group. Although not members of the Clapham Sect there were a number of other Evangelicals of note such as Thomas Gisborne, divine and moral philosopher, John Newton, the slave trader turned cleric, and the sometime minister of state, Lord Dartmouth, described by Cowper as 'he who wears a coronet and prays', and, with reservations, William Cowper himself. In addition (and following convention they will be termed 'evangelicals' when referred to separately) there were men of very similar views in the nascent Methodist connection led by John and Charles Wesley, and in the ranks of dissent.

The world-view of Evangelicals was primarily theological and it was distinctive. None the less it had more affinities with the thought of the eighteenth century as a whole than is commonly supposed. The similarities and the differences can both be seen in their view of Providence, a doctrine which undergirded so much of their thought. On Providence, in the sense of the continuing moral government of the world, they had common ground with the general run of the theology of their age. Thus Wilberforce, arriving at his view of Providence from a study of the judgement of God as seen in Scripture, concludes:

> The apprehensions, which must be excited by thus reading the recorded judgements and awful language of Scripture, are confirmed to the inquisitive and attentive mind, by a close observation of the moral constitution of the world. Such a one will find occasion to remark, that all which has been suggested of the final consequences of vice, is in strict analogy to what we may observe in the ordinary course of human affairs, wherein it will appear, on a careful survey, that God has so assigned to things their general tendencies, and established such an order of causes and effects, as (however interrupted here below by hindrances and obstructions apparently of a temporary nature)

[2] Sir James Stephen, *Essays in Ecclesiastical Biography* (London, 1849) II 312–22; James Stephen, *Memoirs*, ed. Merle M. Bevington (London, 1954) 14.

loudly proclaim the principles of his moral government, and strongly suggest, that vice and imprudence will finally terminate in misery.[3]

It is not for nothing that Wilberforce refers the reader of this passage in his *Practical View* to Butler's *Analogy*, for it is clearly on Butler's classical eighteenth-century contribution to the doctrine of Providence that Wilberforce is partly drawing. Such statements are frequently found in the writings of Evangelicals and in one such Cowper specifically relates Providence to the role of Britain and the other powers in the American War of Independence,[4] whilst in 'Table Talk', written during the course of that same war, Cowper speaks of a Providence acting to punish the nation's sins.

> Nineveh, Babylon, and ancient Rome,
> Speak to the present times and times to come;
> They cry aloud, in ev'ry careless ear,
> Stop, while ye may, suspend your mad career;
> O learn from our example and our fate,
> Learn wisdom and repentance ere too late.
>   Not only vice disposes and prepares
> The mind that sweetly slumbers in her snares,
> To stoop to tyranny's usurp'd command,
> And bend her polish'd neck beneath his hand,
> (A dire effect, by one of nature's laws
> Unchangeably connected with its cause)
> But providence himself will intervene
> To throw his dark displeasure o'er the scene.
> All are his instruments; each form of war,
> What burns at home, what threatens from afar,
> Nature in arms, her elements at strife,
> The storms that overset the joys of life,
> Are but his rods to scourge a guilty land,
> And waste it at the bidding of his hand.

[3] W. Wilberforce, *Practical View of the Prevailing Religious System of Professed Christians in the Higher and Middle Classes in the Country contrasted with Real Christianity* (Dublin, 1801) 32–3. See also ibid. 350–53 and his private letter to Zachary Macaulay of 29 Sept 1796 (*Life of Wilberforce*, II 173).

[4] Cowper to John Newton, 26 Jan 1783, in Cowper, *Poetry and Prose*, ed. Brian Spiller (London, 1968) 681.

He gives the word, and mutiny soon rears
In all her gates, and shakes her distant shores;
The standards of all nations are unfurl'd,
She has one foe, and that one foe, the world.[5]

This general theme recurs constantly – on every other page one could almost say – in the Evangelical journal, *The Christian Observer*, and usually in such a way as to imply that, in relating Providence to human events, the journal was merely making for its Evangelical readers specific connections but that of the principle involved those readers needed no persuasion.[6] Granville Sharp wrote extensively on the theme of Providence and the moral government of the world. He firmly believed that the hand of Providence could be discerned very specifically – so specifically, indeed, as sometimes to seem quaint to the late twentieth-century mind. Thus he was convinced *'that the late* fall of THE PAPAL Power in France, *as well as* the overthrow *of the* political state (*the* Crown, or "HORN OF THE BEAST,") *by which that most baneful and intolerant faction*, THE PAPACY, *had long been supported in that nation, were really effected by* Divine Providence.'[7]

[5] Ibid., 195. Note also the primary importance which Stephen attached to Providence. 'Among all the blessings I enjoy the first is my knowledge, my *certain* knowledge from long experience, that "verily and indeed there is a God who governs the world"' (Stephen, *Memoirs*, 205).

[6] See a long article in the 'View of Public Affairs' section of *The Christian Observer*, no. 1, vol. ɪ (Jan 1802) 53–62. See also 'View of Public Affairs: Reflections on the Danger arising from National Sins', ibid., no. 12, vol. ɪɪ (Dec 1803) 764–7; ibid., no. 11, vol. ɪɪ (Nov 1803) 638. These are random citations. Note also that the proceedings of the Eclectic Society, the gathering of Evangelical ministers in London, both trace the foundation of *The Christian Observer* to a discussion in the Society and include, among the objects of the journal, attention to 'historical events of the month, with a particular reference to Providence'. Josiah Pratt (ed.), *Eclectic Notes; or, notes of discussions on religious topics, at the meetings of the Eclectic Society, London, during the years 1798–1814* (2nd ed, London, 1865), 93–4. In its meetings the Eclectic Society not only gave particular attention to each annual national fast-day, as it approached, but frequently returned to such themes as the lessons to be learned from the dispensations of Providence (ibid., 75–8); 'What have been the signal Interpositions of Providence in favour of Britain during the late war?' (239–40); and 'What may we infer of the designs of God from the Dispensations of His Providence?' (393–4).

[7] G. Sharp, *A COLLECTION OF POLITICAL PAPERS concerning the*

Not all Sharp's readers understood the meaning of 'Horn of the Beast', and their Book of Revelation, as well as Sharp. Thus when he was pressing the abolitionist case on Charles James Fox, whose biblical knowledge his best friends would not have rated highly, by urging that Britain's toleration of slavery ranked her among the 'existing *Horns of the Beast*', Fox, if one may be allowed the solecism, was quite foxed, 'for he answered with apparent surprise – "*The Beast! – What is that? – What is that?*".'[8] The literal way in which Sharp approached Scripture might seem to suggest that his view of Providence was merely idosyncratic.[9] In fact in *The Law of Retribution, A serious Warning to Great Britain and her Colonies, founded on unquestionable Examples of God's Temporal Vengeance against Tyrants, Slave-holders and Oppressors* (1776) he provides a coherent interpretation of the operation of Providence in periods of Old Testament history. At considerable length the Scriptures are expounded so as to demonstrate how 'the *Divine Law* was revealed in a more particular manner to *that People*, and to others *only through them*, so the

[8] *Sharp Transcripts* (*J.A.W.*), Granville Sharp to Capel Lofft, 2 Oct 1806.
[9] For instance in *The Law of Retribution* pp. 319–40 Sharp identifies the actions of the prophet Oded, who, as the reader may need to be reminded, found four chiefs of the House of Ephraim to support him in a protest against an act of enslavement, with his own appeal to four bishops, in default of four English noblemen (i.e. chiefs) to come forward in opposition to the slave trade. Certainly Sharp's literary style was idiosyncratic. Not only were the titles of his works essays in themselves, but Sharp could not resist pursuing several hares at once. Thus the reference to the English episcopate in his appeal *à la* Oded led him into a footnote on his views on episcopacy which ran over eight pages, reducing the main text to two lines per page, and which spawned subsidiary footnotes of his own.

———————

most dangerous factions that have annoyed mankind within the last twelve centuries; and the necessity of guarding against their influence in all CHRISTIAN STATES by requiring an acknowledgement of the CONSTITUTIONAL FOUNDATIONS OF POLITICAL AND RELIGIOUS LIBERTY as the TEST OF A LEGAL QUALIFICATION for the due exercise of SUFFRAGE, TRUST, OR AUTHORITY, IN ANY SUCH STATE (London, 1797) v. The title itself tells one a good deal about Sharp's style. See also G. Sharp, *Mémoire sur les causes des Calamités Publiques qui règnent à présent partout l'Etendue de l'Ancien Empire Romain* (Privately printed, 1776) passim, in which he sees these misfortunes as the result of the spread of the Roman Church, and acceptance by the temporal powers of practices contrary to the faith and practice of the early church.

effect even of their Disobedience was an exemplary demonstration, from time to time, of God's Vengeance, as well as of his *Mercy*'.[10]

Evangelicals responded similarly to other of the century's values: liberty, happiness and benevolence – these they accepted and transposed. In his *Practical View*, Wilberforce with difficulty restrains himself from enlarging on the 'unrivalled excellence' of the British Constitution[11] – implicitly because it is a proven safeguard of civil and political liberty. The foundation of this liberty, however, lies ultimately in that Christian liberty which is essentially freedom from sin. A similar transposition is evident in Cowper:

> 'Tis liberty alone that gives the flow'r
> Of fleeting life its lustre and perfume,
> And we are weeds without it. All constraint,
> Except what wisdom lays on evil men,
> Is evil; hurts the faculties, impedes
> Their progress in the road of science; blinds
> The eyesight of discovery, and begets,
> In those that suffer it, a sordid mind
> Bestial, a meagre intellect, unfit
> To be the tenant of man's noble form.
> . . .
> But there is yet a liberty unsung
> By poets, and by senators unpraised,
> Which monarchs cannot grant, nor all the powers
> Of earth and hell confed'rate take away
> A liberty which persecution, fraud,
> Oppression, prisons have no power to bind,
> Which whoso tastes can be enslaved no more.
> 'Tis liberty of heart, derived from heav'n,
> Bought with HIS blood who gave it to mankind,

[10] Ibid., 11–12.

[11] Wilberforce, *Practical View*, 290. Wilberforce attested his commitment to English institutions generally by his somewhat insular condemnation of foreign ones. When on a visit to France in 1783, with his friends Pitt and Edward Eliot, he recoiled firmly from underdone roast beef, suggested that Louis XVI was 'so strange a being (of the hog kind) that it is worth going a hundred miles for a sight of him', and returned to England 'better pleased with his own country than when he left it' (*Life of Wilberforce*, I 39, 42, 44).

> And seal'd with the same token. It is held
> By charter, and that charter sanction'd sure
> By th'unimpeachable and awful oath
> And promise of a God. . . .
> . . .
> He is a freeman whom the truth makes free,
> And all are slaves beside. There's not a chain
> That hellish foes, confed'rate for his harm
> Can wind around him, but he casts it off
> With as much ease as Samson his green wyths.[12]

Happiness too is a laudable object. It 'is the end for which men unites in civil society', wrote Wilberforce approvingly,[13] and 'it is the duty of every man to promote the happiness of his fellow-creatures to the utmost of his power';[14] John Newton wrote to his wife that 'I know nothing that is required of us as a duty, but what is both consistent with our happiness, and has a tendency to promote it'.[15] But, as with the Evangelical view of Liberty, there is an important qualification, namely that although true happiness is a proper aim it is only achieved when it is recognised that:

> Thou art the source and centre of all minds,
> Their only point of rest, eternal word.[16]

The approach to benevolence is similar, and again Wilberforce sums it up. This great principle of the age is accepted but criticised for its insufficiency unless informed by Christian love and humility. 'Benevolence, indeed, when not originating from Religion, dispenses but from a scanty and precarious fund; and therefore if it be liberal in the case of some objects, it is generally found to be contracted towards others. . . .'[17] The benevolence of true Christianity, on the other hand, is so much more comprehensive because it is an effect of faith and of the rooting out of 'our natural selfishness'. 'Benevolence, enlarged, vigorous, operative benevolence, is her master principle . . . and humility . . . lays the deepest

[12] Cowper, *The Task*, book v.
[13] Wilberforce, *Practical View*, 290.
[14] Ibid., vii.
[15] Newton, *Letters to a Wife*, 30.
[16] Cowper, *The Task*, book v.
[17] Wilberforce, *Practical View*, 286.

and surest ground for benevolence.'[18] Granville Sharp put his view of the matter in the observation that the 'glorious maxim . . . "THOU SHALT LOVE THY NEIGHBOUR AS THYSELF" ' was 'the sum and essence of the whole Law of God',[19] whilst Thomas Scott – author of *Scott's Commentary on the Holy Bible*,[20] a work of immense influence among Evangelicals – spoke frequently but quite simply of 'the law of love'.

The Evangelical, then, had a heightened consciousness of the operations of an awful Providence and whilst accepting the age's concepts of liberty, benevolence and happiness, gave to them a more profound dimension. Distinguished from his fellows in these respects, the most radical distinction, and the root of his whole world-view, lay in his conviction of sin and redemption, of personal sin and personal redemption, and in the readiness for complete dedication to God which was the product.

Such a theology was, of course, not original but was, rather, a part of the heritage of the Church through the ages. The Established Church in the eighteenth century may not normally have much emphasised it, but nor did she completely neglect it, whilst both within her ranks and in the life of dissent, there were always men who saw personal salvation and commitment as the essential character of Christianity.[21] Two such, Philip Doddridge (1702–51) and William Law (1686–1761) were in their own right important formative influences upon the Evangelical Movement and are amongst the more systematic of the authorities to whom the Evangelicals looked for spiritual food.[22] Doddridge was a dissenting

[18] Ibid., 291.

[19] G. Sharp, *The Law of Liberty, or Royal Law by which all Mankind will certainly be judged* (London, 1776) 20–21, 26. (The B.M. catalogue gives 1788 as the date of the first edition.)

[20] The Commentary was written in serial form, however, and according to Scott's biographer was not completed until 1792, the year to which the B.M. catalogue assigns the second edition (A. C. Downer, *Thomas Scott the Commentator. A Memoir of his Life* (London, 1909) 70).

[21] For an important aspect of this see notably, J. D. Walsh, 'The Yorkshire Evangelicals in the Eighteenth Century: with Especial Reference to Methodism' (University of Cambridge unpublished Ph.D. thesis, 1956) passim.

[22] Wilberforce, for instance, set store on Pascal's *Pensées*, on Fenélon, and on a number of seventeenth- and eighteenth-century works of biographical piety, such as Burnet on Leighton and on Lord Rochester (*Life of Wilberforce*, i 90, v 308, and Wilberforce, *Practical View*, 336 n.

divine and scholar.[23] His *Rise and Progress of Religion in the Soul* (1745) is an intensely lucid appeal to the nominal Christian to realise his true, sinful, condition, accept the free grace of Christ, and, by diligence in discipline and devotion, to live out a life of full obedience to him. An important characteristic of this school of theology is shown in the preoccupation, spanning nearly the first quarter of the book, with a state of sin.

The 'careless sinner' must first be awakened by reminding him of the nature of God, of the personal obligation to God, and of the danger of neglect of him when 'considered in its aspect as a future state'. Once awakened the sinner is urged to immediate consideration of the claims of religion on grounds ranging from 'the Excellency and Pleasure of the Thing itself' to the danger of God withdrawing his spirit. Arraignment and conviction of the sinner follows; he is shown to be in rebellion against God by appeal to the reader's conscience, to the knowledge of favours received and to his resistance to the strivings of the spirit of God in the heart. The sinner is then stripped of his pleas, such as that he had always shunned the gross immoralities – the appeal was primarily to the person of outwardly blameless life rather than to the man who was a sinner in the less sensitive parlance of the world – and 'shaken over the Pit' as a necessary means to persuade him to seek salvation from a damnation which must otherwise be his fate. 'You must feel the Execution of it [the sentence of Law], if the Gospel does not at length deliver you; and you must feel something of the Terror of it, before you can be excited to seek to that Gospel for Deliverance.'

In that situation news of possible salvation is brought to the condemned man in terms which are at once a statement of Evangelical faith. Confronted with the sin of man, God

> determined to enter into a Treaty of Peace and Reconciliation . . . in a certain Method, which His Infinite Wisdom judged suitable to the Purity of his Nature, and the Honour of his Government. . . . Accordingly, at such a Period of Time as Infinite Wisdom saw most convenient, the *Lord Jesus Christ* appeared in Human Flesh; and after he had gone through incessant and long continued Fatigues, and borne all the preceding Injuries, which the Ingratitude and Malice of Men could

---

[23] See Caroline Robbins, *Eighteenth-Century Commonwealthman*, 254–7.

inflict, he voluntarily *submitted himself to Death, even the Death of the Cross*; and having been *delivered for our Offences, was raised again for our Justification.* After his Resurrection, he continued long enough on Earth to give his Followers most convincing Evidences of it, and then *ascended into Heaven in their sight*; and *sent down his Spirit* from thence *upon his Apostles* to enable them . . . to preach the Gospel . . . that through the Righteousness he has fulfilled, and the Atonement he has made, we might be accepted by God as righteous, and be not only pardoned, but received into his Favour.

This pardon man can receive on the sole condition that he appropriate it by faith.[24] So ends the first half of Doddridge, the part in which he has treated of the *rise* of religion in the soul. The remaining fifteen chapters are devoted to the nurture of the convert, the maintenance of his spiritual health and to his new-found duties in the world.

Law's *Serious Call* is written to a different plan. It lacks the systematic step by step development of Doddridge's argument but has common ground in its lengthy and profound advice on the spiritual life. Perhaps the most distinctive characteristic of the book is the simple demand on the true Christian for complete devotion.

If there is an infinitely wise and good Creator, in whom we live, move, and have our being, whose providence governs all things in all places, surely it must be the highest act of our under-standing to conceive rightly of Him; it must be the noblest instance of judgement, the most exalted temper of our nature, to worship and adore this universal providence, to conform to its laws, to study its wisdom, and to live and act everywhere, as in the presence of this infinitely wise and good Creator.[25]

Although the religion of both Doddridge and Law was, in a sense, a religion of the heart, it was also both systematic and rational. Doddridge's book is a model of lucidity; Law wrote an incisive treatise on the limitations – and importance – of Reason, entitled *The Case of Reason* (1731) in reply to the Deist, Toland,[26]

[24] P. Doddridge, *The Rise and Progress of Religion in the Soul*, chaps. i–xv passim. The two longer quotations are from pp. 51 and 71–3.

[25] Wm Law, *A Serious Call to a Devout and Holy Life* (London, Everyman ed. 1967) 350–1.

[26] See Cragg, *Reason and Authority in the Eighteenth Century*, 93–8.

and in his *Serious Call* is breathtakingly and frighteningly reasonable in his delineation of what flows from a conviction of sin and
from salvation. Take for instance his section on the obligation of
benevolence in his sense of that term.

> Our obligation to love all men . . . is founded upon many
> reasons. First, upon a reason of equity; for if it is just to love
> ourselves in this manner, it must be unjust to deny any degree of
> this love to others, because every man is so exactly of the same
> nature, and in the same condition as ourselves.
>
> If, therefore, your own crimes and follies do not lessen your
> obligation to seek your own good, and wish well to yourself;
> neither do the follies and crimes of your neighbours lessen your
> obligation to wish and seek the good of your neighbour.
>
> Another reason for this love is founded in the authority of
> God, who has commanded us to love every man as ourself.
>
> Thirdly, we are obliged to this love in imitation of God's
> goodness, that we may be children of our Father which is in
> Heaven, who willeth the happiness of all His creatures, and
> maketh his sun to rise on the evil, and on the good.
>
> Fourthly, Our redemption by Jesus Christ calleth us to the
> exercise of this love, who came from Heaven and laid down
> His life, out of love to the whole sinful world.
>
> Fifthly, by the command of our Lord and Saviour, who has
> required us to love one another, as He has loved us.
>
> These are the great, perpetual reasons, on which our obliga-
> tion to love all mankind as ourselves is founded.
>
> These reasons never vary or change, they always continue in
> the full force; and therefore equally oblige at all times, and in
> regard to all persons.[27]

Both Doddridge and Law insist upon a reasoned and systematic,
even meticulous, approach to the devotional life of the true
Christian. If Law, rather quaintly, insisted on the need to sing,
rather than merely say the Psalms in one's daily devotions – a
practice which Granville Sharp improved by chanting them to
the accompaniment of a traverse harp which he had made himself[28]
– it was, according to its premises, both commonsense and
rigorously logical.

[27] Law, *Serious Call*, 287–8.
[28] Prince Hoare, *Life of Granville Sharp* (London, 1828) II 218, 292.

Here then was a religious system which profoundly challenged men and in which a reasoned system of devotion complemented and sustained an act of faith. Because it incorporated reason as well as faith it could appeal to the well-read, educated men that the leading Evangelicals were. There were differences between Law and Doddridge – notably in Law's emphasis on private benevolence almost to the exclusion of public duty, contrasted with Doddridge's belief in the secular vocation of Christians[29] – but in their central insistence on the syndrome of conviction of sin, offer of salvation in Christ, acceptance in faith, and life of devotion and practical benevolence, they were as one. In this, too, they were both a considerable influence on the Evangelicals – Wilberforce spoke of 'the excellent Doddridge'[30] whose writings so greatly helped him; Stephen referred to 'the doctrines which that excellent man taught';[31] Scott, in his *Commentary,* frequently invoked him and Zachary Macaulay acknowledged his debt to him.[32] Law, for his part, was a particular influence on John and Charles Wesley, Whitfield, Thomas Scott, Henry Venn and Newton.[33]

Just as Doddridge and Law between them inspired the true language of the Evangelical heart so they well depict the Evangelicals' spiritual progress. Stephen, for instance, in his early life, although there was the countervailing influence of his mother, was subject to many circumstances inimical to 'real Christianity'. His father seems to have suffered alike from a deficient business sense and the ill-faith of others, and the son's education and upbringing clearly suffered from the straitened circumstances of the

[29] Doddridge, *Rise and Progress of Religion,* 281.

[30] Wilberforce, *Practical View,* 336 n. and *Life of Wilberforce,* especially I 76–7 and 101–2.

[31] Stephen, *Memoirs,* 66. See also *The Christian Observer,* no. 5, vol. 1 (May 1802) 319–20 for a eulogy of Doddridge, *Rise and Progress of Religion.*

[32] Knutsford, *Life and Letters of Zachary Macaulay* (London, 1900) 155.

[33] M. J. Quinlan, *Victorian Prelude: A History of English Manners, 1700–1830* 38. The leaning to mysticism and the declining emphasis on churchmanship and the sacraments in Law's later years made him in a measure vulnerable in the minds of Evangelicals but *The Christian Observer* in 1807, coupling him with Taylor, saw the continuing value of Law's writings as consisting in 'their minute details and lively illustrations of the Christian character, in their anatomy of the human heart, and in their formal exhortation of the practice of all godliness . . .' (*Christian Observer,* VI, no. 11 (Nov 1807) 735). See also ibid., no. 10, vol. I (Oct 1802).

parent – straitened for a period in the literal sense that he spent
some years in the Fleet prison for non-payment of debts. The son
shared his father's confinement and during these years, enlivened
by his irrepressible father's leadership of a gaol break-out and
subsequent argument, in the courts, that imprisonment for debt
was unlawful, was subject to the dubious influences of prison life.
Even in periods when his father was not thus restrained the young
Stephen's education was subject to the somewhat anomalous influences first of the noted Deist, Peter Annet, and subsequently
of a cheesemonger who had failed in business. In his teens and
early twenties the always passionate Stephen became involved in
a highly complex love affair, the particular object of Stephen's
interest being Anna Stent (Anna was her real Christian name,
but Stephen himself always called her 'Nancy'), the sister of a
friend, Thomas. The friendship was not welcomed by Anna's
parents, and its development suffered many interruptions. Eventually a mode of arranging meetings notwithstanding suggested
itself when Thomas Stent was called away to sea. Himself strongly
enamoured of a girl to whom Stephen gave the fictitious name of
Maria Rivers, who was also known to Anna, young Stent proposed that Stephen should contrive to share the same lodgings
as the strikingly beautiful Maria, and in this way would be able
both to press the claims of his friend, the absent sailor, and because
of the friendship between Anna and Maria would have abundant
opportunity for meetings with the object of his own devotion.

> This judicious scheme led to difficulties. When, after a time,
> Stephen began to speak to Maria on behalf of Stent, the lady
> at last hinted that she had another attachment, and, on further
> pressure, it appeared that the object of the attachment was
> Stephen himself. He was not insensible, as he then discovered, to
> Maria. 'I have been told,' he says, 'that no man can love two
> women at once; but I am confident that this is an error.'

Leslie Stephen goes on to give a brief indication of the outcome
of this understandably delicate situation in terms of Stephen being
'only able to decide that if either of them married he was bound
to marry the other'.[34] In fact – and this is the object of the biographical excursion – what in the pages of the apostate but still

[34] Leslie Stephen, *The Life of Sir James Fitzjames Stephen* (London, 1895)
8 ff.

filial Leslie Stephen appears as a harmless subject for his engaging wit was to James Stephen a much more searing and guilt-laden affair. In his own unfinished memoir of his life, written, he tells us, for the warning and guidance of his children, James Stephen reveals both that he had a child by Maria – not to mention an affair with a 'Mrs B' – and a devastating cycle of exaltation, remorse and rationalisation which, with its attendant shifts and subterfuges, for some time tore him, before he eventually married Anna. Clearly Stephen saw this episode as only a striking manifestation of that bondage to sin from which, gradually, he was to escape. In his own words:

> I became a great sinner before God; . . . I was in consequence plunged into a labyrinth of guilt and misery from which my extrication was to human eyes almost impossible: and, but for the infinite mercy of God, I should at this moment have been the Author of the destruction, the temporal destruction at least, if not the eternal, of more than one fellow being who fondly loved me, and whom I fondly loved, and should have been justly regarded as one of the worst and most perfidious of mankind. From all these dreadful consequences the gracious Providence of God has wonderfully rescued me. He chastised me indeed, long and severely chastised me, but it was chiefly by the anguish, remorse, and terror of which I was the victim, and the privation of happiness that I might otherwise have enjoyed; and in the midst even of this correction he remembered mercy. At length these bitter fruits of sin, and a sense of dependency on his Providence for the averting those dreadful consequences with which others were imminently threatened, brought me to true repentance and gave me a victory over those guilty passions by which I had been so long enslaved.

Despite the excellent health of his old age – he celebrated his seventieth birthday by walking twenty-five miles to his office to begin the day's work – Stephen did not live long enough to complete his memoir and so we do not know the detail of that religious conversion which was to lead him heart and soul into membership of the Clapham Sect. Clearly, however, he went through the very process postulated in his mentor, Doddridge.[35] So also did Wilberforce – but in his case his biographers tell us more about it.

[35] Stephen, *Memoirs*, passim. The quotation is from p. 313.

As a young man, both at Cambridge and subsequently at the hub of London society, Wilberforce's religion, as he later termed it, was that of the nominal Christian. He refrained from the grosser vices,[36] subscribed to the doctrines of his religion and feared any touch of enthusiasm. Humanly speaking, Wilberforce saw his spiritual salvation as beginning with Isaac Milner – Wilberforce's companion on their continental journey of 1784–85. At that time, we are told, Milner was 'deficient in practical religion'[37] but readily agreed to undertake with Wilberforce the serious study of Doddridge's *Rise and Progress of Religion* which chance had attracted to Wilberforce's attention on the Continental journey. This led them to probe for themselves those Scriptures which Doddridge cited as his authority[38] and to a spiritual crisis for Wilberforce in 1785 and 1786. For a time he was torn between the old ways and the new. At Spa, a resort of English and Continental society, he joined freely in most activities but began to disassociate himself from certain diversions. Mrs Crewe, of whose glittering circle he had for some time been a coveted adornment, 'cannot believe that I can think it wrong to go to the play' and was surprised that it was at his wish that his party avoided travelling on the Sunday.[39] At the same time he was being wracked by a growing sense of sin and yet by a sense of dullness of heart which prevented him alike from realising his true condition and the saving grace of Christ. His diary records his torment and his exertions. He must be longer at prayer, decides to keep a spiritual diary, resolves to keep Doddridge's rules of practical devotion, reads Pascal's *Pensées* and Butler's *Analogy* – the latter being recommended to him by his friend Pitt.[40] In old age Wilberforce could telescope the anguish of months into a still powerful and moving statement.

> At length, however, I began to be impressed with a sense of the weighty truths, which were more or less the continual subjects

[36] John Ehrman (*The Younger Pitt*, London, 1969, 17) cites no authority for his observation, made upon the fact that Pitt's Cambridge circle 'was not a dissolute set', 'which was why Wilberforce, soon to be one of Pitt's closest friends, saw little of it'.

[37] *Life of Wilberforce*, I 76.

[38] Ibid., I 76 ff.

[39] Ibid., I 88.

[40] Ibid., I 87–112 passim.

of our [Wilberforce and Milner] conversation. I began to think what folly it was, nay, what madness, to continue month after month, nay day after day, in a state in which a sudden call out of the world, which I was conscious might happen at any moment, would consign me to never-ending misery, while at the very same time I was firmly convinced from assenting to the great truths taught us in the New Testament, that the offers of the gospel were universal and free, in short that happiness, eternal happiness, was at my option. As soon as I reflected seriously upon these subjects, the deep guilt and black ingratitude of my past life forced itself upon me in the strongest colours. I condemned myself for having wasted my precious time, and opportunities, and talents; and for several months I continued to feel the deepest convictions of my own sinfulness, rendered only the more intense by the unspeakable mercies of our God and Saviour declared to us in the offers and promises of the Gospel. These however by degrees produced in me something of a settled peace of conscience. I devoted myself for whatever might be the term of my future life, to the service of my God and Saviour...[41]

In his *Practical View,* as one might expect, Wilberforce demonstrated to his readers this same need to be convicted of sin and to receive the Gospel, a task he carries out in the context of an attempt 'to point out the scanty and erroneous system of the bulk of these who belong to the class of orthodox Christians, and to contrast their defective scheme with a representation of what the author apprehends to be real Christianity'.[42] And so it is with all the Evangelicals, an intense conviction of sin followed by the assurance of redeeming grace, often the culmination of a long spiritual agonising as, for instance, with John Wesley at the Aldersgate Street chapel. A contemporary statement of the Evangelical position is contained in the first number of the Evangelical journal, *The Christian Observer,* and is made in the context of the opposition between Calvinism and Arminianism.

With regard, then, to our own views upon the points in controversy between Calvinists and Arminians, we take this occasion of stating, once for all, that though on the full disclosure of

[41] Ibid., 1 381–2, Memorandum dictated by Mr Wilberforce.
[42] Wilberforce, *Practical View,* ix.

our private sentiments, some of us would be claimed by the one party and some of us by the other, yet, we would rather desire to lose the two appellations altogether in the more catholic term of Bible Christians, and would give the right hand of fellowship, as to true believers and true churchmen, so far as these points are concerned, to all who unequivocally and with the heart regard SALVATION AS ORIGINATING WHOLLY IN GRACE, APPLIED THROUGH THE INSTRUMENTALITY OF THAT FAITH WHICH IS THE GIFT OF THE HOLY SPIRIT, AND WHICH BRINGS THE BELIEVER INTO A STATE OF ACCEPTANCE WITH GOD, BY MAKING HIM PARTAKER OF THE MERITS OF CHRIST, AND PREPARES HIM FOR HEAVEN BY MATURING HIM IN LOVE AND OBEDIENCE.[43]

A further element in the Evangelical world-view made a particular contribution to a comportment in the world which was nothing less than dynamic. To apprehend this is to come back again to the idea of Providence but to a different form of it, that which the Evangelicals knew as particular Providence. What they meant by this was the particular direction of the individual godly man's

---

[43] *Christian Observer*, no. 1, vol. i (Jan 1802) 10. In understanding the Evangelicals the Calvinist/Arminian dichotomy is perhaps not as important as such a basic theological controversy might suggest. After all, Evangelicals are here claiming common ground and in practice they seem usually to have been successful in preventing the issue from becoming divisive. Dr John Walsh suggests that division amongst Evangelicals was between what he terms 'mediatists' and 'immediatists'. The former believed that God normally acted 'mediately', that is through the Church the sacraments, the mind attuned to him, etc.; the latter asserted a direct leading through direct and particular revelations. Dr Walsh further suggests that most Anglican Evangelicals were in the former category, many, if not most Methodists in the latter. Fighting on another front, Evangelicals within the Church of England had to assert that they were the true believers, the repositories of traditional orthodoxy. For a notable defence of this position see John Overton, *The True Churchmen Ascertained: or An Apology for those of the Regular Clergy of the Establishment who are sometimes called Evangelical Ministers*, 2nd ed. (London, 1802). For numerous insights into Evangelical theology and practice see Pratt, *Eclectic Notes* since the gatherings of the Eclectic Society were a forum for the exchange of views, as well as for mutual encouragement and it took in Evangelicals both within and outside the Established Church.

life by God. Stephen put it in this way when relating the significance of his *Memoirs* as he saw it. 'The great truth' to be learned from the story of his life 'is the superintendence of a wise and just, tho' most merciful and gracious Providence, in all the concerns of human life.'⁴⁴ Stephen explored the nature of particular Providence at some length in the introduction to his *Memoirs* just as earlier he (like Granville Sharp) had closely examined the nature of the general Providence of God. Not all the Evangelicals concerned themselves to the same degree with the theology of particular Providence but a firm belief in the operation of it characterised them all. Wilberforce, for instance, more than once reflected on Providence's particular direction of his own life in a passage in his spiritual journal.

'The singular accident, as it seemed to me, of my asking Milner to go abroad with me in 1784. How much it depended on contingencies! – coming to Hull with his brother; being known to my grandfather; distinguishing himself, etc. If he had been as ill as he was afterwards, or if I had known his character, we should not have gone together. Doddridge's 'Rise and Progress' having fallen in my way so providentially whilst abroad, given by Unwin [of Cowper's circle] to Mrs Smith, thence coming to Bessy, and by her taken abroad. My being raised to my present situation just before I became acquainted with the truth, and one year and a half before I in any degree experienced its power. This, humanly speaking, would not have taken place afterwards. What a mercy to have been born an Englishman, in the eighteenth century, of decently religious parents, with a fortune, talents, etc. Even Gibbon felt thankful for this; and shalt not thou praise the Lord, O my soul? My being providentially engaged in the Slave Trade business. I remember well how it was – what an honourable service. How often protected from evil and danger

and so on, the dangers being exemplified in physical illness and the threats of violence made to him by various defenders of the slave trade.⁴⁵

⁴⁴ Stephen, *Memoirs*, 26.
⁴⁵ *Life of Wilberforce*, II 165–6. In a memorandum dictated in old age Wilberforce elaborated on his reasons for seeing the hand of Providence in initiating him into political life before his conversion. 'That gracious

There is a particular implication of the Evangelical conviction that one's life was so directed as to be called to particular tasks which it takes William Law, the mentor of so many of the Evangelicals, to draw out. Scripture clearly tells us, he says, 'that the time and manner of every man's coming into the world is according to some eternal purposes and direction of Divine Providence, and in such time, and place, and circumstances, as are directed and governed by God for particular ends of His wisdom and goodness'.[46] The inescapable logic of such a conviction is not only that one is called to do certain things but that there is an inescapable commitment to them, once they are defined, a divine command to pursue them whatever the obstacles and dangers, disappointments and discouragements. Here is an important reason for the sheer dogged persistence of these men in the task to which, they unfailingly believed, Providence had called them – the abolition of the slave trade. On the narrowest temporal definition, it is worth recalling, their commitment was constant for two decades. But was Evangelical religion purely emotional, purely a matter of the heart? Did it have any place, apart from acceptance of certain of its values, for the moral philosophy by which the eighteenth century set so much store?

John Wesley, though he advocated 'a religion founded on reason and everyway agreeable thereto',[47] though he was intensely rational in the way he proceeded from premisses, though they

[46] Law, *Serious Call*, 232.
[47] Quoted in Cragg, *Reason and Authority*, 158.

Providence which all my life long has directed my course with mercy and goodness, and which in so many instances known only to myself has called forth my wonder and gratitude, was signally manifested in the first formation of my parliamentary connexion with the county of York, and in its unintermitted and long continuance. Had the change in my religious principles taken place a year sooner, humanly speaking I never could have become member for Yorkshire. The means I took, and the exertions I made, in pursuing that object, were such as I could not have used after my religious change; I should not have thought it right to carve for myself so freely, if I may use the phrase (to shape my course for myself so confidently), nor should I have adopted the methods by which I ingratiated myself in the good-will of some of my chief supporters; neither after my having adopted the principles I now hold, could I have conformed to the practices by which alone any man would be elected for any of the places in which I had any natural influence or connexion . . .' (Ibid., I 383).

were partly the premisses of Revelation, said of Hutcheson, for instance, that 'I know both from Scripture, reason and experience that his picture of man is not drawn from life'[48] and more generally, that 'so far as you add philosophy to religion, just so far you spoil it'.[49] The Evangelical was in fact bound to oppose the some-what naïve view of human nature which is found, for instance, in Hutcheson's *System of Moral Philosophy* and in Adam Smith's *Theory of Moral Sentiments*: none the less, just as in an earlier generation Law had been led to enter the lists against Toland, so, *mutatis mutandis*, Gisborne was led by Paley's use of the principle of happiness as the guide to utility to propound an alternative scheme of moral philosophy. More precisely, Gisborne attacks Paley's teaching that, when Scripture gives no clear guidance 'the method of coming at the will of God concerning any action, by the light of nature, is to inquire into the tendency of that action to promote or diminish the general happiness'.[50] This approach, says Gisborne, is wrong because – and clearly he is influenced by Burke – the expediency principle is subject to various shortcomings, especially error and personal vagary, reflecting the fact that men do not have the understanding always to judge correctly what makes for happiness. 'General expediency is an instrument not to be wielded by a mortal hand. The nature of general con-sequences is too comprehensive to be embraced by human under-standing, too dark to be penetrated by human discernment'.[51] Justice should rather be the operative principle; it gives less scope for error in speculation and abuse in practice. Gisborne goes on to establish rights and obligations 'from Reason and Revelation'. Quite apart from 'any social engagement . . . every man finds himself possessed of existence, of various bodily powers, and mental faculties'. Because 'he must become convinced that these blessings are the gifts of a gracious Being' these gifts have a divine sanction and so burgeon into rights. Everyman 'may therefore be assured that he has a right to the undisturbed enjoyment of them as long as it shall seem meet to God who bestowed them'.[52] From this

[48] Quoted in ibid., 162.
[49] Quoted in ibid., 160.
[50] T. Gisborne, *The Principles of Moral Philosophy*, 2nd ed. (London, 1790) 11–12.
[51] Ibid., 52.
[52] Ibid., 72.

characteristic angle Gisborne has no difficulty in elaborating a conventional enough catalogue of natural rights, including, we might note, 'a right to freedom from personal injury and from personal restraint'.[53]

Qualitatively, it would seem that Gisborne's importance lies in the way in which he emphasises justice as the criterion of action and the manner in which he is wholly prepared to invoke revelation as a support for his system at the same time as he uses the empirical method. It was not profound philosophy but one may surmise that his book would have given considerable satisfaction to those who, wholly prepared to admit the authority of revelation, still wanted deductions from it to cohere with the fruits of empirical reasoning.[54]

A similar concern perhaps lay behind Evangelical embracing of another philosopher – not himself of their school – who none the less 'believed that his talents could not be so usefully employed as in combating the schemes of those who aimed at the complete subversion of religion, both natural and revealed'.[55] This was Thomas Reid (1710–96), with Hume, the most intellectually distinguished member of the Scottish moralist school, whose philosophy seems to have constituted a kind of associated dimension of the Evangelical world-view. This must surely be not least because Reid stood forward as the avowed opponent of Hume's scepticism.

Hume's views on religion may in part have been inspired by a hatred of the corruptions of Christian churches; his refusal to dogmatise his scepticism may serve to qualify his attack on religion; and we may notice the doubts he had about his own scepticism: but in his own day he was without doubt seen as an arch subverter of religion and morality.[56] His intellect was too formidable for his

---

[53] Ibid., 194.

[24] To cite evidence gleaned at random, Gisborne is cited thrice in the *Christian Observer*, 1805, and in a mode which assumes familiarity with him. Sir James Stephen wrote of Gisborne: 'He was the expositor of the "Evangelical" system to those cultivated or fastidious readers who were intolerant of the ruder style of his less refined brethren' (*Ecclesiastical Biography*, II 302–3).

[55] Dugald Stewart, 'Account of the Life and Writings of Thomas Reid D.D.' in Sir Wm Hamilton (ed.), *The Works of Thomas Reid* (Edinburgh, 1880) I 32.

[56] None the less he seems to have been most commonly known at second and third hand and his direct influence in the eighteenth century was

work to be ignored by the well-read men that the leading Evangelicals were, and it is reasonable to suggest that, like Stephen,[57] they may have turned to one who could meet Hume on his own ground, namely Reid. For in Reid there was a philosophical rebuttal of Hume, compatible with their evangelical convictions – and their convictions as men brought up in the rational tradition of the eighteenth century.

Another member of the Scottish school of philosophers, James Beattie, fulfilled something of a similar role for Evangelicals. The title of his *Essay on the Nature and Immutability of Truth, in Opposition to Sophistry and Scepticism* (1770), though the work was not so intellectually distinguished as Reid's, explains its appeal to Evangelicals. 'To Dr. Beattie', wrote the *Christian Observer* after his death, 'the world has long looked up as a friend and champion of the Christian cause'.[58]

Before we examine more closely the Evangelical dynamic in regard to abolition it will be convenient to look at their attitude to other public questions. Wilberforce set out the comportment in the world which must be the fruit of the faith of true Christians in the *Practical View*.

> Let them boldly assert the cause of Christ in an age when so many, who bear the name of Christians, are ashamed of Him; and let them consider as devolved on Them the important duty of suspending for a while the fall of their country, and perhaps of performing a still more extensive service to society at large

[57] Stephen, *Memoirs*, 202. 'Dr. Reid's *Essays on the Human Mind* have of late years been my favourite guides on such subjects [metaphysical writings] and seem to me to deserve even more celebrity than they have attained.' Stephen is here referring to Reid's *An Inquiry into the Human Mind on the Principles of Common Sense* (1764). His two other major works were *Essays on the Intellectual Powers of Man* (1785) and *Essays on the Active Powers of Man* (1788).

[58] *Christian Observer*, June 1807, 389–96, and July 1807, 466–73. The contributor went on to stricture Beattie as having been shown to have been insufficiently devout, but this was subsequently contested by another contributor (ibid., July, 473–9).

apparently not great. Lois Whitney (*Primitivism and the Idea of Progress*, (New York, 1965, 326) reminds us that his books were notoriously bad sellers in that century and quotes Hume's own lament that his *Treatise of Human Nature* 'fell dead-born from the Press'.

. . . that sure and radical benefit of restoring the influence of Religion, and of raising the standard of morality.[59]

The most obvious expression of this commitment was Wilberforce's foundation of the Proclamation Society in 1787, a body which he formed to take action against offences specified in the Royal Proclamation from which the body took its name – 'profamation of the Sabbath, swearing, drunkenness, licentious publications, unlicensed places of public amusement, the regulation of licensed places, etc.'[60] For most of the years in which he was involved in the abolition, at any rate, Wilberforce himself seems not to have given much time to his brainchild, but after its reconstitution in 1802, as the Society for the Suppression of Vice, the association became a characteristic outworking of Evangelical zeal. Although a partial explanation of the measure of success which it achieved was that membership included churchmen of all shades, its attempt to reform society by the use of the laws – usually by way of prosecutions – was of chiefly Evangelical inspiration.[61]

Evangelicals active in public life believed themselves called to that station. Occupying it, they believed they had necessarily to make up their minds on public matters. The attitudes which they took up provide a part of the context of their attitude to the slave trade. By and large they were sensitive to the claims of liberty, as they interpreted it, and to the call of benevolent measures. Wilberforce was personally friendly with parliamentary reformers like Cartwright and Wyvill, and to a lesser extent with the eccentric Stanhope. Wilberforce supported Pitt in the Prime Minister's unsuccessful parliamentary reform bill of 1785, hastening back from Nice especially to do so;[62] and when that failed, took over from Stanhope, on the latter's succession to the Lords, the management in the lower house of a bill, which passed the Commons but was thrown out by the Lords, designed to curb corruption at elections.[63] In 1809, in the same line of conduct, he supported Curwen's bill

[59] Wilberforce, *Practical View*, 350.

[60] Wilberforce to William Hey, 29 May 1787 in *Life of Wilberforce*, I 134.

[61] For the two societies, see a well-documented account, albeit from a somewhat modern perspective, in Ford K. Brown, *Fathers of the Victorians* (Cambridge, 1961) passim, and especially 83–8 and 428–45.

[62] *Life of Wilberforce*, I 77–9.

[63] Ibid., I 113–14.

for making the sale of parliamentary seats illegal.[64] In 1792 and 1793, with only a few reservations, Wilberforce supported Wyvill in what Wilberforce himself termed 'a temperate parliamentary reform'[65] and though he opposed Grey's reform bill of 1797 as 'too bold'[66] he declared himself still in favour of moderate parliamentary reform 1817 and 1831, and voted for it in 1822.[67] In 1795, on the other hand, Wilberforce supported two repressive measures, the Treasonable Practices Act and the Seditious Meetings Act, repeating this pattern in 1817–19 when he defended the new Seditious Meetings Bill, the suspension of Habeas Corpus and the Six Acts.[68] He believed that revolution threatened at both these periods and that if it prevailed the traditional liberties of Englishmen would be no more. Wilberforce, of course, was never a political radical, never a democrat. Interestingly, however, his opposition to continuation of the war with France after the fall of Robespierre in 1794 led not only to temporary estrangement with Pitt in 1795[69] but to suspicion that Wilberforce had French sympathies. ' "Your friend Mr Wilberforce", said Mr Windham to Lady Spencer, "will be very happy any morning to hand your ladyship to the guillotine." '[70] Wilberforce's reasons for, after much heart searching,[71] supporting the union with Ireland show the cast of his political thinking as well as anything. They were 'to widen the basis of political power, and so destroy that predominant influence of a few great families, by which Ireland had been long misgoverned'.[72]

The strand of Christian benevolence in the political conduct of the Clapham Sect led Wilberforce, in 1801,[73] to deplore the failure

[64] E. M. Howse, *Saints in Politics: The Clapham Sect and the Growth of Freedom*, 2nd English impression (London, 1971) 130. House delineates very well the multifarious activities of the Clapham Sect.

[65] *Wrangham MSS*, Wilberforce to Wyvill, 31 May 1792; *Life of Wilberforce*, II 2, 9. But Wilberforce did not actually vote for Grey's reform bill of 1793.

[66] Ibid., II 442.

[67] Howse, *Saints in Politics*, 130.

[68] Ibid., 117–8.

[69] Ibid., 52–3.

[70] Quoted in *Life of Wilberforce*, II 72, n.d.

[71] *Crawford Muniments*, Wilberforce to Muncaster, 3 Dec 1798.

[72] *Life of Wilberforce*, II 326

[73] Ibid., III 13.

to relieve the poor 'in not granting a liberal supply out of the public purse'[74] – a measure backed by *The Christian Observer*, to sponsor (unsuccessfully) the Surgical Subject Bill of 1786 whereby the bodies of certain deceased felons might be made available for dissection[75] and warmly to support Sir Robert Peel's Factory Acts of 1802 and 1818, and the case of the chimney boys.[76] He also devoted fair attention to penal reform, an interest which brought him into contact with Bentham whose plan for the famed Panopticon he spent much time in furthering. (Interestingly, we learn that Wilberforce was intimate with Bentham as far, as Wilberforce's biographers rather nicely put it, 'as the disagreement of their tastes rendered possible'.)[77] Indeed, in Wilberforce's advocacy of more generous welfare provision, in his views on penal reform, in his doubts about 'the barbarious custom of hanging'.[78] and in his support of measures against bull-baiting[79] we have a possibly unexpected adumbration of a more modern syndrome.

Of the small number of Evangelicals who were also members of Parliment, Henry Thornton was a shade more radical, as seen notably in his support of Grey's parliamentary reform bill of 1797.[80] Outside Parliament Granville Sharp was much more radical. He had been a leading figure in the Association Movement and consistently leaned further to the left. In sum, and in the period up to the abolition of the slave trade in 1807, the predominant Evangelical political posture is of support for a variety of measures of moderate reform. Of course, wide-ranging philanthropic and religious schemes were at least as important to Evangelicals as parliamentary activity. But as regards political attitudes Sir James Mackintosh said of Wilberforce that though he was a

[74] *Christian Observer*, no. 7, ɪɪ (July 1803) 429–30. For Evangelical recognition of the inadequacy of the existing Poor Law, see ibid., ɪ (Apr 1802) no. 4 240.

[75] Ibid., ɪ 113–4. In the winter of 1796 Wilberforce also gave much time to reforming abuses at St Thomas's Hospital (Ibid., ɪɪ 180).

[76] Howse, *Saints in Politics*, 131.

[77] *Life of Wilberforce*, ɪ 131; ɪɪ 170–72, 183.

[78] Quoted in *Life of Wilberforce* ɪ 131.

[79] *Christian Observer*, no. 8 ɪ (Aug 1802) 548–9. For the delight which Marianne Thornton shared with Hannah More in some undisclosed victory over bull-baiters see *Thornton MSS*, *Wigan Letter Book*, Marianne Thornton to Hannah More, 8 July 1802. See also an excellent assessment in Coupland, *Wilberforce*, 335–70.

[80] *D.N.B.*

Tory by predilection, by action he must be judged 'liberal and reforming'. Perhaps that description is also true of the political attitudes of the Clapham Sect as a whole.[81]

Whatever their involvement in other reforms, however, Evangelicals had no doubt that the slave trade was greater than any other evil. Stephen, who had known near-poverty himself, could not see the situation of the poor in England as comparable for, as he put it, 'in no other part of the globe are the poor and helpless so well protected by the laws, or so humanely used by their superiors. . . . Can it be alleged that there is any contemporary provocation [of Heaven] that bears any proportion to the slave trade?'[82] And when Wilberforce was challenged with the criticism that the slave trade should be dealt with in the same way as domestic evils, he replied:

> What evils my Noble Friend can possibly allude to, I cannot conceive. There certainly are none, that have any affinity with the Slave Trade, which have existed in this country since those days of gloomy bigotry and furious fanaticism, from the horrors of which we are now most happily exempt. The greatest evil of our condition that I know is, the continuance in our name of a Traffic in Human Beings, the reproach of which we ought no longer to endure.[83]

Beilby Porteus, a bishop sympathetic to Evangelicalism and an ardent abolitionist, was quite specific in his conviction 'that the lowest of our labourers were much happier than the negro slaves

[81] Howse, *Saints in Politics*, 131; Sir J. Stephen, *Ecclesiastical Biography*, II 260.

[82] Stephen, *Dangers of the Country*, 186, 211. The passage continues: 'If other sins of the same heinous species could be justly charged upon us; if "the sorrowful sighing of the prisoner, the complaint of the poor oppressed, and the cry of innocent blood", had gone up against us from other regions than Africa, and the West Indies; still it ought to be shewn, that in those other cases, as in this, the crime had been aggravated by equal obduracy, and extended with equal perverseness, after the open exposure of its guilt, and solemn calls for reformation. But in these respects, as well as in its magnitude, and its cruel effects, the slave trade stands alone among our national offences; defying, like Satan, in the foremost rank, the wrath of the Almighty.'

[83] *Substance of the Debates on a Resolution for Abolishing the Slave Trade*, 1806 (London, reissue by Dawsons, 1968) 36.

in the West Indies'.[84] Nor should one expect the judgement to have been otherwise: the problem of the poor and oppressed was not a problem conceived primarily in terms of economic theory – because economic theory made only an indirect contribution to the solution of that problem – but one conceived in terms of liberty and benevolence. And Christian benevolence heard the most clament call from those who on any reckoning were lowest in the scale of liberty.

[84] *Porteus MS. 2103*, f. 158. Diary of 13 Apr 1787. Porteus is actually reporting the verdict of an informant with direct West Indian experience, but clearly signifies his own agreement. For Sharp's similar view see pp. 242–3 below.

8 Evangelical Theology and Abolition

The Evangelical leaders of the abolition campaign, as will be noticed, became aware of slavery as an evil in a variety of adventitious ways. But notwithstanding, the exploration of Evangelical theology must be taken further for it is in it that another element of the Evangelicals' spiritual dynamic is found, namely a specific theological inspiration which demanded of them that they direct the point of their sword at the slave trade, and that they persist in their attack until victory be gained.[1] Firstly, in this further theological exploration, we must notice that the Old Testament is studied not only to discover a pattern of providential judgement on wickedness, but to demonstrate that slavery and slave trading were major expressions of that wickedness. Nothing could be clearer than this intention in Granville Sharp's *The Law of Retribution* (1776). He sets out to prove 'from Holy Scripture some plain examples of God's vengeance upon that particular nation [the Jewish], expressly for this kind of *Oppression;* which, I hope, will

[1] For an illuminating examination of the relationships between the idea of slavery and sin before this period see Davis, *Problem of Slavery*, 76, 78, 83–90, 291–2, 299, 307, 383, 492–3. For a discussion of the Christian abolitionist, including the Evangelical view of 'what *kind* of men the Africans were' and of African culture see Curtin, *Image of Africa*, 52–7; for Wilberforce's view on these and kindred matters see W. Wilberforce, *A Letter to the Gentlemen, Clergy, and Freeholders of Yorkshire* (London, 1807) 54, where he denies that Negroes are 'an inferior race of beings' and asserts that 'a position so shameless, and so expressly contradicted by the Holy Scriptures, could not long be maintained in plain terms'. See also ibid., 83–5, and W. Baker, 'William Wilberforce on the Idea of Negro Inferiority', *Journal of the History of Ideas*, xxxi (1970), no. 3, 433–40. For the view of the Rev. James Ramsay, another notable abolitionist, see his *Essay on the Treatment and Conversion of African Slaves in the British Sugar Colonies* (London, 1784), described by Curtin as 'the best anti-racist tract of the eighteenth century' (*Image of Africa*, 55).

sufficiently prove that *slavery* was ever detestable in the sight of God'[2] (and that it is therefore vital for England, which is in the same condemnation, to repent). A judgement on Sharp's success in his task, as on Stephen who made a more modest attempt at it, might be that it enjoyed real, but limited success. Certainly, for instance, Sharp could convincingly cite the third chapter of the book of the prophet Joel, where, *inter alia,* the nations, and especially Tyre and Sidon – for Sharp the analogy with Liverpool and Bristol was irresistible – were condemned for selling God's chosen people into slavery;[3] equally the prophet Amos' condemnations could be drawn upon to the same effect,[4] and the people of Jerusalem itself could be shown as guilty in the judgement of God because they 'dealt by oppression with the stranger'[5] [Ezekiel 22:7]. Also brought convincingly under tribute is Jeremiah 34:8–22 and the judgement upon the Chosen People, in the form of the Babylonian captivity, because 'Ye have not hearkened unto me in proclaiming liberty every one to his brother, and every man to his neighbour'.[6]

In one sense the effect of such exegesis on men whose faith *and* whose frame of human history was rooted in Scripture cannot be exaggerated: but the anti-slavery message in the Bible was not as explicit as the citation of texts, however compelling in themselves, might suggest. Frequently the condemnation of slavery is a part of a condemnation of social injustice as a whole, and so to that extent the sense of the evil is diffused.[7] Again, the really central condemnations of slavery seem to be reserved for the enslavement of Hebrew by Hebrew, and, literally construed, had no relevance

[2] Sharp, *Law of Retribution*, 2–3.

[3] Ibid., 217–20; Stephen, *Dangers of the Country*, 184 n.

[4] Sharp, *Law of Retribution*, 244–50.

[5] Ibid., 32–3.

[6] Ibid., 126–7, 169–84; Stephen, *Dangers of the Country*, 184 n.

[7] Stephen, for instance, broadens the canvas by asking 'What can be . . . the causes which are most frequently assigned in scripture for the chastisement of sinful nations? They are, for the most part, the sins of oppression, injustice, and violence towards the poor and helpless.' He then goes on to quote, as one reverse illustration, the exhortation of Jeremiah: 'Execute ye judgment and righteousness, and deliver the spoiled out of the hand of the oppressor; and do no wrong, do no violence to the stranger, and the fatherless, nor the widow, neither shed innocent blood' (Stephen, *Dangers of the Country*, 182–3).

to the enslavement of Negroes by Europeans. Yet again, the under-lining of the function of the Babylonian captivity as a punishment for slaveholding, together with the instruction to the Israelites in Leviticus 25:44 to purchase slaves from surrounding nations, even if explained by the fact that they were 'an abandoned race of people',[8] can only have suggested to the reflective but still literal mind that slavery had a place in the divine economy. For all Granville Sharp's extensive pleading, for all Stephen's conviction that the clear word of Scripture condemned slavery, the Bible as interpreted by most contemporaries must have been seen as speaking less than conclusively. Although Scripture depicted slavery and the slave trade as generally opposed to the will of God, the stated exceptions, together with the role of slavery as punish-ment for sin, meant that no incontrovertible condemnation of the institution could be deduced from the literal word of Scripture.[9] It would have been surprising had this been the case; after all, the generations of believers who had found in the ambivalence of Scripture, literally interpreted, warrant for their own ambivalence had included many men as devout as the Evangelicals.

The difference, and it is great, came when Holy Writ was inter-preted from an Evangelical perspective. That perspective had four elements: the first was the manner in which, the metaphor by which Evangelicals apprehended the doctrine of salvation. It may be true to say of twentieth-century Evangelical theology that it conceives salvation to be the *summun bonum* and that its attain-ment is described by the metaphors of the ritual sacrifice – pro-pitiation, expiation and atonement; of the law court – justifica-tion; and of emancipation from slavery – redemption. All these terms, being biblical terms, are used by Evangelical commentators of the eighteenth and early nineteenth centuries, but it soon be-comes apparent that 'redemption' and, after that, 'atonement' are central. Wilberforce, in *A Practical View*, his critique of pre-vailing religious practice in the light of Evangelical faith, makes this clear. His list of (fourteen) leading 'Scripture Doctrines' has

[8] G. Sharp, *The Just Limitation of Slavery in the Laws of God* (London, 1776), 3–4.

[9] It is significant that John Wesley, in 'Thoughts upon Slavery', *The Works of John Wesley* (London, 1872) xi 59–79, does not ground his strong denunciation of slavery on Scripture but principally on an appeal to justice and liberty, mercy and compassion.

as its very beginning: 'That "God so loved the world, as of his tender mercy to give his only Son Jesus Christ for our redemption" ';[10] the whole range of belief and infidelity relate to 'the doctrine of Redemption of Christ';[11] it is the 'contemplating the work of Redemption' which shows us 'our natural darkness, and helplessness, and misery',[12] whilst 'a single thought of the great work of Redemption will be enough to fill us with compunction'.[13] *A Practical View* also makes a number of references to atonement – the 'atoning blood', the 'atoning death', 'the atonement of the Saviour', etc.[14] More importantly, the relationship between atonement and redemption is spelt out in a most illuminating phrase, the 'scheme of redemption by the atonement of Christ',[15] a phrase which is paralleled by the Rev. Thomas Scott, the commentator, when he writes of 'redemption as the purchase of his [Christ's] atoning blood'.[16] In short, whilst the two most influential (Anglican) Evangelical writers speak of justification, propitiation and the other salvation concepts, the bedrock concept is of redemption as the quintessential blessing which is made possible by the atoning work of Christ. Moreover, both Scott and Wilberforce frequently use 'redemption' as a synonym of 'salvation', and 'Redeemer' as a synonym of 'Saviour'.

The second perspective stems naturally from this focus on the individual's salvation, and redemption from sin. Men with such a focus could not but regard the Old Testament account of the deliverance of the Chosen People, the working out of God's covenant with them, and which they understood as the outward sign,[17] the typology of their own salvation experience, with a sharpened attention as deep calling unto deep. And when they did so regard that account, they saw it not just as collective deliverance but in

[10] Wilberforce, *Practical View*, 43.

[11] Ibid., 86.

[12] Ibid., 244.

[13] Ibid., 242. For other references to redemption see pp. 81, 84, 89, 91–3, 106, 112, 240, 259 and 319.

[14] Ibid., 23, 91, 231; see also pp. 43, 94, 101 and 253.

[15] Ibid., 40.

[16] Scott, *Commentary*, VI, Comment on Epistle to the Colossians, Chap. I, v.v. 9–14.

[17] 'The mercies shewn to Israel, in their deliverance from bondage and captivity, were external signs of that redemption afforded in all ages to the remnant of believers, on setting them free from the bondage of sin and Satan' (Scott, *Commentary*, III, Practical Observations on Psalm LXXXV).

the very clear mould of redemption from physical bondage. The attestations which they read were, as the writer of Exodus put it, 'I am the Lord thy God which have brought thee out of the land of Egypt, out of the house of bondage' (20:2), or, as we find it – yet more positively – in Leviticus (26:13): 'I am the Lord your God, which brought you forth out of the land of Egypt, that ye should not be their bondmen; and I have broken the bands of your yoke, and made you go upright.' Such assertions are repeated time and time again,[18] whilst the subsequent Babylonian captivity is also, ultimately and for the righteous remnant, in the pattern of God's redemption of his people from subjection. God's whole redemptive purpose is placed firmly in the context of physical slavery and liberation.

The third fresh perspective from which Evangelicals interpreted Scripture was that of the law of love, that important outworking of their theology. Granville Sharp, implicitly, and Scott explicitly, so work this concept into the theme of God's deliverance of his Chosen People from bondage as to find in Scripture a command to godly men to show humanity to slaves precisely because mercy had been shown to the Chosen People in their captivity. By referring to a number of passages, Sharp argues that the Israelites

> were reminded of their *Bondage in Egypt:* for so the almighty *Deliverer* from *Slavery* warned his people to limit and moderate the *bondage,* which the Law permitted, by the remembrance of *their own former bondage* in a foreign land, and by a remembrance also of his great mercy in *delivering them* from that *bondage:* and he expressly referred them to *their own feelings,* as they themselves had experienced the intolerable yoke of Egyption Tyranny! 'Thou shalt not oppress a Stranger; for ye know the heart of a *stranger,* seeing ye were strangers in the land of Egypt' (Exodus 23:9). And again: 'Thou shalt remember that thou wast a *Bond-man* in the land of Egypt, and the Lord thy God redeemed thee' (Deuteronomy15:15)[19]

The same point, together with explicit invocation of the law of love, is made by Scott, the commentator – specially significant because

---

[18] See Exodus 13:8, 13:14; Leviticus 19:36, 23:43; Deuteronomy 5:6, 5:15, 6:12, 7:8, 8:14, 13:5, 15:15; Joshua 24:17; Judges 6:8; Psalm 81:10.

[19] Sharp, *The Just Limitation of Slavery in the Laws of God* (London, 1776) 6–7; see also ibid., 56–8.

his *Commentary on the Holy Bible* (1792) had a tremendous influence on the development and propagation of the theology of
the Evangelical movement.[20] Commenting on Deuteronomy
15:12–15, the passage in which the Jews were required to eman-
cipate Hebrew slaves after six years, he wrote: 'This addition to
the law . . . is likewise a divine interpretation of the law of love,
which was enforced upon the Israelites by the consideration of
their redemption from the Egypt bondage, and the prosperity
to which the Lord had advanced them'.[21]

Once the law of love is invoked as the supreme criterion, slavery
stands condemned. A breakthrough is achieved, leaving no doubt
where the faithful Evangelical's duty lay, as Scott's comment on
Exodus 21:2–11 makes clear:

> Slavery was almost universal in the world; and though, like
> wars, it always proceeded of evil, and was generally evil in
> itself, yet the wisdom of God deemed it better to regulate, then
> to prohibit it; we should not, however, judge of the practice
> itself by these *judicial regulations,* but by the *law of love.* Slavery,
> like war, may in some cases, in the present state of things, be
> lawful: for the crime which forfeits life, no doubt forfeits liberty;
> and it is not inconsistent even with the moral law, for a criminal
> to be sold and treated as a slave, during a term of time propor-
> tioned to his offence. In most other cases, if not in all, it must
> be inconsistent with the law of love.

Evangelicals, then, apprehended salvation primarily through
the concept of redemption; when they related the idea of redemption, in its existential, individual application, to God's great redemptive purpose as made known in the Old Testament they saw
that, historically, redemption was not least a redemption from
physical bondage; whilst thirdly, Sharp and Scott so interpreted
scriptural passages on the treatment and emancipation of slaves
owned by the Hebrews that the hesitancy and ambivalence of the
scriptural record was cut through and virtually all forms of slavery

[20] 'Scott was their interpreter of Holy Scripture' (Sir J. Stephen,
Ecclesiastical Biography, ii 99). Stephen designates Scott as one of the four
clerical leaders of the first generation of Evangelicalism; others were
John Newton, Joseph Milner and Henry Venn.
[21] Scott, *Commentary,* i see under Deut. 15:12–15. The 1852 edition,
used here, is not paginated. The second (first complete) edition was in
1792.

condemned at the bar of the law of love. Fourthly, the whole linkage between the physical slavery of the 'captive' and 'our hateful and ruinous bondage', and between 'liberty to the captive' and 'freedom in the service and favour of God',[22] is a constant in the Evangelical mind. This linkage appears time and time again in Evangelical theology, literature and hymns – this last, of course, being a favourite medium of expression. Wilberforce in *A Practical View*, for instance, makes numerous references to the slavery of sin: 'How is he [the sinner] a slave to the meanest of his appetites!'; again, as unregenerate men, 'instead of deploring our miserable slavery, we have too often hugged, and even gloried in our chains' – the use of the metaphor is frequent.[23] Numerous hymns of Charles Wesley, the great hymn-writer of the evangelical revival, use this image. Representatively, we may cite one of his still popular hymns:

> Long my imprisoned spirit lay
> Fast bound in sin and nature's night;
> Thine eye diffused a quickening ray –
> I woke, the dungeon flamed with light;
> My chains fell off, my heart was free....[24]

Significantly, an eminent student of the Wesleys, W. F. Lofthouse, tells us that 'the central fact for Charles Wesley, as for his brother, was that he was a slave redeemed from death and hell'.[25] Men

[22] The terms are Scott's as he develops precisely this theme in *Commentary*, I, 'Practical Observations' on Exodus 21.2–11.

[23] Wilberforce, *Practical View*, 18 and 25. See also pp. 26, 30, 33, 75, 93, 234, 250, 351.

[24] The most readily available, extensive collection of Charles Wesley's hymns is in the *Methodist Hymn Book* (London, 1933). The hymn quoted is no. 371.

[25] W. F. Lofthouse, 'Charles Wesley', *History of the Methodist Church in Great Britain*, vol. I, ed. Rupert Davies and Gordon Rupp (London, 1965) 133. See also E. Routley, *Hymns and the Faith* (London, 1955) 132. The basis of these images is, of course, the New Testament. In the Epistle to the Romans 8:21 St Paul contrasts the 'bondage of corruption' with the glorious liberty of the children of God', whilst in the Epistle to the Galatians, 5:1, the infant church is enjoined: 'Stand fast therefore in the liberty wherewith Christ has made us free, and be not entangled again with the yoke of bondage.' St John, in turn, affirms that 'Whosoever committeth sin is the servant of sin ... but ... if the Son shall make you free, ye shall be free indeed' (St John's Gospel 8:34–36). So familiar, indeed, is the metaphor, so much can appropriation of it be assumed, that

who saw their spiritual condition in these stark terms could not but condemn, by metaphoric association as well as by conviction, physical slavery as the analogue of sin; and they could only see emancipation and freedom as physical analogues of redemption and the liberty of the Christian man.

It may be objected, that, however important the concept of redemption was, spiritual redemption was unfailingly regarded as more important than physical. This was certainly the case. In Scott's words, if . . . deliverance from outward captivity be so valued, and rejoiced in, how ought we to value redemption from the wrath to come, and from the power of sin and Satan!'[26] But to argue from this that the biblical teaching on slavery, as interpreted by evangelicals, was solely relevant to the interior life would be an error, would be to ignore Evangelical psychology in its innermost depths. A perceptive appreciation of the Evangelical's psychology and theology must rather suggest that it was precisely because of his predominantly spiritual concern that he was so sensitive to the slavery issue – and, after all, the question at issue is not why the Evangelical did not devote himself to the attack on physical slavery, but why he did. For him there was a necessary externalisation of the polar opposites of his own religious experience at its deepest level, and that externalisation could only give to his anti-slavery zeal a drive which few men, concerned as humanitarians but lacking the tension and the analogues which the Evangelical knew so well, could generate. For us the circle is squared; contradiction softens to paradox.

A final reason why Evangelical theology marked down slavery and the slave trade as objects of particular and sustained attack lay in the limited range of Evangelical theological concern. A belief in Providence, general and particular, in the law of love and a profound concern with the concepts relevant to salvation – the range did not extend more widely. Evangelical theology, said Sir J. Stephen, 'revolved so much on a very few central points'.[27] But the very narrowness lent intensity, and a concern with redemption,

[26] Scott, *Commentary*, III, 'Practical Observation' on Psalm 126:1–3.
[27] Sir J. Stephen, *Ecclesiastical Biography*, II 170.

St Paul can on occasion reverse it as when he says 'being made free from sin [ye] became servants to God'. See also, *inter alia*, Romans VIII[15] and Galatians IV[9].

so dominant that it frightened, alarmed or amused contemporaries, could only have the most galvanic effect on attitudes to physical, to Negro, slavery. Moreover, the Evangelical experience of redemption from the slavery of sin into the freedom of the children of God, and the association of spiritual slavery with physical bondage, had come with a newness and revelatory force which constituted its own compulsion to this first generation of Evangelicals.[28]

Evangelicalism, it may be objected, did not always and necessarily, in comparable situations, involve anti-slavery zeal. In particular, Donald G. Mathews has shown that many American Methodists from the War of Independence onwards, persuaded themselves that they had no divine summons to campaign for abolition, or to liberate their own slaves.[29] This objection, however, is wide of the mark – British Evangelicals just were not put to the same test as were American Methodists. The summons to devoted abolitionist activity, stemming from their personal experience of liberation and their lively sense of the God of the Old Testament as the liberator from bondage, could not find in the economic and socio-

---

[28] Cf also a recent extended definition of the idea of Redemption in Christian theology: 'This Old Testament evidence may be summarised by saying that (1) the theme of redemption is embodied in every part of the literature and informs the whole course of Israel's history; (2) emphasis is laid upon the divine initiative in redeeming and ransoming man; (3) redemption is primarily from material perils and hardships . . .; (4) the redemptive activity is usually directed towards the whole people [i.e. has a group reference]. . . . In the N.T. [New Testament] . . . perhaps the most interesting passage to consider . . . reads ,'the Son of Man came not to be ministered unto but to minister and to give his life a ransom for many' . . . The verse as a summary of the character and purpose of the ministry of Jesus asserts (1) the voluntariness of the act as a deliberate sacrifice of self; (2) the costliness of it, using the word employed to describe the price to be paid for the release of prisoners or the manumission of slaves; (3) something done for the many which they could not do for themselves. . . . Other points call for some comment. (1) The results of redemption, on which so much emphasis is laid especially in the Epistles, are to cleanse men from the guilt and power of sin . . . (2) The recollection of the price paid by Christ to secure the redemption of men is set forth as the dynamic of Christian service' (F. J. Taylor, 'Redeem', *A Theological Word Book of the Bible*, ed. Alan Richardson (London, 1950) 185–7; see also F. J. Taylor, 'Bond', ibid., 36–7).

[29] *Slavery and Methodism: A Chapter in American Morality 1780–1845* (Princeton, N.J., 1965).

logical circumstances of Evangelicals any check to hinder its free course.

It should now be evident that Evangelical theology, by reason of the very elements which composed it, had to mark down slavery and, in the immediate, the slave trade, as the object of attack. An important consequence followed: the heightened Evangelical sense of providential judgement on national wickedness came necessarily to be focused on the slave trade as the most crying national sin. The mode was, naturally, to make the analogues from Scripture specific. Thus in *The Law of Retribution* Sharp, after reference to the Israelites' own deliverance from the bondage of slavery, emphasises their own sin in taking slaves as a major cause of the afflictions they suffered from a righteous God, and goes on to represent the Babylonian captivity as punishment for the Chosen People's breach of their promise to liberate their captive servants and handmaids.[30] Of course Sharp is explicit about the inference he is drawing, that because 'Slavery was ever detestable in the sight of God . . . a speedy Reformation is absolutely necessary . . . if we mean to entertain the least hope of escaping a severe *National Retribution*'.[31] This emphasis upon what he elsewhere termed 'the political necessity of Righteousness'[32] is a constant theme in Sharp's writings and correspondence, and usually in connection with slavery and the slave trade.

The presentation of the slave trade as an affront to the moral government of God, and as an evil which had necessarily invited his wrath and which must be ended lest still worse national tribulations befall, henceforth became an important theme in Evangelical thought and writing. Gisborne, as the peroration of his appendix on the slave trade, which he included in the fifth edition of his *Principles of Moral Philosophy* (1798), asked if any happy issue of the nation's afflictions could possibly be expected whilst she set justice and religion at defiance.[33] Wilberforce, in what proved to be the last tract he had to write against the British slave

[30] Sharp, *Law of Retribution*, 169–84.

[31] Ibid., 2.

[32] *Sharp Transcripts* (J.A.W.), Granville Sharp to Bishop of Peterborough 12 Mar 1781 (copy).

[33] T. Gisborne, *The Principles of Moral Philosophy, 4th edition, to which is added a New Edition, being the fifth, with an Appendix, of Remarks on the late decision of the House of Commons respecting the Abolition of the Slave Trade* (London, 1798) 466.

trade, cradled his whole case in the conviction that the trade was an affront to Providence, inviting retribution unless amendment were made. Interestingly he finds support for his view that 'it is . . . most commonly by the operation of natural causes, and in the way of natural consequences, Providence governs the world' in the history of ancient Rome,[34] that area of history which had so attracted those concerned with the pathology of states. Much more developed was James Stephen's tract, *The Dangers of the Country* (1807). He starts by founding his general principle in natural and revealed religion and by making the already familiar distinction between the meting out of individual and collective justice – all in a manner owing much to Butler.

> What indeed can be more consonant to our views of the divine government, whether derived from revealed or natural religion, than such retributory justice? Kingdoms have no world to come; communities of men will not, as such, stand collectively before the judgement seat of Christ. If then, it pleases the Almighty in his temporal providence, often to punish and reward in a re-markable manner, the vices and virtues of individuals; we may reason from analogy (that best natural interpreter of the unseen works of God) to the probability that Nations, will sometimes be made to illustrate in the same way, his justice, power, and mercy.[35]

Stephen then adduces the specific cause of the divine wrath:

> What are the causes which are most frequently assigned in scripture for the chastisement of sinful nations? They are, for the most part, the sins of oppression, injustice, and violence towards the poor and helpless; and the shedding of innocent blood.[36]

Stephen then shows by an interesting process of elimination, that if rapine, oppression, violence to the poor, the stranger, and the destitute, dishonest gain, and the effusion of innocent blood, be put in inquest against England, where will they be found but in

[34] W. Wilberforce, *A Letter on the Abolition of the Slave Trade Addressed to the Inhabitants of Yorkshire* (London, 1807) 4–6, 348–51.
[35] James Stephen, *The Dangers of the Country* (London, 1807) 180.
[36] Ibid., 182–3.

the Slave Trade; except indeed in its associated iniquity, the dreadful slavery of our colonies?[37]

Whatever may be said about British treatment of the inhabitants of the East Indies, Britain is guiltless in that region of oppression and slavery alike, 'unless the condition of a few domestic life servants, may deserve the name'.[38] Nor, our author continues, in a way which gives an invaluable insight into what men like Stephen regarded as evils – and he had known poverty himself[39] – is there domestic oppression.

> If we cast our eyes around us in this happy island, there is still less matter of charge against the national conscience on the score of violence and oppression. In no other part of the globe, are the poor and helpless so well protected by the laws, or so humanely used by their superiors ...
>
> If therefore we are suffering for such offences as have usually provoked the scourge of the Most High, if it be as the protector of the poor and destitute, that God has entered into judgement with us, we must, I repeat, look to Africa, and to the West Indies, for the causes of his wrath. But the magnitude of the crimes of the Slave Trade, still more than their specific character, will conduct us to the same conclusion.[40]

The nation's guilt, Stephen continues in a passage where the eighteenth century's concern with liberty and happiness peeps out, is terrible enough in itself, but is compounded when all that the country owes to a 'benignant providence' is recalled.

> Who are the people that have provoked God thus heinously, but the same who are among all the nations of the earth, the most eminently indebted to his bounty? He has given to us an unexampled portion of civil liberty; and we in return drag his rational creatures into a most severe and perpetual bondage. Social happiness has been showered upon us with singular profusion; and we tear from oppressed millions every social, nay almost every other comfort. In short, we cruelly reverse in our treatment of these unhappy brethren, all the gracious dealings

[37] Ibid., 185.
[38] Ibid., 185–6.
[39] See James Stephen, *Memoirs*, passim.
[40] Stephen, *Dangers of the Country*, 187.

of God towards ourselves. For our plenty we give them want; for our ease, intolerable toil; for our wealth, privation of the right of property; for our equal laws, unbridled violence and wrong. Science shines upon us, with her meridian beams; yet we keep these degraded fellow-creatures in the deepest shades of ignorance and barbarity. Morals and manners have happily distinguished us from the other nations of Europe; yet we create and cherish in two other quarters of the globe, an un-exampled depravity of both. A contrast still more opprobrious remains. God has blessed us with the purest effulgence of the Gospel; and yet we dishonour by our slave trade the christian name; and perpetuate the darkness of paganism among millions of our fellow-creatures.[41]

Pausing to ask the reader if 'we shudder at the idea of those calamities which a successful invasion would bring upon our country'[42] – Napoleon was unambiguously cast as the agent of retributive justice – Stephen gives a particular twist to his argu-ment by warning the nation that if it persists in an evil after it has been laid bare, then it would be committing that same aggra-vation as has brought avenging fire upon Sodom, after the warning of Lot, and plagues upon Egypt after the cautions of Moses and Aaron. Moreover, the volume of the British slave trade had in fact increased since the initiation of the abolition campaign.[43]

Can it be denied then, that we have in this great national offence, an adequate cause of the displeasure of Heaven, and of the calamities which have fallen upon the country? Or can it be alleged, that there is any contemporary provocation that bears any proportion to the slave trade.[44]

Author and reader alike are then transposed into visitors from another planet so that the connection between the iniquity of the slave trade and of Britain's loss by foreign war can be clearly seen. As visitors we are

impressed with our present ideas of the divine Government, but ignorant of the History of Europe since the year 1787, and

[41] Ibid., 195.
[42] Ibid., 196.
[43] Ibid., 197–211.
[44] Ibid., 211.

informed alone of the Parliamentary discussions on the Slave Trade, and of those iniquities which England has since committed against the African race, we might naturally be disposed to inquire, 'Has no scourge from Heaven yet appeared? Have no calamities, indicatory of Divine wrath, overtaken that guilty land?' But should we next take up a history of the French Revolution, and of the fatal wars that have ensued; and learn how strangely the prosperity, the peace, and the security of England have been subverted by them, what singular evils we have endured, ever since our first refusal to abolish the slave trade, and by what still greater evils we are at this moment threatened; it would be impossible, I conceive, not to recognise with wonder and awe, the chastising hand of God. The only difficulty would be, to comprehend how the living witness both of the provocation and the punishment, could possibly be unobservant of the visible connection between them.[45]

Drawing his argument towards a conclusion Stephen substantiates his correlation of Britain's evil and the judgement on her by passing in review the recent history of a number of other European states which 'have also drunk, and hitherto much deeper than ourselves of the phial of divine wrath poured out in the French Revolution?'[46] It is striking, he concludes, that they have all, independently, provoked the divine justice by participation in the slave trade or by other kinds of injustices as, for example, the oppression of Poland.[47] Conversely, 'has not the hand of Providence distinguished some portion of the earth, with blessings equally unusual?' And is this not because the country in question, the United States, has seen every state in the union save one abolish the slave trade with the result that Americans have 'done much to redeem themselves from those sins to which, I chiefly ascribe the calamities of Europe'.[48] *The Dangers of the Country* was written with the particular purpose of influencing voting on the motion for general abolition of February 1807 and so it concludes with a

45 Ibid., 211–12.
46 Ibid., 216.
47 Ibid., 216–22.
48 Ibid., 222–3. Stephen assessed too charitably the significance of what the various States had done, but we shall have occasion to note the importance in the abolitionists' assessment of the foreign slave trade, and hence of their tactics, of Stephen's view of the American trade.

final appeal that the vote should be positive rather than signify 'a new apostacy, worse by far than any former provocation of the same kind'.[49] So ended a notable piece of historical and biblical exegesis highly important to the understanding of the Evangelical mind. Reflecting that mind *The Christian Observer* both expressed the Evangelical belief in a superintending Providence, and mirrored the specific relation made by Stephen and others between national participation is the sin of the slave trade and the danger of a providential judgement.[50]

All in all the Evangelical mind was a dynamic thing. It accepted much of the moral philosophy of the day – notably the belief in liberty as a cardinal virtue, in benevolence as the duty of men and in happiness as a proper goal. But the first the Evangelical deepened by seeing true liberty as founded only on the freedom of the sons of God, the second he saw as only erratically effective unless fortified by the Pauline conviction that 'we love because he first loved us', and the third he believed vain if sought as an object in itself. Their ability to transpose, to supercharge, these values stemmed from a desolating conviction of their own sin, the assurance that that sin was forgiven and could be overcome by the grace of God, and by the consequential assurance that they could overcome the sin of and in other men by that same grace. Anterior to this was a greater sense of the horror of evil just because they had come to see its enormity in themselves. They believed in Providence as a divinely sustained moral order, which included judgement on the nation that sinned, and this belief gave them a satisfying and coherent philosophy of history, whilst their lively sense of a particular Providence ruling and directing their own lives was also their inescapable summons to mould the world to a righteousness which would avert deserved national disaster, relieve the mundane sufferings of men, and pave the way for the salvation of their eternal souls. Nor was their thought incompatible with, at any rate, a dominant current of the philosophy of the age – that of Reid and other members of the Scottish school – whilst it found more direct philosophical support from a member of the sect itself, Thomas Gisborne.

[49] Ibid., 226. See also Stephen to Wilberforce, 22 Aug 1797, quoted in *Life of Wilberforce*, II 256–7.

[50] See *The Christian Observer*, e.g. no. 10 II (Oct 1803) 620; and no. 12, II (Dec 1803) 766–7.

There were various immediate reasons why the individual Evangelical took up the cause of abolition. As we shall see, Sharp's involvement began with the discovery at his brother's surgery of the ill-treated black, Jonathan Strong; Wesley is approached by Benezet; Stephen is horrified by the mockery of the Barbadian slave trial; Wilberforce, for reasons of which we are ignorant, had first been disturbed by slavery when in his teens. Furthermore, in their passionate concern for Evangelism Evangelicals could only regard the slave trade and slavery as an obstacle to missionary work in Africa and the West Indies. But what must be emphasised is the imperative to seize upon the slave trade as the object of attack deriving from the deeper, the theological level which we have just explored. Thus the Evangelical came to have in abolition a focus for his response to the mercy which God had shown him, and for the payment of the debt which, as a redeemed sinner, he must discharge. All this, *and* a philosophy of history whose lesson was that the nation was in danger of the judgement, was stamped upon the Evangelical's heart and mind and combined to make him a formidable force when he turned to political action against the slave trade.

9 Origins of Quaker Action Against the Slave Trade

The faith of the Evangelicals, we have seen, was a powerful dynamic for action in the world: its proving ground was the abolition campaign of the late 1780s and onwards. Paradoxically, however, this dynamism was released by the abolitionist enthusiasm of Quakers, members of a denomination in which Quietism had always been an important element. The reasons for this lie, in their turn, in Quaker theology, in the internal dialogue of eighteenth-century Friends and in the deep political, religious and psychological stresses which American Friends underwent in the period from the French and Indian war[1] to the Confederation.

The internal dialogue of which we have spoken was not merely or even primarily a dialogue between Friends on one side of the Atlantic or the other. What is so striking about the Society of Friends in the eighteenth century is that it was a veritable Atlantic community. At the beginning of the century there were estimated to be at least 50,000 Friends in Britain and, at 40,000, almost as many in the Western hemisphere, the great majority in British North America, with Pennsylvania as the heartland. And despite the fact that the Society had neither tightly-drawn creed nor visible head, and no rigid institutional structure, it was, in Rufus Jones' words, 'a living group'. The ability to be so derived initially from George Fox's concern to maintain links with Friends overseas and his creation of a system of monthly, quarterly and yearly meetings, comprehending all Quakers. As one might expect, the London Yearly Meeting, in which Friends from all over the British Isles were represented, and the Philadelphia Yearly Meeting, re-

[1] In the language of European international relations this was the Seven Years War (1756–63).

presenting Pennsylvania, New Jersey and Delaware, soon came to have a recognised primacy on their respective sides of the Atlantic, and the London Meeting a recognised primacy in the movement as a whole. But, to repeat, it was an informal primacy. The living sense of one Anglo-American community of Friends was sustained in part by correspondence between London and American Yearly Meetings, and by the frequent and numerous letters which Friends wrote to one another whether on the Lord's business or as the business partners which they sometimes were.

Perhaps more vital was the constant travelling back and forth across the Atlantic to which Friends felt, as they described it, a 'drawing'. Professor Frederick B. Tolles has compiled a list, which he believes to be incomplete, of 148 British Friends who travelled in America even before the close of the seventeenth century whilst the Quaker literature of the eighteenth reveals Friends as engaged in a constant criss-crossing of the Atlantic. For the most part Friends engaged in such voyaging obtained a certificate of authorisation from their own monthly meeting, an endorsement which elevated them into a kind of itinerant ministry. Nor did the visitation stop at London, Bristol or Liverpool, at Philadelphia, Newport or Providence, but was commonly a lengthy tour through a large area of the British Isles, or a group of adjoining colonies, such that the humblest Friend in a small Meeting would share fellowship with the visitor from across the Atlantic, and feel himself joined to those like-minded with him across the sea.[2]

As in every credible creed, there were internal tensions in Quakerism and particularly between the quietism which was so pronounced amongst the sect, and the call, in accordance with the

[2] One amongst many indications of the importance of these visitations is the lament of the London Meeting for Sufferings – the term derives from the committees originally set up to aid Friends who suffered persecution during the reign of Charles II – during the War of American Independence that, 'brotherly intercourse is so much interrupted in the way of personal visits, heretofore so frequent and edifying, as well as of epistolary correspondence' (*Friends House MSS.*, Letters between the London and Philadelphia Meetings for Sufferings, 1757–1815, London to Philadelphia, 29 Dec 1780). For the sometimes unappreciated dimensions of eighteenth-century Quakerism as an Atlantic community see *inter alia* Michael Kraus, *The Atlantic Civilisation: Eighteenth Century Origins* (Ithaca, 1949); F. B. Tolles, *Quakers and the Atlantic Culture* (New York, 1960); Anne T. Gary, 'The Political and Economic Relations of English and American Quakers', Oxford University D. Phil thesis, 1935.

illumination of the Inner Light, to change the world. Rufus Jones sees in Woolman's *Journal* an excellent indication of the quietistic attitude:

> Being thus humbled and disciplined under the cross, my under-standing became more strengthened to distinguish the pure spirit which inwardly moves upon the heart, and which taught me to wait in silence sometimes many weeks together, until I felt that rise which prepares the creature to stand like a trumpet, through which the Lord speaks to his flock.[3]

Whatever the latent potential for action in this world of this kind of spirituality it clearly does not emphasise involvement in worldly affairs with a view to changing them. Indeed the outgoing activity of the individual Friend seemed often to be restricted to the articulation of relationships with other Friends and the harmony and good order of the Society, locally and at large. A preoccupation with 'birthrightism', the near-automatic conferment of membership on the children of Friends, as a means of maintaining numbers and keeping the purity of the faith, would seem to evidence this limited vision. For all this the outgoing concern of the 'first publishers' of the founding years was not completely eclipsed. An itinerant preacher like John Griffith would still expound the Gospel to all who would listen, whilst Friends generally still sought to bring about such change in the world as was implied in works of compassion.

It would seem that the very fact that they were an Atlantic community led some Friends to an awareness of a category strikingly deserving of their compassion – Negro slaves. Friends resided in the West Indies as well as on both borders of the Atlantic and although most of these Friends who were involved in some dimension or another of the slave economy or of the slave trade satisfied themselves with the traditional justifications of slavery, participation led to a troubled mind in a few. Significantly the first Quaker agitators of the slave question were predominantly European born. The first anti-slavery resolution of all came from the descriptively named Germantown in 1688 and the other agitators were mainly of English origin; that is to say, they were men more likely to be challenged by the newly experienced sight

[3] Quoted in Rufus Jones, *The Later Periods of Quakerism* (London, 1921) ɪ 813. See pp. 57–103 for an exposition of quietism.

and touch of slavery than those brought up amongst it. But if it was their European origin which so often lay behind this quickened conscience, it was their membership of an international community which gave the opportunity to expound their new and disturbing convictions in centres where slavery was in one form or another a part of the way of life. Thus William Edmundson, John Farmer, Ralph Sandiford and Benjamin Lay all grew up in England, and all save Farmer derived their fundamental revulsion from slavery from residence in the West Indies. Their crusade against it, however, was carried on in North America, and especially Pennsylvania.

Although George Fox, the founder of Quakerism, had condoned slavery, reflecting the orthodox Christian position of the mid-seventeenth century, the inner logic of Quakerism was bound to condemn slavery once even a few minds – and some of those highly idiosyncratic, whilst Farmer and Lay were somewhat unbalanced[4] – began to engage with the question. That logic stemmed from the basic proposition that Christ died for all men, so postulating a fundamental equality between them, and from the call to Quakers to love all men. Serious reflection on the institution of slavery soon revealed that the obtaining of slaves (since it was believed usually to involve warfare), the constraint which kept slaves in subjection, and the separation of families which was the common accompaniment of slavery, ran directly counter to basic Quaker convictions about the immorality of engaging in war (even if only vicariously by buying slaves already enslaved), of dealing in stolen goods and countenancing adultery. At the same time the belief in the Inner Light as direct personal illumination made it impossible not to listen to such Friends as were 'straitened in their minds' to develop anti-slavery testimonies. Qualifying this tendency was a deeply felt conviction that the unity of Friends must be sustained and that though sin could properly attract a white heat of condemnation, a fellow Friend must be spoken to in love.

The first outcome of these countervailing tendencies was that the point of anti-slavery testimony amongst Friends might sometimes be deflected from its target because accompanied by the kind of personal attack on Friends involved in slavery that was made

---

[4] But note David Davis' comment: 'If Benjamin Lay was not quite sane, one should remember that the sanest minds found excuses for Negro slavery' (*Problem of Slavery*, 321).

in Sandiford's *A Brief Examination of the Practice of the Times* ... (1729) and Lay's *All Slave-Keepers, that Keep the Innocent in Bonudage, Apostates* ... (1737).[5] But despite this, despite a disposition to reject the testimony of Friends disowned – and Southeby and Farmer, Sandiford and Lay all were disowned – and despite the proneness of Meetings of Friends to put off painful decisions until other Meetings had been consulted and uniformity of decision obtained, the Quaker testimony against slavery did make progress in the first half of the eigthteenth century. Certainly the first step was the least painful (and it was the first for precisely this reason) for the withdrawal of Quakers from participation in the import slave trade demanded least sacrifice. But taken the step was, and in the classic two stages of advice and discipline. The Philadelphia Yearly Meeting made avoidance of slave trading a matter of advice as early as 1696 and of discipline in 1719.[6] London advised in 1727 and went the rest of the way in 1761 whilst the other American Yearly Meetings were mostly well advanced in the two-stage process by 1760. The next step was to end the purchase and sale of slaves once imported. The Philadelphia Yearly Meeting led the way here, advising with increasing vigour against the practice in the thirties, but not making slave dealing a matter of discipline until 1774. By this time, however, in the mid-fifties, to be precise, the whole Quaker attack on slavery had been broadened. In the last quarter of the seventeenth and first half of the eighteenth centuries, the pressure had come mainly from Friends of English origin, backed by the London Meeting's pronouncement of 1727, following a discreditable refusal to commit itself in 1712, and increasingly firm rulings in 1713, 1715 and 1720, and by such works as the English Quaker John Bell's winsome injunction to treat slaves kindly in *An Epistle to Friends in Virginia, Barbadoes, and other Colonies and Islands in the West Indies where any Friends are* (1741) which set in train amongst American Friends soul searching on the actual keeping of slaves. In mid-century the American, and especially Pennsyl-

[5] Even in an age of verbose titles Benjamin Lay surely excels in the 116-word title of his book. (See Bibliography.)

[6] Some Pennsylvania Friends none the less continued to deal in slaves up to the 1750s, but they were relatively few and risked disownment (Darold D. Wax, 'Quaker Merchants and the Slave Trade in Colonial Pennsylvania', *Pennsylvania Magazine of History and Biography*, LXXXVI (April, 1962) 157–9).

vanian, testimony was to produce two striking figures, John Woolman and Anthony Benezet, and was to develop into a broadly
based attack on slave holding by Friends and by others. In itself,
this development falls outside our concern, but the new testimony
had as a subsidiary effect new initiatives against the British slave
trade. To these two figures, and to the traumatic shock which set
Pennsylvania Quakers on a new course in the 1750s, we must
now turn.[7]

John Woolman was born in up-country New Jersey in 1720 and
from the age of twenty managed a village store which he subsequently bought. The original owner taught him tailoring, and
Woolman after 1756 restricted himself to this trade in conjunction with farming and conveyancing, feeling, as he expressed it, 'a
stop in my mind' as the business became 'too cumbersome'. This
was an early indication of an asceticism which he was to carry
to extremes – he conceived a moral objection to dyestuffs, for
instance, and refused to wear clothes that had been so treated.
It was in the course of his conveyancing that his uneasiness about
slavery was first aroused, for his employer simply told him one
day to write out a bill of sale for a slave in his household, a woman
whose very acceptance in the household up until that time had
masked the harsher face of slavery. 'Through weakness', as he
subsequently recorded, he complied, but 'I was so afflicted in my
mind that I said before my master and the Friend [who was purchasing her] that I believed slavekeeping to be a practice inconsistent with the Christian religion'. Soon afterwards Woolman refused to write an 'instrument of slavery' when requested to do so
by a young Quaker,[8] and, his concern about slavery now aroused,
he undertook a tour of colonies to the south partly in order to
investigate slavery in colonies where, as plantation slavery, it was
more widely and deeply implanted. As a result of his tour Woolman, in 1746, wrote *Some Considerations on the Keeping of*

[7] For the development of the Quaker anti-slavery testimony up to the
mid-eighteenth century, see Thomas E. Drake, *Quakers and Slavery in
America* (New Haven, 1950) 2–51; Sydney V. James, *A People Among
Peoples: Quaker Benevolence in Eighteenth-Century America* (Cambridge, Mass.,
1963) 103–32; Davis, *Problem of Slavery*, 299–332; Gary, *Relations of English
and American Quakers*, 170–88.

[8] Phillips P. Moulton (ed.), *The Journal and Major Essays of John
Woolman* (New York, 1971) 32–3. For biographical detail about Woolman see Janet P. Whitney, *John Woolman: American Quaker* (London, 1943).

Negroes but was not sufficiently sure of himself to submit it for publication for another eight years.[9] During this period Woolman not only further extended his knowledge of slavery but formed a lasting friendship with Anthony Benezet, a Quaker schoolmaster in Philadelphia and one like-minded with him, and the two began to raise the question of slavery with leading Friends in the Philadelphia and other Meetings. In both Woolman and Benezet there were ingredients of a more powerful anti-slavery appeal than ever the abrasive Sandiford or Lay could achieve. At one level Benezet shared Woolman's engaging asceticism, manifesting it for instance, in his reaction to a display 'of fine goods and fancy articles' when 'he pleasantly exclaimed . . . "What a number of beautiful things are here which I do not want" '.[10] More fundamental was a Christlike quality in both of them which enabled them to expound their cause without attacking – and alienating – their opponents. Their underlying faith, too, was of a similar cast, as is particularly clear in a passage in a letter from Benezet in which he acknowledged his debt to Woolman, and manifested a common inspiration.

> The world is sinking away from us, and we shall very soon be forgot by its foolish inhabitants. And Oh the advantage, the unexpressible advantage to labour honestly, sincerely and diligently to get rid of selfishness and carnality of every kind. . . . The reading John Woolman's journal gives me a prospect of it. When we honestly labour that our ease, our profit, a name amongst men, even those who are esteemed religious is not suffered to come in competition with the purity of our hearts, the honour of God, and the good of our fellow men, we are in the true track of happiness and holiness. . . . To be rid of all selfishness, of indulgence to our weakness, those plagues of our own heart, to be content to be thought little of, for doing our duty in a steady dependence on the promise 'I will be with thee. I will never leave thee' etc., is indeed the most exalted state a human being can arrive at.[11]

[9] i.e. in 1754 at Philadelphia. A second part of this essay was likewise published in Philadelphia, in 1762.

[10] Deborah Logan to Roberts Vaux, *c.* 1825, in G. S. Brookes, *Friend Anthony Benezet* (London and Philadelphia, 1937) 469.

[11] *Allinson MSS.* (Quaker Collection at Haverford College), Benezet to Samuel Allinson, 14 Dec 1773.

Woolman, in the presentation of his anti-slavery witness, stressed the incompatibility of slavery with the will of God, as revealed, he believed, both in the Old and New Testaments, and at the same time sought to bring home to his readers, by such means as inviting them to imagine a reversal of roles, a sense of horror at slavery. To persist in slave owning or slave trading was therefore self-will, the destruction of peace of mind and happiness. Nor did Woolman spare his hearers and readers from the assurance that judgement must fall on societies which persisted in iniquity.[12]

All was done, however, in a complete absence of rancour and vituperation, and in a community such as was the Society of Friends this, as much as his arguments, was probably the cause of their appeal. The tone of his whole approach is seen in the peroration to the second part of his *Considerations on the Keeping of Negroes* (1762).

Negroes are our Fellow Creatures, and their present Condition amongst us requires our serious Consideration. We know not the Time when those Scales in which Mountains are weighed, may turn. The Parent of Mankind is gracious; his Care is over his smallest Creatures; and a Multitude of men Escape not his Notice. And though many of them are trodden down, and despised, yet he remembers them; He seeth their Afflictions, and looketh upon the spreading, increasing Exaltation of the Oppressor. He turns the Channels of Power, humbles the most haughty People, and gives Deliverance to the Oppressed, at such Periods as are consistent with his infinite Justice and Goodness. And whenever Gain is Preferred to Equity, and wrong Things publicly encouraged, to that Degree that Wickedness takes Root, and spreads wide amongst the Inhabitants of a Country, there is real Cause for Sorrow to all such whose Love to Mankind stands on a true Principle, and who wisely consider the End and Event of Things.[13]

That Woolman should have struck this last note was particularly significant because it chimed in perfectly with the heart-searching that afflicted Pennsylvania Friends in the aftermath of Indian raids

[12] See Woolman, *Journal*, passim, for many such references.

[13] John Woolman, *Considerations on the Keeping of Negroes*, Part II, printed in Moulton, *The Journal and Major Essays of John Woolman*, 237. Part I of the *Considerations* (Philadelphia, 1754) is printed in ibid., 198–209.

in the mid-fifties, and which was to lead them to take upon themselves the rooting out of slavery as part of a more general programme of moral reform.

We have already seen something of the tensions in eighteenth-century Quakerism but an interpretation merely at that level conceals important truths about the Society. As Sydney V. James has ably shown,[14] these tensions were also more complex and were so pronounced as to constitute contradictions. Firstly, by the beginning of the eighteenth century Quakers in most countries had an accepted place in society as a minority sect. With the ending of serious persecution, and, no doubt, with the diminishing fervour which often characterises a movement in the second or third generation, there was a marked weakening in the original concern to publish the truth and a tendency to regress into a simple quietism. Although in Quakerism there was also a concern both to preserve the integrity, harmony and good order of the gathered community *and* a residual concern to propagate truth and institute secular reforms, the first of these predominated to such an extent as to lead to the adoption of 'birthrightism', the practice whereby the children of Friends were near automatically deemed members. Originally conceived out of filial affection, the effect of this custom was both to weight the balance in favour of inward-lookingness and to negate the spontaneity and directness of the classical Quaker concept of the Inner Light. Finally, Quakers retained the belief in temporal catastrophe as the harbinger of upheavals which would lead all men into the possession of Truth – a notion, that is, which in its concept of the flooding in of outsiders into the one true church was in conflict with the idea of the society as a hereditary corporation.

If these contradictions were common to Friends everywhere in the first half of the eighteenth century, Pennsylvania Friends laboured under yet another. In other colonies, as in Europe, Friends accepted a role as a permanent minority group, hoping for toleration from the state: in Pennsylvania, on the other hand, they had come as the founders of a new community which was to be at once a religious and a political community – Penn's 'Holy Experi-

---

[14] James, *People Among Peoples*, passim, and Sydney V. James, 'The Impact of the American Revolution on Quakers' Ideas about their Sect', *William and Mary Quarterly*, 3rd series, xix (1962) 360–65. I do not claim to have followed James in every particular.

ment'. In the event the first utopian hopes had hardly survived
the passing of the seventeenth century, and Friends, as they became more and more of a minority in the community, and less and
less able to command the moral as well as the numerical weight
to implement their policies, increasingly rested their political power
on the shifts and compromises which are the necessary stuff of
politics. In particular, Friends in the provincial assembly compro-
mised their peace testimony by condoning taxation for military
purposes – as long as those military purposes were not flaunted in
their faces. In short the particular situation of Pennsylvania made
the contradictions within Quakerism particularly acute by the
middle of the eighteenth century. No less important, a group of
Friends centring on Israel Pemberton and including Woolman,
Benezet, Samuel Fothergill and John Churchman, saw the incon-
sistencies of their sect's behaviour with its true testimony and were
anxious to root out worldliness and purify the brotherhood.[15]

Before 1755, however, this reform movement had attained
neither coherent purpose nor direction. But in that year a soul-
searching was forced upon Pennsylvania Quakers by a climactic
event, and out of it came both a clear sense of direction and the
means of giving the reform movement a broad base in the Society
generally. The climactic event was Indian raiding, backed by the
French, into the province itself. Appropriately accompanied by
a (minor) earthquake in Philadelphia – earthquakes were of
course an accepted mark of divine displeasure – the whole Quaker
record in Pennsylvania was called into question. Until this time it
had been possible for the more unreflecting Friends to believe that
the province was still a Christian experiment: but now it seemed
both that the peace testimony was no longer the assurance of security from the Indians that it had long appeared to be and that injustice to the Indians had brought its own retribution. The spiritual
and moral crisis also had a political dimension, one which brought
events to a head. This was because the danger in which the colony
stood urgently demanded fresh taxation for fortifications and
troops. What were Friends in the Assembly to do? To turn realist,
vote military expenditure, but deny the peace testimony? Or

[15] James, *People Among Peoples*, 142–3, 152–9; James, 'Quakers' Ideas
about their Sect', 360–66; John J. Zimmerman, 'Benjamin Franklin and
the Quaker Party, 1755–1756', *William and Mary Quarterly*, 3rd series,
XVII (1960) 291–3.

withdraw from the Assembly, remain faithful to the pacifist position but be excluded from public life? After much agonising during and after the 1755 Yearly Meeting, and a walk-out by the compromisers, some twenty members set the tone by signing a declaration that payment of war taxes was unjust. Later, when Quaker lobbying in London had obtained an understanding that if Quaker assemblymen could be persuaded to resign their office the Government would do its best to stop office being permanently closed to them,[16] and when war had been declared on the Delawares, seven Friends, led by James Pemberton, resigned from the Assembly. Others refused to stand again when their terms of office expired: the compromisers remained.

It is clear that associated with the stand against military taxes was a more general moral stand which included condemnation of the treatment of true Quakers, of the Delaware Indians and of Negro slaves by assemblymen and magistrates. But moral protest of this kind, even if informed by the increasingly widely shared conviction that the province's troubles were a judgement not only for its treatment of the Delawares but for its oppression of Negroes also,[17] would have left only a limited mark had it not developed into a reform programme which was to give not only Pennsylvania, but also American Quakerism generally, a new direction and a new role. The first concern of the reformers was to purify the sect itself and, apart from a drive to end slave-holding among Friends, steps were taken at least to minimise the baneful effects of birth-rightism by scrutinising membership rolls more carefully, and to provide better schooling for the children of Friends. But Pennsylvania Friends also needed a role in society at large to replace the formal public role which they had lost and one which could enable them to make a respected contribution to society when they were under attack for a pacifism which seemed to open the frontier to the raiding Indian and even the French grenadier. As a logical development of their conviction that retribution followed

[16] By stopping any attempt to end the privilege of affirmation, on which Friends set such store.

[17] See e.g., Samuel Fothergill's reaction to his visit to Maryland in November 1756; 'Maryland is poor; the gain of oppression, the price of blood is upon that province – I mean their purchasing, and keeping in slavery, Negroes – the ruin of true religion the world over, wherever it prevails' (George Crosfield, *Memoirs of the Life and Gospel Labours of Samuel Fothergill, with Selections from his Correspondence* (New York, 1844) 282.

the commission of evil they entered on courses designed to demonstrate – indeed to cause to happen – the obverse, namely that righteousness exalteth a nation. An area which clearly cried out for the application of righteousness was the Indian problem, and to seek a just solution Friends founded in 1756 the self-explanatory Friendly Association for Regaining and Preserving Peace with the Indians by Pacific Measures. Six years later, if not before, it is clear that the venture had merely entangled Quakers in the same worldliness as that from which they were seeking to extricate themselves. Better success, if undramatic, was achieved with a number of philanthropic activities such as the provision of relief for a group of Acadian deportees from Nova Scotia, the founding of the Philadelphia Bettering House as a relief institution, and the Pennsylvania Hospital. But more important than any of these achievements of the Quaker revival was a determination amongst Pennsylvania Friends, which then spread into other Meetings, to act more effectively against slavery, both within the sect and in the community at large. To this impulse we now turn, for in addition to having important consequences in America this element in the Quaker revival was to play an important part in initiating a campaign against the British slave trade.[18]

The important initial step in the more thoroughgoing attempt to end slave-holding by Quakers was the decision of the Philadelphia Yearly Meeting in 1758 to exclude from participation in the business affairs of the church any Friends who continued to buy or sell slaves and to urge Friends to set at liberty any slaves that they might own. To this end the Meetings accepted the offer of a number of Friends, of whom Woolman was one, to visit all slave-holders within the limits of the Yearly Meeting the better to urge them to manumission. Slowly these approaches bore fruit or, alternatively, slave-owning Friends contributed negatively to purification of their sect by leaving it. In 1776 the Yearly Meeting went the further stage of prescribing disownment for any who still kept slaves and followed this three years later with agreement that proper compensation should be paid to emancipated slaves in respect of the deprivation of liberty which they had suffered.[19]

[18] James, *People Among Peoples*, 163–215; Tolles, *Quakers and the Atlantic Culture*, 88–9.
[19] But Pennsylvania Friends were only completely free of slave-holding after the passage of an emancipation bill in the state legislature in 1780

Other Yearly Meetings followed the Philadelphia pattern. First the question of slave-holding received the 'weighty consideration' of the Meeting; an effort was then made to obtain voluntary manumissions and this was eventually followed by the ultimate Quaker disciplinary power of disownment, and obligatory provision for compensation. The process was most difficult in the south and for obvious reasons – the liberation of eighty slaves is reputed to have cost Robert Pleasants of Virginia £3,000. Here the completion of the process was longer drawn out, but American Friends had substantially freed themselves from the sin of slave-holding by the close of the War of Independence.[20]

No sooner was Quaker participation in slavery and the slave trade ended than American Friends turned their attention to obtaining the end of the import slave trade by legislative action, either by outright prohibition of fresh imports or through the imposition of prohibitively high import duties. From 1772 onwards[21] and, more effectively, after the Revolution, Friends applied strong pressure upon the separate state legislatures and had a part in securing the piecemeal ending of the import slave trade by a majority of states in the twenty years after 1788. Friends also lobbied unsuccessfully in the Constitutional Convention for the immediate prohibition of the import of slaves.[22] Our concern, however, is not with the detail of these attempts, nor even with the already related successes of the American Quaker anti-slavery movement for their own sakes. There was, as we saw earlier, an Atlantic dimension to the Society of Friends, and, important as the American Quaker anti-slavery reform movement is in the history of American anti-slavery achievement, we must now draw out the importance of that movement in spurring British Friends into action against the British slave trade, a trade considerably greater than the American.

For Quakers the essential condemnation of slavery and the slave trade was that they were incompatible with Christian truth,

[20] For delineation of this process see Drake, *Quakers and Slavery*, 60–84, and James, *People Among Peoples*, 216–31.

[21] *Sharp Transcripts* (*J.A.W.*), Granville Sharp's Diary, 3 Jan 1773 ff. passim.

[22] Drake, *Quakers and Slavery*, 85–113.

(*Pennsylvania Abolition Society MSS.*, Am. S.001, Wm J. Brick, *Manuscript History of the Pennsylvania Abolition Society*).

and love, and it was therefore largely in these terms that the original Quaker appeal was made. But even when Friends had their sights firmly set on the purification of their own Society, chance encounters with people outside necessarily made Friends consider the grounds for a wider appeal. Thus when Woolman became involved in discussion with a thoughtful captain of militia on the subject of slavery the Quaker declared to him, not the religious argument that stirred him to the roots of his soul, but the proposition that 'liberty was the natural right of all men equally'.[23] Five years later in 1762 in the second part of *Considerations on the Keeping of Negroes,* Woolman develops a little the theme that 'Liberty is the right of innocent men',[24] though, as one would expect from knowledge of the man, it was the religious argument that predominated. In the thought of the American Quaker revival generally, however, as James has pointed out,[25] increasing recourse was made to natural-rights arguments as a basis for the reform programme, coupled with an appeal to other great concepts of the century, especially benevolence, and the concept of a moral sense. The extent and the limits of this recourse to the favoured ideas of the age is further assessed by James:

Friends did not pioneer in the development of the phrases and ideas of eighteenth-century humanitarian ethics; they adopted them at the same time that many others did. Nor did the Quakers abandon older ideas, practices, and formulations in embracing the new. Their advocacy of ideas of natural liberty in the Revolutionary period and their application of them to the Negroes similarly followed current intellectual fashion. In both instances, using contemporary ideas helped Quakers to express their virtues in ways which could be appreciated by the general public. . . . Humanitarianism among Friends was sincere; but it was not the totality of the religious outlook of their church. It gave them a bond, which they cherished, to the ideas and political conditions surrounding them.[26]

[23] Woolman, *Journal* (Moulton Edition), 61.
[24] Woolman, *Considerations on the Keeping of Negroes, Part II* (Moulton Edition) 236.
[25] James, *People Among Peoples*, 222–5, 321–9.
[26] Ibid., 324. James also quotes an interesting early case of a Friend, Israel Pemberton, the younger, exhibiting 'an impressive array of the common terms of humanitarian morality' in a letter to his brother, John,

No American Quaker of the century gives evidence of wider awareness than Benezet, the man who also took the lead in urging both English Friends and a range of notable Englishmen to act against the British slave trade. It is in his writings that we find a rounded case against slavery, of which the inspiration is Quaker but, being directed to the non-Quaker world, also brings into service the moral philosophy and the sentiments of the age.

Benezet set out to show, as he put it in the opening pages of *A Caution to Great Britain*, that the slave trade was 'inconsistent with the plainest Precepts of the Gospel, the dictates of reason, and every common sentiment of humanity'.[27] The religious ground was simplicity indeed. It rested in the fact that the slaves whom the planter (or slave captain) oppresses 'are undoubtedly his brethren, his neighbours, the children of the same Father, and some of those for whom Christ died, as truly as for the planter himself'.[28] For proof of the religious, but not necessarily Christian, proposition that 'God . . . imposed no involuntary subjection of one man to another' Benezet invoked legal and moral philosophy. 'The truth of this Position has of late been clearly set forth by persons of reputation and ability', the first of whom to be invoked

[27] A. Benezet, *A Caution to Great Britain and her Colonies in a Short Representation of the Calamitous State of the Enslaved Negroes in the British Dominions* (London, 1784) 5. The first edition appeared in 1766.

[28] A. Benezet, *Some Historical Account of Guinea, Its Situation, Produce, and the General Disposition of Its Inhabitants with an Inquiry into the Rise and Progress of the Slave Trade, Its Nature, and Lamentable Effects* (London, 1788); Cass. reissue, 1968) 79. The first edition appeared in 1771.

in 1750. In it Israel praised the 'spirit of universal benevolence to mankind, and the real pleasure arising from our being conscious of this being the spring of our actions, [which] so farr [sic] surpasses any gratification in our common pursuits and engagements that those may truly be called Happy, who devote their time and strength to the discharge of their duties, from this principle' (ibid., 323–4). So rhapsodic a piece as this would surely have delighted Hutcheson and Ferguson, and James' further indication that similar sentiments came subsequently to be more and more in the mouths of Friends raises the interesting question of the reception of European thought of the eighteenth century by American Quakers. Their intellectual awareness is commonly regarded as low, but their familiarity with the fashionable sentiments of the age suggests that, by mid-century, American Quakers were being influenced by European moral philosophy.

is George Wallis [*sic*], *System of the Laws of Scotland*, in which it is shown that governments are instituted for the good and happiness of mankind and cannot dispose of their subjects. 'Besides, no man has a right to acquire or to purchase them; men and their Liberty are not either saleable or purchaseable (so) . . . every one of those unfortunate men, who are pretended to be slaves, has a right to be declared free . . . This', Wallace triumphantly concludes 'is the Law of Nature.' If Wallace was most apt for Benezet's purpose, because most direct, Benezet could also effectively quote from others, as from the anonymous author of a pamphlet *An Essay in Vindication of the Continental Colonies of America* for his assertion 'that the bondage we have imposed on the Africans is absolutely repugnant to justice . . . (and) highly inconsistent with civil policy . . . shocking to humanity, violative of every generous sentiment', quite apart from being 'abhorrent utterly from the Christian religion'. Francis Hutchinson [*sic*], *System of Moral Philosophy*, and 'the noted Baron Montesquieu' are likewise invoked, the latter not as tellingly as he might have been, and, at greater length, the – in that age – probably equally well-known James Foster in his *Discourses on Natural Religion and Social Virtue*. Foster is cited as declaring the slave trade 'to be a criminal and outrageous violation of the natural right of mankind', and is quoted for his (somewhat unhistorical) argument that if the admired Greeks and Romans had traded in their own species they would stand condemned as 'entire Strangers to Virtue an Benevolence'; the slave trade, for Foster, also 'spurns at all the principles both of natural and revealed Religion'.[29]

Benezet confined his recourse to moral philosophy almost entirely to the pages of *A Caution to Great Britain*, but a significant part of the *Historical Account of Guinea* demonstrated how the slave trade was an affront to 'the dictates of reason' in another way. His immediate reason for embarking on what was a novel line of argument was the need which he felt to rebut that defence of the trade which held that it saved the lives 'of . . . captives in war, who would otherwise have been sacrificed to the implacable revenge of their conquerors'.[30] Benezet's method was to give an

---

[29] Benezet, *Caution to Great Britain*, 28–35. Montesquieu, alone of moral and legal philosophers, is also very briefly quoted in the *Historical Account of Guinea*, 62.

[30] Benezet, *Historical Account of Guinea*, xv.

account of the African coast from Senegal to Angola, section by section, and to conclude from

> The most authentic relations of . . . early times, the natives were an inoffensive people, who, when civilly used, traded amicably with the Europeans. . . . And from the same relations there is no reason to think otherwise, but that they generally lived in peace amongst themselves; for I do not find, in the numerous publications I have perused on this subject, relating to these early times, of there being wars on that coast, nor of any sale of captives taken in battle, who would have been otherwise sacrificed by the victors.[31]

The ills of Africa resulted mainly from the advent of the European-directed slave trade, whose horrors, together with the evils of American and Caribbean slavery, Benezet went on amply to demonstrate.

This approach of Benezet was important for a number of reasons. Firstly it was authoritatively carried out, for the author based his work on most of the authorities then available. James Barbot's *Description of Guinea,* William Smith's *Voyage to Guinea,* Francis Moor(e)'s, *Travels into Different Parts of Africa,* Adanson's *A Voyage to Senegal,* William Bosman's, *Description of the Coast of Guinea*, together with Brue, Jobson, Thomas Philips and others via the pages of Astley's and Churchill's *Collection of Voyages,*[32] all were called into service and used in a way that was quite new. The impression was certainly given, just as Benezet undoubtedly believed, that the work of authors for the most part themselves engaged in the slave trade wholly supported Benezet's conclusions. Secondly, the slave trade was shown to be an offence against reason, because it was unjust in the context of African history, and, though this was a line of argument that Benezet did not seriously develop, because a much more profitable trade could be done with Africa if the slave trade were ended. Thirdly, the essential inhumanity of the trade was elaborated. If we broaden

[31] Ibid., 50–51. The ingenious conclusion that there were no wars on the coast before the coming of the Europeans is modified in the author's introduction where he admits that 'wars, arising from the common depravity of human nature, have happened, as well among the Negroes as other nations' (xiv).

[32] The spellings and titles are as Benezet rendered them.

our view to take in the two principal anti-slavery works together
we find yet further importance in Benezet, for, reflecting the
Quaker revival in America, he brings the moral philosophy of the
age, with all its appealing emphasis on liberty, benevolence, happiness, justice, and so forth, to the support of a position reached on
religious grounds,[33] and so makes a more comprehensive and compulsive case to the world at large. Here one may infer the reaction
of readers to have been was an advocate who brought not only
piety, but religion generally, the fruits of recent moral philosophy
and the authority of African voyagers to the support of his case.
Finally, there is a further important note in Benezet's anti-slavery
appeal, the constant striking of which is the index of its importance.
It is this: the slave trade is seen in the context of that providentially
sustained moral order in which not only devout men, but men of
the time generally, believed. Time and time again Benezet returns
to this theme. It is the inhabitants of Christian Europe who have
caused the woes of Africa and perpetrated the cruelties of the
Americas. Theirs is the guilt and not a guilt to be merely noted
and shrugged off, for, quoting Las Casas, 'the blood of *one* man
unjustly shed calls loudly for vengeance'.[34] Richard Baxter, Woolman and others are all invoked to the same purpose of showing that
evil, when persisted in, brings national retribution. Now that the
slave trade for the first time, on such a scale, had been examined
and found wanting by the moral philosophy and the ethnographi-
cal knowledge of the age, as well as by the piety of a few and the
religion of nearly all, the effect of some of Benezet's warnings must
have been distinctly chilling.

Do we indeed believe the truths declared in the Gospel? Are
we persuaded that the threatenings, as well as the promises

[33] Important and original though this marshalling of moral philosophy
was, the choice of quotation, and spelling variations, e.g. Wallis for
Wallace, Hutchinson for Hutcheson, make one doubt that Benezet had
first-hand acquaintance with the authors in question. He may not, in
other words, have been as different from the generality of unlearned
American Friends as the court connections of his French Huguenot
mother, his fluency in French, and the fact that the historian Rapin de
Thoyras was his great-uncle, might suggest. This, however, is not a
necessary conclusion. The biographical section of Brookes, *Friend Anthony
Benezet*, is not informative on Benezet's reading and scholarship, and he
has attracted relatively little biographical attention.

[34] Benezet, *Historical Account of Guinea*, 43.

therein contained, will have their accomplishment? If indeed we do, must we not tremble to think what a load of guilt lies upon our nation generally, and individually so far as we in any degree abet of countenance this aggravated iniquity?[35]

Benezet's development of the anti-slavery case was an outstanding contribution to the Quaker anti-slavery role as a whole. To see how Quaker anti-slavery pressure was brought to bear on the British slave trade we must return to the study of the dialogue within the Anglo-American community and note also an extension of that dialogue which took in a wide variety of other Englishmen opposed to the slave trade. By the time the Quaker reform movement was getting under way in America in the later fifties, the London Yearly Meeting, it will be remembered, had still not made the advice of 1727, that trading in slaves was wrong, a matter of discipline. Save for John Bell's *Epistle* of 1741 to colonial Friends which, as we saw, induced further heart-searching among its recipients, British Friends appear not to have concerned themselves at all with further agitation of the abolition question.[36] This must surely have been largely because a considerable number of Quakers were still involved in the British slave trade. In any event, as of 1756, Dr Gary lists no less than eighty-eight whom she deems to have been engaged in the slave trade in virtue of their membership of the Company of Merchants Trading to Africa.[37] Assuming these men were real Quakers, as distinct from the type of 'wet Quaker', to use the term applied to Philadelphia Quakers

[35] Benezet, *Caution to Great Britain*, 42. See also ibid, 37 and 43–5, and Benezet, *Historical Account of Guinea*, 64 n., 71, 78, 109–10, 115. For an explicit statement of Benezet's underlying notion of national retribution note this passage in his pamphlet *Observations on the Enslaving, Importing and Purchasing of Negroes with some Advice thereon extracted from the Yearly Meeting Epistle of London for the present year* (Germantown, 1759) 3: 'Evils do not arise out of the dust, nor does the Almighty willingly afflict the Children of Men; but when a people offend as a nation, or in a publick capacity, the justice of his moral government requires that as a nation they be punished, which is generally done by War, Famine, or Pestilence.'
[36] There is no reference to the slave trade in this period in *Epistles from the Yearly Meeting of Friends in London to the Quarterly and Monthly Meetings in Great Britain, Ireland and elsewhere from 1675 to 1857 inclusive* (London, 1858). All major concerns of Friends found expression in these epistles. See also *London Yearly Meeting, Meeting for Sufferings Minutes* (Friends House), vol. xxx 95, 15 July 1757.
[37] Gary, 'English and American Quakers', 506.

who went the way of the world at this very period,[38] they were overridden remarkably quickly, once the question again came before the London Yearly Meeting. Come it did at the 1757 Yearly Meeting[39] but who was responsible for raising the matter is not apparent. It may have been the result of an initiative of Samuel Fothergill the English Friend, who at this very time had just returned from a visit to America where he had been much seized with a sense of the iniquity of slavery. He was particularly well connected, being the brother of Dr John Fothergill, a leading Quaker and royal physician, as well as being influential in his own right.[40] Certainly John Fothergill was a member of the committee of the Meeting for Sufferings which was appointed, as a result of the fear expressed at the Yearly Meeting that Friends were still engaged in the slave trade, to look out previous epistles of guidance and circulate them among Friends in Britain and abroad.[41] The committee duly reported that they could find nothing since the advice of 1727, whereupon the Meeting for Sufferings referred the question to the next Yearly Meeting with the recommendation 'to take that practice into their serious consideration'.[42] The result though it still stopped short of disownment, was a strong injunction in the 1758 annual epistle that Friends everywhere 'be careful to avoid being any way concerned in reaping the unrighteous profits arising fom the iniquitous pratice of dealing in Negroes and other slaves'.[43]

The Philadelphia Meeting for Sufferings welcomed this recent London advice,[44] and in 1761, when informing the London Meet-

---

[38] Tolles, *Quakers and the Atlantic Culture*, 89.

[39] *London Yearly Meeting, Minute Book* (Friends House), vol. xi 271, 4 June 1757.

[40] Samuel Fothergill actually attended the 1757 Yearly Meeting (Crosfield, *Memoirs of Samuel Fothergill*, 309.)

[41] *London Yearly Meeting Minutes*, vol. xi 271, 4 June 1757; *London Meeting for Sufferings Minutes*, vol. xxx 86, 17 and 24 June 1757; Drake, *Quakers and Slavery in America*, 60.

[42] *London Meeting for Sufferings Minutes*, vol. xxx 95, 15 July 1757.

[43] *Epistles from the London Yearly Meeting*, i 307–8. The minutes of the 1758 session of the Yearly Meeting contain no indication of any discussion on the question. Gary, 'English and American Quakers', 192–3.

[44] *MS Letters which passed between the Meeting for Sufferings in London and the Meeting for Sufferings in Philadelphia, 1757–1815* (Friends House), Philadelphia to London, 1 Feb 1759. Gary, 'English and American Quakers', 193.

ing of the recent passage in the Pennsylvania Assembly of a law imposing a duty on slaves imported, expressed the hope that 'should attempt be made to obtain a repeal of the law . . . there will be a care and proper concern rest upon some Friends to use their endeavours to prevent it in such manner as the Wisdom of Truth may direct'.[45] Less than two months later the London Yearly Meeting actually took the decisive step of making persistence in slave trading punishable by disownment.[46]

The explanation of the consummation of the step initiated back in 1727 is not entirely clear but all the indications point to the importance of quiet pressure from Philadelphia Friends. Part One of Woolman's *Considerations on the Keeping of Negroes* and the Philadelphia Yearly Meeting's *Epistle of Caution and Advice concerning the Buying and Keeping of Slaves* (1754), which was Woolman's work, had almost certainly been read by a number of English Friends;[47] Samuel Fothergill was only one of many channels by which the rising anti-slavery zeal of American Friends was likely to have been relayed to London; finally, the request of the Philadelphia Meeting for Sufferings that London Friends should lobby against any attempt to disallow the bill levying a tax on slaves imported, can only, in logic, have placed pressure on English Friends to complete the putting of their own house in order.[48] Yet it is still surprising that, if Dr Gary's list of eighty-eight Quakers involved in the slave trade is accurate, and contains for the most part the names of Friends in good standing, the London Meeting should have moved so quickly and apparently effortlessly, once the matter had been raised in 1757. Probably the cause of the rapid – at the last – English Quaker response to American pressure is a compound of Quaker readiness to put principle above interest, once there was a sharp and disseminated sense of what the pursuit of interest involved, and of the fact that the reform

[45] *MS. Letters between London and Philadelphia*, Philadelphia to London, 24 Mar 1761.

[46] *London Yearly Meeting Minutes*, vol. xii 205, 14 May 1761.

[47] Whitney, *Woolman*, 181–2; Drake, *Quakers and Slavery in America*, 56.

[48] The Philadelphia letter of 24 March 1761 may not have reached London in time to be considered at the Yearly Meeting in early and mid-May, but the numerous correspondence between English and American Friends must surely mean that English Friends are likely to have known what they were to be officially asked to do.

movement had spread to English Friends by this time,[49] facilitated by the effects upon the Society of Friends of the Seven Years War. The opposition of English Friends to the war, Dr Gary suggests, in that it led to some persecution, both purged the Society of some of its weaker members and had a refining effect on the Society as a whole.[50]

For the minority sect which the English Quakers were, there was a sense in which their proper duty was now completed. For English Friends it was not a self-evident step that they should now proceed to gird themselves for a general onslaught on the slave trade. Certainly the London Meeting, in the yearly Epistle of 1763, renewed its exhortation to Friends to keep completely clear of the slave trade,[51] apparently without prompting from America, but more extended action by London had to await the slow ferment of ideas implanted by American Friends. It seems to have been Benezet who, in 1763, first sought to draw English Friends along this new course when he wrote to two eminent English Friends, John Fothergill[52] and Joseph Phipps. In his letter to Phipps he requested him to read some recently published pamphlets which he enclosed – they probably included the Second part of Woolman's *Considerations on the Keeping of Negroes* and his own *Short Account of that Part of Africa Inhabited by the Negroes: With Respect to . . . the Manner by which the Slave Trade is Carried on*, both of which had been published in 1762 – for he explained that because of the deep engagement of the British in the slave trade, made worse by the recent acquisition of Senegal, 'a proper check must come from amongst you'. Specifically, Benezet urged that 'if the treatise [he appears to have meant his own] was reprinted amongst you with such amendment as might be thought necessary, and dispersed amongst those in whose power it is to put a restraint upon the trade etc., particularly if our gracious King, his counsellors and each member of both houses of

[49] James, *People Among Peoples*, 379 n.

[50] Gary, 'English and American Quakers', 200.

[51] *Epistles from the London Yearly Meeting*, 1763, i 328. 'We . . . renew our exhortation that Friends everywhere be especially careful to keep their hands clean of giving encouragement, in any shape, to the slave trade, it being evidently destructive to the natural rights of mankind, who are all ransomed by one Saviour'.

[52] *Haverford Quaker MSS.*, File 852. Note appended to Benezet to Joseph Phipps, 28 May 1763 (copy).

Parliament had one put in their hands, might it not with Divine
Assistance answer some good end?'[53] The approach to Phipps and
Fothergill brought no evident response and Benezet himself was
uncertain what could be done when he raised the matter with
David Barclay in 1767.[54] At about that same time, however, John
Fothergill brought to the London Meeting for Sufferings a letter
from the kindred body in Philadelphia suggesting the reprinting
of one of Benezet's pamphlets – apparently his *Observations on the
Enslaving, Importing, and Purchasing of Negroes*. The Meeting
for Sufferings responded by ordering 1,500 copies and arranging
for their distribution to include every member of both Houses of
Parliament.[55]

Not until 1772 did London Friends go beyond propaganda, and
this again was in response to American Quaker initiatives, initially
one by Benezet. Evidently the American Quaker view that the
British slave trade was the principal evil had hardened for Dr
Benjamin Rush, the friend and collaborator of Benezet [though
not a Quaker himself Rush was close to the leading Pennsylvania
Friends and a champion of anti-slavery], wrote to Granville Sharp
in May 1773 that 'nothing of consequence . . . can be done here
till the axe is laid to the root of the African Company'.[56] Starting
in about January of that year Benezet wrote privately to a number
of influential English Friends, amongst whom were John and
Henry Gurney, Thomas Corbyn, John Elliott, Mark Beaufoy,
David Barclay, Thomas Wagstaff and John Fothergill.[57] In his
letters he doubtless put the strictly religious case against the slave

[53] *Haverford Quaker MSS.*, File 852, Benezet to Phipps, 28 May 1763
(copy).

[54] Benezet to David Barclay, 29 Apr 1767, quoted in Gary, 'English
and American Quakers', 194.

[55] *London Meeting for Sufferings Minutes*, vol. xxxiii 68, 22 May 1767 and
69, 29 May 1767. It was reported to the Meeting three years later that
many copies of the tract were still on hand and it was decided that the
Committee on Friends Books should be asked to distribute them amongst
London merchants and elsewhere as they thought fit (ibid., vol. xxxiii
408, 31 Aug 1770. Benezet's, *Caution and Warning to Great Britain* (1766)
was also distributed widely in Britain (Gary, 'English and American
Quakers,' 190).

[56] Rush to Sharp, 1 May 1773, in L. M. Butterfield (ed.), *Letters of
Benjamin Rush* (Princeton, 1951) I 80–81.

[57] Benezet to Franklin, 27 Apr 1772, Brookes, *Friend Anthony Benezet*,
287–90.

trade – including an emphasis on the judgement which must follow if the evil were persisted in – which he put in his long letter to the Gurneys,[58] but he also urged upon his correspondents, as he told Benjamin Franklin, 'whether it might not be the duty of our Friends, either as a body or some particulars joining, to lay the iniquity and dreadful consequence of the slave trade before Parliament, desiring a stop may be put to it'.[59] According to Benezet's subsequent recollection his correspondents, save for Fothergill, did not reply,[60] but they were not allowed to drop the question for in midsummer 1772 John Woolman, with other American Friends, was present at the London Yearly Meeting, having felt a call to visit Friends in England. By this time Woolman was far gone in sartorial singularity stemming mainly from his feeling against dyes, for in the words of a contemporary account, 'His dress was as follows – a white hat, a coarse raw linen shirt, without anything about the neck, his coat, waistcoat and breeches of white coarse woolen cloth with wool buttons on, his coat without cuffs, white yarn stockings, and shoes of uncured leather with bands instead of buckles, so that he was all white'.[61] There was at first almost a revulsion against the presumed oddity of one so quainty attired, but his contribution soon came to be valued. There is no direct evidence that Woolman spoke on the question of the slave trade, but it seems likely that a man so concerned about the slave trade as to dictate during his last illness, less than four months later, a dream about the iniquity of the slave trade, and its interpretation,[62] would have missed this opportunity.

A specific cause in which English Friends were to be asked to exert themselves was soon made known to them – very possibly on Benezet's initiative. Benezet had been arousing opposition to the slave trade in North Carolina and Virginia, amongst other colonies.[63] At the end of July a letter from the Virginia Yearly Meeting was received, requesting that London Friends 'use their

[58] Benezet to John and Henry Gurney, 10 Jan 1772 in ibid. 283–7.

[59] Benezet to Franklin, 27 Apr 1772, in ibid., 287–8.

[60] Benezet to George Dillwyn, n.d. [1783], and Benezet to Fothergill, 28 Apr 1773 in Brookes, *Friend Anthony Benezet*, 302–3 and 324.

[61] Contemporary account quoted in Whitney, *John Woolman*, 370.

[62] Whitney, *John Woolman*, 369–74; Woolman, *Journal* (Moulton ed.), 191–2. Woolman also wrote a pamphlet on the slave trade in the last months of his life (ibid., 20).

[63] Brookes, *Friend Anthony Benezet*, 103.

endeavours with those in authority' in support of an address to
the king by the Virginia House of Assembly requesting an end of
the slave trade.[64] The following February an epistle from the
Yearly Meeting of North and South Carolina was brought to the
London Meeting for Sufferings.[65] After deliberating for some weeks
on the first request a committee of the London Meeting for Sufferings was appointed to look into the matter. Eventually in
February of the following year David Barclay reported 'that the
first Lord of Trade had been waited upon' and that he had expressed the view that the slave trade should be discouraged.[66]
When the Carolinas' submission was received members of the
ad hoc committee applied to 'persons in power on this subject'[67] –
despite the chill intimation given them in their interview the previous months that further action by Friends 'did not appear
necessary',[68] an indication, surely of the difficulties in political
lobbying.

Nothing came of the Virginia petition and further agitation of
the slave trade question was made more difficult by crisis and then
war.

During the War of American Independence Friends suffered
considerable hardship as a result of the fighting, and significant
persecution as a result of their refusal to take sides. Much of the
correspondence between London and Philadelphia Quakers was
consequently taken up with such matters as the relief of distressed
Friends (for which English Friends made generous provision):
but a persistent element in that correspondence is recurring pressure from Philadelphia that English Friends should bestir themselves against the British slave trade. Philadelphia reopened the
question in 1777. Pennsylvania Friends have long been disturbed
by the slave trade and opinion against it is now near universal in
the Yearly Meeting and the cause is gaining ground outside but
'as this crying evil principally originates from the trade carried on
by Great Britain, it is our ardent desire that our brethren there

[64] *London Meeting for Sufferings Minutes*, vol. xxxiii 127–8, 31 July 1772;
Gary, 'English and American Quakers', 221.
[65] *London Meeting for Sufferings Minutes*, vol. xxxiii 221, 12 Feb 1773;
Gary, 'English and American Quakers', 216, 221.
[66] *London Meeting for Sufferings Minutes*, vol. xxxiii 153–4, 25 Sept, and
218, 5 Feb 1773; Gary, 'English and American Quakers', 222.
[67] *London Meeting for Sufferings Minutes*, vol. xxxiii 235, 26 Mar 1773.
[68] Ibid., vol. xxxiii 218, 5 Feb 1773.

may so attend to this important consideration' as to avoid compli-
city in it even of an indirect kind.[69] To this the London Meeting
for Sufferings did not immediately reply but referred the matter
to the next Yearly Meeting – which did nothing. Eighteen months
after the Philadelphia letter, however, London informed Philadelphia that 'few, if any, under our name' gave even indirect
support to the trade but the intimation received from Philadelphia
is being brought to the notice of English Friends.[70] The next year
Philadelphia went a step further, for the Philadelphia Meeting
for Sufferings strongly hinted that English Friends should now
initiate national action against the slave trade. The opening of
the Philadelphia plea surely contains a reproach.

> May a pious solicitude effectually prevail on your side of the
> Atlantic where the desire of gain has very materially streng-
> thened and upheld the cruel traffic. It is indeed a subject highly
> worthy of the serious and deliberate attention of the Rulers in
> your Nation, and now [here the Quaker preoccupation with
> Providence and the moral order asserts itself] when trouble
> and distress so surround that the very foundations of a mighty
> empire appear to be shaken, ought not an enquiry individually
> and as a nation to go forth – Why is it thus with us? Is there not
> a cause?[71]

Nine or ten months after receipt London rather blandly replied
to this letter,[72] and Philadelphia's next went no further than to
observe that it was 'most safe to dwell and move in the fear of the
Lord, rather than suffer the fear of men so to prevail, as, by
temporising, to give any countenance or strength to the iniquity'.[73]
But in August of the following year, 1782, Philadelphia is forthright, encouraged, perhaps, by recent progress on manumissions
in their own province:

> Now as through the favour of divine Providence the Light of
> Truth hath evidently broken forth in many places amongst
> those whom temporal considerations and long accustomed pre-

[69] *MS Letters between London and Philadelphia*, Philadelphia to London, 21 Nov 1777.
[70] Ibid., London to Philadelphia, 2 Apr 1779.
[71] Ibid., Philadelphia to London, 20 and 21 Jan 1780.
[72] Ibid., London to Philadelphia, 29 Dec 1780.
[73] Ibid., Philadelphia to London, 15 Nov 1781.

judices have held in obdurate blindness, and much of the cruel
traffic of enslaving those objects of Christian compassion has
originated, and the trade to the African coast is still supported
by authority on your side, while this continues to be the case,
Great Britain cannot be clear of pollution, the effects whereof
are so justly to be dreaded. We therefore beseech you brethren,
that a consideration of this crying enormity may have such
weight in your minds, as to engage you to embrace all opportunities of promoting the discouragement . . . and . . . gradual
extirpation of this so great, and extensive iniquity.[74]

In the vocabulary of Quaker dialogue a preamble which claimed
that Providence had already begun to make the light of truth
prevail, and a request which 'besought' fellow Friends to take
action could not but be taken seriously. For the first time in nine
years the Meeting for Sufferings went seriously into the matter,
appointing a committee[75] which met many times through the
winter of 1782–83. Then on 4 April 1783 the Meeting both
agreed to 'acknowledge the Christian propriety of your call to us'[76]
and to lay the matter before the next Yearly Meeting.[77] It is clear
that the zeal for reform of a number of American Friends was such
that they resolved to intervene directly in the discussion of the slave
trade question at the London Yearly Meeting in June 1783.[78] The

[74] Ibid., Philadelphia to London, 15 Aug 1782.

[75] *London Meeting for Sufferings Minutes*, vol. xxxvi 317, Nov 1782 et seq.

[76] *MS Letters between London and Philadelphia*, London to Philadelphia,
4 Apr 1783.

[77] *London Meeting for Sufferings Minutes*, vol. xxxvi 385, 4 Apr 1783. See
also ibid., 394–5, 16 May 1783.

[78] The content of, and nuances in, a letter of 19 July from the influential Philadelphia Quaker reformer, James Pemberton, to his brother
John, who had just begun a visit to Britain, are most informative. 'I
expect there are letters now on the way, which when received will give us
the desirable intelligence how you have fared at the late yearly meeting,
and particularly in what manner Friends have been led in the interesting
affair of taking upon them the declaration and furtherance of our testimony against the iniquitous African trade, which we wish may have
impressed them with a sense of the weight and importance it justly requires, so that they may be amenable to a united exertion of their endeavours for the abolition of that inhuman commerce, from whence
immeasurable evils and calamities originated. In our Epistle from our
Meetings for Sufferings on fifth day last in answer to one lately received
from them, a fresh paragraph on this very interesting subject was unitedly

concern with the outcome of the discussion which James Pemberton displayed in a number of letters he wrote in the summer of 1783,[79] Benezet's renewed epistolary offensive at the same time,[80] together with the fact that both were members of the Philadelphia Meeting for Sufferings, indicate that the initiative probably came from them. There is less information, however, on which American Friends attended the London Meeting but John Pemberton certainly, and Nicholas Waln probably, did so. As to what happened there the minutes of that Meeting, and of the Committee for Sufferings at that period, merely tell us that the Yearly Meeting appointed a committee to prepare an address to the king, but that this instruction was then revised, when it was learned that there was at that very time a bill to regulate the African trade before the House of Commons, and the petition addressed to the Commons instead.[81] Behind this bare report, however, lay a debate considerably more impassioned than was common among Friends, as a strongly-worded private letter from David Barclay to his friend and business associate, James Pemberton, makes clear.

> Our yearly meeting being ended . . . I think it not wholly improper to say to thee that I have been not a little pained that it has fallen to my lot to openly dissent from the opinions of thy countrymen, and to express the sentiments of some of our most weighty valuable Friends, and I believe I may mention the names of Isaac Sharples, Thomas Corbyn, Isaac Wilson, William Rathbone, Edmund Gurney with safety, and very many others. I found with concern thy well meaning countrymen are come

[79] See n. 78 above and n. 84 below.

[80] See n. 84 below.

[81] *London Yearly Meeting Minutes*, vol. xvii 281, 13 June 1783, and 298–307, 16 June 1783; *London Meeting for Sufferings Minutes*, vol. xxxvi 408–13, 17 June 1783. The Bill was merely to prevent servants of the Crown engaging in the business of the Royal African Company.

> agreed to, as necessary to encourage their assiduous attention to it; and I wish our American Friends now on that side may be present when it is taken under consideration in order to obviate the objections which temerity and ill grounded fears may suggest in any to impede its progress, and I hope our Friend N. Waln is by this time safely landed and will be strengthened to unite in the service, which I believe he is desirous may be successful having laboured honestly therein here! (*Pemberton MSS* (Pennsylvania Historical Society) vol. xxxix, James Pemberton, Philadelphia, to John Pemberton, 19 July 1783)

here as *Reformers* with an impetuosity that several of our most valuable Friends have termed over driving and are of opinion that the means pursued will defeat the end they wished for.

Barclay goes on to explain that the Americans had raised four contentious points. One was to urge that, contrary to the usual practice of Friends, they should not pay 'mixed' taxes, i.e. taxes of which some part was devoted to military expenditure, another was a reform in order and discipline, both views being pressed from the conviction that 'the present day is more enlightened than those of our ancient Friends'. The remaining two points related to the slave trade, but the reformers had contrived to introduce along the way an attack on no less a Quaker luminary than William Penn himself. 'I have been told,' Barclay related with horror, 'not to quote William Penn because he had dealt or approved the dealing in slaves!' More fundamentally,

> I had a most uncomfortable opposition on the 7th day of our yearly meeting on a proposition of thy countrymen to address the King to *use his influence* with his Parliament to discountenance that trade, and that proposition *stamped so high* by themselves, and some few others, that a committee was appointed to draw up so improper an address, which the King must treat with that mark of disapprobation as to give no answer to it, however he might approve our sentiments, and consequently it would be put into the bag of commonplace petitions, and heard no more of.

Barclay goes on to indicate that his discovery that a bill to regulate the African trade was already before the Commons enabled him to persuade the committee to vary its approach, but ended with the terse observation that he hoped 'Friends will be wise enough to submit with propriety to the powers placed over them or that such as do not approve thereof will leave the country'.[82]

The reason why Barclay, a Quaker with more knowledge of the political world than most Friends,[83] attached more importance to the question of who was to receive the petition was presumably

[82] *Pemberton MSS.*, vol. xxxix, David Barclay to James Pemberton, 2 July 1783.

[83] David Barclay, or his family before him, had received all three Georges at their house in Cheapside (Gary, 'English and American Quakers', 455).

that, in the then state of constitutional evolution, ministers would take amiss a petition to the king as something which might seem to exalt his power. In the event Quaker charity, though evidently under severe strain, held and the London Yearly Meeting, including its more conservative members, not only allowed itself to be carried along by the American reformers but kept doggedly to the new course. Certainly during the summer of 1783 Benezet and Pemberton, and possibly others, saw to it that English Friends should not sink back, by writing to a variety of them, urging persistence in the lobbying of Parliament and on occasion enclosing copies of the anti-slavery books and pamphlets published in the United States and urging that they be republished by the London Meeting for Sufferings.[84]

The London Yearly Meeting set to work with characteristic Quaker thoroughness. An *ad hoc* committee of the Yearly Meeting appears to have drafted the petition to the Commons, but the promotion of the petition was then entrusted to the Meeting for Sufferings, and two groups of Friends added to that Meeting, the one to assist it generally in the matter of agitation against the slave trade, and the other to concern itself specifically with the furthering of the petition.[85] These slightly untidy origins in fact marked the birth of a permanent slave trade Committee of the Meeting for Sufferings. Eventually in mid-June the petition was duly presented and, Barclay reported, was 'very favourably received'.[86] The petition was a plea for the total abolition of the slave trade on the grounds that it was inconsistent not only with Christianity, but also with humanity, justice and the natural rights of mankind generally.[87] Interesting as a demonstration of the

[84] Benezet to George Dillwyn, n.d. (1783) (saying he has written to David Barclay and Thomas Wagstaffe, also Granville Sharp); Benezet to John Gough, 29 May 1783; Benezet to William Dillwyn, 20 Aug 1783, printed on 372–7, 381–4 of Brookes, *Friend Anthony Benezet*; *Pemberton MSS.*, vol. xxxix, James Pemberton to John Pemberton, 19 July 1783; James Pemberton to Daniel Mildred, 21 July 1783; and Benezet to John Pemberton, 10 Aug 1783.

[85] *London Yearly Meeting Minutes*, vol. xvii, 281 13 June 1783 and 298–307, 16 June 1783; *London Meeting for Sufferings Minutes*, vol. xxxvi 408–13, 17 June 1783. The Minute of 20 June in ibid., records a further group of Friends who had been asked to assist in the work.

[86] Ibid., xxxvi 417, 20 June 1783.

[87] The text of the petition is reproduced in ibid., xxxvi 408–13, Minute of 17 June 1783.

readiness of English Quakers to follow American Quaker reformers and invoke the support of natural rights, it had no immediate result. Friends therefore decided to lobby the King and
Queen and ministers of state and to print and distribute copies of
a revised edition of a succinct pamphlet by Benezet, first published
in 1783,[88] *The Case of our Fellow-Creatures the Oppressed
Africans, respectfully recommended to the Serious Consideration
of the Legislature of Great Britain by the People called Quakers.*
The lobbying took the form of the presentation of a copy of the
revised edition of this pamphlet to the King, Queen and Prince of
Wales, through intermediaries, and to leading ministers by a deputation of two members of the slave trade committee.[89] *The Case of
the Oppressed Africans* was forthright in its major premiss that
'the Righteous Judge of the whole earth chastiseth nations for
their sins . . . and can it be expected that he will suffer this great
iniquity to go unpunished' but added to this and the natural rights
plea a brief outline of the argument that abolition would be sound
national policy. However, as the London Meeting for Sufferings
later reported to Philadelphia, 'Our application to Government
only produced an approbation of our benevolence, while but little
prospect appears of success'.[90] The main weight of the committee's
exertions had therefore to be applied to propaganda – but the
effort was impressive. Eleven thousand – possibly more – copies of
The Case of the Oppressed Africans were printed and distributed
not only to members of both Houses of Parliament but to justices
of the peace, clergy, merchants and others.

   A consequence of the sheer need to place the copies in the right

[88] Brookes (*Friend Anthony Benezet*, 197) attributes authorship to Benezet.
The reversed edition was credited with no author as such, but was signed
by John Ady, as clerk to the London Yearly Meeting.

[89] Ibid., vol. xxxvii 51–3. The ministers waited on were Lord Thurlow,
Earl Mansfield, Earl Gower, William Pitt, Lord Howe, Lord Carmarthen,
Lord Sydney and Speaker Cornwall.

[90] *MS. Letters between London and Philadelphia*, London to Philadelphia,
3 Nov 1786. Ministers were reported as declaring 'their hearty concur-
rence with our society in thus liberally taking the part we have done, but
thought the time was not yet come to bring the affair to maturity, which
they nevertheless wished and are ready to promote it, when opportunity
offers' (*London Meeting for Sufferings Minutes*, vol. xxxvii 51–3, 28 May
1784). This may seem merely a devastatingly urbane *non possumus* but it
must be remembered that Pitt came quite soon to give the abolition cause
his warm support.

hands was the creation of a network of Quaker correspondents in the provinces – some 150 had been named by December 1784 – and in this way propaganda led to the foundation of an embryonic national organisation.[91] One sally was to discover from American Friends 'a few well authenticated facts of the benefit of manumission' with a view to persuading 'the uninfluenced part of the public' of the advantages of abolition.[92] This produced few conclusive cases, but it did produce at least one interesting testimony to Negro intelligence, namely the achievements of one Thomas Fuller, a slave of about seventy who could neither read nor write. But 'upon being asked how many seconds a man has lived, who is 70 years, 17 days and 12 hours old, he answered, in a minute and a half, 2,210,500,800'. One of the two men interviewing him then told Fuller his anwer was too large, but he broke in with 'Stop Massa, you forget de leap year'. Fuller clearly had the best of the encounter in every way for when one interviewer observed to the other that it was a pity the Negro had received no education, he interposed 'No Massa, it is best I got no learning, for many learned men be great fools'.[93]

In March 1787 the Meeting for Sufferings accepted the recommendation of the committee on the slave trade to make another application to Parliament,[94] but before anything could come of this an important watershed in the anti-slavery movement was reached. On 19 May the devoted abolitionist William Dillwyn entered in his diary: 'Went to town on my mare to attend a committee of the Slave Trade now instituted.'[95] He was in fact going to a meeting of what was to come to be known as the London

---

[91] *London Meeting for Sufferings Minutes*, vol. xxxvii passim, especially p. 65, 18 June 1784 and pp. 91–3, 27 Aug 1784; *London Meeting for Sufferings Committee on the Slave Trade, Minute Book, 1783–1792*, Minute of 28 Dec 1784, and list of recipients of *The Case of the Oppressed Africans* at end.

[92] *MS. Letters between London and Philadelphia*, London to Philadelphia, 3 Nov 1786. *London Meeting for Sufferings Minutes*, vol. xxxvii 225, 7 Oct 1785.

[93] *Pennsylvania Abolition Society MSS. Am.* S.01, Minutes of 19 Jan 1789 containing text of letter of 12 Nov 1788 to London Abolition Society. For subsequent co-operation between British and American Abolitionists see Betty Fladeland, *Men and Brothers* (Urbana and London, 1972) 144–79.

[94] *London Meetings for Sufferings Minutes*, vol. xxxvii 379–80, 2 Mar 1787.

[95] *Calendar of the Diaries of William Dillwyn*, vol. ii, 19 May 1787.

Abolition Committee, a non-sectarian and important abolitionist pressure group. Although the Meeting for Sufferings – and its slave trade committee until 1792 – still concerned themselves with the slave trade, though on a declining scale, and although nearly all the new committee's founder members were Friends,[96] the epoch when agitation against the slave trade had been exclusively a Quaker preserve had passed. With 1787 a national movement began.

Close examination of the relations between English and American Friends over the anti-slavery question therefore abundantly confirms Rufus Jones' more instinctive judgement that English Friends 'were stirred to greater action by sensitive American Friends who visited them, or who reached them through direct correspondence, or through Yearly Meeting Epistles'.[97] Aware of the evil of slavery and the slave trade because more directly confronted with them, the concern of American Friends to lead their English brethren to a similar concern clearly owed much to the inspiration of the Quaker Reform Movement. The pressure of American Friends was clearly evident in 1761, in 1772 and in 1783–84 – all three of the occasions in the later eighteenth century when English Friends took a new initiative in the matter of the abolition. No less important a fruit of American Quaker zeal against the slave trade were the arguments developed by Woolman and especially Benezet. To the orginal Quaker position, based on the simple logic of love, was added the assertion of natural right and the sanction which resulted from bringing slavery and the slave trade within the orbit of providentially sustained retributory justice. And to complete this broader appeal the manner in which Benezet used ethnography was such as to evoke response in an age susceptible to the ideal of the noble savage. Benezet's writings had two particunlarly important effects. John Wesley's pamphlet, *Thoughts on*

---

[96] *B.M. Add. MSS. 21254*, Minute of 22 May 1787. The original meeting is here described as taking place on the 22nd. Dillwyn's diary is quite clear, however, and perhaps the discrepancy lies in the fact that Sharp attended for the first time on the 22nd (as Dillwyn himself noted).

[97] Rufus Jones, *Later Periods of Quakerism*, I 320. For a valuable study of this question see Michael Kraus, 'Slavery Reform in the Eighteenth Century: An Aspect of Transatlantic Intellectual Co-operation', *Pennsylvania Magazine of History and Biography*, LX (1936) 53–66 (or alternatively the second part of Chapter vi of Kraus, *The Atlantic Civilisation (Eighteenth Century Origins)*.

Slavery (1774), was inspired by a reading of Benezet's *Historical Account of Guinea* whose text it closely follows in places.[98] And it was of no little importance that a man of Wesley's standing and influence should come out with a trumpet blast against, as he termed it, 'that execrable sum of all villainees, commonly called the slave trade'. Even more important was the influence of the *Historical Account of Guinea* on Thomas Clarkson. When preparing his Cambridge prize essay on the question of the morality of enslavement he found himself very short of material until he accidentally noticed a newspaper advertisement for the book. So important was this discovery that Clarkson 'to lose no time, hastened to London to buy it' and in the reading of it, or of the authors to whom Benezet led him, he became so oppressed by the slave trade that his essay 'became now not so much a trial for academical reputation, as for the production of a work, which might be useful to injured Africa'.[99]

By 1787, then, English Quakerism had emerged as a sect with a clear testimony against the slave trade. We have earlier noticed the dynamic implications of the creed of another religious party, the Evangelicals. As we shall see, the co-operation of Quakers and Evangelicals in the campaign against the slave trade was of critical importance, and is the more easily understood when we realise the nature of their theological relationship. As Dr Frank Baker has shown, there was a blend of attraction and repulsion in the relations between Methodists (the Evangelicals with whom Quakers had most to do) and Quakers. John Wesley accepted what he termed the 'main principle' of Friends, that men are led by the Spirit to worship God in spirit and in truth. He also had a tremendous admiration for Quakers like William Edmundson,[100] whilst there was much common ground in the debt which Friends and Methodists, like Evangelicals generally, owed to mystics like Madame de la Motte Guyon,[101] Fénelon and William Law. Of course there were differences: Wesley had qualifications about

---

[98] Brookes, *Friend Anthony Benezet*, 84–6; Wesley, *Works*, xi 59–79.

[99] Clarkson, *History of the Abolition of the Slave Trade*, i 207–9.

[100] Frank Baker, *The Relations between the Society of Friends and Early Methodism* (London, 1949; reprinted from the *London Quarterly and Holborn Review*), 4–11 passim; Jones, *Later Periods of Quakerism*, i 269–70.

[101] A large number of the so-called Olney hymns of the Evangelical poet, William Cowper, are translations from Madame Guyon.

Robert Barclay's view of justification and declared Barclay's influential *Apology* to be but a 'solemn trifle,'[102] whilst there are clear limits to a harmony between a movement 'born in song' and one which, to adapt F. B. Tolles' phrase, demanded that its members be born tone-deaf. But even the occasions of difference could bring a moving together. A noted instance of this was Mary Dudley's forsaking of Methodism for Quakerism despite Wesley's strong attempts to keep her in the fold: but although drawn by the mystical approach to worship in Quakerism, Mary Dudley had such an evangelical passion that her ministry, joined to that of ministers like Rebecca Jones, who laboured in America, and who had had a similar spiritual pilgrimage, brought Quakerism closer to Evangelicalism by making it more Evangelical.[103]

Rufus Jones discerns two dominant tendencies in Quakerism between 1775 and 1825, 'a clearly marked tendency to mould and formulate Quaker thought in the direction of Evangelical doctrine', and, at the same period, a strong current towards 'an excessive reaffirmation and reinterpretation of the principle of inward Light as the sole and sufficient basis of religion and thus in a somewhat anti-Evangelical direction'.[104] But just because of the mystical heritage common both to Quakers and Evangelicals even the second tendency was still within the mental and theological conspectus of Evangelicals, whilst the first tendency produced a clear rapprochment. Thus we can conclude that the two dominant developments in Quakerism were such as either not greatly to impede a movement towards Evangelicalism, or positively to bring it on. The upshot, in Frank Baker's words, was that the last quarter of the eighteenth century witnessed 'the beginnings of a profound spiritual transformation, when a large proportion of the Friends were carried over from a mystical to an evangelical basis', one formulated by William Tuke in *The Faith of the People called*

---

[102] Baker, *Friends and Early Methodism*, 10–11; Jones, *Later Periods of Quakerism*, I 269. Jones saw Wesley as 'firmly opposed to the main tenets of Quakerism' but Baker's more thorough study of this point stresses the important extent of the common ground between Wesley and Quakerism.

[103] Ibid., I 277–87. For an example of a marked Evangelical quality in a leading Quaker minister of the time see Jonathan Evans (ed.) *Journal of the Life, Travels and Religious Labours of William Savery* (London, 1844).

[104] Jones, *Later Periods of Quakerism*, I 275. A third, and much more limited tendency, was towards rationalism.

Quakers in our Lord and Saviour Jesus Christ, and *Principles of Religion, as professed by the Society of Christians, usually called Quakers,* as early as 1801 and 1805 respectively.[105]

Nor was this the extent of the important degree of theological consanguinity between Quakers and Evangelicals. Just as Evangelicals surmounted the problem of the absence of a clear, specific and universal prohibition of slavery in Scripture by appeal to the law of love, the Golden Rule, so Quakers had earlier, if undramatically, achieved the same breakthrough. A Woolman might attempt a scriptural justification of anti-slavery but the heart of the Quaker appeal is found, for instance, in the religious argument (the only religious argument, one should note) that Benezet uses in so central an anti-slavery tract as his *Historical Account of Guinea.* Speaking of the West Indian planter and his treatment of slaves, he asks rhetorically: 'Can we restrain our just indignation, when we consider that they [slaves] are undoubtedly *his brother! his neighbours! the children of the same Father, and some of these for whom Christ died, as truly as for the planter himself.* Let the opulent planter, or merchant, prove that the Negro Slave is not his brother, or that he is not his neighbour, in the scripture sense of these appellations.'[106]

There were thus abundant grounds for Quaker and Evangelical co-operation in realising the abolitionist tendencies of eighteenth-century moral philosophy. Their role was indeed central in the inspiration and conduct of a political campaign against the slave trade.

[105] Baker, *Friends and Early Methodism,* 23; Jones, *Later Periods of Quakerism,* 285.

[106] Benezet, *Historical Account of Guinea,* 79.

PART FOUR

PART FOUR

10 The Transition to Political Agitation

It was the aim of the second section of this book to argue that by the 1770s the content of received wisdom had so changed that educated men in Britain, including the political nation, were likely to regard slavery as morally and philosophically condemned. What one must now again emphasise is that the issue was not one which men judged solely by theoretical criteria. For a few, but only for a few, direct, personal interest was involved: for the wider number it was rather that the national interest had to be kept in view. Men in this category were disposed to support abolition but needed, first, to be assured that the national interest would not be harmed by it, or at any rate not seriously harmed. None of these mundane considerations affected the minority, made up of Quakers, Evangelicals, other radical Christians and most political radicals who were active abolitionists on principle. We have already considered the dynamic quality of Evangelicalism and Quakerism. But how was this dynamism transposed into a national campaign for abolition? That is the concern of the present chapter, whilst in subsequent chapters we shall ask how the abolition campaign impinged on the political process, why the campaign was for so long unsuccessful, and why it eventually carried the day.

It was Benezet who made the first calculated attempt to encourage action against the slave trade by non-Quakers. Some time between 1758 and 1768 he solicited the support of the Archbishop of Canterbury,[1] and in 1767 of the Society for the Propagation of the Gospel (S.P.G.).[2] More fruitful was the approach Benezet made to the founder of Methodism. By May 1772 Benezet could

[1] Benezet to Thomas Secker, n.d., in Brookes, *Friend Anthony Benezet*, 273–4.
[2] Benezet to S. P. G., 26 Apr 1767 in ibid., 272–3.

refer to 'my friend John Westly' and it was as a result of Benezet's approach, as it was certainly informed by Benezet's writings and sources, that Wesley produced his important pamphlet, *Thoughts on Slavery* (1774). Wesley had read *Oronooko* in 1726 or 1727 but his feelings against slavery were only aroused with the perusal of Benezet from 1772 on.[3] Over the last two decades of his life Wesley maintained his witness against slavery. We find him, in 1774, bringing up to Benezet the case of the kidnapping of a number of Negroes at Old Calabar 'by order of one Captain Bevan of London'.[4] But the chief significance of Wesley's stand was that he preached and wrote against slavery. In 1788 he preached a sermon at Bristol fiercely denouncing the slave trade. The strength of that denunciation may be gauged from the much more widely influential *Thoughts on Slavery*.

'I would to God it [the slave trade] may never be found more: that we may never more steal and sell our brethren like beasts; never murder them by thousands. Oh, may this worse than Mohammedan, worse than pagan abomination be removed from us for ever. Never was anything such a reproach to England, since it was a nation, as the having a hand in this infernal traffic.[5]

When the Abolition Committee came to be formed in 1787 Wesley lent it all support[6] and it is significant that his last, or one of his last letters was one of encouragement to Wilberforce in his parliamentary campaign.[7] Considerable importance lay in the fact that

[3] 'Sometime ago the Rev^d Mr. Westley [sic] signified to me by letter, that he had a desire to write against the Slave Trade; in consequence of which I furnished him with a large bundle of Books and Papers on the Subject; and a few days ago he sent me his Manuscript to peruse; which is *well drawn up*, and he has reduced the substance of the Argument respecting the gross iniquity of that Trade, into a very small Compass: *his Evidence*, however, seems chiefly extracted from the Authors quoted in your several publications' (*Sharp Transcripts (J.A.W.)*, Sharp to Benezet, 7 Jan 1774). V. H. H. Green, *John Wesley* (London, 1964) 156. Wesley's Journal, 12 Feb 1772, *Works*, III 453.

[4] *Sharp Transcripts (J.A.W.)*, Benezet to Granville Sharp, 18 Nov 1774.

[5] Quoted in Green, *Wesley*, 156.

[6] Clarkson, *History*, I 446–8, 451–2; Prince Hoare, *Life of Granville Sharp* (London, 1828) II 229.

[7] As Robert and Samuel Wilberforce put it, their father 'received an

Wesley 'was the earliest religious leader of the first rank to join the protest against slavery'.[8]

The relevance of Burke's writings for anti-slavery thought we have already seen but the direction of his attention specially to Negro slavery as a subject for political action appears to have been another fruit of Benezet's approaches. In June 1772 Benezet drew the attention of a notable Irish Friend, Richard Shackleton, to the iniquity of the slave trade and especially because 'our dear friend Samuel Neale . . . tells me that thou art closely connected with a person of judgement and weight in the English Parliament, who may be a good instrument in forwarding an inquiry into this potent evil'.[9] Certainly from 1772 Burke began to interest himself in the anti-slavery cause[10] and, as we have seen,[11] drafted a scheme for gradual emancipation. He was deterred from proceeding further, however, 'from the conviction that the strength of the West India body would defeat the utmost efforts of his powerful party, and cover them with ruinous unpopularity'.[12]

[8] *D.N.B.*
[9] Benezet to Richard Shackleton, 6 June 1772 in Brookes, *Friend Anthony Benezet*, 293–6.
[10] Jones, *Later Periods of Quakerism*, I 319.
[11] See p. 108 above.
[12] *Life of Wilberforce*, I 152.

---

animating charge traced upon the bed of death by the faltering hand of the venerable Wesley'.

Feb. 24 1791.

My dear Sir,

Unless the Divine power has raised you up to be as Athanasius contra mundum, I see not how you can go through your glorious enterprise, in opposing that execrable villainy which is the scandal of religion, of England, and of human nature. Unless God has raised you up for this very thing, you will be worn out by the opposition of men and devils; but if God be for you who can be against you. Are all of them together stronger than God? Oh be not weary of well-doing. Go on in the name of God, and in the power of His might, till even American slavery, the vilest that ever saw the sun, shall vanish away before it. That He who has guided you from your youth up may continue so to strengthen you in this and all things is the prayer of,

Dear Sir,
Your affectionate servant,
JOHN WESLEY

(R. I. and S. Wilberforce, *The Life of William Wilberforce* (London, 1838) I 297.)

A third Englishman approached by Benezet had a most marked propensity for being deterred by nothing. This was Granville Sharp who had, of course, already entered the lists against slavery and the slave trade, but had his resolution 'confirmed and enlarged', as Prince Hoare, his biographer, put it, by the correspondence with Benezet.[13] It is entirely proper that Sharp should have had a virtually important role as a 'linkman' in the earlier stages of the political campaign for abolition for he was a 'link man' in the different sense that so many of the religious and philosophical inspirations of anti-slavery came together in him. Liberty, as Prince Hoare rightly said, was his subject's 'darling object'[14] but Sharp's basis for this golden principle, as set out in *The Law of Liberty, or Royal Law* (1776) was scriptural and not philosophical. Sharp's passion for liberty involved him in strong support for the American cause,[15] in strict resistance to the practice of impressment which the conduct of the War of Independence brought with it,[16] in a leading role in the Association Movement[17] and in advocacy of parliamentary reform. Given a feeling for liberty and reform so strong that he believed 'God's last kingdom on earth will be Democracy or popular power',[18] Sharp nevertheless saw Negro slavery as infinitely worse than any domestic evil. Advocates of the slave trade, he complained to Beilby Porteus, Bishop of London,

> are continually vaunting the superior condition of the colonial slaves to that of the *labouring Poor* in England! But the comparison is as unjust as it is odious, because the English labourer

[13] Hoare, *Life of Sharp*, I 172. On Benezet's introduction, Benjamin Rush of Philadelphia also engaged in correspondence with Sharp, on slavery and other questions, from 1773 onwards (see John A. Woods, 'The Correspondence of Benjamin Rush and Granville Sharp, 1773–1805', *Journal of American Studies*, I, no. 1, 1–38).

[14] Hoare, *Life of Sharp*, II 384.

[15] Hoare, *Life of Sharp*, passim. It was to support colonial claims that Sharp wrote, *A Declaration of the People's Natural Right to a Share in the Legislature* (London, 1774).

[16] Hoare, *Life of Sharp*, I 239–55.

[17] Sir George Onesiphirus Paul believed that Sharp's extremism was one cause of the decline of the Association Movement in 1781–82 (E. C. Black, *The Association: British Extra-Parliamentary Political Organisation, 1769–1793* (Cambridge, Mass., 1963) 83.

[18] *Sharp Transcripts (J.A.W.)* 'Remarks on the Answer of a learned Writer to Mr. King's "Signs of the Times",' 1799.

is protected at least from all personal ill usage and outrage by equal laws, and when the scanty pittance of wages (though not half that is due from his Employers) is [insufficient?], he is entitled to demand some additional support for his Family from the parish where he lives.[19]

Benevolence, again from a Christian inspiration, had an exceptionally positive meaning for Sharp. As he once expressed it:

> The same benevolent principles – viz. *universal love and charity* – founded on the great commandment, 'Thou shalt love thy neighbour as thyself' which obliges the true Christian most disinterestedly to forgive all personal injuries, and pass over every affront offered to his own person, will necessarily engage him, on the other hand, as disinterestedly to oppose every degree of oppression and injustice which affects his brethren and neighbours, when he has a fair opportunity of asserting them.[20]

We have also seen that Sharp had a particularly emphatic sense of a providential system of government – indeed, that he had himself contributed to the heightening of that concept. He was also, as behoved an adoptive member of the Clapham Sect, devout. On rising, we are told, 'his first employment was either reading the Holy Scriptures or chanting a portion of the Hebrew Psalms to his harp'.[21] The harp – a traverse harp which Sharp had built himself – might be a devotional vehicle but it was no less to be played for enjoyment in the Sharp family orchestra. Instrumental music was matter for some suspicion amongst both Quakers and Evangelicals, but for the Sharps, whether in one of the family houses in London, or slowly navigating up and down the Thames in the *Appollo* or *Union,* two of the family fleet of small vessels, and entertaining on board even royalty itself, it was sheer delight. Nor did Granville Sharp seem to agonise over his spiritual condition in quite the same way as other Claphamites. He was also, as has already been indicated, politically more radical than almost any of the Evangelicals. Personally Sharp was a

---

[19] *Sharp Transcripts* (*J.A.W.*), Granville Sharp to Bishop of London, 14 Jan 1795. Sharp went on to say that it was none the less very unjust that the industrious man should, by becoming a pauper, lose his elective right as a householder.

[20] Quoted in Hoare, *Life of Sharp*, II, p. 382.

[21] Hoare, *Life of Sharp*, II 292.

delightful man. Certainly he had 'a settled conviction of the wickedness of our race' but this was 'tempered by an infantile credulity in the virtue in each separate member of it'.[22] surely an amiable contradiction. A mild eccentricity characterised Sharp – as, for instance, in his proposal 'at once to diminish the waste of human life in the Peninsula [campaign] and to aide the depressed workmen in England'. The manufacture of 'portable woolpacks' was Sharp's remedy. Evident enough as a mode of reducing unemployment, we must have recourse to Sir James Stephen's rotund but teasing phrase to discover the more humane function of this strange device: 'under the shelter of [these] ever-ready intrenchments' we are told 'our troops might without the least danger to themselves, mow down the ranks of the oppressors of Spain'.[23] Sharp also argues tirelsssly for the revival of King Alfred's frank pledge as the healing salve for all social and political wounds, be it in America, England or Sierra Leone. But if Sharp was eccentric, his very persistence was a primary cause of his success as an abolitionist.

Sharp's original involvement in the slavery question was, of course, in respect of slaves in England – and was accidental in its origins. Beginning in 1765 with the chance discovery of a Negro, Jonathan Strong, waiting at the door of brother William Sharp's house for medical attention for some savage wounds inflicted by his West Indian master, Sharp sought in this and other cases over the next seven years to prevent various West Indians from forcibly removing their slaves from England. In the famed climax, the case of the slave James Somerset in 1772, the point of law resolved dealt with the right of a master forcibly to remove his slave out of the country; what Lord Chief Justice Mansfield ruled was that there was no such right. His decision was therefore less than that prohibition of slavery on English soil which it is commonly believed to have been: it none the less, not least through misunderstandings in the courts themselves, opened the way for the quite rapid demise of slavery in England.[24] In any event the victories

[22] Sir J. Stephen, *Ecclesiastical Biography*, II 312.
[23] Ibid., II 320.
[24] James Walvin, *Black and White: The Negro and English Society, 1555–1945* (London, 1973) 117–31. I am also indebted to David B. Davis' chapter, 'Anti-Slavery and the Conflict of Laws', in his forthcoming *The Problem of Slavery in the Age of Revolution, 1770–1823*. In this chapter will

in the various cases, and above all in the Somerset case, were an outstanding achievement, for Sharp had to devote himself to intensive legal study in order to justify his conviction that accepted legal opinion on the legality of Negro slavery in England was wrong. The achievement is the more credible when one recalls that Sharp had earlier mastered Greek and Hebrew, respectively, in order to counter a Socinian and a Jew in theological debate, and had, as an apprentice, so worked up the claim of one of his masters, Mr Willoughby, to a barony as to propel him into the House of Lords as Lord Willoughby de Parham.[25] To take an accepted legal opinion and win, and in a matter widely recognised to be of great significance was a spectacular achievement and one which brought Sharp national renown.

Collaboration between Sharp and Benezet took the form of the exchange of some of their writings[26] whilst Sharp lent his support to an early attempt, inspired by American Quakers, to obtain action against the American import slave trade – both by petitioning the King that it be disallowed and by persuading colonial legislatives to impose prohibitive import duties on slaves imported.[27] Sharp's role in this was to urge upon Lord Dartmouth, the Evangelical Secretary of State, a favourable response by the Privy Council to these colonial initiatives.[28] Dartmouth was personally sympathetic but Sharp attributed delay in London to 'the opposition of persons interested in the African Trade, whose extraordinary influence on Administration astonishes me'.[29] No result seems to have come from these moves, and the question of securing Privy Council approval was rendered irrelevant by the outbreak of the Revolutionary War in 1776.

An overlooked initiative by Sharp was his attempt to draw attention to the iniquity of the slave trade, and even to have it

---

[25] See Hoare, *Life of Sharp*, i, 43–139.

[26] See p. 242 above.

[27] Benezet to Sharp, 14 May 1772, and Sharp to Benezet, 21 Aug 1772 in Brookes, *Friend Anthony Benezet*, 290–93, 418–22.

[28] *Sharp Transcripts (J.A.W.)*, Granville Sharp Diary, 1773, n.d., 25 Mar 1773, 7 June 1773, 7 Jan 1774; Granville Sharp to Benezet, 7 Jan 1774.

[29] Ibid., Sharp to Benezet, 7 Jan 1774.

---

be found the most thorough examination of the complex issues raised in the Somerset and preceding cases.

stopped, by getting the issue raised in a House of Commons Committee appointed in 1779 to examine into the British African trade. To do this, Sharp built upon his growing acquaintance with the bench of bishops – he had sent them copies of *The Law of Retribution* two years previously. During the spring of the year Sharp canvassed twenty-two out of the twenty-six bishops and archbishops and with promising results: 'Both the Archbishops, and the Bishops of Durham, London, Oxford, Litchfield, Bristol, Norwich, Llandaff, Ely, Bangor, Worcester, St Asaph and Lincoln expressed themselves very handsomely on the occasion, and seemed very desirous of putting a stop to the evil.' The Bishops of St Davids and Peterborough, Sharp added, were particularly earnest about the matter. Here indeed was an impressive and enthusiastic phalanx which 'gave me reason to hope that they would publicly oppose any further encouragement of the Slave Trade, had it come before them in the House of Lords', but this not unimportant episcopal condemnation could not be uttered for whilst the Committee was considering the slave trade question, news was received of 'the capture of our African settlements [and] the Committee, it seems, had directions from the Ministry not to proceed in their report'.[30]

In the spring of 1783 Sharp unsuccessfully attempted to prosecute in the Court of Admiralty those responsible for throwing overboard slaves from the slaver *Zong* but he would only seem to have taken any further significant action in regard to abolition by becoming chairman of the Abolition Committee when it was brought to birth out of the womb of the Meeting for Sufferings of the London Quakers in 1787. On first appearances the terms on which Sharp became chairman meant, paradoxically, that he was less active in the abolition cause than before, for as he tells us:

[30] Hoare, *Life of Sharp* i, 275–8. 'Sharp enjoyed close relations with at least two of the bishops. On 25 May 1781 he recorded in his diary: 'Bishop of Peterborough called twice to Day when I was from home and left a Note desiring me to spend a few Days with him at Cambridge – and also a Proposal in writing relating to West India Slavery on which he desired my opinion'. And on 17 Dec Sharp recorded: 'In the Park I was accosted by the Bishop of Chester . . . Had much talk with the Bishop . . . as also on the Slave Trade.' (*Sharp Transcriptions* (*J.A.W.*), Diary.) As will subsequently be seen, the majority of bishops were always ready to support abolition, but they mostly waited to be mobilised.

The Committee of Gentlemen associated for the abolition of the Slave Trade have thought proper to choose me their Chairman, and much business has *been done in my name,* tho' I have never yet been in the Chair, nor attended the Meetings, but have only signed the letters that have been sent to me: for I previously told the Gentlemen that it would be impossible for me to undertake any additional trouble; and they answered, that they would only desire the use of my name and signature, and would among themselves in rotation undertake to write all the Letters; and they gave me a reason which was excellent considering from whom it came, *being chiefly Quakers.* They wished to write in the *ordinary style,* and to lay aside every peculiarity which might seem to belong to a particular Sect; for they hoped to have the Society consist of all denominations of Christians; and therefore they would write the Letters just as if they were formed by myself; this is a great concession![31]

It was nevertheless of great significance that Sharp became chairman of the Committee and in practice he relented and became very active in the Committee's work. No others at that time could have brought such lustre to the anti-slavery cause in Britain, such was his achieved reputation. In addition to Sharp and the Quaker contingent, the enlarged Abolition Committee included from the beginning another recruit of great future importance – Thomas Clarkson.

Clarkson's involvement in the abolition was the result of a conjunction of influences. As a recent Cambridge graduate (he was a Johnian) he sought, in the ordinary way of scholarly attainment, an essay prize on the subject of 'Is it right to make slaves of others against their will?' The subject had been set by the vice-chancellor, Dr Peckard, who had long been a warm advocate of civil and religious liberty and who had preached a university sermon against the slave trade in 1784. In it liberty as a natural right and the prospect of providential justice upon such iniquity were equally invoked. However, the young Clarkson conceived the essay subject as pointing directly to the African slave trade 'and more particularly as I knew that Dr Peckard, in the sermon which I have mentioned, had pronounced so warmly

[31] *Sharp Transcripts (J.A.W.),* Granville Sharp to Rev. Dr. Sharp, 3 Nov 1787.

against it'.[32] But Clarkson found himself confronted with a dearth of material which various contacts could not wholly supply. Rescue came from a source whose ubiquity we have already noticed.

> I still felt myself at a loss for materials, and I did not know where to get them; when going by accident into a friend's house, I took up a newspaper then lying on his table. One of the articles, which attracted my notice, was an advertisement of Anthony Benezet's *Historical Account of Guinea*. I soon left my friend and his paper, and, to lose no time, hastened to London to buy it. In this precious book I found almost all I wanted. I obtained by means of it, a knowledge of, and gained access to the great authorities. . . .[33]

But with the reading of Benezet and the sources to which that led, Clarkson became emotionally involved, became oppressed with the enormity of the slave trade. As a first step, and after winning the first prize for his essay, Clarkson resolved to translate his essay from the Latin and to publish it in expanded form. When seeking a suitable publisher he accidentally encountered James Phillips, a member of the London Quaker Abolition Committee, and a publisher. This secured for Clarkson not only his immediate object, but an introduction to other Friends, especially William Dillwyn – who in his person epitomised Anglo-American Quaker abolitionism – and to Granville Sharp and the Rev. James Ramsay. Ramsay was a force in the dissemination of abolitionist sentiments in his own right. He had conceived an hostility to slavery, as an affront to humanity and as inhibiting missionary activity, following nineteen years' residence in the West Indies. As rector of Teston, in Kent, he was encouraged by Bishop Porteus, who held the nearby living of Hunton and spent much of the year there, and who was himself led by Ramsay to a resolve to take action against the horrors of the slave trade, to publish his material.[34] Ramsay's patron, Sir Charles Middleton (later the first Lord Barham), Comptroller of the Navy and a robust but devout naval officer, and his

[32] Clarkson, *History*, 1 207.
[33] Ibid., 1 207.
[34] *Porteus MS*. 2104, ff. 94–5, Diary, 16 Mar 1807. 'Those facts [in Ramsay's MS.] made a most forcible impression on my mind.' Porteus reveals here, and elsewhere in the diary (ibid., 2103, f. 25, Diary, 10 July 1789), that he had taken various opportunities of checking Ramsay's facts and had always found them corroborated.

lady, were also powerfully influenced by Ramsay. Ramsay's two pamphlets of 1784 – *An Essay on the Treatment and Conversion of the African Slaves in the British Sugar Colonies* and *An Enquiry into the Effects of the Abolition of the Slave Trade* – had a great effect in arousing public feeling against the trade,[35] but an important individual consequence of his testimony was its effect upon (among others) Clarkson for it was as a result of discussion with the Middletons, to which a visit to Ramsay naturally led, that Clarkson resolved to give up his considerable prospects of ecclesiastical preferment and devote himself to the abolitionist cause. What moved Clarkson appears to have been the enormity of the evil and the call of Christian benevolence.[36] It was therefore natural that the Quaker abolition committee should be broadened to take in Clarkson, Sharp (as we have seen) and one other non-Quaker, and so the basis of a nationwide agitation had been laid with the formation of that committee in April 1787.[37]

Important though their role was to be, abolitionist zeal was not confined to the twelve members forming the Abolition Committee. In the months before its formation, and following his visit to Ramsay and the Middletons, Clarkson had begun to canvass for support amongst men of note likely to be sympathetic to abolition. In one or two cases there was previous acquaintance to build

[35] Ibid., 2103, f. 25, Diary, 10 July 1789, speaks of the *Essay* as the work which 'first excited the attention of the Public to that important question'; *Life of Wilberforce*, I 148 speaks of *The Essay* as 'the work from which sprung the long and bitter controversy which brought the treatment of the Negro race before the public eye'.

[36] 'I urged to myself, that never was any cause, which had been taken up by man in any country or in any age, so great and important; that never was there one in which so much misery was heard to cry for redress; that never was there one, in which so much good could be done; never one, in which the duty of Christian charity could be so extensively exercised; never one, more worthy of the devotion of a whole life towards it; and that, if a man thought properly, he ought to rejoice to have been called into existence, if he were only permitted to become an instrument in forwarding it in any part of its progress' (Clarkson, *History*, I 228–9).

[37] This account of Clarkson's involvement in the cause is based on his *History*, I esp. pp. 100–04 and 58. Clarkson (p. 256) gives the members of the Committee as Granville Sharp, William Dillwyn, Samuel Hoare, George Harrison, John Lloyd, Joseph Wood, Thomas Clarkson, Richard Phillips, John Barton, Joseph Hooper, James Phillips and Philip Sansom. The third non-Quaker was Sansom.

upon; in other cases there were introductions from sympathisers like the Middletons whom he had already met; in any event the presentation of a copy of his *Essay on the Slavery and Commerce of the Human Species* constituted a basis for an approach. In this way, in the months from mid-1787 onwards, Clarkson enlisted the support of men such as Bennet Langton, a respected man of wide acquaintance and one of Dr Johnson's circle, of Lord and Lady Scarsdale, of Dr Baker, an influential London rector, and of members of Parliament who included Sir Herbert Mackworth, Sir Richard Hill, the Hon. J. C. Villiers and Mr Thomas Powys (later Baron Lilford).[38]

Far the most important of all those with whom Clarkson became acquainted at this time was William Wilberforce, but Clarkson's was the only one influence which drew Wilberforce to the leadership of the abolition campaign. Why Wilberforce's attention was first drawn to the subject of slavery we do not know. As a boy of fourteen he had, in 1773, written to a York newspaper condemning the slave trade,[39] and seven years later he specifically asked a friend travelling to Antigua to collect information on the condition of the slaves with the hope 'that some time or other I should redress the wrongs of those wretched and degraded beings'.[40] In 1783 he had some conversation on slave conditions with Ramsay[41] and it must surely have been soon after its publication in 1784 that Wilberforce read Ramsay's *Essay on the Treatment and Conversion of the Africa Slaves in the British Sugar Colonies.* Bishop Porteus, indeed, writing in 1807 believed the influence of Ramsay's book on Wilberforce to have been considerable:

> It very soon excited a considerable sensation in the public mind; and particularly made a strong impression on Mr Wilberforce, who told me (if I recollect right) that it gave him the first idea, or at least confirmed him in the resolution of bringing the question of the slave trade before Parliament.[42]

In any event, as Wilberforce later confided to Stephen, 'it was the condition of the West Indian slaves which first drew my attention, and it was in the course of my inquiry that I was led to Africa and

[38] Clarkson, *History*, 231–54.
[39] Coupland, *Wilberforce*, 78; *Life of Wilberforce*, I, 9, 147.
[40] Ibid., I, 149–50.
[41] Ibid., I, 148.
[42] *Porteus MS.* 2104, f. 95, Diary, 16 Mar 1807.

the abolition'.[43] Throughout 1786 Wilberforce was busy inquiring into the slave trade amongst the African merchants themselves – at that time ready enough to give him information freely[44] – but 1787 was the year of real decision. Not only were there the Clarkson and Ramsay impulses; not merely an approach in 1786 from that same Lady Middleton who had inspired Clarkson:[45] the question of taking up the abolition cause probably came up with the revered John Newton,[46] whose pastoral counsel – he was now Vicar of St Mary, Woolnoth – Wilberforce sought during the protracted crisis of his conversion.[47] Certainly he discussed the matter with his friends Pitt and W. W. Grenville (who had succeeded to the peerage in 1790) and it was in conversation with them in the earlier months of 1787 that, after Pitt had urged him to take up the abolition, 'I resolved to give notice on a fit occasion in the House of Commons of my intention to bring the subject forward'.[48] This decision he publicly avowed at a dinner party given by Bennet Langton and at which Clarkson had hoped to obtain just such a declaration.[49] Now the crisis of Wilberforce's spiritual coversion, which had begun with these long discussions with Milner as their coach bumped over the indifferent highways of France, had come to a climax which endured from the latter part of 1785 to the spring of 1786.[50] It is therefore reasonable to accept the clear view of Robert and Samuel Wilberforce that the real cause of their father taking up the abolition 'was the immediate consequences of his altered character'. His previous interest in the condition of West Indian slaves now led to practical exertion. He felt called upon to undertake the abolition cause as 'a sacred charge'.[51]

[43] Wilberforce to Stephen, 15 Jan 1817, quoted in *Life of Wilberforce*, I 149.

[44] Ibid., I 149–50.

[45] Ibid., I 147.

[46] R. I. and S. Wilberforce (eds.), *The Correspondence of William Wilberforce*, I x.

[47] *Life of Wilberforce*, I 96–7, 101, 103–4. Wilberforce had been in touch with Newton since c. 1777 (private communication from David B. Davis on evidence of *Wrangham MSS*).

[48] *Life of Wilberforce*, I 150–51.

[49] Ibid., I 150; Clarkson, *History*, I 252–4.

[50] *Life of Wilberforce*, I 89–113.

[51] Ibid., I 147–9.

The man called – alike by the small group of abolitionists and by his God – to lead the struggle was, even by mundane standards, superbly equipped for the task. Wealth, ability and charm – all were his. Natural talent meant that academic work, first at school and then at St John's College, Cambridge, came easily to him, and though as an undergraduate he was never in danger of working hard – indeed, he later confessed that 'from seventeen to twenty-one, when I ought to have been under that strict and wholesome regimen which the peculiar diseases of my intellectual powers seemed to require, I was strengthening these natural maladies'[52] – he never completely succumbed to the advice of his instructors at Cambridge that he was too clever to need to do anything. By the time he went down his considerable personal charm had brought him a circle of acquaintances and, with wealth and family position in the town, secured him a parliamentary seat at Hull in 1780. Translated to London, his charm and his conversation opened the way to every political hostess's dinner table.

Sir James Stephen reported Madame de Stael's judgement of Wilberforce as 'the most eloquent and the wittiest converser she had met in England'[53] and, more largely, develops the insight that 'society was not merely his delight or his passion; it was the necessity of his existence'.[54] Like Granville Sharp, 'he thinks badly enough of human nature in the abstract but in the individual always too favourably',[55] – which can only have made him more likeable. At the same time 'his unrivalled dramatic powers',[56] despite his slight figure and occasional propensity for his voice to rise to a whine, soon brought him acclaim in the House of Commons as an orator. Wilberforce also possessed considerable wit but kept it on a tight rein in his speeches and was particular never to show personal animosity, nor display sarcasm – save on one occasion, described by Brougham, which throws a deal of light

[52] Ibid., III 58.

[53] Sir J. Stephen, *Ecclesiastical Biography*, II 286.

[54] Ibid., II 217.

[55] *Macaulay MSS* (Huntington Library), Box 3, MY 803, James Stephen to Z. Macaulay, 8 Oct 1808.

[56] Sir J. Stephen, *Ecclesiastical Biography*, II 270. Stephen gives an excellent biographical portrait of Wilberforce as does Henry Brougham, *Historical Sketches of Statesmen who flourished in the Reign of George III, Collected Works* (London and Glasgow, 1855) III 343–9. Coupland also provided a good general evaluation of his subject's character in his *Wilberforce*.

on Wilberforce and the respect with which he must have been treated.

When a well-known popular member thought fit to designate him repeatedly, and very irregularly, as the *'Honourable and religious gentleman'*, not because he was ashamed of the Cross he gloried in, but because he felt indignant at any one in the British senate deeming piety a matter of reproach, he poured out a strain of sarcasm which none who heard it can ever forget. A common friend of the parties having remarked to Sir Samuel Romilly, beside whom he sat, that this greatly outmatched Pitt himself, the great master of sarcasm, the reply of that great man and just observer was worthy to be remarked, – 'Yes', said he, 'it is a most striking thing I almost ever heard; but I look upon it as a more singular proof of Wilberforce's virtue than of his genius, for who but he ever was possessed of such a formidable weapon, and never used it?'[57]

Brought into close intimacy with Pitt, whom Wilberforce had not really known at Cambridge, it was natural for Wilberforce to become a leading member of Goosetree's, the new and select political club where Pitt's followers congregated. A rise to influence that was already rapid was taken further in 1784. In the political crises following the dismissal of the Fox–North coalition Wilberforce secured one of the seats for the county of York in virtue of a brilliant oratorical intervention (carried further at a hard-drinking dinner) which reconciled the disparate factions of the opponent of the coalition – Tory squires and Yorkshire Association men – and humbled their powerful Whig magnate opponents. Building on this success, the new member was assiduous in the county's business, the business of the premier county in England as, politically, all reputed it. A moderate reformer, he symbolised the union between Pitt and Wyvill. Charming, popular, gifted and supremely well-connected the new leader of the abolition cause had the requisite qualities and attainments to an astonishing degree.[58] It was deemed politic that Wilberforce should not at

[57] Brougham, *Historical Sketches. Works*, III 345.
[58] Ibid., 1–64. Coupland, *Wilberforce*, 1–30; For the political events of 1783–84 see also Black, *The Association*, 105–6; J. R. Christie, *Wilkes, Wyvill and Reform* (London, 1962) 201–3; and J. C. Colquhoun, *Wilberforce, His Friends and His Times* (London, 1866) 40–50.

once openly take membership of the Abolition Committee, but from the very evening of the Langton dinner party it was agreed that that Committee should work closely in Wilberforce's support.[59]

From 1787 onwards, then, the campaign against the slave trade can be said to have been 'in business'.

[59] Clarkson, *History*, I 254. See ibid., I 272–3 for Clarkson's assessment of the unique importance of Wilberforce's qualifications: 'And what could the committee have done without the parliamentary aid of Mr. Wilberforce? . . . there was never yet one, who appeared to me to be so properly qualified, in all respects, for the management of the great cause of the abolition of the Slave-trade, as he, whose name I have just mentioned.'

For a recent biography of Wilberforce which appeared whilst this book was in the press, and which makes significant use of MS sources, see Robin Furneaux, *William Wilberforce* (Hamish Hamilton, 1974). A further biography, no less well founded, by John C. Pollock is shortly to be published by Constable. I am grateful to Constable and Mr Pollock for allowing me to read this latter in typescript.

11 The Campaign for Abolition, 1787–1796

By mid-1787, then, the abolition lobby was coming to possess a broader base than ever the sectarian Committee for Sufferings could provide. Principally through the agency of Clarkson, recruits had been brought in from the political and society world whilst others, like the Middletons, and above all Wilberforce, had had their consciences quickened by their religious convictions. When to this was added the adhesion of men like Grenville and the prime minister himself, each of whom had come to oppose the slave trade largely, it would seem, as children of their age, the possibility of carrying the all-important legislation against the slave trade began to look real indeed. Even conceding the limitations of the Prime Minister's authority in such matters as abolition – of which more anon – it was surely matter for considerable encouragement that it was Pitt, head of the ministry since 1783, who, with Grenville, had specifically urged Wilberforce to take up the abolition cause.

The aims of the abolition movement were succinctly stated by the London Committee at an early meeting.

> Our immediate aim is, by diffusing a knowledge of the subject, and particularly the Modes of procuring and treating slaves, to interest men of every description in the Abolition of the Traffic; but especially those from whom any alteration must proceed – the Members of our Legislature.[1]

The decision to concentrate all energies on the slave trade and not to make the institution of slavery itself an object of attack was not reached without some debate in the early weeks of the new Committee's life. According to Clarkson, 'it appeared soon to be the sense of the committee, that to aim at the removal of both would

[1] *B.M. Add. Mss.* 21254, Abolition Committee Minutes, 17 July 1787.

be to aim at too much, and that by doing this we might lose all'. Theoretically, so reasoning in the Committee continued, it did not matter which evil should be selected for attack, for each would be vitally weakened by a successful onslaught on the other. In practice, however, the slave trade was the more promising target 'for, by aiming at the abolition of the slave trade, they were laying the axe at the very root'. But this was not the only reason: if the attack were made on slavery, the cry would be raised that property was being attacked and that 'an irritated race of beings' would be let loose, whilst it was doubtful whether action against slavery could be taken without overriding the colonial legislatures. An attack on the slave trade, on the other hand, would be in the acceptable province of the imperial government's right 'to regulate or abolish any of its branches of commerce'.[2] For Granville Sharp, and probably for him only, this self-denial was not acceptable for he declared to the Abolition Committee, probably at this time, that 'with respect to myself, *individually*, when acting with them, professing that my own opposition is aimed not merely against the *slave trade*, but also the toleration of slavery itself'.[3]

The abolition campaign was to last twenty years and it will be convenient to consider it in two parts, with 1796 as the point of division. Within the earlier period a further division marks off the years up to and after mid-1792 as suitable segments for study. Beyond the acceptance by the Abolition Committee of the necessity of a parliamentary motion, the promise of Wilberforce to sponsor it, and a realisation by the Committee of the need to arouse public opinion – in the restricted eighteenth-century sense – no clearly conceived strategy had been formulated.

To arouse what Wilberforce's biographers termed 'the general moral feeling of the nation',[4] literature must be distributed. Here the Committee worked along three lines. It arranged for the production and distribution of pamphlets on a relatively large scale, for the more restricted dissemination of special editions of larger works (both categories usually published by James Phillips, the

[2] Clarkson, *History*, I 282–8.

[3] *Sharp Transcripts* (*J.A.W.*), Sharp to David Barclay, 28 May 1807 (Notebook 12). Most abolitionists probably hesitated to brand slavery as having the same infamy as the slave trade; some also believed in the practicality of amelioration of slavery.

[4] *Life of Wilberforce*, I 153.

bookseller and member of the Committee), and for favourable notice in the Press. It was natural that a start should have been made with a pamphlet by Clarkson, *A Summary View of the Slave Trade and of the Probable Consequences of its Abolition* (London, 1787). This was a boiling down of the author's *An Essay on the Slavery and Commerce of the Human Species, particularly the African* and an anticipatory summary of his forthcoming *An Essay on the Impolicy of the African Slave Trade.*[5] Other pamphlets included an apt letter by the Rev. R. B. Nicholls, Dean of Middleham, Yorkshire, in which it was argued that, given humane treatment, the supply of plantation labour could be maintained by natural increase; and *Thoughts on the African Slave Trade* by the revered John Newton, in which he effectively attacked the trade in which he had once participated. In the more substantial category were editions of Benezet's *Some Historical Account of Guinea* and of Clarkson's full-length works. Such was the scale of the propaganda effort that in fifteen months £1,106 19s. 9d. had been spent on the 'printing of books' in quantities ranging from 15,050 copies of the *Summary View* to 1,500 of Benezet's *Historical Account*.[6] As to newspaper publicity, it seems that, just as the 1787 Committee had taken over, generally, from where the Quaker committee had left off, so it inherited some readiness on the part of the *General Evening Post, Lloyd's Evening Post* and of a number of provincial newspapers to publish items favourable to the abolition.[7] Arrangements with London newspapers were taken further by the Committee.[8]

In addition to literature directly inspired or disseminated by the Abolition Committee, the very existence of a campaign against the slave trade led sympathisers to take up their pens, sometimes quite independently, sometimes at a request perhaps indirectly relayed. A notable example of this type was *The Wrongs of Africa*, anonymously written in 1787 by the none the less courageous

[5] Clarkson, *History*, I 277–8.

[6] Clarkson, *History*, I 454–99 passim; *B.M. Add. MSS.* 21255, Abolition Committee Minutes of 12 Aug 1788.

[7] Clarkson, *History*, I 125; E. M. Hunt, 'The North of England Agitation for the Abolition of the Slave Trade, 1780–1800' (Manchester University M.A. Thesis, 1959), 9–10 and passim.

[8] E.g. *B.M. Add MSS.* 21255, Abolition Committee Minutes of 3 June 1788 and 27 Apr 1790. *B.M. Add. MSS.* 21256, Abolition Committee Minute, 22 Mar 1791 and Hunt, 'North of England Agitation' 232.

Liverpool abolitionist, William Roscoe. Roscoe was a man with literary gifts and there is a kind of measured grace about such lines as:

> Form'd with the same capacity of pain,
> The same desire of pleasure and of ease,
> Why feels not man for man.[9]

In the following year Hannah More felt impelled to produce *Slavery*, subsequently entitled *The Black Slave Trade* (1788). Though she – undeservedly – came to have later the reputation of a prim Evangelical spinster (Boswell, by contrast, reports that at Johnson's ambiguous utterance that a certain woman had 'a bottom of good sense' Hannah More's countenance became sufficiently mobile for her to take refuge behind another's back) the likely influence of her poem must be assessed against the circumstance that she was in the eighties an adornment of London literary society in her own right and a woman of whom Johnson thought highly.[10] The authoress had no illusions but that the poem was written too hurriedly to be good. It is significant, however, because of the way in which at one and the same time it manifests Evangelical receptivity to the values of the age, and Hannah More's sense of what chords to evoke in her readers' minds.

The religious appeal, apart from the assurance that slaves are within the redemptive purpose of God, is little more than the conventional eighteenth-century appeal to the retributory justice of God upon the slave trade:

> Yet the last audit shall reverse the cause;
> And God shall vindicate his broken laws.

Then the noble savage ideal is invoked:

> Perish the illiberal thought which would debase
> The native genius of the sable race!

and likewise sensibility:

> Tho' few can reason, all mankind can feel.

Liberty, however, is a note frequently struck, notably in the appeal to the tradition of England as the home of liberty:

[9] Clarkson, *History*, I 279–82; Sypher, *Guinea's Captive Kings*, 181–3.
[10] Boswell, *Life of Johnson* 1139, 1141, 1278.

> Shall Britain, where the soul of Freedom reigns,
> Forge chains for others she herself disdains?
> Forbid it, Heaven! O let the nations know
> The liberty she tastes she will bestow;[11]

Another Evangelical – the poet Cowper – at first refused to write poems, but in the event wrote five, three of them at least being both written and first published in 1788. The quality – and literary limitations – of these are suggested by the opening lines of the best known of them *The Negroe's Complaint:*

> Forc'd from home, and all its pleasures,
> Afric's coast I left forlorn;
> To increase a stranger's treasures,
> O'er the raging billows born.

But just as this poem was set to a popular tune and evidently designed as a propaganda jingle, so they should all be judged in this light. Less known now but perhaps equally effective was his *Pity for Poor Africans* in which the poet expresses shock at the purchase of slaves but goes on to express the various inconveniences of ending it. For instance,

> If foreigners likewise would give up the trade,
> Much more in behalf of your wish might be said;
> But while they get riches by purchasing blacks,
> Pray tell me why we may not also go snacks?[12]

Nor was it necessary for the poetry to be the work of an acknowledged poet: a polite society with literary pretensions was as like to be influenced by *On the Slave Trade by a Young Lady at School* and numerous counterparts. All in all the propaganda value of a poem is likely to be in inverse proportion to its poetic merit. Of course the degree of dissemination is also important, and E. M. Hunt has discovered that abolitionist poetry, and

[11] Hannah More, *Works*, i (1818) 371–90; Sypher, *Guinea's Captive Kings*, 193–5. Hunt, 'North of England Agitation', 207–8.

[12] 'The Morning Dream' was the third poem to be written and published in 1788. 'Sweet Meat has Sour Sauce, or, the Slave-Trader in the Dumps', though written in 1788 was not published until 1836 and 'Epigram (Printed in the Northampton Mercury)' was not published until 1792. All are to be found in Cowper, *Poetical Works*, 4th ed. (Oxford, 1967), 371–6. See also Hunt, 'North of England Agitation', pp. 208–10, and Sypher, *Guinea's Captive Kings*, 186–9.

especially Cowper, were much reproduced in provincial newspapers.[13]

Widely disseminated, especially perhaps amongst an almost captive audience, the Methodists, was Wesley's *Thoughts upon Slavery,* of which, as he offered the Abolition Committee in 1787, he had a new edition published.[14]

Just as Clarkson's writings began with condemnation of the immorality of the slave trade and progressed to demonstration of its impolicy, so the Abolition Committee soon concluded that the general, moral case against the slave trade had been made and that the way to induce a positive readiness to end the trade was to demonstrate that it was impolitic as well as unjust and inhumane. In a (second) letter of support to the Committee, considered on 30 October 1787, John Wesley urged that care to be taken 'that the question should be argued as well upon the consideration of interest as of humanity and justice, the former of which he feared would have more weight than the latter.'[15] By the New Year the Committee had taken the point and reported that 'they have more particularly directed their attention to the plea of political necessity which is frequently urged to justify . . . this traffick'.[16] Here was the first assertion of a conscious balance in advocacy which was henceforth to be frequent in the whole abolition campaign.

If propaganda was vital, some kind of grass-roots organisation was no less so. At a meeting of 17 July 1787 the members of the Abolition Committee drew up a list of men who, in virtue of knowledge of their suitability possessed by one or other of the members, would be likely to agree to serve as correspondents and who would disseminate publications forwarded by the Committee and generally promote the cause in their areas. It is hardly surprising that a committee in which Quakers still predominated numerically should have found the great majority of its correspondents amongst the Society of Friends – indeed the provincial organisation of the Committee for Sufferings seems largely to have been taken over. Thomas Fox, a manufacturer of Wellington, Somerset,

[13] Hunt, 'North of England Agitation', 210–14. For a thorough survey of anti-slavery poetry, drama and fiction from the 1780s onwards see Sypher, *Guinea's Captive Kings,* 181 ff.

[14] Clarkson, *History,* I 448.

[15] Clarkson, *History,* I 451–2.

[16] *B.M. Add. MSS.* 21254. Abolition Committee Minutes of 15 Jan 1788.

Dr Fothergill, Robert Barclay, William Tuke – these are representative of the list. Within two months of its formation the Committee had correspondents in 35 of the 40 English counties whilst names had been suggested for Edinburgh and Glasgow.[17]

The abolition movement, as well as adding more Quakers, quite soon came to broaden its base yet more; James Martin, a humanitarian and reformer,[18] and William Morton Pitt, a relation of the Prime Minister,[19] were the first two members of Parliament to be added – on 1 January 1788.[20] Not for another three and a half years did Wilberforce surrender what was initially felt to be the advantage of not being openly enrolled[21] – in fact he was constantly involved in the Committee's work[22] – but he was eventually co-opted in April 1791[23] together with his intimate friend Lord Muncaster,[24] with William Smith, the Unitarian reformer, who had at the very beginning offered his services to the Committee[25] and who was exceptionally active in the cause for twenty years, and with no less than Charles James Fox himself. Henry Thornton followed the next month and Sir William Dolben, L. A. Grant and Matthew Montagu at about the same time[26] whilst the same period saw the adhesion of a number of men of note, not members of Parliament, such as David Hartley, a man of letters and a scientist of note, committee member of the Yorkshire Association and earlier an M.P., who had joined with Sir George Savile in the abortive abolition motion of 1776[27] William Burgh, yet another

[17] *B.M. Add. MSS.* 21254, Abolition Committee Minute of 17 July 1787; Clarkson, *History*, I. 444–5; P. C. Lipscomb, 'William Pitt and the Abolition of the Slave Trade' (University of Texas Ph.D. thesis, 1960) 112–13.

[18] L. B. Namier and J. Brooke, *The Commons 1754–1790* [History of Parliament Series], (London, 1964), I, 156–57.

[19] Ibid., III 302.

[20] *B.M. Add. MSS.* 21254, Abolition Committee Minutes, 1 Jan 1788.

[21] *Life of Wilberforce*, I 152.

[22] On 30 Oct 1787 a sub-committee was appointed specifically to keep in touch with Wilberforce (*B.M. Add. MSS.* 21254, Abolition Committee Minutes, 30 Oct 1787).

[23] *B.M. Add. MSS.* 21256, Abolition Committee Minutes, 26 Apr 1791.

[24] *Life of Wilberforce*, passim.

[25] *H. of P.*, III 452–3; Clarkson, *History*, I 443–4.

[26] *B.M. Add. MSS.* 21256, Abolition Committee Minutes of 10 May 1791; Clarkson, *History*, II 341.

[27] *H. of P.*, II 252; *D.N.B.*, I. R. Christie, *Wilkes, Wyvill and Reform*, 121, 134; Clarkson, *History*, I 84–5; II 28.

close friend of Wilberforce, and a leading member of the Yorkshire Association,[28] and Bennet Langton.[29] Most of the hard work of the London Abolition Committee continued to be done by the original Quaker nucleus – William Dillwyn's diary, though only occasionally informative on particulars, is instructive in showing the sheer constancy of his labours[30] – but it is clearly significant of the abolition movement's development into a national movement that its central committee is augmented by men of the kind we have noticed. Taking one with another, there is a reformist tinge about the new recruits, and when we examine a second category of those who write in to the Committee offering their services and support, or were ready to give some special assistance, we find this characteristic is often repeated. Major Cartwright, T. W. Coke, M.P., of Holkham, Norfolk, William Frend, Fellow of Jesus College, Cambridge, Joshua Grigby, M.P., Capel Lofft, the Duke of Richmond, Lord Mahon, Samuel Tooker of Rotherham, and the Rev. Christopher Wyvill[31] – all coupled a positive abolitionist enthusiasm with a (varying) commitment to reform.

There was sometimes, though less often, a commitment to political reform on the part of those who were active in forming and running abolition committees in the provinces (a category not always distinguishable from those just named). Such is the case, for instance, with John Chubb of Bridgewater. A political friend of Fox he had been chairman of the Bridgewater Reform Committee in 1780 and readily rallied to the support of the abolition in 1787.[32] A comparable figure in the East Midlands was the Rev. George Walker, a Unitarian minister, advocate of parliamentary and other reforms, and most energetic of the Nottingham aboli-

---

[28] *B.M. Add. MSS.* 21256, Abolition Committee Minutes, 26 Apr 1791; *Life of Wilberforce*, passim; Christie, *Wilkes, Wyvill and Reform*, 207; *D.N.B.*

[29] Clarkson, *History*, I 497.

[30] Vol. II of the *Calendar of the Diaries of William Dillwyn* (1 Jan 1781– 31 Dec 1790) (transcribed by the National Library of Wales and available there) shows some 100 attendances on slave business, mostly committee meetings between May 1787 and the end of 1790. In addition some 40 entries from 1781–87 show his assiduousness in the work of the earlier Quaker Committee.

[31] Clarkson, *History*, I 453, 497, 456, 460, 493, 465; *B.M. Add. MSS.* 21255, Abolition Committee Minutes of 6 May 1788 (Cartwright) and 24 Feb 1789 (Richmond and Mahon).

[32] Clarkson, *History*, I 321; Black, *Association*, 92; Lipscomb, *Pitt and Abolition*, 120.

tionists.[33] It was in Manchester, however, and only in Manchester, that we find a provincial committee of which the radical members, though a minority on any reckoning, were for a time able to determine its proceedings. This was evidently because Thomas Walker, acknowledged leader of Manchester radicals by 1791, and substantial merchant, together with Thomas Cooper, charter member of the Society for Constitutional Information, seem usually to have been supported by the important Whig faction on the thirty-one member committee. By 1790 the minority of politically radical abolitionists had probably come quite to dominate the committee.[34] The Manchester Committee, we shall see, was quickly to be responsible for the development of abolitionist tactics nationally in a popular direction.

It would be wrong, however, to exaggerate the importance of the adhesion of most reformers to the cause of abolition.[35] Study of Clarkson's lengthy lists of adherents and of Hunt's valuable work on North of England abolitionists makes it clear that support for the cause was much more broadly, if imprecisely based. One must insist upon the primary importance of the Quakers who were to be found working doggedly for abolition in nearly all corners of the realm. Where a Literary and Philosophical Society existed it was commonly strongly represented in the ranks of local abolitionists. There was a good sprinkling of Fellows of Oxford and Cambridge Colleges and a number of professors of Scottish Universities, including John Millar. East of the Pennines, and to some extent elsewhere, dissenting ministers were important, attesting the influence both of the dissenting academies and of the Scottish universities. A few Methodist laymen and preachers – like the colourful John Murlin of High Wycombe who pulled down the figure of an angel and trumpet that had injudiciously been erected

[33] Clarkson, *History*, ii 352; Hunt, 'North of England Agitation', 126; *D.N.B.*

[34] Clarkson, *History*, i 452–3; Black, *Association*, 118 n., 176–8 and 208; G. S. Veitch, *The Genesis of Parliamentary Reform* (London, 1913), 183; Hunt, 'North of England Agitation', 60–79, 100–02; James Walvin, 'How Popular was Abolition? Popular Dissent and the Negro Question, 1787–1833' (Unpublished article kindly communicated by the author).

[35] Not all reformers were abolitionists; notable amongst reformers who positively opposed abolition were the Earl of Abingdon and, in the Commons, Henry Cruger, Crisp Molineux, John Sawbridge and Brook Watson.

over his pulpit, Thomas Thompson, a Hull banker, and Samuel
Bradburn of Manchester who was active in the boycott of slave-
grown produce – followed in the path charted by their founder.
In parts of Yorkshire, in particular, Evangelicals like William Hey
of Leeds played an important part whilst there was an infusion
of clergy of the Established Church sufficient to make this group
the largest after the Quakers. They were headed by four bishops:
Bathurst of Norwich, Hinchcliffe of Peterborough, Porteus of
London and Watson of Llandaff. There were very many, doubtless gentry and merchants, who cannot readily be classified, and
often the categories overlap. And there was at least one original,
Lord Gardenstone, Lord of session and philanthropist who became chairman of the Scottish Abolition Committee.[36] In Gardenstone's striking resemblance to P. G. Wodehouse's Lord Emsworth
(for Gardenstone had a propensity for keeping a pig in his bed-
room) he is almost one's favourite abolitionist.

The creation of local committees had in part been spontaneous,
but it also owed something to the initiative of Clarkson who, on
behalf of the London Committee and not primarily for this purpose, had engaged on a journey to Bristol and Liverpool, but also
taking in certain inland cities, notably Manchester in the summer
of 1787. His main purpose had been to obtain more information
on the slave trade in anticipation of that public inquiry into the
trade which, he asserts, the Abolition Committee were already
persuaded was probable. With some prescience Clarkson saw the
advantage of beginning his inquiry before passions became heated
and before 'interest felt itself biased to conceal the truth'. This was
in fact the first of several journeys of investigation (some of the
friuts of which we have already noticed): Clarkson was concerned
to learn more of the manner of carrying on the trade – one forgets
that relatively little published information on this subject existed –
to discover more of the prospects for trade in African produce and
to inquire into the condition of seamen engaged in the slave trade.
Taken as a whole, Clarkson's journeys were of great importance,
comparable with his writings against the slave trade, for probably

[36] The major sources for this assessment are *B.M. Add. MSS.* 21254,
Abolition Committee Minutes, 15 Jan 1788; *B.M. Add. MSS.* 21255,
Abolition Committee Minute of 26 Aug 1788. Clarkson, *History*, passim,
and Hunt 'North of England Agitation', passim, supplemented by the
D.N.B.

only by such means could the abolitionists have learned the weaknesses of the institution they had set out to destroy. Clarkson's inquiries, as his purpose became known, brought serious threats against his life – he once narrowly escaped being pushed off the dock at Liverpool; his *coup de théâtre* was the discovery from the study of ships' muster rolls that mortality amongst seamen in the trade was greater than in any other. Clarkson tabulated his findings – his sample was of no less than 20,000 seamen – in considerable detail in his *Essay on the Impolicy of the African Slave Trade* and in his evidence to the Privy Council Enquiry[37] which, as we shall see, was initiated early in 1788, but the gist of it is amply contained in the succinct observation 'that more persons would be found dead in these slave vessels from Bristol, in a given time, than in all the other vessels put together, numerous as they were, belonging to the same port'. The significance of Clarkson's researches into this question is that the supporters of the slave trade could thereafter only speak of the trade as a nursery of seamen as a kind of ritual incantation; all conviction had gone from the proposition. At least as valuable a fruit of Clarkson's journeys was that he discovered men who would give evidence before official inquiries, as well as finding out an immense amount about the slave trade. Between 1787 and 1794 he made seven journeys in Britain and covered 35,000 miles.[38]

At first Wilberforce and the London Abolition Committee had no more precise aims than to generate feeling in support of abolition, to discover more evidence about the slave trade in anticipation of an inquiry, and to bring on a parliamentary motion against the trade. It was the Manchester Abolition Committee which sought to give abolitionist public opinion a cutting edge by the organisation of petitions to Parliament, a constitutional device which had been widely used during the campaign for

---

[37] *A. & P.*, 1789, xxvi (646a) pt ii, Clarkson to Lords of Committee of Privy Council, 27 July 1788. He demonstrates conclusively that the deaths among the ships' companies of slave ships amounted to one-quarter to one-fifth of the whole; Clarkson, *Essay on the Impolicy of the Slave Trade*, pp. 53–83. Clarkson's conclusions were later officially confirmed. See Minutes of the Evidence of the Commons Committee, *A. & P.*, 1790–91, xxxiv (748) 276–81.

[38] The journeys are described in Clarkson, *History*, i 292–440, and ii 2–11, 169–78, 349–51, 462, 466 and 470. The quotations in the above sections are from ibid i, 289 and 326.

parliamentary reform. Certainly Clarkson, having accidently heard that Bridgwater had petitioned against the slave trade in 1785, had privately urged at Bridgwater, Bristol, Gloucester and elsewhere that petitions should be organised but says that he made it clear that his suggestion was without the knowledge or consent of the Committee.[39] Manchester abolitionists, however, quite independently resolved at the very end of December 1787 to circulate a petition in Manchester and went on to urge 'many respectable individuals [and] . . . the chief magistrate of every principal town in Great Britain' to do likewise.[40] A number of provincial newspapers in the weeks immediately following attested the positive influence of the Manchester initiative.[41] So effective was it that by later January the London Committee were being advised by correspondents throughout the country of an intention to petition Parliament.[42] This development led the London Committee to endorse the tactic by circularising the mayors of all corporate towns that had not yet petitioned.[43] By June of 1788 the Commons had received over 100 petitions requesting it to take the slave trade into its consideration.[44]

In London, however, this first and moderately strong expression of a national opinion in favour of the abolition failed to exercise the leverage of which it was capable – the requisite force just was not applied to the lever. This was partly, it would seem, because of a certain over-confidence in the abolitionist camp, leading to insufficiently tight direction of the agitation, and partly because the political and constitutional obstacles in the way of a speedy abolition had not been properly appreciated. The likely effect of Pitt's support may also have been exaggerated.

Given that the anonymous author of *An Apology for Negro Slavery* (London, 1786) could speak of himself as 'stepping forward against a nest of foes, the single champion of a very uncommon and unpopular doctrine', given that one who submitted

[39] Ibid., I 320–21, 415–6.

[40] Hunt, 'North of England Agitation', 79–80. See also Clarkson, *History*, I 415–6.

[41] As did an expenditure of *c.* £180 on postages and newspaper insertions (Hunt, 'North of England Agitation', 79–81).

[42] Clarkson, *History*, I 467–8.

[43] *B.M. Add. MSS. 21254*, Abolition Committee Minutes of 22 Jan 1788; Hunt, 'North of England Agitation', 27–28.

[44] Ibid., 31. See also Lipscomb, *Pitt and Abolition*, 152–66.

evidence to the Privy Council Committee could write in February 1788 that 'the abolition of the slave trade is demanded by a great part of England',[45] Wilberforce's optimism is perhaps understandable. 'There is no doubt of our success', he assured Sir William Eden on 18 January;[46] 'I trust there is little reason to doubt of the motion for the abolition . . . being carried in parliament', he writes to Wyvill on the 25th.[47] Some petitions to make specific what the great majority of men had already demanded, so Wilberforce's thoughts seem to have run – and in the very same letter he was asking Wyvill to generate petitions in Yorkshire – were all that was required to bring Parliament to swift and decisive action. But more sobering thoughts evidently supervened almost immediately, for sometime towards the end of January, or early February, Pitt and Wilberforce agreed that more factual information, which, they automatically supposed would necessarily discredit the slave trade, must be sought.[48] Pitt, as prime minister, was able to choose the means, and he chose the Privy Council acting through a committee. A major delay in the placing of a substantive parliamentary motion against the slave trade was a necessary result of this stratagem. The Privy Council could hardly report in less than several months – in the event it was not until April 1789 – and by definition of the stratagem no substantive motion could be put until the evidence which was to justify it had been laid on the table. No one in abolitionist circles – including perhaps in his still considerable optimism, Pitt himself – seems to have realised the extent of the likely delay, and the effect of reference to the Privy Council was in fact clouded by the serious illness of Wilberforce from March onwards. By the end of the month, say his biographers, 'his disorder had now assumed the character of an entire decay of all the vital functions', and a friend predicted that he could not last three weeks.[49] In this situation, Pitt immediately

---

[45] *A. & P.*, xxvi (1789), pt i, no. 13, 'W. J.' (London) to Committee of Trade, 27 Feb 1788.

[46] The Bishop of Bath and Wells (ed.), *The Journal and Correspondence of William Lord Auckland* (London, 1861–62) i 307, Wilberforce to Eden, 18 Jan 1788.

[47] Quoted in *Life of Wilberforce*, i 160.

[48] Wilberforce's biographers imply that the essential decision was Wilberforce's (*Life of Wilberforce*, i 166) but John Ehrman that it was Pitt's (*The Younger Pitt*, 392–3).

[49] *Life of Wilberforce*, i 169.

carried out a promise he had made to Wilberforce at the beginning of his illness and took over the direction of affairs, promising to do all that was politically possible that session, and until Wilberforce recovered.[50] He had already actively involved himself as a member of the Privy Council Committee.[51] Now on 21 April Pitt summoned Granville Sharp, as chairman of the Abolition Committee, and told him, in Sharp's own words:

> His heart was with us – that he had pledged himself to Mr W[ilberforce] that the cause should not suffer – but believed that the best way would be to give time to collect all possible evidence and to obtain an order of the present session, if the Rules of the House would permit, of which he would inform himself, and to resume the business early in the next session.[52]

This programme Pitt carried through. With the help of Bishop Porteus, W. W. Grenville and Clarkson witnesses were brought before the Privy Council Committee who could effectively make the case for abolition – and counteract the Liverpool witnesses who had in the earlier stages of the inquiry held the floor.[53] As to the parliamentary resolution, Pitt soon confirmed that it was constitutionally permissible[54] and arranged for it to be brought on on 9 May. By April a number of abolitionist supporters had grown restive at the absence of any parliamentary action,[55] but Pitt's

[50] A. M. Wilberforce, *The Private Papers of William Wilberforce* (London, 1897), 177–8; *Life of Wilberforce*, I 169–70.

[51] *Porteus MS.* 2103, f. 16, Diary, 12 Feb 1788.

[52] *Sharp Transcripts* (*J.A.W.*), Diary, 21 Apr 1788. See also *B.M. Add. MSS. 21255*, 22 Apr 1788, Minutes of Abolition Committee, for the reporting of Pitt's statement.

[53] *Life of Wilberforce*, I 170; Clarkson, *History*, I 471–91. In February 1788 the Liverpool Common Council and the African Merchants of Liverpool appointed a delegation to concert opposition to the abolition proposal. They were able to feed numerous witnesses with actual experience of the slave trade into the Privy Council Committee and were thus able to gain an initial advantage. In Clarkson's view, the advantage began to swing the other way when the abolitionists brought the Swedish scientists and travellers, Charles Wadstrom and Andrew Spaarman, before the Committee (Frank Sanderson, 'The Liverpool Delegates' and Sir William Dolben's Bill', *Transactions of the Historic Society of Lancashire and Cheshire*), vol. 124 (1973) 61–9.

[54] *B.M. Add. MSS. 21255*, Abolition Committee Minutes, 29 Apr 1788. The confirmation was conveyed through William Morton Pitt.

[55] Clarkson, *History*, I 491–502; *Life of Wilberforce*, I 170.

scheme for a parliamentary resolution meant that a channel now opened up for the display of these frustrated energies. When, at a meeting of the Committee on 6 May, it was announced that Pitt was proposing his resolution in three days' time a lobbying of M.P.s was immediately put in hand. Interestingly – and perhaps significantly – Walker and Cooper were present at the committee meeting as Manchester delegates. Major Cartwright also attended. In the lobbying which then commenced Walker and Cooper took part, along with Sharp, Clarkson and three other committee members, whilst Cartwright also lent assistance.[56] The debate on Pitt's resolution duly took place and the resolution that the House would bind itself to take the slave trade into consideration the next session was eventually passed *nem con*. It was noteworthy that the defenders of the trade reserved their defence. They could afford to, for although there was a commitment to consider the question, it was no more than that, and ensured delay for a further year.[57]

These exertions, however, were not the whole of Pitt's activities during his period as *locum tenens* for Wilberforce. During May, Dolben, the member for Oxford University, and who had spoken in support of Pitt's resolution, was so horrified at what he saw of a slave ship which he visited in dock that he moved a bill to ameliorate the conditions on a slave ship by restricting the number of slaves that could be carried per ton and by providing for bounties for the captain and surgeon on slaves landed alive. The bill was hotly contested by the defenders of the trade both in Lords and Commons but the significance of it – beyond the sharp fall in mortality which it eventually occasioned[58] – was that Pitt threw his weight behind the bill both as man *and* minister. The opposition made effective use of the delaying tactic of hearing evidence and conjured up in the Lords an alarming number of supporters. This potentially decisive obstacle Pitt broke by apparently stating in Cabinet that if the bill were defeated in the Lords 'the opposers of it and myself cannot continue members of the same

[56] *B.M. Add. MSS. 21255*, Abolition Committee Minutes of 6 May 1788; Clarkson, *History*, I 503.

[57] The debate is in *Parliamentary History*, XXVII (1788–89), Cols. 495–506, 576–99 and 638–52, and is summarised in Clarkson, *History*, I 504–24 and Coupland, *Wilberforce*, 92–3.

[58] See pp. 30–1 above, and Appendix 1.

Government'.[59] Here was a measure of trade regulation on which
the Prime Minister could insist at least on not being decisively opposed. The episode attests Pitt's toughness and resolution but it
may, as John Ehrman suggests, have strengthened his disposition as a politician and prime minister, to make sure of his ground
before supporting major change.

By May 1788, remarkably, Wilberforce had substantially recovered and began again to advise the London Committee. The
London Abolition Committee as such had taken no part in the
promotion of Dolben's bill fearing 'lest any interference on our
part towards the support of *Regulations* in this Commerce should
be construed as an admission if its principles'.[60] However, it continued the task of lobbying members of Parliament, hurriedly
begun in connection with Pitt's resolution. Apparently a good deal
of effort was devoted to this task:[61] in any event by the end of the
year it could be reported 'that the list of Members of Parliament
has been perused and marked by the members of this committee'.[62]
This more considered approach to the task of influencing parliamentary opinion in readiness for the motion the following year
had been accompanied by the positive fostering of local committees. The London Committee had at one time, indeed, been prepared to call a general meeting of the Society but when Wilberforce, by letter, advised against this, apparently on the ground
that a national as distinct from a local meeting could be deemed
subversive, and thus harm the cause, the idea was abandoned.[63]
A sub-committee was, however, formed at the end of July 1788
to 'correspond and advise with Mr Clarkson' who was despatched
on another journey partly to found new committees, and 'paying

[59] Historical Manuscripts Commission, *Report on the Manuscripts of J. B.
Fortescue Esq, preserved at Dropmore* (London, 1892 ff), I 342. Pitt to Gren-
ville, 29 June 1788. The episode is surveyed at length in Clarkson, *History*,
I 527–61, and more briefly, and from the point of view of Pitt's career, in
Ehrman, *Life of Pitt*, 393–5. For an important testimony to Pitt's exertions
over Dolben's Bill see H. B. Wheatley (ed.), *Historical and Posthumous
Memoirs of Sir Nathaniel William Wraxall* (London, 1884) v 138–49.

[60] *Philadelphia Abolition Society, Am. S.01*, Sharp to Philadelphia Abolition Society, 30 July 1788, reproduced in minutes of 6 Oct 1788.

[61] *B.M. Add. MSS. 21255*, Numerous minutes of Abolition Committee
from May to Dec 1788.

[62] Ibid., minutes of 23 Dec 1788. This marked list, which would be
invaluable, has not survived with the minute books.

[63] Ibid., Minutes of 1 and 15 July 1788; *Life of Wilberforce*, I 183–4.

regard to the advice contained in Mr Wilberforce's letter . . . of the 8th July to avoid giving any possible occasion of offence to the legislature by forced or unnecessary Associations'.[64] It does not seem that more than three new provincial committees were established as a result of this journey or, indeed, independently.[65] In February of the new year, however, when the London Committee learned that Wilberforce was hopeful of bringing on the abolition question within weeks, it sprang to a renewed lobbying and assiduously pressed the case, by personal interviews, on a number of leading members of both Houses, and at the same time urged provincial correspondents and committees to act likewise.[66] Meanwhile Wilberforce, with Clarkson, devoted considerable and often anxious attention to obtaining good witnesses for the Privy Council committee and to preparing himself for the abolition motion which eventually came on on 12 May 1789, following publication of the Privy Council report towards the end of April.[67]

The debate of 12 May and the adjourned debate of 21 May[68] were fundamentally non-events. This was not the fault of the care and skill with which Wilberforce prepared and delivered his speech, nor of any lukewarmers on Pitt's part – he, rather, made positive suggestions about the mode of proceedings[69] – nor of a deficient support from leading members and supporters of abolition, notably Fox and Burke. The case quite simply was not argued substantively but shelved on the ground that the Commons must hear their own evidence on the matter – and this *despite* the very lengthy and thorough report of the Privy Council. In reluctantly acceding to this demand for evidence to be heard at the Bar of the House, Wilberforce and his supporters believed that the delay would be only until the next year. The aptness of some of their opponents at obstruction, however, and the length of time taken by a number of weighty West Indian witnesses, were such that the substantive motion was unable to be put until April 1791 – the

[64] *B.M. Add. MSS. 21255*, Minutes of 29 July 1788.
[65] Clarkson (*History*, II 3–11) lays more stress on the fact-finding purpose of this journey. The three committees were at Poole, Plymouth and Exeter.
[66] *B.M. Add. MSS. 21255*, Abolition Committee Minutes of 24 Feb. 3, 10, 24 and 31 Mar, 6, 14, 21 and 28 April, and 5 May 1789.
[67] *Life of Wilberforce*, I 202–18 passim.
[68] *Parliamentary History*, XXVIII, cols. 41–101.
[69] *Life of Wilberforce*, I 214–6.

abolitionists had even had to fight to secure a hearing for their witnesses before the Commons Committee.[70] Most of the abolitionists' exertions during this period were devoted to the discovery – not least by Clarkson – and examination of witnesses before the Commons Committee. To muster sixty abolition witnesses, even though some were unsatisfactory, was a considerable feat, considering the great reluctance to testify which was encountered,[71] and Wilberforce, together with William Smith and Dolben, put in long hours in the examination of witnesses.[72] By early 1790, too, those whom Pitt jokingly called his 'white Negroes', the Abolition Committee, were dining weekly with Wilberforce.[73]

As in every stage of the abolitionist campaign, Wilberforce used the friends both from his old and his new life. Spiritually, his diary reveals, he was torn by the problem of how far he should mix in the world, but duty, and, one suspects, a continuing unadmitted pleasure, took him into society. Certainly his popularity paid unforced dividends for one secret of such triumphs as the abolition movement gained was Wilberforce's popularity and connections. For instance in recruiting men to appear before the Commons Committee, 'he enticed a reluctant witness through the resistless influence of the Duchess of Gordon'[74] – at whose London house he frequently visited and which constituted the social centre of the Government party.[75] Finally, under Wilberforce's supervision a

[70] Ibid., I 265–7; Clarkson, *History*, II 178·80.

[71] Clarkson, *History* 168–206.

[72] *Life of Wilberforce*, I 295. For the systematic nature of Wilberforce's questioning see list of questions in *Clarkson MSS* (Huntington Library), CN 191, 'Questions to be asked Witnesses before Parliament on the subject of the Slave Trade'.

[73] *Life of Wilberforce*, I 255.

[74] Ibid., I 222.

[75] *D.N.B.* The Duchess was an exceedingly feminine woman who possessed great beauty, family ambitions, good nature and wit – marred by coarseness of speech. One can credit that she was resistless for she is said to have raised a Scottish regiment by giving each recruit his shilling with her lips. Did the still unmarried Wilberforce perhaps succumb a little to her spell – woven, doubtless, without any coarse thread? She features numerous times in his diary in 1789 and when Lord Calthorpe spent a Sunday at her home in 1801 (when 'she fell asleep . . . while I was reading to her part of Leighton's *Commentary* and awoke with lively expressions of admiration at what she had not heard') he wryly reported to Wilberforce that he 'had found the warnings against her fascinations very necessary' (*Private Papers of Wilberforce*, 103).

selective *Abstract of the Evidence* was produced at astonishing speed in the autumn of 1790[76] and then distributed to all members of (the new) Parliament.[77] But at the provincial level, and as a reform movement, the abolition campaign was clearly running out of steam, nothing significant being done to sustain it during this period. When the motion for abolition came in April 1791 it was certainly argued on its merits but was defeated – 'the character, talents and humanity of the House were left in a minority of 88 to 163'.[78]

With this defeat a kind of way-stage had been reached. Despite the early activity of the Manchester Committee and the London Committee's endorsement of Manchester's efforts to spread the agitation, the main thrust of the abolitionists had been to work on the 'political nation' and in this way to produce a favourable vote in Parliament. This approach, after suffering numerous delays and setbacks, only really came to the test in April 1791, the first time on which the abolition was discussed on its merits, and was found wanting. Wilberforce now decided – or was persuaded, we do not know – to alter his approach. Certainly the London Committee continued along the old line of seeking to influence individual members of Parliament,[79] but it was resolved to go beyond this. 'It had now become evidently necessary to appeal to the justice and humanity of the nation for that redress which was denied by the policy of parliament'.[80] The first expression of the new approach was to despatch Clarkson, subsequently aided by Dr Dickson and Campbell Haliburton as regards Scotland, on a tour to arouse opinion by disseminating the *Abstract of the Evidence* and the kindred *Substance of the Late Debate*.[81] By the late autumn Wilberforce had advanced further along this path, as he told Muncaster in an important letter of late November. 'I mean to bring on the slave business within a month after parliament meets, that we may then, being defeated, sound the alarm throughout the land (*provoco ad populum*), get petitions, etc. and carry

[76] Clarkson, *History*, II 207; *Life of Wilberforce*, I 280–83.
[77] *B.M. Add. MSS. 21256*, Abolition Committee Minutes of 19 Apr 1791.
[78] *Life of Wilberforce*, I 299. The debate is in *Parliamentary History*, XXIX (1791–92), cols. 250–359.
[79] *B.M. Add. MSS. 21256*, Abolition Committee Minutes of 24 May 1791.
[80] *Life of Wilberforce*, I 300.
[81] Ibid.

something important before the session is over.' Reviving interest in the abolition cause led him to modify this intention, as he explained to Wyvill on 19 December:

> I have considered and talked over with several friends, our future plan of operation, and we are all at length pretty well agreed, that the best course will be to endeavour to excite the flame as much as possible in a secret way, but not to allow it more than to smother until after I shall have given notice of my intention of bringing the subject forward. This must be the signal for the fire's bursting forth. We hope by that time to have laid all our trains, and that by proper efforts the blaze will then be universal.[82]

As the caution 'as much as possible in a secret way', and the assurance of Wilberforce's biographers that 'this was no appeal to the political impulses of the multitude',[83] suggest, the appeal *ad populum* must still be seen in the restricted sense of 'People'. None the less the bid for support was a bid over the heads of Parliament, it was conducted with great energy, and it could not be prevented from sometimes running along radical channels. Wilberforce devoted much time to writing to his friends urging them to secure petitions from county meetings or in other ways;[84] so did the London Abolition Committee.[85] Clarkson helped to found the Newcastle-on-Tyne and Nottingham, and Dickson the Glasgow abolition societies, whilst many other societies sprang up during the winter months.[86] The unavoidable association with radicalism came because the Manchester committee, at any rate, became more radical at this time – and produced a petition with no less than 20,000 signatures,[87] and because nothing could prevent some

[82] Both quoted in ibid., I 333–4.

[83] Ibid., 334.

[84] Ibid., I 334–7. Wilberforce, as so often, brought his political astuteness into play observing to Gisborne, for instance, that if Dudley Ryder's father, a local political magnate, 'were to see reason to believe, that his coming forward would be likely to attach to him Wedgwood, and all the Abolitionists in Staffordshire, it might operate wonderfully' (quoted in ibid., I 337).

[85] *B.M. Add. MSS. 21256*, Abolition Committee Minutes of 24 Jan and 28 Feb 1792.

[86] Clarkson, *History*, II 349–54.

[87] Hunt, 'North of England Agitation', 104–6, 109.

of the petitions being couched in somewhat radical terms.[88] A number of abolitionists also renounced the use of sugar at this time, an action regarded as radical,[89] especially when commended in the kind of extreme terms used by Rev. Samuel Bradburn of Manchester in his *Address to the People called Methodists concerning the Evil of encouraging the Slave Trade* (Manchester, 1792).[90] But whatever the inconveniences of this more popular appeal it brought results in a way that had not been previously achieved by the abolitionists – 519 petitions for the total abolition of the slave trade.[91] Nor were the Committee's traditional methods neglected. A sub-committee was set up to 'wait upon' potential supporters in the Commons 'in order to strengthen our interest previous to the decision of the Question of the Slave Trade on the 29th instant'.[92]

The new methods appear to have paid off. Wilberforce and his friends did not obtain the total and immediate abolition for which they had striven but they did secure agreement in the Commons for the immediate ending of the supply of slaves to foreigners and the termination of the remainder of the British trade in 1796. It seemed at first that a major, albeit not complete, victory had been won, but it soon proved that the Lords were of a different temper. They had barely been constrained to a regulatory measure in 1788: now they were confronted with a more fundamental measure and with Pitt unable, in a matter on which the right of private judgement was admitted, to use the methods adopted on that earlier occasion. Resort was made to the old ploy of hearing evidence – to the belated distress of the Archbishop of Canterbury who had originally supported this procedure in the belief that it would not occasion delay[93] – and then the hearings were put off to the next

[88] E.g. at Rotherham (*Life of Wilberforce*, I 339–40).

[89] Clarkson, *History*, II 349–50. For Wilberforce's rejection of this measure as likely to alienate moderate men see *Life of Wilberforce*, I 338–9.

[90] Hunt, 'North of England Agitation', 107–9. The pamphlet included the statement: 'if moderate men ... had been attended to in France, ... the Bastille had still remained'.

[91] Clarkson, *History*, II 355.

[92] *B.M. Add. MSS. 21256*, Abolition Committee Minutes of 13 Mar 1792.

[93] *PRO 30/8/161* (Chatham MSS.), Archbishop of Canterbury to Pitt, 9 May 1792 (kindly communicated by Dr Grayson Ditchfield).

session.[94] They in fact passed over the horizon for good for by the next session the political scene had changed radically as a result of the further progress of the French Revolution and Britain's entry into the war. The irony of the abolitionists' situation was that the technique of a wider agitation which they had begun to use successfully was no longer, in that changed situation, open to them.

The French Revolution, as such, and its Caribbean consequences, had no significant effect on the abolition cause until the autumn of 1791. The flight of Louis XVI to Varennes did not take place until June 1791 and the news of the terrible slave rising on San Domingo was only received in the Autumn whilst the first wave of killings in France was a year later. But the Revolution of course much encouraged radicalism in England and, already during the petitioning campaign preparatory to the 1792 motion, the leading abolitionists felt weakened by the support of radicals who saw in abolition merely one of numerous necessary political and social reforms of a more radical kind than any seriously envisaged before. 'It is certainly true,' wrote Wilberforce in this period, 'and perfectly natural, that these Jacobins are all friendly to the Abolition; and it is no less true and natural that this operates to the injury of our cause.'[95] By the late winter or early spring the prejudicial effect of the San Domingo rising was such that many well-wishers, including apparently, though perhaps momentarily, Pitt himself, urged the postponement of the motion until the next year.[96] In the April 1792 debate itself, such had been the rise of

[94] The whole discussion was, procedurally, somewhat complex but is exhaustively summarised in Clarkson, *History,* II 355–460.

[95] Wilberforce to William Hey, n.d., quoted in *Life of Wilberforce,* I 343. See also extracts from Wilberforce to Muncaster, Oct, n.d., Milner to Wilberforce, n.d., and Dundas to Wilberforce, 18 July 1791, in ibid, I 343–4; and Samuel Hoare to Wilberforce, 20 Feb 1792, *Correspondence of Wilberforce,* I 89–90.

[96] *Life of Wilberforce,* I 340–41. The phrase in Wilberforce's diary customarily taken as evidence of Pitt's attitude is 'Pitt threw out against Slave motion on St. Domingo account'. I am not persuaded that the transcription is accurate. Apart from the *non-sequitur* implied by the immediately preceding sentence in the published diary 'Called away after dinner to Slave Committee' (Pitt, was, of course, not a member of the Committee), consultation of the original diary in the *Wrangham MSS.* leaves me unconvinced that the accepted rendering is accurate. Wilberforce's hand is so difficult to read, however, that I am unable to suggest an alternative.

political radicalism in England, many speakers referred to the association of abolition with levelling principles as a reason for opposing it.

From that time onwards, however, the storm could not be ridden. A pamphlet, of the summer, or later, of 1792 could speak of 'the JACOBINS OF ENGLAND, the Wilberforces, the Coopers, the Paines and the Clarksons', and could go on to ask:

By what motives the promoters of the Abolition have been actuated? The answer is plain, Fanaticism and False Philosophy had exalted their imagination, and obscured their reason; and in what they affected to call a Reform in the Constitution, they saw the means of establishing such a Government as best suited their wild ephemeral theory.[97]

Doubtless most people dismissed this extravagant identification of Wilberforce with Jacobinism but what gave colour to the accusation, and could not be denied by late 1792, was that radical political societies had become the most vociferous champions of abolition in the country generally. The ability of Walker and Cooper to urge the Manchester Abolition Committee along more radical channels has already been seen: in the same period the Society for Constitutional Information had begun, from 1787, 'to register strong abolitionist as well as reforming tremors'. More significant was the foundation of the London Corresponding Society in January 1792 by Tom Paine, Thomas Hardy and the S.C.I. So marked was the concern of the L.C.S. and kindred provincial societies with abolition that, for instance, the motif chosen for the membership card of the Melbourne, Derbyshire Corresponding Society represented the enslavement of Africans whilst by the summer of 1792, such was the concern of Corresponding Societies with anti-slavery, that Hardy began to express concern lest they be side-tracked from parliamentary reform, their primary objective. By 1792, as a result of the emergence of radical societies,

---

[97] Anon., *A Very New PAMPHLET indeed! Being the TRUTH addressed to THE PEOPLE AT LARGE containing some strictures on the ENGLISH JACOBINS and THE EVIDENCE OF LORD McCARTNEY, and others, Before the HOUSE OF LORDS, respecting THE SLAVE TRADE.* (London, 1792) 3–4.

abolition indeed spoke with 'a new, if somewhat coarser, voice';[98] by 1793 that voice was so coarse and so strong that, as one of Wilberforce's Hull correspondents told him: 'People connect democratical principles with the Abolition of the Slave Trade and will not hear it mentioned. This is, I hear, precisely the case in Norfolk.'[99] 'I scarcely need say that the abolitionists here stand forward also in the class of Reformers', William Rathbone wrote from Liverpool to William Smith. 'Both causes are unpopular.'[100]

In this situation the struggle would have to be waged exclusively in Parliament and a new phase in the abolition movement began.

The parliamentary campaign during the next four years cannot have seemed to hold much hope of success, but Wilberforce felt driven on by a conviction that to fight on was his duty to his God.[101] Stephen Fuller, Wilberforce's West Indian opponent, made the same point rather differently: 'it will be necessary to watch him [Wilberforce] as he is blessed with a very sufficient quantity of that enthusiastick spirit which is so far from yielding, that it grows more vigorous from blows'.[102] In February 1793 he sought to hasten proceedings in the House of Lords by a further motion in the Commons seeking a renewal of its decision of the previous year. The Abolition Committee renewed their approaches to their parliamentary supporters, but the measure failed by eight votes –

[98] Based on Walvin, *How Popular was Abolition?*, 1–8. The quotations are from pp. 5 and 2 respectively. The complete sentence containing this last quotation is 'By 1792, with the emergence of the radical societies, led by the London Corresponding Society, abolitionism found a new strength and a new, if somewhat coarser, voice', and is in the context of the thesis that 'in the three distinct phases of abolitionist pressure (1787–1807) against the slave trade; in 1814 in favour of effective international abolition, and finally between 1828–1833 in the final push for total emancipation, popular opinion, drawn from a wide social front, was instrumental in promoting the cause of black freedom'.

[99] Quoted in *Life of Wilberforce*, II 18. See also Capel Lofft's information from Suffolk in the same year: 'Of collective applications in any shape I see not now any probability in this country, though I well know what great numbers in it, and how respectably composed, were earnest for the Abolition, but a damp and odium has fallen on these collective applications' (quoted in ibid., II 18–19).

[100] *William Smith (Duke) MSS.*, Rathbone to Wm Smith, 3 Feb 1793.

[101] *Life of Wilberforce*, II 21.

[102] *Fuller Letterbook*, II, Fuller to Jamaica Committee of Correspondence, 5 July 1791.

and there was further postponement in the Lords.[103] Wilberforce then tried another tack, taking up a proposal that had come up in the 1792 debate, namely that the supply of foreigners by British slavers be forbidden. At first carried in a small House by a small majority (41 to 34), it failed on the third reading.[104] Attempted again in the following year, Wilberforce got it through four divisions in the Commons, only to have it put off in the Lords where he suffered the added mortification of finding that the ordinary supporters of abolition in that House deserted the cause, and that even Grenville declined to support the bill whilst their Lordships were still hearing evidence on the general motion.[105] The 1793 and 1794 motion had, however, one particularly interesting feature for the singling out of the supply of foreigners was effected partly, as Sharp explained, to 'facilitate the future general abolition of *the trade*, by cutting off a considerable part of the interested opposition against us'.[106] The tactic[107] did, indeed, produce a result of some potential significance, for it eventuated in that division in the West Indian camp which was one of its avowed aims. Some influential West Inidans, including Vaughan and

[103] *Life of Wilberforce*, II 19–20; *B.M. Add. MSS. 21256*, Abolition Committee Minutes of 29 Jan 1793; Clarkson, *History*, II 463–4.

[104] *Life of Wilberforce*, II 23. Some lobbying of members of both Houses was evidently undertaken. See Granville Sharp's letter of 7 June 1793, quaintly addressed, in his editor's version, to 'his Grace the Archbishop of . . .', in which, true to the writer's belief in the particular role of bishops he urges his correspondent both to support the bill and to suggest that absent bishops leave their proxies with 'your Grace, or with any Bishop friendly to our cause' (Hoare, *Memoirs of Granville Sharp*, II 247–8). Of course, the bill never reached the Lords.

[105] *Life of Wilberforce*, II 48–51; Clarkson, *History*, II 466–8. The hearing of witnesses in the Lords ceased, without any conclusion, a few days later.

[106] Sharp to Archbishop of . . . 7 June 1793, 'printed in Hoare, *Memoirs of Granville Sharp*, II 247.

[107] Debrett, *Parliamentary Register*, XXXVII, Commons 1794, 500–01, has totally misled us by printing as a 'List of the Minority who voted against Mr. Wilberforce's Motion on the Slave Trade Bill' on 7 March 1794 what William Woodfall, *An Impartial Report of the Debates that occur in the Two Houses of Parliament* (London, 1794) II 214, terms 'Names of the Minority in the House of Commons on Mr. Whitbread's Motion [on the war and foreign policy], March 6, 1794'. The point is that the two lists are identical, including the same tellers and the same non-alphabetical order in which the names are listed. An error is the more explicable in that the two days are adjoining days.

Foster Barham in 1794, voted for the bill,[108] whilst in the previous year, Fuller reported a West Indian as asserting in the Commons 'that it would be for the benefit of himself and the rest of the Planters as they should have their slaves at a cheaper rate'.[109] Reviewing the events of 1793, Stephen Fuller, the Agent for Jamaica who was co-ordinating the West Indian opposition, re ported that the 'very great majority' of West Indian merchants and planters believed 'that the exclusion of the supply of Foreigners will interfere with our own', but that none the less the lack of unanimity meant that 'we have not the wished for weight'.[110] The following year Fuller observed that this division in West Indian opinion, in the strict sense, implied a more serious division 'between the Planters and the African Merchants, which may possibly, if it should take place, be fatal to the cause, as the African Merchants have many friends in the House who will certainly leave us if we leave them'. He has, therefore, 'excited every nerve' to keep them united.[111]

Wilberforce did not further utilise this divisive tactic in 1795 but attempted another general motion in the Commons. He was defeated by 78 votes to 61 on 26 February.[112] The London Abolition Committee seem to have felt that there was nothing more that could be done for the time being. As Samuel Hoare, one of their number, wrote to Philadelphia abolitionists later in the year;

Since the commencement of our correspondence which has been so agreeable to us, we have never addressed you under circumstances of greater discouragement, as to the attainment of the object of our institution, than at present. The acts and sophistry of interested men have been proved sufficient to induce the House of Commons to desert a duty the incumbency of which after a long investigation it had solemnly acknowledged. Although fully disposed to renew . . . [our] . . . exertions when-

---

[108] *Life of Wilberforce*, II 48–9.

[109] *Fuller Letterbook*, II, Fuller to Jamaica Committee of Correspondence, 5 June 1793.

[110] Ibid.

[111] Ibid. II, Fuller to Jamaica Committee of Correspondence, 4 Mar 1794.

[112] *Life of Wilberforce*, II 83–4. Clarkson, *History*, II 472, gives the minority as 57, but Fuller (*Letterbook*, II, Fuller to Taylor, 1 Mar 1795) has 61.

ever opportunities may encourage them; the Meetings of this Committee are now held only occasionally.[113]

Discouraged they might be, but Wilberforce found in an adventitious circumstance an opportunity of renewing his attack the next year. This circumstance was the enhancement of his reputation following upon the discredit it had incurred in many minds by his alleged association with Jacobinism and his support of efforts to terminate the war. The episode blew up quite unexpectedly when the opponents of the Ministry proposed a county meeting at York to arouse feeling against the Treason and Sedition Bills. Wilberforce broke his usual rule by starting, on a Sunday, a breakneck dash to York where his intervention was the climax of a massive demonstration of Freeholders in support of the bills, which, when hastily reported in Westminster, had great effect. As Fox was wont to say, 'Yorkshire and Middlesex between them make all England'.[114] On 14 January the London Abolition Committee resolved that country supporters be asked to solicit the attendance of likely parliamentary friends to the forthcoming motion by methods appropriate in each case. Not surprisingly, in view of past defeats, Wilberforce opened his speech for leave to bring in a bill 'coldly and indifferently', but his subject warmed him and support was better than expected. After three successful divisions, however, it was lost – and by a majority small enough to be really

[113] *Philadelphia Abolition Soc., Am. S. 081*, Hoare to Philadelphia Abolition Society 14 Aug 1795. Sharp had written similarly soon after the defeat: 'As our long continued labours, expenses, and best exertions have thus far proved entirely fruitless with respect to the Legislature, we are entirely at a loss how to proceed farther with any reasonable hope of success, at least from that quarter? (Ibid., Sharp to Pemberton, 20 Mar 1795). See also *Crawford Muniments*, Gisborne to Muncaster 5 Mar 1795.

[114] The episode is described in *Life of Wilberforce*, II 112–33. 'Last year you had not half the advantages you now possess', wrote Dr Burgh from York immediately after this episode, on 12 December 1795. 'To what nonsense were my ears then a frequent witness. Your desire to terminate the war was a result, forsooth, of dissenting principles, principles hostile to all good government, and your zeal to abolish the slave trade was of course included in the same silly charge. But as yet nothing has faded upon the memory of those who heard you here; and this, therefore, is the moment to bring your question under the protection of your renewed reputation while in its bloom, with all its honours hanging thick upon it' (quoted in ibid., 134–5).

mortifying, 74 to 70. 'Ten or twelve of those who had supported me', Wilberforce confided in his diary, 'absent in the country, or on pleasure. Enough at the Opera to have carried it.'[115]

Who were the MPs who supported the abolition campaign? Unfortunately only a partial, tentative and indirect answer can be given to this question. In the absence of the list of MPs which the members of the Abolition Committee so diligently marked, we have to make do with a partial list of those who voted for abolition in 1791[116] and a nearly complete list of those who supported abolition in 1796.[117] In the former case 47 out of 88 names are listed; in the latter case 64 out of 70. Collation of these lists reveals that 26 of those known to have voted for abolition voted for it on both occasions and can on that account perhaps be defined as committed abolitionists. If we make the contentious assumption that the unknown voters in 1791 voted for abolition in both motions in the same proportion as the known voters we have a figure of 49 as the limit of the hard-core abolitionist vote. The 26 certainly strike one, however, as approximating very closely to the list that could be constructed on evidence other than division lists. They are:

Henry Bankes	Wm Pitt
J. P. Bastard	W. Plumer
J. Courtenay	Lord Carysfort
Wm Dolben	Hon. Dudley Ryder
E. J. Eliot	R. B. Sheridan
R. Fitzpatrick	Wm Smith
C. J. Fox	Thos Steele
Ph. Francis	Henry Thornton
Charles Grey	Robert Thornton
James Martin	Samuel Thornton
R. S. Milnes	S. Whitbread (Jun.)
M. Montagu	Wm Wilberforce
Lord Muncaster	Wm Windham

To this list of those who gave a double vote the following might be added on the grounds of known exceptional exertions in the abolitionist cause.

[115] *Life of Wilberforce*, II 139–42; Clarkson, *History*, II 473; *B.M. Add. MSS. 21256*, Abolition Committee Minutes, 14 Jan 1796.
[116] In Clarkson, *History*, II 338 n.
[117] *Parliamentary History*, XXXII, 901–2.

Henry Beaufoy (d. 1795)
I. M. Browne
Henry Duncombe
Wm Morton Pitt
S. Whitbread (Senr)

The presumption must therefore be that the number of committed abolitionists falls much nearer to the lower than the higher end of the theoretical mathematical range and may therefore be said to have numbered about thirty in the period up to 1796. Further analysis of this group readily reveals that three – Bastard, Martin and Henry Thornton – together, possibly, with Beaufoy – are best termed Independents; that nine – Courtenay, Fitzpatrick, Francis, Grey, Plumer, Sheridan, Smith and the two Whitbreads – were attached to Fox; that the remaining sixteen were followers of Pitt. The division between Foxite and Pittite abolitionists – to use terms that are really too specific – is not, however, significant. (An apparent Foxite division against Wilberforce over his Foreign Slave Trade bill in 1794 proves, on examination, to be an error in Debrett.) There was no party basis to the abolition cause.

If a party correlation has little significance there is some positive correlation between the eighty-three known to have voted at least once for abolition in 1791 and 1796 and the support of parliamentary reform. This limited correlation can best be expressed as five propositions:

1.– Of the eighty-three known to have voted at least once for abolition in 1791 and 1796, forty-seven were in Parliament at the time of Pitt's 1783 Reform motion. Of the forty-seven, thirty (63·8 per cent) voted for reform and made up 19·9 per cent of the minority vote for reform.

2. Of the eighty-three, fifty-four were in Parliament at the time of Pitt's 1785 Reform motion. Of the fifty-four, twenty-nine (53·7 per cent) voted for reform and made up 16·7 per cent of the minority vote for reform.

3. All eighty-three were in Parliament at the time of Grey's 1793 Reform motion. Of the eighty-three, thirty (36·1 per cent) voted for reform and made up 73·2 per cent of the minority vote for reform.

[118] See p. 279, n.107 above.

4. Of the eighty-three, sixty-eight were in Parliament at the time of Grey's 1797 Reform motion. Of the sixty-eight, twenty-nine (42·6 per cent) voted for reform and made up 31·2 per cent of the minority vote for reform.

5. The average percentage of those known to have voted at least once for abolition, and who were in Parliament at the relevant time, and who supported the parliamentary Reform motions, was 49·1. On average they constituted 35·3 per cent of the minority vote for reform. Or, in other words, an average of 35·3 per cent of those who voted for reform are known also to have voted for abolition at least once between 1791 and 1796.[119]

A sixth proposition, making the somewhat different correlation between votes cast for abolition and votes cast for repeal of the Test and Corporation Acts in 1787 and 1789, supports the view that there was a significant reformist component in the abolitionist vote. It is this:

Of the eighty-three known to have voted at least once for abolition, fifty-four were in Parliament at the time of the 1787 and 1789 Repeal bills. Of the fifty-four, twenty-nine (53·7 per cent) voted for repeal at least once, and made up 26 per cent and 23·1 per cent respectively, of the vote for repeal.[120]

The significance of all these conclusions is of course prejudiced

[119] The Minorities in support of parliamentary reform in 1783, 1785, 1793 and 1797 are taken, respectively from Wyvill, *Political Papers*, II 255–6; *Stockdale* (1785), V 359–62; *Parliamentary History*, XXX, col. 925; and *Debrett*, (Commons 1797, 3rd series) II 656–7. It has been assumed that all those who are known to have voted for abolition in at least one of the 1791 and 1796 motions were in Parliament in 1793.

There is, as one might expect, a pretty negative correlation between votes cast against abolition and attitudes to parliamentary reform, demonstrating that supporters and opponents of abolition were markedly different in their attitudes to parliamentary reform. The average percentage of those who voted against abolition in 1796, and who supported parliamentary reform motions which came on during their membership, was 7·8% and constituted 2·3% of the minority vote for reform.

[120] Dr Ditchfield kindly allowed me to use the lists of those who voted for repeal in 1787 and 1789, from the *Odgers MSS.*, contained as an appendix in his as yet unpublished article, *The Parliamentary Struggle over the Repeal of the Test and Corporation Acts, 1787–1790*.

by one glaring *lacuna* – our ignorance of the names of forty-one of those who supported abolition in 1791 (as well as of six of the seventy supporters of the cause in 1796). One would surmise that knowledge of the missing names would be likely to strengthen the positive correlation between abolition, and parliamentary reform and the Repeal of the Test and Corporation Acts.

To anticipate for a moment, it is striking that the West Indian interest enjoyed the parliamentary support of two loose but significant groupings of MPs over and beyond those representing the slave-trading ports. The abolitionists, on the other hand, had no such allies. There may, of course be more profound senses in which abolition expressed the emergence of an ideology of Free Trade: but of parliamentary support from any new interest group representing the rising forces in the economy – indeed of the existence of any such groups – there is at this time not a trace.

12 The Opposition to Abolition to 1796

The most likely explanation of the defeats suffered by the abolitionists in the period up to 1796 is, surely, that the West Indian interest, conjoined with the African merchants, was able to muster superior parliamentary strength. If Thomas Fowell Buxton could assert, in 1823, that the 'West India interest could put forth a phalanx of 200 members in the House of Commons',[1] must one not conclude that that interest would have been at least as strong before 1807, before the West Indian position in the scheme of things had begun to be eroded? No less a statesman than Edmund Burke had seriously considered pressing a scheme for gradual abolition of the slave trade in 1780, but had abandoned the attempt 'from the conviction that the strength of the West Indian body would defeat the utmost efforts of his powerful party, and cover them with ruinous unpopularity'.[2] But can we more precisely probe the strength of the West Indians? And what was their organisation and achievement in the struggle against abolition?

According to the important analysis of parliamentary membership by G. P. Judd, the West Indians in the Commons, planters and merchants combined, numbered twenty in the 1784 Parliament and twenty-nine in its successor.[3] This was not the full

[1] *Parliamentary Debates*, XIII, col. 607, quoted in B. W. Higman, 'The London West India Interest, 1807–1833', *Historical Studies*, XIII, no. 49 (Oct. 1967), 2.

[2] *Life of Wilberforce*, I 152–53.

[3] G. P. Judd, *Members of Parliament, 1734–1832* (New Haven, Conn., 1955). These totals were derived from Judd's overall list of West Indians on p. 94. His summary totals on p. 89 are lower, in respect of the 1790 Parliament (and indeed, for others) because, to avoid double counting, he only places a member in one category. In his own words, 'I have not made multiple entries for men stated to be "merchants" in addition to another form of trade. That is, if a man is stated to be a banker and a

extent, however, of those who might normally be expected to oppose abolition, for up to ten more members, representing constituencies in which the slave trade and West Indian trades were felt to be important interests, seem normally to have opposed abolition. These constituencies were, predictably, Bristol, Liverpool, Lancashire and London. Contemporaries seem often to have described all the opponents of abolition as West Indians. This was doubtless because the essential interest concerned was the West Indian slave-based economy and because the West Indians had a social and political position more elevated than that of the hardnosed slave trader.

The institutional heart of the West India interest was the Society of West India Planters and Merchants, a body which represented an amalgamation of the London West India planters with the London merchants trading to the West Indies. Its activities were financed by a levy on imports into the port of London. Between 1782 and 1784 an executive committee, the Standing Committee, came into existence; it did not meet regularly, but as business required. There appear also to have been lesser West India societies at Liverpool, Lancaster, Glasgow and Bristol – ports with major West Indian connections.[4]

It was therefore natural that the lead in opposing abolition should be taken by the London Society of Planters and Merchants. A leading member of that body, Stephen Fuller – a planter in his own right, and at the same time Agent for Jamaica, the largest Caribbean colony – reported to the island legislature's Committee of Correspondence on 5 December 1787 that abolition was to be raised in Parliament.[5] By the end of January of the new year Fuller

[4] Lillian M. Penson, 'The London West India Interest in the Eighteenth Century', *E.H.R.*, xxxvi (July 1921) 373–92

[5] *Fuller Letterbook*, i, Fuller to Jamaica Committee of Correspondence, 5 Dec 1787.

merchant, he appears only once, as a banker. This distinction escaped me in a footnote on the strength of the West Indian interest in my 'A Re-Interpretation of the Abolition of the British Slave Trade, 1806–07), *E.H.R.*, lxxxvii (April 1972) no. 343, 324. Namier and Brooke also give a figure for West Indians in the 1784 Parliament – 9 only. Their definition, however, is more tightly drawn, namely 'those who were born in the islands or had resided there' (L. B. Namier and J. Brooke, *The Commons 1754–1790* [History of Parliament series] (London, 1964) 156–57 (henceforth *H. of P.*).

had written to Lord Hawkesbury[6] and Lord Sydney urging upon them opposition to abolition.[7] The pace then quickened: a report reached Fuller that 'Mr Wilberforce had opened his plan for the abolition of the slave trade to Mr Pitt and that Mr Pitt had declared his resolution to give him full support'. Immediately Fuller besought Lord Sydney, Home Secretary in Pitt's Administration and 'the firmest and warmest Friend we have' to inquire if the report were true – to learn, in other words, what kind and degree of backing the Prime Minister was going to give to Wilberforce.[8] It may be that it was the West Indians' realisation of Pitt's stake in the question – 'it appears to me that Mr Pitt means to support any motion of Mr Wilberforce for an inquiry into the African slave trade'[9] – that jogged them into a realisation that counteraction must be taken. In any event Pitt's referral of the slave trade question to the Privy Council at this very time meant that the West Indian watchdog must rouse up, and it was at a meeting of the Standing Committee of the West India Planters and Merchants on 7 February that it was decided to appoint a sub-committee to take all necessary action in the matter of 'the present application to Parliament on the subject of Negroes'.[10] Although Lord Penrhyn, the chairman of the Standing Committee, was chairman also of the sub-committee, much of the hard work seems to have been done by Stephen Fuller. Fuller had already made his own assessment of the odds – and with an intriguing note of self-

[6] Charles Jenkinson had been created Baron Hawkesbury in 1786 and was to be made 1st Earl of Liverpool in 1796, in which year R. B. Jenkinson assumed the title of Hawkesbury. Up until 1796, therefore, a reference to Hawkesbury is to Charles Jenkinson, and after 1796 to R. B. Jenkinson.

[7] Ibid., i, Fuller to Jamaica Committee of Correspondence, 30 Jan 1788.

[8] Ibid., i, Fuller to Jamaica Committee of Correspondence, 6 Feb 1788.

[9] Ibid.

[10] *West India Planters and Merchants, Minutes*, vol. 3, Minutes of Standing Committee, 7 Feb 1788. (The volume numbers are those pencilled in on the spine of the bound volumes; the sequence includes some volumes which are minutes of the Merchants only, and will be so referred to). The twelve members were Lord Penrhyn, Messrs. Neave, C. Arcedeckne, Edward Long, Beeston Long, Baillie, John Ellis, James Gordon, Spooner, Braithwaite, Fuller and Stanley – the last four were Colonial Agents (Ibid.). Henry [?] Dawkins was evidently added to the sub-committee very shortly afterwards (*Fuller Letterbook*, i, Fuller to Jamaica Committee of Correspondence, 20 Feb 1788).

mockery. 'The stream of popularity runs against us; but I trust nevertheless that common sense is with us, and that wicked as we are when compared with the abolishers, the wisdom and policy of this country will protect us.'[11]

The way to see that 'wisdom and policy' would sustain the West Indian cause was, of course, to bring influence to bear on the Privy Council Committee and to lobby members of both Houses. Fuller's reports to the Jamaica Assembly are full of efforts to bring favourable witnesses before the Privy Council Committee and reports with delight such *bons mots* as that Admiral Lord Rodney had testified before it that 'he never saw any Negro flogged with half the severity that he had seen an English schoolboy'.[12] Whether from effective lobbying, or because of predisposition, the West Indians could claim an impressive bloc of support at this time. At the beginning of July Fuller counted Lord Thurlow, the Lord Chancellor, Earl Bathurst, Lords Sandwich, Rodney, Heathfield, Morton, Brownlow, Buckinghamshire, Galloway, Lonsdale, Cadogan, King (?), the Duke of Chandos and the Bishop of Bangor.[13] Sydney can only have been omitted from the list in error and we know that Hawkesbury should also be numbered amongst the supporters of the West Indian cause.[14] How far Penrhyn, Fuller and their sub-committee had some responsibility for arousing a significant phalanx against abolition in the Lords remains obscure. As regards the Commons, separate general meetings of West India planters and of West India merchants agreed on petitions to that House at the end of April 1789[15] whilst at the same time, evidently anticipating that the opponents of abolition would be able to insist upon evidence being heard at the bar of both Houses, it was agreed by the planters that the levy on West

[11] Ibid., I, Fuller to Jamaica Committee of Correspondence, 30 Jan 1788.

[12] Ibid. I, Fuller to Jamaica Committee of Correspondence, 6 May 1788, and *Letterbook*, passim. There are numerous representations hostile to abolition which were submitted to Hawkesbury, the effective chairman of the Privy Council Committee, in the *Liverpool Papers, B.M. Add. MSS. 38416*, passim.

[13] Ibid., I, Fuller to Jamaica Committee of Correspondence, 1 July 1788.

[14] Wraxall, *Memoirs*, 143; *Life of Wilberforce*, 293–4.

[15] *W.I. Planters and Merchants, Minutes*, vol. 3, Minutes of General Meeting of Planters, 24 Apr 1789 and of Merchants, Mortgagees, Annuitants etc. 24 Apr 1789, and of Planters and Merchants, 26 Apr 1789.

Indian imports into London should be increased from 1d. to 6d. 'per hogshead and puncheon and so in proportion for all other articles', so as to defray expenses of legal representation.[16] In May the opponents of abolition *did* carry their insistence that evidence be heard and in the next session of Parliament a General Meeting of Planters and Merchants appointed a committee to prepare and select evidence for the Commons inquiry.[17] The West Indians were for some time able to maintain a strong front in the examination of witnesses, John Stanley, together with the Liverpool and Bristol MPs, being particularly effective.[18]

It was only natural that the MPs for Liverpool and Bristol should have been active in the examination of witnesses, for the slave-trading interest was more immediately threatened by abolition than were the West Indians. Liverpool had begun to bestir itself against the threatened abolition early in February 1788 – at much the same time as Fuller commenced his exertions. Liverpool first grew alarmed when John Tarleton reported on a long interview he had had with Pitt at the very beginning of February, in which the minister had made clear that 'particularly with respect to his situation as the Minister of a great commercial country . . . his present sentiments were for *the Abolition of the Slave Trade* – and that I had authority from him to communicate them immediately to my friends in Liverpool'.[19] The reaction of the mayor of Liverpool, in consultation with the African merchants, was to ask Tarleton to remain in London to head an official Liverpool delegation whose other members came to include Robert Norris,

[16] Ibid., vol. 3. Minutes of General Meeting of Planters, 24 Apr 1789.

[17] Ibid., Minutes of General Meeting of Planters and Merchants, 11 Feb 1790. The members were Messrs. Neave, Long, Beckford, Thos. Boddington, Baillie, Robert Mine [?], H. Manning, Bettesworth, G. Hibbert, Willock, A. Douglas, Johnson, Hankey, Casamajor, B. Long. The committee met on 12, 16 and 26 Feb 1790.

[18] *Wrangham MSS.*, Wilberforce's MS Memoir of his life. See also *Fuller Letterbook*, I, Fuller to Jamaica Committee of Correspondence, 2 June 1789 and 25 Jan 1790. The *Annual Register* for 1790, pp. 95–6, describes the process of calling evidence which it regards as an important reason for the check to abolition.

[19] *Tarleton Papers*, 920 TAR 4/5 (Liverpool Public Libraries), John Tarleton to Clayton Tarleton, 5 Feb 1788, quoted in Sanderson, 'Liverpool Delegates and Dolben's Bill', 61–2, to which source I am indebted for this paragraph on the Liverpool contribution to the campaign against abolition.

James Penny, Lt. John Matthews, RN, and Archibald Dalzell. These Liverpool delegates appear to have been most active in providing and grooming witnesses for the Privy Council Committee. Initially this initiative had considerable effect,[20] but it appears that though Liverpool and its delegates exerted themselves in various ways up until 1792, they were not after that date distinguishable from the general West Indian opposition.

In the early months of 1791, in the new Parliament, Fuller becomes despondent. 'We have lost so many of our friends in the House of Commons at the last General Election,' he records on 2 February;[21] 'we are miserably attended at the Committee,' he laments on the seventeenth.[22] When the abolitionists had managed to secure a hearing for their witnesses, few West Indians would appear to examine them.

> The subject is so completely exhausted that even the members who have property in the colonies seldom or ever attend. Sir William Codrington has endeavoured to persuade them to attend by rotation, one at a time, on a day fixed for each, but he has not prevailed; and I know by what I have tried myself, that he will find it no easy matter to get one single member to sit four hours in a morning at that committee, where he would be sure to find at least three to keep him in order. We have had an irreparable loss in Lord Penrhyn, Sir Peter Parker, and Mr. Dickinson's not being in Parliament, and in the illness of Mr. Stanley, member for Hastings, the best man we had.[23]

It is significant in the explanation of why the abolition cause was for so long unsuccessful that it could not prevail in the debate of March 1791 even despite the serious weaknesses in the West Indian parliamentary representation. Whether because of that weakness, or because, with the termination of the Commons inquiry into the evidence, a close hand was no longer called for, or because it was felt that the abolitionists could not be allowed to remain unchallenged

[20] See p. 268 above.
[21] *Fuller Letterbook*, II, Fuller to Earl of Effingham, 2 Feb 1791.
[22] Ibid., II, Fuller to Edward Long, 17 Feb 1791.
[23] Ibid., II, Fuller to Jamaica Committee of Correspondence, 2 Mar 1791. 'Fuller repeats his lament two years later . . . it being impossible to keep our friends in Town who are not immediately interested in the question, and God knows they are very few in the House of Commons' (Ibid., II, Fuller to Jamaica Committee of Correspondence, 5 July 1793).

in their propaganda campaign, the West Indians made their greatest effort to influence public opinion in 1792 and 1793. In barely over twelve months from the beginning of March 1792 they spent £2,096 on propaganda,[24] and although this was only half the amount they paid out for the presentation of their case at the bar of each House of Parliament – £4,031 for an undisclosed period up to May 1794 – a sum of over £2,000 betokens a major effort and was almost double that of the Abolition Committee on propaganda in a comparable period.[25] The publicity campaign was conducted by the slave trade sub-committee set up in 1788 but which for some reason appears to have been inactive until January 1792 when its membership was augmented.[26] During the remainder of that year, and well into 1793, the sub-committee met frequently and devoted itself to two main objects. Firstly, it sought to secure favourable publicity in the newspapers, national and provincial, by the provision of material and by letters to the editor. In late March 1792, as the time for Wilberforce's motion of that year drew close, members of the sub-committee attended daily at Ibbotson's Hotel between twelve and three to peruse the newspapers so that 'what may be therein inserted by the Favourers of the abolition of the slave trade' could be picked up and controverted. In the presentation of the West Indian case, it was noted at the same time, the *Public Ledger, Star, Whitehall Evening Post* and *Argus* would be of great service for they were 'open to the directions of the Committee'.[27] These weeks were the high point of the sub-committee's activity, but it continued to give much attention to newspaper insertions at its subsequent frequent meetings.[28] The sub-committee also sponsored the writing and dis-

[24] *W.I. Planters and Merchants, Minutes of Slave Trade Sub-Committee*, vol. 3A, summary on flyleaf.

[25] Ibid., vol 3A, Minutes of Sub-Committee, 28 May 1794. Efforts to obtain financial help from the outports seem to have been disappointing, the only remittance noted being one of £430 from Bristol in 1790 (Ibid., 3A, Minutes of Sub-Committee, 30 Apr 1792).

[26] Added on 19 Jan were Geo. Hibbert, Alex Douglas, Wm Innes, Robt. Milligan, Thos. Betterworth, Benjamin Vaughan & Gilbert Francklyn; in March, Richard Crewe; on 19 June, Simon Taylor, ? Sharp, Alex. Campbell, James Wildman and Nath Phillips; and during 1794, Wm Mitchell and Edmund Thornton (Ibid., vol. 3A, List on first page).

[27] Ibid., vol. 3A, Minutes of Sub-Committee, 22 Mar 1792.

[28] Ibid., vol. 3A, Minutes of Sub-Committee, passim.

tribution of pamphlets. Something along this line had already been done. For instance, the Resolutions of a General Meeting of West India Planters and Merchants, held in May 1789, had been published. There was no attempt at moral justification of the slave trade – a most telling indication of the change in moral and intellectual attitudes to slavery which had taken place – but simply the assertion that it had existed 'as a Condition of Mankind in Africa, from the earliest Times' and that the slave trade only took off those already slaves or convicts and prisoners of war who would be massacred. The rest of the case was made in terms of national interest, of a long-standing national commitment to the support of the Caribbean plantation system, and of the sheer economic importance of the sugar-colonies.[29] One pamphleteer, perhaps Stephen Fuller, added a gloss to this kind of presentation in the peroration of his *Remarks on the Resolution of the West India Planters and Merchants* (1789).

In certain vast regions of the Africa Continent, where the Arts are almost as little known, of rural as of civil cultivation, inhabitants grow faster than the means of sustaining them; and Humanity itself is obliged to transmit the supernumeraries, as objects of traffic, to more enlightened, or less populous countries; which, standing in constant need of their labour, receive them into property, protection and employment. Whatever branch of commerce contributes thus to the mutual convenience, and even subsistence, of Nations . . . must insensibly . . . interchange intellectual cultivation with the culture of the ground.[30]

The sub-committee, in 1792, continued along the same lines, its principal efforts being the printing and distribution of *An Abstract of the Evidence favourable to the Africa trade* – the concern to refute the abolitionists' *Abstract* is very evident – by G. Francklyn, one of its members. Five thousand copies of this pamphlet were ordered to be distributed on 22 March 1792[31] whilst within a week

[29] The pamphlet's heading is simply *At a General Meeting of the PLANTERS, MERCHANTS, and Others, interested in the WEST INDIES, held at the LONDON TAVERN, May 19, 1789.* (Copy in *Wm Smith (Duke) MSS.*)

[30] *Remarks on the Resolutions of the West India Planters and Merchants* (1789), Copy in *Fuller Letterbook,* i.

[31] *W.I. Planters and Merchants, Minutes of Slave Trade Sub-Committee,* vol. 3A, Minutes of Sub-Committee, 22 Mar 1792.

the pamplet of one Jesse Foot, *A Defence of the Planters in the West Indies* was ordered to be distributed to Members of Parliament.[32]

The publications so far mentioned were inspired by the Society of West India Planters and Merchants. Two other contributions of different origin deserve notice as, unusually, attempting to justify slavery and the slave trade on non-material grounds. The first had been published just before the abolition campaign proper began and was a reply to Ramsay. In *An Apology for Negro Slavery: or the West India Planters vindicated from the Charge of Inhumanity*,[33] George Turnbull went beyond the conventional defences by asserting it to be justified by Providence and by seizing upon one of the possibilities inherent in that important concept of the eighteenth-century, the Great Chain of Being.

> Negro slavery appears, then, to be, as far as reason can judge, one of those indispensable and necessary links in the great chain of causes and events which cannot, and indeed ought not to be broken; or, in other words, a *part* of the stupendous, admirable, and perfect *whole*, which, if taken away, would leave a chasm, not [to] be filled up by all the wit or the wisdom of erring and presumptuous man.[34]

The author went on to espouse a tactical argument, but one couched, ingenuously or disingenuously, in the language of the age's values. After speaking of the harsh condition of the 'poor peasant' and 'indigent mechanic', he goes on:

> Humanity has no need to visit distant regions, or to explore other climates, to search for objects of distress in another race of men! Here at her very door, there are enough – here let sensibility drop her tear of generous pity – here let charity stretch forth her liberal hand – and here let benevolence, whom Heaven has blessed with the means, exert her noblest power, indulge her sweetest gratification, and enjoy her highest and most delicious luxury.[35]

[32] Ibid., vol. 3A, Minutes of Sub-Committee, 28 Mar, 1792.
[33] Anon (By the Author of Letters to a Young Planter [George Turnbull] (London, 1786).
[34] Ibid., 34–5.
[35] Ibid., 63.

The other justification of the slave trade was the Rev. Raymond Harris, *Scriptural Researches on the Licitness of the Slave Trade. Shewing its Conformity with the Principals of Natural and Revealed Religion. Delineated in the Sacred Writing of the Word of God* (London 1788). This was an apologia for the slave trade in which the author – though, or, as some said, because a Jesuit – took his stand four-square on Scripture, deducing from it that slavery was nowhere declared intrinsically unlawful. The demands of the law of love, moreover, could not be invoked in support of anti-slavery since they could as well be invoked against any form of subordination. If Harris had in this last particular anticipated a major long-term significance of abolition, the immediate effect was to make a case which was very hard to answer, and which abolitionists were not very successful in meeting.[36]

At the other extreme the opponents of abolition, like the abolitionists, also saw the value of doggerel. Of this J. Walker, *A Descriptive Poem of the Town and Trade of Liverpool* (1789), is an example, as the following excerpt suggests:

> Let none too rash condemn the Afric trade,
> Till once the subject they have duly weighed;
> The Moors are purchased from their native shore,
> And sold for slaves, were they not as before?
> 'Tis proved their state is better'd – not made worse,
> Then slav'ry is a blessing, not a curse.
> Oh, might the Muse, her suffrages subjoin,
> To those who've thank'd Lord Penrhyn and Gascoyne,
> Who stood to staunch to prop the Afric trade,
> When Wilberforce its condemnation read.[37]

All in all the propaganda of the West Indians was not of the volume[38] and quality, and could not possess the moral fervour, of that of the abolitionists. As with the abolitionists, the intensity of the West Indian agitation diminished from 1793 onwards. None

[36] For an extended consideration of Harris' *Scriptural Researches* see Chapter 10 of David Davis' forthcoming *The Problem of Slavery in the Age of Revolution, 1770–1823.*

[37] Quoted in Hunt, 'North of England Agitation', 161 n.

[38] Dale M. Porter has reminded us that Ragatz located only 47 pamphlets published in defence of the slave trade, but 109 against it (*The Abolition of the Slave Trade in England, 1784–1807* (Hamden, Conn., 1970) 87).

the less the Society of Planters and Merchants kept a watching brief, notably in seeking assurances from Pitt, through Lord Carhampton, about the foreign slave trade bill of 1793,[39] and by circulating opponents of abolition in March 1796 requesting their attendance in the abolition debate then shortly coming on.[40]

In the period ending in 1796, as far as the possibility of a general, immediate abolition was concerned, the current was flowing the way of the West Indians – though the narrow margin by which the 1796 motion was lost in the Commons must have caused concern. The division in the West Indians' ranks resulting from the abolitionists' introduction of abolition of the foreign slave trade as a separate measure has already been noticed, and had, as we shall eventually see, considerable significance for the future. But the period drew to a close with the confident assertion by Fuller that 'of the absurd attempt of abolishing the slave trade . . . I think we shall hear no more . . ., even in the House of Commons after the next General Election'.[41]

The role of the West Indians in preventing the passage of the Abolition Bill in the years 1787–96 should now begin to emerge as both more and less credible than we had supposed. It is more credible because able to be spelled out in some detail. But the traditional notion of the West Indian role, namely that the West Indian vote was of itself sufficient to prevent abolition is rendered less credible. When we turn to the study of the solitary anti-abolition division list that appears to exist we gain further illumination on the nature and strength of the anti-abolition vote.

The list in question is found only in Debrett[42] and Woodfall and is unsatisfactory only to the marginal extent that it totals the Noes at the accepted figure of seventy-four, but then goes on to list seventy-seven names as opposing abolition – though this does include the two tellers. With this reservation, however, the list is invaluable as the only list we have of votes cast against aboli-

[39] *W.I. Planters and Merchants*, vol. 4, Minutes of General Meetings of 25 and 28 May 1793.

[40] Ibid., vol. 4, Minutes of Standing Committee, 8 Mar 1796; Ibid., vol. 3A, Minutes of Slave Trade Sub-Committee.

[41] *Fuller Letterbook*, ii, Fuller to Jamaica Committee of Correspondence, 31 Mar 1795.

[42] *Debrett*, xliv 323–4 and Woodfall, *Debates*, iii (1796) 453–5. I owe my awareness of this list to the kindness of my colleague, Dr Grayson Ditchfield.

tion at any time between 1787 and 1807. What is immediately surprising about the list is that it contains only six – J. Foster Barham, Edward Lascelles, W. Lushington, J. Nesbitt, G. M. Rose and R. M. Trench Critwell – of the twenty-four West Indians who, by Judd's list, were in Parliament in 1796. However, the strength of the West Indian component of the vote does not remain at this low figure because a strong case can be made out for increasing the West Indian interest from the twenty-four listed by Judd (as of 1796)[43] to thirty-four[44]. Of this extra ten,[45] nine are included in the 1796 majority against abolition.[46] If our increase in the number of West Indians is accepted, therefore, fifteen out of thirty-four West Indians voted against abolition – but only fifteen. Again, however, we can augment what at first sight seems to be the full extent of the 'interest' group, for eight more of the seventy-four in the majority can be identified as having a business or constituency involvement in the slave trade.[47] Again, and somewhat dubiously, we can count as having a stake in the West Indies three who sat in Sir James Lowther's interest,[48] since Lowther had West Indian property. Of course, a few of the remaining members who voted against abolition may have had West Indian or slave trading connections which do not appear from the biographical information about them but such unknown connections

[43] Judd's list, apart from those just named, comprises Richard Beckford, R. Cunningham-Graham, E. H. East, C. R. Ellis, S. Estwick (the younger), F. Ford, James Gordon, Wm Pulteney, G. F. Lyttleton, Wm Macdowall, Wm Manning, Ralph Payne, M. Sloane-Stanley, John Stanley, Geo. Thomas, C. Tudway, B. Vaughan and Geo. White-Thomas.

[44] Cf. Sir L. Namier, *England in the Age of the American Revolution* (London, 1963) 234–45, for acceptance of the view that in an extended definition there were about 40 West Indians in Parliament in the 1760s.

[45] On a variety of evidence, particularly in *H. of P.*, the following appear, by property background, family or business connection, to have had significant stakes in the West Indies: R. Barclay, D. Davidson, J. Dawkins, Sir R. G. Gamon, B. Lethieullier, Charles Long, R. Mackreth, G. Rose, John Sargent and Sir William Young. It should be emphasised that the criteria for inclusion are not always as rigorous as Judds.

[46] The exception is Long.

[47] J. Blackburne, J. Dent, Bamber Gascoyne, Lord Somerset (Marquis of Worcester), Lord Sheffield, Thomas Stanley, Sir Banastre Tarleton and John Tarleton.

[48] J. Anstruther, J. Baynes Garforth and R. B. Jenkinson. It is by no means certain that the first and last would obey Lowther in a matter of this kind by 1796, and both had other reasons for opposing abolition.

are unlikely to have been numerous or substantial enough to add significantly to the list.[49] As the list stands then, no more – and our criteria are broad, demanding no more than some species of known connection with the West Indies – than twenty-six out of the seventy-four can reasonably be termed 'West Indians'. And if an extra ten is allowed for unknown West India connections, the total only rises to thirty-six.

What is immediately striking about this modest total is that it is approximately the same as our previously calculated estimate of 'hard-core' abolitionists. The last vestiges of an explanation of the failure of abolition in terms of a powerful West Indian group able to determine the Commons' decision therefore fall away. It is instructive to proceed further with a comparison between the abolitionist and anti-abolitionist votes. If one compares the more extended categories of the number who usually supported, and usually opposed abolition, we have, again two not very dissimilarly sized groups. In 1791 the abolition vote mustered eighty-eight. In 1792 the advocates of immediate abolition numbered 125.[50] In 1796, as we have seen, Wilberforce reckoned that ten or a dozen over and above the seventy who actually voted for abolition were absent. To this extended, looser group of abolitionists of, say, ninety, we can oppose an anti-abolitionist counterpart somewhat higher. Votes against abolition of 163 in 1791, eighty-seven in 1792 and seventy-four in 1796 point to an average of something over 100. These extended groups, however, are less constant, more volatile, and in two senses. Firstly, they were prone to erosion – be it by the lure of the opera, as Wilberforce complained, or by the attraction of the countryside as the parliamentary session neared its end, as Fuller lamented.[51] They were volatile in the second

[49] The *History of Parliament* of course only covers the years up to 1790 and therefore contains no entries for men who were first elected in 1790. The deficiency can be partly made up from the *D.N.B.* and miscellaneous sources, especially Sir Chas. Elphinstone Adam (ed.), *The Political State of Scotland in the Last Century, A Confidential Report on the Political Opinions, Family Connections and Personal Circumstances of the 2662 County Voters in 1788* (Edinburgh, 1887). Analyses of members' interests and of voting patterns in the Parliaments of 1790 onwards will be much facilitated by publication of the next volume of the *History of Parliament*.

[50] T. Gisborne, *Principles of Moral Philosophy*, 5th ed. (London, 1798) 400–02 (Appendix on 'the late decision of the House of Commons respecting the abolition of the Slave Trade'); Clarkson, *History*, II 449.

[51] *Fuller, Letterbook*, II, Fuller to Jamaica Committee of Correspondence,

sense that they were subject to really massive increase or diminution. This becomes apparent if we look ahead to 1807. By that time the nuclear abolitionist group does not appear to have been significantly larger – five votes for immediate abolition in 1804 and 1805 and a notable Resolution about Abolition of 1806 averaged ninety-nine,[52] whereas they would surely have increased markedly if the core-group had grown significantly larger – and yet the final abolition motion which followed as soon afterwards as 1807, was carried by 283 to sixteen. The critical question which therefore emerges is that of the composition of what can crudely be termed the floating vote and the influences and constraints upon it.

Why, first of all, was this a question for a free vote? Why was it not, rather, one in which the Prime Minister, the warm supporter of abolition, could command the votes of his supporters? Surely he could wield such authority after years of continuous power – thirteen years by 1796. Brougham, indeed, believed that it was in Pitt's power to have done just this, and that he was culpable for having failed to do so.

> But I fear the worst remains to be urged against the conduct of this eminent person. No man felt more strongly on the subject of the African slave trade than he; and all who heard him are agreed that his speeches against it were the finest of his noble orations. Yet did he continue for eighteen years of his life, suffering every one of his colleagues, nay, of his mere underlings in office, to vote against the question of abolition, if they thought fit; men, the least inconsiderable of whom durst no more have thwarted him upon any of the more trifling measures of his Government, than they durst have thrust their heads into the fire.[53]

[52] *Life of Wilberforce*, III 168, 174, 178, 212, 263.
[53] Lord Brougham, 'Historical Sketches of Statesmen who flourished in the Reign of George III', *Collected Works* III 283–4. Cf. also Stephen's charge, made in 1797, that 'Mr. Pitt unhappily for himself, his country and mankind, is not zealous enough in the cause of the Negroes, to contend for them as decisively, as he ought, in the Cabinet any more than in Parliament' (quoted in *Life of Wilberforce*, II 225). See also Francis'

5 June 1793. Absenteeism 'will always be the case so late in the session; it being impossible to keep our friends in Town who are not immediately interested in the question'.

This is a serious allegation, made by a political opponent of Pitt's party, yes, but no less by one informed about the abolition campaign because active in the later stages of it. Wilberforce himself was concerned to vindicate Pitt from the charge of inconstancy, and the memorandum which Wilberforce dictated in his retirement both does this and, what is more important for our immediate purpose, explains Pitt's conduct in the light of the conventions of the Constitution. A consequence, said Wilberforce, of the abolition question

> not being brought forward by a member of Government and the judgement of the Administration not having been taken upon it, every official man was at liberty to act as he saw fit and here it may be proper to enter into some explanation on this head. Mr. Pitt's enemies [have] called in question his sincerity as a friend of the abolition but certainly without any just ground though not without plausibility especially in the instance of those who are unacquainted with the actual practice of Parliament. It is the established system that all official men vote with their principal, but . . . the Minister is not considered as being entitled to require the votes of the inferior members of Government except on political questions or those in which the credit or stability of the Government be fairly supposed to be in some

---

urbanely vicious attack on Pitt in 1796 in reference to the recent close defeat of abolition: 'And does he think it possible that the country, that any rational being should give credit to a proposition so extravagant and so monstrous, that the all-powerful minister of the crown, with all his eloquence, and with all his influence, and with the accession of thirty voices from his [sic] side of the House, should not have been able to engage more than seventy votes in a favourite question of his own, if, in earnest and *bona fide*, he had designed to carry it. Is there nothing in his mind to elevate him for a moment above the level of his station?' (*Parliamentary History*, XXXII, cols. 949–50). It must be remembered that Francis was an ardent Foxite. A further edge may conceivably have been lent to his feelings about the slave trade because his abolitionist stand had, he once told the Commons, been at the cost of considerable personal expectations. Debrett's report is significantly different. At the critical point it says: 'With the aid of seventy voices, to which he [Pitt] was usually indebted in the votes of that House, he was not able to muster about seventy members on the side of the question which he espoused!' (*Debrett*, XLIV 398). This confirms the suspicion that the *Parliamentary History* should read: 'with the accession of thirty voices from *this* side of the House'.

measure at stake. . . . For instance when Mr. Pitt brought forward his measure for improving the poor laws, many of his warmest political adherents opposed his measure without its being supposed by any one that they were less attached to him than before – in short what shall and what shall not be a Government question is not an abitrary arrangement, nor is it dependent on the Minister's will, it turns in fact on the answer to the question: 'Is the credit or stability of an administration at stake?' In the instance therefore of my motion for abolishing the slave trade every one was perfectly at liberty to vote as he should see fit – It was in no sense a party question.

At this stage Wilberforce made, in effect, a partial concession to Brougham's charge by arguing that the abolition question should have been construed as a national question to be furthered by government.

Yet it must be owned that the question considered in relation either to the commercial interest of the country or to the personal security of a large mass of its population was of great importance and there is the more reason to regret the narrow view that was taken of it because it prevented Government taking the measure (as they ought to have done) into their own hands and associating it as they must have done with a plan for improving the condition of the Negro slaves and gradually transmitting them into a free peasantry. Unhappily this just view of the case was not taken.

With the coming of war, Wilberforce continued, 'it must be confessed that other questions and other interests occupied more his thoughts and feelings . . . I can truly however declare that he . . . never produced in my mind any suspicion of luke warmness in his opinion or feeling on the question', a feeling shared by William Smith who, as a Foxite, at any rate after the mid-nineties, was unlikely to be disposed in Pitt's favour.[54]

[54] *Wrangham MSS.*, William Wilberforce, MS Memoirs of his Life, n.d. A short part of the memoir is quoted in the *Life of Wilberforce*, I 165, and in a manner which does not make the extent of editorial intervention clear. We ourselves have amended the punctuation of the extract given above since, as a dictated piece, it has many syntactical deficiencies. Clarkson's verdict on Pitt is 'But though Mr. Pitt did not carry this great question, he was yet one of the greatest supporters of it. He fostered

It therefore emerges from Wilberforce's defence of Pitt that in Wilberforce's view it would have been a proper alternative for Pitt to have made the abolition a government matter, but the very context of Wilberforce's criticism makes clear not only that Pitt's sincerity in the cause is not thereby impugned, but that it was in accord with the conventions of the Constitution, even that the weight of these conventions would on balance demand, that abolition be not treated as a government question. Any tendency Pitt may have felt to stretch the Constitution over this issue must have been countered by the known opposition to that particular measure of Cabinet colleagues of the stature of Thurlow (in the Cabinet until mid-1792), Dundas and Liverpool, and later Portland. The accession of the Portland Whigs meant that more opponents of abolition now entered the Cabinet, of whom the Duke of Portland himself and Lord Loughborough were the longest serving members.[55] It is likely indeed that the accession of Portland's following may have been on the same condition as one (amongst others) discussed in abortive negotiations in 1792 and noted by Lord Malmesbury, one of the group, in his diary, in these terms: 'On Lord Loughborough's observing to him that . . . the strong manner in which he (Pitt) had promoted the abolition of the Slave Trade,

---

[55] Earl Fitzwilliam was also an opponent of abolition; but he left the Cabinet at the end of the year to be replaced by the Earl of Mansfield (Viscount Stormont until he succeeded to his uncle's title in 1793). Mansfield had been in the Cabinet since 1794 and left it in September 1796. See also Porter, *Abolition*, 92–3.

---

it in its infancy. If, in his public situation, he had then set his face against it, where would have been our hope? He upheld it also in its childhood, and though in this state of existence it did not gain from his protection all the strength which it was expected it would have acquired, he yet kept it from falling' (Clarkson, *History*, II 506). That Wilberforce was right about Smith's judgement of Pitt is shown in Smith's remarks on 10 June 1806 in the Commons (*Substance of the Debates on a Resolution for abolishing the Slave Trade* (London, 1806; reissue 1968, Dawsons of Pall Mall) 67–8.' Canning also is on record as supporting Pitt's view of his limited powers over the abolition. 'Pitt allowed his most intimate & attached friends to differ from him [over abolition], without remonstrance. We are come to fine times if Mr A's [Addington's] government is to impose a restraint upon liberty of conscience, which Mr Pitt never ventured to think adviseable' (Canning to Sturges, 7 Feb 1802, *Canning Papers*, quoted in Patrick C. Lipscomb, 'Party Politics, 1801–1802: George Canning and the Trinidad Question', *The Historical Journal*, XII (1969) no. 3, 457).

would require some explanation, he said certainly some concessions must be made . . .'.[56] And once war had begun, the dangers
and hazards of wartime did not merely engage most of Pitt's attention, but because of the greater premium they put on Cabinet unity,
made it significantly more difficult to put that unity at risk by
seeking to convert the abolition into a government matter. Recent
work by constitutional and political historians supports the view
of the tendency of constitutional conventions which Pitt took.
Professor Pares has pointed out that reform measures such as
Catholic emancipation, parliamentary reform – and abolition –
were not in this period measures which could be cabinet measures,
given the convention that Cabinet measures were confined to
'matters of government, as government was then understood'.[57]
In a similar vein, Professor Aspinall has shown that there was no
possibility of commanding ministerial agreement on 'open' questions,[58] whilst John Ehrman's comment is specifically on abolition. 'The abolition of the slave trade was at best a marginal
subject for a Government motion, and Pitt's ministry at that
time [the early 1790s] would certainly not have accepted it.'[59]

We find a striking example of ministerial obstruction of Pitt if
we look ahead to 1799. Canning, a rising politician and star in the
abolition firmament, had originally thought to move a bill limiting slave importations to the amount of the annual decrease, but
was happy to resign this to Pitt and Grenville who had come to
feel that the recent opposition in the Lords to two regulatory bills
was 'utterly indecent and improper'.

> Pitt and Lord Grenville have in consequence set seriously about
> mustering a sufficient strength to carry measures to which they
> are personally pledged in opinion. It has been felt also (and

[56] Diary, 17 June 1792, *Diaries and Correspondence of James Harris, First
Earl of Malmesbury* (London, 1844) II 463–4. See also *P.R.O. 30/8C11*,
Pitt to Chatham, 29 May 1799; Lipscomb, *Pitt and Abolition*, 344; and
Porter, *Abolition*, 92. Porter quotes Malmesbury's diary extract but does
not make clear that it dated from June 1792.

[57] Richard Pares, *King George III and the Politicians* (Oxford, 1953) 164–5.

[58] A. Aspinall, 'The Cabinet Council, 1780–1832', *Proceedings of the
British Academy*, XXXVIII (1952) 223–4.

[59] Ehrman, *The Younger Pitt*, 392. Cf. T. Steven Watson. *The Reign of
George III, 1760–1815* (Oxford, 1960) 301: 'His [Pitt's] advocacy [of
abolition] was not insincere, but it was not carried to the point of dis-
rupting his political system.'

it is high time it should) that the state in which the whole slave
trade question has been suffered to remain, hung up under
pretence of an examination of evidence in the House of Lords,
and brought in and lost annually, against the declared opinion
and wish of a Minister who generally *can* carry a question in
the House of Commons, is at best ridiculous, if not disgraceful.
And a resolution has therefore been taken, to bring the matter
to a point, to discuss it regularly in Cabinet; form a Government
opinion upon it, and bring that forward next session with
ministerial authority.[60]

But what in fact happened? Pitt tried to persuade Lord Liverpool
that he might feel able to agree to support a measure resting 'almost
wholly on political grounds' rather than on the general principle.
Only imports sufficient to maintain the existing population would
be permitted, the supply of foreign possessions should be stopped
and of conquered islands[61] either stopped or severely limited.[62] On
the same day a Cabinet was held – Liverpool was absent through
illness – but Pitt, if Canning is correct in attributing firmer intentions to him, had already come to believe they could not be persisted in. Aware of the continuing opposition of Dundas, Portland
and Lord Westmorland, Pitt told the Cabinet that he was not
proposing his measure as a Cabinet measure.[63]

It is possible that royal hostility to any Cabinet endorsement of
abolition may also have been a specific cause of Pitt's retreat on
this occasion.[64] Certainly it cannot be overstressed that the mon-
arch, and especially George III, still possessed a considerable
voice in government at this time. George III was firmly opposed
to abolition, doubtless because he saw it as a threat to the well-
being of that kingdom which it was his duty to preserve. 'The King
did not like the measure', Pitt himself told Loughborough in

[60] Canning to Wilbraham, 7 June 1799, Josceline Bagot (ed.), *George
Canning and His Friends* (London, 1909) i 151.

[61] 'Where we are at present pouring in English capital only to create
(in the event of their being restored at the Peace) future rivals to our
own possessions.'

[62] *B.M. Add. MSS. 38192* (Liverpool Papers), f. 102, Pitt to Liverpool,
9 July 1799.

[63] *B.M. Add. MSS. 38191*, f. 245, Portland to Liverpool, 12 July 1799.
For this episode see also Porter, *Abolition*, 103–5.

[64] *B.M. Add. MSS. 38190*, f. 108, Duke of Clarence to Liverpool, 23
July 1799.

1792,[65] whilst Lord Liverpool, as Hawkesbury became in 1796, wrote in 1799 that he understood from the Duke of Clarence 'that it was the King's determination that any business of this sort [a proposal for limitation of the slave trade] should never be made a cabinet measure'.[66]

D. G. Barnes, in the light of his exhaustive study of the correspondence between George III and Pitt, makes an informed speculation on the significance of the conjunction of opposition to abolition from members of the Cabinet with opposition from George III. Pitt, he says,

> had no desire to sacrifice his place at the head of the ministry by attempting to make George III and his fellow ministers accept the measure by a threat that he would resign. Thus while Pitt could secure the reluctant acquiescence of his cabinet on small measures by threatening to make the King choose between him and the dissenting ministers, evidently he felt that he could not secure the King's approval of the major reforms by threatening to resign, or it seems likely that he would have tried it. In short, there was a no-man's land between George III and Pitt. The King might have forced Pitt to resign rather than give way on what he considered a major issue; but at the same time he was very anxious to retain his chief minister and was willing to make such concessions as allowing minor reforms to be passed or as permitting members of the cabinet who became distasteful to Pitt to be ousted. Neither George III nor Pitt seemed anxious to find precisely where the line of demarcation was in this no-man's land.[67]

In the opposition of George III to abolition we therefore find a further powerful reason why it could not become a Cabinet measure. Less important, but still highly significant, was the hostility of the Duke of Clarence. Opposed in much else, father and son shared an hostility to the ending of the slave trade and the Duke took a tireless part in resisting the measure in the

[65] Malmesbury, Diary, 17 June 1792, *Diaries and Correspondence of Lord Malmesbury*, ii, 464

[66] *B.M. Add. MSS. 38416*, f. 312, Liverpool to Duke of Clarence, 10 July 1799 (copy).

[67] D. G. Barnes, *George III and William Pitt, 1783–1806* (London, 1965) 180–81. See also Clarkson, *History*, ii 506.

Lords.[68] We know, too, of one occasion when the Duke was used by Liverpool as a channel for informing the King of a proposal by Pitt for limiting the trade, and of Liverpool's own opposition to the measure.[69] On that occasion there was no need of royal buttressing of dissident ministers, but the reality of such a union was always latent.[70]

Given that it was politically impossible for abolition to become a government matter, what determined how MPs voted? The short answer, at one level, is their principles and their prejudices. What is surely one of the more agreed conclusions of historians of the period about the political behaviour of members must here be stressed. It has been aptly restated in precisely our context by R. A. Austen and W. D. Smith.

> While there were plenty of specific interests represented in the Commons, of which the West Indian slave holding interest was one of the more important, when a question at issue touched neither a Member's particular concerns nor those of his party he could be expected to vote according to his conceptions of 'principle' and the national good.[71]

Our question therefore becomes: how did conceptions of principle and the national good bear upon the abolition question in the thinking of men beholden, in this matter, neither to government nor opposition?

We can assume from the evidence already adduced of the major shift in attitudes to slavery, that what has been termed the extended abolition vote came from men who were behaving as children of their age – or, more precisely, who either believed that abolition would be beneficial in all its effects or who could not see

[68] Note the vote of thanks for his exertions against abolition proferred by the Society of West India Planters and Merchants in 1804 (*W.I. Merchants Minutes*, vol. 8, Minutes of Meeting of Merchants, 11 Sep 1804).

[69] *B.M. Add. MSS. 38416*, f. 312, Liverpool to Duke of Clarence, 10 July 1799 (copy).

[70] For an extended assessment of the evidence regarding Pitt and Abolition see Patrick Lipscomb, 'William Pitt and the Abolition Question: a Review of the Historical Controversy'. *Proceedings of the Leeds Philosophical and Literary Society*, XII, pt IV (1967) 87–128.

[71] R. A. Austen and W. D. Smith, 'Images of Africa and British Slave Trade Abolition: The Transition to an Imperialist Ideology, 1787–1807', *African Historical Studies* II (1969), no. 1, 72–4.

that any harm which might result from abolition was as important as the good to humanity which would ensue. There is, as one would expect, testimony enough in the speeches delivered in the debates of the influence of considerations of humanity and justice. Yet it is obvious that members not themselves interested in the continuation of the slave trade and slavery believed that there were principles which demanded a vote against abolition. A part of the evidence for the nature of these principles is found by analysis of the list of opponents of abolition in the division of 1796. It is, first of all, striking that a group of twenty-three had in common strong colonial and especially East India connections.[72] They were proprietors, nabobs, retired officers or officials or connected with these by close family or business ties. One (Jenkinson) was a member of the Board of Control. The only one of the twenty-three whose colonial connection was not East Indian was Scrope Bernard. Bernard was, however, a son of a former Governor of Massachusetts and notable upholder of the imperial connection. Here, we may reasonably infer, was a group of men who might have varying views on how Empire should be run, who might see it either as oyster, or, more rarely, trust, but whose lives, beliefs or fortunes, were so involved with India, the second great centre of the old Empire, that they instinctively felt that an attack on any part of the accepted imperial order must be resisted.[73] The credibility of this inference is indirectly reinforced by the discovery in

[72] R. Barwell, Scrope Bernard, P. Benfield, A. Brodie, J. Callander, Wm Clive, Sir A. Fergusson, Sir J. Frederick, Sir E. Impey, W. Keene, J. Langston, D. Scott, General R. Smith, G. Steward, H. Strachey, Geo. Sumner and Sir Mark Wood, plus J. Anstruther and R. B. Jenkinson, who have already and very dubiously been categorised as dependants of patrons, and W. Lushington and R. Mackreth who have been included as West Indians (see p. 297 above), and J. Blackburne and J. Dent who, we have seen, represented 'interested' constituencies. Major sources for this list are *H. of P.*, Judd, *Members of Parliament*, 92–3, and C. H. Philips, *The East India Company 1784–1834* (Manchester, 1961) 340–47. According to the extensive, but not always clearly particularised list of East Indians in this last source, 10–14 East Indians voted for abolition in 1796.

[73] See the speech of Gen. Smith, the only one of the group of 17 to speak in the 1796 debate. It includes a warning that a result of the passage of abolition would be that 'we might be threatened with the loss of the colonies, to the utter ruin of England' (*Parliamentary History*, XXXII, cols. 868–9).

the 1796 anti-abolition vote of a further group of no less than eleven members more or less closely connected with Dundas.[74] We have abundant evidence of Dundas' conviction of the need to maintain and defend the Empire. Early in his political life he had been a strong opponent of conciliating the Americans[75] and by 1794 believed that abolition would 'be considered by the colonies as an encroachment upon their legislative rights, and they will not submit to it unless compelled'. In his immediately following sentence, he said that it was 'upon this ground' that he had used all the influence he possessed to prevent the abolition question being raised at any rate whilst the nation was at war.[76] To provoke the Caribbean legislatures to rebellion, after all, would be to threaten the Empire in its wealthiest part. Dundas, even more than most men, had strong convictions about the value of the old Empire in general and the Caribbean possessions in particular, and increased his stake in those convictions by successfully imposing on Pitt and the Government a war strategy whose main exertions were in the West Indies.[77] It was only to be expected that his speech in the 1796 debate should give significant attention to the

[74] Wm Dundas, Robert S. Dundas, J. Ferguson, W. Garthshore, P. Horne, Ch. Ross, Wm Wenyss together with R. Barclay, already categorised as a West Indian, A. Brodie and D. Scott and Sir A. Fergusson, already categorised as East Indians. P. Heron should possibly be added to this list. He was member for Kircudbright Stewartry but it is unclear whether or not he was one of the few Scottish M.P.s whom Dundas had not brought into line (see *Political State of Scotland*, 199). Major sources for this list are *H. of P.*, *D.N.B.*, and *Political State of Scotland*.

[75] *H. of P.*

[76] Dundas to Wilberforce, n.d. (?1794), qouted in *Life of Wilberforce*, II 49–50.

[77] *Wrangham MSS.*, Wilberforce MS Memoirs of his Life, 'Under an idea of executing his declared purpose of not making peace with France without indemnity for the past and security for the future he [Pitt] was seduced by Mr. Dundas then the War Minister into West Indian expeditions . . .' On the confusion attending the conduct of colonial policy in wartime, note Windham's remark, of the winter of 1795–96, just after he had become Secretary at War, and Holland Rose's following comment: '"The fault, I am persuaded, is not that any one [of the Ministers] has thought or acted wrong, but that they have not thought at all." The remark throws a flood of light on what is dignified by the name of colonial policy' (J. Holland Rose, 'The Conflict with Revolutionary France, 1793–1802', *C.H.B.E.* II (Cambridge, 1961) 61.

commercial, fiscal and maritime value of the British West Indies and to the estimated £70 m–80 m of property invested there.[78] The nature of the attachments which produced the bloc of Dundas voters raises an interesting point. Dundas, of course, was not a patron with a following but, rather, Government election agent and dispenser of patronage for Scotland.[79] All of those opponents of abolition in 1796 who have been identified as members of his 'clan' sat for Scottish constituencies, save for Garthshore – and he was Dundas' private secretary. Given the particularly tight hold, and the independent authority, which Dundas exercised in Scotland there is no doubt that when he told Wilberforce that he had 'used all the influence he possessed' against the raising of the abolition question, this included not least his interest with Scottish members who were supporters of Administration. In other words, because of the special nature of Dundas' influence in Scotland, the votes of Scottish supporters of government were being mobilised against abolition. This would also explain the charge made by Philip Francis in 1796 that placemen had been mobilised against abolition.[80]

There remain twenty-nine of the seventy-four anti-abolition voters of 1796 about whose connections and 'interest' we for the most part know little. Had they possessed an obvious 'interest' in the slave trade and West Indies it is reasonable to conclude that this would normally have emerged. With a few tentative exceptions, therefore, we may see this group as made up of men who simply voted on the merits of abolition as they saw them, concluding that the national interest demanded the continuation of the slave trade. The possible exceptions are, firstly, a group of clients. S. Haynes had come in in the Duke of Bridgwater's interest, R. Hopkins and

---

[78] *Parliamentary History*, XXXII, cols. 874–81. 'He . . . for some years . . . disposed of the votes in Parliament of nearly the whole Scottish commoners, and of the whole Peers' (Brougham, *Historical Sketches, Collected Works*, III 309).

[79] Holden Furber, *Henry Dundas, First Viscount Melville, 1742–1811* (Oxford, 1931) 201–67.

[80] *Parliamentary History*, XXXII, col. 950. 'Allow me to tell you a short story, from good authority; but whether it be true or not is immaterial. A member of this honourable House was asked how he voted on the last question of abolition. "Sir, I voted with my friend the minister." How so? I thought you had divided against the bill – "Very true; I certainly divided against the bill; but I voted with my friend the minister".'

perhaps W. Keene in the Duke of Grafton's, T. Wildman[81] in H. Gough Calthorpe's (the latter himself voted against abolition in 1796, but we have no knowledge of any particular reasons), and H. Walpole in the Duke of Portland's. Of these patrons, only Portland is known to have been an opponent of abolition, presumably on policy grounds and because he had obtained the reversion of several valuable offices in the West Indies for relations,[82] and it is conceivable that this was the case with other patrons. Secondly, there was a group of three bankers – J. Langston, W. Praed and G. Steward – and two London merchants, J. Trevanion and Sir J. M. Vanneck. It is possible that their businesses gave them particular or general reasons for supporting the West Indian cause.

Dundas, however, is not only significant as a political patron whose views demanded that he call out his phalanx to help vote down abolition. Nor is it the sole significance of the East Indian vote that so many East Indians did vote as a bloc. For both the Dundas group and the East Indians, in the concern for maintenance of the Empire which can reasonably be imputed to them, constitute a pointer to the kind of influences which shaped the independent vote on abolition motions. The seeming paradox of the many votes against abolition begins with the fact that no serious defence of the slave trade on grounds of justice and humanity is attempted by the opponents of abolition. 'I am most averse to a traffic of men, termed a slave trade' – thus spoke the West Indian, Sir William Young, in 1791.[83] The African slave trade was 'founded upon injustice and inhumanity', the words are those of Dundas in 1796.[84] Others met the question – and avoided the real issue – in some such manner as Mr Grosvenor in the 1791 debate: 'He acknowledged it was not an amiable trade, but neither was the trade of the butcher an amiable trade, and yet a mutton chop was, nevertheless, a very good thing'.[85] But although there is a failure to attempt a defence of the trade on moral or legal grounds,

[81] It is possible that Wildman should be classified a West Indian for the name is not very common and a James Wildman was active in the Society of W.I. Planters and Merchants.

[82] A. P. Thornton, *The Habit of Authority* (London, 1966) 121, cited in Porter, *Abolition*, 100.

[83] *Parliamentary History*, XXIX, col. 295.

[84] Ibid., XXXII, col. 874.

[85] Ibid., XXIX, col. 281.

there are numerous defences of it on political and economic grounds. Thus Lord Penrhyn in 1789:

> There were mortgages in the West India islands to the amount of seventy millions; the fact therefore was, if they passed the vote of abolition, they naturally struck at seventy millions of property, they ruined the colonies, and by destroying an essential nursery for seamen, gave up dominion of the sea at a single stroke.[86]

And Mr Molineux later in the same debate:

> The abolition of the slave trade would destroy the West India trade. What were they about to do? Did they mean to swallow all the property of the planters in order to gratify a humane disposition towards the Africans? Before they were humane to these, he thought they should be tender of their own subjects, whom they had seduced to hazard their property in this trade.[87]

Mr Rolle, also, 'entreated them to pause and seriously consider the fatal tendency of the measure to our commerce, and to our importance as a political nation'.[88]

Mr Cawthorne said in 1791: 'In deciding on a question which involved the abolition of the slave trade, they would do well to recollect what was required by justice to the islands, by humanity to themselves, and by general policy.[89] Sir William Young's defence of the slave trade included a defence on general national grounds:

> The slave trade, he said, again in 1791, derives from its connection with them [the West Indian colonies] an importance touching the very existence of the British Empire. Should the motion of this night be adopted, I presume not to measure the extent of ruin in the islands, and decay in their commerce as dependent for a time on that with Africa. How little in such case the West Indian commerce might become, I dread to think of! How great that commerce acually is, I will show briefly and in part only....[90]

[86] Ibid., xxviii, col. 78.
[87] Ibid., xxviii, col. 98.
[88] Ibid., xxviii, col. 82.
[89] Ibid., xxix, col. 332.
[90] Ibid., xxix, col. 311. See also, *inter alia*, the speeches of Dempster, Sawbridge, Drake and Newnham (ibid., xxvii (1789), cols. 77–8, 79,

To the defence of the trade on the score of political and economic necessity was often added the plea that, even if the slave trade was wrong, the consequences of stopping it would be harmful to Africans. 'If they could not be sold as slaves, they would be butchered and executed at home,' said Sawbridge.[91] If no longer bought by British slavers, they would be purchased by foreigners who had a higher mortality aboard their ships, said Jenkinson.[92]

Not only were important national and private interests represented by speakers in the debates as demanding prior consideration; not only was the ending of the morally indefensible slave trade represented as none the less likely to harm its intended beneficiaries. One frequently reiterated school of thought contrived to square the circle: it gratified its humanity by condemning the slave trade but served what it saw as the national interest by urging the postponement of abolition until some time in the future, an advocacy often coupled with the proposal of regulations to govern the trade meanwhile. The effect was a vote against abolition. Mr Burden, for instance, in the 1791 debate largely agreed with Wilberforce, but he wished to go gradually: 'A judicious physician would follow nature, and produce a gradual recovery of his patient, by administering gentle alternatives, rather than hazard the death of a patient by giving strong and violent medicines all at once.'[93] That immediate abolition would harm vital national interests but that it should come some time in the future; that, meanwhile, regulations should ameliorate the lot of the slave – these were arguments deployed by Jenkinson,[94] Addington[95] and, above all, Dundas.[96]

The abolitionists, as one might expect, sought to counter the argument from political and economic interest. With proper encouragement a slave population could reproduce itself, there would be no need of expensive slave imports, and there was no threat to

[91] Ibid., xxvIII, col. 79.
[92] Ibid., xxIX, cols. 1126–7.
[93] Ibid., xxIX, col. 286. See also ibid., xxvIII, cols. 95–6, Mr. Cruger, and ibid., xxIX, col. 315, Lord John Russell.
[94] Ibid., xxIX, cols. 1124–33.
[95] Ibid., xxIX, cols. 1110–13.
[96] Ibid., xxIX, cols. 1104–10 and xxxII, cols. 874–81.

79–80 and 80–81); Grosvenor, Cawthorn and Drake (ibid. xxIX (1791), cols. 381–2, 332–3 and 358; Baillie (ibid. xxIX (1792), cols. 1079–83).

the plantation owner and to the West Indian plantation economy. Africa's national produce would be an alternative quest for the slave trader; the slave trade was not as important for Liverpool and Bristol as it had been made out to be; the slave trade, far from being a nursery of seamen, was their cemetery; it was not certain that other nations would take up that part of the trade which we laid down. There are various modes of assessing the persuasiveness of the rival arguments in this area of political and economic interest. As to the abolitionists' arguments, it must be said that they were too often hopes and calculations rather than demonstrable truths.[97] And there was, perhaps, too much of a limitation in the scope of the abolitionists' reassurances. Wilberforce himself, though he always developed non-moral arguments for abolition of a kind which did not, as he often said, weigh much with him personally, perhaps indicated a still too limited concern with this kind of argument when in 1791 he said that 'surely no man, however free he might deem himself to decide on grounds of expediency, would require more at his hands than that he should show that the measure [abolition] would not prove absolutely ruinous to the West Indies'.[98] Again, there was perhaps an absence of cutting edge, and positive cause for alarm in the custodians of the metropolitan interest, in his assurance to the West Indians that, even if his various arguments about the economic practicability of abolition were wrong, 'that the increase of price will make up their loss, and is a clear ultimate security'.[99]

In addition to this assessment of the limited persuasiveness of abolitionist arguments at this level, there is one particularly valuable indication that it *was* widely feared that abolition would have just those fatal consequences which its opponents predicted. The accounts of parliamentary speeches at this time scarcely ever notice reactions to speeches. The following extract from Wilberforce's 1789 speech is therefore noteworthy and makes an important point

I have in my hand the extract from a pamphlet which states, in very dreadful colours, that thousands and tens of thousands

[97] The notable exception was the abolitionist case on mortality amongst slavers' crews.

[98] *Parliamentary History*, xxix, col. 259.

[99] Ibid., xxviii, col. 54. See also a portion of his 1792 speech (ibid., xxix, col. 1065).

will be ruined; how our wealth will be impaired; one third of our commerce cut off for ever; how our manufactures will droop in consequence, our land-tax will be raised, our marine destroyed, while France, our natural enemy and rival, will strengthen herself by our weakness (*A cry of assent* [*was*] *heard from several parts of the House*) [my italics].[100]

We know, furthermore, that the most skilful and influential exponent of all the political and economic dangers of immediate abolition – Dundas – intervened both in 1792 and in 1796 to considerable effect, an effect greater than indicated in his already noticed ability to bring out a Scottish phalanx to vote against abolition in 1796. The evidence is, quite simply, the informed assessment of the abolitionists in respect of 1792[101] – though the case there is obvious in any event – and of abolitionists and West Indians in regard to 1796. In March of that year the Society of West India Planters and Merchants passed a vote of thanks to Dundas 'for his able and constitutional speech in the House of Commons on Tuesday the 15th instant, and for the effectual opposition he thereby gave to the Bill for the Abolition of the Slave Trade'.[102]

The bearing of Dr Burgh's letter of 19 March 1796 to Wilberforce is equally clear. 'Such wretches as T [Tarleton?] and D [Dent?] may be consigned to mere contempt. Sir William Young by his insincerity entitles himself to as much attention as may frustrate a shallow trick, but against Dundas I recommend, and will cultivate in myself, a propensity to direct hostilities.'[103] Burgh might be pompous about Dundas: Robert and Isaac Wilberforce made the more piercing thrust that 'oppression could not find a kinder advocate, or abuses a more honest patron'.[104] When the Minister of War, using his considerable presence and parliamentary gifts, could draw on the authority of his office to declare, as

[100] Ibid. This reference to the pamphlet was in fact a rhetorical ploy. Wilberforce immediately went on to say that it had been written in 1774 and that he had cited it to show 'how men in a desponding moment will picture to themselves the most gloomy consequences, from causes by no means to be apprehended'.

[101] *Life of Wilberforce*, I 350–51.

[102] *W.I. Planters and Merchants*, vol. 4, Minutes of Standing Committee. 22 Mar 1796.

[103] Quoted in *Life of Wilberforce*, II 142.

[104] Ibid., I 351.

he did in 1796, that 'prohibition of the trade with Africa . . . if passed into a law in the present distracted state of the colonies, would throw them entirely into the power of the enemy',[105] the abolitionists were right to acknowledge Dundas, as in effect they did, as the most important cause of the failure of immediate abolition in the Commons in the period up to 1796.

To offer an explanation of the defeat of abolition in the Commons is not, of course, completely to explain the parliamentary failure of abolition, for, as we have seen, the compromise motion for gradual abolition passed the Commons in 1792 but ran into the ground in the Lords. Likewise the Foreign Slave Trade Bill of 1794, after successfully passing the Commons, was lost in the Lords. Were the reasons for the failure there the same as the causes of failure in the Commons? The absence not only of Cabinet agreement on abolition, but of individual ministers prepared to support it, was even more harmful in the Lords than in the Commons. In the Commons there was always the outstanding oratory of Pitt to counter Dundas: in the Lords formidable debaters like Thurlow (also enjoying the particular confidence of the King) and considerable orators like Lord Stormont[106] confronted situations where ministers mostly sat silent; where, as in Dolben's Bill, the Duke of Richmond might defend the measure, in Wraxall's words, 'with zeal if not ability',[107] or where Lord Stanhope, persuaded, it would seem, that a cause was only ever really right if he found himself its sole champion, did his loyal but – to his cause – damaging best. Beyond this, we see as an ingrained attitude in the Lords the same kind of instinctive concern for traditional imperial interests as was evident in the Commons. Thurlow had been inflexible over the rights of the mother-country in America and now professed a tender concern for the plight of British West Indian traders and planters; the Duke of Clarence was convinced of the importance of the West Indies, evidently as a result of his naval service there.[108]

[105] *Parliamentary History*, xxxii, col. 752. On Dundas' role see also Clarkson, *History*, ii 486–8; *Life of Wilberforce*, ii 17; *Fuller Letterbook*, ii, Fuller to Sewell, 9 Mar 1795.

[106] A. S. Turbeville, *The House of Lords in the Age of Reform, 1784–1837* (London, 1958) 89. Stormont succeeded his distinguished uncle as Lord Mansfield in 1793.

[107] Wraxall, *Memoirs*, 143–4.

[108] *Parliamentary History*, xxix, cols. 1351–2, 8 May 1792, and ibid., col. 1350, 3 May 1792.

Lord Heathfield, the saviour of Gibraltar, had had West Indian experience as well as Lord Rodney, the victor of the Saints. The opposition to abolition of them both can be construed as inspired by a concern to maintain that Empire which they had so conspicuously defended.[109] Sydney, until his resignation in mid-1789, could not but implicitly invoke the authority of his office (for colonial affairs then came under the Home Secretary) for his view that 'the question of the slave trade was too serious to be frequently agitated',[110] whilst it is significant that when, in May 1792, Stormont put his motion for inquiry to be made – by evidence to be heard at the Bar – into the slave trade, he added: 'and also into the nature, extent and importance of the sugar trade, and into the general state and condition of the West India islands, and the means of improving the same'.[111] Indirect support for the view of the House of Lords as hostile to abolition, because of a concern for the traditional imperial trading system, is found in the numerous fears voiced a little earlier, in 1784–85, when Pitt sought to liberalise Irish trade as part of an attempt to reform Anglo-Irish relations, fears of the harm that would be done to the West Indian and other imperial trades.[112]

At another level, it may be argued, much conspired to induce their Lordships to see themselves as defenders of a traditional imperial interest, just because events since the constitutional crisis of 1783–84 had cast the Lords in the role of defenders of the traditional constitutional order.[113] When Fox attacked them as enemies of the people and a menace to constitutional government[114] their natural reaction was to emphasise their role as defenders of the established order. When George III appealed to the Lords, through Pitt, 'to prevent either the Crown or the Commons from encroach-

---

[109] 'Exceedingly important were the West India islands to our commerce and navigation, and he [Rodney] could appeal to the noble Lord (Heathfield) behind him, whether he did not think the Bill unnecessary, and likely rather to introduce evils than benefits' (ibid., xxxii, col. 639, 25 Jan 1788).

[110] *Parliamentary History*, xxvii, col. 646, 25 Jan 1788.

[111] Ibid., xxix, col. 1350. This account of the views of leading opponents of abolition in the Lords includes their attitudes to Dolben's Bill, a regulating and not an abolition bill. But if such a measure as this is opposed, then, *a fortiori*, so must the abolition be opposed.

[112] See ibid., xxv, cols. 820–85 passim.

[113] Turberville, *The Lords in the Age of Reform*, 68–70.

[114] Ibid., 59.

ing on the rights of each other',[115] the response elicited was essentially the same. In one specific respect, the insistence that evidence be heard before the Bar of the House, this 'strict construction' approach, may well have owed something to the Lords sense of their role as defenders of the constitution.[116] The Duke of Clarence made an explicit connection between the role of the Lords as guardians of the constitution and their proper attitude to abolition: 'Another circumstance had great weight with him, namely, that an implicit obedience to the House of Commons, much as he respected that House, would render the House of Peers useless, and thus the national and constitutional balance in the constitution would be endangered.'[117]

It is not unreasonable to postulate a carry-over of attitudes from the constitutional area to that of trade and Empire. In any event we cannot fail to discern in the Lords an even more hostile reaction to the French Revolution than in the Commons. After all, the aristocracy was the subject of total attack and its reaction was therefore the stronger. And whilst a generally conservative stance, a 'spontaneous dislike of all change', as Pares simply termed it,[118] demanded opposition to change in the established imperial system, the evident connection between Jacobinism and abolition (perhaps accentuated in the Lords by Stanhope's prominent role in the abolition) must demand resistance to abolition. The Earl of Abingdon expressed the connection perfectly in 1793:

For in the very definition of the terms themselves, as descriptive of the thing, what does the abolition of the slave trade

[115] Quoted in ibid., 59.

[116] Bishop Porteus gives the names of the members of the Lords who voted in the minority in the Bishop of Rochester's unsuccessful motion of 10 March 1794 to have the evidence taken in a Committee room above stairs: 'The Abp. of Canterbury, The Bishops of London, Durham, Lichfield, Exeter, Rochester, Norwich, Duke of Montrose, Lords Grenville, Radnor, Spencer, Guilford, Holland [?], Morton.' To these 14 were opposed 42, of whom only the Bishops of Bangor, Ely, Oxford and St. David's are named (*Porteus MS. 2103*, Diary entry of 10 Mar 1794).

[117] *Parliamentary History*, xxix, col. 1350, 3 May 1792. See also Stormont's speech in the continuation of the same debate attesting the right of the Lords to alter and modify Commons resolutions (ibid., col. 1350).

[118] Pares, *George III and the Politicians*, 42. See also Walvin, *How Popular was Abolition*, 9, where the slightly different version of the speech that appeared in the *Annual Register* of 1793 is quoted.

mean more or less in effect, than liberty and equality? What more or less than the rights of man? And what is liberty and equality, and what the rights of man, but the foolish fundamental principles of this new philosophy.[119]

The available evidence, then, suggests that attitudes to abolition in the Lords were determined principally by recoil from Jacobinism, by an awareness of what imperial interests demanded yet more heightened than in the Commons, and by the less able presentation than in the Commons of the abolition case. Of the role of interest there is even less evidence than in the Commons. Stephen Fuller, as we have seen, might enumerate peers committed to the support of the West India cause:[120] but evidence of attachment by the strong bond of interest is rarely to be found. On present knowledge it would seem that only a handful fall in this category. The Duke of Chandos, we have seen, had come into substantial property in Jamaica through what had come to his duchess from her first husband;[121] Rodney was related to the Chandos family;[122] Lord Lonsdale's West Indian interest is recalled when we recall his commoner title of James Lowther; Lord Cadogan had a close family connection with the Sloane family, a real West Indian clan.[123] Doubtless there are other connections. But had they been much more numerous, the tip of the iceberg would surely be larger.

Examination of the composition of the votes for and against abolition provides much of the explanation in both Lords and Commons for the failure of the abolition movement up to 1796. More speculatively, reflection on the course and context of the abolition campaign suggests other possible reasons for failure. It is, for instance, conceivable that had the abolitionist leaders realised the extent of their opponents' delaying tactics, and learned their lesson about the need to cultivate outside pressure a little earlier, they would have been able so to time their grand heave as to come on, say in 1791 or 1792, without letting enthusiasm dissipate, and before the French Revolution ruled out of court the possibility

[119] *Parliamentary History*, xxx, col. 654.
[120] See p. 289 above.
[121] Wraxall, *Memoirs*, 144.
[122] *D.N.B.*
[123] *D.N.B.*

of generating pressure from 'without doors'.[124] And if immediate abolition had not been gained, the conjoined concern to act according to the dictates of humanity and not to harm accepted national interests is so evident as to suggest that gradual abolition might possibly have been carried in Lords, as well as Commons, in 1791 or 1792. Porteus, at any rate, thought so. He reports the protracted Commons debate on the date for the implementation of abolition, in April 1792, resulting in a majority for 1 January 1796 instead of the originally proposed first day of 1800, in these terms:

> This alteration I most sincerely regret, as I fear it will occasion the entire loss of the Question. The term of 8 years is a reasonable term *and would probably have prevented further opposition. Mr. Dundas himself told me that the West India Planters and Merchants would have acquiesced in the annihilation of the trade in the year 1800* [my italics].[125]

Porteus may have been too gullible an auditor of Dundas and Dundas may have been wrong in his report of West Indian attitudes. Moreover, it was the general sense of the Lords that had to alter rather than the attitude of the West Indian interest group. On the other hand, Porteus is entitled to respect for his opinion of the prospects in the House of which he was a member, and, if Dundas was right in his statement of West Indian attitudes, then it would have been much harder for the disinterested opponents of abolition, even though constituting the majority of anti-abolitionists, to have continued the fight when the ranks of interest had broken and abandoned the field.

But of course they had not done so. It was, rather, and as the *New Annual Register* regretfully put it in 1796, that 'the narrow views of interest and policy prevailed over every consideration of religion and justice'.[126] Put another way, a majority of members in both Houses had brought policy to the support of interest, in itself a puny creature, and enabled both to triumph over humanity justice and religion. Too many shared the view of Mr Grosvenor – he of the mutton chop analogy: 'He must acknowledge that the

---

[124] Cf. Clarkson, *History*, II 347.

[125] *Porteus MS. 2100*, 57–8, Diary 25 Apr 1792. *MS. 2100* is an early nineteenth-century transcript of the original which, in this case, for reasons not clear, gives a fuller account than the original.

[126] *New Annual Register*, 1796, 180.

slave trade was an unamiable trade; but he would not gratify his humanity at the expense of the interests of his country, and he thought we should not too curiously inquire into the unpleasant circumstances with which it was perhaps attended.'[127]

John Wesley had earlier characterised this attitude even more succinctly by invoking words attributed to a mid-century statesman when speaking to another policy question: 'D—n justice; it is necessity'.[128]

[127] *Parliamentary History*, xxix. col. 282.
[128] Wesley, *Works*, xi 72.

13 The Progress of Abolition, 1796–1804

Both from the viewpoint of the abolitionists themselves, and in the context of the whole history of abolition, the years 1796–1804 may appear barren and sterile. Eight years are a long time when one is living them, especially when they follow an earlier eight years of unrewarded exertion, and when there is disproportionately little achievement to record. Yet the events of the eight years after 1796 both reveal the reasons why the abolition still was not achieved and contain the seeds of developments in abolitionist thinking and tactics which were shortly to be important ingredients of success.

The obvious, accepted abolitionist tactic was the motion for general and immediate abolition, and Wilberforce moved such a motion in 1797, 1798, 1799 and 1802, though in this last year the motion was introduced too late in the session to achieve anything. It was for tactical reasons, as we shall see, that Wilberforce refrained from his annual motion in 1800 and 1801, and could only introduce it too late for effective action in 1802, whilst in 1803 the imminent threat of invasion led him to stay his hand.[1] As speakers in the debates from time to time apologetically pointed out, there was little fundamentally new that could be said about the issue: what was new stemmed from the passage of events or the accession of new members to Parliament. Byran Edwards, intellectually the most distinguished of all the West Indians of his time, became a notable addition to their parliamentary ranks in 1796 and Canning, who entered Parliament at the same time, a

---

[1] 'You can conceive what would be said by Lord Hawkesbury if I were to propose the Abolition now, when the whole attention of government is justly called to the state of the country ... I don't think ... we should have above thirty or forty supporters' (Wilberforce to Babington, 22 Mar 1803, quoted in *Life of Wilberforce*, III 87–8.)

sparkling augmentation of abolitionist debating strength. The former excelled as the able, sensible man who wished, or professed to wish, 'most sincerely that the slave trade was suppressed' – but gradually:[2] the latter excelled by his wit as well as by his outstanding ability.[3]

During this period Pitt continued to play his unavoidably ambivalent role. In April 1798 he told the Commons that the importation of new slaves was such a threat to 'internal tranquility' that he must 'now press the necessity of our immediate and total abolition for the salvation of these very islands'[4] – an argument, incidentally, which surely demonstrates that it was not because abolition was inherently unfit to be a government matter, but because ministerial colleagues and royal influence prevented it being so, that Pitt had to content himself with acting as a private man. Wilberforce, for his part, being led by events to brood on the state of the nation, increasingly related the evils which afflicted, and the dangers which confronted it, to continuation in the slave trade.[5] What might have happened in the Lords to a bill bereft of full ministerial backing is easy to predict, but Wilberforce's general motions came tantalisingly close to victory in the Commons: seventy-four to eighty-two in May 1797;[6] eighty-three to eighty-seven in April 1798;[7] and fifty-four to eighty-four in March 1799.[8] Respectable as these votes in favour of abolition were, the political obstacles to a general abolition continued to be insuperable. Up to the peace of 1801, identification between the French Revolution and abolition was still made, whilst periods of intense national crisis, as in 1797 where there were mutinies at Spithead and at the Nore, and as when invasion threatened, compounded unreadiness to see the abolition agitated. Wilberforce (assuming, as we may, that his biography owes its observation to its subject) believed that 'the House of Commons which was returned in 1796, when this fear [of French principles] was at its height, had been unreasonably but deeply prejudiced against any change in our Colonial

---

[2] *Parliamentary History*, xxxii, col. 1386 (3 Apr 1798).
[3] See esp. ibid. xxxiv, cols. 537–60.
[4] Ibid., xxxii, cols. 1399–1402.
[5] Ibid., xxxiii, cols. 278–9 (6 Apr 1797) and 1385 (3 Apr 1798).
[6] Ibid., xxxiii, col. 576.
[7] Ibid., xxxiii, col. 1415.
[8] Ibid., xxxiv, col. 565.

system'.[9] It was therefore even more ready than its predecessor to heed such a plea as Sir William Young's, in April 1798, 'to consider the West India islands as an integral part of the British empire, and to pay that attention which was due to the body of West-India planters'.[10] Many must have reacted as did Lord Ellenborough, who told Wilberforce in 1802 that he had always felt 'a great abhorrence' of the slave trade and doubted whether sound policy could ever grow out of a vicious system, but was 'frightened at the consequences of any innovation upon a long established practice, at a period so full of danger as the present'.[11] As for the committed, there was little change on either side. West Indian parliamentary strength seems to have diminished, but only slightly,[12] whilst Wilberforce's comment to Gisborne in 1802 suggests a comparable slight weakeneing in the ranks of the abolitionists: 'They adhere to the party . . . not all of them, alas! [Windham is the leading defector whom Wilberforce must have had in mind] be it what it may, which they originally joined, and give a languid support, as if by prescription.'[13]

An attempt to secure international agreement on abolition was an obvious enough adjunct of the campaign for total, national abolition. Evidently abolition by other powers would be a good in itself but its more particular value was that it would enhance the prospects of carrying abolition in Britain by removing the fear that British self-denial in the carrying of slaves would merely be others' gain. Moves to bring about international action had been attempted as early as 1786–87 when Pitt had instructed William Eden (later Lord Auckland) to try for some agreement on ending the slave trade in the negotiations for a commercial treaty with France. Wilberforce himself was privy to this attempt and hoped to improve it by embarking on a similar negotiation with Spain. As he explained to Charles Grey, in what may have been one of

[9] *Life of Wilberforce*, III 163.

[10] *Parliamentary History*, XXXIII, col. 1402.

[11] Ellenborough to Wilberforce, 27 June 1802, quoted in *Private Papers of Wilberforce*, 124.

[12] Taking Judd's calculations – we have already argued that they are on the low side – the number of West Indians who sat in the Commons at any time in the Parliaments of 1790, 1796 and 1802 was 29, 27 and 24 respectively (*Members of Parliament*, 94).

[13] Wilberforce to Gisborne, 20 Sept 1802, quoted in *Life of Wilberforce* III 70–71.

various private approaches to inhibit domestic opposition to such a design,

> It is my firm belief that it would be for the interest of both those powers to abolish the Slave Trade; but what I should depend on still more for the success of the proposal, would be the shame and scandal of refusing, when the main grounds of the objection that has been urged should be thus taken away, the Trades being carried on by other and Rival powers in case they should relinquish it.[14]

Wilberforce followed up these exertions by offering, in December 1787, to go to Paris himself, accompanied by Grenville, to lend further assistance but the whole negotiation, as far as the abolition was concerned, was sterile since the French were completely un-accommodating.[15] Some months later, as Pitt told both Grenville and Wilberforce, Pitt had hopes that Necker's accession to power 'will prove very favourable to this object':[16] but this hope, too, was abortive. A year later, and seeking to capitalise upon revolutionary fervour, the Abolition Committee sent Clarkson to Paris: but despite initial high hopes, and the exertions of Mirabeau, Lafayette, Brissot and others, canvasses of the National Assembly revealed that a majority could only be obtained 'if England would give an unequivocal proof of her intention to abolish the trade'[17]

Intensification of the Revolution ruled out further approaches until 1797 when Lord Malmesbury was entrusted with peace feelers. Wilberforce believed that here was a return of opportunity and was deeply hurt with Pitt over his refusal – possibly because of the difficulty of obtaining the agreement of the Cabinet – to include the subject of abolition in the peace negotiations.[18]

[14] *Grey Papers* (Durham), box 57, file 4, Wilberforce to Grey, 17 May 1787.

[15] Bishop of Bath and Wells (ed.), *The Journal and Correspondence of William, Lord Auckland* I 304–8; Williams, *Capitalism and Slavery*, 246; Coupland, *Wilberforce*, 85–7; *Life of Wilberforce*, I 155–8.

[16] Pitt to Wilberforce, 1 Sept 1788, quoted in A. M. Wilberforce, *The Private Papers of William Wilberforce*, 24; Pitt to Grenville, 29 Aug 1788, in Historical Manuscripts Commission, *The Manuscripts of J. B. Fortescue Esq preserved at Dropmore* (London, 1892–1927) I 353.

[17] Clarkson, *History*, II 122–66 (the quotation is from p. 163); *Life of Wilberforce*, I 224–32.

[18] Wilberforce to Pitt, n.d., quoed in Coupland, *Wilberforce*, 185; *Life of Wilberforce*, II 224–5.

Wilberforce made two other attempts towards an international abolition. In 1800, he wrote to F. Hare Naylor, an intimate of Fox and a member of the Duchess of Devonshire's brilliant circle, who was personally acquainted with Napoleon, asking him to use his influence with Napoleon to have the matter of a general abolition raised in the forthcoming peace negotiations, where virtually all the powers involved in the trade would be represented. Wilberforce explained that such were the different opinions in the Cabinet that he feared he would be unable to get agreement that the initiative should come from the British side. But, as for Napoleon,

> there would be the less reason against his bringing forward the proposition, because even granting (what I utterly deny) that on the most abstracted mercenary principles, the slave trade is profitable to a nation having West Indian colonies, the state of the French islands precludes their being contaminated with such bloody profit.[19]

Interestingly, Wilberforce sought another intermediary in the shape of Rufus King, the United States minister in London, himself sympathetic to abolition and on quite close terms with Wilberforce. Writing to King in September 1801, Wilberforce said that he had 'been reflecting with much Solicitude on the grand project I suggested to you of effecting a *general abolition* of the Slave Trade by a convention to be made in the negotiations for peace. Would King feel able to assist by arranging a confidential interview with Otto, the French representative in London (though the peace preliminaries were near, Britain was still at war with France) who 'tho' a Frenchman, may I suppose be deemed capable of keeping a secret.'[20] King's response to this delicate request is unclear but may have been positive for King committed to paper a long conversation he had had with Wilberforce on the prospects of including an abolition article in the definitive peace treaty when the two sat together at dinner with Prime Minister Addington in late November 1801.[21] In the new year Wilberforce was encouraged by the intimation from the French minister in London

[19] Wilberforce to Hare Naylor, 5 July 1800, quoted in *Life of Wilberforce*, II 369–70.
[20] Wilberforce to King, Sept 1801, Private, *The Life and Correspondence of Rufus King* (New York, 1894–1900) III 510–13.
[21] Memorandum Book, 27 Nov 1801, ibid., 21.

'that if our government would propose to negotiate for the Abolition, theirs would probably consent to it',[22] and yet again used his political position and personal acquaintance to urge Addington, the new Prime Minister, and Hawkesbury 'to negotiate for a general abolition of the slave trade'.[23] Finally Wilberforce wrote a long letter to Addington reminding him of his support of gradual abolition in 1792 and of Dundas' advocacy at that same time of negotiations with the powers. A general abolition would meet a strong objection to abolition, namely 'that of other nations carrying on the Trade, if we should discontinue it'. All the powers engaged in the trade will be at Amiens and the ascendancy of Britain and France would enable them to give a lead. A similar opportunity might not recur and if it is left for Britain eventually to abolish unilaterally, the benefit to Africa will be infinitely less than if all the European powers were to abolish by common consent.[24] Neither Addington or Hawkesbury, however, could be persuaded.[25] Even so, Wilberforce did not quite give up, for in September he wrote at length to Fox 'instigating' him 'to urge Buonaparte on the Abolition'.[26] One consequence of these attempts was that Wilberforce refrained from putting down a general abolition motion in 1801 in order that possible failure therein should not prejudice his bid for a general convention.[27]

Indeed such a balancing of tactical considerations had to be a keynote of abolitionist conduct in this period. Complete British abolition remained the goal but Wilberforce withheld a motion on this in years when to introduce such a motion might prejudice a wider purpose, such as a general convention, or when some partial measure had a better chance of success. In fact, for a time, the opponents of abolition stole this intermediate ground by an initiative of April 1797. Dale H. Porter has shown how the moderate West Indians sought to offer concessions to attract uncommitted M.P.s. The initiative was Sir William Young's and in the winter of 1796 he worked out in some detail the case for

[22] Wilberforce, Diary, 3 Jan 1802, quoted in *Life of Wilberforce*, III 26.
[23] Wilberforce, Diary, 21 Jan 1802, quoted in *Life of Wilberforce*, III 35.
[24] Wilberforce to Addington, 2 Jan 1802, quoted in *Life of Wilberforce*, III 28–34.
[25] *Life of Wilberforce*, III 35.
[26] Ibid., III 70.
[27] Ibid., III 26.

moderation and persuaded twenty-one of the West Indian M.P.s. of its merits.[28] Three of the clauses of a statement of the case which Young made to the Leeward Islands Assembly are perceptive and significant

> That many persons of great weight and character, tho' conscious of the danger to be apprehended from the measure proposed by Mr Wilberforce, have supported, and will continue to support them, because no mode of conduct at all compatible with their ideas of humanity has been proposed as an alternative.
>
> That on the other hand many persons who have hitherto opposed the measures of Mr Wilberforce will feel themselves under the necessity of submitting to them, unless some plan of regulation shall be brought forward . . .
>
> That . . . for the joint purposes of opposing the plan of Mr Wilberforce, and establishing the Character of the West India body, it is essential that they should manifest their willingness to promote actively the cause of Humanity by such steps as shall be consistent with safety to the prospects of Individuals, and the general interests of the Colonies.[29]

C. R. Ellis, another West Indian, agreed to be responsible for initiating action, namely a 'Humble Address to the King', asking him to urge West Indian Governors and Assemblies to adopt such measures as would obviate the causes which have impeded natural increase, encourage the slave population to become self-reproducing and so 'gradually . . . diminish the necessity of the slave trade, and ultimately . . . lead to its complete termination'.[30] Measures should also be taken to effect the moral and religious improvement of the slaves, and to give them due protection under the law. Wilberforce opposed the proposal out of sheer distrust that West Indian Assemblies could really be prevailed upon to do anything effective, and reminded the Commons that in 1792 they had voted for abolition in 1796 and that it was therefore utterly inconsistent to support a spurious gradual abolition in 1797.[31] Most committed abolitionists supported Wilberforce but Ellis' proposal

---

[28] Porter, *Abolition*, 96–9.
[29] *C.O. 152/78*, Young to Leeward Islands Assembly, quoted n.d. in Porter, *Abolition*, 97–9.
[30] *Parliamentary History*, xxxiii, cols. 251–69.
[31] Ibid., cols. 276–9; *Life of Wilberforce*, ii 195–6.

could only but appeal to those members torn between humanity
and justice, on the one hand, and policy on the other. The clinch-
ing clue to why the resolution passed by ninety-nine to sixty-three
votes is surely contained in Dundas' observation that 'the motion
afforded him an opportunity of agreeing to a final abolition,
through the medium of a prudent and preliminary regulation'.[32]
Prudence, then, need not affront conscience and conscience need
not tax prudence. Even a number of abolitionists were, at this time,
prepared to countenance some species of amelioration, regulation
or gradual abolition. Porteus had urged Wilberforce before the
introduction of the 1796 motion 'not to press an *immediate* abolition (which I always thought inadvisable and impracticable) but
to give a reasonable time for its discontinuance which I was confident would be the only way to ensure success in both Houses,
especially in that of the Lords'.[33] Porteus now agreed to support
Ellis' proposal – interestingly the Bishop of London's backing had
been specifically sought by Mr Knox, the agent for Dominica.[34]
Soon after the failure of Wilberforce's 1796 motion, so forthright
an abolitionist as Philip Francis had introduced his own motion
for amelioration,[35] whilst when the news of Ellis' forthcoming
motion was first bruited, Pitt – Wilberforce confided to his diary –
'wanted me to close with it modified'.[36] If committed abolitionists
could see tactical wisdom in regulation, it is not surprising that
men who could not make up their minds not only found Ellis'
motion appealing, but also persisted in seeing amelioration as an
alternative approach to abolition which should be given a trial for
a few years. Canning was evidently putting his finger on this
feeling when, as the peroration of his speech in the 1799 debate,
he asked rhetorically whether the measures taken by the Jamaican

[32] *Parliamentary History*, xxxiii, col. 293.

[33] *Porteus MSS.* 2103, Diary, 14 Feb 1796.

[34] Ibid., 2103, Diary, 8 Apr 1797. An evident consideration for Porteus
was that the measure would further the giving of religious instruction to
the slaves, a concern which Porteus had had since 1783.

[35] *Parliamentary History*, xxxii, cols. 944–992.

[36] Diary 1 Apr 1797 quoted in *Life of Wilberforce*, ii 196. Wilberforce
adds that when he refused to take this course Pitt 'stood stiffly by me'.
Pitt's speech in the debate, however, though not outstanding was in its
concluding paragraph forthright. 'He decidedly objected to the motion,
because he considered it to be only a substitute for that abolition which
the honour of the country and the safety of the islands so loudly called
for (*Parliamentary History*, xxxiii, cols. 288–9).

Assembly as a result of Ellis' motion (and on which he had poured scorn) were sufficient to bring about the termination of the slave trade instead of themselves taking the necessary steps to that end.[37]

But if Wilberforce was in a measure forced upon this intermediate ground there were areas of it where he could take the initiative. In the development of tactics he seems to have come to owe a good deal in this period to James Stephen. This is not to suggest that the influence of other close abolitionist friends like Henry Thornton, Thomas Gisborne, Thomas Babington and William Smith became less, but that Stephen had a particular contribution to give. We have already seen something of Stephen's early career and how in those precarious years his life was much involved, and simultaneously, with Nancy Stent and 'Maria'.[38] It was through them that Stephen first came to his anti-slavery convictions. The girls had asked him to take them to a public debate on slavery at Coachmakers Hall and, in the hope of impressing both girl friends at once, as he later confessed, he prepared a major speech for the occasion. The result was that by the time the evening came anti-slavery was, as he remarked a trifle ingenuously, 'a cause that I had sincerely embraced'.[39] Subsequent residence in the West Indies, and particularly the travesty of a slave trial which he witnessed at Barbados, confirmed his hatred of slavery; religious conversion confirmed his resolve to fight it. From 1789 onwards he supplied Wilberforce with valuable information, first as a West India resident, and from 1794 onwards, after his permanent return to England, he spoke not only as former resident but with what came to be the increasingly relevant authority – for reasons which we shall see – of a lawyer practising in the Prize Appeals Court of the Privy Council. From August 1797 he was ready openly to identify himself with the abolition cause[40] and the intimacy with Wilberforce to which this led was

[37] *Parliamentary History*, xxxiv, cols. 559–60.

[38] See p. 169 above.

[39] Stephen, *Memoirs*, 277. The presence of one beloved is, no doubt, sufficient to inspire most men: with two present, Stephen gave what in old age he believed to be the best speech of his whole life and secured a 50:1 majority in an audience of 1500–2000.

[40] Ibid., passim; *Life of Wilberforce*, I 202–3, II 255–6; *D.N.B.*; Stephen, *Memoirs*, 12–13.

naturally cemented by Stephen's marriage – he was by then a widower – with Wilberforce's widowed sister.[41]

What kind of measures, then, short of complete abolition did Wilberforce and his friends seek to implement? They can be placed, typologically, in a kind of ascending order of actual or potential effectiveness, and start with a Slave Carrying Bill of 1799[42] which sharply reduced the number of slaves per ton allowed to be carried from the levels prescribed by Dolben's original Act, and its successors, principally by stipulating more headroom between decks. William Smith fathered this bill[43] – no doubt in the tradition now established that Wilberforce himself should not overtly take the lead in measures which could be construed as condoning the slave trade. The way had been paved by an earlier measure of 1798,[44] and the subsequent measure may have played an important part in sharply reducing the profitability of the British slave trade in the years which followed.[45]

We have only limited information about the bill's passage (the *Parliamentary History* and *Debrett* substantially ignore it) but it was introduced in the Commons on the 19 April and passed the third reading without a vote on the 7 May.[46] In the Lords the Duke of Clarence led the opposition to it in a long speech and in a second intervention added that 'it had been the study of [a]

---

[41] Wilberforce's observations on this event are worth repeating. 'I trust it will please God to bless the union. Stephen is an improved and improving character, one of those whom religion has transformed, and in whom it has triumphed by conquering some strong natural infirmities. He has talent, great sensibility, and generosity. My chief objection was, that it seemed like my sister's beginning life again, and going to sea once more in a crazy vessel' (Wilberforce to Miss Mary Bird, 19 May 1800, quoted in *Life of Wilberforce*, II 367). The new Mrs Stephen was a character in her own right. She wore only old clothes in order to be able to give away all but £10 of her £350 allowance. All other efforts to persuade her to buy new clothes having failed, Gisborne on one occasion – which must have been fairly riotous by Evangelical standards – tore her skirt from top to bottom saying, 'Now Mrs. Stephen you must buy a new dress'. But, the chronicler records, she merely stitched it up again (Stephen, *Life of Sir James Fitzjames Stephen*, 8 ff).

[42] 39 Geo. III c. 80.

[43] *Life of Wilberforce*, II 331.

[44] 38 Geo. III c. 88. See also *Life of Wilberforce*, II, 279–80.

[45] See Appendix 1.

[46] For the progress of the bill see *The Senator or Parliamentary Chronicle* (1st series) XXIII 1368, 1434, 1442, 1461, 1463, 1538, 1600–02, 1732–34.

great part of his life to gain information respecting it [the slave trade][47] – an observation which perhaps strengthens the evidence for royal hostility to abolition as a significant influence. Grenville[48] and the Bishop of Rochester spoke very ably in support of the bill, however, and doubtless the revelation that space between decks could be under three feet helped produce what the *Parliamentary Chronicle* quaintly terms a majority of — two for the Duke of Clarence.[49] Porteus adds that it was a close-run thing and gives the division list.[50]

Thornton took control of another partial measure of 1799, the Slave Trade Limitation Bill. Intended to prohibit the export of slaves from a substantial northerly portion of the West African coast, the measure was several times obstructed by West Indians in the Commons but eventually passed on the Third Reading by fifty-nine to twenty-three on 2 May.[51] In the Lords as in the Commons the bill had to surmount the old obstacle of the examination of witnesses at the bar of the House. As with the Slave Carrying bill the outcome was a close-run thing. Pitt exerted himself greatly over the bill – which, after all, could be seen as regulatory and so a matter for ministerial unanimity – even going to the lengths of reprimanding a hostile colleague in full Cabinet, and was wholeheartedly backed by Grenville.[52] As *The Times* put it, 'the question was canvassed in its progress with greater interest and zeal than any that has occurred since the Regency. The votes of the Peerage were solicited out of doors with as much spirit and perseverance as if it had been a party question'[53] The journal added, four days later, 'Many expresses were sent and many

[47] Ibid., xxiii 1734.

[48] For an indication of the help Granville was giving to the cause at this time see *Wm. Smith MSS.* (Duke Collection), Grenville to Smith, 22 Feb and 10 June 1799.

[49] *The Senator or Parliamentary Chronicle*, xxiii 1734.

[50] *Porteus MSS. 2103*, Diary, 20 June 1799.

[51] *Parliamentary Chronicle* (1st series), xxiii, 1321, 1351, 1359, 1365, 1368, 1434, 1442, 1350.

[52] *Life of Wilberforce*, ii 331–40 passim.

[53] *The Times*, 8 and 12 July 1799, quoted in *The Later Correspondence of George III*, ed. A. Aspinall (Cambridge, 1967) iii, no. 1983 n. The report of 12 July also included this comment: 'The late conduct of Administration in the business of the slave trade is the fullest refutation of all those malicious censures to which they have frequently been exposed for not *pressing, insisting,* and using the whole of their *influence* in its support.'

proxies given and withdrawn, in a manner that will sufficiently prove in what light Government has regarded this question'. On the other side of the question, however, was not only that distrust of abolition which we have previously noticed, but also the opposition of four royal dukes, including the Duke of Clarence, who, yet again, took a leading part in the debate but for some reason did not vote in the division. The King may well also have exerted himself against the bill. Certainly Wilberforce noted in his diary: 'Slave Limitation Bill not popular at Court'.[54] Here is a possible reason why Pitt, who presumably felt that to use his influence on behalf of a partial bill of this kind was in any event the most he could do, could do no more. To do so, on this hypothesis, would have involved a confrontation with the King.[55] Finally a disastrous error was made about proxies. 'Grenville says we had fourteen more, but for mistakes about proxies', wrote Wilberforce.[56] The outcome was the loss of the bill on its second reading by some half-dozen votes only. The importance of the bill in abolitionist strategy is perhaps indicated by Wilberforce's comment in his diary: 'Never so disappointed and grieved by any defeat'.[57]

Limitation could, however, operate in yet another way, and one which arose out of conquests made in the war. This project of limitation was that action should be taken against the supply of slaves to Trinidad, captured early in 1797, and to St Vincent, made available for cultivation following deportation of the Carib inhabitants of this former French island as punishment for a rising they had made in 1795. Partly at Stephen's strong, scarcely temperate urging[58] Wilberforce made private approaches to Pitt early in 1798 to thwart an order-in-council permitting the supply

[54] Diary, 4 June 1799, quoted in *Life of Wilberforce*, II 337.

[55] See pp. 304–6 above.

[56] Diary, 8 July 1799, quoted in *Life of Wilberforce*, II 340.

[57] Diary, 6 July, 1799, quoted in *Life of Wilberforce*, II 340. For information on the course of this measure see also Viscountess Knutsford, *Life and Letters of Zachary Macaulay*, 216–30 passim. There are at least three different versions of the Division List: the most reliable, that of the Clerk Assistant of the House of Lords, is printed in *Later Correspondence of George III*, III, no. 1983.

[58] Wilberforce, Stephen told him, ought to have been more outspoken, 'because those high priests of Moloch, Lord Liverpool and M. Dundas, are your political, and Mr Pitt also your private friend' (n.d., quoted in *Life of Wilberforce*, II 265).

of slaves to these conquered islands from the older British islands, the resulting deficiency in the latter then being made up by an increased slave trade; on 1 April Wilberforce was able to report that he had 'at last got the proclamation about slaves rescinded.[59] This was only a partial success, however, for British slavers were certainly continuing to supply what were variously described as 'new lands'[60] or 'new settlements'[61] which can only have been the conquered colonies which, however, also came to include Demerera and Surinam.[62] Indeed, Wilberforce is unlikely to have been wrong when he wrote in 1800 that importations into the new settlements constituted about three-quarters of the British slave trade.[63] Wilberforce and Stephen did not cease to worry at this problem. By August 1800 they had come to believe (Stephen may have had a local informant) that the Customs returns did not reveal 'one-eighth' of the slaves imported into the conquered colonies. Imports on such a large scale were major cause for concern, certainly: but they also suggested to Wilberforce a tactic which the abolitionists were to use more than once, namely to press 'on those who are unassailable by higher principles, that the British ought not to invest much capital in colonies, which may probably have to be surrendered on the return of peace'.[64] That Wilberforce attached importance to this stratagem is made clear by the urgency of his request to Stephen to provide in usable form information confidentially given of slave imports into the conquered islands over the preceding two or three years. 'I earnestly beg you not to lose a moment in the commission.'[65]

Before any use was made of this stratagem the Peace of Amiens supervened. All the conquests except Trinidad were returned – Wilberforce regretted the retention of Trinidad[66] – and the aboli-

---

[59] Ibid., II, 257–65.

[60] Wilberforce, Diary, 8 June 1799, quoted in *Life of Wilberforce*, II 337.

[61] Wilberforce to Stephen, 25 Aug 1800, quoted in ibid., II 377.

[62] For the course of the conflict in the West Indies see J. Holland Rose, 'The Conflict with Revolutionary France, 1793–1802', *C.H.B.E.*, II 37–82 passim.

[63] Wilberforce to Gisborne, 6 June 1800, quoted in *Life of Wilberforce*, III 368.

[64] Wilberforce to Stephen, 25 Aug 1800, quoted in *Life of Wilberforce*, II 377–8.

[65] Ibid.

[66] Ibid., III, 19.

tionists now sought to obtain limitation of slave imports into this new and virgin possession. In January 1802 Wilberforce wrote to Addington, the new Prime Minister (he had succeeded Pitt in March 1801 mainly because Pitt's conviction of the necessity of Catholic Emancipation made him no longer acceptable to the King), with whom the abolitionist leader was on quite close personal terms, pressing various facets of the abolition case, including the urgency of not allowing slaves to be used in the work of opening up Trinidad.[67] Wilberforce also engaged Pitt in the task of putting pressure on Addington[68] and then, as his diary for 8 February records, 'went after Canning'.[69] Canning was still 'staunch and warm for Abolition' and also because, as we shall see, Wilberforce's purpose went hand in hand with a political objective of Canning's own, he agreed to move against opening up Trinidad by new slave importations from Africa.[70] Canning's motion eventually came on on 27 May. The timing meant, incidentally, that Wilberforce's general motion that year was aborted because, after anxious consideration, he had concluded that Canning's motion should precede his own, as having a better chance, and no success could attend a major question like general abolition introduced so late in the session.[71] In itself, however, Canning's speech of his motion was a masterly achievement and deserves attention as the first major attempt by the abolitionists to achieve significant lessening of the slave trade specifically to British possessions on grounds other than the general principle.

Canning's approach is low key. His concern is that the nation should gain maximum advantage from its new acquisition. He would not deny that his attention to the possibility that Trinidad be peopled with an army of new slaves had been aroused because of his concern with the question of the African slave trade in general, but went on to affirm that he had been led to his view of the case as much by policy considerations as by 'the fear of that danger and that shame which would attend the enormous exten-

[67] Wilberforce to Addington, 2 Jan 1802, quoted in *Life of Wilberforce*, II 28–34.

[68] Ibid., III 35–7. The original of the letter from Pitt to Wilberforce, 4 Feb 1802, reporting a successful meeting with Addington (p. 37) is in *Wilberforce MSS*. (Duke).

[69] *Life of Wilberforce*, III, 38.

[70] Ibid., III, 37–8.

[71] *Life of Wilberforce*, III, 38–50 passim.

sion of the slave trade, or rather the creation of a new slave trade for this express purpose'. He believed, and he spoke here from a non-party stance, that Trinidad could be better developed by other means than by slavery, and he brought the matter before the House because of reports that plans for the sale of unclaimed Trinidadian lands were already well advanced. 'My object is delay only' in order to prevent precipitate action which would prevent Parliament subsequently coming to a considered view of the matter. Canning then became more subtle by arguing that the Commons resolution of 1792 that the slave trade ought to be gradually abolished constituted one proof that the House was pledged not 'to create a new slave trade'. The other proof was the passage of Ellis' motion in 1797, for Canning saw – or perhaps professed to see in this motion that

> the object of this address was to give to parliament and the country the assurance that the West Indians themselves laid claim to the continuance of the slave trade only till such time as they should be able to continue their cultivation on the then existing scale without it; not to increase the slave trade beyond its actual bounds, still less to uphold the principles or defend the justice of it; but, on the contrary, to give a pledge of their desire gradually to diminish, and ultimately to abolish it. . . . Such was the object of that address.

Canning then took disingenuousness yet further. He took advantage of the fact that Ellis, a personal and political friend, was sitting near him to observe that

> the benevolence and ingenuousness of the character of him whom they selected to bring it forward were undoubtedly the best securities that could be offered to the House for the sincerity of those who promoted and those who concurred in it. I appeal then to my hon. friend, whether or not, on the principle of the address which he then moved, he does not feel himself bound, and not himself only, but all those whose sentiments he spoke, and all whose concurrence he obtained on that occasion, to vote in support of a measure, the object of which is not only strictly conformable to the spirit, but falls much within the letter of his address.

In citing the second of these 'proofs', Canning had at one and the same time made his appeal to the West Indians. He then turned to a section of what we have already seen to have been the vitally important uncommitted group, what he termed the 'moderate men', whom he went on to define as the declared supporters of gradual abolition and asked 'with what face they can stand up and defend a plan for cultivating a new island with new importations'. Other groups remained, and for one the rapier was briefly unsheathed.

> The first, a small, I hope, and select class, those who admire the slave trade for itself, who dream of it, as those did of virtue, that it requires only to be looked at to be beloved. . . . With men holding that opinion I can have no argument. It requires a degree of fellow-feeling to be able even to differ in discussion to any purpose . . . but such persons must have their minds altogether so differently constituted, their sentiments, affections and passions must be so unlike anything that I can conceive, that I avow my incapacity to understand them and my despair of making them understand me. To their opposition, therefore, I must make up my mind.

The next group to which he turned was the convinced abolitionists to whom he made what was surely a contrived appeal (for it would fortify his posture as the reasonable man in the middle), not to oppose a partial measure from the belief that this would be to condone the essential evil. This gave Canning his opportunity to estimate the enormity of allowing Trinidad to be developed by slave labour – it would demand at least one million slaves, and would be against the manifest interest of 'the established West Indian planter'.

Canning was not done yet. He went on to address himself to those whom, again, we have already discerned as important, those who had hitherto opposed abolition not from interest but from policy,

> to those gentlemen unconnected with the West Indies themselves, who had yet always made West Indian interests the plea and pretence for their votes in favour of the slave trade. This day afforded a test of their sincerity also. Was it indeed true that they had always hitherto been compelled to give a reluctant consent to the continuance of the slave trade, only because they felt themselves bound in justice to take care that the vested in-

terests of the colonies should receive no injury by a hasty abolition? Did they endure an evil they abhorred, only because its continuance was indispensably necessary for the protection of an interest which they regarded? What would be their plea now? Now that the interest of the established West Indian was to be prejudiced by the very same act that created an enormous extension of the evil?

Canning now proceeded to drive a wedge between support of the slave trade and of the West Indian connexion in a rhetorical flight of some power. There were

> those moderate men who have hitherto supported the West India interest and the slave trade together. As long as they went together all was well. The slave trade was to be tolerated because its ally, the West Indian interest, was to be supported. But the alliance was now dissolved: the West Indian interest points one way; the slave trade another. Which will you follow? No disguise; no equivocation now. It is not slave trade *and,* but slave trade *or,* the old West Indian interest that you must support – slave trade in all its naked charms, without the cloak of a pretended West Indian interest to hide them. If, in this choice, you take the road which leads to the enormous increase of the evil, which you pretended to deplore, and abandon the interests for whose sake alone you pretended, while you deplore, to endure it, what shall be said? What can be believed but that your affected tenderness for the colonists was all mere hypocrisy and that at all times, in all periods of the discussion, while regard for colonial interests was on your lips, the secret devotions of your heart were paid to the slave trade.

Canning, then, in a long speech of power, clarity and verbal felicity had presented his project for delay as something which all sections of the House, save the inveterate supporters of the slave trade, could and must support. His positive proposals for Trinidad – settlement by a free peasantry, and perhaps its development into the emporium of British and South American commerce – were sketchy. The principal resolution in his proposed Address to the King was that regulations should be laid which would prevent settlement of Trinidad by slaves from Africa until Parliament had further considered the matter.[72]

[72] *Parliamentary History*, xxxvi, cols. 854–76.

In his reply, Addington was unable, not surprisingly, to forbear from observing 'that the motion now before the House was not strictly conformable to the expectation which had been formed from his notice', and criticised a number of Canning's arguments and assumptions, but went on to deny that any decision to open up Trinidad in such a way as would justify Canning's apprehensions had been taken, to inform the House that Commissioners had been appointed to survey the island and report to assure the House that no grants of land would be made until the subject was again brought before the House.[73] Given these 'public declarations and pledges' as he termed them, Canning was perfectly prepared to withdraw his motion.[74]

Dr Patrick Lipscomb has recently demonstrated[75] that there was more to Canning's intervention than meets the eye. His commitment to abolition does not have to be questioned; it is just that he saw the pressure on Addington which his own motion constituted as one means of fulfilling his wider political aim of forcing Pitt to repudiate the promise he had made, on grounds of principal, of general support for the Addington ministry, and to drive him into opposition. A desirable crisis between Pitt and Addington could come over the Trinidad question because Addington was a lukewarm gradual abolitionist who hoped to augment the national treasury by sales of conquered lands in Trinidad whereas Pitt, on the other hand, was firmly opposed to the *extension* of cultivation in Trinidad which land sales would encourage since this would lead to massive new importations of slaves. For Canning the beauty of so pressing Addington was that the scheme, implicitly or overtly, must align Pitt against Addington whilst, on the principle of free voting on the abolition question, many others would respond likewise. Moreover, Canning was probably assured of the support of moderate West Indians – through C. R. Ellis, a personal and political friend of Canning, whom we have seen to be one such – since they apparently chose to see their interests as planters on the older islands as likely to suffer from the competition of virgin Trinidad. Most important of all, if Addington yielded, it would be because of the threat of open opposition by Pitt: if he did not, then a break between Pitt and Addington would be much closer.

[73] Ibid., xxxvi, cols. 876–81.
[74] Ibid., xxxvi, col. 881.
[75] Lipscomb, 'Canning and the Trinidad Question', 442–66.

Canning's reasoning is particularly clearly spelt out in two letters, the first to J. H. Frere in November 1801:

> But there is still another point, upon which I was most anxious to ascertain how he [Pitt] felt – and I find he feels right. And it is one of which much may be made. Trinidad, you know, is almost uncultivated. Hawkesbury etc. etc. vaunt its fertility, and capacity for cultivation and the West Indians I *know* have conceived, and I believe have been diligently taught to conceive the question of the *Slave Trade* as settled for ever by the acquisition of such a tract of land, which it would be madness not to make the most of, and to make the most of which will require an annual importation of Negroes beyond that of all our old Islands put together. I asked P[– itt] whether he was prepared to consent to this? He said, No...[76]

The second letter was written after Addington had given notice that the Government was planning the sale of the Trinidad lands and, though a letter to an intimate, the Rev. John Sneyd, perhaps shows rather too well why many regarded Canning as too clever by half.

> I observed the foolish notice he [Addington] gave before the holidays, but I said not a word. 'Snug', quoth I to myself, 'the time will come.' So he went on and on, and I asked Pitt amicably, quite cool and good-natured, 'What a Devil, he [Addington] was doing?' and Pitt could not tell so I said nothing, and only looked and watched, till at last Pitt came here a fortnight ago, as it might be this day fortnight, and I asked him what the Doctor [Addington] meant, and he could not tell – but he was against the slave trade (he, Pitt) just the same as ever. 'So,' says I, 'I will go up and ask the Doctor himself. Marry!' will I! So Pitt had nothing to say but to look foolish, and not to be able to help it. 'I will go up and give notice of a motion,' says I, 'and oppose the Doctor upon this business, and *you* shall support me.' Then Pitt saw what a scrape the Doctor had got into, but could not help it. Now, the Doctor was an ass. Adieu.

Elsewhere in the same letter Canning had added, making his anticipatory delight painfully clear, that Addington would be

[76] Canning to Frere, 21 Nov 1801, *Canning Papers*, quoted in Lipscomb, 'Canning and the Trinidad Question', 449.

hounded 'like a polecat and all in good humour, at least on our part'.[77]

In the event, Addington's substantive yielding meant that Canning could not extract from the episode the satisfaction of an open break between Pitt and Addington: but (quite apart from Canning's satisfaction on the outcome of the Trinidad issue itself) it was clear to all that it was Pitt's determination to support the motion if Addington had opposed it that had forced Addington to give way. The whole episode was somewhat out of the mainstream of abolitionist tactics in virtue of Canning's dominant role in it and because abolition had become involved in the politics of party – or of faction. None the less, an important holding action had been fought and won for the sale of the extensive Crown lands on Trinidad and St Vincent would have constituted a veritable magnet for vast new slave importations.[78]

Another partial measure which would have had considerable effect, had it ever been implemented, was suspension. In 1808, the first occasion when this was talked of, the prospect was sufficiently alluring for Wilberforce to put off his annual motion.[79] This approach seems to have grown out of the abortive attempt of Pitt to make a comprehensive measure of limitation a Cabinet matter in 1799.[80] Even though Pitt was defeated on this, he continued to support Wilberforce in the project of gaining a suspension of the trade, and the West Indians may have felt that they would be wise to combine some amenability to the minister with what was arguably in their interests anyway. A five- or seven-year suspension was talked of but Pitt, with Wilberforce, was eventually denied West Indian support, save for Sir William Young, when at a public meeting of the West India body the rank and

[77] Canning to Sneyd, 10 Feb 1802, in Bagot, *George Canning and His Friends*, i 188–9, quoted in Lipscomb, 'Canning and the Trinidad Question', 449.

[78] There was no undertaking to end *all* imports into Trinidad, and Customs returns show that 4332 slaves were imported directly from Africa in 1802 and 3952 in 1803 (*A. & P.*, 1806, xiii (777–781). Wilberforce seems to have hoped for something even more positive from Addington and laments its absence. Puzzlingly, Canning's motion was 'sadly too short' and the 'House flat' (Diary, 27 May 1802, quoted in *Life of Wilberforce*, iii 48–9).

[79] *Life of Wilberforce*, ii 367.

[80] See pp. 303–5 of previous chapter.

file disavowed what their leaders had proposed. They reasoned, no doubt, that a suspended trade might well never revive. Wilberforce urged Pitt to continue with his bill notwithstanding, but Pitt presumably felt that in view of what had happened in the Cabinet the previous year, he had no hope of success without the help of the West Indians and, in the Cabinet, at least of Dundas, who rejected Wilberforce's attempts to persuade him to back it.[81] Virtually the same cycle of events was repeated in 1804, for when Wilberforce first indicated he planned to bring up the general question, some West Indians began to urge suspension, avowedly out of fear of the competition of the superior soils of the lands conquered again since the resumption of the war. Wilberforce unsuccessfully tried to persuade Addington to father the measure; the general body of West Indians opposed it, and Pitt did not feel that the support of a few 'sensible West Indians' was enough to warrant him making the attempt himself.[82]

By mid-1804 the abolition campaign had been in progress for seventeen years and disappointments had been numerous and frequent. It was apparent that although the West Indian interest sometimes manifested division in its ranks, and even when united had no more chance than ever it had had to prevent abolition, independent members of Parliament were still too often judging the question on policy grounds, as it effected colonial interests traditionally conceived. Well might abolitionists have agreed with Fox when he wrote to William Smith in 1802 that he saw no prospect of abolition being achieved in the lifetime of George III.[83] Yet even from the perspective of the time there were grounds for encouragement: no serious attempt was any longer being made to defend the slave trade in principle; the Commons had in 1792 declared itself in favour of gradual abolition; the trade was effectively regulated as a result of the measures of Smith and Dolben; and limits had been placed on the supply of slaves to Trinidad which might otherwise well have become the most important market for the British slave trade. Moreover, the abolitionists were already flexing their muscles on strategies which wove significant

[81] *Life of Wilberforce*, II 367–8; *Macaulay MSS.* (Huntington Library), box 22, Z. Macaulay to Babington, 19 Apr 1800 (Copy).
[82] *Life of Wilberforce*, III 163–7; Wilberforce to Hannah More, 21 Feb 1804, *Correspondence of Wilberforce*, I 299.
[83] Lipscomb, 'Canning and the Trinidad Question', 450.

measures of abolition into the received wisdom of national interest. In the next three years, aided by a change in government which enhanced the degree of ministerial support, they were helped by events and their own insights to develop a strategy which by 1806 was to end up two-thirds of the British slave trade, basically by appeal to national interest. This made easier, but does not fully explain, the triumph of humanitarian principle in 1807.

14 Wind of Change
May 1804–February 1806

After the failure to secure a temporary suspension of the slave trade in the early months of 1804, Wilberforce addressed himself yet again to bringing on a motion for general abolition. Changed circumstances offered some encouragement.[1] Since in France democracy had now turned to despotism the damaging taunt that abolition was founded on French democratic principles now fell wide of the mark.[2] France, in any event, was swinging back in favour of the slave trade and so, as hostilities had recommenced in May of the previous year, support of abolition could almost bear the colour of patriotism. A further favourable development was that most of the Irish members newly arrived at Westminster saw in abolition a cause worthy of their support,[3] whilst since some West Indians could contemplate suspension, there was clearly some weakening in their ranks. All these encouraging omens doubtless moved the members of the Abolition Committee to meet again – they had last done so in 1795 – a development which in itself improved further the prospects of the abolition. Notable additions to the revived Committee in 1804 were – understandably – James

---

[1] Wilberforce's biographers err in suggesting that 'the substitution of a Cabinet in which it [abolition] had many warm friends, for one almost wholly hostile, was a favourable circumstance' (*Life of Wilberforce*, III 163). Certainly the only real abolitionist in Addington's Administration was Lord Hobart, but at the beginning of Pitt's Second Administration one can only rate Pitt himself, Lord Harrowby and the Earl of Camden as abolitionists, and they were opposed at least by the Earl of Westmorland, the Duke of Portland, Lord Eldon, Lord Hawkesbury, and Viscount Melville (formerly Dundas) and Lord Mulgrave.

[2] 'In France, democracy had assumed the less attractive features of military despotism, . . . and Jacobinism was too much discredited either to render to the Abolition her destructive aid, or supply a convenient reproach for its supporters' (*Life of Wilberforce*, III 163).

[3] Clarkson, *History*, II 490.

Stephen; Zachary Macaulay, now returned from the governance of the Sierra Leone settlement and editor of the recently founded Evangelical monthly, *The Christian Observer;* and Henry Brougham, still with his way to make in public life but cutting his political teeth on colonial questions and on the abolition. Another accession of strength came from the return to the Committee of Clarkson who, broken in health by his exertions, had been compelled to leave the committee in 1794, whilst Stephen and Henry Brougham became more and more active in the cause. Correspondence between the London and Pennsylvania Abolition committees also seems to have revived at this time.[4]

Wilberforce introduced his 1804 bill on 30 May and by 25 June it had successfully passed through all three readings in the Commons. The voting was 124 to 49, 100 to 42 and 99 to 33. After the first reading, Wilberforce and the abolitionists believed success was within their grasp. On that first reading the new Irish members voted en bloc for the motion and apparently continued to support abolition in both successive readings.[5] The anti-abolition vote, however, compared with what had been mustered between 1796 and 1799 – 82 on average – had almost halved. Certainly the Lords were still to be feared although it was ground for mild encouragement that Grenville, with whom Wilberforce's relations had for some time been distinctly cool, apparently was very ready to take charge of the bill in the Lords.[6] But the old obstacles of the lateness of the session and the insistence of the upper house on hearing evidence in a matter of this kind remained insuperable. Both Grenville and Porteus advised that if a division were forced the vote was likely to go against abolition and the cause would, furthermore, be prejudiced thereby were a fresh motion introduced the next session.[7] When Pitt added his weight to that pressure but at the same time told Wilberforce that it had been agreed

---

[4] *B.M. Add. MSS. 21256*, Minute of Abolition Committee, 29 Apr 1805, containing list of members of the Committee: Clarkson, *History*, II 490; Fladeland, *Men and Brothers*, 69.

[5] *Life of Wilberforce*, III 168–78.

[6] Ibid., III 178–80. In his journal, 25 May 1806, Wilberforce speaks of Grenville 'to whom always rather hostile till of late years, when I heard he was more religious' (quoted in ibid., III 261–2). Pitt had once said to Wilberforce, 'You don't like Grenville and Grenville knows that you don't' (quoted in ibid., III 262 n.).

[7] Ibid., III 180–81; *Porteus MSS.* 2104, f. 32, Diary, 3 July 1804.

in Cabinet that the cause ought to be put off until the next year when it could be 'regarded as a new question, on the ground of the danger of the colonies',[8] there was surely an indication that the abolition would, or at least might, become a government measure. Wilberforce, in any event, felt he had to submit; the mild euphoria which followed the successful first reading had evaporated but he allowed himself the cautious comfort, as he put it to Muncaster, 'that we are somewhat advanced on our way'.[9]

Indeed, the portents for the success of a general measure in 1805 were surely good, but at the very outset Pitt drew back. Far from giving official support, if that is what the hope had been, Pitt urged Wilberforce to postpone his motion in order to avoid division in the ranks of the Prime Minister's political friends.[10] This Wilberforce could not do, partly, perhaps, because he felt confident of victory in the House of Commons. Parliamentary preparations were made, including the appointment by the revived Abolition Committee of a strong sub-committee 'to procure the support of the members of both Houses of Parliament'. At the same meeting a deputation was appointed to wait on Fox and 'request the honour of his advice and co-operation' and a further sub-committee was created to publish and circulate abolitionist literature.[11] The bill was duly read a first time on 19 February but was then defeated on the second reading by seventy to seventy-seven.[12] Anxious inquiry soon revealed what had gone wrong. Only nine of the Irish members had supported the bill, others having been persuaded by the West Indians that abolition was a threat to property; nine committed abolitionists who had over

[8] *Life of Wilberforce*, III 180–81.

[9] Ibid., III 181–2.

[10] This episode remains puzzling. The *Life* is the source here and simply says 'Mr Pitt felt that his majorities were feeble, and wished to put aside all questions which could divide his friends' (ibid., III 211). Wilberforce, of course, was a most influential county member and, though not a party man, normally a supporter of Pitt. Conceivably Pitt felt that a contentious question, even as agitated by a private person, could weaken his own position, since his usual supporters would be divided on the issue. A more credible explanation is that in 1805 Pitt was on the brink of making the abolition a policy and hence a government matter, but was fearful of dividing his followers by officially taking up Wilberforce's motion at that time.

[11] *B.M. Add. MSS. 21256*, Abolition Committee Minutes, 22 Jan 1805.

[12] *Life of Wilberforce*, III 211–12.

long years never wavered in their support had preferred other engagements in the conviction that their cause was safe;[13] what Wilberforce terms 'some Scotch', presumably directed by Dundas, had opposed the motion, whereas the previous year they had remained neutral;[14] and the opponents of abolition had canvassed very strongly[15] – which last finds confirmation in the strong hostile reaction to Wilberforce's intended measure at a general meeting of West India Planters and Merchants on 14 February 1805 and the appointment of a strong committee to take all appropriate steps.[16]

The implications for the abolitionist cause of the failure to carry general abolition in 1804 and 1805 are immediately clear to the historian, blessed with hindsight, and quite quickly became clear to the abolitionist leaders themselves. Although the political climate was much more in favour of general abolition from 1804 onwards than previously, the securing of the cause in the Commons, despite the deceptively comfortable and consistent victories of 1804, had still not been effected. Enemies had only to exert themselves more, and friends less, and the day was lost. Nor, especially after failure in the Commons, could the abolitionists be sanguine of success in the Lords. Matters might well have been different in both Houses had Pitt felt able to exert himself as minister in 1805 in the way he was *perhaps* intending to do in 1804. But he had not so felt.

Confronted with failure on their main front the abolitionists, as in earlier years, turned (indeed had begun to do so in July 1804) to a partial measure. This time they sought to halt the supply of slaves by British slavers to the fertile, barely opened, and newly conquered Dutch Guiana. This angle of approach, when developed further, was to bring great rewards within less than two years. This was essentially because the abolitionists consistently used the argument of national interest, in support of particular measures of abolition.

Their first move, in this period, was ordinary enough. When hostilities had been resumed in 1803 a number of enemy Caribbean possessions had quickly fallen to British arms. The most

---

[13] Clarkson, *History*, ii 499–500; *Life of Wilberforce*, iii 212–3.

[14] Diary, 28 Feb 1805, quoted in *Life of Wilberforce*, iii 212.

[15] Ibid., iii 212, and Clarkson, *History*, ii 499.

[16] *West India Committee Minutes* (*Feb 1805–Mar 1822*), Minutes of General Meeting of Planters and Merchants, 14 Feb 1805.

important of these were Essequibo, Demerera and Berbice, which together comprised Dutch Guiana. Containing much virgin soil and eminently suitable for an extensive sugar cultivation, only slaves were lacking and some British capitalists began to import new slaves into Guiana in order to take advantage of its rich soils. There were two powerful arguments from national interest against permitting these slave imports. The first was succinctly put by the Attorney-General when referring to Guiana in a later debate: 'It was evidently against the policy of this country, that great importations of slaves should take place in settlements which perhaps might be restored at the conclusion of peace'.[17] Recent precedent abundantly supported this reasoning, for at the Peace of Amiens all conquests save Trinidad had been returned, much enriched by British capital.[18] The other argument from national interest was that there was already abundant evidence that enhanced supplies of British plantation sugar were unwelcome. As produce of a conquered territory, Guiana's exports enjoyed access to the British market and there merely added to an existing crisis. This crisis was relatively recent.[19] Although a number of serious problems had come to afflict the British West Indies since the American War – the slave rising on San Domingo in 1791, and the consequent collapse of its economy in turmoil and anarchy, had been a boon to the British West Indies. This was because the British plantation economy had always depended for its health on Britain's ability to re-export a proportion of the tropical produce imported into the mother country.[20] The volume of this re-export was a major determinant of the price tropical produce could fetch in the British market. In the decade before 1791 the extensive production of the rich soils of San Domingo had dominated the Continental market,

[17] *Parliamentary Debates*, VI col. 598, 31 Mar 1806.

[18] 'In the last war we lodged eighteen millions of property there [in the conquered territories]' Wilberforce to Muncaster, n.d., 1805, quoted in *Life of Wilberforce* III 234.

[19] For this sketch of the West Indian economy after 1783 I follow Ragatz, *Fall of the Planter Class*, 204–38, 286–94, and Porter, *Abolition*, 108–18.

[20] 'If ever . . . it could happen, that Great Britain should become the sole consumer of sugars imported from our islands, by her inability to find a vent for the superfluity of foreign markets, this event cannot happen without the desolation of some of our islands . . .' (E. Long, *History of Jamaica*, I 526–7). For the relative volume of sugar imports and re-exports, 1700–1772, see Pitman, *The Development of the British West Indies*, 169.

the principal market for British re-exports: conversely the collapse
of San Domingo was the opportunity for the re-exporter of British
sugar and the principal reason for the boom which British sugar
enjoyed, with one major break in 1799, until the end of 1800. But
other tropical sources were now increasing their supply – notably
Brazil, Cuba and the East Indies – and the recapture of Guiana
soon after the resumption of hostilities meant that its sugar came
to the British market when that market was overstocked with
British grown sugars, and when a world oversupply of sugar, and
the obstacles of wartime, combined to make re-exportation difficult. Save in the limited sense that oversupply of the market
kept down prices to the metropolitan consumer, the national
interest was harmed by oversupply. A closed tropical empire
was still regarded as vital to the nation's security and low returns
rendered it unviable. It was not only the national interest which,
in these two ways, was harmed by the supply of slaves to
Guiana: the planters of the old West India possessions also
felt themselves threatened[21] for reasons which should now be
obvious.

When the stopping of the Guiana slave trade was first proposed,
Pitt, Wilberforce said in his diary, 'positively said he had no doubt
of stopping the trade by Royal Proclamation. Very strong on this,
and against any vote of Parliament'.[22] But despite persistent pressure from Wilberforce, Pitt delayed and delayed, presumably
because of other preoccupations and perhaps from fear of raising
what might have proved a contentious issue.[23] Wilberforce, however, kept at it, declaring to his friend Muncaster that 'if we
cannot stop the whole of this accursed traffic, it is much to stop
half of it; and I am resolved to do what I can, I repeat it.'[24] It was
only, it would seem, as a result of Wilberforce in effect threaten-
ing Pitt with the parliamentary motion which, as we have seen,
he was anxious to avoid, that Pitt eventually, but belatedly, carried
out his promise in an order-in-council of 15 August 1805.[25]

[21] Wilberforce to Grenville, 27 June 1804, quoted in *Life of Wilberforce*,
III 180–81.

[22] Diary, n.d., (July 1804) quoted in *Life of Wilberforce*, III 184.

[23] Wilberforce's biographers term this delay 'the great blot in all
Mr. Pitt's treatment of this cause' (*Life of Wilberforce*, III 184).

[24] Wilberforce to Muncaster, 4 Mar 1805, quoted in ibid., III 214–16.

[25] See pp. 358–9 below. The Order is in *The Commons Journal*, LXI,
Appendix 763.

Important though this measure was – Wilberforce may have been right in supposing that the stopping of the Guiana trade, though a partial measure, would save 12,000–15,000 slave exports annually[26] – it was a straightforward measure of partial abolition. Another abolitionist tactic at this same time likewise sought to harness the abolitionist cause to the chariot of national interest, but did so in a much more sophisticated way.

James Stephen, we have already noticed, had given great support to the abolition cause, especially since his return to England in 1794, and had grown even closer to Wilberforce since marrying Wilberforce's sister. His livelihood he gained by a legal practice in the Prize Appeal Court of the Privy Council where he had come to have a large share of the leading business.[27] He had also become an author of note – and not just of abolition tracts – for in 1802 he had published *The Crisis of the Sugar Colonies*. This work was written at the time when Napoleon's expedition to reconquer lost islands in the French West Indies was being prepared. Stephen's concern was to consider the consequences for the security of the British West Indies of all likely outcomes of the French expedition, from total failure to complete success. Whatever happened, he reasoned, the result would be a massive threat to the British Caribbean possessions either from an enlaged French army in the Caribbean, backed by locally recruited legions, or by coloured armies grown bold on destruction of the French. To prevent insurrection by the slaves within her own gates, Britain must put in hand an immediate programme of amelioration of slavery, whilst the slave trade itself should be limited by prohibiting the introduction of slaves to the newly acquired, unopened lands of Trinidad. That island must, rather, be opened up by free labour. Publication of *The Crisis of the Sugar Colonies* attracted considerable notice – it was reviewed at length in the *Edinburgh Review*,[28] for instance, albeit in a hostile manner – and established Stephen as an authority on colonial questions.

During 1805 – he may possibly have commenced it in the previous year – Stephen turned to the production of another work. Although by the robust standards of the age what left the presses as a work of 252 pages was frequently described as a pamphlet,

---

[26] *Life of Wilberforce*, III 234.
[27] *D.N.B.*
[28] Vol. I (Oct 1802) 216–37.

the *War in Disguise, or the Frauds of the Neutral Flags* (1805)
was a substantial work in every way. Its burden was to demonstrate
that in the present conflict, as in earlier conflicts, the colonial trade
of France and other enemies had been thrown open to neutrals
to the clear, generally unrealised detriment of British interests.
France had first made recourse to this expedient during the Seven
Years War. With her own merchantmen driven from the seas, she
had thrown open her normally closed colonial trade to neutrals.
But on that occasion her action had been rapidly and decisively
countered. This was effected through a decision of the British prize
courts which took up the plain ground that a neutral had no right
to relieve a belligerent from the pressure of its enemies by engaging
in a trade with it from which that neutral was debarred in time
of peace. This, in a word, was the so-called 'Rule of 1756'. During
the American War, partly because France, since 1763, had somewhat relaxed her colonial monopoly and partly because Britain
lacked naval power, the Rule of 1756 was not fully enforced. In
1793, however, France had immediately thrown open the trade of
her colonies to neutrals but the initial British counter stroke, reversion to the Rule of 1756, was soon deprived of much of its
effect by an expedient yielding to neutral pressure, especially
American. When hostilities were resumed in 1803 essentially the
same blunted approach was once more adopted – neutrals were
permitted to carry on trade between enemy colonies and their
own shores.

The effect of this indulgence, Stephen went on to point out,
was that the enemy's colonies enjoyed untrammelled intercourse
with their mother-country. This was effected by shipping a cargo
of colonial produce on board a neutral vessel in the name of a
neutral consignor. If the vessel belonged to a European neutral,
her papers were made out to show the European mother-country
of that neutral as the destination. Vessel and cargo were thus
immune from seizure until European coastal waters were reached,
when it was a simple matter to slip into a port of the appropriate
belligerent – France, Holland, or, after December 1804, Spain.
If the neutral was American – and the great majority were so –
this device could not, for obvious reasons, be used: instead, the
cargo was shipped to the United States and then re-consigned as
American produce to an enemy port on the continent of Europe.

Outward cargoes were carried by the reverse process. The extent of the abuse, Stephen demonstrated, was prodigious.

> France and Holland have totally ceased to trade under their own flags, to or from the ports of any of their colonies; and have apparently assigned the whole of these branches of their commerce to the merchants of neutral states.
>
> Spain, though with more hesitation, and by gradual advances, has nearly made as entire a transfer of all her trade with her colonies on the Atlantic . . . [including] the . . . important commerce of the Havannahs, and of Cuba in general.

In short, for all Britain's enemies,

> it may be truly affirmed that neutrals have been their only carriers. The mercantile colours of their respective countries, and of their confederates, have been absolute strangers in their ports. . . .
>
> Though to the generality of my readers this proportion may seem extraordinary, and perhaps too strange to be believed, yet it forms only part of a still more comprehensive and singular truth – *With the exception of a very small portion of the coasting trade of our enemies, not a mercantile sail of any description now enters or clears from their ports in any part of the globe, but under neutral colours*

An important consequence of this recourse to the neutral flags has been a great augmentation of the enemy's colonial resources.

> Buonaparte has recently boasted, that Martinique and Guadaloupe are flourishing, in despite of our hostilities. . . . The Spanish Government is not so ostentatious; but its colonies are quietly reaping the fruit of that fortunate revolution, the suspension of their prohibitory laws. The neutral flag gives to them not only protection, but advantages before unknown. The gigantic infancy of agriculture in Cuba, far from being checked, is greatly aided in its portentous growth during the war, by the boundless liberty of trade, and the perfect security of carriage. . . . In short, all the hostile colonies, whether Spanish, French, or Batavian, derive from the enmity of Great Britain, their ancient scourge and terror, not inconvenience but advantage: far from being impoverished or distressed by our hostilities, as formerly, they

find in war the best sources of supply, and new means of agri-cultural, as well as commercial prosperity.[29]

Serious as the effects of the rise of the neutral flag on the develop-ment of the enemy's colonies were, Stephen discerned two princi-pal ways in which further harm was done. The first was implicit in the 'frauds' of the neutral flags, for it permitted enemy colonial produce to be brought unimpeded to Europe *and,* because un-impeded, more cheaply than by British West Indiamen. British Caribbean produce was much subject to the danger of the still rampant French privateers and this danger, because it meant delay in waiting for convoys and higher insurance rates, sharply raised the cost of the British product and made it uncompetitive in the Continental market.[30]

> While our colonies, and our colonial commerce, are labouring under great and increasing burthens, those of the enemy, com-paratively unencumbered, are thriving at their expense. While freight, war duties, and insurance, are advancing in England, the expense of neutralization [i.e. the carriage of enemy produce to Europe in neutral bottoms] is daily diminishing in France, Holland and Spain. Competition, and the safety of neutral carriage, are reducing it every day.[31]

This is a serious matter, for 'the consumption of West India pro-duce in Europe has natural limits; and the Jamaican Assembly has satisfactorily shown that those limits are scarcely now wide enough to receive the actual supply at such prices as the British planter can possibly afford to accept'.[32]

The second way in which the abuse of the neutral flag harmed Britain's interest was more directly military – or, more precisely,

[29] James Stephen, *War in Disguise, or the Frauds of the Neutral Flags,* 58–64, 212–3, 'The [American] re-export trade expanded, . . . spectacularly, from an infinitesimal amount in 1791 to $60 million in 1806. In 1806, 47 million pounds of coffee, more than 146 million pounds of sugar, and nearly 2 million pounds of cotton imported into the United States were re-exported to Europe' (Bradford Perkins, *Prologue to War: England and the U.S. 1805–1812* (Berkeley, 1961) 30).

[30] Of course the fact that the British export of tropical produce was a re-export trade further added to its costs whilst the initial cost of pro-duction was usually higher also.

[31] Stephen, *War in Disguise,* 166–7.

[32] Ibid., 171–2.

naval – and consisted in the deleterious effect which the toleration of the carriage of enemy produce in neutral vessels had on the relative balance of naval power. Stephen elaborated at length on this, but the essence of his contention was that

> While he [the enemy] is preparing the means of active maritime enterprizes, we are reduced at sea, as well as on shore, to a mere defensive war. . . . The hostile navies are nursed, augmented, and reserved in safety for a day of advantageous trial; while our own is sustaining all the most laborious duties of war, with scarcely any of its ancient encouragements; our seamen, also, are debauched into foreign employ, to carry on the trade of our enemies.[33]

The misuse of neutral flags, then, damaged British interests to a surprising extent and in unsuspectedly complex ways. The remedy, however, was simple – a return to that Rule of 1756 which had brought such good results during the Seven Years War. If neutrals were denied access in war to trades from which they were debarred in peace, neutral sailings to and from enemy colonies would cease; neutral vessels would no longer be the same lure for British seamen; the enemy's economy would suffer; and his navy would be drawn into desired combat, if it sought to protect a colonial trade which had hitherto been made over to neutrals.

No one seems to have doubted the accuracy of Stephen's analysis of the existing situation.[34] They could not easily do so, given that Stephen's law practice in the Prize Court gave him what few others possessed – the insights which enabled him to penetrate the clouds of obscurity and dissimulation which masked the real flows of wartime trade. (Disagreement there was, but over the propriety, in international law, of the Rule of 1756 and over the possible American reaction to such a move, Stephen being confident that such reaction would not go so far as a declaration of war.) Thus far, therefore, Stephen was seen to be making a powerful appeal to the national interest. But in what way was the cause of abolition being attached to that interest? Stephen makes

[33] Ibid., 166–7.

[34] For that situation, and the debate upon it, see Bradford Perkins, *Prologue to War;* R. Horsman, *Causes of the War of 1812* (Philadelphia, 1967); A. T. Mahan, *Sea Power in its Relations to the War of 1812* (Boston, 1905); E. Heckscher, *The Continental System* (Oxford, 1922); F. Crouzet, *L'Economie Britannique et le Blocus Continental, 1806–1813* (Paris, 1958).

a specific connection only in one place. When speaking of the tremendous expansion of agriculture in Cuba, which had been so much aided 'by the boundless liberty of trade, and the perfect security of carriage', he went on:

> Even slaves from Africa are copiously imported there, and doubtless also into the French islands, under American colours. America indeed has prohibited this commerce, and wishes to suppress it; but our enemies can find agents as little scrupulous of violating the law of their own country, as the law of war; and so wide has been our complaisance to depredation on our belligerent right, that even the slave trading smuggler has been allowed to take part of the spoil.[35]

It is fair to say that in this passage, given the context of the argument of the book as a whole, Stephen was indicating that one branch of the neutral carrying trade which a return to the Rule of 1756 would destroy would be the import of slaves into enemy colonies by neutral slavers. Yet, when one recalls Stephen's abolitionist passion, there is something curiously incidental in his citation of this branch of the slave trade and in the fact that this is the sole significant mention of the slave trade in the whole book. Indeed any mention at all of the slave trade has, rather, the quality of a Freudian slip, once we understand that Stephen believed that the abolition cause *would* be well served by the measures against neutral carriers which he was urging but that the very avowal of such an abolitionist object was likely to prejudice its fulfilment. The vital evidence of Stephen's design is contained in an obscure footnote in the *Life of Wilberforce*. The text asserts that by 1805 'the colonies of Holland, France, and Spain could only be supplied [with slaves] under the neutral colours of America', and to this the footnote adds the following important comment: 'Mr. Stephen aiming only at its [i.e. the neutral slave trade's] suppression published a masterly pamphlet (*War in Disguise*) upon the rights of neutral powers. *Fearing if he mentioned the slave trade, that the effect of his arguments might be diminished by a suspicion of his motives, he confined himself entirely to the general question*' (my italics).[36]

[35] Stephen, *War in Disguise*, 62–3.

[36] *Life of Wilberforce*, III 234–5. The footnote begins with the sentence 'The "Orders in Council" were, by a curious connexion, the offspring of

Now we have seen that the claim that Stephen 'confined himself entirely' to the general principle is not literally true; but it is true in essence since the only mention of the slave trade is brief and incidental. It does not matter, for our purposes, whether the assertion that Stephen was aiming 'only' at the suppression of the slave trade is true:[37] what is clear is that Wilberforce's biographers[38] are right in attributing to Stephen a conscious, major concern to promote abolition by the advocacy of measures whose overt appeal was that they served the national interest, and to avoid *prejudicing* the abolition cause by yet another appeal to a humanity which, after nearly two decades of campaining, still had not melted enough hearts. The measures against neutrals which Stephen so powerfully urged would, it must be stressed, have an unsuspectedly wide effect and would go much beyond the interdiction of the supply of slaves to enemy possession by neutral slave traders. For in addition to this, both imports into enemy colonies from the metropolitan country, and exports to it, in neutral bottoms, would be prohibited. Supplies and manufactures from Europe would not reach enemy colonies: exports of tropical produce to Europe would not leave them. And if such interdictions could be enforced – and Britain's naval supremacy was total save for French privateers (news of Trafalgar which set the seal on this supremacy, reached Stephen as he was correcting his proofs) – the whole economy of the enemy's colonies would collapse with, as a major consequence, a total inability to purchase any more new slaves.

[37] Stephen's strong and continuing advocacy of tougher measures against neutrals *after* both the British and the American abolition suggests that Stephen held this cause near to his heart on general patriotic grounds. But it would be entirely typical of Stephen, and of the Evangelical mind, to assume a necessary consonance between a morally justified national policy and the furtherance of abolition. He had made just such a link – but overtly – in *The Crisis of the Sugar Colonies.*

[38] We know that the *Life* was read in manuscript by Stephen's son (David Newsome, review of Brown, *Fathers of the Victorians* in *Historical Journal*, VI (1963) 303 – I am indebted to Dr Tom Barron for this reference) and it may be that the footnote was added as a result.

this trade', and concludes with the clause, 'and from the abstract principles he was thus led to lay down, the celebrated "Orders" were subsequently drawn'. This is a reference to Stephen's acknowledged role as advocate, and possibly originator, of the tougher measures against neutral shipping introduced by Orders-in-Council from 1806 onwards.

Application of the Rule of 1756 had yet another implication: it would damage a sector of the *British* slave trade, namely the supply of French and Spanish possessions with slaves, commerce which had continued, despite hostilities, by such expedients as landing cargoes at the Danish islands of St Croix and St Thomas, for onward shipment to enemy colonies.[39] For one effect of damaging the economy of the enemy's tropical possessions would be that they would no more be able to afford to buy new slaves from British slave traders than from neutral.

By the end of 1805, therefore, the abolitionists had obtained a stop of the supply of slaves to the most important of the enemy possessions conquered since the resumption of hostilities. In addition to this the measures proposed by Stephen against neutral shipping would, if applied, cut off both the neutral and British slave trades to enemy possessions.[40] Whilst the war lasted, at least, this would leave as the principal remaining sectors of the Atlantic slave trade the Portuguese supply of South America, principally Brazil; American importation into her own southern colonies which though it revived from 1804 onwards was by 1806 mooted as likely to end by federal prohibition in 1808; and the British slave trade to her older West Indian islands, commonly reckoned as about one-third of the total British slave trade. The various partial measures of abolition, which cumulatively added up to a good deal, had largely – sometimes entirely – been urged on national interest grounds, the whole constituting an able acting-

[39] See, e.g., speeches by the Attorney-General, the Duke of Clarence and the Earl of Westmoreland in the debates on the Foreign Slave Trade Bill of 1806, *Parliamentary Debates*, VI, cols. 597–8; VII 227–9 and 230.

[40] *War in Disguise* was widely noticed and read. It was reviewed, for instance, in the *New Annual Register*, 1805 (p. 333) and again in 1806 on the appearance of third and fourth editions (342–4). There was a particularly long notice in the *Edinburgh Review* in April 1806 (VIII, no. 15, 1–35). Doubtless Lord Holland's comment on it to Fox was but one of many in private correspondence (*Fox MSS.*, *B.M. Add. MSS. 47575*, Holland to Fox, 3 Jan, 1806) – and one should note that, although Holland dismissed the book as 'abominable and mischievous', the Ministry of which he was a part began the implementation of a more rigorous policy against neutrals. James Monroe, who was in London on the Monroe–Pinckney mission at the time, sent copies to two correspondents in November 1805 (J. Monroe to James Bowdoin, 13 Nov 1805 and to General Armstrong, 14 Nov 1805, in S. M. Hamilton (ed.), *The Writings of James Monroe* (New York, 1900) IV 366, 369).

out of the injunction in Matthew 10.16 to be 'wise as serpents', an inspiration which Stephen, particularly, would surely have been happy to own. Had a Ministry whose leading members were sympathetic to abolition, not come to power in February 1806, on the unexpected death of Pitt, a sizeable segment of the slave trade would still have been destroyed, at least for as long as the war endured. The measures against the trade to conquered islands operated ever more widely as conquest followed conquest and could scarcely have been repealed during wartime, whilst the years from 1806 onwards saw the successively more rigorous application of the measures which Stephen had proposed. But the death of Pitt – paradoxically, because he supported abolition to the end – paved the way for a more direct abolitionist attack.

The principal reason why Pitt's unexpected death made such a difference was that the coalition ministry which came to power was dominated by men who favoured abolition. Some indeed, including the two leading men, Grenville, the titular head of the ministry, and Fox, had been committed to the cause since its infancy. Not all were as enthusiastic for abolition of the slave trade to the older islands as for the ending of other branches of the British slave trade, but it appears that only Windham was opposed to abolition in all its proposed forms. There were, in addition, political reasons why this uneasy coalition might find in abolition a cause round which most of its members could unite. Even though many of their energies had to be devoted to conducting the war – in measure as their hopes of concluding a peace came to be disappointed – the administration could hardly feel comfortable without some reforming cause to espouse, especially as the largest single group in it were Foxites. But, as J. Steven Watson has pointed out, time had eroded the appeal of so many once glorious principles. Since the 1790s and their acute social and political discontents talk of parliamentary reform would rouse a spectre indeed, whilst Pitt had stolen the Foxite's clothes by his measures, albeit limited, of economical reform. All that remained as unifying causes were Catholic emancipation – and abolition.[41] The former so largely

---

[41] Watson, *Reign of George III*, 435–40. Cf. Holland's words to Fox on 20 Feb 1804: 'I shall only say that three great questions seem to be ripe for discussion . . . I mean the Catholic question, the abolition of the slave trade, and the Prince. . . .' (*Fox MSS., B.M. Add. MSS. 45775*).

united them that they eventually fell together over a very modest instalment of it: the latter cause, particularly, Grenville and Fox would obviously espouse with enthusiasm. Only Addington, the head of the third group which made up the coalition, would be unhappy, just as he broke from his colleagues in the last stages of the extremely limited measure of relief to Catholics.

The Talents Ministry, then, found that abolition was an issue which would give substance to their coalition whilst more basic was the commitment of its leading men to ending the slave trade: but in the tactical handling of the matter the abolitionists themselves had a vitally important role to play. That they could do so demands explanation because, even though abolition was in a sense not a party question, the abolitionist leader had been, whilst retaining his independence, the single most influential supporter of the minister with whom Foxites, Grenvillites and Addingtonians had been at odds. We have already noticed that, to obtain the order-in-council stopping the British slave trade to Guiana, Wilberforce had, in effect, to threaten Pitt. If the fact of the threat had some immediate significance, the form of it had real significance for the future. It will be remembered that Pitt had confidently promised in July 1804 that the Guiana trade could be stopped by order-in-council, and that he was firmly opposed to the matter being raised in Parliament,[42] presumably because he wished to avoid all occasion of division in the ranks of his supporters. The order was promised week after week but despite a number of pleas from Wilberforce[43] nothing effective was done until the following March. On 6 March 1805 Wilberforce wrote again, and strongly, to Pitt and at an interview three days later, as Wilberforce confided to his diary: 'I declared that I must positively bring it into the House, and with opposition – concert, and combination, as also foreign slave trade and Trinidada'.[44] Here was a clear threat to join with the opposition and it induced Pitt to declare 'that

[42] Wilberforce, Diary, n.d. 3 July 1804, quoted in *Life of Wilberforce*, III 184.

[43] Ibid., III 184; Wilberforce to Pitt, 14 Sept 1804, *Correspondence of Wilberforce*, I 311–12; Wilberforce to Stephen, 2 Oct and 18 Nov 1804, ibid., I 331–2, 341.

[44] Wilberforce, Diary, n.d. [9 Mar 1805], quoted in *Life of Wilberforce*, III 216.

government did unanimously agree to stop that trade [the Guiana trade], and that he wished me to prepare regulations'[45] None the less, Wilberforce felt that Pitt's record of procrastination was such that he was justified in keeping up the pressure. The next development was a meeting at the house of the rising Whig politican, Lord Henry Petty, at the end of March at which, Wilberforce noted in his diary, 'Opposition preponderated'.[46] There was agreement that the measure with the best chance of success was the prohibition of the Guiana trade, and it was decided that Pitt should be pressed by the meeting – threatened, indeed – on the question. As Wilberforce described it to his friend Muncaster,

> Bankes and I were expressly commissioned from the meeting, to ask Pitt whether he wished to take this service on himself or not, that we might determine whether Lord Henry Petty should give notice of it, or of some other measure. We had an interview with Pitt soon after, and were directed by him to report his answer to the meeting . . . which had been adjourned for five days to give time for receiving it . . . that he would himself stop the Guiana Trade.[47]

Pitt was still dilatory, but the order was eventually laid on 13 September 1805. That Wilberforce, in concert with opposition abolitionists, had threatened Pitt is clear, and in the view of Robert and Samuel Wilberforce it was the threat that produced the action.[48] Yet the really significant thing is that Wilberforce, a continuing friend of Pitt, and normally his political supporter, had drawn closer to the opposition on the cause which was, after all, the one closest to Wilberforce's heart. This move was purely a pragmatic one and Pitt's decline which was to lead to his death early the next year was, apart from his growing tendency to procrastination, still not apparent. But die Pitt did on 23 January 1806, and it is striking that Wilberforce took an early opportunity to cement those links with the erstwhile opposition, now the 'new

[45] Wilberforce, Diary, 11 Mar 1805, quoted in ibid., III 216.
[46] Wilberforce, Diary, 29 Mar 1805, quoted in ibid., III 216–17.
[47] Wilberforce to Muncaster, n.d., quoted in ibid., III 232–4. Wilberforce's account of the meeting at Lansdowne House is contained partly in this letter to Muncaster and partly in the diary entries quoted in ibid., 216–17.
[48] Ibid., III 185.

men', which he had so fortuitously begun to forge in the spring of the previous year.

The occasion arose because of a by-election in the Cambridge University constituency in February 1806, where Wilberforce, as a Cambridge man of considerable political standing, enjoyed considerable influence amongst University voters. With a double irony, since Wilberforce's friendship with Pitt had been close – and within recent days Wilberforce had been a pall-bearer at the state funeral[49] – and since the seat in question was that for which Pitt himself had sat, Wilberforce supported the Whig candidate, Lord Henry Petty. (Indeed, there was a triple irony in Wilberforce's decision since the opposing candidate was the youthful Lord Palmerston who in mid-century was to do so much to crush the remaining branches of the Atlantic slave trade.) This unexpected attitude evoked annoyance, indeed grief, amongst some of his friends and the terms in which his old friend and mentor, Isaac Milner, the Dean of Carlisle and now President of Queens' College, reproved him are the measure of this forceful reaction.[50]

I have very great doubts [wrote Milner] *of the effect* which this step of yours will have on *your general character*. My objection does not arise from your joining with what may be called the old opposition on a single point or two or more. . . . My objection arises from what *will be deemed* (explain it as you please) a hasty change of political principle upon the unexpected death of the great leader. I seem myself to foresee this, that the dissenting, low, party, now the governing party, will be very glad to receive you on their side, but . . . they will only make a temporary use of you. Then the old party (if any of them be indeed left) will look on you in their hearts as an apostate, and timeserver, or at best one whose attachments to the establishment are but weak.

Milner went on to make clear that part of his criticism of Wilber-

---

[49] The official invitation is in the *Wilberforce (Duke) MSS*.

[50] *Wrangham MSS.*, Milner to Wilberforce, 7 Feb 1806. There is a version of this letter in the *Correspondence of Wilberforce*, II 67–9, but it exemplifies early nineteenth-century editing at its worst, and quite blunts the force of Milner's criticism. The editors of Wilberforce's letter do, however, print a letter from Milner to Wilberforce the previous day (ibid., 64–7) which is somewhat more pointedly critical of Wilberforce. I have not discovered the original of the letter of 6 Feb in the *Wrangham MSS*.

force's attitude stemmed from Petty's religious beliefs, from the fact that he was 'intimately acquainted with notorious Socinians and unbelievers of the Scriptures'. Altogether, Milner was extremely upset with Wilberforce; 'I am', he said, *'vexed to the heart'* (Milner's italics throughout). All this notwithstanding, Milner hinted at Wilberforce's motives well enough, when he wrote: 'I fervently wish you may find Lord H.P., and Fox, etc., as true friends to the Abolition as you have reason to suppose them'.[51] Wilberforce himself recorded the episode in his diary thus:

> My suddenly promising Lord Henry Petty (which done too hastily, partly from not thinking I had any interest, partly from being found in a state of wishing to show Lord Henry how much both I and the cause felt indebted to him), has produced a sad degree of rufflement. Dear Dean [Milner] much hurt about it for my sake ...[52]

Wilberforce saw himself as acting consistently with his habit of supporting the King's government whenever possible, but so preserving his independence as to oppose it when necessary.[53] In a letter to Gisborne written at this time he attests the good which the Cambridge University election had done to the abolition cause – and somewhat disingenuously refrains from specifically mentioning the super-added zeal for abolition which his support for Petty, the new Chancellor of the Exchequer, must have engendered in the successful candidate. He goes on to survey the likely attitudes of members of the Cabinet, and to point up once more the importance of the royal family's opposition.

> Our great cause has been considerably accredited by what has passed at the Cambridge election. Lord Henry Petty got a great deal of support, owing to his known zeal in it. His opponent, Lord Palmerston, lost much owing to his being supposed, mistakenly I believe, to be our enemy; and numbers declared they would not, though satisfied in all other points, vote for an anti-abolitionist. So far well. The Chancellor of the Exchequer [Petty] comes from Cambridge in a good state of mind *quoad hoc*. Fox a decided friend, Grenville ditto. Lord Spencer I

[51] *Wrangham MSS.*, Milner to Wilberforce, 7 Feb 1806.
[52] *Life of Wilberforce*, III 256.
[53] Ibid., III 255.

believe favourable, but not very strong. Lord Moria I doubt; Sidmouth, Ellenborough, Erskine talking friendly to me, but always absenting himself. Lord Fitzwilliam I am not quite sure, but I think favourable. Windham contra. But the great point would be to get if possible the royal family to give up their opposition.

Wilberforce goes on to make clear that he means to try to secure all the rewards of support of the ministry without the impropriety of a specific bargain.

Stephen had a plan suggested by his warm zeal, that we should send a deputation to the new ministry, to make a sort of contract that we would befriend them as we did Pitt, i.e. give them the turn of the scale, etc. if they would promise us to support the Abolition as a Government measure.[54] The idea is inadmissable, both on grounds of rectitude and policy (the two parties would infallibly have different ideas of the practical extent of the obligation, and mutual misunderstanding would ensue), yet I think we ought to contrive that the effect intended by it may be produced; and though I dare scarcely be sanguine when I recollect with whom we have to do, yet I cannot but entertain some hopes that the wish to nullify, and even conciliate, a number of strange unpracticable and otherwise 'uncomeatable' fellows by gratifying them in this particular, may have its weight; at least it will tend to counteract the fear of offending the West Indians.[55]

In the period of less than two years since May 1804, when the attempt to secure total abolition had been resumed, the abolition cause had passed from high optimism to frustration and to the dawning of new hope. At another level the abolitionists had come to manifest considerable sophistication in their use of the national

[54] This statement must not be taken at its face value – i.e. that the abolitionists, as a bloc, had supported Pitt (still less, of course, that Pitt had ever made the (general) abolition a government measure). What is meant is that Pittite and independent abolitionists might make this overture. Foxite and Grenvillite abolitionists would support the new ministry on abolition anyway.

[55] Wilberforce to Gisborne, 11 Feb 1806, quoted in *Life of Wilberforce* III 256–7.

interest ploy as a cover for their coveted object. With the accession to office of the Talents Ministry, and with the surprisingly warm relations with the leading men that Wilberforce had come to enjoy, a new prospect of advancing the abolitionist cause had indeed emerged.

15 Abolition: 1806

During later February and much of March, as the new ministry was settling into office, there was initially a good deal of inconclusive discussion between ministers and leading abolitionists about how to proceed. Brougham, who was now gaining access to the higher councils of the Whigs, reported to Wilberforce, probably in March, that he had had lengthy discussions with Petty and Lord Holland, at one of which Fox was present, and gave it as his opinion that the abolition question 'cannot, or at least will not, be taken separately from the general American question'[1] – an interesting indication that not only Stephen, but ministers also, saw a connection between abolition and Anglo–American relations. Wilberforce himself had 'many interviews' with Fox, and, warmed to him as they again took up their acquaintance.[2] At first, though, there was an ominous note, as well as encouragement.

> Consulting about Abolition [runs Wilberforce's diary on 5 March], Fox and Lord Henry Petty talked as if we might certainly carry our question in the House of Commons, but should certainly lose it in the House of Lords. This looks but ill, as if they wished to please us, and yet not forfeit Prince of Wales' favour, and that of G.R. [the King] and other anti-abolitionists.[3]

But shortly afterwards, there were grounds for more optimism on this important question of the Prince's attitude. William Smith was the means of initiating a change. Smith had been valuable as an intermediary with abolitionists of politically radical inclination and now, because of his intimacy with Fox, Grey and other Whig

[1] Brougham to Wilberforce n.d. [? March 1806], *Correspondence of Wilberforce*, II 78. See also Brougham to Wilberforce, n.d. [? March 1806], ibid., II 79–80.
[2] *Life of Wilberforce*, III 259.
[3] Diary, 5 Mar 1806, quoted in ibid, III 259.

leaders, was to perform his most important services for the abolition.[4] 'Our slave business rather mends. William Smith saw Lord
Moira, who will confer with the Prince of Wales'.[5] As a result,
though after what lapse of time is unclear, the Prince promised
that he would not 'stir adversely' in the matter.[6] In mid-March
there were 'many conferences' on the abolition question with Grenville, Sidmouth, Stephen, Fox and Petty, and it is clear from a
letter of Wilberforce to Grenville of 24 March that the result was
agreement that Wilberforce should put down yet again his motion
for a general abolition but this time with the strong support of
many of the leading men in the Cabinet. Due to the nature of the
issue and the continued opposition of at least two ministers,[7] the
abolition could still not become a government question, but its
prospects were evidently substantially better than ever before – at
any rate in the Commons – precisely because Grenville, Fox, Grey
and Petty, particularly, were heart and soul behind the motion.[8]

Whether those prospects were sufficiently improved to ensure
victory was another matter. In any event second thoughts supervened before notice was given of Wilberforce's motion. They
originated with Stephen and are revealed in a vitally important
letter from Wilberforce to Grenville of 24 March. That letter lays
out a sophisticated strategy entirely worthy of the author of *The
War in Disguise*, and must be reproduced in full.

> Since I had the pleasure of seeing your Lordship the other day,
> an idea has been suggested by Mr. Stephen (whom your Lord-

[4] Davis, *Dissent in Politics*, 111 ff. Especially when it is remembered that
Smith was a Unitarian and a Whig there was a surprising intimacy
between Wilberforce and Smith. Smith was one of the very few whom
Wilberforce addressed by his Christian name, and in a letter to Smith
of 20 Feb 1798 (*Smith MSS.* [Duke]) Wilberforce bares his soul on both
political and religious questions – he ends the letter with the injunction
'let me beg you to burn this, lest it should ever fall into any hands but
yours' – in a manner which attests the depth of the relationship, and is
very revealing of Wilberforce's moral and spiritual strength, and of his
charity to opponents.

[5] Wilberforce, Diary, 13 Mar 1806, quoted in *Life of Wilberforce*, III 259.

[6] Wm Smith to Wilberforce, 17 Nov 1806, quoted in ibid., III 259.

[7] Ibid., III 262. Windham and either Fitzwilliam or Sidmouth, probably
the former, were presumably meant.

[8] Lord Holland, who was very warm in the cause, did not enter the
Cabinet until the autumn.

ship may probably have heard when at the Cockpit[9]) which has prevented my giving notice according to the intention I then stated. This is, that an Act of Parliament has often, or even generally, been found necessary for rendering an order of his Majesty in Council really effectual; and that in the instance of the order for stopping the supply of slaves to Dutch Guiana, issued about last August, an act of Parliament is peculiarly requisite. The next step to which we were led, was, that on the very same principles as those on which the Guiana Order[10] and the proposed act for rendering it effectual would rest, the British slave trade for supplying all foreign colonies ought also to be prohibited. And as the order was supported by those members of administration who were most adverse to abolition principles, we thought that a further measure grounded on the same principle might probably without difficulty obtain the support of all the members of the present administration. Being also officially introduced (for I scarcely need remark to your Lordship that it must be a Government measure) it would meet with little or no opposition in Parliament, especially as at the moment the foreign slave trade is all but quite extinguished by the War,[11] though, during Peace, it may again become, as it has been

[9] The colloquial term for the Prize Appeal Court of the Privy Council.

[10] 'It seems highly desirable that the principle of the measure should be distinctly laid down in the front of the Order; and if such of your Cabinet as are friendly to our cause mean honestly to join in preventing British capital from going to Guiana, they will surely least of all object to the assertion of a principle, which will render it impossible for any one to suppose that justice and mercy have had any share in dictating the measure, and thence to charge them with inconsistency in not being governed by those principles on the main question' (Wilberforce to Pitt, 25 May 1805, quoted in *Life of Wilberforce*, III 231–2).

[11] The suggestion that the 'foreign slave trade is all but quite extinguished by the war' is puzzling, for the clear weight of other testimony is that it continued to be important. See e.g., *Parliamentary Debates*, VI, cols. 597–8, 31 Mar 1806, Attorney-General; J. A. Picton, *Memorials of Liverpool, Historical and Topographical* (Liverpool, 1907), I 277, who gives a figure of 13,800 slaves landed in foreign colonies in 1804; and *S.P.*, 1806, XIII (265), no. 6, from which a figure of 11,500 sold to foreigners in the year ending 10 October 1805 may be inferred (see n. 39, p. 376 below). Conceivably Wilberforce was being disingenuous by suggesting that because the nation was at war no one would feel able to acknowledge the existence of a trade to foreigners, who were for the most part enemies, and, *a fortiori*, not be able to defend it.

heretofore, a large proportion of the whole. It is obvious, however, that as the stopping of the foreign slave trade may be justified even to the satisfaction of the opponents of General Abolition, it would be imprudent to embark them both in the same
bottom, and therefore it would be highly desirable that Government should give notice of the measure I have suggested, before
my motion is made which would include the foreign slave trade
as part of the whole.

I have this afternoon had some conversation on this subject
with Mr. Fox as I had before with Lord Henry Petty: I understood they would take the earliest opportunity of conferring with
your Lordship, which renders it unnecessary for me to trouble
your Lordship with any more particular detail. I am persuaded
I need not say anything as to the Importance of the object in
question and I will only again take the liberty of stating, that
the measure ought to proceed my motion, which however, is
now full late and cannot be much longer delayed.[12]

What Wilberforce, prompted by Stephen, was proposing is
clear: rather than start the new campaign with Wilberforce's
general motion, albeit with more support from ministers than
ever it had known before, let a measure be first introduced to end
two important segments of the British slave trade, namely the
supply of conquered islands and the supply of foreigners. Since
such a measure could be presented as a policy matter it would,
indeed must, be an official measure, and because of its avowed
basis it would not be difficult to obtain the assent of the minority
of ministers still hostile to the principle of abolition. More than
this the reference to the principles on which the Guiana Order was
justified abundantly confirms that 'justice and mercy', as motives
were to be kept discreetly in the background. After nearly twenty
years the appeal to humanity and justice still had not brought
success: perhaps more could be done behind the cloak of national
interest. What else might follow from this strategy we shall see in
due course. What was immediately important, of course, was
Grenville's reaction, and the promptitude with which it came is
an indication of what it was. Grenville promised to take 'the first
moment possible' to discuss the proposal with Fox and Petty 'and
I need not say how happy I shall be, if I can in any way promote

[12] *Dropmore MSS.* (*W.B.H.*), Wilberforce to Grenville, 24 Mar 1806.

the objects you mention'.[13] Nor were these just fair words, for within less than a week – a quite remarkably short time, probably possible only because Wilberforce had either assured ministers that Stephen knew precisely how the bill should be drafted, or because Stephen actually drafted it himself[14] – the Attorney-General gave notice of his intention to introduce the bill. Within a further week, namely by early April, the new strategy had been further clarified, as Wilberforce describes in his diary: 'Lords Grenville and Henry Petty wish my general abolition bill not to come on, till the Attorney-General's bill carried through. I believe they are right, and at all events must give way to their wish.'[15]

Sir Arthur Piggott introduced his motion by saying that it 'was one in which humanity and sound policy were united' but thereafter made no further reference to the humanitarian aspect of the bill but outlined the manner in which the national interest would be served by ending the supply of slaves to foreigners in British ships and by strengthening, by statute, the royal proclamation of 15 August 1805 which prohibited, with exceptions, the supply of slaves to conquered colonies.[16] In the debates at the various stages of the bill it was argued, particularly by George Rose, Sir R. Peele, Sir C. Price and General Tarleton, that the bill would injure British industry and commerce by the reduction in exports to West Africa which would ensue. Rose and Gascoyne played upon fears of a breach with America by arguing that certain provisions

[13] Ibid., Grenville to Wilberforce, 25 Mar 1806 (copy). Also printed in *Correspondence of Wilberforce*, II 84–5 where, however, its point is blunted since the letter to which it is a reply, together with the great bulk of the critically important Wilberforce–Grenville correspondence, is not included.

[14] My reasons for this conclusion are contained in Wilberforce to Grenville, 8 May 1806 (*Dropmore MSS*. [WBH]). 'I have learned from certain authority, that the opponents of the measure, despairing of opposing us with effect on the general principle, mean to defeat us by obtaining such modifications in the Committee as would render it altogether inoperative. *Mr. Stephen authorises me to declare to your Lordship in the most positive manner, that the provisions have been lowered down to the lowest extent which the case will bear, and that therefore it would be ruinous to weaken them*' (My italics).

[15] Diary, 5 Apr 1806, quoted in *Life of Wilberforce*, III 260.

[16] *Parliamentary Debates*, VI, cols. 597–8, 31 Mar 1806. The Attorney-General, in the report of his speech, is made to give 15 August 1804 as the date of the Guiana order-in-council. It was, of course, 15 August 1805.

in the bill, especially those relating to foreign slavers fitting out in British ports, would antagonise the United States.

Tarleton and General Gascoyne, the two Liverpool members, defended the slave trade on grounds that were merely repititious, but added that any British withdrawal from the trade would be matched by American advance in it, a point also argued by Rose. Mr Brooke, however, considered the measure 'as beneficial to the West India merchants' whilst Sir William Young looked on the bill 'as a boon' to his fellow West Indians 'and thanked the learned gentleman for having brought it forward'. The only speaker in the Commons who dilated on the humanitarian overtones of the bill was Fox. Clearly, a man who had once dismissed Political Economy as 'that most nonsensical of all sciences'[17] was hardly likely to expatiate on the politico–economic purposes of the bill, but, even so, he kept to the agreed approach and gave nothing away. To begin with, indeed, there was a decent dissimulation: 'As to the bill having an operation gradually to abolish the slave trade, as some gentlemen seemed to apprehend, he owned he could not flatter himself in the hope that it would produce such a consequence'. And there was nothing really remiss when he added, 'and if he thought it would have such a tendency, instead of that being with him an argument against the bill, it was one which would render him ten times more enamoured of it'. Even when he went on to nail his humanitarian colours to the mast[18] he still gave nothing away about the strategy agreed between the abolitionists and the ministry. Wilberforce, indeed, who sat silently through all the debates, positively evaded a challenge in this area. Both Tarleton and Gascoyne pressed him as to whether

---

[17] *Fox MSS., B.M. Add. MSS. 47575*, Fox to Holland, 29 Mar 1804. His literary interests are, rather, and as one might expect, conveyed by a comment to his nephew ten days later that he had recently read very little 'just a play or two of Euripides' (Ibid., Fox to Holland, 9 Apr 1804).

[18] 'He ... and several of those with whom he had the honour to act ... still felt it [total abolition] as one involving the dearest interests of humanity, and as one which, however unfortunate this administration might be in other respects, should they be successful in effecting it, would entail more true glory upon their administration, and more honour upon their country, than any other transaction in which they could be engaged.' But such a motion might be brought on by Wilberforce and he, Fox, would support it warmly whenever Wilberforce thought fit to bring it forward.

he intended to bring on his annual motion that session. But, as the parliamentary reporter tells us, on the second occasion, 'Mr. W. took no notice of the question put to him by the hon. general'.

The real testimony to the success of the agreed strategy, of low-key approach, was not just the successful result on 1 May – thirty-five to thirteen on the third reading – but the small size of the vote.[19] It is as if, helped by the fact that this was an issue which the West India body did not wish to contest[20] (that they should have no interest in doing so was a further testimony to the new strategy), the impression had been successfully propagated that here was a routine matter of government business, but self-evidently serving the national interest, regarding which the generality of members need feel no concern to attend. There is significance in Wilberforce's choice of adverb when he wrote in his diary on 5 April: 'The Foreign Slave Bill is going quietly on'.[21]

What might happen in the Lords, however, was another matter. Already before the bill was out of the lower House, Wilberforce was expressing alarm to Grenville in a letter which once more underlined the principle upon which the Foreign Slave Trade Bill was being urged.

> I happened to hear lately from certain authority that the Duke of Clarence had declared it to be his fixed intention to oppose the Attorney-General's Bill in the warmest manner. I have therefore thought it right to communicate that intelligence . . . to your Lordship, that a strong party may not be formed against the Bill in the House of Lords under the mistaken idea that it rests on general abolition principles or is grounded on justice and humanity, an interpretation which I am aware would prove fatal to it.[22]

[19] For the Commons debates on the bill see *Parliamentary Debates*, VI, cols. 597–9, 805, 917–9, 1021–5.

[20] At a General Meeting of Planters and Merchants on 11 Apr 1806 it was recommended that the Standing Committee should examine the bill closely and 'take such measures as they shall find expedient in opposition to any of the provisions thereof which may tend to the prejudice of the interests of the British West India Colonies' (*West India Committee Minutes Feb. 1805–March 1822*, Minutes of General Meeting, 11 Apr 1806). This is the only reference to the bill.

[21] Diary, 5 Apr 1806, quoted in *Life of Wilberforce*, III 260.

[22] *Dropmore MSS. (W.B.H.)*, Wilberforce to Grenville, 23 Apr 1806.

Grenville's reply was immediate and invoked that shadow of fear at the consequences of opposition from the royal family which the abolitionists had perceived in their early discussions with ministers: 'I grieve at the intelligence contained in your note, as if that Standard be raised against us in the House of Lords, I know too well that neither reason nor justice will avail much against it. We must however do the best we can, and I need not say that no endeavours will be wanting on my part.'[23]

As Grenville prepared himself for the fray in the Lords the pervasive role of Stephen was again manifested. Writing to Grenville on 2 May Wilberforce, with exquisite tact, opened by saying that the nature of the Foreign Slave Trade Bill for various reasons 'has never been fully stated in our House, nor the arguments in favour of it argued'. It might therefore save Grenville trouble if he, Wilberforce, sent him 'a paper or two written by my relation Mr. Stephen (who is thoroughly acquainted with all West Indian questions) on some points which are most likely to come in dispute'.[24] 'I should be most particularly obliged to Mr. Stephen,' replied Grenville, accepting the so tactfully professed help, 'whose abilities and knowledge of this subject I am well acquainted with, for any information on the subject of the bill.'[25] When the day for the second reading of the bill came Grenville opened the debate with a speech that reflected Stephen's whole approach.

Nothing he had heard . . . had tended to convince him that the principle of the bill was erroneous or impolitic; on the contrary, he still believed it to be a measure which was called for by every dictate of sound policiy. The islands in the West Indies were now nearly all of them in the possession of this country, or of our enemies; and, it was a clear and obvious policy that we should not give advantages to our enemies, it was surely equally clear that we should not supply their colonies with slaves, whereby affording them additional means of cultivation, contributing to increase the produce of their islands, and thus enabling them to meet us in the market upon equal terms of competition, or perhaps to undersell us. This appeared to him so obvious that he thought it unnecessary to argue it. The first object of the

---

[23] Ibid., Grenville to Wilberforce, 25 Apr 1806 (copy).
[24] Ibid., Wilberforce to Grenville (Private) n.d. [2 May 1806].
[25] Ibid., Grenville to Wilberforce (copy), 5 May 1806.

bill, therefore, was to prevent British subjects from supplying foreign colonies with slaves. The same principle was also applicable to the supply of colonies captured from the enemy, and only held until peace. In the islands captured last war, and which were given up at the peace, British capital was employed to so great an extent, that the exports from those islands equalled the exports from Jamaica. All this went to benefit and enrich the enemy, and to increase their means of rivality. Another object of the bill, therefore, was to enforce the order of council, issued to restrain this species of trade, enacting, at the same time, additional regulation, in order to prevent the importation of slaves into the islands thus conquered from the enemy, and the consequent investiture in them of a large portion of British capital.

Towards the end of his speech, Grenville permitted himself a brief word about the morality of abolition. 'No consideration relative to our commerce or our navigation could induce him to think that the slave trade ought to be continued. He considered it as a cruel and unjust traffic, which ought to be abolished.' But he went on to conclude his speech by coming back on course with a neat linkage.

If, however, it was to be continued, it ought to be carried on under those regulations which might at least render it less revolting, by making it conduce to the benefit of our navigation. The third object of the bill, therefore, was to prevent British subjects from carrying on the slave trade in any other than British vessels.[26]

The debate on the second reading was brief, with battle clearly being reserved for the Committee stage, in which Hawkesbury declared his intention of moving several amendments, and, if necessary, for the third reading. Hearing of the likelihood that the opponents of the bill would seek to whittle it down by amendments, Wilberforce wrote Grenville again on 8 May citing Stephen's firm opinion that no concessions could be made and adding that Stephen was ready to elaborate on that opinion verbally if Grenville so wished.[27] 'No,' replied Grenville, the next

[26] *Parliamentary Debates*, vii, cols. 32–3, 7 May 1806.
[27] *Dropmore MSS.* (*W.B.H.*), Wilberforce to Grenville, 8 May 1806. See also n. 14, p. 368 above where a part of this letter is quoted.

day, there was no need for that. He was well aware that no amendments could be admitted and Stephen's paper, already at hand,
told him all he needed to know.[28] The debate on the third reading
was, as a consequence of the successful resistance to amendments
in Committee, relatively long. Of Cabinet members, Ellenborough
and Sidmouth supported the measure; none of course opposed it,
and Moira had supported the bill in the brief second reading
debate. The principal opposition came from the Duke of Clarence
and Lord Sheffield and was based on much the same reasons. The
duke was mainly opposed to the ending of the supply of slaves to
foreigners, because there was a clear balance of advantage in that
trade, but never actually moved the amendment which he
threatened. In contrast to Clarence, another royal duke, Gloucester,
in a maiden speech, not only supported the measure under consideration but also the principle of abolition. The only two bishops
who spoke – London (Porteus) and St Asaph – predictably supported the bill.

Grenville's intervention in the third reading debate had a two-
fold importance. He went out of his way to counter the suggestion
that the measure of abolition proposed would merely transfer
that segment of the slave trade to foreigners, as Eldon, for one,
had argued.

> Did not the noble and learned Lord (Eldon) see, that if we gave
> up the trade, it was not possible for any other state, without our
> permission, to take it up? Did we not ride everywhere unrivalled
> on the ocean? Could any power pretend to engross this trade,
> while we commanded from the shores of Africa to the western
> extremities of the Atlantic? America had been represented as
> likely to succeed us in the trade; but were not noble lords aware,
> that there was a majority of the United States decidedly hostile
> to this traffic . . . In such circumstances little vigour was to be
> expected in a trade so contrary to the principles and feelings
> of the majority of that people.

Grenville's other departure, surprisingly, was to attest his wish
to see a general abolition. Indeed he showed little reserve, and
waxed eloquent.

> When the advantages of traffic and commerce were opposed
> to the horrors of peculation and murder, he had no hesitation in

[28] Ibid., Grenville to Wilberforce, 9 May 1806 (copy).

deciding his judgement. His lordship said that this bill had been represented as abolition in disguise. Were this true, he should be glad indeed, not of the disguise, but of the abolition. It would be an event most grateful to his feelings to witness the abolition of a traffic that was an outrage to humanity, and that trampled on the rights of mankind. But he could see no reason for disguise on such a subject. He had heard of fraud in disguise, of injustice and oppression in disguise; but justice and humanity required no disguise. Those who felt those virtues would also be proud to acknowledge them.[29]

This surprising taking up of moral ground is explained by the fact that between 5 May and 9 May Grenville's assessment of the chances of success had changed decisively. Whereas on the fifth, before the second reading of the bill, he told Wilberforce that 'we may have no little difficulty in carrying it',[30] on the ninth, immediately after the Committee stage had been surmounted without concessions, Grenville believed that 'for the remaining stages we are quite secure' partly, at least, because proxies could be used in those remaining stages.[31] In consequence, as he told Wilberforce in reference to his speech in the debate on the third reading on 16 May, 'I saw our strength and thought the occasion was favourable for launching out a little beyond what the measure itself actually required'.[32] The Prime Minister was quite right to have scented victory, for the division – it is significant that more members voted than in the much larger Commons – was forty-three to eighteen.

Within less than two months the new strategy of the abolitionists and their ministerial supporters had already achieved a striking triumph. Stephen had been its architect and the approach had been low key with all the emphasis on the national policy arguments. Lord Auckland's informed comment to Grenville, when writing on the eve of victory, was that 'the opposition to the Slave Bill is much broken by the manner in which we have quietly forwarded it to the third reading',[33] whilst Stephen observed some

[29] The Lords debates are in *Parliamentary Debates*, VII, cols. 31–4 and 227–36.

[30] *Dropmore* (*W.B.H.*), Grenville to Wilberforce (copy), 5 May 1806.

[31] Ibid., Grenville to Wilberforce (copy), 9 May 1806.

[32] Grenville to Wilberforce, 17 May 1806, quoted in *Life of Wilberforce*, III 261.

[33] H.M.C., *Report on the Fortescue Manuscripts*, VII 1039–4, Auckland to

months later 'that with many supporters of that great measure, its principle was purely political'.[34] One of two of the opponents of abolition had realised something of the bill's importance. As Tarleton aptly put it, 'As the measure could not be carried in its general form, they [the abolitionists] were now coming by a side wind on the planters'.[35] Now the cannonade which can follow from an approach by a side-wind can be as strong as from ships of the line bearing down under full sail. Tarleton, as a slave trader, must have realised that the Foreign Slave Trade Bill would cut off a really large part of the British slave fleet; but it is not clear that the abolitionists, Stephen probably apart, realised the full importance of the throw which they were making. It is possibly significant that nowhere in their correspondence with each other up to mid-May did abolitionists and their ministerial sympathisers attempt to quantify the volume of the British slave trade to conquered and foreign possessions,[36] whilst Wilberforce, in the immediate aftermath of victory, persisted in terming the general measure, whose timing had now urgently to be considered, 'the main question'.[37] Whether or not they were aware of the full importance of what they were doing, the abolitionists calculated in due course that 'nearly two-thirds' of the British slave trade had thus been brought to an end.[38] In fact hindsight suggests that the proportion

[34] James Stephen, *New Reasons for Abolishing the Slave Trade, being the last section of a larger work, now first published, entitled the Dangers of the Country* (London, 1807) 51.

[35] *Parliamentary Debates*, VI col. 919, 25 Apr 1806.

[36] In the debate on the third reading the Duke of Clarence made the somewhat muddled observation 'that out of upwards of 38,000 slaves more than 22,000 were afterwards exported from the British islands to foreign colonies and settlements' (*Parliamentary Debates*, VII col. 228).

[37] Diary, 18 May 1806, quoted in *Life of Wilberforce*, III 261.

[38] The estimate given in *The Christian Observer* (Zachary Macaulay, ed.), May 1806, 326. In a pamphlet headed *Society for Effecting the Abolition of the Slave Trade*, dated 30 July 1806, the Abolition Committee expressed the converse: 'nearly one half of this cruel commerce still subsists and flourishes, under the national sanction'. Fox said in the Commons on 10 June 1806 that the Foreign Slave Trade bill had 'abolished more than one half of the whole' (*Substance of the Debates on a Resolution for Abolishing the Slave Trade which was moved in the House of Commons on the 10th June 1806, and in the House of Lords on the 24th June, 1806* (London, 1806) 8,

Grenville, 14 May 1806. Nevertheless Auckland went on to submit 'the propriety of circular notes for an attendance on Friday'.

was more like three-quarters.[39] In any event the episode was a triumph. It was a triumph for Wilberforce with his consummate handling of ministers, and especially of Grenville. It was a triumph for Grenville, backed especially by Fox and Lord Henry Petty, who displayed amenability towards the abolitionists and resolution in Parliament. And it was a triumph, not least, for what enemies would doubtless have termed Stephen's deviousness, for what he would doubtless have claimed was merely emulation of the serpent, as enjoined in Holy Writ, and for what the cruder terminology of a later age might fairly term the 'soft sell'. As regards this episode, at any rate, Brougham's comment that Stephen was 'gifted with . . . an ingenuity which was rather apt to err by excess than by defect'[40] must be stood on its head.

When Grenville wrote to Wilberforce in the immediate aftermath of triumph in the Lords, the Prime Minister observed: 'I really think a foundation is laid for doing more and sooner than I have for a long time allowed myself to hope'.[41] If Grenville could seemingly contemplate the possibility of rapid follow-up action, still more could Wilberforce, who, after all, had originally hoped to introduce his general motion before the session ended. 'We are now deliberating whether we shall push the main question', he noted in his diary on 18 May[42] Stephen – could it be otherwise? –

[39] According to the estimates made in my 'Volume and Profitability of the British Slave Trade', some 32,000 slaves were imported in British slavers in 1805. In the year ended 10 Oct 1805 net imports into the old British West Indies and Trinidad were approximately 7,500 (8924 imported and about 1500 re-exported to foreign possessions). Some 13,000 were imported into the conquered lands, leaving a balance of 10,000 (plus the 1500 re-exports) as the total sold to foreigners. Thus the 1806 bill, confirming and extending the 1805 Order-in-Council, had actually brought to an end just over three-quarters of the British slave trade. (*A. & P.*, 1806, XIII (265), no. 6.)

[40] Quoted in Sir J. Stephen, *Ecclesiastical Biography*, II 330. Cf. Hochstetter, *Abschaffung*, 84–103, for an interpretation of the 1806 measure.

[41] Grenville to Wilberforce, 17 May 1806, quoted in *Life of Wilberforce*, III 261.

[42] Wilberforce, diary, 18 May 1806, quoted in ibid., III 261.

Fox. Ever since the American War, and possibly earlier, only about one-third of the British slave trade had been for the supply of the older British islands. Cf. James Jones, a well-informed British merchant, observing to Hawkesbury on 14 Feb 1788 that 'full two-thirds of the Negroes purchased by the British ships go to the French, Spanish, and Dutch Settlements' (*B.M. Add. MSS.* 38416, ff. 20–1).

was his principal co-adjutor, but, through William Smith, Fox was also drawn in.[43] Fox, as we know from Brougham, and as Brougham told Wilberforce, was 'extremely sanguine 'about the prospects of the general question, apparently if moved before the session ended.[44] The outcome was a letter to Grenville on 20 May in which Wilberforce urged that 'the present time' was 'less unfavourable' for the general motion 'than possibly next year will be'. But, Wilberforce continued, he felt convinced the motion would be better brought forward by Fox, for 'the circumstances of your patronizing the measure in the House of Lords and Mr. Fox in the House of Commons will have, I trust, great weight in neutralizing some, who might otherwise be active enemies, and in converting into decided friends, some who might otherwise be neutral'.[45] Grenville wrote back on the same day.

I have read and very carefully considered both your letter and Mr. Stephen's paper, and both before and since I received them I have conversed on the subject with Mr. Fox. I am very far from being insensible to the risks of delay – indeed I feel them so strongly that if I could ever bring myself to think that the chances of success or failure this year were equal I should be for trying the experiment. But I fear that is not the case. Much of our force in the H. of Lds. depended upon our having been able to separate the last measure from the question of immediate and total abolition, and altho' I think much ground was gained towards that object by the triumphant manner in which we carried our bill yet I fear matters are not yet ripe for so strong a course as that of abolition brought forward in May, and therefore carried (if at all) thro' both Houses in the most summary way. And if we fail now we do irretrievable mischief to the cause.

As an alternative Grenville urged two courses of action. It should be possible to do something that session about the Trinidad slave trade (though the fruit of conquest, Trinidad had been conquered

[43] H.M.C., *Report on Fortescue Manuscripts*, VIII 146, Wilberforce to Grenville, 20 May 1806.

[44] *Wilberforce MSS*. (Duke Collection), Brougham to Wilberforce, n.d. [19 May 1806]. Brougham added that not only he himself, but Holland and Petty were anxious to be employed in furthering the general abolition.

[45] H.M.C., *Report on Fortescue Manuscripts*, VIII 146–7, Wilberforce to Grenville, 20 May 1806.

in the previous war and so did not rate as a conquered island, in contemporary terminology. It was sometimes referred to as a ceded island but its status was essentially the same as a regular British possession) and to restrict the slave trade to the reduced volume necessary to supply the older islands. The actual reduction was to be by two-thirds, a figure reached, interestingly, on the basis of the Duke of Clarence's estimate of the size of the British slave trade to the older islands and Trinidad.

> We were told [*sic*] the other night that we had stopped the export from Africa of 22,000 out of 38,000 slaves annually carried from thence to the West Indies. If this is true, and they are bound to admit what they have asserted, it follows of necessity that one third of the present supply (or a little more) will be equal to the future demand of our People – and if we strike out Trinidad we might I suppose simply take it at one third.

Grenville was confident that both these partial measures could be achieved that session – a stop of the Trinidad trade would be welcomed by 'all indeed except those who love the slave trade for its own beauty' –

> and we should then come at the beginning of next session to consider the most advantageous way of bringing forward the rest of the subject, either moved as a Govt. measure by Mr. Fox (if on full consideration that is thought best for the success of the thing which I well know is what you will most regard) or brought forward as before by you, and supported by a previous decision of the Cabinet, supposing that can be obtained.

Grenville concluded with an interesting display of deference to what Wilberforce might think which can hardly have been common in him. 'If however on consideration you should see reason to differ from the opinions I have stated here you will certainly command every possible exertion of mine, both in and out of Parliament to forward this business in whatever shape you propose it.'[46]

[46] *Wilberforce MSS* (Duke Collection), Grenville to Wilberforce, 20 May 1806. Of some historiographical interest is the comment scribbled on this letter by 'S.W.' (Samuel Wilberforce): 'I think this is dull.' This sentiment signifies Robert and Samuel's deficient understanding of their father's vitally important dealings with Grenville in the twelve months

Interesting though this lengthy letter is as an indication of Grenville's thinking, judgement, and amenability towards the abolitionists, further discussions between abolitionists and sympathetic minister led, within days, to agreement on a different course for the remainder of the parliamentary session. Fox, retaining the leading role which had been assigned him in the proposal for a general motion, was to move in the Commons a resolution binding the House[47] in these terms:

> That this House, considering the African slave trade to be contrary to the principles of justice, humanity, and sound policy, will, with all practicable expedition take effectual measures for the abolition of the said trade, in such manner, and at such period, as may be deemed advisable.[48]

Before the motion could come on, Grenville came up with another suggestion, that abolition could be achieved by the imposition of high duties on slave imports. Wilberforce duly pondered this, but rejected it on the advice of Stephen.[49] Meanwhile, however, Grenville had proposed just this measure to Sidmouth as a concession which would secure the support of that most gradual of all gradual abolitionists and thus enable the abolition to become a Cabinet measure, or, as Grenville put it, for 'Government . . ., if possible,

---

[47] *Life of Wilberforce*, III 261.

[48] *Substance of the Debates on a Resolution for Abolishing the Slave Trade which was moved in the House of Commons on the 10th June 1806 and in the House of Lords on the 24th June 1806* (London, 1806) 10, Fox. The account in this source is much fuller than in *Parliamentary Debates*, VII, cols. 580–603 and 801–9, and I have therefore preferred it.

[49] 'The objection to the plan . . . did not so forcibly strike my own Mind, but Mr. Stephen, who is better acquainted than any man I ever knew with all West Indian matters in their practical operation and connections, has lately convinced me that the plan is in the highest degree objectionable and that it would prove in fact altogether ineffectual to its purpose' (*Dropmore MSS. (W.B.H.)*, Wilberforce to Grenville, 2 June 1806, Private).

---

from March 1806. In the biographers' failure of understanding must have originated the general lack of appreciation, on the part of historians, of Grenville's role. But note Professor Pares comment: 'Grenville has not been given enough credit for the abolition of the slave trade' (Pares, *George III and the Politicians*, 42 n.), a view abundantly shared on the basis of exhaustive study of the *Dropmore MSS.* by the late Professor W. B. Hamilton (personal communications). See also Lipscomb, 'Pitt and the Abolition Question, 116–18.

to form a united and well considered system of conduct'. Grenville emphasised that this was to proceed more slowly than either he or Fox wanted, but none the less made it clear that the duty per slave would be so steep in the second year of implementation that the yield, and the volume of the trade, would rapidly fall off.[50]

On 5 June Wilberforce had another suggestion to make to Grenville as a result of further discussion with one or two friends, namely that Parliament should be moved to present a humble address to the King 'that he would be graciously pleased to embrace the most suitable opportunity of negotiations with Foreign Powers with a view to the General Abolition of the Slave Trade'. The political advantage of this commitment to such overtures would be that it would outflank the traditional, but now newly reiterated objection 'that if we should abolish the slave trade, it would be taken up, in a proportionately greater degree, by foreign nations'. The absolute advantage would be that it would, hopefully, lead to abolition 'by all foreign countries'. Wilberforce had already put the suggestion to Fox and the latter had no objection to the humble address being moved at the conclusion of the debate on his own motion on the Resolution. The letter concluded with a postscript urging that at the peace negotiations which were shortly to open, the favourable opportunity for an agreement on abolition should not be overlooked.[51]

The debates on the Resolution for Abolishing the Slave Trade took place in the Commons on 10 June and, success achieved, in the Lords on 24 June. Fox, in proposing the motion, explained its purpose. The lateness of the session rendered inexpedient the bringing of a bill for immediate and total abolition but it was highly desirable 'not to pledge the House to any particular measure,

---

[50] H.M.C., *Report on Fortescue Manuscripts*, VIII 168–70, Grenville to Sidmouth, 1 June 1806. The tax, apparently £10 per head in the first year and £20 per head in the second, was seemingly to be imposed on slave ships as they cleared out from the British port.

[51] *Dropmore MSS. (W.B.H.)*, Wilberforce to Grenville, 5 June 1806. Wilberforce's assessment of the auguries, in his postscript, was excessively, and ungrammatically, optimistic: 'all the powers by which the slave trade is carried on being more or less concerned in it [the peace negotiation] – France, Spain, Portugal, Sweden, Denmark and America have or will have abolished.' See also ibid., Wilberforce to Grenville, 7 June and 10 June 1806.

to any particular time, to any particular course, but to show that this House is determined not to abandon, but on the contrary to follow up, the question of the Abolition of the African Slave Trade'. But both in this speech and in his winding-up speech Fox made it abundantly clear that the three qualifications did not mean very much and that the clause in his motion which would bind the House to 'all practicable expedition' meant that, if the Lords agreed, the abolition question would be taken in hand in the *next* session of Parliament. Even if they did not agree, there would be nothing to prevent the Commons from attempting all that it was open to it to attempt. There was little new in Fox's justification of abolition as demanded by 'justice, humanity and sound policy': but there was all his debating thrust and sparkle though with a concurrent concern to rally opinion, as instanced in his praise for Pitt's conduct over abolition. There was, finally, his political testament which has the great poignancy in hindsight since this was the last occasion before his death that Fox could support abolition in Parliament. He had, he said, sat for thirty–forty years in the House and 'if I had done nothing else, but had only been instrumental in carrying through this measure, I should think my life well spent'. For, he added later in the debate, 'there never was a time in which any other evil existed that was comparable to that of the African Slave Trade'.[52]

It would be too much to expect much originality in the speeches of other contributors to the debate, either in the Commons or the Lords. It is noticeable that the defenders of the slave trade felt at a disadvantage when opposed, as Wilberforce said, by 'nearly all the most considerable men for talents and respectability on both sides of this House', and were reduced to sheltering behind gradual abolitionists, such as Castlereagh, or arguing that policy need not necessarily point in the same direction as justice and humanity, or that war was a bad time to tamper with an allegedly important trade. In the Lords, Grenville, now free to elaborate on his conviction that the slave trade was primarily a moral evil, for which, he said, 'there is nothing comparable . . . to be found in the whole history of this world, ancient or modern', made what must have been one of the most appealing speeches that proud man ever delivered. Amongst other things, Grenville, in true eighteenth-century style, condemned the slave trade as incompatible with

[52] For Fox's speeches see *Substance of the Debates*, 1–10, 71–85.

happiness and freedom, and, in an interesting passage, with the protection of property.[53] He was less forthright than Fox only in that, though making abundantly clear his own yearning for immediate abolition, he explicitly stated that assent to the resolution was compatible with the advocacy of gradual abolition when the substantive consideration came on. This caution was evidently induced by a desire to carry Sidmouth along if at all possible, but in the event it was only Sidmouth, of all members of the Cabinet, who signified his intention of voting against the resolution. Fitzwilliam, likewise, did not approve of it but in the event neither seems to have voted against it.[54] Windham, surprisingly, gave assent in principle. Erskine, Ellenborough and Spencer, of whom Wilberforce had for one reason or another been doubtful, supported the resolution.

The division, when it came, gave a clear affirmative not only in the Commons but, a fortnight later, in the Lords, the voting being 114 to 15 and 41 to 20 respectively. The sense one has is that nearly all of those who voted for the resolution in the Commons favoured immediate abolition but that the affirmative vote in the Lords included more gradual abolitionists. But, in any event, it is difficult not to believe that the abolition cause had gained important ground in both Houses, as a result firstly of the Foreign Slave Trade bill and then of the Resolution. Given such strong favourable votes, it was almost a formality that the humble address to the King on the opening of negotiations with foreign powers went through, in both Houses, without a division.[55]

It was precisely in the matter of negotiations with foreign powers that further action could first be taken. We have seen that both for the sake of the object itself, and on tactical grounds, the thoughts of the abolitionists had never been long removed from the slave trade of other nations. Wilberforce had hoped something might be done by representations to Napoleon, and at the peace negotiations which culminated in the Peace of Amiens; the

[53] (*Substances of the Debates*, 99–100, Grenville.)

[54] 'Lord Fitzwilliam and Lord Sidmouth did not approve the Resolution, but I think they did not vote against it' (*Porteus MS. 2104*, Porteus, Diary, 24 June 1806).

[55] The Commons debate is on pp 1–85 of *Substance of the Debates* and the Lords on pp. 87–154.

point of Stephen's sword in the *War in Disguise* had been directed at the neutral slave trade. The abolitionists' other recent foray in this direction had taken place on Brougham's initiative. He had volunteered to make use of a Continental tour – on which, with a nice disdain of French hegemony on the Continent, he embarked in 1804 – to sound out prominent men in Holland on the possibilities of Dutch abolition. What he came to believe he could offer was Dutch abolition in return for a somewhat improbable 'private and individual' expression of view by Pitt that such an abolition would remove a major obstacle to the restoration of Guiana to Holland at the peace. Brougham was most assiduous in the business but was distrusted by Stephen and Thornton, the latter believing, in addition, that the Dutch had duped him. The whole business came to nothing.[56]

An early result of the Humble Address was, on the other hand, that official overtures to foreign states were soon made. Within days, on 1 July, the Earl of Yarmouth, who was engaged in tentative peace preliminaries in Paris, presented Talleyrand with a copy of the humble address. Talleyrand's initial response was temporising[57] but Yarmouth was pressed by Fox not to let any opportunity slip of reverting to the subject of common action against the slave trade.[58] On the ninth Talleyrand assured Yarmouth that Napoleon would discuss such common action when the major points in negotiation had been agreed,[59] but by the 24th the French position had somewhat hardened, Yarmouth being told that France would negotiate on the slave trade once peace was made but that the trade could not figure in the treaty as the question had not been adequately considered in France.[60] The Earl of Lauderdale, who was also involved in these *pourparlers*, was

[56] For this episode see *Life of Wilberforce*, III 195–6; Wilberforce to Lord Harrowby, 29 Sept 1804, *Correspondence of Wilberforce*, I 328–31; *Wrangham MSS.*, Brougham to Wilberforce, 30 Aug 1804, and n.d. [27 Dec. 1804]; *Wilberforce MSS.* (*Duke Collection*): Brougham to Wilberforce, n.d. and 9 (?) Dec 1804; Stephen to Wilberforce 22 Sept 1804 ('I would wish too that he had chosen some other ladder than a cause which ought to be held too sacred to be the instrument of any self-interested purpose'); Thornton to Wilberforce, 24 Sept 1804.
[57] Yarmouth to Fox, 1 July 1806 in *S.P.* 1806–07, Lords XIV (165).
[58] Fox to Yarmouth, 5 July 1806 in ibid.
[59] Yarmouth to Fox, 9 July 1806 in ibid.
[60] Yarmouth to Fox, 24 July 1806 in ibid.

prodded by Grenville, just as Yarmouth had been prodded by Fox. Grenville's note, being private, has the additional interest of constituting a commentary on what his motives in the whole question were.

> If discussions should proceed, pray do not overlook the slave trade. I think it appears clearly that Bonaparte is not much influenced by the motives of justice or humanity on which we act, and indeed how should he be? But I really think we might shame him by an official note so as to make it very difficult for him to refuse his concurrence, supposing other things adjusted.[61]

Of course nothing came of the approach to France on the slave trade since the peace negotiation did not get anywhere but the next approach, to the United States, had a somewhat more positive outcome. Negotiations for an Anglo-American treaty had been going on for some time when on 15 October, Holland and Auckland wrote to their American counterparts, telling them of the humble address. The British negotiators added: 'They cannot help expressing their Confidence, as it is their earnest Wish, that Mr. Monroe and Mr. Pinckney will be disposed to co-operate with them in the most cordial Manner for effectually promoting the objects of that Address'.[62] In the event a short – and, it must be said, toothless – article (No. XXIV) engaging the parties to procure the co-operation of other powers in finally extinguishing the slave trade was included in the Monroe-Pinckney treaty, signed in December 1806.[63] Apart from the dubious value of the clause, the treaty itself was never ratified. In any case events had overtaken the aspiration expressed in the humble address since in June 1806, or possibly earlier, it became apparent in England that there was every likelihood that the United States would herself abolish the slave trade from January 1808.[64] Common action with the United

[61] H.M.C. *Report on Fortescue Manuscripts*, VIII 262, Grenville to Lauderdale, Private 8 Aug 1806 (copy).

[62] Holland and Auckland to Monroe and Pinckney, 15 Oct 1806 in *S.P.* 1810, Lords, XXXVII (149).

[63] Printed in *S.P.*, 1808, XIV, Correspondence with the United States, July to October 1807.

[64] Fox made this point in the debate on the Resolution which immediately preceded the motion for a Humble Address (*Substance of the Debates*, 83, Fox). I have not so far come across any clear indication that U.S.

States regarding the British and American slave trades was, therefore, doubtless not believed to be worth serious attention. Certainly the slave trade received little attention in the negotiations.[65] It was neither opportune nor apposite to raise the matter of the slave trade with any other power.[66]

The result of the successful passage of the measures against the slave trade of early summer may have been, as Robert and Samuel Wilberforce believed, that people generally now believed the abolition cause to be gained.[67] Certainly there was some further encouragement to abolitionists in the successful passage in July 1806 of a short bill designed to prevent any massive increase in the supply of the West India colonies with slaves pending a further measure of abolition.[68] But nothing resulted from discussions on the interim measures which Grenville had proposed against the Trinidad slave trade, partly, at least, because there was disagreement between the Law Officers on what could be done,[69] whilst it was clear to Wilberforce, from interviews he had with Grenville in the period up to Wilberforce's departure for Lyme Regis in mid-August, that the Prime Minister, though 'very open and friendly' still wished to abolish 'by high and increasing duties'.[70] Wilberforce, indeed, was by no means sure that a straightforward measure of total abolition would succeed, as he made clear in a letter to William Smith on 18 August.[71]

Wilberforce was surely right to entertain such doubts, for the debate culminating in the passage of the Foreign Slave Trade Bill,

---

[65] *F.O.* 95/515, passim.

[66] *Parliamentary Debates*, VIII, col. 432, 12 Jan 1807, Grenville.

[67] *Life of Wilberforce*, III 270.

[68] See *Dropmore MSS.* (*W.B.H.*), Grenville to Wilberforce, 10 July 1806 (copy), and Wilberforce to Grenville, 9 July 1806; *Parliamentary Debates*, VII, cols. 1143–45.

[69] *Dropmore MSS.* (*W.B.H.*), Wilberforce to Grenville, Private, 25 July 1806.

[70] Wilberforce, Diary, 12 Aug 1806, quoted in *Life of Wilberforce*, III 271.

[71] *William Smith MSS.* (Duke Collection), Wilberforce to Smith, 18 Aug 1806.

---

intentions on this score were known in Britain before June 1806. See also W. E. Dubois, *The Suppression of the African Slave Trade to the United States of America, 1638–1870* (New York, 1896), 91–107 and Mary S. Locke, *Anti-Slavery in America, 1619–1808* (Boston, 1901), 149–56.

had been mainly fought out on the chosen ground of national interest, and the Resolution against the slave trade, though its passage
gave marked cause for encouragement, was still only a declaration
of intent. What was now different was that whereas the British
slave trade to foreigners and conquered islands could be dressed
up as a violation of evident national interest, the remaining sector
of the British slave trade, the supply of the older islands and Trinidad, could not. To transpose the issue into the terms in which a
number of historians have chosen to see the question, the argument
that overproduction demanded abolition[72] can plausibly be applied
to the approach which found its consummation in the Foreign
Slave Trade Bill, for that measure (in conjunction with the
approaching American abolition) could be regarded as effectively
cutting off the supply of Britain's competitors. But to apply the
overproduction argument to the 1807 measure is utterly fallacious.
In an admitted condition of global overproduction of sugar, it
scarcely requires argument to prove that one does not cut down on
one's own production when one believes one has the means to
check production of those who are not merely rivals but enemies.
In other words, the overproduction argument neither has now,
nor had then, any plausibility as a serious ground for ending the
remaining sector of British slave trade.[73] And if overproduction

---

[72] See (1) Eric Williams' statement: 'Overproduction in 1807 demanded abolition' (*Capitalism and Slavery*, 152). It is interesting that Williams
fails to see that such *prima facie* case for the overproduction argument as
exists, exists in respect of the 1806 bill; (2) Porter, *Abolition*, 142–3.

[73] In this whole context, note two highly significant passages from reports of parliamentary committees of 1807 and 1808 on various aspects of,
and remedies for, West Indian distress. 'It has appeared obvious to your
Committee that effectual relief to the West Indian Colonies was only to
be expected in one of three following ways: a change of their staple
commodity Sugar for some more lucrative produce; a reduction of the
Expenses attending its Cultivation and Sale; or an advance of Price,
whether effected by an increase of the Demand or a diminution of the
Supply. . . . As to a diminution of the Supply, it could not be effected
without loss, except by the discovery of some profitable mode of employ-
ing the labour of the Negroes, which . . . has not yet been devised'
(Fourth Report of the Committee on the Distillation of Sugar and
Molasses, *S.P.*, 1808, IV (318), 394).

'The result of all their enquiries . . . have brought before their eyes one
grand and primary evil, from which all the others are easily to be deduced; namely the facility of intercourse between the hostile colonies and
Europe, under the American neutral Flag, by means of which not only

cannot be invoked, nor can contemporaries be credited with the discernment of any other compulsive economic consideration which demanded the final stage of abolition. Two policy arguments could be, and were, invoked, but both were less than compelling: there was danger, it was said, in allowing the slave population to increase by continued importations, whilst a creole-born self-producing population would constitute a cheaper cost of production. But whereas neither of these propositions was provable, the crushingly obvious definition of Britain's national interest lay in maintaining the slave trade to her own possessions whilst denying it to her enemies and competitors.[74]

[74] The abolitionists had previously considered the possibilities of the argument that ending the supply of slaves to one's own colonies would either not harm, or even benefit them, in relation to their competition with rivals still carrying on the slave trade. Thornton and Stephen disagreed with Wilberforce on this question, believing that it was cheaper to seize slaves 'ready made' than to 'fabricate' them as one would have to do with a slave labour force that would have to be self-reproducing. Thornton illustrated his argument with the story of one dishonest broomseller who said to his rival (I summarise): 'I steal the hafts, I steal the brushes,

the whole of their Produce is carried to a market, but at charges little exceeding those of Peace, while the British Planter is burthened with all the inconvenience, risk and expense, resulting from a state of war. . . . In order to counterbalance, in some degree, the advantages thus enjoyed by the hostile colonies, to the detriment of the British Planter, it has been recommended, that a blockade of the Ports of the Enemy's Settlements should be resorted to; such a measure, if it could be strictly enforced, would undoubtedly afford relief to our Export Trade. But a measure of more permanent and certain advantage would be the enforcement of those restrictions on the trade between Neutrals and the Enemy's Colonies, which were formerly maintained by Great Britain, and from the relaxation of which the Enemy's Colonies obtain indirectly, during War, all the advantages of Peace; while our own colonies . . . are deprived of the advantages under which in the present War, by means of our decided Naval superiority, would have amounted to the exclusive supply of the whole of Europe; and when those extraordinary measures are taken into consideration which have been adopted to exclude the British Colonial produce from the European market, it appears to your Committee to be a matter of evident and imperious necessity to resort to such a system, as by impeding and restricting, and as far as possible preventing the Export of the produce of the Enemy's Colonies from the places of its growth, as shall compel the Continent to have recourse to the only source of supply which, in that event, would be open to it (Report . . . on the Commercial State of the West India Colonies, *S.P.*, 1807, iii (65) 5–6).

Thornton, in the summer of 1806, saw very clearly that the last stage of the abolition could only be based on the appeal to humanity and justice. 'We want parliament and the country,' he wrote to Wilberforce on 26 August, 'to practice a notable piece of self-denial, and to do a magnificent act of justice – to pass a kind of self-denying ordinance; and we can only hope that a parliament will do this heroic deed in some fit of heroism.'[75] Wilberforce, in fact, arrived at the same conclusion. In a long and important letter to William Smith on 18 August, in which his first concern was to make it known that Grenville was still in favour of abolition by high duties, he had also rehearsed various arguments against the efficacy of such a measure.[76] Then in a subsequent letter of 5 September, Wilberforce added a yet more compelling argument.

But I own another argument has been continually growing in magnitude in my mind which I had thought of before I conferred with Lord G. tho' I did not state it to him. Babington also feels it forcibly. I mean that supposing we were to carry the Measure of an increasing Scale of Duties, we should have no security for its continuance or even against its being rescinded. On the contrary I have scarce a doubt, or rather I have no doubt, it would at least be suspended before it had risen to any very high amount. I own, now that the probability of our carrying our great question has led me to look more distinctly and particularly into the consequences, I foresee a perfect hurricane on the other side of the Water and such a number of hard cases will be stated that nothing would enable us to resist the application that would be made to Parliament to rescind or at least suspend the measure but the disgrace which Parliament would incur in the face of the whole world by reversing on grounds of interest a Measure which it had expressly declared to have adopted on principles of Religion, Justice and Humanity. Our

[75] Thornton to Wilberforce, 26 Aug 1806, quoted in *Life of Wilberforce*, III 272 n.

[76] *Wm Smith MSS.* (Duke Collection), Wilberforce to Smith, 18 Aug 1806.

and I steal the twine to tie the hafts to the brushes, and yet you still sell your brooms more cheaply.' 'Yes,' said his rival, 'but I just steal the brooms' (*Wrangham MSS.*, Thornton to Wilberforce, 15 Dec 1804, Transcript).

obtaining this recognition will alone enable us to withstand the torrent we shall have to encounter.[77]

Wilberforce, then, was sure that immediate abolition based on grounds of 'Religion, Justice and Humanity' was what the abolitionists must go for, even though he had specifically accepted in his earlier letter that abolition by prohibitory duties would be easier to carry than their own preferred measure. Moreover, Grenville's mind was not irrevocably made up. 'From all that passed I am clear that Lord G. will give way to us very handsomely if we cannot bring ourselves to come over to his opinion.' Wilberforce went on to stress the importance of 'all of us whose opinions are likely to have most weight[78] to make up their minds on the two modes of proceeding and communicate the result to Grenville direct. Moreover, Grenville had already intimated the possible desirability of new tactics. 'If we should adopt the other Plan of passing a penal Law against the Slave Trade . . . it might be best to bring the Question forward first in the House of Lords . . . at the very opening of the Session.'[79]

The fact remained that though Grenville was prepared to defer to the abolitionists, if they confirmed their opposition to prohibiting duties, the same obstacle remained as had originally, in Wilberforce's view, induced Grenville to favour the gradual abolition by high duties. When we recall Grenville's concern to accommodate Sidmouth and his following, expressed in his letter to Sidmouth of 1 June, Wilberforce's words convey a wealth of meaning.

> Lord G. did not state the Arguments on which his opinion in favour of the Plan rested. He seemed however, if I mistake not, to be chiefly influenced by the greater ease with which we could carry it than any direct prohibitory Law. Lord Sidmouth and

[77] Ibid., Wilberforce to Smith, 5 Sept 1806. Wilberforce reveals the unusual sense in which he used 'probability', namely as 'possibility' or perhaps 'likelihood', when he said, in his preceding letter of 18 Aug: 'Our Plan, though I clearly see the probability of Defeat is much greater . . .'.

[78] Wilberforce enumerates the group as Smith, Clarkson, Babington, Gisborne, Stephen, and Macaulay. Thornton can only have been ommitted by oversight. Four of the eight – Wilberforce himself, Clarkson, Babington and Gisborne – had been at St John's College, Cambridge.

[79] *Wm Smith MSS.* (Duke Collection), Wilberforce to Smith, 18 Aug 1806.

his friends would support it and probably others also who would oppose our penal Law.[80]

In short, the obstacle to the introduction of a final and complete measure of abolition, based explicitly on religion, justice and humanity, and which the abolitionists believed essential and which Grenville would prefer if politically possible, was Sidmouth. Within a very short time, however, the effectiveness of that obstacle was, by an unexpected political development, to be decisively reduced.

[80] Ibid.

16 The Kill

'So poor Fox is gone at last. I am more affected by it than I thought I should be.' So wrote Wilberforce to Sidmouth on 19 September[1] in comment on an event which was to have a significant, if indirect, bearing on the roles which writer and recipient were to play in the further progress of abolition. Whilst he lived, Fox, by his personality and charm, had continued to give to the ministry a unity which surprised its friends almost as much as it disconcerted its enemies. But after his death matters did not go so smoothly. The agreement which a gifted personality could secure found an indifferent alternative in elaborate discussions and bargains. In October 1806, therefore, Grenville resolved on a General Election in an only slightly belated, conventional attempt to ease the task of government by securing the return of a House of Commons more friendly to the still new ministry. The main result of that election was that there was a significant gain to the Government of forty-six seats.[2] But more significant for our purpose were the losses suffered by Sidmouth's personal following of some thirty politicians. Grenville had used the traditional pressures in a traditional way and, in this case, had given preference to Foxites in the safe government boroughs. As a consequence there were no safe seats left for Sidmouth's followers. Independent though they and their leader believed themselves to be, their recent manoeuvrings made them look like run-of-the-mill, unscrupulous politicians and they suffered accordingly when standing, as they had to, in independent-minded constituencies. 'The effect of this loss of support,' says Steven Watson, 'was to make Sidmouth a much more difficult colleague. Sidmouth now felt that he must,

---

[1] Wilberforce to Sidmouth, 19 Sept 1806, quoted in *Life of Wilberforce*, III 274.

[2] Watson, *Reign of George III*, 438. Of course, this was not an age of well-defined and docile parties and, as Steven Watson points out, there was not necessarily any permanent recruitment of this size.

for self-protection, insist upon his particular point of view and refuse to be treated as a negligible wasting asset.'[3] But if less co-operative than previously, Sidmouth could only, with the reduction in his following, be less obstructive. Conversely, Wilberforce's relations with Grenville were even closer for their co-operation had been sealed by the way in which Grenville offered, and actively used, his influence on Wilberforce's behalf in the Yorkshire election.[4] The simple circumstance of the blow to Sidmouth's standing would suggest that after the General Election Grenville would drive on with much less regard for Sidmouth than before,[5] but such firmer direction in the post-election period is abundantly attested. A letter from Grenville, already clearly confident of the result of the General Election, to Wilberforce, early in November, when Grenville had evidently just heard news that Wilberforce's opponent, Lascelles, had withdrawn, leaving Wilberforce and his ally Fawkes to secure the nomination, both bespeaks the warmth of the Prime Minister's attachment to Wilberforce, and announces his plans for the abolition.

> I cannot resist the expressing to you the great pleasure I have derived both from your letters and from the events which the last communicates.
>
> I felt most warmly interested in your success, and heartily congratulate you upon it.

[3] Ibid., 439. The preceding section is based on ibid., 438–9.

[4] *Dropmore MSS.* (*W.B.H.*), Grenville to Wilberforce (copy), 23 Oct 1806; Wilberforce to Grenville Private, 1 Nov 1806 (says Grenville's 'liberal and friendly manner ... has made a deep impression on my heart, and made me feel in return a more than political attachment to you'); H.M.C., *Report on Fortescue Manuscripts*, VIII 406, Grenville to Earl Fitzwilliam, 28 Oct 1806; E. A. Smith, 'The Yorkshire Election of 1806 and 1807: A Study in Electoral Management', *Northern History*, II (1967) 66–7.

[5] This point is well taken by Porter, *Abolition*, 136, but he errs in speaking of the *December* election. It was the late W. B. Hamilton who first pointed out to me the significance of the November General Election for Grenville's conduct of the abolition. In a personal communication, Hamilton wrote – in his inimitable style: 'Whatever the reason – may be he just decided the Doctor, as he used to call him with contempt before he was united with him, had not much bite after the November 1806 elections – by the time he came to move in the new Parliament, now full master in his own Government, he wanted simple, plain, quick abolition and no foolishness.'

When you return to town which, however, I suppose cannot be quite immediately, I should be glad to talk with you about our slave trade proceedings. My idea is (as I believe I mentioned to you) to present to the House of Lords within the first days of meeting a bill simply abolishing the trade and declaring the being engaged in it to be a misdemeanour punishable as such at law.

Grenville goes on to say that this procedure would allow time for a fresh inquiry if their opponents insisted upon it and asks Wilberforce whether the subject 'should be . . . at the same time entered upon in the House of Commons? I rather think yes – but that I should wish you to decide for us'.[6] Grenville followed up this approach by sending a draft of the bill for abolition to Stephen some time before the 14th of the month.[7] Wilberforce, for his part, warmly thanked Grenville for his friendly letter and said he was at the minister's command for further discussion on the next steps.[8]

At the end of November the pace quickened again. On the 29th Wilberforce wrote to Grenville that Clarkson had suggested the advantage of persuading the bishops 'to support the Abolition as a Question in which Religion is concerned and on which it therefore became them as the Guardian of Religion to take a decided part'. Wilberforce favours the idea but what does Grenville think?[9] Grenville evidently approved for, judging from extant replies from the Bishops of London, Lincoln and Durham, he applied to a number of bishops.[10] As we shall see, the bench of bishops voted virtually en bloc for abolition when the motion came on. It was natural that Grenville should devote most of his attention to the House of Lords, the chamber in which the motion was to be first introduced and in which the most resolute opposition had hitherto

[6] *Dropmore MSS.* (*W.B.H.*), Grenville to Wilberforce, 5 Nov 1806 (copy). A part of this letter is reproduced with minor inaccuracies in *Life of Wilberforce*, III 286–7.

[7] *Macaulay MSS.* (Huntington Collection), Box 22, Communication (to Macaulay?] from an unknown source, 14 Nov 1806.

[8] *Dropmore MSS.* (*W.B.H.*), Wilberforce to Grenville, 22 Nov 1806.

[9] Ibid., Wilberforce to Grenville, 29 Nov 1806.

[10] The record of the episcopal bench on abolition was in fact good, the point of thus discreetly whipping them being evidently to make sure they gave in their proxies if they could not attend personally. The source is *Dropmore MSS.*, but indirectly, through Professor Hamilton's summary notes kindly transmitted to me.

been encountered. Doubtless Grenville was further spurred to action by news from Wilberforce, in mid-December, that the sixteen Scottish representative peers were, in general, hostile to abolition.[11] We certainly know of approaches to the Earl of Leicester, and Lords Rivers, Carlisle and Willoughby de Broke, the approach in the last three cases being in the form of the enclosure of blank proxies in the belief that the recipients would be unable to attend the debate.[12] On New Year's Day, Thornton wrote to Patty More (Hannah More's sister) that 'Lord Grenville was sanguine, but is now a little nervous on the subject [of abolition].[13] At the end of January there was some alarm in the camp of the abolitionists and their great ministerial supporter. On the 30th, wrote Wilberforce, 'Grenville told me . . . he could not count more than fifty-six, yet had taken pains, written letters, etc. The Princes canvassing against us, alas.'[14] The next day Wilberforce writes in some alarm that a number of peers who were expected to come up for the debate and vote for abolition had not yet come, and as Holland was ill should not the debate be put off?[15] On 2 February Grenville agreed to postponement till the 4th – Spencer was also ill – adding: 'Any votes that you can get in the interval pray do'.[16] By the next day, the 3rd, however, Grenville had gone 'over the list of peers, and was sanguine, counting on above seventy in all'.[17] But what had the defenders of the trade been doing?

The West India Planters and Merchants, having become aware early the previous June with 'deepest concern and astonishment' that the question of total abolition was about to be revived, agreed

[11] *Dropmore MSS.* (*W.B.H.*), Wilberforce to Grenville, 18 Dec 1806, Private.

[12] Unparticularised information from *Dropmore MSS.* kindly communicated by Professor Hamilton.

[13] *Wigan Letter Book*, Thornton to Patty More, 1 Jan 1807.

[14] Wilberforce, Diary, 31 Jan 1807, quoted in *Life of Wilberforce*, III 291. The *Life* adds, 'the Dukes of Clarence and of Sussex declared openly against the Bill, speaking, as it was understood, the sentiments of all the reigning family'. But it appears that the Prince of Wales, faithful to his undertaking, did not move against the Bill.

[15] *Dropmore MSS.* (*W.B.H.*), Wilberforce to Grenville, 31 Jan 1807.

[16] Ibid., Grenville to Wilberforce, 2 Feb 1807 (copy).

[17] Wilberforce, Diary, 3 Feb 1807, quoted in *Life of Wilberforce*, III 291–2. But see *Wigan Letter Book*, Thornton to Patty More, 4 Feb 1807: 'We . . . are not without fear of a weak attendance of our friends in the House of Lords.'

to oppose the measure, and voted the sum of £500 for propaganda.[18] On 10 December they reaffirmed their opposition[19] and at a well attended general meeting on 21 January resolved upon a petition to the Lords against Abolition[20] in which proceeding they were subsequently joined by the merchants of Liverpool, by Liverpool corporation and the trustees of the dock at that port, and by the merchants and planters of Jamaica[21] and Trinidad. The exertions of the anti-abolitionists were serious: 'the friends of the slave trade . . . made unusual exertions to procure votes against the Bill', commented John Allen at Holland House.[22] On the eve of the Lords second reading debate, however, Thornton told Patty More that the 'slave traders are very low in spirits, but', he added cautiously, 'we suspect them to be affecting to underestimate their own strength'.[23]

When the debate came on, then, Grenville was reasonably, but not entirely confident, and just what the opponents of abolition, aided by failure to turn out on the part of some of the friends of the measure, might yet contrive was unclear. The most notable feature of the debate was a speech by Grenville lasting nearly three hours, and which was widely acclaimed as outstanding.[24] If there was little new that could be said, the abolition case could now rest four-square on justice, on a justice which 'imperiously calls upon your lordships to abolish the Slave Trade', a justice to the planters themselves, which would in no way harm their true interests, but a justice due principally to the inhabitants of Africa. Moreover, such an act of justice could not be threatened with ineffectiveness by foreign rivals since they lacked either the inclination or the ability to take up Britain's share of the trade. But the voting was the important thing. In the Foreign Slave Trade Bill the division

[18] *West India Planters and Merchants*, Minutes, Feb 1805–March 1822, Minutes of Standing Committee, 9 June 1806.
[19] Ibid., Minutes of General Meeting, 10 Dec 1806.
[20] Ibid., Minutes of General Meeting, 21 Jan 1807.
[21] *Parliamentary Debates*, VIII, col. 613.
[22] *B.M. Add. MSS. 52194. (Holland House Papers)*, John Allen, Journal, 26 Feb 1807. See also *B.M. Add. MSS. 38416* (Liverpool Papers), f. 317, Chalmers to Lord Liverpool, 16 Jan 1807. I owe both these references to W. B. Hamilton.
[23] *Wigan Letter Book*, Thornton to Patty More, 4 Feb 1807.
[24] *Porteus MS. 2104*, f. 86, Diary, 5 Feb 1807; *Christian Observer*, Feb 1807, 143.

in the Lords had been 43 to 18; on the Resolution against the slave trade 41 to 20; now it was 72 plus 28 proxies against 28 plus 6 proxies – 100 to 34.[25]

Here was a famous victory and it was, as anticipated, confirmed, after passing through the committee and report stages on the 6th and 9th, by passage of the third reading, without a division, on 10 February. On the same day the first reading was moved in the Commons, but though its successful passage there was probable, it was not assured. As Grenville wrote to William Smith: 'Still I fear we are not quite at the end of our labours, for I see many symptoms of much opposition to it in the House of Commons'.[26] The day for the all-important debate on the second reading was set for 23 February and in anticipation of this, as its formal minutes tell us, the Abolition Committee set itself to the classical lobbying occupation of drawing up lists of members known to be friendly and known to be hostile, with a view either to exhort them to be diligent in attendance or to urge on them a change of mind.[27] Mrs Henry Thornton, in a letter to Patty More, adds some flesh and blood to the bones of the minutes. A large party have hired a house in Downing Street and meet every day. Each has a list of members to whom he can have access for the purpose of recommending the subject and prevailing on them to attend.[28] Following the meeting on the 13th, Wilberforce noted: 'A terrific list of doubtfuls. Lord Grenville not confident on looking at Abolition list; yet I think we shall carry it'.[29] When the

[25] The Lords Debates are in *Parliamentary Debates*, VIII, cols. 257–9, 431, 601–2, 612–8, 657–72, 677–83, 691–3, 701–3; IX, 146–7, 168–70. The quotation is from Grenville's speech on the Second Reading (ibid., VIII, col. 657). The names of the 72 Ayes are contained in *Porteus MS.*, *2104*, f. 85.

[26] *Wm Smith MSS.* (Duke Collection), Grenville to Smith, 11 Feb 1807. Cf. also Wilberforce to Muncaster, 11 Feb 1807, printed in *Life of Wilberforce*, III, 293–4, 'Our opponents are making their utmost exertions, and by what I hear, are proceeding with considerable art and plausibility, so that I am afraid of the steadfastness of such of our friends as may not be rooted in principle'.

[27] *B.M. Add. MSS.* 21256, Abolition Committee Minutes, 10, 11, 13, 17 and 20 Feb 1807. At this period Zachary Macaulay was also keeping the newspapers informed of the progress of the American Abolition Bill (Fladeland, *Men and Brothers*, 75).

[28] *Wigan Letter Book*, Mrs. Henry Thornton to Patty More, 21 Feb 1807.

[29] Wilberforce, Diary, 13 Feb 1807, quoted in *Life of Wilberforce*, III, 295

great day of the second reading – 23 February – arrived, the main speech in favour of the motion was made by Grey, now Lord Howick. In contrast to Grenville in the Lords, most of Howick's speech was devoted to the 'sound policy' argument that West Indian planters and merchants, and even the merchants and ports engaged in the slave trade, would not merely not be harmed, but would positively benefit from abolition. All this involved Howick in a certain disingenuousness and the eventual landslide vote showed, given the weakness of some of his arguments, that he had misjudged the mood of the House in choosing, as he specifically said, to pass over the argument from justice as already made, and to devote himself to the argument for policy. That mood was made conclusively clear by the remarkable and spontaneous ovation accorded to Wilberforce as a result of the tribute made him in the debate by Romilly. Wilberforce was reduced to tears by what was, as his friend William Hey prosily observed, 'an unprecedented effusion of approbation'.[30] In such an atmosphere, few ventured to speak in support of the slave trade, and the vote, when it came, was much more overwhelming than anyone had predicted – 283 to 16. Even so there remained some hurdles. There was further debate, and many-sided discussion, involving *inter alia* Romilly, Stephen, Smith, Wilberforce, Grey and Grenville, on the penal provisions which were added, on a proposed amendment to postpone the operation of the bill for five years, and on the antiabolitionists' last fling – excision from the preamble of the bill of reference to justice and humanity as being two of its three bases.[31] The whole process was complicated by the need to secure the approval of the Lords to amendments, and threatened in mid-March, by the imminent resignation of the Ministry over relief for Irish Catholic officers. In fact, the crucial decision having been taken and by strong majorities, there was no disposition to defeat the bill by procedural obstacles, or by allowing it to fall between governments; and so after the bill had been passed by the Lords on the 23 March, the day on which it was returned to them, it

[30] Hey to Wilberforce, 28 Feb 1807, quoted in ibid., III 297.

[31] In *Grey MSS.* (Durham), Wm. Smith to Grey, 9 Mar 1807, Smith argued strongly that the point should not be conceded, as resting the bill only on 'sound policy' would be to base it on the most disputable ground. The concession, though made, was more apparent than real, for the preamble of the bill cited instead the *threefold* justification of the Resolution against the Slave Trade (47 Geo. III, c 36).

received the royal assent on 25 March.[32] The entire British slave trade was abolished with effect from 1 May 1807.

The immediate explanation of the passage of the 1807 bill lies in systematic abolitionist lobbying, and, much more importantly, the political pressure which Grenville did not hesitate to exert. We have already seen the pains he went to to get votes in the Lords, where the danger was greater; and we have earlier noticed how much more prepared he was than either Pitt had been, or constitutional conventions easly permitted, to try to make the general abolition bill a government measure, that is, one for which the support of ministers and their political supporters could be demanded. Grenville had written to Wilberforce on 20 May 1806:

> We should then come at the beginning of next session to consider the most advantageous way of bringing forward the rest of the subject, either moved as a Government measure by Mr Fox (if on full consideration that is thought best for the success of the thing . . .) or brought forward by you, and supported by a previous decision of the Cabinet, supposing that can be obtained.[33]

We know that he was not in the event able to make the bill a government measure – Sidmouth,[34] Windham and probably Fitz-

[32] For the debates in the Commons see *Parliamentary Debates*, VIII, cols. 717–22, 829–38, 939–43, 945–95, 1040–53; IX, 59–66, 114–40. The best summary of this final stage is in Coupland, *Wilberforce*, 276–83. For varied correspondence on the bill during the Commons stage see *Dropmore MSS.* (*W.B.H.*), Wilberforce to Grenville, 7 Feb 1807 and Grenville to Wilberforce, 7 Feb 1807, Wm. Smith to Grenville, 10 Feb 1809, Private and encl.; Stephen to Grenville, 18 Feb and 20 (?) Feb 1807; Grenville to Stephen, 19 Feb 1807 (copy); *William Smith MSS.* (Duke Collection), Grenville to Smith, 11 Feb 1807. (A copy is in the *Dropmore MSS.* (*W.B.H.*) *Wigan Letter Book*, Mrs. Henry Thornton to Patty More, 21 Feb 1807; *Grey MSS.* (Durham) Wilberforce to Grey, 23 Feb 1807, Wm. Smith to Grey, 9 Mar 1807. For other evidence on the later stages of the bill see *Life of Wilberforce*, III 203–302.

[33] *Wilberforce MSS.* (Duke Collection), Grenville to Wilberforce, 20 May 1806.

[34] Sidmouth had spoken against the final measure. This final inconsequence led Wilberforce to quip 'that Lord Sidmouth's speech on the Slave Trade consisted of a medley of ideas, one cribbed from every person with whom he had ever conversed on the subject. He was like a man who, going through the Haymarket, stole a wisp of hay from every wagon, and then said "Who will buy *my* hay"' (*Wigan Letter Book*, Thornton to Patty More, 4 Feb 1807).

william remained intransigent,[35] and the conventions of the constitution permitted them to do so – but it appears that the political pressures Grenville personally applied may have been the stronger precisely because the general abolition bill could not formally be a government measure. Richard Ryder, who was a supporter of abolition, had a highly significant comment to make on the methods used to whip up the vote:

> Nobody expected this great question to be carried with so high a hand. I cannot but rejoice at it; but unless one is to suppose that a *sudden* and complete revolution has taken place in the public mind without any new or assignable cause upon this subject, and that not confined to one but extended to both Houses of Parliament, it is to one who holds my opinion both disgusting and alarming to observe that the present Administration can do so much more than Pitt could accomplish in the plenitude of his power. I call it alarming because there is no knowing to what length or to what subjects this reluctant acquiescence (for reluctant it has been) to the will of Government may be carried in the future.[36]

The other evidence gives a good deal of support to Ryder – 'the decision of the slave trade shows what a Government *can* do if it pleases', commented Canning[37] – as of course does the sheer disparity between the 'yea' and 'nay' votes – 100 to 34 in the Lords and 283 to 16 in the Commons.[38] But Ryder's assertion of a 'reluc-

---

[35] Fitzwilliam appears to have remained silent on the issue after June 1806, but it is likely that he also opposed abolition in Cabinet. It is significant that Clarkson, in dedicating his *History of the Abolition* to *inter alia* nine out of twelve of the members of the Talents Ministry, excludes Fitzwilliam as well as Sidmouth and Windham.

[36] Ryder to Harrowby, 27 Feb 1807, extract in *English Historical Documents*, XI, *1783–1832*, edited by A. Aspinall and E. A. Smith (London, 1959) 803. Interestingly, the extract continues: 'No one is more surprised than Wilberforce himself. He attributes it to the immediate interposition of Providence.' The extract quoted above also appears in W. B. Hamilton, 'Constitutional and Political Reflections on the Dissmisal of Lord Grenville's Ministry', *Canadian Historical Association Report*, 1964, 92.

[37] N.d., quoted from *Harewood MSS.* in *Later Correspondence of George III*, IV, no. 3380, n.

[38] I would also like to quote a characteristic personal communication from the late W. B. Hamilton. 'And the final job may have been a pushover . . . but Grenville didn't know it would be. What you have here for

tant acquiescence' must be qualified in the light of the voting on
the Resolution, the declaration of intent, the previous June, when
the measure passed by 41 to 20 in the Lords and 114 to 15 in the
Commons. Certainly the majority of ministers supported the bill
on that occasion but there is no evidence of resort to the methods
which Ryder so deplored in 1807. Must one not therefore conclude
that a significant shift of opinion had already taken place by the
middle of 1806? There are, after all, credible reasons why this
should have happened. The most immediate is that Stephen's
masterly tactic of concentrating first on the abolition of those
branches of the trade which could be represented as harming the
national interest in time of war, and the way in which this measure
was played down, meant that the political nation was confronted
all of a sudden with the fact that it had abolished what was believed
to be nearly two-thirds of the British slave trade almost without
realising it. William Cobbett, a strong opponent of abolition,[39]
saw that the Foreign Slave Trade Bill was but an instalment and
warned the readers of his *Political Register* accordingly.[40] But no
amount of warning could have prevented the slave trade to Trinidad and the older British West Indian islands becoming more
vulnerable in virtue of the simple fact that the 'national interest'
argument could more readily contemplate ending the supply of

[39] 'So often as they agitate this question, with all its cant for the relief
of 500,000 blacks; so often will I remind them of the 1,200,000 white
paupers of England and Wales' (*Cobbett's Political Register*, ix, 7 June
1806, cols. 844–5).

[40] Ibid., ix, 10 May 1806, cols. 687–93, 'Slave Trade Bill'. This is not
actually an article by Cobbett but a letter by 'W. W.'. However, Cobbett
endorses it by saying, 'Every argument that I have heard in favour of the
Slave Trade Bill is, in my opinion, completely answered in a letter which
immediately follows below'.

the first time was Government headed by men who, by Heaven, were
going to abolish. Pitt has *said* he was for abolition, but he didn't throw
himself into it. . . . And note that Grenville was making this fierce and
sustained effort in the midst of cooking up a (silly) financial and tax plan,
making a treaty with the United States (aborted by the latter), contend-
ing with a damned fool, Windham, in his War Office and cabinet, and
shaping the measure for the Irish Catholics that was to cost him Office.'
See also *Dropmore MSS.* (*W.B.H.*), Wilberforce to Grenville, 25 Feb 1807,
'It is no more than justice to yourself to say, that to yourself and to the
tone you have taken and the exertions you have made, our success is
mainly to be attributed.'

slaves to the British West Indies if the supply of slaves to Britain's competitors had first been curtailed. The decision to go first for the ending of the British slave trade to foreigners, by an appeal to sound policy, and then to introduce the wavering ranks of independent men gently to a total abolition, based additionally on justice and humanity, by means of a declaration of intent, was of immense importance. But nothing makes the essential difference in the basis on which the final abolition bill was founded more clear than the terms in which the abolitionists and their ministerial supporters hailed the event in their personal notes and communications – not those designed for publication – with one another. 'I am truly thankful to Providence for permitting me to see this great Work brought to a conclusion', wrote Porteus in his diary;[41] Romilly spoke to Smith of the final abolition as 'that great act of natural justice[42] and Sir James Mackintosh wrote to Wilberforce that 'the benefit that he has conferred on the world' was 'the greatest that any individual has had the means of conferring.[43] William Smith was less rhetorical when he wrote to Grey, pleading that the citation of justice and humanity should not be removed from the preamble of the 1807 bill

> And shall we now be afraid to state in the preamble the ground of the Enactment? . . . Will you now hesitate to speak out as before? . . . Will it not seem like abandoning our strongest, our unexpungable ground? . . . The only reasons for Abolition are the Trade being adverse to J^{ce} and H^{ty} [Justice and Humanity], and to *sound Policy*. If at last You refuse to declare its contrariety to the former, it may be argued that You in fact rest on the latter ground; and who would willingly chuse the most disputable, however good in itself he might think it? . . . The true principle of the Abolition [is] . . . broadly and explicitly laid down in the present preamble.[44]

For one of the ministers involved, Holland, his share in the passage of the 1807 act was 'the greatest gratification of his publick life'[45] whilst Grenville invoked the memory of Fox and the respon-

[41] *Porteus MS*. 2104, f. 91, Diary, 16 Mar 1807.

[42] *Wm. Smith* MSS. (Duke Collection), Romilly to Smith 5 Mar 1807.

[43] Mackintosh to Wilberforce, 27 July 1807, quoted in *Life of Wilberforce*, III 302.

[44] *Grey Papers* (Durham), Smith to Grey, 9 Mar 1807.

[45] *Wrangham MSS*., Brougham to Wilberforce, n.d.

sibility of office as he wrote to congratulate Grey on the result of the second reading in the Commons

> I most heartily congratulate you on the glorious count of last night. Come what will, we may now put the sentiment which Fox so often expressed, that we have not been called in vain to the stations which we occupy. How much it is to be regretted that he did not live to feel the pleasure of such an event.[46]

Grenville could hardly have put it better. And even though the method which abolitionists and their ministerial supporters had had to adopt had, at a decisive stage and for the sake of that majority of uncommitted men concerned about the national interest, cloaked humanity with interest, the public comment which Grenville made to the Lords was no less justified. Parliament, he said, had 'performed one of the most glorious acts that had ever been done by any assembly of any nation in the world'.[47]

[46] *Grey Papers* (Durham), Grenville to Grey 23 [?24] Feb 1807.
[47] *Parliamentary Debates*, ix, col. 170, Grenville, 23 Mar 1807.

17 Conclusion

This book began with the study of the slave trade as an economic phenomenon. The slave trade of the European nations with Western Africa was a commerce which reached its peak in the half-century before British abolition and which manifested considerable sophistication but also much hazard for those who ventured in it. To describe the trade primarily as a theme in economic history had a double purpose; it enabled us to study the matter dispassionately and, in doing so, we were led to the frightening awareness that most of those involved in the slave trade saw their involvement as an 'honourable' and even 'genteel' pursuit. The normal run of men, in other words, could contemplate with equanimity practices which later generations would zealously condemn. Here, rather than in justified condemnation, is the most profound moral commentary on the slave trade. Nor is moral commentary only significant for what it is, for it seems that an attribution of exceptional wickedness to those involved in the slave trade is integrally related to the popular belief that the trade was consistently and immensely profitable. To put it another way, it is supposed that for such wickedness to have existed the rewards must have been vast. It has been demonstrated that overall they were not, even though individuals may have made fortunes. Moreover slave traders tolerated surprisingly modest yields. A low return in the largest Dutch slaving company, an only very moderate one in the French slave trade, had nothing to do with the eclipse of the Netherlands and France as slaving nations, whilst a return of rising 10 per cent in the British trade was distinctly good by the standards of the time. Any significant contribution to the provision of capital for the Industrial Revolution, on the other hand, would have required a profit level vastly greater than this. This qualification here is that, on certain assumptions, there could have been some meaningful contribution to capital development in the Liverpool hinterland, where, of course, the rapid expansion of the cotton industry was concentrated. In all this calculation, however, it must be remembered that the question of the provision of new capital from outside the new industries is no longer regarded by economic historians as being so important a dimension of the overall explanation as once it was.

But of course the slave trade, viewed either as economic phenomenon or dark commentary on the human condition, had considerable implications for Africa. As to its impact in the crudest sense, this investigation has confirmed and quantified the movement eastward and southward in the coastal regions which yielded up most slaves. The direct economic reach in to the interior of even the stronger coastal peoples was limited; they had to link up with internal trade networks, usually through intermediaries. Even a quite powerful coastal kingdom, Dahomey, could gain no permanent prosperity from the slave trade because she was denied access to the interior trading networks. A regional trading network like the Aro, or that which Lunda power made possible, was essential if the slave trade was to command a continuing supply of slaves. At another level the peoples who profited from the slave trade were those whose political institutions were either of themselves or by adaptation appropriate to it: small segmentary societies were usually losers. At the personal level there was much misery but no calculus enables us to quantify it. Population-wise one of the two most important slave-exporting regions, the Bight of Biafra hinterland, seems to have been well able to sustain heavy slave exports without net population loss, but in Congo/Angola the slave export trade probably was an important cause of population decline.

In the examination of eighteenth-century ideas and theology as they affected anti-slavery four threads can be distinguished: a group of concepts in moral and legal philosophy which had a latent anti-slavery implication; numerous and specific denunciation of Negro slavery on philosophical grounds; notable developments in theology which sharpened the conception of how fellow human beings should be treated, which strengthened sanctions on conduct, and which quickened the notion that progress and hence reform was a part of the divine plan; and, fourthly, attitudes latently or specifically hostile to slavery in literature. What we see in the important group of philosophers at whom we have looked is that liberty is extolled, and slavery thereby condemned; happiness becomes the great principle of utility, and slavery, thereby, can only be found wanting; the duty of benevolence is asserted and induces a heightened response to the need of the poor and outcast; and Negro slavery is almost always specifically denounced. All in all changes in ideas have been shown to be both more and less important than is commonly supposed: more important, because the marked anti-slavery tendency of eighteenth-century thought, and the change in the intellectual climate which resulted, have been demonstrated with some thoroughness; less important, because a change in ideas has been shown to have been unable of itself to end the slave trade, let alone slavery. The relevance of theological developments to anti-slavery reform lay in the theological origins and religious dimension of the powerful idea of benevolence; in the reinforcement of belief in a providential order as a sanction on conduct; and in that important root of the idea of progress which consisted in the belief in revelation as progressive with the necessary corollary that the Christian was called to new commitment as he received new revelation. Literature for its part, mainly through the anti-slavery implications of developments of the noble savage theme, combined with ideas of liberty, humanity and happiness, to sharpen and extend awareness of the problem of slavery.

The summary examination of eighteenth-century philosophy, theology and literature was undertaken not only for its own sake but in order to make clear the cultural inheritance of Christian abolitionists, both as an influence which helped to form them and as a body of largely shared assumptions which enabled them to speak a language which their age understood. In assessing the role firstly of Evangelical abolitionists one must keep in tension that they did share many of their age's assumptions *and* that they had an extraordinary and positive dynamic of their own. They accepted much of the moral philosophy of their day, the emphasis on liberty, benevolence and happiness, but transposed them into a religious key; from the assurance that their sin was forgiven through the grace of God in the redemptive work of Christ, they knew not only that they could overcome the evil in their own hearts but also that they could conquer those evils in the world which they felt called to combat. They believed especially powerfully in Providence as the sustaining power in the moral order and this belief gave them a satisfying and coherent, albeit disturbing, philosophy of history. Equally their lively sense of a particular Providence directing their own lives was also their inescapable summons to mould the world to a righteousness which would avert national catastrophe, relieve the earthly sufferings of men and pave the way for the salvation of men's eternal souls. Finally, in the very warp and woof of Evangelical faith, slavery, of all social evils, stood particularly condemned, and because slavery and freedom represented the externalisation of the polar opposites of the Evangelicals' inmost spiritual experience, they were impelled to act in the cause of abolition with a zeal and a perseverance which other men could rarely match.

The Quaker role in the abolition was theologically less dramatic but had profound importance in the slow chemistry whereby conviction was turned into action. The dialogue within the Anglo-American Quaker community, and the pressure on English Friends which stemmed from the American Quaker reform movement, building on the Inner Light and the law of love, and broadening latterly into a theology much tinctured with Evangelicalism, constituted Quakerism's ideological contribution. But Quakers also made up the first anti-slavery lobby in Britain and by the approaches they made to widely varying men outside their ranks played a major part in the formation of a national abolition lobby.

A point easily overlooked is the novelty of the concept of a national lobby, that it was quite unprecedented for such a campaign as the abolition campaign to be set on foot. Even the abolitionists themselves seem in the early stages not to have realised the unprecedented nature of what they were doing and hence to have underrated the difficulties. But as Sir James Stephen put it, from the perspective of the late 1830s, 'in later days, agitation for the accomplishment of great political objects has taken a place among social arts. But sixty years since, it was among the inventions slumbering in the womb of time, taught by no professors, and illustrated by no examples'.[1]

There is therefore much significance in the simple fact that twenty years elapsed between the foundation of the London Abolition Committee and the final accomplishment of its object. Such a delay also underlines the truth that an intellectual climate favourable to abolition, though important, was in no way sufficient

[1] Sir James Stephen, *Essays in Ecclesiastical Biography*, II 234.

to secure it. But difficult and unprecedented as the task was, it was as a political campaign that abolition had to succeed, for it was only by means of the political process that pressure could be translated into the necessary legislation. As a pressure group the abolitionists were, for their day, unexampled; their leadership was outstanding, and their organisation was impressive, whilst their mistakes are easier to discern with hindsight than they were evident at the time. We have remarked that early success was thwarted by the full explosion of the French Revolution and its inhibiting effect on all British reforming activity, at precisely the time when the abolitionists were on the verge of a broadly based national campaign; we have noticed the variety of measures attempted when total abolition seemed unattainable, and the importance of the arch-conservatism of the Lords; we have analysed Pitt's role and the constitutional conventions governing the abolition; we have sought to quantify the West Indian (in the extended sense) opposition, to identify members of the core-group of abolitionists, and have urged that West Indian opposition in itself was never remotely strong enough to arrest the progress of abolition. A more generalised but deep-rooted sense of the importance of the West Indies for British prosperity amongst the political nation, especially as represented in Parliament, was the critically important obstacle: and it was this which made Stephen's discernment of how the cause of abolition could be linked to the chariot of national interest so important. (And here, although our argument has demanded only that a majority of informed, uncommitted men should have *supposed* that the West Indies were still highly valuable to the imperial economy, we must repeat that we accept Drescher's demonstration that they *actually* were so.) The key to the eventual passage of abolition is the way in which the abolitionists conceived the tactic of so using a particular, fortuitous conjunction in Britain's politico-economic position, brought about by war, as to present the abolition of up to two-thirds of the British slave trade as an elementary dictate of the national interest in time of war. To this tactic Grenville, in particular, gave wholehearted and vital support. With the supply of foreigners and conquered islands ended by the 1806 abolition bill, the West Indians were like shorn lambs to the wind of a humanity which now blew cold indeed. For in the situation which Grenville and the abolitionists had so ingeniously contrived – and which is perhaps the harder to discern because one is so conditioned to expect interest to masquerade as altruism that one may miss altruism when concealed beneath the cloak of interest – the mass of independent members of Parliament were ready, against all the evidence of the West Indies' importance to the nation, to act as the children of the later eighteenth century, with its manifest anti-slavery convictions, that they really were.

There is a further and broader significance in the use of this tactic, consisting in its indication of the relationship between ideas and reform. It was argued in Part Two of this book that a clear fruit of the philosophy of the eighteenth century was the appearance of a marked anti-slavery testimony but that the indications of a readiness actually to effect reform in institutions, to make practice accord with theory, though clear, are less strong. In fact the back of the problem of carrying abolition was broken without the political nation having to gird itself to the necessary pitch of resolution to make a major social reform on principle. It was still early days for reformers; the Burkean hand that tremblingly sought reform so trembled that it could write little that was new in the statute book. Parliamentary reform, save in very limited respects, Catholic Emancipation, repeal of the Test and Corporation Acts, Poor Law Reform, all had failed. What is striking is the way in which the abolitionists, without theorising about the problem, pragmatically adjusted to it by effecting the bulk of the abolition under the guise of a regulatory wartime measure and not a measure of principle. Of course they fought hard and in the end with substantial success for the 1807 bill to be based openly on justice and humanity, as well as sound policy, but the greater part of the trade had already been abolished without, to repeat, the need to extract from Parliament a reform on principle, and one more extreme and significant than anything that had ever gone before, and which Parliament had many times refused to enact. In short, a major reform was achieved without a major frontal breach of the still stubborn tradition that reform of institutions on principle was not lightly to be ventured upon. The paradox remains that, once achieved, abolition was immediately viewed as a whole – after all the entire British slave trade was comprehended in the 1807 Act – and as a measure of principle, and not merely as the initiative of committed abolitionists, private men and ministers, which it undoubtedly was.

As for the abolitionists themselves, they are not only to be credited with consummate tactical skill. Their organisation was masterly and their doggedness surpassing. Behind the political activity of the religiously inspired men who constituted the core of the abolition lobby[2] was a theology of a profoundly dynamic kind, and one which, especially through the particular way in which the concept of redemption was worked out and applied, had profound significance both in the development of a theology of anti-slavery, and for future social reform.

[2] In that it stressed these important characteristics of abolition, the 'Coupland school' was absolutely right.

18 Some Reflections

The abolition is normally regarded as, at least, eccentric to the process of reform which burgeoned in nineteenth-century Britain. Dr Oliver Macdonagh's work is of course essentially concerned with the years after 1815 but it is interesting that when he observes of his model of the reforming process that it applies 'peculiarly to the half-century 1825–75', he also excludes from that model 'a few important exceptions such as slavery reform. None the less the abolition does constitute a possible limited application of the model: the origin of abolition did lie in the 'exposure of a social evil', an exposure which was the work of abolitionist investigation and propaganda; there is, further, a sense in which the abolition was applied in stages; 'executive officers', though not specifically appointed for the purpose, did supervise the operation of the regulations imposed from the time of Dolben's Act onwards; certainly here was a situation where there was a discordance between 'time and timing' – the failure of 1792 when the atmosphere generated by the French Revolution inhibited abolitionist recourse to a 'popular' campaign springs conspicuously to mind; and without any doubt 'the character of the beneficiaries [of abolition] was such that little or nothing could be left to their own unassisted efforts':[1]

But to apply Macdonagh's model as any kind of overall explanation would be to strain his categories and the history of the abolition alike. In particular the various measures of regulation and curtailment were never regarded by their sponsors as other than palliatives very incidental to the abolitionists' central aim, whilst the abolition question at no stage created the phenomenon of enforcement officers who developed into a force for further

[1] See Oliver Macdonagh, *A Pattern of Government Growth, 1800–1860* (London, 1961), especially 320–36, and Oliver Macdonagh, 'The Nineteenth-Century Revolution in Government: A Re-Appraisal,' *The Historical Journal*, I (1958) no. 1, 52–67 and especially 58–61.

change. Macdonagh's work does, however, provide valuable insights and, additionally, provokes us to consider anew the whole relationship of abolition to reform.

First of all there has to be some ground-clearing. Given the tradition, starting with Cobbett,[2] and Hazlitt,[3] later evident in the Hammonds[4] and C. E. Raven,[5] and in recent days in E. P. Thompson,[6] that the abolitionists either had nothing to do with domestic reform, or actively opposed it, it is generally supposed that abolition was at best eccentric to the general movement of reform. Now we have already remarked the record on other reforming measures, including, as some may suppose, the blemishes, of the group conveniently described as the Clapham Sect. But reflection on the successful accomplishment of abolition can tell us something more profound, sometimes involving paradox,[7] about reform in the later eighteenth and earlier nineteenth centuries: we draw out this deeper significance in a series of propositions:

First: Eighteenth-century philosophy so developed as to include a latent attack on slavery, and contained numerous specific – and of course philosophically based – condemnations of Negro slavery. Side by side there developed a philosophical acceptance of the possibility and desirability of reform of institutions, but this was a less sturdy plant.

Second: There was a prolonged and seemingly necessary period of gestation for anti-slavery *action* in the bosom of a religious community, the Anglo-American Quaker community; internal dialogue over the best part of a century was the condition of the eventual American Quaker pressure on their English brethren to initiate action against the British slave trade.

Third: The focus on the slave trade as the age's cardinal evil

[2] William Cobbett, *A History of the Last Hundred Days of English Freedom*, ed. J. L. Hammond (London, 1921) 18, 107–8, 114.

[3] William Hazlitt, *The Spirit of the Age: or Contemporary Portraits* (London, 1825) 356–63.

[4] See e.g. J. L. and Barbara Hammond, *The Village Labourer, 1760–1832* (3rd ed., London, 1920) 99–100, 118–19, 154 n., 198–9, 308.

[5] C. E. Raven, *Christian Socialism* (London, 1920) 12.

[6] E. P. Thompson, *The Making of the English Working Class*, 3rd ed. (London, 1970) 60–61, 141, 160–61, 442–3, 779. See also on this general point Howse, *Saints in Politics*, 116–37.

[7] On this see David Spring, 'The Clapham Sect: Some Social and Political Aspects', *Victorian Studies*, Sept 1961, 35–48.

was, for the politically most effective abolitionist group, the Clapham Sect, a direct function of Evangelical theology. In developing such a focus Evangelicals – and Quakers by returning to a rich source in their own tradition – broke out of the long theological ambivalence regarding slavery and emancipation.

Fourth: Reform of this kind and extent was previously unheard of.

Fifth: The abolition campaign in Parliament had to operate within the limitations of contemporary conventions of the constitution and especially the inability of the prime minister to command the support of King, of ministers and of parliamentary supporters for reforming measures.

Sixth: Radicalism in France, San Domingo and Britain checked the progress of abolition; the blocking of abolition in the House of Lords was the most serious manifestation of the inhibition of reform which fear of radicalism engendered.

Seventh: The aboliton campaign could not prevail in Parliament as long as the numerous uncommitted members believed that abolition would seriously impair the position of the West Indies as a vital support of the imperial economic system.

Eighth: It was an unpredictable and fortuitous conjunction of politico-economic circumstances in 1806–07, and brilliant discernment by the abolitionists of the opportunity, which enabled them, with the vital political support of most leading ministers, and especially Grenville, to persuade M.P.s first that action long sought on grounds of humanity and justice was now demanded by national interest, and, in 1807, that action on moral principles which they accepted must prevail even over national interests which they valued. This strategy also meant that men did not have to bring themselves to such a degree of acceptance of institutional reform as is implied in one comprehensive measure of abolition, avowedly based on principle.

Ninth: Outside Parliament abolitionists broke new ground in the extent to which they developed a national organisation for the advocacy of a reforming cause.

Tenth: There was a logic in the success of abolition pregnant with future consequences: the techniques of abolition could be applied to other reforming causes whilst the object of abolition, a defenceless group, was a bridgehead through which Evangelicals and others initiated domestic reforms. Moreover, the raising of the slavery question in any form necessarily raised the whole question of the limits of authority over other men, with all the implications that follow.

The abolition, then, is not only important for its own sake, and that was important enough: it is an episode the study of which illuminates the further investigation of reform in the nineteenth century and which will provide not least a major component of a model of the role of religion in reform, or, perhaps, of 'The Salvation Ethic and the Spirit of Reform'.[8]

[8] Cf. Max Weber, *The Protestant Ethic and the Spirit of Capitalism* (1904).

Appendix 1

Mortality in the Slave Trade 1761–1810

Three principal sources were used. Captains and others in the slave trade were closely questioned on mortality by the Privy Council Committee of Enquiry into the slave trade and, although they sometimes spoke from memory, and on occasion in round numbers, their evidence constitutes a large random sample, spanning the years 1769–87 (*A. & P.*, 1789, LXXXIV (646a), pt II). For 1789 mortality on large samples of cargoes arriving in the British West Indies was recorded. (*A. & P.*, 1795–96, XLII, Slaves imported into British West Indies, 1789–95.) For 1791 to 1795 there is a resumption of the 1789 B.W.I. arrivals sampling, whilst for 1791–97 we have worked out figures from the collated logs of masters and surgeons (*Lords A List*). For the period in which these last two sources overlap, the mean has been drawn. Figures for blank years are bracketed and based on *ad hoc* derivation from adjacent years. There seem to be no mortality figures for 1798 onwards.

One puzzle obtrudes and one conclusion suggests itself. It is curious that in 1789, when Dolben's regulating Act is in force, the mortality rate is higher than in the preceding period of unrestricted packing, and that it remains at virtually the same higher level in the well-attested year 1791. Although there is a drop in 1792 a sustained lower rate only begins in 1793. It is difficult not to think that the varied provisions of Dolben's Act did not cause the reduction in mortality, but there is no evident explanation of why this effect was delayed. The nature of the evidence does not always permit, and when it permits, does not always require, that we arrive at detailed percentages of loss in the slave trade of other carriers, when seeking to estimate the total number of slaves exported by the other nations engaged in the trade. But we know a loss of 10 per cent of those loaded to be the approximate level in the French slave trade (Curtin, *Census*, 177–9) whilst the figure

	Loaded	Died	% Mortality	% Mortality or mean mortality
1761–68	—	—	—	[8·5]
1769–87	12,792	1085	8·5	8·5
1788	—	—	—	[9·6]
1789	11,014	1053	9·6	9·6
1790	—	—	—	[9·6]

B.W.I. Imports Sample				Sample based on Logs and Journals			
	Loaded	Died	% Mortality		Loaded	Died	% Mortality	% Mortality or mean mortality
1791	15,108	1397	9·2	1791	19,978	1945	9·7	9·5
1792	26,971	2468	9·2	1792	26,705	2040	7·6	8·4
1793	11,720	859	7·3	1793	10,043	376	3·7	5·5
1794	14,611	394	2·7	1794	11,864	434	3·7	3·2
1795	7157	224	3·1	1795	7605	164	2·2	2·7
				1796	8317	283	3·4	3·4
				1797	11,433	480	4·2	4·2
				1798–	—	—	—	[4·0]

Notes:

1. There is a marked discrepancy in the two overlapping lists in one year only, 1793.

2. No allowance is made for mortality accruing from ship loss.

3. There was great variation in mortality according to the coastal region of loading. The breakdown in the B.W.I. imports sample is R. Senegal to R. Volta, 4·1%; R. Volta to Gaboon, 13·1%; Loango to Angola, 2·8%. The coastal divisions are not identical, but this mortality distribution is reflected in insurance rates payable on slave consignments to Jamacia in 1788.

From Calabar	15%	From Windward Coast	7%
From Bonny	10%	From Gold Coast	5%

(*Stephen Fuller MSS. Letter Book I,* Fuller (Agent for Jamaica) to Jamaica Committee of Correspondence, 20 Feb 1788.)

of 12·3 per cent over 106 voyages of the Middleburg Company[1] suggests a figure for the Dutch slave trade as a whole. There is no reason to believe that other nations matched the reduction achieved by the English from the early 1790s onwards, since no other nation restricted cargoes. For national sectors of the slave trade on which evidence of mortality is deficient, a 10 per cent loss in transit should be assumed.

[1] Unger, 'Bijdragen', II 110–13.

Appendix 2

Slave Prices – Gross and net

We have thirty-four indications of gross sale price in the 1760s, forty-four in the following decade and twenty-nine in the next. In both the nineties and the period 1801–07 we possess only seven each. Our basic method has been simply to average those indications over the separate decades, but the individual indications have been adjusted if there was evidence that a given cargo was obviously unbalanced by age or sex whilst allowance was also made if one colony appeared to feature too largely in any decade, e.g. South Carolina in the sixties and seventies. The resulting decennial averages are: 1761–70: £29; 1771–80: £35; 1781–90: £36; 179–1800: £50; 1801–07: £60.

Note the compatibility of the estimates for the first three decades with the opinion of Norris, the Liverpool slave trader, who told the Privy Council Committee in 1789 that the average price commanded by new slaves in the West Indies between 1763 and 1788 was £28–£35, and with the evidence of Evan Baillie, a West Indian slave factor, that the average value of cargoes before the American War was £25–£33, that this had increased to £30–£40 thereafter and to £42–£50 in 1789–90. It is for the 1790s and particularly the years 1801–07 that the number of good indications is too few to be really satisfactory. Sources for sale prices are: *A. & P.*, 1789, xxvi (646a), pt iii, Answers of Witnesses from the various islands to Q. 29; ibid., pt iv, nos. 17 and 18; *A. & P.*, 1790, xxix (698) 94, 194, 199, 230, 305 and 637–8; L. J. Ragatz, *The Fall of the Planter Class in the British Caribbean, 1763–1833* (reissue, New York, 1963) 191; Francis E. Hyde, Bradbury B. Parkinson and Sheila Marriner, 'The Nature and Profitability of the Liverpool Slave Trade', *Economic History Review*, 2nd series, v (1952–53), 370, 375–6; Bradbury B. Parkinson, 'A Slaver's Accounts', *Accounting Research,* vol. ii (1951) 148–9; Michael Craton and James Walvin, *Jamaica Plantation: the History of*

Worthy Park, 1670–1970 (London, 1970), 131 (together with a private communication from Dr Craton); Stanley Dumbell, 'The Profits of the Guinea Trade', *Economic Journal*, II (1931) 256; J.H. Hodson, 'The Letter Book of Robert Bostock, a Merchant in the Liverpool Slave Trade, 1789–92', *Liverpool Bulletin*, III (1953) 41, 45, 47, 57; *The Commerce of Rhode Island*, vol. I (Massachusetts Historical Collections, 7th series, IX, Boston, 1914) 338–9, 346, 398, 425, 461 and ibid., vol. II (Boston, 1915), 14; Elizabeth Donnan, *Documents*, III 190–91, 195, 196, 199, 242, 286, 309; IV 383 n, 383, 399 n, 403, 421, 431, 440, 450 and 451; Charles R. Hand, '*The Kitty's Amelia*, The Last Liverpool Slaver', *Proceedings of the Lancashire and Cheshire Historic Society*, LXXXII (1930) 72–3; *A. & P.*, 1847–48 (536), Slave Trade Select Committee, 3rd Report, paras. 5653–4, 5690–4, Evidence of Thomas Tobin; sundry voyage accounts from Liverpool sources, especially from the *Leyland Papers* (Picton Library) kindly communicated by Mr Frank Sanderson: *Davies-Davenport MSS* (University of Keele), numerous voyage accounts in RR 57/1, 3–5, 8–10.

It is next necessary to determine the percentage deduction to be made from the gross sale price in respect of expenses incurred in the West Indies or other place of sale. These were, notably, the captain's, mate's, and surgeon's commissions, the commission payable to the slave factor and on the remitting home of the bills of exchange given in payment for the slaves, and various disbursements made by the ship's captain. The problem is that only in a few cases are the deductions of the place of sale given clearly and unambiguously. In six cases, however, the case is clear and, small though the sample is, the range is impressively limited – 20·2 per cent, 19·4 per cent 19·1 per cent 18·9 per cent and 16 per cent (*Liverpool and Slavery*, 108; Accounts of two voyages of the *Hawke* (Hyde *et al*, *Profitability of the Liverpool Slave Trade*, 375–6; of the *Lottery* (1798–99) (*Leyland Papers* in the Picton Library); and of the *Emilia* (*A. & P.*, 1790, XXIX (698) 637–9). Finally we have Tarleton's 'Estimate of African Voyage on basis of two Negroes per ton', in *BT* 6/7. In four further voyages from 1798 onwards deductions averaged 20·7 per cent but it is likely that it was payment of duty which was responsible for the higher rate of deduction (Voyages of the *Earl of Liverpool* (1798 and 1799), *Lottery* (1798–99) and *Enterprise* (1806), kindly communicated by Mr Frank Sanderson). Where it is indicated that such duty payments were included in the gross sale price (for other evidence of this practice see Howe, *Mount Hope: a New England Chronicle*, 121 and W. Robert Higgins, 'Charles Town Merchants and Factors dealing in the External Negro Trade, 1735–1775', *South Carolina Historical Magazine*, LXV (Oct 1961) 205–6) this has been allowed for by reducing the gross figure accordingly, and leaving the deductions made at the place of sale at the 'normal' level of 18 per cent.

Appendix 3

The Outset

The largest sample of ship, outfit and cargo costs is Norris' detailed tabulation of all the ships engaged in the Liverpool slave trade in 1790 (*A. & P.*, 1792, xciii) and which is invested with the authority of his considerable local knowledge, and familiarity with the trade. When the components of the list are adjusted to exclude tenders on the African coast and other items which evidently distort, we are left with a valuation – ship, outfit, cargo and 6 per cent insurance – of £45·5 per ton. Now this estimate was in the period after Dolben's Act of 1788, which regulated the size of slave cargoes and when the outset cost *per ton* must necessarily have been lower than before regulation. (This results from the fact that whilst the ship and outfit component of cost per ton remains constant, the cargo cost per ton must decline because that ton is not permitted to carry as many slaves, and so does not require to carry out as much cargo.) We can quite easily project a cost per ton figure for the pre-Dolben period by applying to the cargo component of the figure of £45·5 per ton (at 65 per cent, justified below, this is £29·6) the ratio of average number of slaves per ton landed in the period before and after Dolben, i.e. 1·85:1·43 (see p. 47 above). The result is that the cargo component must be increased to £38·3 and the revised overall outset figure becomes £54·2 per ton. But we do not only depend on projection, for we have summary estimates of outset costs in 1787, before regulation. Figures provided by Tarleton, a leading Liverpool slave trader, give the average value of 80 Liverpool slave ships, totalling 14,028 tons, with their cargoes, as £47·1 per ton, whilst another account accords to thirty Bristol African ships of 4,195 tons a value of £57·2 per ton (*A. & P.*, 1789, xxvi (646a) pt. iv, no. 3). We also possess three voyage calculations or accounts for this pre-Dolben period which give outset per ton figures of £52·5, £53·6 and

£58·5 respectively (*B.M. Add. MSS 38416* (Liverpool Papers),
f.23, James Jones to Hawkesbury, 14 Feb 1788; *B.T.* 6/7, General
Calculations respecting the effect of Sir William Dolben's Bill,
and Tarleton and Backhouse's estimate of profits of voyage of
Eliza). Since these last three figures include insurance at 6 per
cent, as does the projection, we should assume that the summary
Bristol figure of £57·2 also includes insurance, but that the summary Liverpool figure of £47·1 per ton does not. This evidence
is not good enough to justify strict averaging, but we are perhaps
erring on the conservative side if we postulate an outset figure,
including 6 per cent insurance, of £52 per ton for 1787. We are
not, however, justified in taking the peacetime insurance rate for
every years up to – or for that matter after – 1788, since 1761–62,
1776–80, and 1781–82 must be regarded as wartime years in
which insurance can be taken as increased to 12 per cent. These
wartime years must therefore be debited with an outset cost of
£55 per ton. There is the added problem that neither Norris'
Liverpool list, nor the Liverpool and Bristol summaries, are specific about whether wages have been included in the outfitting cost
– an item probably averaging £4·6 per ton at this time. We have
assumed that wages were included, an assumption which perhaps
underlines the conservatism of our £52/£55 per ton figure for
outset cost. What one might in modern terms call 'remuneration
for management' (or 'taking a salary out of the business') has not
been included in outset cost. (Even at, say, £100 per voyage the
profit figure would, as we shall see, be reduced appreciably by inclusion of an allowance for this item.)

Dolben's Act came into force during 1789 and so the years 1761–
88 will be costed on a 'pre-Dolben' basis. The ensuing period 1789–
99 inclusive forms a unity. We have already observed that cost
per ton, at a 6 per cent insurance rate, runs out at £45·5 per ton
in a given year (1790) in this period. However, the years 1793–99
inclusive were wartime years and a 12 per cent insurance rate
raises the cost per ton to £48·1. The last year of this decade, also
a year of war, is subject to yet another complication stemming from
a further measure of restriction in 1799, which will be taken as effective from 1800 onwards. This additional restriction on slaves
licensed per ton necessarily reduced still further the cost per ton
since still less cargo per ton would be required for the yet smaller

number of slaves allowed. From the exhaustive Norris sample we discover that the cargo constituted 65 per cent of the total valuation in the early post-Dolben years, and we already know that whereas slaves per ton allowed from 1789 were 1·60, there were only 1·03 from 1800. The cargo percentage (65) must there be reduced by $\frac{·57}{1·60}$ as compared with the cost per ton figure for a year in the 1790s. This same further limitation of course lasted for the remainder of the life of the British slave trade. Of the final part decade, 1801–02 will be taken as years of peace, and 1803–07 as years of war. The final complication that we must take account of is the price changes over the years, since our projections so far have been on a constant price level basis. In contrast to the long middle years of the eighteenth century, prices in the Revolutionary and Napoleonic war period rose sharply, and it will be necessary to adjust the rates per ton which we have established by reference to the Schumpeter–Gilboy index of consumer prices (B. R. Mitchell and Phyllis Deane, *Abstract of British Historical Statistics* (Cambridge, 1962) 469. After careful consideration we have used the Consumer Goods index rather than the index of Consumer Goods other than Cereals. This second index trails behind the first and the effect of using it would be to lower outset costs and hence improve profitability. The only period in which there is a really striking difference is 1801–07 – profits of nearly 9 per cent as compared with 3·3 per cent – but the aggregate profit, 1761–1807 merely rises from 9·5 per cent to around 12 per cent. It is, of course, necessary to remember that when the Norris valuation was taken the price index stood at 124, whilst the 1787 estimates were made when the index stood at 117). The outcome of these various calculations is as follows:

	Outset cost per ton p.a. at constant prices	Price change factor	Outset cost per ton p.a. adjusted for price changes	Decennial average
1761–62 (War)	£55	$\frac{94}{117}$	£44·2	
1763–70 (Peace)	£52	$\frac{104}{117}$	£46·2	
1761–70				£45·8
1771–75 (Peace)	£52	$\frac{114}{117}$	£50·7	
1776–80 (War)	£55	$\frac{112}{117}$	£52·6	
1771·80				£51·7
1781–82 (War)	£55	$\frac{116}{117}$	£54·5	
1783–88 (Peace)	£52	$\frac{122}{117}$	£54·2	
1789–90 (Peace) First post-Dolben period begins	£45·5	$\frac{119}{124}$	£43·7	
1781–90				£52·2
1791–92 (Peace)	£45·5	$\frac{122}{124}$	£44·8	
1793–99 (War)	£48·1	$\frac{146}{124}$	£56·6	
1800 (War) Second post-Dolben period begins	£36·9	$\frac{212}{124}$	£63·1	
1791–1800				£55·0
1801–02 (Peace)	£35·0	$\frac{202}{124}$	£56·7	
1803–07 (War)	£36·9	$\frac{175}{124}$	£52·1	
1801–07				£53·4

The validity of a per ton figure in the £45–£55 range for the British trade up to 1788 is borne out by the fact that a per ton figure for ninety-eight voyages of the Middleburg Co. 1741–1800 is £58·3 (Sterling) per ton. When this is adjusted to reflect the apparently different composition of that Company's balance sheet, compared with what we assume to have been included in the British estimates, and with insurance at 6 per cent added, the result is at the very least £50 (Sterling) per ton. This is a crude measure only since detailed comparison of how the two national calculations were made is not possible. Also the Dutch 'Last' is taken as two tons, but whether they were measured tons, as with the British, or, as is perhaps more likely, tons burden, it is not possible to say. If the Dutch 'Last'/Tonnage ratio is to tons burthen, the Dutch outset cost in terms of tons measurement must be higher (see Table 7 and Unger, 'Bijdragen', II 87–9, 107–10).

No attempt has been made to adjust cargo values for the years before and after 1787–90 to take into account the fact that slave prices on the African coast were rising throughout the period. It appears that they may have increased by about 25 per cent during our period (P. Curtin, 'The Atlantic Slave Trade, 1600–1800', *The History of West Africa*, vol. I ed. J. F. Ajayi and Michael Crowder (London, 1971) 255 and information kindly supplied by Dr Richard Bean from his unpublished Ph.D. thesis, 'The British Trans-Atlantic Slave Trade, 1650–1775', (University of Washington, 1971)). However, our evidence about cargo values comes from years not long after the mid-way point of our period. A further limitation of our calculations is that there is no evidence specific enough to allow us to build into the cost per ton figure an allowance for the fact that crew wages increased much more sharply than the price index in the wartime years – sometimes to as much as four or five times pre-war rates (cf. e.g. *B.T.* 6/7, Estimate of African voyage on basis of two Negroes per ton, on the one hand, and Crow, *Memoirs*, 90, together with Charles R. Hand, '*The Kitty's Amelia,* the last Liverpool Slaver', 75–6, on the other).

The reason why the insurance rate of 6 per cent must be increased to 12 per cent for the war years is simply that in wartime insurance was necessarily higher. At points in the Revolutionary and Napoleonic Wars insurance for slave ships rose as high as 20 per cent (*A. & P.,* 1847–8 (536), para 5670 (Evidence of Thomas Tobin) 135–6), but a conservative figure of 12 per cent for the years of warfare will be adopted. This figure is also analogically compatible with insurance rates for vessels engaged in the out-and-back West India trade contained in Richard Pares, *A West India Fortune* (London, 1950) 223. It does not concern us whether or not slave traders actually insured. If one includes insurance, no deduction for ship losses has to be made. In fact wartime losses could be quite high – fifteen Liverpool slavers out of ninety-seven in 1800 for example (information kindly supplied by Mr Frank Sanderson).

Appendix 4

*Deduction from Outset cost in respect of Trade in
African Produce*

Since slavers frequently did an incidental trade in the purchase of
African produce it is necessary to attribute a percentage of voyage
capital to this trade. To arrive at such a figure we must inquire
into the value of this commerce. *A. & P.*, 1789, xxvi (646a), pt. iv,
no. 2 gives the alleged number of ships bringing imports directly
from Africa, together with their tonnage and the value of their
cargoes, in the period 1761–87, as follows:

Period	Ships	Tons	Value of Cargo (£)
1761–70	290	29,004	451,150
1771–80	445	45,448	682,090
1781–87	193	30,417	555,912

A difficulty about this list is that it gives a figure for the number of
ships in the direct trade far higher than all the other evidence
about the out and back trade warrants – an average of 45 a year
between 1771 and 1780, for instance, with 69, 66 and 71 in three
of those years. Yet the captain of a ship in this direct trade told
the 1789 committee that he reckoned the number of ships employed in it as 12–14 in each of the two previous years (ibid., pt.
iv, Appendix to no. 2), whilst Gomer Williams attests that less than
5 per cent of Liverpool African ships, namely 5–8, were employed
in the direct trade (Gomer Williams, *Liverpool Slave Trade*,
Appendix xiv). If one builds on the evidence of a Bristol merchant
in the direct trade, also given to the 1789 committee (*A. & P.*, 1789,
xxvi (646a), pt. iv, Appendix to no. 2) that about half of the ivory
(the second most valuable commodity after redwood) brought from
Africa was carried in slave ships, and applies this proportion to

all African produce, and if we assume that the return mentioned above really did refer to imports directly from Africa, we must conclude that, in the decade 1771–80, for example, slave ships carried another £682,099 worth of African produce, demanding another 45,448 tons of shipping. But this is not credible, for total tonnage of slave ships in the decade was 120,168 and all other evidence is against the necessary implication that that African produce amounted, tonnage wise, to 38 per cent of the capacity of slave ships. The alternative procedure would be to assume that the figures given for direct importation from Africa really relate to imports direct *and* in slave ships, and to assume that half of these by value came in slave ships as part cargo and half in out and back ships. In other words, the value of produce brought in slave ships in the sample decade 1771–80 is either £682,099, or one half of this sum, £341,050. As percentages of the sum of the value of the produce and the gross sale value of the slaves, these figures are 8·2 per cent and 4·3 per cent respectively. If the second assumption is applied to the exiguous evidence about imports in the period after 1787 (S.P., 1808, xi (94) British Imports and Exports, 1805–07, App. A1) the percentage results are, for the decades before and after 1771–80, 2·6, 3·5, 2·8 and 3·8. This assumption is to be preferred since the alternative involves accepting an implausibly high number of ships as engaged in the direct trade, but the percentage figure will be rounded up to 5, and applied to each decade.

Bibliography

Documentary Sources and Contemporary Official Publications are listed first and second; the remainder of the bibliography is divided between sources relating to the slave trade itself, the theme of Part One of this book, and to abolition, the theme of Parts Two to Four. The date of books listed is of the edition used but the date of the first edition has been added when desirable. Since most poems are available in several editions it has usually been sufficient to give date of first publication alone. London is the place of publication of books unless otherwise stated.

MANUSCRIPT SOURCES

British Museum:

  Add. MSS. 21254–21256. Minute Books of the Committee for the Abolition of the Slave Trade, 1787–1819, in the British Museum.
  Add. MSS. 38190–94, 38223, The Liverpool Papers.
  Add. MSS. 41267A (Clarkson MSS).
  Add. MSS 47559 63/65/68/69/71–75/91. Fox MSS.
  Add. MS 52194 Holland House Papers.
  Dropmore MSS. Photocopies made available to me by the late W. B. Hamilton; the Collection has subsequently been acquired by British Museum and is currently being prepared for public use.

Perkins Library, Duke University:
  Stephen Fuller MSS.
  William Smith MSS.
  Wilberforce MSS.

University of Durham:
  Grey Papers.

Friends House Library, London:
  Society of Friends. London Yearly Meeting, Minutes; London Yearly Meeting, Meeting for Sufferings, Minutes and Minutes of Meeting for Sufferings Committee on the Slave Trade; Letters which passed between the Meeting for Sufferings in London and the Meeting for Sufferings in Philadelphia, 1757–1815.

Haverford College:
  Quaker MS Collection incl. Allinson, Cadbury, Evans and Howland

Collections and Microfilm of letters which passed between the Meeting for Sufferings in London and the Meeting for Sufferings in Philadelphia, 1757–1815.

House of Lords Record Office, '[Manuscript] Return to an Order of the Right Honourable the House of Lords dated the 10th of July 1799', containing one extensive list of slave ship itineraries (*Lords A List*) and one list of clearances (*Lords B List*).

Henry E. Huntington Library, San Marino California:
Clarkson MSS.
Macaulay MSS.

Keele University Library:
    Davies Davenport MSS. in the Raymond Richards Collection of Miscellaneous Historical Material.

Lambeth Palace Library:
Porteus MSS. Diary and Transcripts.

National Library of Wales:
Calendar of the Diaries of William Dillwyn.

Historical Society of Pennsylvania:
Pemberton MSS.
Pennsylvania Society for Promoting the Abolition of Slavery. Minute Books, Correspondence, Letter Books.

Public Record Office, London:
*BT6/*1–9, 185, 187/88. On African Trade.
Chatham MSS. P.R.O. 30/8.
H.C.A. 10/31 Dutch Prize Assignation Book.

John Rylands Library, Manchester: *The Crawford Muniments.*

Sharp Transcripts (*J.A.W.*) Transcripts from the Granville Sharp Collection (in the possession of Miss Lloyd Baker, Hardwicke Court, Glos.), kindly made available by Dr J. A. Woods.

Society of West India Planters and Merchants, Minute Books.

Wigan Public Library:
Thornton MSS.

C. E. Wrangham Esq. Collection of Wilberforce Papers, cited as *Wrangham MSS.*

CONTEMPORARY OFFICIAL AND SEMI-OFFICIAL PUBLICATIONS

(A) Great Britain:
    (i) Parliamentary Papers: *Accounts and Papers/Sessional Papers.*
    A. & P. 1789, xxiv (633).
        Minutes of the Evidence taken before a Committee of the Whole House on Regulation of the Slave Trade.

A. & P.   1789, xxvi (646a)
        Report of the Privy Council Committee on the Slave Trade.
    ,,   1790, xxiv (698);
    ,,   1790, xxx (699). Minutes of the Evidence: Select Committee
        on the Slave Trade.
    ,,   1790–91, xxxiv (748), Abstracts of Muster Rolls.
    ,,   1792, xxxv (769) Vessels cleared out to the Coast of Africa
        for Slaves.
S.P. 1806–07, iv (83), Report from the Sugar Distillery Committee.
  ,,   1807, iii (65), Report of the Committee of the House of Commons
    on the West India Colonies.
  ,,   1808, iv (178, 278, 300, 318).
    Committee on the Distillation of Sugar and Molasses and Relief of
    Sugar Growers of the West Indies, Four Reports.

(ii) Parliamentary Debates.

William Cobbett (ed.), *The Parliamentary History of England from the
Earliest Times to the Year 1803*, continued as
T. C. Hansard (ed.), *The Parliamentary Debates from the Year 1803 to the
Present Time.*
J. Debrett, *Parliamentary Register.*
The Senator or Parliamentary Chronicle.
Substance of the Debates on a Resolution for Abolishing the Slave Trade, 1806
(Reissue, 1968).
William Woodfall, *An Impartial Report of the Debates that occur in the
Two Houses of Parliament.*

(B) United States.
Annals of Congress, 1789–1808.

WORKS RELATING WHOLLY OR PRIMARILY TO
THE SLAVE TRADE AND ITS AFRICAN IMPACT

(a) Memoirs, Letters, Pamphlets, Periodicals and other Contemporary
Materials:
    J. Adams, *Sketches taken during Ten Voyages to Africa between the Years 1786
    and 1800* (1822).
    The African Institution, *Reports of the Directors* (1810–1819) 57–75.
    An African Merchant, *A Treatise upon the Trade from Great Britain to
    Africa, humbly recommended to the Attention of Government* (1772).
    *American Convention for Promoting the Abolition of Slavery and Improving the
    Condition of the African Race.* Minutes of the Proceedings of the First
    to Fourth Conventions, 1794–1797 and Ninth Convention, 1804.
    Hugh Crow, *Memoirs* (reissue London, 1970; 1st ed. 1830).
    Bryan Edwards, *The History Civil and Commercial of the British Colonies
    in the West Indies*, 3 vols. (3rd ed., 1801).
    Equiano's Travels, ed. Paul Edwards (1967).
    A. Falconbridge, *An Account of the Slave Trade on the Coast of Africa* (1788).

Joseph Hawkins, *History of a Voyage to the Coast of Africa and Travels into the Interior of that Country* (Troy, N.Y., 1797).

Patrick Kelly, *Universal Cambist and Commercial Instructor being a General Treatise on Exchange including the Monies, Corns, Weights and Measures of all Trading Nations and Colonies*, 2 vols. (London, 1811)

P. Labarthe, *Voyage au Senegal pendant les Années 1784 et 1785* (Paris, 1802).

E. Long, *The History of Jamaica, or the General Survey of the Ancient and Modern State of that Island*, 3 vols. (1774).

John Matthews, *A Voyage to the River Sierra Leone* (reissue 1966, 1st ed. 1788).

[John Newton], *An Authentic Narrative of Some Remarkable and Interesting Particulars in the Life of **** communicated in a Series of Letters to the Reverend Mr. Haweis* (5th ed. 1782).

John Newton, *Letters to a Wife* (1793).

———— *Journal of a Slave Trader*, ed. B. Martin and M. Spurrell (1962).

Nicholas Owen, *Journal of a Slave Dealer: a View of Some Remarkable Accidents in the Life of Nics. Owen on the Coast of Africa and America from the year 1746 to the year 1757*, ed. Eveline C. Martin (1930).

Sir William Young, *West India Common Place Book* (1807).

(b) Secondary Works:

Africa South of the Sahara, 1971 (Europa Year Book, 1971).

I. A. Akinjogbin, *Dahomey and its Neighbours, 1708–1818* (Cambridge, 1967).

E. J. Alagoa, 'The Niger Delta States and their Neighbours, 1600–1800', *The History of West Africa*, ed. J. F. Ade Ajayi and Michael Crowder (1971), I 269–303.

———— 'Long-Distance Trade and States in the Niger Delta', *J.A.H.*, XI (1970) no. 3, 319–29.

Roger Anstey, 'The Volume and Profitability of the British Slave Trade, 1761–1807,' in *Race and Slavery in the Western Hemisphere: Quantitative Studies*, ed. Stanley L. Engerman and Eugene D. Genovese (Princeton, N.J., 1974), 3–31.

T. S. Ashton, *An Economic History of England: The Eighteenth Century* (1955).

T. S. Ashton (ed.), *Letters of a West African Trader, Edward Grace, 1767–70* (1950).

David Birmingham, *Trade and Conflict in Angola: the Mbundu and their Neighbours under the Influence of the Portuguese 1483–1790* (Oxford, 1966).

Pierre H. Boulle, 'Slave Trade, Commercial Organisation and Industrial Growth in Eighteenth Century Nantes', *Revue Française d'Histoire d'Outre-Mer*, LIX (1972) no. 214, 70–112.

George E. Brooks, Jr., *Yankee Traders, Old Coasters and Middlemen* (Boston, 1970).

The Commerce of Rhode Island, 2 vols, Massachussetts Historical Collections, 7th ser. (Boston, 1914–15).

R. Craig and R. Jarvis, *Liverpool Registry of Merchant Ships*, Chetham Society, xv, 3rd series (Manchester, 1967).

Michael Craton and James Walvin, *Jamaica Plantation: the History of Worthy Park, 1670–1970* (1970).

I. Cunnison, 'Kazambe and the Portuguese, 1798–1832', *J.A.H.*, ii (1961), No. 1, 61–76.

Philip D. Curtin, *The Atlantic Slave Trade: A Census* (Wisconsin, 1969).

——— 'The Atlantic Slave Trade, 1600–1800', in *The History of West Africa*, i, ed. J. F. Ajayi and M. Crowder (1971) 240–68.

Philip D. Curtin and J. Vansina, 'Sources of the Nineteenth Century Atlantic Slave Trade', *J.A.H.*, v (1964) no. 2, 185–208.

Basil Davidson, *Black Mother* (1961).

K. G. Davies, 'The Origins of the Commission System in the West India Trade', *Transactions of the Royal Historical Society*, 5th ser., ii (1952) 89–107.

——— *The Royal African Company* (1957).

——— 'Essays in Bibliography and Criticism, xliv, Empire and Capital', *Economic History Review*, 2nd ser., xiii (1960–61) 105–110.

Ralph Davis, *The Rise of the English Shipping Industry in the Seventeenth and Eighteenth Centuries* (1962).

Phyllis Deane and W. A. Cole, *British Economic Growth, 1688–1959* (Cambridge, 1964).

Noel Deerr, *A History of Sugar*, 2 vols. (1949–50).

Hubert Deschamps, *Historie de la Traite des Noirs de l'Antiquité à nos Jours* (Paris 1971).

K. O. Dike, *Trade and Politics in the Niger Delta, 1830–1885* (Oxford, 1956).

Elizabeth Donnan, *Documents Illustrative of the History of the Slave Trade to America*, 4 vols. (New York, 1929).

W. E. Dubois, *The Suppression of the African Slave Trade to the United States of America, 1638–1870* (New York, 1896).

Stanley Dumbell, 'The Profits of the Guinea Trade', *Economic Journal*, ii (1931) 254–7.

Stanley L. Engerman, 'The Slave Trade and British Capital Formation in the Eighteenth Century: a Comment on the Williams Thesis', *The Business History Review*, xlvi, no. 4 (Winter 1972), 430–43.

J. D. Fage, 'Slavery and the Slave Trade in the Context of West African History', *J.A.H.*, x (1969), no. 3, 393–404.

M. W. Flinn, *Origins of the Industrial Revolution* (1969).

Daryll Forde (ed.) *Efik Traders of Old Calabar* (1956).

Christopher Fyfe, *A History of Sierra Leone* (1962).

M. Goulart, *Escravidăo africana no Brasil* (São Paulo, 1950).

Richard Gray and David Birmingham, 'Some Economic and Political Consequences of Trade in Central and Eastern Africa in the Pre-Colonial Period', *Pre-Colonial African Trade: Essays on Trade in Central and Eastern Africa before 1900*, ed. Gray and Birmingham (1970) 1–23.

Sv. E. Green-Pedersen, 'The Scope and Structure of the Danish Slave

Trade', *The Scandinavian Economic History Review*, XIX (1971), no. 2, 149–97.

P. E. H. Hair, 'The Enslavement of Koelle's Informants', *J. A. H.*, VI (1965) no. 2, 193–203.

Charles R. Hand, '*The Kitty's Amelia*, the Last Liverpool Slaver'. *Proceedings of the Lancashire and Cheshire Historic Society*, LXXXII (1930), 69–80.

Franz Hochstetter, Die wirtschaftlichen und politischen Motive für die Abschaffung des britischen Sklavenhandels im Jahre 1806/1807 (Leipzig, 1905).

J. H. Hodson, 'The Letter Book of Robert Bostock, a Merchant in the Liverpool Slave Trade, 1789–1792', *The Liverpool Bulletin*, III (1953), 37–59.

Francis E. Hyde, Bradbury B. Parkinson and Sheila Marriner, 'The Nature and Profitability of the Liverpool Slave Trade', *Economic History Review*, 2nd ser., V (1952–53) 368–77.

L. Jadin, 'Relations sur le Royaume du Congo de P. Raimondo da Dicomano, Missionaire de 1791 à 1795', *Bulletin de l'Académie Royale des Sciences Coloniales*, III (1957) no. 2, 307–37.

C. L. R. James, *The Black Jacobins: Toussaint l'Ouverture and the San Domingo Revolution* (New York, 1963; 1st ed. London, 1938).

Marion Johnson, 'The Ounce in Eighteenth Century West African Trade', *J.A.H.*, VII (1966) no. 2, 197–214.

G. I. Jones, *The Trading States of the Oil Rivers* (1963).

Gertrude S. Kimball, *Providence in Colonial Times* (Boston and New York, 1912).

Herbert S. Klein, 'The Trade in African Slaves to Rio de Janeiro, 1795–1811: Estimates of Mortality and Patterns of Voyages', *J.A.H.* X (1969) no. 4, 533–49.

—— 'The Portuguese Slave Trade from Angola in the Eighteenth Century', *The Journal of Economic History*, XXXII, no. 4 (Dec 1972) 894–918.

A. J. H. Latham, 'Currency, Credit and Capitalism on the Cross River in the Pre-Colonial Era', *J.A.H.*, XII (1971) no. 4, 599–605.

—— *Old Calabar 1600–1891: The Impact of the International Economy upon a Traditional Society* (Oxford, 1973).

R. C. C. Law, 'The Constitutional Troubles of Oyo in the Eighteenth Century', *J.A.H.*, XII (1971) no. 1, 25–44.

E. Phillip LeVeen, 'British Slave Trade Suppression Policies, 1821–1865: Impact and Implication' (Univeristy of Chicago Ph.D. Dissertation, 1971).

Liverpool and Slavery: an Historical Account of the Liverpool-African Slave Trade. Was it the Cause of the Prosperity of the Town? By a Genuine 'Dicky Sam', (reissue Newcastle-upon-Tyne 1969; 1st ed. Liverpool, 1884).

P. C. Lloyd, *The Political Development of Yoruba Kingdoms in the Eighteenth and Nineteenth Centuries* (Royal Anthropological Institute Occasional Paper, no. 31, 1971).

Averil Mackenzie-Grieve, *The Last Years of the English Slave Trade, Liverpool, 1750–1807* (1941).

D. Mannix and M. Cowley, *Black Cargoes* (New York, 1962).

P. Mantoux, *The Industrial Revolution in the Eighteenth Century* (New impression, 1962; 1st French Ed., 1906).

Gaston Martin, *Nantes au XVIIIᵉ Siècle: l'Ere des Négriers* (1714–1774) (Paris, 1931).

Phyllis M. Martin, 'The Trade of Loango in the Seventeenth Century and Eighteenth Century', in *Pre-Colonial African Trade*, ed. Richard Gray and David Birmingham (1970) 139–61.

——— *The External Trade of the Loango Coast 1576–1870: the Effects of changing commercial relations on the Vili Kingdom of Loango* (Oxford, 1972).

J. E. Merritt, 'The Triangular Trade', *Business History*, III (1960) 1–7.

Jean Meyer, 'Le Commerce négrier nantais, 1772–1792', *Annales, Economies, Sociétés, Civilizations*, xv (1960).

——— *L'Armement nantais dans la Deuxième Moitié du XVIIIᵉ Siècle* (Paris, 1969).

Joseph C. Miller, 'The Imbangala and the Chronology of Early Central African History', *J.A.H.* XIII (1972) no. 4, 549–74.

W. E. Minchinton, *The Trade of Bristol in the Eighteenth Century* (re-issue, Bristol, 1966).

B. R. Mitchell and Phyllis Deane, *Abstract of British Historical Statistics* (Cambridge, 1962).

P. Morton-Williams, 'The Yoruba Kingdom of Oyo', *West African Kingdoms in the Nineteenth Century*, ed. Daryll Forde and P. M. Kaberry (reissue, 1971), 36–69.

——— 'The Oyo Yoruba and the Atlantic Slave Trade, 1670–1830', *Journal of the Historical Society of Nigeria*, III, no. 1, 1964, 25–45.

C. W. Newbury, *The Western Slave Coast and its Rulers* (Oxford, 1961).

David Northrup, 'The Growth of Trade among the Igbo before 1800, *J.A.H.*, XIII (1972) no. 2, 217–36.

Richard Pares, 'The Economic Factors in the History of the Empire', *Economic History Review*, VII (1936–37) 119–144.

Bradbury B. Parkinson, 'A Slaver's Accounts', *Accounting Research*, II (1951) 144–9.

C. N. Parkinson, *The Rise of the Port of Liverpool* (Liverpool, 1952).

K. David Patterson, 'Early Knowledge of the Ogowe River and the American Exploration of 1854', *International Journal of African Historical Studies*, v (1972) no. 1, 75–90.

F. W. Pitman, *The Development of the British West Indies, 1700–1763* (reissue, 1967).

Karl Polanyi, 'Sortings and "Ounce Trade" in the West African Slave Trade', *J.A.H.*, v (1964) no. 3, 381–93.

——— *Dahomey and the Slave Trade* (Seattle and London, 1966).

Johannes Postma, 'The Dimension of the Dutch Slave Trade from Western Africa', *J.A.H.*, XIII (1972) no. 2, 237–48.

Margaret Priestley, *West African Trade and Coast Society: a Family Study* (1969).

L. J. Ragatz, *The Fall of the Planter Class in the British Caribbean, 1763–1833* (New York, 1928).

D. Rinchon, *Le Trafic Negrier* (Paris and Brussels, 1938),

——— *La Traite et l'Esclavage des Congolais par les Européens* (Brussels, 1929).

——— *Les Armements Négriers au XVIIIᵉ Siècle d'après la Correspondance et la Comptabilité des Armateurs et des Capitaines nantais* (Brussels, 1956).

Walter Rodney, *A History of the Upper Guinea Coast, 1545–1800* (Oxford, 1970).

Simon Rottenberg, 'The Business of Slave Trading', *South Atlantic Quarterly*, LXVI, no. 3 (Summer 1967) 409–23.

A. F. C. Ryder, *Benin and the Europeans, 1485–1897* (1969).

Frank Sanderson 'Bibliographical Essay: Liverpool and the Slave Trade: A Guide to Sources', *Transactions of the Historic Society of Lancashire and Cheshire*, Vol. 124 (1973) 154–76.

R. B. Sheridan, 'The Commercial and Financial Organisation of the British Slave Trade, 1750–1897', *Economic History Review*, 2nd Ser., XI (1958) no. 2, 249–63.

——— 'The Wealth of Jamaica in the Eighteenth Century', ibid., 2nd ser., XVIII (1965) 292–311.

——— 'A Rejoiner', ibid., 2nd ser., XXI (1968) 46–61.

R. P. Thomas, 'The Sugar Colonies of the Old Empire: Profit or loss for Great Britain?', *Economic History Review*, 2nd ser., XXI (1968) 30–45.

The Transatlantic Slave Trade from West Africa, ed. Christopher Fyfe. (Centre of African Studies, Edinburgh University, duplicated, 1965).

W. S. Unger, 'Bijdragen tot de Geschiedenis van de Nederlandse Slavenhandel: (i) Beknopt Overzicht van de Nederlandse Slavenhandel in het Algemeen', *Economisch-historisch Jaarboek* (The Hague), vol. XXVI (1965) 133–74, and (ii) De Slavenhandel der Middelburgsche Commercie Compagnie, 1732–1808, ibid., XXVIII (1961 3–148.

J. Vansina, *The Kingdoms of the Savanna* (Madison, 1966).

———'Long-Distance Trade Routes in Central Africa', *J.A.H.*, III (1962) no. 3, 375–90.

J. L. Vellut, 'Relations internationales du Moyen-Kwango et de l'Angola dans la deuxieme moitié du XVIIIᵉ Siècle', *Etudes d'Histoire africaine*, I (1970) 75–135.

Pierre Verger, *Bahia and the West Coast Trade, 1549–1851* (Ibadan, 1964),

Perry Viles, 'The Slaving Interest in the Atlantic Ports, 1763–1792'. *French Historical Studies*, VII, 4 (Autumn 1972) 529–43.

A. P. Wadsworth and Julia de L. Mann, *The Cotton Trade and Industrial Lancashire* (Manchester, 1931).

Darold D. Wax, 'Negro Imports into Pennsylvania, 1720–1766', *Pennsylvania History*, XXXII (July 1965) 254–87.

W. B. Weeden, *Economic and Social History of New England, 1620–1789*, 2 vols. (Boston, 1890).

Ivor Wilks, 'The Mossi and Akan States, 1500–1800', *History of West Africa*, I 344–86.

Gomer Williams, *History of the Liverpool Privateers and Letters of Marque with an Account of the Liverpool Slave Trade* (1897).

Christopher Wrigley, 'Historicism in Africa', *African Affairs*, LXX, no. 279 (April 1971) 113–24.

WORKS RELATING WHOLLY OR PRIMARILY TO THE INTELLECTUAL AND
RELIGIOUS ORIGINS, AND POLITICS OF ABOLITION

(a) Memoirs, Letters, Pamphlets, Periodicals and other Contemporary Materials:

An Abstract of the Evidence delivered before a Select Committee on the House of Commons in the years 1790 and 1791 on the part of the Petitioners for the Abolition of the Slave Trade. London 1791. Published by J. Phillips.

Sir Charles E. Adam (ed.) *The Political State of Scotland in the Last Century, A Confidential Report on the Political Opinions, Family Connections and Personal Circumstances of the 2662 County Voters in 1788* (Edinburgh, 1887).

The Annual Register

Anon (By the Author of Letters to a Young Planter) [George Turnbull], *An Apology for Negro Slavery: or the West India Planters vindicated from the Charge of Inhumanity* (1786).

Anon., *A Very New PAMPHLET indeed! Being the TRUTH addressed to THE PEOPLE AT LARGE containing some strictures on the ENGLISH JACOBINS and THE EVIDENCE OF LORD McCARTNEY, and others, Before the HOUSE OF LORDS, respecting THE SLAVE TRADE* (1792).

Anon., *A Second Address to the Right Reverend the Prelates of England and Wales on the Subject of the Slave Trade* (1795).

A. Aspinall (ed.), *The Later Correspondence of George III*, 5 vols. (Cambridge, 1963–66).

James Beattie, *Elements of Moral Science*, 2 vols. (3rd ed., Edinburgh, 1817; 1st ed. 1790–93).

Aphra Behn, *Oroonoko: The Royal Slave* (1688: various subsequent versions).

A. Benezet, *Observations on the Enslaving, Importing and Purchasing of Negroes with some Advice thereon extracted from the Yearly Meeting Epistle of London for the Present Year* (Germantown, 1759).

—— *A Caution to Great Britain and her Colonies in a Short Representation of the Calamitous State of the Enslaved Negroes in the British Dominions* (1784; 1st ed. 1766).

—— *Some Historical Account of Guinea, Its Situation, Produce and the General Disposition of its Inhabitants with an Inquiry into the Rise and Progress of the Slave Trade, Its Nature and Lamentable Effects* (Reissue, 1968; 1st ed. 1771).

—— *Serious Reflections affectionately recommended to the well disposed of every religious Denomination, particularly those who mourn and lament on account of the Calamities which attend us.* (Philadelphia 1778).

————— *The Case of our Fellow-Creatures the Oppressed Africans, respectfully recommended to the Serious Consideration of the Legislature of Great Britain by the People called Quakers* (1783).

G. Berkeley, *Works*, 2 vols. ed. A. C. Fraser (Oxford, 1871).

Bishop of Bath and Wells (ed.) *The Journal and Correspondence of William, Lord Auckland*, 4 Vols. (1861–62).

Wm Blackstone, *Commentaries on the Laws of England*, 4 vols. (Reissue 1966 of 1st ed. with supplement, Oxford, 1765–69).

James Boswell, *Life of Johnson* (Oxford Standard Authors ed., London, 1965).

Henry Brougham, *Historical Sketches of Statesmen who flourished in the Reign of George III*, in *Collected Works* (London and Glasgow 1855), III.

————— *Inquiry into the Colonial Policy of the European Powers*, 2 Vols. (1803).

————— *A Concise Statement of the Question regarding the Abolition of the Slave Trade* (1804).

Edmund Burke, *Collected Works* (1852 ed.) vol. v.

Joseph Butler, *The Analogy of Religion Natural and Revealed to the Constitution and Course of Nature* (2nd ed. *1736*; 1st ed. *1736*).

L. M. Butterfield (ed.) *Letters of Benjamin Rush*, 2 vols (Princeton, 1951).

The Christian Observer, 1802–1807.

Thomas Clarkson, *The History of the Rise, Progress and Accomplishment of the Abolition of the African Slave Trade by the British Parliament*, 2 vols. (reissue 1968; 1st ed. 1808).

————— *An Essay on the Impolicy of the African Slave Trade* (1788).

————— *An Essay on the Slavery and Commerce of the Human Species, particularly the African* (1786).

Wm Cobbett, *A History of the Last Hundred Days of English Freedom*, ed. J. L. Hammond (1921).

Cobbett's Political Register.

Wm Collins, *Ode to Liberty* (1746).

Wm. Cowper, *Poetical Works* (4th ed., Oxford 1967).

————— *Poetry and Prose*, ed. Brian Spiller (1968).

Thomas Day, *The Dying Negro, a Poetical Epistle* (1773).

Philip Doddridge, *Reflections on the Conduct of Divine Providence in the Course and Conclusion of the late War: a Sermon preached at Northampton on April 25, 1749.*

————— *The Rise and Progress of Religion in the Soul* (10th ed. 1771; 1st ed. 1745).

The Edinburgh Review

Epistles from the Yearly Meeting of Friends in London to the Quarterly and Monthly Meetings in Great Britain, Ireland and elsewhere from 1675 to 1857 inclusive (1858).

Adam Ferguson, *Essay on Civil Society* (Reissue, Edinburgh 1966, ed. Duncan Forbes; 1st ed. 1767).

S. M. Hamilton (ed.), *The Writings of James Monroe* (New York 1900), vol. IV.

James Harris, *Diaries and Correspondence of James Harris, First Earl of Malmesbury*, 4 Vols (1844).

Historical Manuscripts Commission, *Report on the Manuscripts of J. B. Fortescue Esq., preserved at Dropmore*, 10 vols. (1892 ff.)

David Hume, *Essays Moral, Political and Literary* (Reissue 1904; 1st ed. 1741–42.

Frances Hutcheson, *A System of Moral Philosophy*, 2 vols, preface by Wm Leechman (1755).

C. R. King (ed.), *The Life and Correspondence of Rufus King*, 6 vols. (New York, 1894–1900).

Benjamin Lay, *All Slave-Keepers that Keep the Innocent in Bondage, Apostates Pretending to lay Claim to the Pure Holy Christian Religion; of What Congregation so Ever; but Especially in Their Ministers, by Whose Example the Filthy Leprosy and Apostacy is Spread Far and Near; It is a notorious Sin, Which Many of the True Friends of Christ, and His Pure Truth, Called Quakers, Has Been for Many Years and Still Are Concern'd to Write and Bear Testimony Against, as a Practice so Gross and Hurtful to Religion, and Destructive to Government, Beyond What Words Ever Set Forth, or Can be Declared of by Men or Angels, and Yet Lived in by Ministers and Magistrates in America* (Philadelphia, 1737).

J. Millar, *The Origin of the Distinction of Ranks* (3rd ed. 1779).

C.-L. de S. Montesquieu, *L'Esprit des Lois* (1748); English trans. by J. V. Prichard and T. Nugent (1878).

Hannah More, *Works*, 2 vols. (1818).

Phillips P. Moulton (ed.), *The Journal and Major Essays of John Woolman* (New York, 1971).

The New Annual Register

Wm Paley, *The Principles of Moral and Political Philosophy* (1785) in *Works* (1828) I.

—— *Natural Theology* (1802) in ibid., II 4–200.

Alexander Pope, *Essay on Man* (1734).

Josiah Pratt (ed.), *Eclectic Notes; or notes of discussions on religious topics, at the meetings of the Eclectic Society, London, during the years 1798–1814* (1856).

James Ramsay, *An Essay on the Treatment and Conversion of African Slaves in the Sugar Colonies* (1784).

—— *An Enquiry into the Effects of the Abolition of the Slave Trade* (1784).

Abbé G. T. F. Raynal, *A Philosophical and Political History of the Settlements and Trade of the Europeans in the East and West Indies*, trans. J. O. Justamond, 8 vols. (1783).

Thomas Reid, *Works*, 2 vols., ed. Sir Wm. Hamilton (Edinburgh, 1880).

William Robertson, *History of America*, 2nd. ed. (1778).

George Rose, *Diaries and Correspondence*, 2 vols., ed. Rev. L. V. Harcourt (1860).

J.-J. Rousseau, *Le Contrat Social* (1762), trans. by G. D. H. Cole as *The Social Contract* (1968).

Ld. John Russell, *Memorials and Correspondence of Charles James Fox*, 4 vols. (1853–57).

Thomas Scott, *Commentary on the Holy Bible* (1792).

Granville Sharp, *A Declaration of the People's Natural Right to a Share in the Legislature* (1774).

——— *Mémoire sur les causes des Calamités Publiques qui règnent à présent partout l'Etendue de l'Ancien Empire Romain* (1776).

——— *The Law of Retribution* (1776).

——— *The Law of Liberty, or Royal Law by which all Mankind will certainly be judged* (1776).

——— *The Just Limitation of Slavery in the Laws of God* (1776).

——— *The Law of Passive Obedience* (1776).

——— *A COLLECTION OF POLITICAL PAPERS concerning the most dangerous factions that have annoyed mankind within the last twelve centuries; and the necessity of guarding against their influence in all CHRISTIAN STATES by requiring an acknowledgement of the CONSTITUTIONAL FOUNDATIONS OF POLITICAL AND RELIGIOUS LIBERTY as the TEST OF A LEGAL QUALIFICATION for the due exercise of SUFFRAGE, TRUST, OR AUTHORITY, IN ANY SUCH STATE* (1797).

Adam Smith, *The Theory of Moral Sentiments*, ed. E. G. West (New York 1919; 1st ed. 1759).

——— *An Inquiry into the Nature and Causes of the Wealth of Nations* (1920, ed. E. R. A. Seligman; 1st ed. 1776).

Society for Effecting the Abolition of the Slave Trade, 30 July 1806 (Title of a pamphlet published by the Society).

James Stephen, *The Crisis of the Sugar Colonies* (1802).

——— *The War in Disguise, or the Frauds of the Neutral Flags* (3rd ed. 1917; 1st ed. 1806).

——— *The Dangers of the Country* (1807).

——— *New Reasons for Abolishing the Slave Trade, being the last section of a larger work, now first published entitled the Dangers of the Country* (1807).

——— *Memoirs*, ed. Merle M. Bevington (1954).

Summary View of the Slave Trade and of the Probable Consequences of its Abolition 1787 (Pamphlet printed by J. Phillips).

James Thomson, *Liberty* (1734–36).

Archbishop Tillotson, *Works*, 3 vols. (9th ed. 1728).

F.-M. A. Voltaire, *Dictionaire Philosophique* (1764), trans. as *Philosophical Dictionary*, 1824.

H. B. Wheatley (ed.) *Historical and Posthumous Memoirs of Sir Nathanie William Wraxall* (1884) v.

A. M. Wilberforce, *The Private Papers of William Wilberforce* (1897).

Robert Isaac and Samuel Wilberforce, *The Life of William Wilberforce*, 5 vols. (1838).

——— *The Correspondence of William Wilberforce*, 2 vols. (1840).

Wm Wilberforce, *Practical View of the Prevailing Religious System of Professed Christians in the Higher and Middle Classes in the County contrasted with real Christianity* (Dublin, 1801; 1st ed., 1797).

―― *A Letter on the Abolition of the Slave Trade; addressed to the Inhabitants of Yorkshire* (1807).

Joshua Wilson, *Biographical Index to the House of Commons* (1806).

Edward Young, *Night Thoughts* (1747).

(b) Secondary Works:

Roger Anstey, 'Capitalism and Slavery: a Critique', *Economic History Review* 2nd Ser. XXI (1968) no. 2, 307–20.

―― 'A Re-Interpretation of the Abolition of the British Slave Trade, 1806–07', *E.H.R.*, LXXXVII (Apr 1972) no. 343, 304–32.

A. Aspinall, 'The Cabinet Council, 1780–1832', *Proceedings of the British Academy*, XXXVIII (1952) 145–252.

A. Aspinall and E. A. Smith (eds.), *English Historical Documents*, XI (1959).

R. A. Austen and W. D. Smith, 'Images of Africa and British Slave Trade Abolition: the Transition to an Imperialist Ideology, 1787–1807', *African Historical Studies*, II (1969) no. 1, 69–83.

Josceline Bagot (ed.), *George Canning and his Friends*, 2 vols. (1909).

Frank Baker, *The Relations between the Society of Friends and Early Methodism* (1949, reprinted from the *London Quarterly* and *Holborn Review*).

W. Baker, 'William Wilberforce on the Idea of Negro Inferiority', *Journal of the History of Ideas*, XXXI (1970) no. 3, 433–40.

D. G. Barnes, *George III and William Pitt, 1783–1806* (1965).

M. C. Battestin, *The Moral Basis of Fielding's Art* (Middletown, Conn., (1964).

Wm Bentley, *Diary of William Bentley D.D.*, 4 Vols. (Salem, 1905–14).

G. F. A. Best, 'The Evangelicals and the Established Church in the Early Nineteenth Century', *The Journal of Theological Studies*, X. (1959), 63–78.

E. C. Black, *The Association: British Extra-Parliamentary Political Organisation, 1769–1793* (Cambridge, Mass., 1963).

G. S. Brookes, *Friend Anthony Benezet* (London and Philadelphia, 1937).

Ford K. Brown, *Fathers of the Victorians* (Cambridge, 1961).

P. A. Brown, *The French Revolution in English History* (Reissue, 1965).

J. H. Brumfitt, 'Scotland and the French Enlightenment' in *The Age of the Enlightenment: Studies presented to Theodore Besterman*, ed. W. H. Barber and others (Edinburgh and London, 1967) 318–29.

Gladys Bryson, *Man and Society: the Scottish Inquiry of the Eighteenth Century* (Princeton, 1945).

J. B. Bury, *The Idea of Progress* (1920).

H. Butterfield, *The Origins of Modern Science* (1950).

John Cannon, *Parliamentary Reform, 1640–1832* (Cambridge, 1973).

S. C. Carpenter, *Eighteenth Century Church and People* (1959).

E. Cassirer, *The Philosophy of the Enlightenment* (Princeton, 1951).

Lord David Cecil, *The Stricken Deer or the Life of Cowper* (1938 ed.)

I. R. Christie, *The End of North's Ministry 1780–1782* (1958).

—— *Wilkes, Wyvill and Reform: The Parliamentary Reform Movement in British Politics 1760–1785* (1962).

A. Cobban, *Edmund Burke and the Revolt against the Eighteenth Century* (1962).

J. C. Colquhoun, *Wilberforce, His Friends and His Times* (1866).

T. W. Copeland, *Edmund Burke* (1950),

R. Coupland, *Wilberforce* (1945; 1st ed., Oxford, 1923).

—— *The British Anti-Slavery Movement* (1933).

—— 'The Abolition of the Slave Trade', *C.H.B.E.*, II 188–216.

C. P. Courtney, *Montesquieu and Burke* (Oxford, 1963).

G. R. Cragg, *Reason and Authority in the Eighteenth Century* (Cambridge, 1964).

R. S. Crane, *The Idea of the Humanities and Other Essays Critical and Historical*, 2 vols. (Chicago, 1967).

Lester G. Crocker, *An Age of Crisis: Man and the World in Eighteenth Century French Thought* (Baltimore, 1959).

F. Crouzet, *L'Economie Britannique et le Blocus Continental, 1806–1813* (Paris, 1958).

Philip D. Curtin, *The Image of Africa: British Ideas and Action, 1780–1850*. (Madison, 1964).

Rupert Davies and Gordon Rupp (eds.), *A History of the Methodist Church in Great Britain*, vol. I (1965).

David Brion Davis, *The Problem of Slavery in Western Culture* (Ithaca, 1966).

—— 'New Sidelights on Early Anti-Slavery Radicalism', *William and Mary Quarterly*, 3rd ser., XXVIII, no. 4 (Oct 1971), 585–94.

—— *The Problem of Slavery in the Age of Revolution, 1770–1823* (Ithaca, 1975).

Richard W. Davis, *Dissent in Politics 1780–1830: the Political Life of William Smith M.P.* (1971).

Thomas E. Drake, *Quakers and Slavery in America* (New Haven 1950).

John Ehrman, *The Younger Pitt* (1969).

W. H. Elkins, *British Policy in its Relation to the Commerce and Navigation of the U.S.A. from 1794 to 1807* (Oxford University D. Phil thesis, 1936).

Hoxie Fairchild, *Religious Trends in English Poetry*, Vol. II (New York, 1958).

R. R. Fennessy, *Burke, Paine and the Rights of Man* (The Hague, 1963).

Betty Fladeland, *Men and Brothers: Anglo-American Anti-Slavery Co-operation* (Urbana and London, 1972).

F. T. H. Fletcher, *Montesquieu and English Politics, 1750–1800* (1939).

A. S. Foord, *His Majesty's Opposition 1714–1830* (Oxford, 1964).

E. M. Forster, *Marianne Thornton, 1797–1877* (1956).

Holden Furber, *Henry Dundas, First Viscount Melville, 1742–1811* (Oxford, 1931).

Anne T. Gary, 'The Political and Economic Relations of English and American Quakers' (Oxford University D.Phil Thesis, 1935).

Peter Gay, *The Enlightenment: an Interpretation. Volume II: The Science of Freedom* (New York, 1969).

Eugene D. Genovese, 'Materialism and Idealism in the History of Negro Slavery in the Americans'. *Slavery in the New World: a Reader in Comparative History*, ed. Laura Foner and Eugene D. Genovese (Englewood Cliffs, 1969) 238–55.

Leo Gershoy, *From Despotism to Revolution, 1763–1789* (New York and London, 1944).

F. C. Gill, *The Romantic Movement and Methodism* (1954).

Thomas Gisborne, *The Principles of Moral Philosophy* (2nd ed. 1790 and 5th ed. 1798).

Norman Goldhawk, 'William Paley: or the Eighteenth Century Revisited', in *Providence*, ed. Maurice Wiles (1969, S.P.C.K. Theological Collections No. 12) 50–61.

V. H. H. Green, *John Wesley* (1964).

E. Halévy, *The Growth of Philosophic Radicalism* (4th ed. 1952).

W. B. Hamilton, 'Constitutional and Political Reflections on the Dismissal of Lord Grenville's Ministry', *Canadian Historical Association Report, 1964.*

A. D. Harvey, 'The Ministry of All the Talents: The Whigs in Office, February 1806 to March 1807', *The Historical Journal*, xv (1972) no. 4, 619–48.

P. Hazard, *European Thought in the Eighteenth Century*, trans. J. Lewis May (1954).

E. Heckscher, *The Continental System* (Oxford, 1922).

B. W. Higman, 'The London West India Interest, 1807–1833', *Historical Studies*, xiii, no. 49 (Oct 1967).

Prince Hoare, *Life of Granville Sharp*, 2 vols. (1828).

R. Horsman, *Causes of the War of 1812* (Philadelphia, 1967).

E. M. Howse, *Saints in Politics: The Clapham Sect and the Growth of Freedom* (2nd English impression, 1971).

A. R. Humphreys, 'The Social Setting' in *Pelican Guide to English Literature* iv: *From Dryden to Johnson*, ed. B. Ford (1970).

E. M. Hunt, 'The North of England Agitation for the Abolition of the Slave Trade, 1780–1800' (Manchester University M.A. thesis, 1959).

Dallas D. Irvine, 'The Abbé Raynal and British Humanitarianism', *Journal of Modern History*, iii (1931) 564–77.

Sydney V. James, *A People Among Peoples: Quaker Benevolence in Eighteenth-Century America* (Cambridge, Mass., 1963).

———— 'The Impact of the American Revolution on Quakers' Ideas about their Sect', *William and Mary Quarterly*, 3rd ser., xix (1962), 360–82.

Russell P. Jameson, *Montesquieu et l'Esclavage: Etude sur les Origines de l'Opinion anti-esclavagiste en France au XVIII Siècle* (Paris, 1911).

Rufus Jones, *The Later Periods of Quakerism*, 2 vols. (1921).

G. P. Judd, *Members of Parliament, 1734–1832* (New Haven, Conn., 1955).

Frank J. Klingberg, *The Anti-Slavery Movement in England* (New Haven, Conn., 1926).

Viscountess Knutsford, *The Life and Letters of Zachary Macaulay* (1900).

Michael Kraus, *The Atlantic Civilisation: Eighteenth Century Origins* (Ithaca, 1949).

—— 'Slavery Reform in the Eighteenth Century: An Aspect of Transatlantic Intellectual Co-operation', *Pennsylvania Magazine of History and Biography*, LX (1936) 53–66.

E. C. P. Lascelles, *Granville Sharp and the Freedom of the Slaves in England* (1928).

Wm Law, *A Serious Call to a Devout and Holy Life* (Everyman ed., 1967; 1st ed. 1728).

P. C. Lipscomb, 'William Pitt and the Abolition of the Slave Trade' (University of Texas Ph.D. thesis, 1960).

—— 'William Pitt and the Abolition Question: a Review of an Historical Controversy', *Proc. of the Leeds Philosophical and Literary Society*, XII pt IV (1967) 87–128.

—— 'Party Politics, 1801–1802: George Canning and the Trinidad Question', *The Historical Journal*, XII (1969) no. 3, 442–66.

Mary S. Locke, *Anti-Slavery in America, 1619–1801* (Boston, 1901).

A. O. Lovejoy, *The Great Chain of Being* (New York, 1965; 1st ed. 1936).

Oliver Macdonagh, *A Pattern of Government Growth, 1800–1860* (London, 1961).

—— 'The Nineteenth-Century Revolution in Government: a Re-Appraisal', *The Historical Journal*, I (1958) no. 1, 52–67.

A. D. McKillop, *The Background of the Seasons* (Hamden, Conn., 1961).

S. Maccoby, *English Radicalism 1786–1832* (1955).

Ed. C. Mack, *Public Schools and British Opinion 1780–1860* (1938).

A. T. Mahan, *Sea Power in its Relations to the War of 1812*, 2 vols. (Boston, 1905).

Bernard Martin *John Newton* (1950).

Donald G. Mathews, *Slavery and Methodism: A Chapter in American Morality 1780–1845* (Princeton, N.J., 1965).

Standish Meacham, *Henry Thornton of Clapham, 1760–1815* (Cambridge, Mass., 1964).

D. Mornet, *French Thought in the Eighteenth Century*, trans. L. M. Levin (Hamden, Conn., 1969).

L. B. Namier, *England in the Age of the American Revolution* (1963 ed.).

L. B. Namier and John Brooke, *The Commons 1754–90*, 3 vols. (History of Parliament Series, 1964).

Chester New, *Life of Henry Brougham to 1830* (Oxford, 1961).

J. H. Overton and F. Relton, *The English Church from the Accession of George I to the End of the Eighteenth Century* (Reissue, 1926).

David Owen, *English Philanthropy 1660–1960*. (Cambridge, Mass., 1965).

Richard Pares, *A West India Fortune* (1950).

—— *King George III and the Politicians* (Oxford, 1953).

Charles Parkin, *The Moral Basis of Burke's Political Thought* (reissue, New York, 1968).

Lillian M. Penson, The London West India Interest in the Eighteenth Century', *E.H.R.*, xxxvi (July 1921) 373–92.

────── *The Colonial Agents of the British West Indies* (1924).

Bradford Perkins, *Prologue to War: England and the U.S. 1805–1812* (Berkeley, 1961).

C. H. Philips, *The East India Company 1784–1834* (Manchester, 1961).

J. A. Picton, *Memorials of Liverpool, Historical and Topographical*, 2 vols. (Liverpool, 1907).

Dale H. Porter, *The Abolition of the Slave Trade in England, 1784–1807* (Hamden, Conn., 1970).

M. J. Quinlan, *Victorian Prelude: A History of English Manners, 1700–1830* (1965).

A. M. Rees, 'The Campaign for the Abolition of the British Slave Trade and its Place in British Politics, *1783–1807*' (University of Oxford B. Litt thesis, 1952–53).

Alan Richardson (ed.), *A Theological Word Book of the Bible* (1950).

Caroline Robbins, *The Eighteenth-Century Commonwealthman: Studies in the Transmission, Development and Circumstances of English Liberal Thought from the Restoration of Charles II until the War with the Thirteen Colonies* (Cambridge, Mass., 1959).

J. Holland Rose, 'The Conflict with Revolutionary France, 1793–1802', *C.H.B.E.*, ii 37–82.

────── 'The Struggle with Napoleon, 1803–1815', *C.H.B.E.*, ii 85–128.

Erik Routley, *Hymns and the Faith* (1955).

Charles Ryksamp, *William Cowper of the Inner Temple, Esq.* (Cambridge, 1959).

Frank Sanderson, 'The Liverpool Delegates and Sir William Dolben's Bill' *Transactions of the Historic Society of Lancashire and Cheshire*, cxxiv (1973) 57–84.

E. D. Seeber, *Anti-Slavery Opinion in France during the Second Half of the Eighteenth Century* (Baltimore and Oxford, 1937).

E. A. Smith, 'The Yorkshire Election of 1806 and 1807: a study in Electoral Management', *Northern History* II, (1967), 62–90.

H. F. V. Somerset (ed.), *A Notebook of Edmund Burke* (Cambridge, 1957).

David Spring, 'The Clapham Sect: Some Social and Political Aspects', *Victorian Studies* (Sept 1961) 35–48.

Sir James Stephen, *Essays in Ecclesiastical Biography*, 2 vols. (1849).

Leslie Stephen, *History of English Thought in the Eighteenth Century*, 2 vols. (3rd ed., 1902).

────── *The Life of Sir James Fitzjames Stephen* (1895).

Wylie Sypher, 'Hutcheson and the "Classical Theory of Slavery"', *Journal of Negro History*, xxiv (July 1939) 263–80.

────── *Guinea's Captive Kings: British Anti-Slavery Literature of the XVIIIth Century* (Reissue, New York, 1969).

Allen C. Thomas, 'The Attitude of the Society of Friends towards Slavery', *American Society of Church History*, Papers, viii.

E. P. Thompson, *The Making of the English Working Class* (3rd ed., 1970).

Mack Thompson, *Moses Brown: Reluctant Reformer* (Chapel Hill, 1962).

Frederick B. Tolles, *Quakers and the Atlantic Culture* (New York, 1960).

A. S. Turberville, *The House of Lords in the Age of Reform, 1784–1837* (1958).

G. S. Veitch, *The Genesis of Parliamentary Reform* (1913).

J. Voisine, *J.-J. Rousseau en Angleterre à l'Epoque Romantique* (Paris, 1956).

J. D. Walsh, 'The Yorkshire Evangelicals in the Eighteenth Century: with Especial Reference to Methodism' (University of Cambridge unpublished Ph.D. thesis, 1956).

James Walvin, *Black and White: The Negro and English Society, 1555–1945* (1973).

W. R. Ward, *Religion and Society in England, 1790–1850* (1972).

J. Steven Watson, *The Reign of George III, 1760–1815* (Oxford, 1960).

John Wesley, 'Thoughts upon Slavery), in *The Works of John Wesley* (1872) XI 59–79.

E. G. West, *Adam Smith: The Man and his Works* (New York, 1969).

Janet P. Whitney, *John Woolman: American Quaker* (1943).

Lois Whitney, *Primitivism and the Idea of Progress* (New York, 1965).

Basil Willey, *The Eighteenth Century Background: Studies on the Idea of Nature in the Thought of the Period* (7th impression, 1961).

Eric Williams, *Capitalism and Slavery* (New York 1961; first published Chapel Hill, 1944).

Wilson E. Williams, 'Africa and the Rise of Capitalism' (Howard University M.A. thesis, 1938).

John A. Woods, 'The Correspondence of Benjamin Rush and Granville Sharp, 1773–1805' *Journal of American Studies*, I, no. 1, 1–38.

Index